Estate Planning Applications

Huebner School Series   *Gary K. Stone, Editor*

Group Health Insurance
Burton T. Beam, Jr.

Readings in Financial Planning
David M. Cordell (ed.)

Fundamentals of Financial Planning
David M. Cordell (ed.)

Readings in Income Taxation
James F. Ivers III (ed.)

McGill's Life Insurance
Edward E. Graves (ed.)

McGill's Legal Aspects of Life Insurance
Edward E. Graves and Burke A. Christensen (eds.)

Group Benefits: Basic Concepts and Alternatives
Burton T. Beam, Jr.

Planning for Retirement Needs
Kenn Beam Tacchino and David A. Littell

Readings in Wealth Accumulation Planning
American College Faculty (eds.)

Fundamentals of Estate Planning
Constance J. Fontaine (ed.)

Estate Planning Applications
Ted Kurlowicz (ed.)

Planning for Business Owners and Professionals
Ted Kurlowicz, James F. Ivers III, and John J. McFadden

Financial Planning Applications
William J. Ruckstuhl

*The Impact of the Political and Regulatory Process
on Life Insurance*
Jon S. Hanson

Financial Decision Making at Retirement
David A. Littell, Kenn Beam Tacchino, and David M. Cordell

The Practitioner's Guide to Advanced Pension Topics
David A. Littell and Kenn Beam Tacchino

Executive Compensation
John J. McFadden (ed.)

Huebner School Series

Estate Planning Applications
Third Edition

Ted Kurlowicz, Editor

The American College/*Bryn Mawr, Pennsylvania*

This publication is designed to provide accurate and authoritative information about the subject covered. While every precaution has been taken in the preparation of this material, the editor and The American College assume no liability for damages resulting from the use of information contained in this publication. The American College is not engaged in rendering legal, accounting, or other professional advice. If legal or other expert advice is required, the services of an appropriate professional should be sought.

© 1995, 1997, 1998 The American College
All rights reserved

Library of Congress Catalog Card Number 98-072484
ISBN 1-57996-007-3

Printed in the United States of America

To my mother

Contents

About the Editor   xiii

1 Forecasting Estate Settlement Costs   1

Costs of Transferring Wealth   2
Issues in Forecasting Estate Settlement Costs   8
Calculating Estate Settlement Costs   21
Final Note   26

2 Life Insurance in Estate Planning   39

Life Insurance Serves Two Purposes   40
Life Insurance Products   42
Transfer Tax Implications of Life Insurance   45
Federal Estate Taxation of Life Insurance   45
Federal Generation-Skipping Transfer Tax   56
Federal Gift Taxation   58
Outright Gifts of Life Insurance Policies   60
Practical Uses for Life Insurance in Estate Planning   62

3 Irrevocable Life Insurance Trusts (ILITs)   75

Advantages of ILIT   76
Gift Tax Planning for ILITs   80
Keeping ILIT Proceeds out of Grantor's Estate   94
Dispositive Provisions of ILIT   97
Concerns about Irrevocability   102
Special Planning Applications for ILIT   107

4 Valuation Principles Used in the Estate Planning Process   113

Valuation Principles   114
Sources of Valuation Rules   117
Fair Market Value   118
Alternative Valuation Date   119

Valuation of Specific Property 121
IRC Sec. 7520: Rules for Valuing Partial Interests 145
IRC Secs. 2701–2704: Valuation of Lifetime
Transfers with Retained Interests 150

5 Gifts to Family Members and Trusts — 151

Outright Gifting Program 152
Transfers to Family Trusts 156
Removal of Life Insurance Proceeds from Decedent-Insured's
Gross Estate 181

6 Estate Freezes for Family Businesses — 185

What Is an Estate Freeze? 185
Estate Freezes through Family Partnerships 192
Estate Freezes through Sales of Family
Businesses to Family Members 201

7 The Basics of Charitable Giving — 213

Charitable Giving in the United States 214
Role of Government in Charitable Giving 218
General Federal Tax Implications of Charitable Giving 218
Federal Estate Tax Treatment of Charitable Giving 223
Federal Gift Tax Treatment of Charitable Giving 227
Federal Income Tax Treatment of Charitable Giving 229
Estate Planning Opportunities in Charitable Giving 237

8 Sophisticated Methods of Charitable Giving — 253

Introduction 254
Donations of Less than Donor's Entire Interest in the Property 254
Charitable Remainder Trusts (CRTs) 259
Planning Applications of CRTs 271
Pooled-Income Fund 281
Charitable Lead Trust 282
Qualified Conservation Donations 284

9 Miscellaneous Estate Planning Issues Stemming from the Marital Relationship — 287

Concept of Intestacy 288
Spouse's Right of Election against the Will 290

Sec. 2034: Dower and Curtesy Interests	292
Federal Estate and Gift Tax Implications of Transfers Incident to Divorce or Separation	293
Division of the Marital Home	295
Ownership of Life Insurance	296
Acquisition and Maintenance of Life Insurance Policies Pursuant to Divorce Decree or Property Settlement	296

10 Community Property—Its Implications on Estate Planning   299

Introduction	300
Historical Background	301
The Basics of Community Property	301
Residence and Domicile	305
Separation or Divorce—Ending the Community	305
Distribution of Property at Death in Community-Property States	306
Disposition of Community Property in Common-Law States Following the Uniform Disposition of Community Property Rights at Death Act	308
Premarital Planning	309
Liability Problems with Community Property	309
Estate Planning Considerations	309

11 Estate Planning for Non-U.S. Citizens   319

Transfer Taxation of Noncitizens	319
Estate and Gift Taxation of Transfers by Nonresident-Aliens	321
Estate Planning for Transfers to a Noncitizen-Spouse	325
Minimizing the Burden of QDOT Treatment for Surviving Noncitizen-Spouses	339

12 Taxation of Trusts   345

Revocable Trusts	346
Transfers to Trusts with Retained Powers; Effect of Grantor Trust Rules	348
Comparison of Income, Gift, and Estate Tax Consequences of Transfers to Trusts with Retained Powers or Control	355
Irrevocable Living Trusts with No Retained Powers or Controls	362
Generation-Skipping Transfer Tax	366
Powers of Appointment	372

13 Estate Planning Implications of Employee Benefits — 377

Estate Planning for Distributions from Qualified Plans and IRAs — 379
Nonqualified Deferred Compensation — 396
Death-Benefit-Only Plans — 400
Group Term Life Insurance (Sec. 79) Plans — 402
Split-Dollar Life Insurance Plans — 405
Sec. 162 Bonus Life Insurance Plans — 410

14 Procedural Principles of Estate Planning (Including a Case Study) — 413

Effective Organization of Written Estate Plan — 413
Case Study — 424

Index — 449

Acknowledgments

The editor is grateful for the contribution of previous authors whose material this textbook still contains. The editor has updated the material substantially and is responsible for any errors in it.

The editor wishes to thank Evelyn Rice for her typing and production skills, which were clearly an integral prerequisite to the completion of this text, and Lynn Hayes for her expertise in the editorial context.

The editor also wants to thank The American College faculty for their gracious and patient assistance with various technical questions and practical recommendations that have added to the quality of the course.

Ted Kurlowicz, JD, LLM, CLU, ChFC, AEP
Professor of Taxation

About the Editor

Ted Kurlowicz, JD, LLM, CLU, ChFC, AEP, is professor of taxation in the Solomon S. Huebner School of The American College. His primary responsibility is course development in the estate, gift tax, and business planning areas.

Estate Planning Applications

1

Forecasting Estate Settlement Costs

Chapter Outline

COSTS OF TRANSFERRING WEALTH 2
    Transfers during Lifetime 2
    Transfers at Death 3
ISSUES IN FORECASTING ESTATE SETTLEMENT COSTS 8
    Estimating Administrative Expenses 8
    Forecasting Federal Estate Taxes 9
CALCULATING ESTATE SETTLEMENT COSTS 21
    Single Clients 21
    Married Clients 22
FINAL NOTE 26

There are many steps in the estate planning process. In its broadest definition, estate planning includes accumulating, preserving, and distributing a client's wealth. It is obvious that many aspects of estate planning must begin long before a client's death if the process is to be successful.

The primary factor in planning a client's estate is the client's goal with respect to the distribution of his or her accumulated wealth. There are many choices available to the client. The planning process should include answering the "who," "how," and "when" questions; that is, the client must establish goals for who will receive his or her wealth, how or in what form the wealth will be transferred, and when the wealth will be distributed to the intended beneficiary.

A number of technical rules will affect the various choices made by the client in planning his or her estate. There are legal issues regarding the form of property ownership and how various forms of property interests can be transferred. Generally, there are costs associated with the transfer of property. There may be legal costs, local transfer taxes, and gift or estate tax costs at the state and/or federal level.

The financial services professional who assists clients in estate planning must have extensive knowledge of the various costs of transferring wealth. The estate planner must know how to forecast these costs based on the various alternatives available to the client. Only with an accurate forecast of the transfer costs can the client make an informed decision in selecting the appropriate estate plan.

COSTS OF TRANSFERRING WEALTH

Transfers during Lifetime

A wealthy client often will—and generally should—begin transferring wealth while he or she is still alive. Clients find lifetime gifts attractive for both tax and nontax reasons. Most individuals find it extremely satisfying to make gifts to younger generation family members while the donor is still able to observe the donee's enjoyment of the gift. In addition, the donor is able to observe the donee's skill in managing the transferred wealth and make decisions about the form of future transfers to such donee, if any. Throughout this text, we will discuss the many transfer tax benefits for lifetime gifts. We will clearly demonstrate that lifetime gifts are the most effective tool for reducing the costs of estate settlement.

Legal Costs Associated with Lifetime Gifts

The legal costs associated with a lifetime gift range from minimal to substantial. For certain types of property, such as real estate, the instruments of transfer may have to be prepared by professionals, who will charge fees. Some local jurisdictions may impose a realty transfer tax. For a gift designed in a more complex form, such as a family trust, extensive legal advice may be necessary to plan and implement the transfer. Financial services professionals should be aware of and be able to make estimates of these costs before recommending lifetime gifts.

Gift Taxes

The federal transfer tax system, which is imposed on the privilege of transferring wealth, provides a unified system of estate and gift taxes; that is, these taxes share one progressive set of tax rates. However, there are many dissimilarities between estate and gift taxes that make lifetime gifts quite attractive. Gift taxes are imposed only if transfers exceed various exemptions, exclusions, deductions, and tax credits. The initial taxable gifts made by a client will be exempt due to the exclusions and/or credits. Once gift taxes become payable, they are imposed by a progressive tax rate structure, with marginal rates ranging from 37 to 60 percent. Paying gift taxes at the lower brackets is advantageous because the estate tax return is cumulative, and a decedent's estate is subject to the highest bracket based on the gross estate at the time of death plus adjusted taxable gifts made (after 1976) while the decedent was alive. The financial services professional must be familiar with the gift tax system to be able to effectively estimate and minimize gift tax costs before recommending lifetime gifts.

Some states also impose a gift tax. Fortunately, such additional gift taxes will be imposed only in a minority of states. The financial services professional should be aware of any state gift taxes before recommending lifetime gifts.

Transfers at Death

Most individuals transfer the majority of their wealth at the time of their death. Unfortunately, substantial costs are generally associated with settling an estate and transferring its assets. Without proper planning, many of these costs are unavoidable once the estate owner dies. Estate settlement costs can be divided into three categories. The first category is the final costs associated with winding up the decedent's affairs and providing for burial; the second is the administrative and legal costs associated with probate; and the third is death taxes imposed on transferring the decedent's wealth.

Decedent's Final Costs

The final costs, consisting of final expenses and burial costs, are fairly predictable and relatively small. The final expenses include the payment of the decedent's debts, which could include regular bills for services incurred before the decedent's death. For example, there may be medical bills, unpaid property taxes, and final federal, state, and local income taxes the decedent owed. The other expense in this category is, of course, the funeral costs for the decedent.

Probate Costs

Probate is the procedure through which the decedent's estate is settled with local court supervision. The court determines if a valid will exists, decides who should represent the decedent's estate as executor or administrator, and approves a plan for distributing the decedent's estate.

The size of the probate or administrative expenses depends upon many factors. One expense, although a relatively minor one, is the court costs associated with settling the estate. There are standard published court fees imposed at the county level in most jurisdictions. The more steps that the executor must take under court supervision, the higher these court costs are. Generally, these costs are higher if the estate is complex and must be kept open for a long period of time.

The highest probate costs are the fees paid to various professionals who settle the estate. These professionals could include the executor of the estate, the attorney who advises the executor, tax preparers, and property appraisers. The amount of these probate costs will depend upon the extent these professional advisers are employed in settling the estate.

Executor's Commission. The personal representative of the estate is either an executor or administrator. An executor is the individual or entity named in the decedent's will. If there is no will or the executor appointed in the will fails to serve, the probate court appoints an administrator for the estate. The executor or administrator does not have to be a professional or corporate entity. Individual family members or friends could be chosen as the personal representative. If a professional individual or a corporate executor is chosen, the executor's fee, often referred to as a commission, generally is established by local practice. The commission is usually based on the size of the probate estate, with the commission percentage declining as the value of the estate increases. The customary charges vary from jurisdiction to jurisdiction. Often, the charges are different in various regions within individual states. A few states, notably California, have commission rates that are set by statute. The California statutory rates are shown in table 1-1. The majority of states have commissions that are approved as customary practice. Table 1-2 indicates the customary charges in one of those states.

Legal Fees. An attorney typically is retained to advise an executor, even if the executor is a professional or corporate entity. The executor's responsibility is to manage the process of settling the estate. The executor is not meant to practice law in the role of executor. Therefore if legal issues need to be resolved in the estate settlement process, an attorney must be retained. Examples of such legal issues include interpreting provisions of the decedent's will, protecting the decedent's estate against legal claims, and interpreting difficult issues with respect to death taxes.

Traditionally, the attorney for the estate was paid on a commission scale similar to that of the executor. Often, the attorney's charges will, in fact, exceed the executor's commission. Many jurisdictions now prefer the attorney's fees to be billed on an hourly basis as opposed to a commission scale. The disciplinary rules for attorneys, governed by the state's bar association, generally provide that fees not be excessive. Fees based on hourly charges that reflect the amount and difficulty of the work performed by the attorney are generally viewed as more reasonable than a commission rate.

Tax Preparer's Fees. Several tax returns may have to be prepared in the estate settlement process. First, the decedent will have a final income tax return. Next, the estate must file an income tax return for every year the estate is open and has taxable income over $600. Often, both a federal and state income tax return must be filed for the estate. Finally, the death tax returns must be prepared. These could include a federal Form 706 estate tax return and a state estate or inheritance tax return. The tax preparation fees are paid to the attorney for the estate or an accountant employed to prepare such tax returns. These fees normally are billed on an hourly basis.

TABLE 1-1
California Statutory Fees and Commissions for Executors and Attorneys

Value of Estate	Executor's Commission	Attorney's Fees
$ 15,000	$ 600	$ 600
50,000	1,650	1,650
100,000	3,150	3,150
150,000	4,150	4,150
200,000	5,150	5,150
300,000	7,150	7,150
400,000	9,150	9,150
500,000	11,150	11,150
600,000	13,150	13,150
700,000	15,150	15,150
800,000	17,150	17,150
900,000	19,150	19,150
1,000,000	21,150	21,150
1,250,000	23,150	23,650
1,500,000	26,150	26,150
2,000,000	31,150	31,150
3,000,000	41,150	41,150
4,000,000	51,150	51,150

TABLE 1-2
Schedule of Executor Fees for Typical Bank & Trust

Principal Fees	
First $200,000	5.0%
Next $300,000	4.0%
Next $400,000	2.5%
Next $4 million	1.25%
On the excess	0.75%
Minimum principal fee	$5000
Income fee	6.0%

Additional services—Bank reserves the right to add additional charges for above-standard services.

Appraisal Fees. Finally, the estate settlement process may necessitate professional appraisal fees. The federal estate and state death tax returns are based on the value of the assets included in the applicable tax base. To determine the tax base, a value must be ascertained for the estate's assets. The valuation of some assets, such as cash or marketable securities, is fairly straightforward. However, other assets, such as personal property, artwork, collectibles, real estate, and closely held business interests, are more difficult to value. Appraisal fees for estates including such items could be substantial. For example, the appraisal of a closely held business could cost $20,000.

The cost of this professional appraisal could be estimated in advance by investigating the type of assets held by the estate owner. In some cases, the financial services professional can minimize these costs through lifetime planning. In fact, this may be one of the estate planning goals in some instances. For example, the business appraisal fee could be avoided if the business is subject to a properly designed buy-sell agreement that effectively establishes the value of the business at the time of the business owner's death.

Federal Estate Taxes

For most wealthy individuals, the federal estate tax will be the largest cost associated with transferring wealth at death. Although federal estate taxes are unified with gift taxes into one transfer tax system, the federal estate tax is far more burdensome in most circumstances.

First, no exclusion that is analogous to the federal gift tax annual exclusion is available for the federal estate tax return. Second, all appreciation on property included in the gross estate is subject to tax. Third, the estate taxes are paid at the highest marginal rate imposed on the decedent's transfers due to the nature of the estate tax calculation. Finally, the federal estate tax is a tax-inclusive system—that is, the federal estate taxes are imposed on all property included in the gross estate, including estate assets that must be used to pay federal estate tax. As we will see later in chapter 5, gift taxes paid on lifetime transfers are not subject to additional transfer tax if they are made more than 3 years before the decedent's death.

The mechanics of the federal estate tax calculation will be discussed further later in the chapter.

Federal Generation-Skipping Transfer Tax (GSTT)

Certain transfers, whether made by lifetime gift or at a transferor's death, are subject to the generation-skipping transfer tax. Generally speaking, the GSTT applies to transfers taxable under either the estate or gift tax system that skip a generation in the transferor's family. (Note that transfers to unrelated transferees are subject to the GSTT if the transferee is more than 37 1/2 years younger than the transferor.)

Every individual has a $1 million (to be indexed for inflation beginning in 1999) cumulative exemption against transfers subject to the GSTT. In addition, there are exclusions for lifetime generation-skipping gifts, with similarities to and differences from the gift tax exclusions.

Generation-skipping gifts or bequests should be planned carefully. Transfers subject to the GSTT are taxed at the maximum federal estate and gift tax rates, currently 55 percent. The financial services professional forecasting estate settlement costs must be aware of the potential impact of the GSTT, especially since it can arise in circumstances that are less than obvious. The GSTT will be covered in detail in chapter 12.

State Death Taxes

All 50 states and the District of Columbia impose some type of death tax for wealth transferred at death. The type of death tax used varies from state to state. The state death tax systems can be categorized as inheritance, estate, or credit estate taxes.

Inheritance Tax. Some states impose an inheritance tax on property received at death. State inheritance taxes are based on a set of tax rates and usually have tax base inclusion rules defined differently from those for the federal gross estate. The tax rates typically vary according to the relationship of the beneficiary to the decedent, with more distant relations paying the inheritance tax at a higher rate. Practically speaking, the problems inheritance taxes cause for the estate are similar to the federal estate taxes because they are imposed on the property transferred.

Estate Tax. Other states have an estate tax similar to the federal transfer tax system. Again, there is a separate set of rates, but the property included in the tax base is defined similarly to the federal gross estate.

Credit Estate Tax or Sponge Tax. This state death tax system imposes a tax equal to the maximum allowable credit against the federal estate taxes for state death taxes paid by the estate. The state death taxes paid are allowable as a credit against federal estate taxes only if they do not exceed a limit set by the federal tax rules. The limit is provided by a tax table based on the adjusted taxable estate, as defined on the federal estate tax return. All states and the District of Columbia impose a credit estate tax. Some states use the maximum allowable state death tax credit as their sole death tax. Other states use the credit estate tax in conjunction with the other state death taxes, making the federal state death tax credit the minimum amount paid for state death taxes.

The financial services professional should be well acquainted with the state death tax systems in states where his or her clients reside or own property. This is particularly important if the states in question impose a special inheritance tax. In many cases, the property subject to inheritance taxes differs from property subject to federal estate taxes. For example, many states exempt life insurance owned by the decedent-insured if paid to a named beneficiary other than the decedent-insured's estate. In addition, the inheritance tax rate imposed commonly varies according to the relationship between the decedent and the beneficiary. The more distant the relationship, the higher the inheritance tax rate generally is; for example, the Pennsylvania inheritance tax rate is 6 percent for lineal descendants but 15 percent for other beneficiaries. This could have a significant effect on the client's choice of beneficiaries or which assets should be transferred to each.

State death taxes are a substantial cost of settling an estate. For estates with assets less than the federal applicable exclusion amount (formerly known as the unified credit equivalent), the state taxes are the only death taxes paid. The state death taxes will often far exceed the maximum allowable state death tax credit against federal estate taxes if the state imposes a separate inheritance or estate tax in addition to a credit estate tax.

ISSUES IN FORECASTING ESTATE SETTLEMENT COSTS

Estimating Administrative Expenses

The administrative expenses and other settlement costs vary based on a number of factors. If the decedent and his or her family had an effective probate avoidance plan, these expenses should be relatively low. If complex estate settlement matters require substantial professional help, administrative fees could be significant. Any special or unique characteristics related to the client's estate should also be considered. For example, if the client has substantial recourse loans—loans where the grantor and/or his or her estate are personally liable—such loans unpaid at the time of the client's death could be an immediate cash expense. Other factors, such as appraisal fees, vary from case to case; for example, an estate containing one or more closely held business interests or unusual personal property necessitates the estimation of significant appraisal fees.

Normally, the administrative expenses and other settlement costs (other than death taxes) are stated as a percentage of the value of the estate. This is generally the case whether the estate forecast is done manually or with computer software.

For simplicity, most planners estimate the administrative expenses as 3 to 5 percent of the estate. Generally, the larger the estate, the lower the percentage for estimated administrative costs. Be aware that part of the estate planning process typically is to reduce the administrative expenses that will ultimately be paid. The forecast of any proposed estate plan should take the reduction in administrative expenses into consideration. Finally, be aware of the special circumstances of an estate that might result in extraordinary administrative expenses.

Forecasting Federal Estate Taxes

Determining the Gross Estate

The first step in forecasting a client's estate settlement cost is determining the amount of the anticipated gross estate. The gross estate for federal estate tax purposes is the total of the items included in the client's estate tax base. This initial step requires the financial services professional to be familiar with the federal estate tax inclusion rules, state property law issues, and basic principles of property valuation. Each of these issues will be examined in later chapters, but we will give a brief description of these subjects here.

The client's gross estate is found by totaling the following items:

- property owned outright by the decedent at the time of his or her death
- certain property interests transferred by gift within 3 years of the decedent's death
- property transferred during the decedent's lifetime in which the decedent retains certain rights
- benefits from qualified retirement plans, IRAs, and nonqualified annuity products purchased by the decedent (or paid for by the decedent's employer) payable to a survivor at the decedent's death
- property jointly held between the decedent and a survivor where the survivor obtains the decedent's interest through rights of survivorship
- general powers of appointment held over property by the decedent during his or her lifetime and/or at the time of his or her death
- life insurance in which the decedent held incidents of ownership (or gratuitously transferred incidents of ownership within 3 years of death) or which was payable to the decedent's executor
- property subject to a life interest held by the decedent in which the decedent's spouse or the executor of such spouse's estate made the so-called QTIP election to require inclusion in the estate of the decedent

Property Owned Outright by the Decedent (Sec. 2033). This broad-based inclusion section (often called the "catchall provision") is designed to cause inclusion of any property owned or held by the decedent at the time of his or her death and transferred by the decedent's will or state intestacy law. This provision causes the inclusion of property owned outright by the decedent regardless of its form; that is, the property could be real property as well as tangible or intangible personal property. The property interest held by the decedent must be a beneficial interest in the property, with more than simple legal title held over the property.

Specifically included in this section are the decedent's home (if titled individually), bank accounts, securities, personal items, and other property interests that can be transferred by the decedent at the time of his or her death. For example, property interests held by the decedent in tenancy in common is an interest, although shared with others, that can be transferred by the decedent at the time of his or her death. Other property interests included in the catchall provision are future interests in property in which the decedent did not have immediate possessory rights at the time of his or her death and income in respect of a decedent (IRD). IRD is income earned by the decedent while he or she was alive but has not been paid at the time of his or her death.

The items included in this section encompass the decedent's probate estate. Thus, the probate estate is a subset of the federal gross estate.

Certain Property Interests Transferred by Gift within 3 Years of the Decedent's Death (Sec. 2035). Most lifetime gifts are not includible in the decedent's gross estate even if transferred within 3 years of his or her death. However, certain property interests receive special treatment under this provision. For example, life insurance given away within 3 years of the decedent-insured's death is included in his or her gross estate. In addition, gift taxes paid on gifts within 3 years of death are included in the decedent's gross estate under this provision. Finally, certain lifetime gifts of property with retained rights are included in the decedent's gross estate if he or she relinquishes such rights within 3 years of death.

Lifetime Gifts with Retained Rights (Secs. 2036, 2037, and 2038). The rules under this provision are fairly complex and will be discussed in detail later in this text. Stated briefly, the decedent's gross estate includes property interests given away during his or her lifetime if the decedent retained (1) a life estate, (2) the ability to revoke, alter, or amend the transfer, or (3) a reversionary interest in the property worth actuarially more than 5 percent of the value of the property at the time of the decedent's death.

Benefits from Qualified Retirement Plans, IRAs, and Nonqualified Annuity Policies (Sec. 2039). The rule for retirement benefits and nonqualified annuity policies is fairly straightforward. First, their value is included only if benefits are paid from the retirement plan or annuity policy to a survivor of the decedent. Thus, a straight-life annuity is not included in the annuitant's gross estate. In addition, the benefits are included in the decedent's gross estate only to the extent the decedent or his or her employer contributed the funds that provide the survivor benefit. According to IRS data, 30 percent of the federal estate tax returns currently filed include some type of retirement plan asset in the gross estate of the decedent. With the growth of qualified and quasi-qualified retirement plans, it is anticipated that this inclusion provision will become far more significant in the near future.

Jointly Titled Property with Rights of Survivorship (Sec. 2040). Property is included in the decedent's gross estate under this provision only if the decedent held the property jointly with rights of survivorship with the surviving joint tenant. Two forms of property ownership are affected by this provision. The first is tenancy by the entireties. This form of property ownership is uniquely available only to married couples. It is a special form of jointly held property in which the surviving spouse receives the entire property interest at the death of the first spouse to die. Under this provision, 50 percent of the property held jointly with the spouse is included in the estate of the deceased spouse.

The second form of property ownership affected by these rules is property titled jointly with rights of survivorship. This form of ownership can be held either with a spouse or with other family members and unrelated parties. In the case of property titled jointly between spouses, the 50 percent inclusion rule again applies. For other jointly titled interests, the deceased joint tenant's estate will include a portion of the property equal to the decedent's proportional contribution to the original purchase price. Thus, if the decedent supplied the entire purchase price, his or her estate includes the entire amount of the property interest that passes to the survivor at the decedent's death.

General Powers of Appointment (Sec. 2041). A general power of appointment is a broad invasion power held over a property interest, generally a trust, by which the holder of the power has the unfettered right to invade the property. Specifically included as a general power of appointment is the power holder's ability to appoint the property to himself or herself, his or her creditors, his or her estate, or the creditors of his or her estate. At least one of these invasion powers must be available for the power to be considered a general power of appointment.

A general power of appointment causes inclusion of the property subject to the power in the power holder's gross estate if he or she holds this power while alive or at the time of his or her death. Property subject to a general power of appointment may be included in surprising circumstances. Normally, the power holder does not have outright ownership of the property subject to the power; in fact, he or she may not be a direct beneficiary of the property interest. However, such broad-based powers to invade the property interest cause inclusion in the decedent's gross estate.

Life Insurance on the Decedent's Life (Sec. 2042). Life insurance is included in the gross estate of an insured-decedent if (1) the decedent held incidents of ownership in the policy at the time of his or her death, (2) the decedent gave the policy away within 3 years of his or her death, or (3) the policy was payable to the decedent's executor. The important rules concerning the inclusion of life insurance in an insured's gross estate will be discussed in chapters 2 and 3. Be aware that life insurance is generally not subject to state inheritance taxes if it is payable to a named beneficiary other than the insured's estate in those states that impose a separate inheritance tax.

QTIP Property (Sec. 2044). Special marital deduction rules permit a transfer of a life income interest to the transferor's spouse to qualify for the federal estate or gift tax marital deduction. This rule applies whether the income interest was transferred when the transferor was alive or at the time of his or her death. However, the transferor or the transferor's executor must make the special QTIP election to qualify the transfer for the marital deduction. This election has an adverse effect on the estate of the spouse who receives the QTIP interest: The property interest, despite its termination at the death of the surviving spouse, must be included in the surviving spouse's gross estate.

Gross Estate Inclusion Rules and Estate Tax Forecasting. A thorough listing of the items included in the decedent's gross estate is essential for forecasting federal estate taxes. Without an accurate estimation of the tax base, any subsequent forecasting calculations will produce erroneous results. The financial services professional should have a thorough understanding of these inclusion rules. In most instances, clients do not have any idea how the federal estate tax will affect their property. In fact, clients will be surprised to learn that certain items, such as their pension assets or life insurance, are subject to federal estate or state death taxes.

The financial services professional should also be aware of the forms of property ownership. The different estate tax effects of jointly held property, life insurance, and general or limited powers of appointment can be seen in the discussion above. Many clients are not certain of the form in which they own their property. For example, spouses rarely are sure whether property is titled jointly with rights of survivorship, titled jointly without rights of survivorship, or individually owned by either spouse. For other items, such as retirement plans, clients typically are unsure of, and have no record of, the selected beneficiary designation. The same may also be true for a client's life insurance. Clients may not remember whether policies were transferred to third parties or the beneficiary designations that were selected.

An essential component of the process of forecasting estate settlement costs is the determination of the property included in the client's gross estate, including resolving the property ownership issues discussed in the paragraph above. It is important that the financial services professional gather thorough and accurate data for each client. A valuable tool in this data-gathering process is a fact-finding questionnaire.

The completion of a fact finder serves several purposes. First, the client gains confidence in the financial services professional who is thorough and knowledgeable regarding the data gathering. Second, the data collected on the client's assets, life insurance, and retirement benefits enable the financial services professional to accurately forecast the estate settlement cost as the client's plan is currently designed. Third, the questions on the fact finder alert the financial services professional and the client to any unusual property ownership interests the client holds that should be given special consideration. Finally, the fact finder helps the client formulate goals, enabling the financial services professional to design and recommend an effective alternative to the client's current estate plan.

Valuing Estate Assets

To accurately forecast a client's estate settlement cost, it is necessary to know not only what assets are included in the estate tax base but also the value of such assets. Chapter 4 provides a complete discussion of valuation techniques. However, a few brief comments should be made here.

Estimating Current Value. The estate settlement costs forecast will be accurate only if appropriate values are estimated for each item included in the client's gross estate. The accuracy of the valuation estimates depends on (1) the appraisal skills of the financial services professional doing the forecast, (2) the input available from the client's other advisers, (3) the types of assets held by the client, and (4) the willingness of the client to pay for accurate property appraisals, if necessary.

Many types of assets lend themselves to immediate accurate valuation. For example, the client's estate could consist of cash, marketable securities, and life insurance. The value of all such items can be determined simply and accurately. Other items, such as real estate, closely held business interests, and special types of personal property (such as artwork), involve more complex and uncertain valuation.

The client may have records at his or her disposal that could assist the financial services professional in estimating the value of specific items. For example, appraisals on certain property interests may have been done in the recent past for credit reports or property and liability insurance. In the case of real estate, the client may have a property appraisal that was performed to obtain a mortgage or in contemplation of selling the property. In the case of a closely held business, the financial statements available from the client or his or her accountant are a good starting point in determining the value. Relatively inexpensive appraisal guides or business valuation software could assist the financial services professional in determining the value of the closely held business interest. The client's accountant or an independent appraiser may have recently performed a business appraisal. The financial services professional should be aware of and obtain a copy of such appraisal reports.

Because clients usually believe that obtaining appraisal reports solely for the purpose of forecasting estate settlement costs is overly expensive and dilatory, they must be made aware that the estate settlement forecast is accurate only if appropriate data are used. With a little patience and effort, the financial services professional can usually obtain or determine reasonable estimates for the value of most or all assets included in the gross estate. However, investigating the value of the client's assets should never be limited to the quick completion of a fact-finding questionnaire or the client's word as to the value of his or her estate, particularly when complex items are involved.

Impact of Inflation. Estate settlement cost forecasts involve projections into the future. A simple "snapshot" approach, which indicates the client's current estate settlement costs, assuming he or she will die today, presents a possibly unrealistic picture of the client's estate settlement problems. The client will rarely die immediately after the forecast. Problems are more evident when the forecast is for the estate settlement costs of a married couple because the additional life extends the mortality assumptions.

The mortality assumptions for the estate tax forecasting depend upon the preferences of the client and the financial services professional. With the availability of sophisticated computer software, several forecasts with different assumptions can be run quickly and inexpensively. When a married couple is involved, different dates of death typically are assumed for each spouse. The author's personal preference is to present a snapshot of the current estate settlement cost, assuming one spouse will die immediately or in the relatively near future. The death of the surviving spouse is assumed to occur somewhat farther down the road to demonstrate the impact of inflation over time. Normally this time frame should be in the foreseeable future, such as 10 or 15 years. Forecasting estate settlement costs into the distant future invariably becomes less accurate for several reasons. First, inflation figures cause enormous growth in the size of the estate if a long time horizon is selected. The client may have difficulty believing the amount of growth in the estate if the forecast extends over a long period. Second, the client may face an emergency or receive a financial windfall that will change the estimate. These possibilities become less predictable in a long-term forecast. Third, the composition of the assets the client holds could change significantly over a long period of time. Finally, unforeseen tax law changes will have a larger effect the longer the time horizon chosen.

Inflation has a significant effect on the forecast of estate settlement costs. If assets included in the client's estate grow with the rate of inflation, probate fees, state death taxes, and federal estate taxes will also increase. The estate is subject to "bracket creep" simply as a result of inflation. The maximum federal estate tax rate of 55 percent applies when the taxable estate exceeds $3 million; there is an additional 5 percent surcharge for taxable estates between $10 million and $21,225,000 (the upper limit to the surcharge range will increase as the applicable credit increases; the figure stated here is for 1998).

When forecasting estate settlement costs over a period of time, inflation should be taken into account. The most accurate method is to use a separate inflation forecast for each asset included in the client's estate. Obviously, this method is less realistic for forecasts over a longer period. It is unlikely that the current composition of assets will be stable over a long time horizon. Assuming different inflation factors for individual assets may result in inaccurate forecasts if assets are transferred and/or the client acquires new assets. For example, the client's estate may currently hold a closely held business interest. The client may be planning to sell the business interest at his or her retirement. An inflation rate assumed for the business interest may be different from the inflation rate for the investment assets purchased by the client with the sale proceeds at retirement.

In some cases, it may be unrealistic to assume that assets will continue to grow at a designated inflation rate until the assumed date of death. For example, with a retirement plan, the account balance in the plan may decline as the client begins withdrawing retirement benefits. At the very least, the required minimum distribution from the retirement plan once the client reaches age 70 1/2 will slow the growth of the account balance.

What inflation rate should be chosen? As we discussed above, the most accurate method of forecasting growth for the purposes of determining estate settlement costs is to select an inflation growth rate for each individual asset. Personal property, marketable securities, real estate, and closely held business interests will all have different growth rates over time. Some assets, such as real estate or closely held business interests, could be subject to wild fluctuations in the rate of growth. Clearly, a decade like the 1980s would have a higher growth rate for real estate than one like the 1990s. To be completely accurate, such trends should be analyzed carefully. However, such pinpoint inflation forecasting is often unrealistic. If the estate forecast is done manually, this type of forecasting could be extremely time-consuming. The benefits achieved in accuracy may not be worth the effort. If the estate forecast is made with the assistance of computer software, the planner should be aware that many software packages do not facilitate the use of separate growth rates for individual estate assets. Quite often, one inflation figure is chosen for the entire estate. This method offers simplicity with, perhaps, very little loss of accuracy. Some items, such as cash or personal property, may have growth rates under the average inflation assumption. Other items, such as marketable securities or business interests, may experience long-run growth in excess of the average inflation factor.

From 1951 to 1991, inflation averaged just over 4 percent, although it has dropped in recent years, averaging below 3 percent from 1991–1995. If we assume that the client's assets share in the growth of the economy, it may be realistic to assume a growth rate on assets slightly higher, for example, 6 percent. However, remember that trends are very important when forecasting. For example, the inflation rate during the 1970s was 7.4 percent, but the current trend is for an inflation rate less than the long-term average.

Most important, we are trying to forecast a client's estate settlement costs to determine whether changes should be made to the client's existing estate plan. If the financial services professional and the client feel the assumptions made are a realistic estimate of the future performance, they will be more confident that recommended changes to the estate plan, if any, are appropriate.

In summary, the following factors should be taken into consideration in forecasting the inflation growth rate on a client's estate assets:

- the composition of assets held in the client's estate
- the expected growth rate for each asset in the estate
- the client's plans, if any, to change the composition of the assets during the period of the estate settlement costs forecast

- the client's income needs both before and after retirement and the effect of those needs on the growth of the client's estate
- the expected inflation rate for the economy

Calculating Federal Estate Taxes

Exclusion for Qualified Family-Owned Businesses. The Taxpayer Relief Act of 1997 (hereinafter TRA 97) created a new exclusion for estates of decedents dying after 1997 for certain closely held family businesses. The provision will allow qualifying estates to exclude the first $1.3 million of qualified family-owned businesses from the gross estate of the business owner. The family-owned business exclusion works in conjunction with the applicable credit amount (formerly the unified credit as discussed below) so that the total $1.3 million exclusion includes the applicable exclusion amount sheltered by the applicable credit amount. For example, the applicable exclusion amount (the amount sheltered by the applicable credit amount) is $625,000 for 1998. Thus, the family business exclusion could result in a shelter of $675,000 from the family business exclusion and $625,000 from the applicable exclusion amount. This results in the total permissible exclusion of $1.3 million. As the applicable credit amount increases between now and 2006, the benefit of the family business exclusion will diminish. (At the time this material was written, Congress was considering technical corrections to TRA 97 that would increase the family business exclusion as the applicable credit amount increases.) The rules for qualifying for the family business exclusion are very complex and will be discussed later in chapter 4.

Determining the Adjusted Gross Estate. The financial services professional involved in estate planning must understand the estate-tax calculation procedure thoroughly. We have already discussed the important first step in the estate tax calculation—determining the value of the gross estate. The estate tax return and the calculation of taxes are not, in theory, markedly different from the income tax return. The gross tax base—the gross estate—is reduced by deductions against the gross estate to arrive at the adjusted gross estate. Deductible items should be included in the estate settlement cost forecast since they will be part of the cash needs of the estate. In addition, they have the effect, as deductible items, of reducing the estimated estate taxes. Items deductible from the gross estate include the following:

- funeral expenses
- unpaid taxes, such as property taxes
- administrative expenses
- recourse debts of the decedent
- creditor claims or other claims against the estate

- losses incurred on estate assets (which are fortuitous, do not occur until the estate is being settled, and are impossible to estimate in the forecast)

Determining the Taxable Estate. The adjusted gross estate determined above is an arbitrary calculation and is used to measure certain thresholds. For example, the eligibility for Sec. 303 redemptions or Sec. 6166 installment payments (both discussed later in the text) is based on a percentage threshold of the *adjusted* gross estate. The adjusted gross estate is further reduced by two important deductions—the federal estate tax marital and charitable deductions—to reach the taxable estate. The rules for these deductions are complex and will be discussed later.

Determining the Tentative Tax Base. At this point, there is a significant departure from the theory behind the income tax calculation. This departure is a result of the unification of the federal estate and gift tax systems. The federal transfer tax base could be perceived as one system applying to all transfers made by the decedent during his or her lifetime and at the time of death. The federal estate tax return could be viewed as the sole unified return. However, since gift taxes must be reported under an annual tax accounting concept, adjustments must be made for gift tax returns already filed at the time of death. If the decedent made taxable gifts during his or her lifetime, such taxable transfers are first sheltered by the decedent's applicable credit amount against gift taxes. After the credit is exceeded, the donor must pay gift taxes during lifetime. Once the taxable estate has been computed, the decedent's adjusted taxable gifts made after 1976 (the date when the estate and gift tax systems were unified) must be added to the taxable estate to determine the *tentative tax base*.

Lifetime gifts are added to the tax base at this point to preserve the theory of unification between the estate and gift tax systems. Thus, the decedent's estate tax return will appear as though all taxable transfers during the decedent's lifetime were made at the time of his or her death. The addition of adjusted taxable gifts in the estate tax return has the effect of placing the decedent in the highest possible federal estate tax bracket based on total taxable transfers, whether made during lifetime or at the time of death.

Determining a Tentative Federal Estate Tax. The progressive tax rate schedules (shown in table 1-3) are applied to the tentative tax base to determine a tentative tax. Since there can be no double-counting of taxes, the federal gift taxes made on such taxable gifts before the decedent's death must be deducted from the tentative estate taxes.

Determining the Net Federal Estate Tax Payable after Credits. After the tentative tax has been reduced by the amount of gift taxes payable on post-1976 taxable gifts, the federal estate tax payable is reduced by certain credits. Specifically, the credits include the following:

- the applicable credit amount against state and gift taxes. Note that this credit is reinstated at this time even if used against lifetime taxable gifts since lifetime taxable gifts have been added back into the calculation. This credit against federal estate and gift taxes was amended by TRA 1997 and will increase pursuant to the schedule in table 1-3. It is now called the applicable credit amount, which is $202,050 for 1998.

TABLE 1-3
Schedule of Applicable Credit Amount

Year	Applicable Exclusion Amount	Applicable Credit Amount	Upper Limit on 60% Surcharge Bracket
1998	$625,000	$202,050	$21,225,000
1999	$650,000	$211,300	$21,410,000
2000 and 2001	$675,000	$220,550	$21,595,000
2002 and 2003	$700,000	$229,800	$21,780,000
2004	$850,000	$287,300	$22,930,000
2005	$950,000	$326,300	$23,710,000
2006 and later	$1,000,000	$345,800	$24,100,000

- credit for state death taxes. State death taxes paid are allowed as a credit against the federal estate tax. However, the state death tax credit is limited by a rate schedule, shown in table 1-5. The credit actually allowed on the return is equal to the lesser of the maximum state death tax credit or state death taxes actually paid by the decedent's estate.
- foreign death tax credit. A credit may be allowed against the federal estate tax for taxes paid by the decedent's estate to a foreign country for estate inheritance or other death taxes. This credit may be available whether the decedent is a citizen of the United States or a resident alien at the time of his or her death. This credit is for foreign death taxes paid on properties located outside the United States that are also included in the decedent's gross estate for federal estate tax purposes.
- credit for gift taxes paid on pre-1977 gifts
- credit for tax on prior transfers. This credit provides relief if property included in the gross estate was inherited from someone who died less than 10 years before the date of the decedent's death. The credit is designed to prevent federal estate taxes from being paid twice on the same asset within a short period of time. The credit is 100 percent of the federal estate taxes paid at the time of the initial transfer reduced by 20

Chapter 1 Forecasting Estate Settlement Costs

percent every 2 years. Thus, if 10 years or more have passed since the property was taxed in the initial estate, the credit is completely phased out.

TABLE 1-4
Unified Rate Schedule for Computing Estate and Gift Tax

If the amount with respect to which the tentative tax is to be computed is . . .	The tentative tax is . . .
Not over $10,000	18% of such amount
Over $10,000 but not over $20,000	$1,800, plus 20% of excess of such amount over $10,000
Over $20,000 but not over $40,000	$3,800, plus 22% of excess of such amount over $20,000
Over $40,000 but not over $60,000	$8,200, plus 24% of excess of such amount over $40,000
Over $60,000 but not over $80,000	$13,000, plus 26% of excess of such amount over $60,000
Over $80,000 but not over $100,000	$18,200, plus 28% of excess of such amount over $80,000
Over $100,000 but not over $150,000	$23,800, plus 30% of excess of such amount over $100,000
Over $150,000 but not over $250,000	$38,800, plus 32% of excess of such amount over $150,000
Over $250,000 but not over $500,000	$70,800, plus 34% of excess of such amount over $250,000
Over $500,000 but not over $750,000	$155,800, plus 37% of excess of such amount over $500,000
Over $750,000 but not over $1,000,000	$248,300, plus 39% of excess of such amount over $750,000
Over $1,000,000 but not over $1,250,000	$345,800, plus 41% of excess of such amount over $1,000,000
Over $1,250,000 but not over $1,500,000	$448,300, plus 43% of excess of such amount over $1,250,000
Over $1,500,000 but not over $2,000,000	$555,800, plus 45% of excess of such amount over $1,500,000
Over $2,000,000 but not over $2,500,000	$780,800, plus 49% of excess of such amount over $2,000,000
Over $2,500,000 but not over $3,000,000	$1,025,800, plus 53% of excess over $2,500,000
Over $3,000,000*	$1,290,800, plus 55% of excess over $3,000,000

*The tentative tax is increased by 5% of the amount (with respect to which the tentative tax is computed) in the range of $10 million to $21,225,000 (for 1998; see table 1-5 for the upper limit on the surcharge range for any given year). This 5% surcharge eliminates the benefit of the graduated rates and applicable credit amount.

TABLE 1-5
Credit for State Death Taxes

If the adjusted taxable estate* is ...	The maximum tax credit is ...
Not over $90,000	0.8% of amount by which taxable estate exceeds $40,000
Over $90,000 but not over $140,000	$400, plus 1.6% of excess over $90,000
Over $140,000 but not over $240,000	$1,200, plus 2.4% of excess over $140,000
Over $240,000 but not over $440,000	$3,600, plus 3.2% of excess over $240,000
Over $440,000 but not over $640,000	$10,000, plus 4% of excess over $440,000
Over $640,000 but not over $840,000	$18,000, plus 4.8% of excess over $640,000
Over $840,000 but not over $1,040,000	$27,600, plus 5.6% of excess over $840,000
Over $1,040,000 but not over $1,540,000	$38,800, plus 6.4% of excess over $1,040,000
Over $1,540,000 but not over $2,040,000	$70,800, plus 7.2% of excess over $1,540,000
Over $2,040,000 but not over $2,540,000	$106,800, plus 8% of excess over $2,040,000
Over $2,540,000 but not over $3,040,000	$146,800, plus 8.8% of excess over $2,540,000
Over $3,040,000 but not over $3,540,000	$190,800, plus 9.6% of excess over $3,040,000
Over $3,540,000 but not over $4,040,000	$238,800, plus 10.4% of excess over $3,540,000
Over $4,040,000 but not over $5,040,000	$290,800, plus 11.2% of excess over $4,040,000
Over $5,040,000 but not over $6,040,000	$402,800, plus 12% of excess over $5,040,000
Over $6,040,000 but not over $7,040,000	$522,800, plus 12.8% of excess over $6,040,000
Over $7,040,000 but not over $8,040,000	$650,800, plus 13.6% of excess over $7,040,000
Over $8,040,000 but not over $9,040,000	$786,800, plus 14.4% of excess over $8,040,000
Over $9,040,000 but not over $10,040,000	$930,800, plus 15.2% of excess over $9,040,000
Over $10,040,000	$1,082,800 plus 16% of excess over $10,040,000

*For purposes of this section, the term *adjusted taxable estate* means the taxable estate reduced by $60,000.

Forecasting Final Settlement Costs

The final estate settlement costs include the following cash needs of the estate:

- federal estate taxes
- state death taxes
- funeral and administrative expenses
- unpaid property and income taxes
- creditor claims

Forecasting the estate settlement costs involves determining and totaling these expenses. If the forecast is for a long-term period, the impact of inflation and the client's lifetime cash needs must be considered. A sample work sheet for calculating a client's estate settlement costs is provided at the end of this chapter.

CALCULATING ESTATE SETTLEMENT COSTS

Single Clients

In many instances, a current snapshot of the client's estate settlement costs is helpful. This is particularly true when planning a single client's estate. The estate planning process should include determining the cash needs of the client's estate, assuming a current date of death. The possibility of immediate death should be foremost among the potential problems facing the client's estate. The financial services professional should attempt to solve the most immediate problems first, or at least to solve today's problems in conjunction with those of the future. The funding of the estate settlement costs for a premature death can be handled quickly with adequate, properly structured life insurance coverage. In many cases, the life insurance coverage that was initially secured goes a long way toward solving the future problems when combined with other estate reduction techniques.

Example: Suzy Shimmer, a 66-year-old widow, has a substantial estate. In the fact-finding process, the value of her gross estate is estimated at $2,850,000. Suzy inherited a vacation home from her sister Shirley this year. Assume the vacation home caused federal estate tax in her sister's estate and would, if Suzy dies within 2 years, result in a $150,000 credit for the tax on the prior transfer. In addition, Suzy made a taxable gift of $600,000—exactly her unified credit equivalent at that time—8 years ago. Assume the probate fees can be estimated at 3 percent of Suzy's gross estate and that Suzy's state imposes estate taxes equal to the maximum state death tax credit allowable against federal estate taxes. Suzy's estate settlement costs should be estimated assuming a current (1998) date of death to start the estate planning process. The current estate settlement costs are shown on completed work sheet 1. (All work sheets follow the sample work sheet at the end of this chapter.) As the calculations demonstrate, her estate settlement expenses would total $1,224,725, and her heirs would actually receive only 57 percent of her gross estate. Of course, Suzy could solve the current problems by purchasing enough life insurance (preferably with a third-party ownership arrangement) to cover the estate settlement costs.

Estate settlement cost forecasts should take into consideration the effect of several years of inflation. This alerts the estate planner and the client that additional planning must be done to reduce the settlement costs or preserve the estate by securing additional funding for these costs.

Example: Assume the same facts as in the previous example. Suzy would like to know what her estate settlement costs will be in 10 years. Assume that she can live on her social security benefits and the income from her invested assets. In addition, assume a growth rate of 4 percent on her estate. This growth rate seems realistic; since Suzy is not reinvesting the income from her investments and some assets may not be growth oriented, the growth rate should be similar to the long-term inflation rate. If Suzy has no unexpected expenses or economic windfalls, her estate settlement costs in 10 years should match the forecast on completed work sheet 2.

Married Clients

Estate planning for a married couple generally involves balancing several goals. The priority of each goal varies among clients. The goals of married clients include the following:

- adequate income during both spouses' retirement. This goal is best accomplished when all marital assets are retained until the second spouse's death without relinquishment of control.
- deferral of death taxes. Again, using the unlimited marital deduction would permit the retention of the lion's share of marital assets until the second death.
- minimum overall tax burden. This goal is generally satisfied if some assets are not left to the unfettered control of the surviving spouse.
- minimum probate costs. This goal normally can be met with advance planning through joint ownership or a revocable living trust.
- maximizing the inheritances of children or other family heirs. This goal is best satisfied if not all assets are transferred directly into the unfettered control of the surviving spouse. This goal is particularly important if the heirs are children from a previous marriage.

- other specialized goals. Individual clients may have specific goals that are not seen in the typical case. For example, the client may have an heir with special needs who must be provided a specific inheritance.

Other clients may have a charity that they would like to provide for. These goals must be balanced with the others to create an effective plan with the client's available resources.

The first priority in assisting married clients is to design a plan to meet their dispositive goals. Creative planning encompasses satisfying these dispositive goals while minimizing the burden of estate settlement costs. To be capable in this arena, the estate planner must (1) understand a myriad of complex technical rules, (2) be aware of the roles of other professional advisers, and (3) be able to explain the process to clients with varying degrees of acumen. Remember, the clients will take action only if they believe the plan best suits their purposes and is worth the trouble in terms of the ultimate cost savings.

Forecasting with Two Mortality Contingencies

The forecast of the estate settlement costs of a married couple generally involves forecasting two estates and combining the results into one summary of family estate settlement costs. The author's preference is to assume one date of death in the current year and the second death in the foreseeable future—for example, in 10 to 15 years. Then the mortality assumptions are reversed to forecast the estate settlement costs assuming that the other spouse survives.

The initial forecast indicates the problems faced by the estate if the plan is not changed for either order of death for the married couple. The problems exposed by this forecast will include the obvious, such as a large overall settlement cost burden that has not been minimized. In addition, the forecast may indicate that the current asset ownership is not optimal; for example, the less wealthy spouse may not have sufficient assets to fund a credit shelter trust (discussed further in chapter 15) if he or she should be the first to die.

Example: Ted and Tammy Taxavoider have decided to begin estate planning. Ted is 65 years old, and Tammy is 63. Their assets are currently structured as follows:

Individually Owned	
Ted	$1,500,000
Tammy	$ 300,000
Tenants by Entireties	
Ted and Tammy	$1,050,000

Their current plan includes a simple will for each, leaving all assets to the surviving spouse. These wills were executed 12 years ago when their assets were less imposing. To give the Taxavoiders an estate settlement cost forecast, assume that Ted dies today (1998) and that Tammy dies in 15 years. Next, reverse the order of deaths. Assume that administrative charges equal 3 percent of the gross estate and that the property will grow at a rate of 5 percent. The results of these forecasts are illustrated in completed work sheets 3–6. Note that all estate taxes are paid at the second death since the estate taxes are eliminated at the first death by the unlimited marital deduction. The forecasted estate settlement costs are slightly different. The difference results from the fact that the administrative charges are higher at the first death if Ted dies first since his estate is larger. In either forecast, the total settlement costs by the second death exceed $2.5 million, as the summary of results shows. Thus we can solve this problem with a survivorship (second-to-die) policy covering the Taxavoiders with a face amount of approximately $2.5 million placed in an irrevocable life insurance trust.

Summary of Results

Ted Dies First

First-Death Expenses
Administrative expenses $60,750

Second-Death Expenses
Administrative expenses $173,960
Federal estate tax $1,922,817
State death tax $465,763

Totals
Administrative expenses $234,710
Federal estate tax $1,922,817
State death tax $465,763

Tammy Dies First

First-Death Expenses
Administrative expenses $24,750

Second-Death Expenses
Administrative expenses $176,205
Federal estate tax $1,954,034
State death tax $474,474

Totals
Administrative expenses $200,955
Federal estate tax $1,954,034
State death tax $474,474

Comparing Plan Alternatives

Estate planning for married couples generally involves a discussion of the proper use of the estate tax marital deduction. The deduction is unlimited for any qualifying property left to the surviving spouse. The technical rules for the marital deduction are discussed in a later chapter. Leaving all property to the surviving spouse maximizes the marital deduction and defers estate taxes until the second death, as seen in the previous example. The maximum marital transfer also gives the surviving spouse the greatest flexibility and access to the funds. As stated before, this is a goal for many married couples.

Unfortunately, the maximum estate tax reduction occurs if the married couple does not maximize the marital deduction at the first death. Assets passed in a manner avoiding the marital deduction are sheltered by the applicable credit amount, covering up to $625,000 (in 1998) of transferred wealth. If each spouse uses the credit fully, a married couple can pass up to $1.25 million (in 1998 and up to $2 million after 2005) free of estate taxes. When the marital deduction is used in conjunction with the applicable credit amount, it still results in a deferral of all estate taxes until the second death. However, total family taxes will be lower.

The tradeoff for the tax savings is reduced flexibility and access of the surviving spouse to the wealth transferred under the credit shelter trust. This marital deduction-applicable credit amount plan is known as an *optimal marital deduction*.

Let's look at a demonstration of this plan in our example with the Taxavoiders. We have already seen the devastating effect of estate settlement costs at the second death. Suppose instead we forecast the results with a new assumption—that each spouse executes an optimal marital formula will. Looking at the forecast for Ted dying now and Tammy 15 years hence, we find the results on work sheets 7–8 to be strikingly improved. Over $700,000 more ultimately ends up in the hands of heirs at the second death.

However, looking at the forecast if Tammy dies first (work sheets 9 and 10) demonstrates a flaw in the Taxavoiders' asset structure that must be changed to get the maximum savings from the proposed optimal marital formula; that is, Tammy does not currently have enough assets in her individual ownership to use the full $625,000 (in 1998) applicable exclusion amount. Thus, some of her applicable credit amount is wasted if she dies first. (With the increase in the applicable credit amount as illustrated in table 1-3, it will become increasingly important to make sure that each spouse has enough to use the growing credit, regardless of the order of deaths.) The family ultimately gets $376,794 less (when compared to the alternative that Ted dies first) due to the failure to use all of the available credit at Tammy's death. Of course, we would generally recommend the transfer of sufficient assets to Tammy as part of the plan. However, this important fact might have been missed if we failed to forecast the estates with either spouse dying first.

FINAL NOTE

A thorough understanding of the technical rules that affect the estate planning process is necessary to forecast estate settlement costs for clients. The rules to be a complete discussion of all technical rules that might apply. Many are discussed in great detail in subsequent chapters. The purposes of this chapter are to demonstrate how to forecast estate settlement costs and to discuss the components that must be considered. It represents a good start on the road to understanding the process of estate settlement cost forecasting.

Most estate forecasting is actually done on one of the several computer software products available to perform this task more efficiently. However, the financial services professional must understand the underlying calculations to ensure that the data entered into the computer are correct. More important, the financial services professional must understand the calculations to be able to explain the forecast to clients and convince them to take action. Readers should review the examples and the completed work sheets in this chapter until they are confident that they could achieve the same results.

Work sheets are on pages 27–37.

ESTATE SETTLEMENT COST WORK SHEET

Name of Client _____
Date of Death _____

(1)		Gross estate	_____
(2)	*minus*	Funeral and administrative expenses estimated as _____% of (probate) (gross) estate	(_____)
(3)	*minus*	Debts and taxes	(_____)
(4)	*minus*	Losses	(_____)
(5)	*equals*	Adjusted gross estate	_____
(6)	*minus*	Marital deduction	(_____)
(7)	*minus*	Charitable deduction	(_____)
(8)	*equals*	Taxable estate	_____
(9)	*plus*	Adjusted taxable gifts (taxable portion of post-1976 lifetime taxable transfers not included in gross estate)	_____
(10)	*equals*	Tentative tax base (total of taxable estate and adjusted taxable gifts)	_____
(11)	*compute*	Tentative tax (from table 1-4)	_____
(12)	*minus*	Gift taxes payable on post-1976 gifts	(_____)
(13)	*equals*	Estate tax payable before credits	_____
(14)	*minus*	Tax credits	
		(a) Applicable credit amount	(_____)
		(b) Allowable state death tax credit	(_____)
		(c) Credit for foreign death taxes	(_____)
		(d) Credit for tax on prior transfers	(_____)
(15)	*equals*	Net federal estate tax payable	_____
(16)	*plus*	Sum of lines 2, 3, and 4	_____
(17)	*plus*	State death taxes paid	_____
(18)	*equals*	Total estate settlement costs	_____
(19)		Net passing to heirs (line 1 minus line 18)	_____

ESTATE SETTLEMENT COST WORK SHEET 1

Name of Client   *Suzy Shimmer*
Date of Death   *Today's date*

(1)		Gross estate	$2,850,000
(2) *minus*		Funeral and administrative expenses estimated as __3__ % of ~~(probate)~~ (gross) estate	(85,500)
(3) *minus*		Debts and taxes	(-0-)
(4) *minus*		Losses	(-0-)
(5) *equals*		Adjusted gross estate	2,764,500
(6) *minus*		Marital deduction	(-0-)
(7) *minus*		Charitable deduction	(-0-)
(8) *equals*		Taxable estate	2,764,500
(9) *plus*		Adjusted taxable gifts (taxable portion of post-1976 lifetime taxable transfers not included in gross estate)	600,000
(10) *equals*		Tentative tax base (total of taxable estate and adjusted taxable gifts)	3,364,500
(11) *compute*		Tentative tax (from table 1-4)	1,491,275
(12) *minus*		Gift taxes payable on post-1976 gifts	(-0-)
(13) *equals*		Estate tax payable before credits	1,491,275
(14) *minus*		Tax credits	
	(a)	Applicable credit amount	(202,050)
	(b)	Allowable state death tax credit	(161,276)
	(c)	Credit for foreign death taxes	(-0-)
	(d)	Credit for tax on prior transfers	(150,000)
(15) *equals*		Net federal estate tax payable	977,949
(16) *plus*		Sum of lines 2, 3, and 4	85,500
(17) *plus*		State death taxes paid	161,276
(18) *equals*		Total estate settlement costs	1,224,725
(19)		Net passing to heirs (line 1 minus line 18)	1,625,275

ESTATE SETTLEMENT COST WORK SHEET 2

Name of Client   *Suzy Shimmer*
Date of Death   *10 years in the future*

(1)		Gross estate	$4,218,696
(2) *minus*		Funeral and administrative expenses estimated as _3_ % of ~~(probate)~~ (gross) estate	(126,561)
(3) *minus*		Debts and taxes	(-0-)
(4) *minus*		Losses	(-0-)
(5) *equals*		Adjusted gross estate	4,092,135
(6) *minus*		Marital deduction	(-0-)
(7) *minus*		Charitable deduction	(-0-)
(8) *equals*		Taxable estate	4,092,135
(9) *plus*		Adjusted taxable gifts (taxable portion of post-1976 lifetime taxable transfers not included in gross estate)	600,000
(10) *equals*		Tentative tax base (total of taxable estate and adjusted taxable gifts)	4,692,135
(11) *compute*		Tentative tax (from table 1-4)	2,221,474
(12) *minus*		Gift taxes payable on post-1976 gifts	(-0-)
(13) *equals*		Estate tax payable before credits	2,221,474
(14) *minus*		Tax credits	
	(a)	Applicable credit amount	(345,800)
	(b)	Allowable state death tax credit	(289,982)
	(c)	Credit for foreign death taxes	(-0-)
	(d)	Credit for tax on prior transfers	(-0-)
(15) *equals*		Net federal estate tax payable	1,585,692
(16) *plus*		Sum of lines 2, 3, and 4	126,561
(17) *plus*		State death taxes paid	289,982
(18) *equals*		Total estate settlement costs	2,002,235
(19)		Net passing to heirs (line 1 minus line 18)	2,216,461

ESTATE SETTLEMENT COST WORK SHEET 3

Name of Client   *Ted Taxavoider*
Date of Death   *Today's date*

(1)		Gross estate	$2,025,000
(2) *minus*		Funeral and administrative expenses estimated as _3_ % of (probate) (gross) estate	(60,750)
(3) *minus*		Debts and taxes	(-0-)
(4) *minus*		Losses	(-0-)
(5) *equals*		Adjusted gross estate	1,964,250
(6) *minus*		Marital deduction	(1,964,250)
(7) *minus*		Charitable deduction	(-0-)
(8) *equals*		Taxable estate	-0-
(9) *plus*		Adjusted taxable gifts (taxable portion of post-1976 lifetime taxable transfers not included in gross estate)	-0-
(10) *equals*		Tentative tax base (total of taxable estate and adjusted taxable gifts)	-0-
(11) *compute*		Tentative tax (from table 1-4)	-0-
(12) *minus*		Gift taxes payable on post-1976 gifts	(-0-)
(13) *equals*		Estate tax payable before credits	-0-
(14) *minus*		Tax credits	
	(a)	Applicable credit amount	(-0-)
	(b)	Allowable state death tax credit	(-0-)
	(c)	Credit for foreign death taxes	(-0-)
	(d)	Credit for tax on prior transfers	(-0-)
(15) *equals*		Net federal estate tax payable	-0-
(16) *plus*		Sum of lines 2, 3, and 4	60,750
(17) *plus*		State death taxes paid	-0-
(18) *equals*		Total estate settlement costs	60,750
(19)		Net passing to heirs (line 1 minus line 18)	1,964,250

ESTATE SETTLEMENT COST WORK SHEET 4

Name of Client   *Tammy Taxavoider*
Date of Death   *15 years from today*

(1)		Gross estate	$5,798,650
(2) *minus*		Funeral and administrative expenses estimated as _3_ % of (probate) (gross) estate	(173,960)
(3) *minus*		Debts and taxes	(-0-)
(4) *minus*		Losses	(-0-)
(5) *equals*		Adjusted gross estate	5,624,690
(6) *minus*		Marital deduction	(-0-)
(7) *minus*		Charitable deduction	(-0-)
(8) *equals*		Taxable estate	5,624,690
(9) *plus*		Adjusted taxable gifts (taxable portion of post-1976 lifetime taxable transfers not included in gross estate)	-0-
(10) *equals*		Tentative tax base (total of taxable estate and adjusted taxable gifts)	5,624,690
(11) *compute*		Tentative tax (from table 1-4)	2,734,380
(12) *minus*		Gift taxes payable on post-1976 gifts	(-0-)
(13) *equals*		Estate tax payable before credits	2,734,380
(14) *minus*		Tax credits	
	(a)	Applicable credit amount	(345,800)
	(b)	Allowable state death tax credit	(465,763)
	(c)	Credit for foreign death taxes	(-0-)
	(d)	Credit for tax on prior transfers	(-0-)
(15) *equals*		Net federal estate tax payable	1,922,817
(16) *plus*		Sum of lines 2, 3, and 4	173,960
(17) *plus*		State death taxes paid	465,763
(18) *equals*		Total estate settlement costs	2,562,540
(19)		Net passing to heirs (line 1 minus line 18)	3,236,110

ESTATE SETTLEMENT COST WORK SHEET 5

Name of Client   *Tammy Taxavoider*
Date of Death   *Today's date*

(1)	Gross estate	$825,000
(2) *minus*	Funeral and administrative expenses estimated as __3__ % of ~~(probate)~~ (gross) estate	(24,750)
(3) *minus*	Debts and taxes	(-0-)
(4) *minus*	Losses	(-0-)
(5) *equals*	Adjusted gross estate	800,250
(6) *minus*	Marital deduction	(800,250)
(7) *minus*	Charitable deduction	(-0-)
(8) *equals*	Taxable estate	-0-
(9) *plus*	Adjusted taxable gifts (taxable portion of post-1976 lifetime taxable transfers not included in gross estate)	-0-
(10) *equals*	Tentative tax base (total of taxable estate and adjusted taxable gifts)	-0-
(11) *compute*	Tentative tax (from table 1-4)	-0-
(12) *minus*	Gift taxes payable on post-1976 gifts	(-0-)
(13) *equals*	Estate tax payable before credits	-0-
(14) *minus*	Tax credits	
	(a) Applicable credit amount	(-0-)
	(b) Allowable state death tax credit	(-0-)
	(c) Credit for foreign death taxes	(-0-)
	(d) Credit for tax on prior transfers	(-0-)
(15) *equals*	Net federal estate tax payable	-0-
(16) *plus*	Sum of lines 2, 3, and 4	24,750
(17) *plus*	State death taxes paid	-0-
(18) *equals*	Total estate settlement costs	24,750
(19)	Net passing to heirs (line 1 minus line 18)	800,250

Chapter 1 Forecasting Estate Settlement Costs

ESTATE SETTLEMENT COST WORK SHEET 6

Name of Client   *Ted Taxavoider*
Date of Death   *15 years from today*

(1)		Gross estate	$5,873,492
(2) *minus*		Funeral and administrative expenses estimated as __3__ % of ~~(probate)~~ (gross) estate	(176,205)
(3) *minus*		Debts and taxes	(-0-)
(4) *minus*		Losses	(-0-)
(5) *equals*		Adjusted gross estate	5,697,287
(6) *minus*		Marital deduction	(-0-)
(7) *minus*		Charitable deduction	(-0-)
(8) *equals*		Taxable estate	5,697,287
(9) *plus*		Adjusted taxable gifts (taxable portion of post-1976 lifetime taxable transfers not included in gross estate)	-0-
(10) *equals*		Tentative tax base (total of taxable estate and adjusted taxable gifts)	5,697,287
(11) *compute*		Tentative tax (from table 1-4)	2,774,308
(12) *minus*		Gift taxes payable on post-1976 gifts	(-0-)
(13) *equals*		Estate tax payable before credits	2,774,308
(14) *minus*		Tax credits	
	(a)	Applicable credit amount	(345,800)
	(b)	Allowable state death tax credit	(474,474)
	(c)	Credit for foreign death taxes	(-0-)
	(d)	Credit for tax on prior transfers	(-0-)
(15) *equals*		Net federal estate tax payable	1,954,034
(16) *plus*		Sum of lines 2, 3, and 4	176,205
(17) *plus*		State death taxes paid	474,474
(18) *equals*		Total estate settlement costs	2,604,713
(19)		Net passing to heirs (line 1 minus line 18)	3,268,778

ESTATE SETTLEMENT COST WORK SHEET 7

Name of Client _Ted Taxavoider_
Date of Death _Today's date_

(1)		Gross estate	$2,025,000
(2) *minus*		Funeral and administrative expenses estimated as _3_ % of ~~(probate)~~ (gross) estate	(60,750)
(3) *minus*		Debts and taxes	(-0-)
(4) *minus*		Losses	(-0-)
(5) *equals*		Adjusted gross estate	1,964,250
(6) *minus*		Marital deduction	(1,339,250)
(7) *minus*		Charitable deduction	(-0-)
(8) *equals*		Taxable estate	625,000
(9) *plus*		Adjusted taxable gifts (taxable portion of post-1976 lifetime taxable transfers not included in gross estate)	-0-
(10) *equals*		Tentative tax base (total of taxable estate and adjusted taxable gifts)	625,000
(11) *compute*		Tentative tax (from table 1-4)	202,050
(12) *minus*		Gift taxes payable on post-1976 gifts	(-0-)
(13) *equals*		Estate tax payable before credits	202,050
(14) *minus*		Tax credits	
	(a)	Applicable credit amount	(202,050)
	(b)	Allowable state death tax credit	(-0-)
	(c)	Credit for foreign death taxes	(-0-)
	(d)	Credit for tax on prior transfers	(-0-)
(15) *equals*		Net federal estate tax payable	-0-
(16) *plus*		Sum of lines 2, 3, and 4	60,750
(17) *plus*		State death taxes paid	-0-
(18) *equals*		Total estate settlement costs	60,750
(19)		Net passing to heirs (line 1 minus line 18)	1,964,250

Chapter 1 Forecasting Estate Settlement Costs 35

ESTATE SETTLEMENT COST WORK SHEET 8

Name of Client _Tammy Taxavoider_
Date of Death _15 years from today_

(1)		Gross estate	$4,499,320
(2) *minus*		Funeral and administrative expenses estimated as __3__ % of ~~(probate)~~ (gross) estate	(134,980)
(3) *minus*		Debts and taxes	(-0-)
(4) *minus*		Losses	(-0-)
(5) *equals*		Adjusted gross estate	4,364,340
(6) *minus*		Marital deduction	(-0-)
(7) *minus*		Charitable deduction	(-0-)
(8) *equals*		Taxable estate	4,364,340
(9) *plus*		Adjusted taxable gifts (taxable portion of post-1976 lifetime taxable transfers not included in gross estate)	-0-
(10) *equals*		Tentative tax base (total of taxable estate and adjusted taxable gifts)	4,364,340
(11) *compute*		Tentative tax (from table 1-4)	2,041,187
(12) *minus*		Gift taxes payable on post-1976 gifts	(-0-)
(13) *equals*		Estate tax payable before credits	2,041,187
(14) *minus*		Tax credits	
	(a)	Applicable credit amount	(345,800)
	(b)	Allowable state death tax credit	(320,406)
	(c)	Credit for foreign death taxes	(-0-)
	(d)	Credit for tax on prior transfers	(-0-)
(15) *equals*		Net federal estate tax payable	1,374,981
(16) *plus*		Sum of lines 2, 3, and 4	134,980
(17) *plus*		State death taxes paid	320,406
(18) *equals*		Total estate settlement costs	1,830,367
(19)		Net passing to heirs (line 1 minus line 18)	2,668,953
			+ 1,299,330 *

*Principal of credit shelter trust reflecting 15 years' growth

ESTATE SETTLEMENT COST WORK SHEET 9

Name of Client *Tammy Taxavoider*
Date of Death *Today's date*

(1)		Gross estate	$825,000
(2) *minus*		Funeral and administrative expenses estimated as __3__ % of (probate) (gross) estate	(24,750)
(3) *minus*		Debts and taxes	(-0-)
(4) *minus*		Losses	(-0-)
(5) *equals*		Adjusted gross estate	800,250
(6) *minus*		Marital deduction	(525,000)
(7) *minus*		Charitable deduction	(-0-)
(8) *equals*		Taxable estate	275,250
(9) *plus*		Adjusted taxable gifts (taxable portion of post-1976 lifetime taxable transfers not included in gross estate)	-0-
(10) *equals*		Tentative tax base (total of taxable estate and adjusted taxable gifts)	275,250
(11) *compute*		Tentative tax (from table 1-4)	79,385
(12) *minus*		Gift taxes payable on post-1976 gifts	(-0-)
(13) *equals*		Estate tax payable before credits	79,385
(14) *minus*		Tax credits	
	(a)	Applicable credit amount	(79,385)
	(b)	Allowable state death tax credit	(-0-)
	(c)	Credit for foreign death taxes	(-0-)
	(d)	Credit for tax on prior transfers	(-0-)
(15) *equals*		Net federal estate tax payable	-0-
(16) *plus*		Sum of lines 2, 3, and 4	24,750
(17) *plus*		State death taxes paid	-0-
(18) *equals*		Total estate settlement costs	24,750
(19)		Net passing to heirs (line 1 minus line 18)	800,250

Chapter 1 Forecasting Estate Settlement Costs

ESTATE SETTLEMENT COST WORK SHEET 10

Name of Client   *Ted Taxavoider*
Date of Death   *15 years from today*

(1)		Gross estate	$5,301,267
(2) *minus*		Funeral and administrative expenses estimated as 3 % of (probate) (gross) estate	(159,038)
(3) *minus*		Debts and taxes	(-0-)
(4) *minus*		Losses	(-0-)
(5) *equals*		Adjusted gross estate	5,142,229
(6) *minus*		Marital deduction	(-0-)
(7) *minus*		Charitable deduction	(-0-)
(8) *equals*		Taxable estate	5,142,229
(9) *plus*		Adjusted taxable gifts (taxable portion of post-1976 lifetime taxable transfers not included in gross estate)	-0-
(10) *equals*		Tentative tax base (total of taxable estate and adjusted taxable gifts)	5,142,229
(11) *compute*		Tentative tax (from table 1-4)	2,469,026
(12) *minus*		Gift taxes payable on post-1976 gifts	(-0-)
(13) *equals*		Estate tax payable before credits	2,469,026
(14) *minus*		Tax credits	
	(a)	Applicable credit amount	(345,800)
	(b)	Allowable state death tax credit	(407,867)
	(c)	Credit for foreign death taxes	(-0-)
	(d)	Credit for tax on prior transfers	(-0-)
(15) *equals*		Net federal estate tax payable	1,715,359
(16) *plus*		Sum of lines 2, 3, and 4	159,038
(17) *plus*		State death taxes paid	407,867
(18) *equals*		Total estate settlement costs	2,282,264
(19)		Net passing to heirs (line 1 minus line 18)	3,019,003
			+ 572,225 *

* *From credit shelter trust reflecting 15 years' growth*

2

Life Insurance in Estate Planning

Chapter Outline

LIFE INSURANCE SERVES TWO PURPOSES 40
    Estate Enhancement Purposes 40
    Estate Liquidity Purposes 41
LIFE INSURANCE PRODUCTS 42
    Single Life Coverage 43
    Multiple Life Policies 44
TRANSFER TAX IMPLICATIONS OF LIFE INSURANCE 45
FEDERAL ESTATE TAXATION OF LIFE INSURANCE 45
    Life Insurance Payable to an Estate 45
    Possession of Incidents of Ownership 47
    Transfers of Policies within 3 Years of Death 50
    Life Insurance and the Federal Estate Tax Marital Deduction 52
    Value of the Policy Includible in the Gross Estate 54
    Responsibility for Payment of Federal Estate Taxes by Life Insurance Beneficiaries 56
FEDERAL GENERATION-SKIPPING TRANSFER TAX 56
    Direct-Skip Transfers 57
    Taxable Distributions and Terminations 57
    Predeceased Parent Exception 58
FEDERAL GIFT TAXATION 58
    Valuation of Life Policies 58
    The Problem of Inadvertent Gifts 59
OUTRIGHT GIFTS OF LIFE INSURANCE POLICIES 60
PRACTICAL USES FOR LIFE INSURANCE IN ESTATE PLANNING 62
    Gifts of Policies to Trusts 62
    Grandparent-Grandchild Trusts 63
    Estate Liquidity 64
    Equity of Inheritance 67
    Nonworking Spouse Insurance 68
    Second-to-Die Policy 69

Life insurance planning is an essential component of the estate planning process for wealthy individuals. For individuals of modest wealth, life insurance coverage often represents the most significant asset that they can leave to beloved heirs. Because of the relative importance of life insurance in an individual's estate plan, it is critical that life insurance planning be performed appropriately.

Several unique aspects of life insurance make the product a vital asset in the estate planning process. For example, some favorable tax rules apply only to life insurance; life insurance enjoys a significant appreciation in value upon the death of the insured; life insurance is self-completing and provides its benefits when estate taxes and other settlement costs have to be paid and the income or other services of the insured must be replaced. Furthermore, life insurance products offer a substantial degree of flexibility in the estate planning process.

In this chapter, we will first cover the basic purposes of life insurance in estate planning. We will then explain the general tax implications of life insurance transactions. Finally, we will review some practical planning applications for life insurance in the estate planning process. Chapter 3 will discuss the life insurance trust, generally regarded currently as the single most powerful estate planning technique.

LIFE INSURANCE SERVES TWO PURPOSES

The goal of life insurance in the estate plan depends on many factors specific to the client. However, the goals for life insurance in general can be divided into two categories: Life insurance can serve either as an estate enhancement or as an estate liquidity device. The goals of a specific client for his or her life insurance planning depend on his or her age, family circumstances, and financial status.

Estate Enhancement Purposes

A vast majority of individuals have the perception that their accumulated estate will not be as substantial as they would like at the time of their death. In many cases, a decedent's estate will not be sufficient to provide for the blasic needs of his or her heirs. This is particularly true for (1) young clients, (2) clients with family members dependent on their income, and/or (3) clients with small to moderate-sized estates.

These clients generally have estate enhancement as the primary goal for their life insurance coverage since they are either too young or have otherwise failed to accumulate sufficient wealth to provide for their heirs. Furthermore, these clients might have their peak earning years in front of them. The basic support needs of their family, such as educational, medical, and retirement savings programs, depend on this income.

It is essential for these clients to investigate their life insurance coverage needs and secure sufficient insurance to enhance their estates to a size that is, at the very least, adequate to handle their dependent family members' basic needs. Since their death will cause the loss of income otherwise available to meet those basic needs, life insurance is the perfect estate enhancement device to replace the financial loss created by premature death.

Estate Liquidity Purposes

For older clients or clients with large estates, estate liquidity planning is the primary goal of life insurance coverage. Their children's support and educational expense needs are usually a thing of the past. In addition, these older clients are nearing the end of their income-producing years, and they should, presumably, have less income to replace. If they have accumulated enough wealth or if they have an adequate retirement plan, these clients' needs for estate enhancement from life insurance should have diminished in importance relative to their estate liquidity needs.

Probate Expense

Although clients with substantial accumulated wealth should have sufficient assets in their estate to provide for the basic needs of their heirs, life insurance planning for such individuals remains critical. Estate settlement costs generally increase with the size of the estate. The cost for professionals, such as executors, attorneys, accountants, and appraisers, to settle an estate is often based on a percentage of the total size of the probate estate. In some cases, settlement costs are incurred even for nonprobate assets. Generally speaking, the larger the estate, the greater the complexity and the need for costly professional help. One advantage of life insurance is that it avoids probate if it is paid to a named beneficiary.

Death Taxes

Federal estate taxes, generation-skipping taxes, and state death taxes also increase with the size of the estate. The federal estate tax and state death taxes in many states are based on a progressive rate schedule. Larger estates are subject to higher transfer-tax brackets. For affluent clients, the shelter offered by the federal estate tax marital deduction and applicable credit amount is inadequate to protect their estates from substantial estate taxes. In many cases, although the marital deduction will shelter all of the estate from taxes at the death of the first spouse, the death of the surviving spouse will often create a substantial tax problem for the family.

State death taxes often follow a different set of rules. In some states a significant first death tax has to be paid to the state even if substantially all property is left to the surviving spouse.

Liquidity Needs

Wealthy clients often face an additional problem. Frequently, their accumulated wealth contains specific assets that are not liquid. For example, wealthy individuals often own closely held businesses that may be unmarketable to outsiders. Wealthy individuals are also likely to own expensive personal property, such as artwork, home furnishings, and automobiles. Death taxes and other estate settlement costs are based on the full value of such assets owned by the estate. The value of these assets may be high for the purposes of the federal estate tax and state death taxes, and substantial death costs may be incurred. Moreover, the assets may be unmarketable, or very difficult to sell, in the finite time period required to settle the estate. Even if the sale of such assets is feasible, the heirs often want to continue to hold their family assets. However, the heirs must pay estate settlement costs in cash relatively soon after the decedent's death. The federal estate tax and most state death taxes are due within 9 months of the date of death.

The problems faced by wealthy individuals' estates and heirs can often be mitigated by life insurance. For these individuals, the goal of life insurance is estate liquidity or wealth replacement. The wealthy client can purchase life insurance to provide death proceeds equal to the size of the anticipated shrinkage of the estate for death taxes and other settlement costs. In addition, because the life insurance benefits are paid in cash, the estate can be settled immediately. Thus, the nonliquid assets can either be retained by the estate to distribute to family heirs or sold later when an appropriate buyer can be found.

Much of the discussion in this and the next chapter concerns the appropriate design of life insurance for estate liquidity purposes. It is important to arrange life insurance coverage appropriately to solve individuals' estate liquidity problems. An inappropriate life insurance plan can lead to the inefficient use of life insurance as an asset in the estate plan. Improperly designed, life insurance will *add* to the estate's settlement costs.

LIFE INSURANCE PRODUCTS

Competitive forces in recent years have caused the insurance industry to produce many types of life insurance products. This discussion will not attempt to examine the intricacies of every type. Only a general knowledge of each type of product is necessary to understand the uses of the products in the estate plan discussions that follow.

Nevertheless, the services of a competent life underwriter are essential to the estate planning process since the selection of the most appropriate product in a particular estate planning case will maximize the efficiency of the client's entire financial plan. For the purposes of the following discussion, the types of life insurance products are separated into single life policies and multiple life policies.

Single Life Coverage

Term Life

Term life insurance provides coverage for a finite period of time. The specified face amount of the policy will be paid to a designated beneficiary if the insured dies during that time period. If the insured survives the time period, the policy expires and the coverage terminates. The finite time period in term insurance policies is expressed as a number of years—for example, one, 5, or 10. Term insurance generally has a premium that increases with the attained age of the insured. If the coverage needs are longer than the specific term, a renewability provision should be considered. This provision allows the insured to renew without providing new evidence of insurability.

Conversion privileges are often included with term insurance policies. This provision permits the insured to change a term policy for a permanent life policy without giving evidence of insurability. Term insurance is generally appropriate for estate planning uses only if the coverage need is temporary. If the coverage need is anticipated to continue for a substantial period of time, a more permanent life insurance policy or, at the very least, a conversion privilege in the term policy is recommended.

Permanent Life Insurance

I have chosen to arbitrarily categorize many types of life insurance as permanent. The main feature of permanent insurance is that the coverage is designed to exist beyond a fixed term for the entire life of an insured. A distinguishing characteristic of permanent insurance is the existence of a cash value or accumulation build-up within the policy. Permanent coverage can be designed either on a fixed-price premium or flexible-premium basis.

Fixed-price premium life insurance, traditionally called whole life insurance, is life insurance coverage in which a constant guaranteed premium is paid for a specific face amount of coverage. Of course, it is not actually that simple. Many contracts are participating; that is, the contract permits the insured to participate in favorable investment and mortality experience that the insurer might actually realize on that specific class of whole life policies. The participation feature provides for policy dividends that can be used to increase the death benefit or offset future premiums. Thus, participating contracts might not actually require the insured to pay a fixed premium for the remainder of his or her life. Or the dividend performance of such contracts might result in an increasing death benefit over the life of the policy.

In flexible-premium life insurance policies (generally referred to as universal life policies), the insured pays a stipulated premium in the first year of coverage. Afterward, the insured may choose to pay whatever amount of annual premium he or she desires. Since flexible premiums provide for a cash-value accumulation similar to fixed-premium policies, the cash value will either grow or be expended to pay required annual policy charges after the first year. The performance of the policy and the size of premiums actually contributed by the insured after the first policy year will determine the growth (or shrinkage) of the cash value. The actual death benefit of a universal life policy is similarly flexible. The amount of the death benefit paid will depend on the actual premiums contributed by the insured and the policy options selected.

Another type of permanent life insurance policy, variable life insurance, gives the policyowner the ability to select the investment vehicle for the cash value of his or her policy. Presumably, by choosing the investment mix for the cash value of the policy, the insured can be protected from inflation and can participate in the growth of the economy. However, the investment risk for the cash value falls entirely on the insured. Both fixed-premium and flexible-premium variable life insurance products are available.

Multiple Life Policies

Survivorship Life Insurance

Survivorship life insurance (also called second-to-die or last-to-die insurance) is a permanent life insurance policy that provides coverage on the lives of two individuals. The death benefit under the survivorship policy is payable upon the death of the survivor of the two insureds. Although survivorship life insurance is suitable for several purposes, it is generally used to provide coverage for a married couple. This coverage works extremely well under the current estate tax rules that allow an unlimited federal estate tax marital deduction at the first death of a married couple.

As with single life policies, survivorship life insurance coverage can be designed in many fashions. For example, fixed-premium or flexible-premium survivorship coverage is available. In many cases, survivorship policies combine some term insurance element with permanent coverage. The estate tax planning benefits of survivorship coverage will be discussed in greater detail below.

Joint Life

Joint life insurance covers the joint lives of multiple insureds. As opposed to survivorship life insurance, joint life coverage provides its death benefit at the first death of the joint insureds. Thus, joint life is often referred to as first-to-die coverage. Joint life insurance is less widely used than survivorship life insurance, but it has significant estate planning implications for co-owners of a closely held business. Joint life coverage is generally used in a buy-sell agreement in which the first death of two or more co-owners of the business will create the need to fund the purchase price required under the buy-sell agreement. The premium required for a joint life coverage is attractive compared to the premiums for separate individual policies on each of the co-owners.

TRANSFER TAX IMPLICATIONS OF LIFE INSURANCE

The financial services professional involved in estate planning must thoroughly understand the estate, gift, and generation-skipping transfer tax implications of life insurance. Often, life insurance planning is specifically driven by the need to provide estate enhancement or liquidity on the most cost-effective basis. Unique tax advantages usually exempt life insurance policy cash-value build-up and death benefits from income taxes. Thus, the potential *transfer* taxes become the most significant costs in life insurance planning.

FEDERAL ESTATE TAXATION OF LIFE INSURANCE

The first step in the estate planning process is to estimate the size of the estate owner's gross estate. Secs. 2033-2046 of the Internal Revenue Code tell us what property interests must be included as part of this gross estate for purposes of imposing the federal estate tax. Frequently, life insurance is the single largest asset or group of assets in the gross estate. Including life insurance can often mean the difference between a federal estate tax liability and no tax liability. For this reason, we should look at the factors that determine when life insurance is included in the decedent-insured's gross estate for federal estate tax purposes:

- Life insurance proceeds payable to the executor (that is, to or for the benefit of an insured's estate) are includible in the estate, regardless of who owned the contract or who paid the premiums.
- A policy is included in the estate of an insured if he or she possessed an "incident of ownership" in the policy at the time of his or her death.
- Because of the unique rules of Sec. 2035, life insurance is included in the gross estate of an insured who transferred incidents of ownership in the policy by *gift* within 3 years of his or her death.

Life Insurance Payable to an Estate

In general, life insurance should not be payable to a decedent's estate. There are many reasons in addition to avoiding federal estate taxation why estate planners seldom recommend such a beneficiary designation. These reasons include the following:

- Insurance payable to a decedent's estate subjects the proceeds to the claims of creditors.
- Insurance payable to a decedent's estate subjects the proceeds to costs of probate administration, such as executor's fees, but provides no corresponding advantages.
- In many states, life insurance proceeds, otherwise exempt from state death taxes (either fully or partially) if payable to a named beneficiary,

become subject to such taxes if they are payable to the decedent-insured's estate.

In some instances, death benefits payable to named beneficiaries are included in an insured's gross estate if the proceeds can or must be used to pay settlement costs. The regulations under Sec. 2042 make it clear that proceeds payable to a named beneficiary (such as a trustee) are includible in the insured's gross estate if the beneficiary has a legal obligation to use the proceeds to pay the settlement costs for the estate. For example, life insurance that is used as collateral for a loan is payable to the estate to the extent that the loan is a debt of the estate.

Failure to make an effective beneficiary designation could also cause the proceeds to be payable to the estate.

Example: Mr. Jones is the designated beneficiary of his wife's life insurance policy. Mr. Jones murders his wife and because of the "slayer's statute" under state law, he cannot collect the proceeds. If no contingent beneficiary is named, the proceeds are returned to the estate, and they are subject to probate expenses and inclusion in Mrs. Jones's gross estate for federal estate tax purposes.

Although Sec. 2042(1) includes policies payable to the executor, this definition should not be interpreted strictly. The spirit of the law indicates that inclusion of the proceeds in the insured's gross estate results when proceeds are paid in a manner to benefit the estate. In contrast, inclusion should not occur under this provision when the proceeds are not intended to benefit the insured's estate.

The case of *Friedberg v. Commissioner,* T.C. Memo. 1992-310, demonstrates that the statute need not be taken literally. In this instance, the designated beneficiary was also, coincidentally, named executor of the insured's estate. Since the policy was payable to the beneficiary in an individual capacity and was not intended to be available to the estate, the court held that the proceeds were not includible.

It should be noted that life insurance is includible in the gross estate, as discussed below, if the insured held any incidents of ownership at the time of death, whether or not such policy is payable to the estate. Thus, it may not cause any harm from an estate tax standpoint if the policy proceeds are paid to the estate.

However, in instances where the insured did *not* own incidents of ownership, it is critical to avoid having the proceeds deemed payable to the estate. In such instances, the planning dilemma is finding a method to permit the proceeds to enhance estate liquidity while avoiding inclusion in the insured's gross estate. Chapter 3 will explain how an irrevocable life insurance trust can be used to meet this goal.

Life Insurance Payable to a Decedent's Testamentary Trust

In addition to problems created by making life insurance payable to a decedent's estate, there are also complications if life insurance is owned by a third party and made payable to a decedent's testamentary trust. The difference between a testamentary trust and a living trust is that a testamentary trust is created in a decedent's will and takes effect only at death.

Depending on the trust law of the particular state, life insurance payable to a decedent's testamentary trust might actually be considered payable to his or her estate. This could cause inclusion of the proceeds in the gross estate and might subject the proceeds to the expenses of probate and the claims of creditors. The result will vary from state to state, and financial services professionals must consult local laws.

Possession of Incidents of Ownership

When insurance proceeds are paid to a named beneficiary other than the insured's estate, incidents of ownership in the policy at the time of death are the key criteria for inclusion. An incident of ownership is broadly defined as any right to the economic benefits of the policy. The regulations provide that incidents of ownership include (but are not limited to) the power to

- change the beneficiary
- assign the policy
- borrow on the policy
- surrender the policy
- exercise any of the other essential contract rights or privileges

Like any other property, the insurance policy is an asset that may be freely assigned by a policyowner in a gift or sale. Thus, it is possible for the policyowner to transfer all right, title, and interest to any other individual or entity. It is also possible to transfer limited interests to others while retaining some of the privileges and rights in the policy. But to remove the proceeds from the ambit of the federal estate tax, the insured must divest himself or herself of all significant rights and privileges under the contract.

Example: James White, a widower, transferred ownership of three whole life insurance policies to his daughter, Mitzi, 6 years ago. However, it was clear at the time of the transfer that James still had the right to borrow against the substantial cash values of the policies and the right to change the beneficiary by written notification to the insurance company's home office. Although James effectively transferred title in the policies to his daughter, the policies' proceeds will still be included in his gross estate for federal estate tax purposes since he retained the right to borrow against these policies and to change the beneficiary. In order to have successfully removed the proceeds from the gross estate, James must not have reserved the rights to borrow and to change the beneficiary.

The issue of incidents of ownership has been involved in a great deal of litigation over the years. This is because the facts and circumstances of a particular situation are often unusual and cannot be easily categorized into one of the traditional ownership rights. It is clear that a directly held incident will cause inclusion, even if the incident is exercisable only with another's consent. In many cases, inclusion will occur even if the insured is unaware that such incidents are held or is incapable of exercising the incidents. The discussion below is not intended to be an exhaustive survey of all possible Sec. 2042(2) scenarios, but it will offer some guidance in using life insurance in many estate and business planning situations. The scenarios that follow examine some hidden incidents of ownership after assuming that the client has effectively transferred all *traditional* ownership rights to a life insurance policy.

Incidents Held by the Insured in a Fiduciary Capacity

The regulations indicate that the IRS's position is that an incident of ownership that can be exercised by the insured as trustee will cause the policy to be included in the insured's gross estate. This rule applies even if the insured is *not* a beneficiary of the trust. This is a unique treatment of life insurance as an asset of the estate. In many other circumstances, the trustee is not deemed to control an asset (other than life insurance) personally if ownership rights can be exercised only in favor of the beneficiaries.

It seems clear, therefore, that the insured should not gift a policy on his or her life to a trust in which the insured will be trustee even if the trust is irrevocable and the insured cannot benefit. In addition, the insured should not have power to become trustee in the future. But there have been mixed results in cases and rulings on this subject. For example, the IRS recently issued a private ruling in which incidents were not attributed to a trustee who obtained ownership of a policy on her life as trustee of her husband's testamentary trust. The husband had previously owned the policy, and the trustee was prohibited from exercising incidents of ownership in the policy. However, the facts of this ruling are unusual, and the prudent approach is to avoid having the insured as trustee (or potentially a successor trustee) of a trust that might acquire a policy on the insured's life.

Right or Option to Repurchase Policy

Several recent rulings have addressed the issue of whether the retention of the right or option to repurchase a policy will cause its inclusion in the insured's gross estate. The cases have involved different facts and circumstances. In one, the insured retained the right to repurchase the policy after making a gift of the policy to a third party. In others, business life insurance used to fund buy-sell agreements was subject to contingent repurchase options.

The IRS's position in these rulings is that an unrestricted right or option to repurchase the policy is an incident of ownership that creates inclusion under Sec. 2042(2). However, an option to repurchase the policy subject to a contingency beyond the insured's control does not create an incident of ownership unless the contingency has occurred and the option is available at the time of the insured's death.

Giving the insured the right to repurchase or reacquire a policy is clearly a planning mistake if the policy was transferred to avoid inclusion in the insured's estate. A better approach might be to remain silent about this matter. Presumably the insured could, at a later date, reach an agreement with the third-party owner to repurchase the policy for fair market value if the insured desires. The insured would then own incidents of ownership but only *if* the repurchase occurs.

Incidents Attributed to Business Owner

The regulations provide that incidents of ownership held by a corporation will, in some circumstances, be attributed to a majority shareholder. Thus, corporate-owned life insurance may cause estate tax problems for an insured shareholder. The incidents are attributed if (1) the corporation owns life insurance on the life of a controlling (greater than 50 percent voting power) shareholder, and (2) the benefits are *not* payable to, or for the benefit of, the corporation.

Although the issue of attributed incidents is confusing, it must be considered whenever business life insurance is contemplated. The life insurance owned by a corporation on the life of a majority shareholder could have a negative impact on the insured-shareholder's estate in either one of two ways. First, the death benefits will be includible in full in the deceased insured majority shareholder's estate if the proceeds are not payable to, or for the benefit of, the corporation. Second, even if the proceeds are payable to the corporation, the regulations indicate that the value of the stock held by the deceased shareholder's estate should be enhanced for estate tax valuation purposes proportionately with the increase in the value of the corporation caused by the receipt of the proceeds.

The regulations offer some guidance as to what is meant by "payable to or for the benefit of the corporation." Life insurance payable to the corporation to fund a corporate need will not cause incidents to be attributed to the insured. Examples of corporate-owned life insurance used to meet corporate needs include the following:

- key person coverage
- funding for stock-redemption agreements
- funding for deferred-compensation plans

Life insurance is also deemed payable for the benefit of the corporation, in some instances, even if it is payable to a third party. For example, life insurance payable to satisfy a business debt will not cause corporate incidents to be attributed to the insured-shareholder. It is not unusual for a creditor to require insurance on a key person when loaning funds to a corporation. Insurance purchased by the corporation on a majority shareholder's life for this purpose will not cause inclusion in the shareholder's estate. However, the value of the stock held by the decedent *will* increase for estate tax purposes to the extent that the corporation's debt is satisfied.

Inclusion should also not occur for life insurance payable to the majority shareholder's named beneficiary under a death-benefit-only (DBO) deferred-compensation plan, provided the plan had been established to meet a legitimate corporate need to compensate the shareholder as a key employee. That is, the life insurance should avoid direct inclusion, but the estate tax value of the corporation should increase since its liability under the DBO plan is satisfied. (Without the insurance funding, the death of the participant in the DBO plan would cause the stock value to drop by the amount owed to the selected beneficiary.)

Finally, the regulations exempt group term life (Sec. 79) insurance from the attributed-incidents rule. Thus, the ability of the corporation to cancel or change the group term policy does not cause incidents to be attributed to the majority shareholder even though the majority shareholder is likely to control corporate decisions.

The IRS has, on occasion, extended the attributed-incidents rule in a troubling manner. In a split-dollar plan, for example, the IRS has taken the position that the corporate-held incidents (such as access to the cash surrender value) will be attributed to the majority shareholder who participates in the split-dollar plan. Although these rulings have been much criticized, the planner should exercise caution in designing a split-dollar plan if the majority shareholder is trying to avoid inclusion of the proceeds in his or her estate. (See chapters 3 and 13 for the use of a life insurance trust to hold the executive's share of a split-dollar plan.)

Another question is "Does the attributed-incidents rule apply to other entities?" In Revenue Ruling 83-147, the IRS answered this question affirmatively with respect to partnerships. Generally, a partnership is treated as an aggregate of its partners. Thus, the partnership's ability to exercise incidents of ownership could be attributed to insured general partners unless the insurance is payable to or for the benefit of the partnership.

Transfers of Policies within 3 Years of Death

Policies are often transferred to others so that they will not be in the decedent-insured's gross estate. Inclusion will still result, however, if the insured dies within 3 years of a gratuitous transfer (Sec. 2035). Under this 3-year rule, life insurance transferred to a third party within 3 years of an insured's death is automatically includible in the insured's gross estate. Transfers made more than 3 years before the insured's death are not normally includible in the insured's estate, assuming the insured has retained no incidents of ownership. In addition, *sales* to a third party for the full fair market value of the policy will not be included under Sec. 2035 even if the sale occurs within 3 years of the insured's death.

The 3-year rule applies differently to life insurance transfers than it does to most transfers of other property. Other forms of property transferred within 3 years of death are generally excluded from the decedent's gross estate. However, if a donor assigns an interest in a life insurance policy on his or her life and dies within 3 years of the assignment, the full amount of the proceeds will be included in the donor-decedent's gross estate. This rule applies if any incident of ownership in the policy is transferred or released within 3 years of death.

The remainder of the material in this and the next chapter focuses on the planning necessary to keep the proceeds of life insurance on the insured's life out of his or her gross estate. Although the 3-year rule applies to transfers of policies in which the insured possesses an incident of ownership, transferring or assigning the policy might still be an appropriate planning step. The insured simply has to live more than 3 years following the transfer to avoid the proceed's inclusion in his or her gross estate. And even if the insured dies within 3 years, he or she will be no worse off from an estate tax standpoint since the policy would have been included in any event had the transfer or assignment not occurred.

Most of the disputes and litigation between the taxpayer and the IRS under Sec. 2035 have involved the question of whether a transfer of the policy has occurred. Usually, these have been cases in which a third party, such as a family member or life insurance trust, has applied for and owned the policy covering the decedent's life. Generally, the IRS has attempted to treat the third-party owner as an agent of the insured for the purpose of acquiring the life insurance by applying the "constructive transfer" theory to the transaction. That is, the IRS has treated the insured as the original owner who is deemed to have transferred the policy to the third-party owner at the time application is made for the policy by the third party.

Another theory the IRS has applied is the "premium payment test." This theory imputes a transfer by the insured if the insured pays premiums on the policy covering his or her life even if the policy is owned by a third party. Thus, any premium payment by the insured within 3 years of his or her death will, if this theory applies, cause inclusion of the full proceeds under Sec. 2035.

Fortunately, the IRS has been largely unsuccessful in litigating these cases because the courts have given the term "transfer" its traditional meaning. Following its loss in circuit court case *Estate of Headrick v. Commissioner,* the IRS announced that it will no longer litigate life insurance cases under Sec. 2035 where the policy covering the decedent's life was owned and applied for by a third party (Action on Decision [AOD] 1991-012). Thus, inclusion of a life insurance policy in the decedent's estate will be avoided if a third party applies for and owns the policy covering the decedent's life, even if the decedent makes premium payments within 3 years of his or her death. (Of course, such premium payments are gifts by the insured and may be taxable under the gift tax rules.)

Although the IRS has backed down on the application of Sec. 2035 to third-party-owned life insurance, planning in this area should still be performed with extreme caution. The facts in the *Headrick* case were extremely favorable to the taxpayer: Headrick, an attorney, had clearly established the third-party ownership from the life insurance policy's inception. No explicit or implicit evidence suggested that the third-party owner was acting as the agent of the insured. In cases where the third-party owner is under the direction of the insured or where the original ownership of the policy is unclear, the IRS may still attempt to invoke Sec. 2035.

For example, a recent private letter ruling involved the application of Sec. 2035 to the conversion of a group term life insurance policy. Under the facts of the ruling, the insured was covered by a group life insurance policy provided by his employer. Since the insured had problems with insurability, he used the conversion privilege in the policy at the termination of his employment and created an irrevocable trust to apply for the permanent policy created in the conversion. The IRS reasoned that the insured had transferred the group term life insurance policy to the trust, and therefore Sec. 2035 should apply to the new permanent contract held by the trust. Two factors make this application of Sec. 2035 seem reasonable. First, the insured had owned incidents of ownership in the group life coverage. Second, the permanent contract would not have been available (because of insurability problems) except for the conversion privilege in the group term life insurance. The insured could have avoided the problem entirely by assigning all rights in his group term life coverage to the trust prior to the conversion, provided the assignment occurred more than 3 years prior to his death.

Life Insurance and the Federal Estate Tax Marital Deduction

Life insurance proceeds payable at the insured's death to the insured's surviving spouse can qualify for the federal estate tax marital deduction. Since the marital deduction is unlimited, the full value of life insurance proceeds payable in a qualifying manner to the surviving spouse will be deductible from the insured's gross estate.

The federal estate tax marital deduction is available only under the following circumstances:

- The property in question must be included in the decedent's gross estate.
- The property in question must pass or have passed from the decedent to the surviving spouse.
- The surviving spouse must be a citizen of the United States or must obtain citizenship before the decedent's estate tax return is due.

(Property left to a resident alien will qualify for the marital deduction only if the property is payable or assigned in a timely fashion to a qualified domestic trust.)
- The property in question left to the surviving spouse must not provide a nondeductible terminable interest. Under the requirements of Sec. 2056, a life interest in property left to a surviving spouse will qualify only if (1) the remainder following the life interest is payable to the surviving spouse's estate, (2) the surviving spouse has a general power of appointment over the property subject to the life interest at the time of his or her death, or (3) the executor of the deceased spouse's estate makes the qualifying terminal interest property (QTIP) election under Sec. 2056(b)(7).

Under these rules, life insurance proceeds payable outright to a citizen surviving spouse as named beneficiary will qualify for the marital deduction. If the surviving spouse is a resident alien, the marital deduction can be preserved by assigning the proceeds to a qualified domestic trust. If the proceeds are payable to the insured's estate, the proceeds will qualify for the marital deduction if the surviving spouse receives the proceeds under the terms of the decedent's will or the state intestacy statute.

Qualification for the marital deduction becomes more complicated if the surviving spouse does not receive the proceeds outright. For example, life insurance proceeds payable to a surviving spouse under available settlement options may or may not qualify for the marital deduction. Some settlement options terminate payment at the surviving spouse's death. If the remaining payments are not payable to the surviving spouse's estate or subject to the surviving spouse's control, the marital deduction will not be available unless the estate is eligible to make the QTIP election.

If the proceeds of a life insurance policy are payable to a trust benefiting the surviving spouse, qualification will depend on whether the trust otherwise qualifies for the federal estate tax marital deduction. Thus, the marital deduction depends on whether the trust remainder interest is payable to the surviving spouse's estate or subject to the surviving spouse's general power of appointment. Absent such provisions, the trust can qualify only if the deceased spouse's executor makes the QTIP election.

In a recent private letter ruling, a husband transferred a policy purchased on his life to an irrevocable life insurance trust benefiting his wife and children. Since the husband transferred the policy to the trust within 3 years of his death, Sec. 2035 caused the proceeds' inclusion in the husband's estate. The terms of the trust provided for the following at the husband's death:

- Fifty percent of the annual trust income would be payable to the surviving wife for as long as she lives.

- Twenty-five percent of the annual trust income would be payable to each of the deceased husband's two children during the wife's lifetime.
- At the wife's death, the trust principal would first be available to pay her estate expenses, with the remaining principal distributed in equal shares to the couple's two children.

Under the terms of this trust, the wife received a terminable interest since her interest would cease at her death. However, if the deceased husband's executor makes the QTIP election, a marital deduction would be available for 50 percent of the proceeds because the surviving wife would have a 50 percent income interest in the trust.

Value of the Policy Includible in the Gross Estate

Policies on the Life of the Decedent

If a life insurance policy must be included in the decedent-insured's gross estate for federal estate tax purposes, the amount that is included is the *face amount* of the policy. The face amount is the death benefit adjusted by (1) deducting any policy loan or other encumbrance and (2) adding any accrued or terminal dividends. Such concepts as cash value, total premiums paid, or reserves in the policy are irrelevant in this context and have nothing to do with the determination as to what amount is to be included in the decedent-insured's gross estate.

The value included in the gross estate would appear, at first, to be unrelated to whether the policy is included under Sec. 2042 or 2035. Obviously, if the decedent-insured owned the policy at the time of his or her death, the full amount of proceeds must be included under Sec. 2042. But *Friedberg v. Commissioner* reveals a different test for inclusion under Sec. 2035. In this case, the decedent had transferred a policy on his life to his daughter. Following the transfer, the daughter paid the premiums as they came due. The insured died within 3 years of the transfer, and therefore the policy was included in his gross estate under Sec. 2035. However, the court concluded that the value of the policy to be included in the gross estate should be the ratable portion of the proceeds attributable to the actual premium payments made by the decedent-insured. For example, suppose the policy provided a death benefit of $1 million and Mr. Friedberg had paid $90,000 in cumulative premiums at the time he transferred the policy to his daughter. If the daughter subsequently paid $10,000 in premiums, only $900,000 or 90 percent of the proceeds should be included in Mr. Friedberg's estate.

Policies Owned by a Decedent on the Lives of Others

Under third-party ownership of life insurance, which has become extremely popular for estate planning, it is quite possible that a policyowner will die before the actual insured. When this happens, a life insurance policy is treated the same way as any other property the decedent owned. That is, the policy is included in the decedent's gross estate at its fair market value (as evidenced on IRS form 712) at the time of the decedent's death. Generally ownership of the policy will pass by the terms of the decedent's will, by intestacy, or by the terms of the insurance policy itself.

According to Treasury regulations under Sec. 2031, the fair market value of the unmatured life insurance policy at a given point in time depends on the type of coverage. If the policy is currently paid up, its value is equal to the sale price of comparable contracts by the insurance company. This typically is the single-premium cost of a similar policy on the life of a person at the insured's attained age.

If the policy does not have a value that is readily ascertainable through the sale of a comparable contract, its value is determined by the rules provided in the Sec. 2031 regulations. Generally, no ascertainable value is available when a contract has been in force for some time and future premium payments must still be made. Under these circumstances, the value is equal to the policy's *interpolated terminal reserve* at the date of the decedent's death *plus* the proportionate part of the *unearned premium* (the amount of premium already paid covering the period after the policyowner's death).

Example: Sally owns a policy with a face amount of $1 million on the life of her father. Sally dies on July 1st of this year, predeceasing her father. The policy reserve was $50,000 on December 31st of last year. The policy reserve would have grown to $70,000 at the end of this year. If Sally had made a timely premium payment of $15,000 on January 1 of this year, the value of the policy included in her gross estate at the time of her death is determined as follows:

Terminal reserve at the end of the current year	$70,000
Terminal reserve at the end of last year	−50,000
Increase in the terminal reserve over the current year	$20,000

• • • • •

One-half of the increase in the terminal reserve (the increase in terminal reserve at the time of Sally's death halfway through the year)	$10,000
Terminal reserve at the end of last year	+50,000
Interpolated terminal reserve	$60,000

• • • • •

Interpolated terminal reserve	$60,000
One-half annual premium (amount unearned at the time of Sally's death)	+7,500
Value of policy at the time of Sally's death	$67,500

However, if the alternate valuation date (6 months after the date of death) is used for purposes of valuing the decedent-policyowner's gross estate and if the insured dies within this 6-month alternate valuation period, the full amount of the death proceeds is includible in the decedent-policyowner's estate and not just the fair market value of an unmatured life insurance policy.

Responsibility for Payment of Federal Estate Taxes by Life Insurance Beneficiaries

IRC Sec. 2206 stipulates that federal estate taxes attributable to life insurance proceeds included in the decedent's gross estate will be recoverable by the executor from the beneficiary of the life insurance policy unless the decedent's will provides a contrary provision for tax apportionment. This rule ensures that an executor will be able to collect estate taxes caused by life insurance even though the life insurance is paid to a named beneficiary and is not subject to the executor's control.

For many reasons, it is recommended that a testator include a tax apportionment provision in his or her will. Without such direction, state law governing probate will generally allocate the expenses of the estate, including federal estate taxes, to the residuary share of the estate. If the residuary share is insufficient to meet these expenses, state law usually gives the executor the authority to collect the estate expenses and taxes from other property transferred to the decedent's beneficiaries. Thus, both federal and state law empower an executor to collect federal estate taxes from the named beneficiaries of life insurance policies included in a decedent's gross estate.

In one case, the court found that the federal statute took precedence over state law in permitting the executor to collect from a named beneficiary the federal estate taxes attributable to a life insurance policy included in the decedent's gross estate. In this instance, state law would have provided for payment of these taxes from the residuary estate, which, incidently, had sufficient assets to pay all taxes. A tax apportionment provision in the testator's will could have prevented confusion and unintended results regarding payment of estate taxes.

FEDERAL GENERATION-SKIPPING TRANSFER TAX

Life insurance is subject to the federal generation-skipping transfer tax (GSTT) in some circumstances. The GSTT is a particularly burdensome tax since it is applied (1) in addition to the federal estate or gift tax applicable to a transfer and (2) at the highest marginal transfer tax rate. Thus, a transfer that is subject to the GSTT might face total transfer taxes in excess of *100 percent* of the amount of the cash or property transferred. Fortunately, all individuals have a $1 million exemption against taxable generation-skipping transfers.

Life insurance proceeds that are payable directly to, or may someday benefit, skip persons might be subject to the GSTT. A skip person is defined as any person more than one generation below the transferor.

Direct-Skip Transfers

A direct-skip transfer involves a gift or bequest of property directly to a skip person, such as a gift from a grandparent to a grandchild. With life insurance, a direct-skip transfer could involve the payment of policy proceeds on a grandparent's life to a grandchild as the named beneficiary. The GSTT could also be applied to a gift of the policy to a grandchild while the insured grandparent is still alive.

Taxable Distributions and Terminations

The GSTT implications of life insurance trusts are more common and, in all probability, more difficult to avoid. Since all individuals have a $1 million exemption from the GSTT, only sizable estates are generally affected. It is critical to avoid inadvertent problems that may result in the GSTT when employing life insurance trusts that *may* benefit skip persons.

The GSTT applies to trusts in two circumstances—taxable distributions and taxable terminations. A taxable distribution occurs if a distribution of trust income or principal is made to a skip (with respect to the grantor of the trust) beneficiary.

> *Example:* Mr. Reed creates an irrevocable life insurance trust for the benefit of his children and grandchildren. At Mr. Reed's death, the trustee is directed to hold the proceeds and to distribute as much income and principal to the various beneficiaries (a general sprinkle power) as the trustee determines in its sole discretion. If the trustee makes a distribution to any of Mr. Reed's grandchildren, a taxable distribution has occurred for GSTT purposes.

A taxable termination occurs when either (1) a trust terminates and all remainder persons are skip persons or (2) all interests in the trust held by nonskip persons terminate.

> *Example:* Assume the facts from the example above. Suppose Mr. Reed had instead provided that the insurance proceeds would be held in trust for his children with all income payable annually to his children in

equal shares. At the death of Mr. Reed's last child, the trust will terminate, and the remainder will be distributed to his surviving grandchildren in equal shares. When Mr. Reed's last child dies and the trust terminates, a taxable termination occurs.

Predeceased Parent Exception

The GSTT rules exempt the skip beneficiary from tax if his or her parent (who is the lineal descendant of the transferor) is deceased at the first time the potential generation-skipping transfer is subject to gift or estate taxation.

Example: Mr. Jones has a daughter, Janice, who is the named beneficiary of a policy on his life. Janice, who has two children, tragically predeceases her father. Mr. Jones then names his two grandchildren the cobeneficiaries of the policy. At the subsequent death of Mr. Jones, the payment of the proceeds to his two grandchildren will not be a direct skip and will avoid the GSTT. However, the proceeds will still be subject to estate taxes.

FEDERAL GIFT TAXATION

Gifts of life insurance are treated in the same way as gifts of any other asset as far as the $10,000 annual exclusion or the split-gift provisions are concerned. In other words, the federal gift tax laws operate the same way regardless of what asset is being gifted. Under the annual exclusion, $10,000 of gifted value per year per donee may be excluded from the gift tax base when life insurance is gifted. Under the split-gift provision, if a donor of a life insurance policy (or any other asset) is married at the time of the policy's transfer, the amount of the annual exclusion will be doubled to $20,000 per year per donee if the nondonor spouse elects to split gifts.

Valuation of Life Policies

To thoroughly understand all the ramifications of federal gift taxation triggered by transferring a life insurance policy for "insufficient consideration in money or money's worth," it is useful to review the principles of life insurance policy valuation.

The value of a life policy that has been gifted is determined in the same manner as discussed earlier for estate tax purposes. If the policy is transferred immediately (within the first year) after its purchase, the gift is equal in value to the gross premium paid to the insurer.

If the policy is paid up at the time it is transferred (or is a single-premium policy), the gift tax value of the policy is the amount of premium the issuing insurer would charge for the same type of single-premium policy of equal face amount on the insured's life, based on the insured's age at the transfer date. (An insured's impaired health is not addressed by the Treasury regulations, but the IRS has argued that the insured's adverse health at the time of the policy gift affects its valuation. This contention is logical since impaired health obviously affects life expectancy. However, the IRS has issued no formal regulations on this subject.)

If the policy is in a premium-paying state at the time it is transferred, the gift tax value of the gift is generally equal to the sum of (1) the interpolated terminal reserve and (2) the unearned premium on the date of the gift.

Often a donor will continue to pay annual premiums, even after an absolute transfer of the insurance has been made. Each premium paid subsequent to the policy's transfer is considered a gift. As long as the transfer is outright to a donee, the gift of the policy is one of a "present interest." Therefore, the $10,000 annual gift tax exclusion will be applicable, not only to the gift of the policy itself but also to the gift of each premium payment as it is made. However, when gifts of life insurance policies are made in trust, the exclusion is forfeited unless the donee has an absolute and immediate power of withdrawal.

Gifts of policies and premiums may also qualify for the gift-splitting privilege, assuming that the donor is married and the donor's spouse consents. The gift tax marital deduction for gifts of life insurance to spouses is also available.

The Problem of Inadvertent Gifts

Sometimes there is an inadvertent gift of policy proceeds. This can happen when a policy that is owned by one individual on another's life matures by reason of the insured's death and a person other than the policyowner is named as beneficiary. For example, if a wife purchases a policy on her husband's life and names her children as beneficiaries, the proceeds that could (and should) have been payable to her are payable instead to her children at her husband's death. It is treated as if the policyowner (the wife) had received the proceeds and made a gift in that amount to her children. Gift splitting is not allowed, since there is no spouse with whom to split the gift.

Another variation of the inadvertent gift problem is demonstrated in the following example:

Suppose a husband is a policyowner and beneficiary of a policy covering his wife. If his wife dies and he irrevocably elects the settlement interest option with the principal payable to his children at his death, he has made a gift (at the time of the election) of the remainder interest that his children will eventually receive. But since he has retained the right to the income for as long as he lives, he has made a transfer with a retained life estate. In addition to the possible gift tax implications, under the rule of Sec. 2036, the principal will be part of his gross estate for federal estate tax purposes when he dies.

Example: John Oxford died last month with a $500,000 universal life insurance policy in force. His wife, Eve, as the named beneficiary of the policy, has irrevocably elected the interest option. The death benefit therefore is to remain with the insurance company, and Eve is to receive monthly checks representing the interest on the principal amount. As part of her plan, Eve has directed that her daughter, Liza, is to receive the $500,000 death benefit after Eve's death. Eve has made a taxable gift (at the time of the election) of the remainder interest that her daughter will ultimately receive. Further, the $500,000 death benefit will be part of Eve's gross estate for federal estate tax purposes because she has retained the right to the income generated by the $500,000 death benefit for as long as she lives. (Fortunately, the estate tax calculation takes into consideration the gift tax that has already been paid earlier, if any, to avoid double taxation.)

OUTRIGHT GIFTS OF LIFE INSURANCE POLICIES

There are many reasons why estate planners recommend a life insurance policy gifting program. Some of the reasons are as follows:

- The donee feels no richer after receiving the life insurance policy and will seldom dispose of it foolishly. Compare this to a gift of stock that may give the recipient an immediate sense of independence and security that is adverse to the donor's intentions. Because the donor no longer controls the purse strings, the donee can sell the stock or convert all or part of it into spendable cash. A gift of securities, cash, land, or other assets, therefore, can sever rather than reinforce the intended bond between the donor and the donee. A gift of life insurance, on the other hand, is often *burdened* with future premium payments, calling for the donor's continued assistance and cooperation between the donor and donee.
- The donor's financial position is not markedly affected by making a gift of life insurance. In fact, there is normally a minimal change in the donor's income. If the donee pays future premiums, the donor has actually increased his or her cash flow. (However, the donor loses the cash value of the policy that would have been available for business or investment planning, emergencies, or opportunities.)
- The gift tax cost to transfer a policy is usually nominal compared to the potential estate tax savings. This is because the policy is transferred at its present value, which is usually much less than the face value used for estate tax purposes. (Of course, the donor has to survive for more than 3 years following the gift to reap the estate tax savings.) Often, making a gift of a life insurance policy can be accomplished with little or no actual gift tax payable. If company policy allows, a contract can be split

into two or more contracts, so that gifts can be spread over 2 or more years and among several donees. Therefore, the donor can maximize the use of the annual exclusion.
- The gift of a life insurance policy is particularly advantageous for older donors whose estate planning concerns have risen in priority in relation to their other financial planning goals. Usually, older insureds can select appropriate beneficiaries with more certainty and are less concerned about a policy's cash surrender value. If a policy is gifted more than 3 years before the donor's death, the transfer tax savings will be substantial.
- The gift of a new policy is perhaps the best estate planning gift available. The most appropriate method to design this gift is to permit a third party, such as the donor's child or an irrevocable trust, to apply for and own the insurance policy. Then the donor-insured merely makes cash gifts to the donee to pay the premiums. (The design and benefits of the life insurance trust will be covered in chapter 3.)

The foregoing advantages notwithstanding, a potential donor should consider one critical point before making gifts of life insurance policies: The gift must be real and not a sham. This means that something beyond a mere formal change in title is necessary. For example, if a man calls his insurance agent, requests an absolute ownership form, signs the ownership form, and then returns the policy to his own safe-deposit box, he has not really made an assignment. The donor should transfer actual possession of the policy to the donee. Furthermore, the donor should not use the policy as collateral for personal loans or retain the right to control the beneficiary designation. If a mother transfers ownership of a life insurance policy to her married son but the father continues as primary beneficiary, the facts tend to indicate that the mother is remaining in control. For a real transfer to have taken place, the son ought to receive premium notices, make actual payments, and behave like a policyowner in all respects.

The IRS scrutinizes the parties' conduct to determine if there has been an actual ownership change or only a change in name. If the contract itself had been the only evidence examined in the leading court case in this area, the decedent, according to the contract's terms, would have been the policyowner. However, the corporation had actually purchased the policy with corporate funds, carried it as a corporate asset on the business's books, and named itself as beneficiary. The court held that the corporation was, in fact, the real owner and that the decedent-insured was merely its nominee. This case is likely to be used by the IRS to attack formal transfers in which the original policyowner continues to be treated as the owner of the policy.

One of the most common problems that occurs when a life insurance policy is assigned is the return of that policy to the insured by inheritance. If a husband transfers a policy to his wife to remove the proceeds from his estate and no precautions are taken, the policy is quite likely to return to him either by the wife's will or through intestacy laws if her death occurs first. One possible solution is for the donee to specify in the ownership designation that the policy, upon the donee's death, is to go to some family member other than the insured.

When larger policies are involved, setting up an irrevocable trust to serve as recipient of the life insurance policy on the husband's life (and other assets) would prevent the policy from returning to the husband. At the same time, it would provide management and investment expertise for the proceeds. This type of arrangement is particularly valuable where minor children are involved as beneficiaries.

PRACTICAL USES FOR LIFE INSURANCE IN ESTATE PLANNING

There are many practical uses for life insurance in the estate planning context. We will now discuss the following:

- gifts of policies to trusts
- grandparent-grandchild trusts
- estate liquidity
- equity of inheritance
- nonworking spouse insurance
- the second-to-die policy

Gifts of Policies to Trusts

One useful estate planning device involves gifting a life insurance policy to a *revocable trust*. Although there are no tax benefits in using the revocable trust approach, it is advantageous because it provides asset management and dispositive flexibility. It should be noted, however, that revocable life insurance trusts do not offer protection from estate taxes, do not shift the burden of income taxes, and generally do not affect state death taxes.

The revocable trust works extremely well in cases where estate tax planning is not the life insurance plan's primary concern. For example, a young couple with minor children might find a revocable trust to be helpful in their plan. If the total family wealth (including policy death benefits) is less than the applicable exclusion amount ($625,000 for 1998), federal estate tax will be avoided, regardless of the life insurance plan design. Even if the couple's wealth exceeds the applicable exclusion amount, the unlimited marital deduction could shield the deceased spouse's estate from immediate taxes. Estate taxes will probably be deferred for many years unless *both* spouses die prematurely, an unlikely event. Under these circumstances, because the primary need for life insurance is estate enhancement, a revocable trust could be created to receive policy proceeds. At the death of the grantor-insured, the trust would become irrevocable. The trustee would then manage the proceeds for the surviving spouse, if necessary, and the minor children.

If it is preferable for the surviving spouse to receive the proceeds outright, the revocable trust could be used as a secondary beneficiary to manage the proceeds for the minor children in the event of their parents' simultaneous death. The revocable trust would permit the proceeds to be paid immediately for the benefit of the minor children and managed according to the grantor's wishes. Otherwise, a guardian of the minor's property would have to be appointed to manage the proceeds and the minor's other inherited property. The appointment of a guardian could cause some delay and confusion. Moreover, the guardian would be unlikely to have clear direction as to the disposition of the proceeds and other property for the minor's benefit. The grantor of the revocable trust could specify all terms for the disposition of the trust assets, including deferring distribution beyond the time the child reaches the age of majority.

Irrevocable life insurance trusts holding policies on the life of the grantor or his or her spouse also offer attractive estate-tax-saving opportunities (even though trust income used to pay policy premiums may be taxed to the grantor for income tax purposes).

Example: Jim Girard has a gross estate of $4.2 million. Approximately $1.6 million of it is attributable to life insurance proceeds included in Jim's estate because he possesses "incidents of ownership" in the policies. By transferring this life insurance into an irrevocable life insurance trust, Jim will enjoy significant savings in federal estate tax liability.

An irrevocable life insurance trust is often the best solution to an estate owner's liquidity problems. In fact, it is generally perceived as the most beneficial and flexible estate planning technique currently available. Because of the importance of the irrevocable life insurance trust, it will be discussed in more detail in chapter 3.

Grandparent-Grandchild Trusts

One commonly used technique is for a grandparent to purchase insurance on the life of a child for the benefit of his or her grandchildren. When the grandchildren are minors, use of a trust rather than an outright gift is preferable. In a typical arrangement, the grandparent creates a funded irrevocable insurance trust with a trustee owning the policy on the child's life. The trustee also pays premiums and designates the trust as beneficiary. The following example should help illustrate this concept.

Example: A grandfather has an estate of $1 million. His annual income is approximately $100,000. His son's income is about the same.

If the grandfather transfers $100,000 of securities to the trust for the ultimate benefit of his grandson (assuming the grandfather has made no prior gifts), the use of the applicable credit amount available under the federal gift tax laws eliminates the need for any out-of-pocket payment. Generally, the $100,000 is still considered in computing the grandfather's ultimate estate tax liability, but any appreciation on the securities will not be brought back into the estate tax computation process. Also savings in administrative costs and state death taxes are likely and could be relatively substantial. If the $100,000 produces a return of 7 percent, it will yield $7,000 per year.

The trustee would be directed to purchase insurance on the life of the son, which eliminates or reduces the need for the son to carry insurance and to pay premiums out of income at his own tax bracket. It may be possible for the trustee to buy more insurance than either the grandfather or his son could otherwise buy from their own after-tax funds since the trust may be in a lower income tax bracket. Another attractive result is that the proceeds will escape estate taxation, since the son has no incidents of ownership in the policy on his life. By authorizing (but not directing) the trustee to purchase assets from or make loans to the son's estate, it is possible to make the life insurance proceeds available for liquidity purposes. Furthermore, the trust could be authorized to distribute corpus to the son for emergencies or opportunities. No tax advantages will be lost as long as the son is a beneficiary only at the sole and absolute discretion of the independent trustee.

In summary, if the grandfather carries out the arrangement just detailed, the trust will do the following:

- provide some reduction of the grandfather's potential estate taxes
- reduce the amount of insurance the son must carry
- keep insurance proceeds out of the son's estate
- enhance the estate the grandson will receive at his father's death

Estate Liquidity

Unless the executor of an estate wishes to go through a series of complex and burdensome requests for an extension, the tax due by an estate must be paid within 9 months of the date of death. If the gross estate is composed of liquid assets, the executor or administrator faces no problem in meeting the 9-month deadline successfully. For example, if the estate is composed of sufficient cash, marketable securities, or life insurance proceeds, there will be ample liquidity to ensure that the tax can be paid within the required time. Conversely, if the federal estate tax liability exceeds the amount of liquid assets available, there will be an estate liquidity deficit. To meet the 9-month deadline, a forced liquidation of assets—invariably at a loss—will be necessary.

Estate liquidity deficits frequently occur when a decedent owns a closely held business interest at the time of death. The fair market value of this asset must be included as part of the decedent's gross estate, which results in a higher federal estate tax liability.

Life insurance is the most effective way to supply needed dollars to meet federal estate tax obligations. First, the dollars, in the form of death proceeds, are free of federal income taxation. Second, if the life insurance is owned by someone (or something) other than the insured, the face amount of the policy will not be included as part of the decedent's gross estate. Finally, the sizable death benefit may be purchased for pennies on the dollar in the form of premium payments.

Few situations are more tragic than a forced liquidation of a family business and other personal assets to pay federal estate taxes. Life insurance is the perfect way to assure a family that this will never be necessary.

Example: Eddy Easystreet is the sole shareholder of Familyco, Inc., his family business. Eddy is divorced with two children, Edna and Eddy, Jr. Eddy has completed his marital settlement obligations with his ex-wife, but the settlement has left him without significant liquid wealth. Eddy has the following assets and liabilities:

Assets

Familyco stock	$1,000,000
Personal residence	650,000
Vacation home	275,000
Business real estate	500,000
Automobiles and personal property	150,000
Cash and liquid investments	200,000

Liabilities

Mortgage on residence	$200,000
Business loans (personally guaranteed by Eddy)	350,000

Eddy has these specific estate planning goals:

- Transfer the stock to his successor, Eddy, Jr.
- Transfer the business real estate to Eddy, Jr.

- Transfer the vacation home to Edna.
- Provide equal estates to Edna and Eddy, Jr.

The following forecast is for Eddy's current estate if he dies today (1998) with no further planning:

Gross estate	$2,575,000
Funeral and adm. exp. (estimated at 5% of probate estate)	128,750
Debts and taxes	350,000
Losses	0
Adjusted gross estate	$2,096,250
Marital deduction	0
Charitable deduction	0
Taxable estate	$2,096,250
Adjustable taxable gifts	0
Tentative tax base	$2,096,250
Tentative tax	$ 827,963
Gift tax payable on post-1976 gifts	0
Estate tax before credits	$ 827,963
Applicable credit amount	202,050
State death tax paid	106,330
Maximum state death tax credit	106,330
Credit foreign death tax	0
Credit for gift tax on pre-1977 gifts	0
Credit for tax on prior transfers	0
Net federal estate tax payable	$ 519,383

The forecast of Eddy's estate identifies several problems, which are as follows:

- Federal estate and state death taxes totaling $625,913 are due within 9 months of Eddy's death.

- The business loan is due at Eddy's death (although there is the possibility that Eddy, Jr., could get more financing).
- The personal residence might be difficult to sell quickly unless priced well below market value.
- As much as $1,104,663 (taxes, expenses, and loan principal) might be needed in cash to settle the estate while only $200,000 of liquid assets are available—a liquidity deficit of $904,663!
- The business, the business property, and/or the vacation home may have to be sold under this scenario.
- The new family business exclusion created by TRA 97 is no help either since the value of the stock is less than 50 percent of the adjusted gross estate. Note how this "all or nothing" provision will be difficult to qualify and plan for even in a somewhat modest estate with major liquidity problems. The details of the family business exclusion will be discussed further in chapter 4.

Suppose instead, Eddy and Eddy, Jr., enter into an insured cross-purchase buy-sell agreement for the Familyco stock, and Eddy, Jr., purchases $1 million in life insurance on his father's life. (Familyco may have to increase Eddy, Jr.'s salary or split-dollar the policy to make the insurance affordable to him.) At Eddy's death, Eddy, Jr., can use the proceeds to purchase the stock from the estate. Now the picture looks like this:

- The estate tax situation remains the same except that the estate has $1.2 million in liquid assets—a positive liquidity balance of $295,337.
- The appropriate property can be left to each child.
- The goal of equality can be realized.

This solution represents only one possibility for using life insurance to solve the problem. However, it demonstrates clearly how life insurance can be used to provide estate liquidity to an otherwise nonliquid estate.

Equity of Inheritance

There are many estate planning situations in which it is the estate owner's wish to equalize inheritances among children. A prime example is when an estate owner has brought some of his or her children into a family business and intends to provide these children with an ownership interest in the enterprise. The plan may be to pass the interest to these children either during his or her lifetime or after death. However, if there are other children in the family who have no contact with the business, the estate owner may wish to provide for them in some other way so that there is equality among the children. Life insurance in this context is appropriate.

> *Example:* Father is president and sole shareholder of Clipper, Inc., a highly successful manufacturer of paper clips. He has four adult children, two sons and two daughters. The two daughters have expressed an interest in taking over the business when Father reaches age 59 1/2. The two sons have no interest in the business since they are both career men in the military.
>
> Father arranges for the two daughters to receive the business at his retirement or death. To equalize the inheritances of his children, Father acquires life insurance on his life in an amount equal to the anticipated fair market value of Clipper, Inc. Father pays the premiums, and the sons are designated equal beneficiaries. Equity of inheritance has been achieved.

Nonworking Spouse Insurance

There are many reasons why insuring a nonworking spouse makes good estate planning sense. If the nonworking spouse is no longer living, someone must be paid for services he or she previously rendered, such as cooking, cleaning, and laundering. Courts have often valued the cost to replace these services—domestic help and caring for the children—and the figure has run into several hundred thousand dollars. Acquiring life insurance to offset those costs and losses should be an essential part of family estate planning.

Although increased domestic expenses will contribute to family expenditures after the death of a nonworking spouse, the impact of additional income taxes, gift taxes, and estate taxes may be even greater. At the death of one spouse prior to the other, a joint return for federal income tax purposes is no longer available to the survivor. While the percentage of increase in the survivor's tax may appear to be slight, the additional amount of income tax can be substantial over a period of years.

Gift taxes may also increase. The availability of the unlimited marital deduction (interspousal gifts may pass gift tax free) and the ability to split a gift are lost at the death of a spouse. This is because both of these favorable provisions are available only if the marital relationship exists at the time of the gift.

For federal estate tax purposes, the death of the less wealthy nonworking spouse before the death of the working spouse can cause a considerable increase in the survivor's estate tax liability and a reduction in the net amount of property passing to children and other family members at the survivor's death. This increase results from the loss of the federal estate tax marital deduction—the deduction for property passing from the decedent-spouse to a surviving spouse. Although the marital deduction is available at the death of the first spouse, the deduction will not be significant if the deceased nonworking spouse has a relatively small estate.

There are further reasons for nonworking spouse life insurance. At least a minimum amount of insurance proceeds should be available to meet the expenses of the nonworking spouse's last illness and death. Furthermore, if the nonworking spouse owns a sizable estate in his or her own name, life insurance will meet the need for liquidity.

In summary, life insurance on the life of the nonworking spouse is valuable for the following reasons:

- to provide money to meet the expense of domestic help and care for minor children
- to replace money lost to increased income taxes
- to provide funds for death costs
- to provide additional estate liquidity

How should life insurance policies on the nonworking spouse be arranged? If the nonworking spouse's estate is nominal compared to the working spouse's estate, the nonworking spouse should own the policy. The nonworking spouse should provide by policy designation that the policy proceeds go directly to a specified adult child or to a trust. If a trust is the beneficiary, the trustee should be given authority to use the proceeds to purchase assets from or make loans to the estate of either spouse.

In cases where the nonworking spouse has a substantial estate of his or her own, either adult children or a trust should own the policies on the nonworking spouse's life.

Second-to-Die Policy

Next, the use of a survivorship (second-to-die) policy should be considered in estate planning for a married couple. The federal estate tax marital deduction is now unlimited in nature and scope. With the advent of the unlimited federal estate tax marital deduction, however, came an increased potential for overqualification for the marital deduction. There is a greater propensity by estate owners to leave their entire estates to their surviving spouses, which assures no estate tax liability at the first death.

There is, unfortunately, a serious flaw in this approach. The concept of the federal estate tax marital deduction is based on a deferral of estate tax liability—it is *never* to be thought of as a complete forgiveness of the estate tax. Although the deduction is unlimited, to use the deduction to its fullest extent creates a stacking of estate taxes at the second death. The estate tax liability from the estate of the first to die is added to the estate of the second to die. The result is a higher estate tax liability overall. If the entire estate of the first spouse to die is not passed to the surviving spouse, the married couple's overall estate tax liability could be less. This might occur for two reasons. First, the applicable credit amount available to the first spouse to die will be wasted if his or her entire estate qualifies for the marital deduction. Second, the family might take advantage of the lower brackets of the federal estate tax rates if all family wealth is not bunched into the surviving spouse's gross estate.

The unlimited marital deduction has created a need for greater planning for the death of the second spouse. That is why the second-to-die policy was instituted. Many life carriers offer a second-to-die policy that jointly insures a husband and wife. At the death of the first spouse, no death benefit is paid; at the death of the second spouse, the policy proceeds are paid to the named beneficiary.

Other life insurance companies, although aware of the need for a second-to-die-type product, have chosen to use a second-to-die rider instead of a second-to-die policy. Attaching a rider to an existing ordinary life contract allows the beneficiary of the existing policy (usually the surviving spouse) two options. One option is, of course, to take the proceeds from the original policy. The other option is to insure another life, usually that of the surviving spouse. That is, the proceeds that could be taken immediately in cash are used to fund a policy on the life of the surviving spouse, generally with a significantly greater death benefit (also referred to as a "benefit increase option" [BIO]). This rider is favored by some planners since it provides maximum flexibility.

Second-to-die coverage is often a perfect fit in a married couple's estate plan. The most common use of second-to-die coverage is in an estate plan in which taking the unlimited marital deduction after the death of the first spouse will result in more substantial death taxes at the death of the second spouse. With second-to-die coverage, policy benefits will be paid when the insured married unit incurs these more substantial taxes—at the second death of the spouses.

However, there are other uses for second-to-die coverage in estate planning. For a large number of two-income couples, there will still be significant income available to the family even after the death of the first spouse. For younger two-income parents, therefore, the greatest need for income-replacement coverage may be at the second death of the two parents. Second-to-die coverage is a relatively inexpensive way to provide this coverage for young two-income parents with a limited insurance budget. Certainly, it is less costly than individual policies covering each spouse.

Second-to-die coverage is also appropriate for the typical simple estate plan. Many married couples often own their property jointly in the form of tenancy by the entireties. This form of ownership gives survivorship rights to the surviving spouse; the property passes automatically by operation of law when the first spouse dies. Automatic transfer avoids probate costs and qualifies for the unlimited estate tax marital deduction. All probate costs and federal estate taxes associated with property held jointly by the spouses will be incurred at the second death—the exact time when second-to-die coverage will provide its cash benefit.

Example: Otto Palindrome, aged 62, and his wife, Anna, aged 60, have a substantial estate. They have two children, Bob and Lil. They currently have the following total assets:

Otto	$2,200,000
Anna	850,000
Joint	1,050,000

For the purposes of illustration, assume that Otto dies in 8 years (2006) and Anna in 22 years (2020) and that all assets appreciate at 4 percent annually. The couple has an optimal marital-formula estate plan. That is, each spouse's will creates a credit shelter trust funded with the applicable exclusion amount at the time of death ($625,000 if death occurs in 1998); the remainder of their estate is sheltered by the marital deduction. If the funeral and administrative expenses are 3 percent of the gross estate, the estate settlement costs are as follows:[1]

Otto's Death 8 Years Later

Gross estate	$3,729,351	
Funeral and administration	(111,881)	
Marital deduction	(2,617,470)	
Taxable estate	1,000,000	
Tentative tax	345,800	
Applicable credit amount	(345,800)	
State death tax credit	0	
State death tax	0	
Federal estate tax	0	All federal taxes absorbed by applicable exclusion amount
Net first death expense	$111,881	

Anna's Death 22 Years Later

Gross estate	$7,791,248
Funeral and administration	(233,737)
Taxable estate	7,557,511
State death tax	713,021
Federal estate tax (net of credits)	2,738,610
Total second death tax	$3,451,631
Total second death expenses	$3,685,368
Net passing to children	$5,837,556

Suppose Otto and Anna are, not all that surprisingly, unhappy with the potential shrinkage of their family wealth to death taxes. If all of the assets are not liquid, imagine the problems that will occur at the second death!

To minimize the devastating effect of the death taxes and other settlement costs, Otto and Anna have their children purchase a second-to-die policy on their lives with a face amount of $4 million. Otto will gift the $40,000 annual premium to the children. While both spouses are alive, the gift of the annual premium can be sheltered by the gift tax annual exclusion and gift-splitting. After the first death, the premium might be reduced by policy dividends, the grandchildren (if any) could be used to add annual exclusions, or the survivor would have to use some of his or her credit against gift taxes each year for the annual premium in excess of the survivor's current annual exclusions—$20,000.

This plan serves the following three purposes:

- The second-to-die proceeds will replace the family wealth lost to death taxes.
- The annual gifts will keep the taxable estate from growing as fast as it otherwise would.
- The life insurance proceeds will escape estate taxes since the children, not the insureds, own the policy.

The results are as follows:

Otto's Death

Admin. expense	$ 105,310

Anna's Death

State death tax	$ 522,155
Net federal estate tax	$2,278,888
Total second death tax	$2,801,043
Total admin. expenses	$ 293,803
Taxes saved by premium gifts	$ 650,588
Net passing to children	$9,025,256

The plan works fairly well for the Palindromes. The second-to-die benefits more than replace the funds lost to taxes and administrative expenses. In addition, there is a tax savings of $650,588 because the premium gifts reduce the growth of the estates. Furthermore, since the death benefit is excluded from the gross estate of the survivor, the children net $3,187,700 more than if no life insurance gift is made.

NOTE

1. The illustrations shown here are based on the assumption that a simple credit estate tax is the state death tax imposed and that no state death tax is due at the first death. In addition, it is assumed that the $40,000 premium is paid as a gift to the trust until the second death and that gift tax annual exclusions will always be sufficient to shelter the gifts.

3

Irrevocable Life Insurance Trusts (ILITs)

Chapter Outline

ADVANTAGES OF ILIT 76
    Gift Tax Advantages 76
    Estate Tax Advantages 77
    Generation-Skipping Transfer Tax (GSTT) Advantages 77
    Probate Expenses and Publicity Are Avoided 78
    Trust Terms Give Grantor Dispositive Flexibility 78
    Irrevocability Concerns Can Be Addressed 79
    Income Tax Consequences Are Minimal 79
    Estate Liquidity Is Enhanced 80
GIFT TAX PLANNING FOR ILITs 80
    Qualifying Gifts to ILIT for Annual Gift Tax Exclusion 80
    Present-Interest Dilemma 81
    "Crummey" Withdrawal Powers 82
    Application of Crummey Power to ILITs 83
KEEPING ILIT PROCEEDS OUT OF GRANTOR'S ESTATE 94
    ILIT Terms Should Avoid Directly Benefiting Insured's Estate 94
    ILITs and Sec. 2035 3-Year Rule 95
DISPOSITIVE PROVISIONS OF ILIT 97
    Providing for a Surviving Spouse 98
    Second-to-Die Life Insurance and ILIT 99
    Creating Estate Liquidity 99
CONCERNS ABOUT IRREVOCABILITY 102
    Retrieving Life Insurance Policy from ILIT 103
    Flexibility to Change Beneficiaries 105
    Policy Replacement by Trustee 107
SPECIAL PLANNING APPLICATIONS FOR ILIT 107
    Generation-Skipping ILITs (Dynasty Trusts) 107
    ILITs and Employer-Provided Life Insurance 109
    Charitable Wealth Replacement Trusts 110

ADVANTAGES OF ILIT

Estate planning applications of life insurance were discussed in chapter 2. Since the ILIT is generally regarded as the most powerful estate planning technique available today, it merits special treatment in this chapter. In the chapters that follow, the ILIT will be explained further in conjunction with other estate planning techniques.

Gift Tax Advantages

As discussed in this book, there are advantages in making lifetime gifts. The ILIT is a particularly advantageous vehicle for making a lifetime gift. Properly designed and administered, the ILIT can permit the grantor to make significant cash gifts for premium payments that are sheltered entirely by the grantor's annual gift tax exclusions.

The annual exclusion is limited to gifts of a present interest up to $10,000 per donee. (Note: The $10,000 limit is subject to inflationary adjustments beginning in 1999.) If the grantor is married and his or her spouse elects to split gifts, the annual exclusion can be increased to $20,000 per donee. Thus, the grantor is able to contribute up to $20,000 for each beneficiary of the ILIT without any gift tax consequences. The annual-exclusion gift is the single most beneficial estate planning technique because the cash or other property that is transferred through the annual exclusions is forever removed from the donor's transfer-tax base.

The donor's applicable credit amount will shelter up to $625,000 (1998 amount) of additional transfers for amounts contributed to an ILIT in excess of the grantor's annual exclusions. If it is feasible for the donor's spouse to contribute to the ILIT (for example, the ILIT will invest in a survivorship life insurance policy on the donor and his or her spouse), a second applicable credit amount of $625,000 is available. Thus, as much as $1.25 million in premiums in excess of the donor's annual gift tax exclusions can be contributed to an ILIT in 1998 without incurring gift taxes.

In the largest estate planning cases, the annual exclusions and applicable credit amount(s) will not entirely shelter the required premium gifts to the ILIT. Nevertheless, the ILIT continues to be a useful planning technique in these cases.[1] The payment of gift taxes on lifetime gifts in excess of the annual exclusions and applicable credit amount might be beneficial for two reasons. First, the gift taxes paid in excess of the credit are based on the progressive unified gift and estate tax rate schedule. Gift taxes will be paid only on gifts in excess of the applicable exclusion amount ($625,000 in 1998). The first applicable gift tax bracket is 37 percent on gifts over $625,000. However, the maximum federal estate and gift tax rates will not be reached until taxable lifetime gifts reach $3 million. Thus, taxable lifetime gifts to an ILIT permit the grantor to take advantage of the lower brackets available under the unified rate schedule.

Second, gift taxes paid on taxable gifts made more than 3 years prior to the grantor's death will be removed from the donor's gross—that is, the gift tax system is tax-exclusive. This means that the donor will not have to pay transfer taxes on gift taxes paid on gifts made more than 3 years before his or her death.

Compare this either to transfers made within 3 years of death or that are transfers made at death. For these transfers, the transferor will pay tax not only on the property transferred but also on the tax payable on the transfer. Thus, the transfer-tax system is tax-*in*clusive for gifts that are made within 3 years of death and for transfers that are made at death. Since lifetime gifts decrease the ultimate size of the taxable estate, even if they are taxable, lifetime gifts will be an effective transfer-leveraging technique.

Estate Tax Advantages

Chapter 2 demonstrated that life insurance death benefits are subject to unique estate tax rules. Since, following the decision in the *Headrick* case, the IRS has retreated from its previous Sec. 2035 opinions on the purchase of life insurance by an ILIT, the ILIT is a safe way to avoid estate taxes with a uniquely appreciating asset. If the ILIT is properly designed and administered, the death benefits payable to the trustee will be completely free of estate taxes.

The ILIT gives the grantor a tremendous transfer-tax-leveraging advantage. As discussed above, the ILIT can be funded with lifetime gifts sheltered by a variety of gift-tax-sheltering techniques. Thus, the trust could be entirely funded with no transfer-tax costs. Since the death benefits are not subject to estate taxes, both the premium payment gifts and the death benefits received by the trust can avoid all transfer taxes.

Of course, the grantor could transfer virtually any property to an irrevocable trust with the same transfer-tax results. However, the unique nature of the life insurance product offers an appreciation potential that exceeds that of all other investments. This is particularly true if the grantor-insured dies prematurely. Even if the grantor-insured lives to or beyond his or her life expectancy, competitive life insurance products will provide a favorable return.

Generation-Skipping Transfer Tax (GSTT) Advantages

Sometimes the ILIT will be used to bypass the next generation and provide benefits for the insured's grandchildren and great grandchildren. In such cases, the ILIT will be immediately subject to the GSTT rules. In other instances, the insured's grandchildren will benefit after, or in conjunction with, the insured's children. In these cases, the GSTT will be applicable when the grandchildren benefit from the ILIT.

Generally, the insured can avoid any GSTT consequences by allocating his or her $1 million GSTT exemption against premium gifts to the ILIT. (Note that the $1 million GSTT exemption will be indexed for inflation beginning in 1999.)

This represents a tremendous opportunity to use an ILIT for transfer-tax leveraging against the GSTT.

Probate Expenses and Publicity Are Avoided

Much has been made recently of the use of living trusts as a probate-avoidance technique. Living trusts are designed to reduce the probate estate held by the grantor of the trust at the time of death. Probate expenses are substantial if professional help is required.

The ILIT is a type of living trust with these probate-avoidance advantages: The death benefits paid to the ILIT avoid the expenses of probate when the grantor-insured dies. In addition, the ILIT is a private nonprobate document, and the beneficial provisions of the ILIT are known only by the grantor, trustee, and trust beneficiaries. Thus, the grantor of the irrevocable life insurance trust has the ability to create a completely private estate that avoids the scrutiny of the grantor's other heirs.

Trust Terms Give Grantor Dispositive Flexibility

The ILIT is a private document that directs a trustee to manage the trust according to its specified terms. To succeed in meeting the transfer-tax planning goals for the ILIT, the grantor can retain no control over the disposition of the trust after the trust is created. However, the trust terms can be designed to give an independent trustee significant flexibility in managing the trust. The ILIT permits the grantor to defer distributions to beneficiaries and empower a mature, competent trustee to make dispositive decisions for the grantor after the grantor's death.

For example, the trustee can be given discretionary powers to sprinkle trust income or principal among the various beneficiaries after the death benefits are paid to the trust. The grantor can specify that his or her children have merely an income interest in the trust during their lives. The remainder of the trust corpus can be distributed according to the dispositive terms specified by the grantor at the time the ILIT is created, or it can be distributed under powers of appointment granted to the trustee or beneficiaries of the trust.

Compare an ILIT's dispositive flexibility with the outright payment of death benefits to the insured's beneficiaries. With an outright payment nobody but the beneficiary is responsible for managing the death proceeds. They could be consumed or given away quickly by the beneficiary or assigned to the beneficiary's creditors. A large death benefit designed to last a lifetime or into the next generation, therefore, could be wasted in a short period of time.

If the life insurance is instead acquired by an ILIT, the grantor's specified terms will provide for the disposition of the asset. Thus, the death proceeds from the life insurance policy will be invested and managed by a selected individual or institution. The payment of any income or principal could be limited by the predetermined terms of an ILIT or placed in the hands of a responsible and reliable trustee.

Irrevocability Concerns Can Be Addressed

The irrevocability of the ILIT is, of course, a disadvantage from the grantor's standpoint. If the gift and estate tax advantages are to be achieved, the ILIT must be a no-strings-attached transfer. The grantor must not have the express ability to control the actions of the trustee or to reacquire the life insurance policy.

However, the grantor can, through careful trust drafting, give the independent trustee a great deal of flexibility in managing the trust. If it is desirable, the independent trustee can transfer the policy from the ILIT. For example, the policy can be distributed to beneficiaries or sold to anyone, including the grantor, provided the trustee exercises independent judgment. Or the grantor can provide a limited power of appointment for another individual to invade the ILIT. This power of appointment can give access to the policy's cash surrender value or provide for the distribution of the life insurance policy.

Income Tax Consequences Are Minimal

The income tax consequences of the typical ILIT are negligible. Under the grantor-trust rules, the grantor is taxed on any portion of the income of the trust that is or may be applied, without the approval of an adverse party, to the payment of premiums on policies insuring the life of the grantor or his or her spouse. This means under most circumstances the ILIT will be a grantor trust. Therefore, any taxable income of the ILIT will be reported on the grantor's individual return. This rule will affect only trusts that have taxable income. In the typical ILIT the grantor will contribute amounts sufficient merely to cover the premium payments and trust expenses. Thus, the "unfunded" trust will not cause the grantor to incur income taxes.

In the case of a funded ILIT, the grantor has contributed substantial income-producing principal to the trust, and the income from the trust can be used to make the premium payments. The grantor is personally responsible for income taxes created as a result of such trust income. But these taxes can be minimized if the grantor funds the trust with tax-exempt securities or the trustee chooses such investment for the trust principal.

The principal of the unfunded ILIT will be the policy itself. If the policy is permanent insurance, cash surrender value buildup will occur. However, the income tax advantage of life insurance is that this policy buildup is tax free. If the policy is overfunded and fails the modified endowment contract (MEC) rules, taxable income will be incurred only to the extent that the trustee actually withdraws or borrows cash from the cash surrender value of the policy.

Estate Liquidity Is Enhanced

An ILIT should not be designed to directly benefit the insured's estate or to pay estate expenses. Under the rules of Sec. 2042, discussed in the previous chapter, proceeds payable to or for the benefit of the estate will be included in the insured's gross estate. However, the trustee of the ILIT can use the policy death benefits indirectly to enhance the liquidity of the estate. But the trustee should exercise caution when using this technique. (Recommended methods for providing estate liquidity from the ILIT will be discussed later.)

GIFT TAX PLANNING FOR ILITs

The gift tax planning involved in creating and funding an ILIT is the most complex aspect of such trusts. It is essential that the trust be created and managed properly to benefit from the available gift-tax-avoidance provisions of the tax rules. For example, the donor should take advantage of every available annual exclusion. The applicable credit amount should be used only as necessary; if the credit is used to avoid gift taxes, it must be used as efficiently as possible.

Most individuals considering an ILIT have substantial estates. They also are generally older on the average than people who purchase life insurance outright. They usually have significant unearned income, their estates are growing larger all the time, and they are using the ILIT to save estate taxes. In many cases, they own closely held businesses or professional practices. These individuals should be considering the use of every gift-tax-saving avenue for the remainder of their lives. If the premium gifts to an ILIT are not designed in the most gift-tax-efficient manner, the grantor will be wasting estate planning opportunities. Any inefficient use of the gift tax shelters will ultimately result in increased estate tax costs and decreased family wealth for the next generation.

Qualifying Gifts to ILIT for Annual Gift Tax Exclusion

Advantages of Annual Exclusion

The annual exclusion was created to prevent taxation of *de minimis* gifts to family members through the gift tax system. Think of the compliance difficulty that would occur if every birthday or holiday present to a child or grandchild were subject to gift tax reporting. However, the annual exclusion creates an estate planning opportunity that goes far beyond de minimis gifts. A wealthy donor can transfer up to $10,000 (to be indexed for inflation beginning in 1999) to any number of individuals without gift tax consequences. Annual-exclusion gifts are not defined as taxable gifts under the unified estate and gift tax system. Thus, such gifts *never* become part of the donor's transfer-tax base.

Taxable gifts (gifts in excess of the annual exclusions and marital deduction) are, on the other hand, returned to the donor's estate tax base as adjusted taxable gifts, even if the taxable gifts were fully sheltered by the applicable credit amount. Therefore, annual-exclusion gifts represent a rare opportunity to avoid the federal tax system entirely. If the grantor makes systematic annual-exclusion gifts to his children and/or grandchildren over a number of years, a significant estate tax savings will result. If the donor is married and his or her spouse elects to split gifts each year, the transfer tax savings can be doubled by increasing the annual exclusion to $20,000 per donee.

Example: Tom Taxplanner, a widower aged 65, has two children and four grandchildren. Tom can make up to $60,000 of total qualifying gifts annually to his children and grandchildren without ever subjecting this property to the transfer tax base. If Tom lives an additional 16 years (his actual life expectancy), he can give away a total of $960,000 and save up to $528,000 of estate tax if his estate is subject to the top 55 percent tax bracket. This savings estimate actually understates the estate tax savings since the appreciation of the property transferred through annual-exclusion gifts is also removed from Tom's gross estate.

The example above demonstrates the tremendous potential estate tax savings if the annual exclusion is used effectively. The savings demonstrated above could be even greater if the annual exclusion gifts are made to an ILIT and invested in a life insurance policy covering the donor's life (or perhaps the lives of the donor and his or her spouse).

Present-Interest Dilemma

Unfortunately, annual exclusion from gift taxes is not available for all gifts. The rules of Sec. 2503 state that the annual exclusion is available only for gifts of a present interest. That is, an annual-exclusion gift must give the donee a present right of enjoyment. Certainly, all outright transfers of cash or property to a donee qualify for an annual exclusion. Even property such as life insurance, which provides for death benefits at a later date, will qualify as a present interest if it is transferred directly to the donee.

A problem arises in creating a present interest when a gift is made to a trust for the benefit of the donee-beneficiaries. If the trust does not provide for immediate benefits and delays income and principal distribution to a future date, the trust provides a future interest to the beneficiaries. An ILIT is a future-interest trust. The grantor-insured of an ILIT has no intention of providing any current benefits to the ILIT's beneficiaries. The beneficiaries are not expected to benefit until the grantor-insured's death when the death proceeds are received by the trustee. Can irrevocable trusts that defer beneficiaries' receipt of benefits be designed to qualify as present-interest gifts sheltered by the annual exclusion? The answer is given below.

"Crummey" Withdrawal Powers

Fortunately, gifts to trusts can qualify for the annual exclusion if they are appropriately designed. However, the trust must provide current enjoyment rights to the donee-beneficiaries. With an ILIT this is accomplished by giving each donee who will receive annual-exclusion gifts the right to receive the gift outright immediately. These withdrawal powers (hereinafter referred to as Crummey powers) are a powerful planning technique, and they will be discussed below.

The Crummey Case

The Crummey doctrine is derived from the case of *Crummey v. Comm'r*, 397 F.2d 82 (9th Cir. 1968). In this case, the taxpayer, Clifford Crummey, created four irrevocable living trusts for the benefit of his four children, aged 22, 20, 15, and 11. Because the transfer of property into the trusts qualified as a taxable gift, the taxpayer took the annual exclusion (at that time, $3,000 per donee) for each child.

The IRS, however, stepped in and disallowed the annual exclusion for those beneficiaries under the age of 21.

IRS Position in the Crummey Case. Because three of the beneficiaries of the trusts that Crummey had created were minors, the IRS asserted that a present-interest gift was not possible. The IRS was applying the doctrine of property law that states that a minor cannot own property in a highly literal and restrictive manner. Because the minors in the Crummey case could not own the gifted property or even "own" the benefits created under the terms of the trust, according to the IRS, present-interest gifts were impossible. Therefore, the annual exclusion was disallowed.

Holding of the Court in the Crummey Case. The court in *Crummey* rejected the IRS's position and held that a present-interest gift had been made because the guardian named by the taxpayer in the trust had been given the power to demand distribution on behalf of the minors. In essence, although the actual *Crummey* case had nothing to do with transfers of life insurance policies into trust, the case has come to stand for the principle that the annual exclusion is available if a power to *demand* the addition to trust property is given to the beneficiaries.

Thus, annual exclusions are available for premiums given to an ILIT as long as the ILIT contains language that requires the trustee to notify the trust beneficiaries that payments to cover premiums have been transferred to the trust and that the trust's beneficiaries have the right to demand distribution of these payments.

Application of Crummey Power to ILITs

The *Crummey* case has taught us that as long as a trust contains a power to demand distribution, a present-interest gift will be considered to have been made. This guarantees the availability of the annual exclusion. Therefore, since there will be a possible federal gift tax created (1) by transferring existing life insurance policies into a trust and/or (2) by gifting premiums to the trustee, the availability of the annual exclusion becomes very important because it is a method to reduce or even eliminate federal gift tax liability. Thus, qualifying gifts to an ILIT for the annual gift tax exclusion is essential if the grantor hopes to maximize his or her potential gift and estate tax savings.

According to the principles set forth in the *Crummey* case, a clause that allows the beneficiary to demand distribution must be included in the ILIT. This is true regardless of whether or not minors and a guardian are involved. As long as the named beneficiaries of the trust have been given ample notice of their right to demand distribution, a present-interest gift is deemed to exist. Therefore, the annual exclusion will be available.

Example: Marvin has created an ILIT and has transferred a life insurance policy into the trust. The face amount of the policy is $300,000, and there is a cash value of $4,700 on the day of the transfer. Premiums of $903 are payable annually on March 1. The beneficiary of the policy is the ILIT, and the beneficiary of the ILIT is Marvin's daughter, Ellen, aged 28. Because Ellen is not a minor, there is no guardian involved. There is a provision in the ILIT that Ellen, as beneficiary, will be notified within 60 days of receipt if Marvin makes any gifts to the ILIT. Furthermore, Ellen has been given the "power to demand distribution" of this gifted property.

When Marvin's next annual premium is due, he makes a gift of an amount roughly equal to the premium amount to the trustee. The trustee notifies Ellen in writing that she has the right to demand this gift. She, of course, does not demand it. The federal gift tax annual exclusion is available for both the cash value of $4,700 when the policy was originally transferred and for the premium payment of $903. Therefore no federal gift tax liability is triggered.

Example: John has created an ILIT and has transferred a life insurance policy into the trust. The face amount of the policy is $100,000, and there is a cash value of $3,100 on the day of the transfer. Premiums of $811 are payable annually on January 14. The beneficiary of the policy is the ILIT, and the beneficiary of the ILIT is John's daughter, Jennifer, aged 3. John's brother, Ed, is named guardian on behalf of Jennifer, and under the terms of the ILIT, Ed is given the power to demand distribution on Jennifer's behalf when John transfers funds to the ILIT.

When John's next annual premium is due, he makes a gift of an amount equal to the premium amount plus anticipated expenses of the trust to the trustee. The trustee notifies Ed that he has the right to demand this gift as guardian for Jennifer. Ed does not demand it. The federal gift tax annual exclusion is available for both the cash value of $3,100 when the policy was originally transferred and for the premium payment. Therefore no federal gift tax liability exists.

Establishing Validity of Crummey Withdrawal Right

The IRS has published several revenue rulings and a multitude of private rulings presenting its opinions on the interpretation of the Crummey power. It consistently takes a restrictive view of the limits of the Crummey power to create a present interest. One reason is that the Crummey power holders virtually never exercise their powers, particularly with respect to ILITs. (The actual exercise of a Crummey power will jeopardize the permanency of the life insurance policy held by the ILIT since the premium dollars would be withdrawn from the trust.) The beneficiaries' systematic lapse of (failure to exercise) their Crummey powers has been interpreted by the IRS to provide evidence that the powers are not really designed to provide a present interest.

The material that follows presents the IRS's position on the Crummey power. The conservative approach is to follow the IRS's strict view to the letter to avoid gift and estate tax audits and eventual litigation. Bear in mind, however, that the IRS's position might not be entirely correct. Several recent cases, *Cristofani v. Comm'r,*[2] *Kohlsaat v. Comm'r,*[3] and *Holland v. Comm'r,*[4] discussed below, reveal that the courts have not interpreted the Crummey power as strictly as the IRS. However, the IRS continues to adhere to its position, and the estate planner should be aware that the IRS has not changed its policy with respect to aggressive use of the Crummey power.

Eligible Crummey Beneficiaries. Provided they receive the Crummey power, all ILIT beneficiaries should be eligible to receive annual-exclusion gifts. This is true whether or not the beneficiary is a minor. Beneficiaries in the *Crummey* case were minors. The IRS has ruled (Rev. Rul. 73-405, 1973-2 C.B. 321) that an annual exclusion is available for Crummey power gifts in trust for minors if there is no impediment under local law to appoint a guardian to exercise the Crummey power for the minor, even if no guardian has actually been appointed.

The IRS's opinion is that only direct vested income and/or principal beneficiaries are eligible to receive annual-exclusion gifts to an ILIT. For example, suppose an ILIT provides an income interest for the surviving spouse with the remainder interest to be divided equally among the grantor's children. If any child predeceases the grantor or the grantor's spouse, the predeceased child's share will go to the child's lineal descendants. The IRS would take the position that only the spouse and the children of the grantor living at the time a gift is made to the ILIT are eligible to receive annual-exclusion gifts.

In a recent technical advice memorandum (TAM 99628004), the IRS indicated that contingent or remote remainder beneficiaries are not eligible to receive current annual-addition gifts to an ILIT. In this ruling, the IRS stated that such beneficiaries were given withdrawal rights only to multiply the number of annual exclusions used by the grantor. The IRS asserted that because no beneficiaries had exercised their withdrawal rights in the absence of any logical reason not to exercise such rights, the withdrawal rights were not "real." The reasoning of the IRS is that a Crummey beneficiary would withdraw if he or she had no other vested and direct beneficial interest in the trust. The lack of withdrawal by a contingent beneficiary, under this reasoning, is evidence of a prearranged understanding by the grantor and the beneficiaries that the Crummey powers will not be exercised.

The IRS's position runs contrary to the direction of the *Crummey* doctrine. As long as the withdrawal power is exercisable by the donee, the lack of exercise should not be evidence that the power does not exist. In fact, the evidence of the *Crummey* case indicates that the minor beneficiaries did not actually have knowledge of the power. Nor did they, as minors, have the individual capacity to exercise the powers. In addition, the fact that beneficiaries are remote or contingent should not affect the Crummey power's ability to create an annual exclusion for such beneficiaries. To qualify for an annual exclusion the beneficiary must have a present right to enjoyment of the property. If the beneficiary, whether remote or not, has the right to vest himself or herself with the property subject to the Crummey power, that beneficiary has an immediate right to enjoy the property.

In the *Cristofani, Kohlsaat, and Holland* cases, the taxpayers succeeded against the IRS in establishing that all Crummey beneficiaries received present-interest gifts. In the most recent of the cases, *Holland*, the court stated that the annual exclusion is available for all Crummey powerholders unless there is some legal impediment preventing the exercise of the withdrawal rights.

The IRS has not completely backed down, however, as a result of these cases. The Service acquiesced in the *Cristofani* case, in result only (Action on Decision CC-1996-010). The IRS stated that it will consider litigating the issue in future cases, when there is "no bona fide gift of a present interest intended." The IRS will infer this lack of intent when the Crummey beneficiary has no future economic benefit from the trust that is likely to be enhanced by failing to exercise the power.

Private letter ruling PLR 8712014 addressed the issue of whether or not the annual exclusion would be available even though a minor beneficiary's guardian is a nondonor-spouse who consents to split gifts to the trust. In this case, the donor intended to create an irrevocable trust for the benefit of her husband, son, mother, and aunt. A local court had previously appointed the donor's husband as guardian of the minor son. Under the terms of the trust agreement, the trustees were empowered to distribute the net income of the trust to the donor's spouse, son, mother, or aunt, if living, and to any of the donor's issue who were alive at the time of distribution. The crucial point here was that the donor's son or his guardian had a Crummey power to withdraw a portion of the property received by the trustees. The donor's son or his guardian could exercise the withdrawal power by delivering written notice of withdrawal to the trustees at any time during the 60 days following receipt of the notice from the trustees. Even though the nondonor-spouse had previously consented to a split gift under Sec. 2513 of the Internal Revenue Code, the IRS took the position that the transfer to the trust would qualify for the annual gift tax exclusion.

This ruling is particularly important for an ILIT that requires substantial premiums. In these instances, gift-splitting is often necessary to increase the amount of the annual exclusion to $20,000 per ILIT beneficiary. If any beneficiaries are minor children of the grantor, it is generally recommended that the nondonor-spouse receive the Crummey power notices on behalf of the minor children. Thus the fact that the nondonor-spouse is both splitting the gifts to the ILIT and capable of exercising Crummey withdrawal powers does not jeopardize the annual exclusion.

Providing Notice to Crummey Beneficiaries. According to the IRS, the Crummey withdrawal power will be illusory unless the right to withdraw is provided through clear notice to the beneficiary. The beneficiary should receive notice each time an addition that creates a Crummey power is made to the ILIT. In the *Crummey* case, the beneficiaries were minors who never received actual notice of their withdrawal rights from the trust. The IRS ultimately agreed with the *Crummey* reasoning, and it appears that a minor beneficiary need not receive actual written notice; it is simply required that state law would permit the appointment of a guardian to exercise the power for the minor. Although it seems that actual notice to minor beneficiaries is not necessary, trustees will frequently send letters to the minors in care of the noninsured parent.

The IRS strictly adopts the stance that actual notice is required for adult Crummey beneficiaries unless the beneficiary is a trustee (or cotrustee) of the ILIT. A trustee would, of course, be aware of his or her withdrawal rights. It is generally recommended that the trustee send letters to each beneficiary indicating his or her rights to withdraw from the trust. The notice should inform the beneficiary of the amount that the beneficiary can withdraw and the method to use to exercise such withdrawal right. For example, the letter could request written notice to the trustee that a beneficiary wishes to exercise his or her withdrawal right. It has often been recommended that beneficiaries execute waivers of their notices, thus alleviating the trustee of this annual (or perhaps more frequent if the premium is paid more often) paperwork burden. The IRS has recently taken the position in a private ruling that such waivers would jeopardize the annual exclusion because a present-interest gift requires actual notice of the Crummey withdrawal right (TAM 9532001).[5]

As discussed below, most Crummey withdrawal rights are temporary; they lapse after a brief period of time. The notice provided to the beneficiary should indicate the time period during which the withdrawal right is exercisable.

Duration of the Crummey Power. In most circumstances, the Crummey withdrawal power will exist for only a short time. Since the grantor of an ILIT hopes that the beneficiary will not exercise his or her right currently, the shortest possible time period is preferred. Presumably, a longer time period would increase the risk that the power will be exercised. Remember, the exercise of a Crummey power could result in the failure of the trustee to pay the annual premium and, perhaps, the lapse of the life insurance policy.

The IRS has stated in revenue rulings that the withdrawal power will be real only if it exists for an adequate period of time for the beneficiary to receive and exercise the notice. For example, the Service has ruled that a power given on December 29 that lapses at the end of the calendar year is insufficient. Although the shortest time period approved by the IRS is 30 days, the time period used in the *Cristofani* case was only 15 days. Thus, the time window in which to exercise a Crummey power should be 30 days if possible; at the very least, the power should be granted for 15 days.

The Crummey power time window creates some unique issues with respect to an ILIT. In the typical scenario, a Crummey power will be created in an ILIT when a grantor contributes cash to the trust for the purposes of paying the life insurance premium. The trustee will generally want to pay the premium to the insurer as soon as possible. This is particularly true when the gift to the trustee is delayed and the premium on the policy is due.

Most policies have a grace period of 31 days following the premium's due date before the policy lapses. The trustee should be concerned about the liability that could arise if the policy is allowed to lapse while funds are available to pay the premium. For example, if the gift to the trust is made at the time the premium is due, it will be difficult to send Crummey power notices and allow the notices to lapse before the end of the policy's grace period. It is the clear opinion of the author that the trustee should pay the premium on a timely basis—that is, pay the premiums as they come due even if the Crummey withdrawal rights of the beneficiaries are still outstanding. The ILIT terminology should clearly explain that when the Crummey withdrawal rights are exercised, they can be either satisfied out of income or corpus of the trust. Although the authority for this position is not clear, it should not matter for the purpose of the annual exclusion whether the Crummey beneficiary's share of the annual addition is provided to that beneficiary from annual cash or property additions to the trust or from the corpus of the trust. If necessary, then, the Crummey withdrawal right could be satisfied from the cash surrender value of the policy held by the ILIT. Of course, if at all possible, the premium gift should be made to the trust early enough for the trustee to give withdrawal notices to the beneficiaries and for their withdrawal rights to lapse before the premium is due.

Size of Crummey Withdrawal Rights. Under the simplest circumstances, the Crummey withdrawal right of each beneficiary should be limited to demand the lesser of (1) his or her share of the annual addition or (2) the greater of $5,000 or 5 percent of the corpus of the trust at the time of the withdrawal right. In the case of an ILIT, the maximum amount the beneficiaries could generally demand is the annual amount donated to the ILIT by the grantor for the purpose of paying the policy premium. If the ILIT has more than one beneficiary, each beneficiary should receive a withdrawal right equal to his or her proportional share of the annual addition.

> *Example:* Gary Grantor creates an ILIT to own a life insurance policy on his life. The trust provides for distribution of income at his death in equal shares to his five children. The policy acquired by the ILIT has an annual premium of $16,000, which is provided to the trustee each year through cash gifts from Gary. The Crummey power gives each beneficiary the right to withdraw his or her pro rata share of $16,000 ($3,200). Rev. Rul. 80-261, 1980-2 C.B. 279.

Gift Tax Consequences to Crummey Beneficiaries. Beneficiaries who receive a Crummey withdrawal right have a current, temporary general power of appointment over the property subject to the withdrawal right. A general power of appointment is tantamount to absolute ownership of the property. Under these circumstances, the beneficiary is clearly transferring property whether or not he or she exercises the Crummey power. If the beneficiary exercises the power, he or she transfers the property to himself or herself. If the beneficiary lets the power lapse, a transfer is made to the trust since the beneficiary is giving up the right to appoint the property to himself or herself.

With an ILIT, a beneficiary is obviously expected to let his or her Crummey power lapse. When a general power of appointment lapses, a taxable transfer has been made to the ultimate recipient of the property. For gift tax purposes, there is no distinction between the exercise of a withdrawal power in favor of a third party and the lapse of a withdrawal power that causes the third party to receive the property. In the case of an ILIT, the lapse of a Crummey power by a beneficiary causes a taxable gift to the *other* beneficiaries of the trust. To make matters worse, it is a transfer of a future interest because the ILIT usually does not provide for current income rights to the other beneficiaries. Thus, the lapse of a Crummey power creates a gift that is not sheltered by the beneficiary's annual exclusion.

Fortunately, Sec. 2514 indicates that the lapse of a power that does not exceed the greater of $5,000 or 5 percent of the property subject to the power is not treated as the exercise of a general power of appointment. Therefore, the lapse of a Crummey power that is limited to the lesser of (1) each beneficiary's proportionate share of the annual addition to the trust or (2) the greater of $5,000 or 5 percent of the trust corpus at the time of the demand will not create a taxable gift by the beneficiary who allows the power to lapse. Note that in an ILIT funded with permanent life insurance, the cash surrender value is generally the only corpus. After the early years, 5 percent of the cash surrender value may exceed $5,000 and will become the lapse limitation. Consequently, many practitioners limit the Crummey power to this amount.

A problem occurs if the grantor of an ILIT must pay premiums that exceed $5,000 each year per beneficiary. In large premium cases, the grantor often hopes to contribute the maximum gift that the annual exlusion can shelter. Thus, the grantor may want to provide a premium gift of $10,000 for each beneficiary ($20,000 if the gift is split with the grantor's spouse). If Crummey powers are given to the beneficiaries to the extent of $10,000 per beneficiary ($20,000 if gift-splitting is in effect), the annual exclusion shelters the grantor from gift tax consequences. However, the amount of each beneficiary's proportionate share of the annual addition to the ILIT in excess of $5,000 could create a tax problem for the beneficiaries. This discrepancy will grow larger as the annual exclusion is indexed for inflation (beginning in 1999), while the $5,000/5 percent limits are not.

> *Example:* Mr. Jones establishes an ILIT that purchases a survivorship or second-to-die life insurance policy to cover Mr. and Mrs. Jones. The policy has an annual premium of $100,000 and each of the Jones's five children will be beneficiaries of the ILIT. At the death of the survivor of Mr. and Mrs. Jones, the trust corpus will be distributed in equal shares to Mr. and Mrs. Jones's then-living children.
>
> Annually each child is given a Crummey withdrawal power for 30 days over his or her proportionate share of the annual addition to the ILIT. After 30 days, the Crummey withdrawal right totally lapses. Therefore, each annual premium gift to the ILIT gives each child a 30-day withdrawal right to $20,000. If Mrs. Jones elects to split gifts with Mr. Jones, the premium gift is entirely sheltered by their annual exclusions.
>
> If all five children allow their withdrawal rights to lapse, each has made a gift to the other children of $20,000. However, because of the provisions of Sec. 2514, the lapse of a general power equal to the greater of $5,000 or 5 percent of the ILIT corpus is not treated as the exercise of a general power. Thus, each child will not be treated as having made a taxable transfer to the extent of $5,000 for each lapse.
>
> But the bad news is that each child will be treated as having made a taxable gift of the remaining $15,000 to the other children. Furthermore, these gifts are not present-interest gifts, and each child will have to shelter the gift by using $15,000 of his or her applicable exclusion amount each year that the full premium is paid.

Fortunately, the material discussed below offers an answer for grantors who wish to create large-premium ILITs.

Providing Annual-Exclusion Gifts in Large-Premium ILITs

For the purpose of this discussion, we are assuming that the grantor of an ILIT wishes to provide maximum annual-exclusion gifts to the ILIT. As discussed above, gifts greater than $5,000 per Crummey beneficiary can create a gift tax problem for the beneficiary. But there are possible solutions to this gift tax problem without limiting the amount of annual premium that can be donated to the ILIT.

Permanent Crummey Powers. To avoid the taxable gift created by the lapse of a Crummey power, one obvious solution is to prevent the power from lapsing. If the Crummey powers are permanent and cumulative, they will be held continuously and never subject to lapse. Despite its simplicity, this technique has several disadvantages. First, the Crummey power will accumulate and will grow quite large if many annual premium gifts are made to the ILIT. For example, if a beneficiary's share of the annual premium donated to the ILIT is $20,000, the beneficiary will hold a cumulative Crummey power to withdraw $100,000 of ILIT assets in 5 years.

Since the Crummey power is a general power of appointment, it is equivalent to outright ownership of the assets by the beneficiary. As the amount grows, it will become increasingly tempting for the beneficiary to exercise his or her withdrawal rights. This is particularly true if the beneficiary has financial troubles. Even if the beneficiary is not inclined to exercise his or her withdrawal powers, the beneficiary's creditors would have full access to any assets over which the beneficiary has a general power of appointment. The results would be the same if the beneficiary becomes disabled and requires extensive or permanent medical care. The state welfare authorities could include the property subject to a cumulative Crummey power as a countable asset of the beneficiary for the purpose of medicaid qualification.

If the beneficiary voluntarily exercises, or is compelled to exercise, the cumulative Crummey powers, this would have a devastating effect on the ILIT. The trustee would be forced to withdraw cash surrender value from the policy to satisfy the beneficiary's demand. This would either reduce the policy's death benefit or endanger the policy's very existence. The grantor may then be forced to make further additions to the ILIT to keep the policy in force. This could cause the grantor to exceed his or her annual exclusion limits for the year and to place additional assets in the hands of the beneficiary who has chosen, for whatever reason, to exercise his or her demand rights.

The permanent, cumulative Crummey power may defer rather than prevent adverse transfer tax consequences to the beneficiaries. Since the Crummey withdrawal power is a general power of appointment, the property subject to the power will be included in the beneficiary's gross estate at his or her death. It would be a direct concern of the beneficiary if he or she should predecease the grantor. Even if the beneficiary survives the grantor, the continuing general power of appointment the beneficiary holds would cause this property's inclusion in the beneficiary's gross estate. This would be of no consequence to the beneficiary if the beneficiary survives the grantor and the insurance proceeds are paid to the beneficiary outright at the grantor's death. However, in many cases an ILIT is designed to provide benefits to the next generation without causing inclusion in these beneficiaries' gross estates. For example, a parent may create an ILIT to provide a life income for his or her to children with the remaining proceeds held for later distribution to the grandchildren. In this situation, the children would not want to have the remaining proceeds includible in their estates. Yet, if the children were to have permanent Crummey powers, some portion of the proceeds would be includible in their estates.

Stacking Crummey Beneficiaries. Another possible solution to this problem is to add sufficient numbers of Crummey beneficiaries to the trust to reduce each beneficiary's proportionate share of the annual addition to $5,000. Therefore, the lapse of a Crummey power by any beneficiary would not result in a taxable gift to the other beneficiaries. The *Cristofani/Kohlsaat/Holland* cases offer some precedent for the use of every available beneficiary of an ILIT, whether contingent or vested, as Crummey beneficiaries eligible to receive annual-exclusion gifts.

> *Example:* Dolores Donor, a widow, has three children, two of whom have two children each. Dolores creates an ILIT, and the trustee purchases a life insurance policy on her life with an annual premium of $35,000. The trust language provides that "at the death of the grantor, divide the trust fund into as many equal shares as there are children of the grantor living at that time and deceased children with living issue." If the Crummey powers are limited to $5,000 each to her three children, Dolores would have to use $20,000 of applicable exclusion amount each year to shelter the premiums in excess of the three Crummey power gifts. However, by adding the four grandchildren as Crummey beneficiaries under the reasoning of *Cristofani et al*, Dolores would be able to increase the available annual exclusions to seven, or $35,000 annually. Even with the Crummey powers limited to $5,000 each, the full amount of the annual premium would then be sheltered by annual-exclusion gifts. As additional grandchildren are born, it is possible to give them Crummey powers beginning with the year of birth.

Be aware that the use of multiple beneficiaries to provide additional annual-exclusion gifts might run afoul of the IRS's position on Crummey powers. The use of contingent beneficiaries or individuals who are not otherwise beneficiaries will place the grantor at some risk of audit and litigation on the gift tax issue.

Conservative Approach. The safest method for conservative grantors is to follow the rules spelled out by the IRS in its various rulings on the subject. That is, only beneficiaries who receive a vested current interest or vested remainder interest at the time death benefits are payable to an ILIT should be used as Crummey beneficiaries.

Cristofani/Kohlsaat/Holland Approach. This approach has been approved by three courts. However, the IRS recently indicated that it still disagrees with *Cristofani*, and it is possible that the IRS will challenge this approach in other circuits, even if the taxpayer is no more aggressive than Cristofani.[6] For example, a typical ILIT might provide for equal shares at the grantor's death to the grantor's children then living and deceased children with living issue. Certainly, all of the grantor's children are vested beneficiaries. However, the issue of a child of the grantor (that is, the grantor's grandchildren or great grandchildren) could benefit from the ILIT if the child predeceases the grantor. Under this approach, any grandchild or great grandchild alive at the time the grantor contributes a premium to the ILIT could be given a Crummey withdrawal right over a proportionate share of the premium gift.

Aggressive Approach. A more aggressive approach is to extend the reasoning in the *Crummey* and *Cristofani* cases to give Crummey powers to the grantor's friends and relatives who do not otherwise have an interest in the ILIT. For example, the grantor could provide in the ILIT instrument that the trustee give withdrawal notices to the grantor's nieces and nephews. These individuals would become beneficiaries of the ILIT only in the most remote circumstances. Since these Crummey beneficiaries would have an actual right to a present interest in the ILIT to the extent of their withdrawal rights, the grantor could reason that such powers would create additional annual exclusions in favor of these individuals. However, it is virtually certain that the IRS would challenge this use of the Crummey power and possibly subject the grantor attempting this approach to costly litigation.[7]

Limited Powers Solution. A currently popular method for solving this problem involves the use of cumulative limited powers of appointment. Under this method, the Crummey beneficiary receives a normal Crummey power with a specified lapse period (for example, 30 days) for the greater of the first $5,000 or 5 percent of the corpus available each year. The remainder of the amount subject to the Crummey power will not lapse each year, preventing the Crummey beneficiary from creating a taxable gift by lapsing the power in excess of the $5,000 or 5 percent of corpus threshold. This excess continues to be held by the beneficiary under a limited power of appointment and accumulates each year as the additional excess Crummey powers are continued with no possibility of lapse.

The excess amount will be exercisable by the Crummey beneficiary only as a limited power of appointment. For example, the ILIT terms may specify that the Crummey beneficiary can appoint the property only at his or her death. The continued power of appointment would limit the Crummey beneficiary to exercising the power only in favor of a limited class of people, generally the grantor's other heirs. The retention of the right to appoint the property prevents the Crummey beneficiary from having made a taxable transfer. This is logical since the property remains subject to the Crummey beneficiary's power of disposition. Because the Crummey power is a limited or special power with respect to the excess amount, it does not create estate tax problems for the Crummey beneficiary, whether or not it has been exercised at the time of his or her death.

The cumulative-limited-power method is popular with clients because it generally has no negative consequences. The limited power would have an impact on the ILIT only at a Crummey beneficiary's death and, even then, only if the deceased Crummey beneficiary specifically exercises the power through his or her will. This is probably a remote risk. If it does occur, the Crummey beneficiary must exercise the power in favor of the grantor's other beneficiaries. The IRS has ruled favorably on this solution in a private letter ruling (Ltr. 9030005).

> *Example:* Sammy Settlor is married and has three children and four grandchildren. He creates an ILIT, and the trustee purchases a survivorship or second-to-die life insurance policy on Sammy and his wife, Sarah. The annual policy premium is $120,000. The ILIT terms read as follows: "At the death of the survivor of the grantor and the grantor's spouse, the trustee will provide as much income and principal as the trustee determines each year for the issue of the grantor. At the death of the survivor of the grantor's children, the ILIT terminates and the corpus is payable to The American College." Including the three children and four grandchildren as Crummey beneficiaries and using gift-splitting will provide seven annual exclusions (up to $140,000). Since the annual premium is $120,000, each Crummey beneficiary will receive an annual Crummey power to withdraw $17,143. However, since it is desirable to limit the amount subject to lapse each year to $5,000 to avoid gift tax problems, each Crummey beneficiary should be given a limited testamentary power over the excess amount of $12,143 each year. That is, the beneficiaries will lapse their Crummey powers to the extent of $5,000 each on an annual basis. The remainder of each beneficiary's share of the annual premium ($12,143) will be subject to the beneficiary's limited power of appointment. Although these amounts will add up quickly, they can be appointed only to the grantor's other beneficiaries at the Crummey beneficiary's death and, even then, only if the power is affirmatively exercised in the Crummey beneficiary's will—a minor risk.

Hanging Powers Solution. This solution is also to prevent the lapse of powers held by a Crummey beneficiary in excess of $5,000. The excess amounts will "hang" over and accumulate each year as general powers. The provisions of the hanging power will allow for the later lapse of such powers to the extent that the lapse in the later year will not create a taxable gift. That is, the amounts will lapse only in a year that the lapsed amounts do not exceed an aggregate of $5,000 per Crummey beneficiary. The hanging powers solution works well in cases where a vanishing premium approach is selected for the policy. The excess amounts will hang over and accumulate each year when a full premium is paid. After the premium vanishes, the excess amounts so accumulated will begin to lapse to the extent of $5,000 per year until the cumulative amounts are completely dissipated.

Since hanging Crummey powers are cumulative general powers, this solution causes many of the same problems discussed above with permanent Crummey powers. That is, a large amount may someday become subject to the cumulative hanging power. In addition, if the Crummey beneficiary predeceases the grantor while holding such a power, the property subject to the power will be included in his or her gross estate. The IRS ruled privately in 1989 that hanging powers violate public policy. Relying on old case law, the IRS indicated that a savings clause in a trust, such as a hanging power clause, would cause uncertain tax results for the beneficiaries and, thus, cannot be given credence for the purpose of determining the size of the withdrawal powers held by the beneficiaries. This ruling has been greatly criticized, and hanging Crummey powers could possibly be drafted to avoid the public policy argument raised by the IRS in the prior ruling. However, hanging Crummey powers should be considered only with the advice of a competent professional.

KEEPING ILIT PROCEEDS OUT OF GRANTOR'S ESTATE

The rules for including life insurance proceeds in a decedent-insured's gross estate were discussed in chapter 2. Life insurance is included in the gross estate under the rules of Sec. 2042 in conjunction with the special rules of Sec. 2035. Under Sec. 2042 life insurance proceeds are included in the gross estate of a decedent-insured if (1) the policy proceeds are payable to the decedent's executor (that is, for the benefit of the decedent's estate), or (2) the decedent-insured owned incidents of ownership in the policy at the time of his or her death. The special rules of Sec. 2035 also cause inclusion in the decedent-insured's estate if he or she made a gratuitous transfer of the policy within 3 years of his or her death.

ILIT Terms Should Avoid Directly Benefiting Insured's Estate

In the typical ILIT, the trustee is the owner and named beneficiary of the policy held by the ILIT. The ILIT terminology instructs the trustee on how investments should be managed and how the death proceeds will ultimately be provided to the beneficiaries. The proceeds could be payable to the ILIT beneficiaries outright at the decedent's death. In most circumstances, however, the ILIT will continue beyond the life of the insured and provide income and/or principal gradually to the beneficiaries. In many instances, the trustee is given a discretionary power to choose the size and timing of distributions to the beneficiaries.

Caution should always be exercised in drafting the terminology of an ILIT. Sample ILIT documents received from insurance companies, banks, or law libraries should be examined carefully to ensure that the terminology will not cause tax problems for the insured. In particular, the ILIT terminology should neither direct nor permit the trustee to use policy proceeds to pay the expenses of the insured's estate. If the trustee is directed to pay the expenses of the estate, the IRS will deem the policy payable to the executor, and the proceeds will be included in the insured's estate. Even if the trustee is given the discretion to pay estate expenses with the proceeds, any amounts so used will be included in the insured's gross estate. Since the typical ILIT is designed to remove the death proceeds from the insured's gross estate, terminology that directs the trustee to use the death proceeds to pay estate expenses would be a costly mistake, while terminology that permits the trustee to use the death proceeds for estate expense purposes should be used only after careful consideration of all the tax consequences.

ILITs and Sec. 2035 3-Year Rule

Existing Policies Owned by Insured

Policies owned by the insured are subject to the 3-year rule regarding gratuitous transfers. That is, the proceeds will be included in the insured's gross estate if the insured's death occurs within 3 years of the policy's gratuitous transfer to a third party. This 3-year rule, of course, applies to transfers of existing policies to ILITs. Regardless of this rule, transferring an existing life insurance policy to an ILIT is an appropriate planning technique under certain circumstances.

Transferring an existing life insurance policy to an ILIT created by the insured is recommended when the estate planning objectives for the transfer are more important than other goals. The transfer of a policy to an ILIT should not be made until after the insured feels comfortable that he or she will not require further access to the policy's cash value. The grantor-insured should be relatively older and financially more secure. Furthermore, he or she should be certain of his or her ILIT beneficiary selections before implementing the transfer. After the transfer, the trustee will become the owner and named beneficiary of the policy, and the proceeds will be distributed according to the ILIT's terms. Since the trust is irrevocable, the grantor-insured will not be able to retrieve the policy or change the trust's terms.

To achieve estate tax advantages a grantor-insured will have to survive more than 3 years following the transfer of his or her policy to an ILIT. However, this transfer is still a useful planning technique since the full amount of proceeds will avoid estate taxation if the grantor-insured survives the 3-year period. Even if the grantor-insured does not survive the 3-year period, his or her estate will be no worse off than if the transfer had not been made. That is, absent the gift of a policy to an ILIT, the insured's estate would already have included the full proceeds because the insured would have continued to hold incidents of ownership in the policy until the time of his or her death.

Avoiding Estate Inclusion with Newly Acquired Policies

Following the decision in the *Headrick* case (discussed in chapter 2), the IRS indicated that it will no longer litigate the Sec. 2035 3-year-rule implications of life insurance policies newly acquired by an ILIT. Thus, a client will be within a safe harbor if an ILIT is created and administered according to the facts of the *Headrick* case. If the ILIT is created and administered in a more aggressive manner, there is a risk that the IRS will deem that the policy newly acquired by the ILIT was, in fact, transferred to the ILIT by the grantor-insured and thus subject to the Sec. 2035 3-year rule. If the IRS is successful in this endeavor, the grantor-insured of the ILIT could have the full amount of proceeds included in his or her gross estate if the grantor dies within 3 years of the acquisition of the policy. Since the facts of *Headrick* give us careful guidance, it is important to review the events of the *Headrick* case in detail here.

> *Example:* Eddie Headrick, an attorney, approached a local bank and trust company and explained his plan to create an irrevocable trust. The trust was executed the same day and funded by a check Eddie wrote to the bank as trustee. The terminology of the trust permitted many types of investments, including the purchase of life insurance on the grantor's life. The trust terminology did not, however, direct the trustee to purchase such insurance. The following day, the bank, as trustee, applied for a life insurance policy on the life of the grantor—Eddie Headrick. Within 10 days, Eddie submitted to a physical examination for the purpose of securing the insurance. Eddie was found to be insurable, and the trust paid the first premium. Within one month after the trust was created a policy was issued. Mr. Headrick died approximately 2 years later, and the IRS attempted to treat the transaction as if Eddie controlled the trustee and, in effect, caused a transfer of a policy on his life in which he had incidents of ownership to the trust. Thus, Sec. 2035 would require that the proceeds be included in Eddie's gross estate since he died within 3 years of this "deemed transfer." The court held for the estate of Mr. Headrick, based on the grounds that no transfer had actually taken place. The trustee was merely investing trust funds irrevocably transferred to the trust by the grantor. Therefore, the policyowner of the life insurance at the time of its purchase was established unequivocally to be the ILIT and not Mr. Headrick.

The facts of the *Headrick* case can be listed in the following steps that are recommended to anyone establishing an ILIT:

Step 1: The ILIT is executed before the final policy application is made and any premium is paid.
Step 2: The grantor transfers funds to the ILIT (and makes further gifts, as necessary, when premium payments are due).
Step 3: The trustee sends notice to the beneficiaries of their Crummey withdrawal rights. (This step is repeated each time additional gifts are transferred to the ILIT.)
Step 4: The trustee applies for the policy on the grantor's life and is named as owner and beneficiary of the policy. (The insured participates in the transaction only for the purpose of establishing his or her insurability and signs only the "insured" signature block on the policy application.)
Step 5: The trustee pays the policy's annual premium to the insurance company when the Crummey powers lapse.

If an ILIT is created and/or administered in a manner different from the steps described above, the insured is increasing the risk that the IRS will attempt to attribute incidents of ownership to him or her.

To summarize the material discussed above and in chapter 2, the insured should employ the following defensive strategies:

- The insured should not pay the policy premium before the ILIT is created.
- The terms of the ILIT should authorize but not direct the purchase of life insurance on the life of the grantor.
- The insured should retain no contractual rights, and there should be no trust provisions permitting him or her to acquire the policy held by the ILIT.
- The insured should not be the trustee and should not retain the power to become the trustee.
- The trustee should exercise clearly independent decision-making authority over the investment and disposition of trust assets.

DISPOSITIVE PROVISIONS OF ILIT

The grantor has full control over the terminology in his or her ILIT. A significant advantage of using an ILIT to own a life insurance policy is the ability to control the disposition of the proceeds after the insured's death. Compared with outright payment of proceeds or the use of policy settlement options, an ILIT places an independent decision maker selected by the grantor in the role of controlling the disposition of policy proceeds. Thus, the management of the disposition of life insurance policy proceeds can be left, within reasonable limits, in the hands of the trustee after the insured's death.

The amount of dispositive discretion left to the trustee is determined by the grantor when the ILIT is created. The grantor can direct the trustee to pay specific amounts of principal and/or income to the ILIT's beneficiaries. Outright disposition of the entire principal can be deferred until such time as the grantor feels is appropriate (for example, the 30th birthday of the youngest beneficiary). In other instances, the trustee can be given broad discretionary powers to sprinkle funds. Under these circumstances, the trustee can use his or her discretion in determining the timing and amounts of income and/or principal to distribute to each beneficiary. The trustee's discretion can be based on a specified standard, such as the support of the beneficiary, or it can be unlimited. The grantor should select which dispositive terminology to use, based on his or her feelings about each beneficiary's needs and the trustee's ability to handle discretionary authority.

Providing for a Surviving Spouse

We learned in chapter 2 that life insurance proceeds paid directly to a surviving spouse qualify for the unlimited federal estate tax marital deduction. However, if policy proceeds are paid to an ILIT benefiting the surviving spouse, the proceeds will qualify for the marital deduction only if the trust complies with the Sec. 2056 rules. But it is rarely the grantor-insured's intent to qualify the proceeds left to an ILIT for the marital deduction. For the proceeds to qualify for the marital deduction, they first must be included in the grantor-insured's gross estate. The goal of an ILIT is to *avoid* inclusion in the grantor-insured's gross estate. Properly designed, the ILIT gives the grantor-insured the opportunity to benefit his or her entire family and to avoid the proceeds' inclusion in the estate of either spouse.

How can life insurance proceeds paid to an ILIT created by the insured spouse benefit his or her surviving spouse without being included in the surviving spouse's gross estate? Commonly, one of the goals of an ILIT is to provide support benefits for the surviving spouse. But the benefits available to other heirs would be greatly reduced if the insurance proceeds were included in the surviving spouse's gross estate. Inclusion in the surviving spouse's estate could result in significant death taxes. Therefore, the ILIT is usually designed to avoid inclusion in the estate of either spouse. To provide for the surviving spouse while avoiding inclusion in such surviving spouse's gross estate, the ILIT's dispositive terminology must be carefully designed. The surviving spouse should not be given a general power of appointment or unlimited invasion rights over the trust assets. These rights would be tantamount to the surviving spouse's full ownership of the assets and would result in their inclusion in his or her gross estate. In addition, the surviving spouse should be prohibited from exercising powers over the trust assets to satisfy his or her legal support obligations. For example, the surviving spouse should not be given the power to invade the trust for the benefit of his or her minor child.

Although the surviving spouse should not be given unlimited invasion powers, he or she could receive significant benefits from the trust without its inclusion in his or her gross estate. For example, the surviving spouse could be given all income from the trust for the remainder of his or her life. The surviving spouse could also be given the noncumulative right to withdraw the greater of 5 percent or $5,000 of the trust corpus each year. This power is explicitly not a general power of appointment. In addition, the surviving spouse could be given the power to consume or invade the trust corpus subject to an "ascertainable standard" relating to his or her health, education, support, or maintenance. A standard is ascertainable if the power holder's duty to exercise the power is reasonably measurable in terms of his or her health, education, support, or maintenance needs. Powers subject to an ascertainable standard are not general powers of appointment, and, therefore, property subject to such a power would not be includible in the power holder's gross estate. Finally, the surviving spouse could be given a special or limited power of appointment over the trust corpus—for example, a testamentary limited power to appoint the remainder of the trust property at his or her death to one or more of the grantor's children.

Second-to-Die Life Insurance and ILIT

The primary difference between a normal ILIT and a second-to-die ILIT is that in a second-to-die ILIT, policy proceeds are not payable until the death of the survivor of joint insureds (usually the surviving spouse). Therefore, the dispositive provisions of a second-to-die ILIT will not include benefits for a surviving spouse. The primary beneficiaries are normally the couple's children or grandchildren. The grantor of the second-to-die ILIT can be either spouse, or the spouses can be cograntors. The premium gifts to the second-to-die ILIT can be sheltered by both spouses' annual exclusions while they are both still living.

Creating Estate Liquidity

The life insurance proceeds from an ILIT cannot be used directly to pay estate taxes or other settlement costs related to the decedent's estate without adverse estate tax consequences. The ILIT should, therefore, be considered an estate liquidity or wealth replacement device rather than a method to pay estate taxes. That is, the ILIT can be used indirectly to provide cash to assist in the settlement of the estate, or it can replace the decedent's wealth used to pay the estate taxes.

Before the life insurance proceeds can be available to assist the estate, there must be careful planning to avoid adverse estate tax consequences. In many cases, the liquid assets created by the life insurance payable to the ILIT are the main source of liquidity for the estate. Perhaps the insured's estate is substantial but contains mostly nonliquid and largely unmarketable assets. Estate taxes imposed on the estate are due within 9 months following the decedent's death. However, the estate settlement process can be lengthy, and it might take significantly more time to convert the nonliquid assets into cash. Fortunately, there are methods to make the insurance proceeds from the ILIT available to the estate without causing the proceeds' inclusion in the insured's gross estate.

Power to Loan Assets to Insured's Estate

One possibility for making the insurance proceeds from an ILIT available to an estate without causing estate inclusion of the proceeds is a bona fide loan from the ILIT to the estate. There are several factors to consider in making such a loan. First, both the executor and trustee are fiduciaries of different entities. That is, the executor has a responsibility to the beneficiaries of the estate, while the trustee has a duty to be loyal to the beneficiaries of the ILIT. Each fiduciary must be sure that making such a loan does not breach this duty of loyalty. The trustee's powers in the ILIT and the executor's powers in the will should give them the authority to transact the loan. The trust terminology should permit such a loan, but it should not direct that the loan be made. A mandatory direction to make the loans would remove flexibility from the trustee and executor and, perhaps, have adverse estate tax consequences.

The terms of the loan are another important consideration. Generally, it is recommended that the loan follow normal commercial standards. That is, adequate interest should be paid and security provided for the loan. Presumably, the estate would have sufficient assets to collateralize any loan received from the ILIT. Income from estate assets might be enough to cover the required interest and principal payments to the ILIT. Again, the terminology in the life insurance trust should specify the standards that the trustee should follow in making the loan.

Finally, it is important to consider how the loan will be paid off. If the loan is to be paid off by the estate over a lengthy period of time, the estate would have to stay open during this period. This could delay the distribution of estate assets to beneficiaries. In addition, the ILIT would probably not be able to make substantial distributions to its beneficiaries until such time as a large portion of the loan is repaid because the estate would use the proceeds of the loan to solve its immediate liquidity problems—that is, to pay estate taxes and other settlement costs. During the extended period that the estate has to remain open while repaying the loan, the executor should attempt to sell some nonliquid estate assets to raise the funds with which to repay the loan. In many instances, nonliquid assets could be sold to estate beneficiaries who want the assets and have sufficient cash to make the purchase.

It is generally not recommended that the ILIT make a loan to the immediate estate on terms more favorable than normal commercial standards. It is also not recommended that the ILIT forgive repayment of the loan. The IRS could attempt to include the life insurance proceeds in the insured's gross estate if the

ILIT appears to benefit the estate, and adverse income tax consequences might result. Forgiveness of the debt or a below-market-rate loan may cause the estate to incur imputed income.

Purchase of Estate Assets by ILIT

Rather than making a loan to an estate, an ILIT may choose to purchase assets from the estate. This transaction might serve two planning purposes. First, purchasing nonliquid assets for cash would provide much needed liquidity for the estate. Second, the ILIT would manage the estate assets it purchases according to its terms, and immediate distribution of the assets purchased by the ILIT to the trust beneficiaries would not be required. An example of an ILIT that serves these two planning purposes is a trust used as a vehicle for continuing the family business while solving the liquidity problems of the deceased business owner's estate.

Example: Ted Entrepreneur is the sole shareholder of Kinco, Inc., a family corporation. Ted's estate contains the following assets:

Kinco stock	$2,000,000
Residential real estate	$500,000
Cash and other liquid securities	$500,000
Commercial real estate	$1,500,000

Ted is divorced and has satisfied all property settlement arrangements with his former spouse. He has two children, a daughter, Christine, aged 25, and a son, Arthur, aged 22. Ted would like his children to continue Kinco after his death or retirement. However, his children are unprepared to take over control of the business at this time. Ted's estate forecast (for death in 1998) is as follows:

Gross estate	$4,500,000
Funeral and administration expenses (3 percent)	(135,000)
Marital deduction	0
Taxable estate	4,365,000
Tentative tax	2,041,050
Applicable credit amount	(202,050)
State death taxes paid (equal to state death tax credit)	(320,480)
Net federal estate tax	$1,519,020
Total death taxes and settlement expenses	$1,974,500
Liquid assets available	500,000
Liquidity shortfall	$1,474,500

This forecast reveals two problems. First, the death taxes that must be paid within 9 months of death are significant. Second, the composition of the estate's assets shows a substantial liquidity shortfall.

One solution to these problems is to create an ILIT funded with $2 million worth of life insurance on Ted's life. The trustee of the ILIT could be a close friend or relative of Ted's who has the skills either to manage the business or to select an appropriate manager. At Ted's death, the ILIT would receive $2 million of death benefits outside of Ted's gross estate. The trustee would purchase the Kinco stock held by the estate for its fair market value of $2 million. The trustee would then manage the trust principal (Kinco stock) for the benefit of Ted's children. The trust could stay in existence for many years, perhaps for the lifetimes of Christine and Arthur. From the standpoint of Ted's estate, the nonliquid family corporation would have been converted into $2 million of cash. This cash would be available immediately to pay the costs of settling Ted's estate.

CONCERNS ABOUT IRREVOCABILITY

Whether an ILIT purchases a life insurance policy on the life of the grantor or the grantor transfers an existing policy on his or her life to an ILIT, one disadvantage of an ILIT as an estate planning technique is that it is irrevocable. Many potential grantors are concerned about their inability to revoke, amend, or control the ILIT and the ultimate disposition of the insurance proceeds. First, a grantor may be reluctant to relinquish control of the policy permanently because of his or her worries that access to the cash surrender value may be necessary at some point in the future.

Second, a grantor may also be reluctant to relinquish dispositive control over a life insurance policy and premium funds because of a concern that his or her dispositive goals may change. For example, the grantor may be concerned about divorce. If his or her spouse is the beneficiary of an ILIT, a divorce subsequent to creating and funding the trust would certainly change the grantor's feelings about benefiting the ex-spouse. Or if the grantor's children are the beneficiaries of an ILIT and the grantor's relationship with one of them sours, the grantor may be less than enthusiastic about that child benefiting from the trust.

Likewise, a beneficiary's personal needs may change after the creation of an ILIT. A grantor may be concerned, too, that a change in the estate or gift tax laws could remove some of the tax advantages that are currently available to an ILIT.

A grantor for whom these concerns are minor is more likely to consider an ILIT. The ILIT is generally recommended for individuals who are older and have substantial wealth. Presumably, they will not need the policy's cash surrender value at a later date. In addition, these individuals are usually more secure in their marriages and their relationships with other potential ILIT beneficiaries.

These older and wealthier individuals may be more prepared to have the trust terms cast in stone.

Some of the techniques discussed below will offer flexibility to the grantor to manage these concerns. Most of the techniques involve careful drafting of the ILIT at its inception. Since the IRS will probably be very aggressive in its attempt to include life insurance in the decedent-insured's gross estate, caution is advised in the use of these techniques to prevent the grantor-insured from having any retained incidents of ownership. The ILIT should be planned, drafted, and implemented only with the assistance of an experienced estate planning attorney and life underwriter.

Retrieving Life Insurance Policy from ILIT

As discussed above, one concern about an ILIT is that the grantor-insured must irrevocably part with dominion and control of the life insurance policy. The policy's cash surrender value will be an asset of the ILIT and will therefore no longer be available to the grantor-insured. Many potential grantors are afraid to part with the policy in case they might need it for financial reasons or want to change beneficiaries in the future. The ILIT may, in fact, be designed and administered to permit the policy to be distributed to the grantor-insured or to another family member.

Supertrust Powers[8]

One possible method to unlock an ILIT and permit the grantor-insured to regain control of a policy that he or she transferred to the trust is to include a limited power of appointment over the trust's principal in the trust's terms. This power would specifically give the right to its holder to appoint the principal of the trust (that is, the life insurance policy). Thus, the life insurance policy held by the ILIT could be removed from the trust by exercising this power.

The holder of this limited power should be someone other than the grantor-insured. The typical arrangement is for the ILIT to give the power to the grantor-insured's spouse or to an adult child of the grantor-insured. Such a limited power would not cause the policy to be included in the gross estate of the individual who holds the power. Because the possible appointees of this limited power would not include the holder of the power, his or her creditors, estate, or the estate's creditors, the power would not be a general power. And since the grantor-insured would not be the holder of the power, he or she should not have any retained incidents of ownership in the policy.

In practice, it is expected that the holder of this limited power would exercise the power in favor of the grantor-insured if the grantor desires to regain control of the policy. However, the power must be exercised through the independent action of the holder of the limited power. There is, therefore, no guarantee that the power would be exercised according to the grantor-insured's wishes. In fact, the policy could be appointed contrary to the goals of the grantor-insured and his or her family.

Distribution by Independent Trustee

An independent trustee can be given the power to invade the corpus of the trust. If the trust terms permit, the trustee may be empowered to distribute the policy to anyone, including the grantor-insured, as long as the trustee is exercising his or her independent judgment. If it appears that the grantor-insured can control the trustee and retrieve the policy at any time, the IRS is sure to attempt to attribute retained incidents of ownership in the policy to the grantor-insured. Even if the trustee is acting independently, he or she may fear legal action by the trust beneficiaries for distributing the policy. The ILIT must be drafted carefully to permit the trustee to safely distribute the policy.

If the trustee is truly independent (for example, a bank and trust company), there should be no rational reason to distribute the policy. Why would an independent trustee who is charged with fiduciary responsibility in favor of the beneficiaries act adversely to their interests? But if the trustee is not truly independent or if the terms of the ILIT remove independent judgment, the grantor-insured would be treated as having retained incidents of ownership in the policy, and adverse estate tax consequences will result.

Purchasing Policy from ILIT

It is clear that the grantor-insured cannot explicitly retain the right or option to purchase the life insurance policy that he or she gratuitously transferred to an ILIT without adverse estate tax consequences. However, there is no reason why the trustee and grantor-insured could not reach an agreement on the purchase and sale of the policy in the absence of an express right or option. A trust's standard trustee powers clause generally gives the trustee broad discretionary investment powers. Therefore, the trustee of an ILIT usually has the right to sell a life insurance policy and to reinvest the proceeds from the sale in some other type of asset.

The trustee should be able to transact business with anyone, including the grantor-insured. What's more, the trustee should have no liability problems, provided any sale of trust assets meets normal commercial standards. Thus, the trustee of an ILIT should be able to sell the life insurance policy to the grantor-insured for its fair market value. (The methods for determining the fair market value of a policy are discussed in chapter 2.) The grantor-insured will not have retained the right to acquire the policy but will merely have reached an arm's length purchase and sale agreement with the trustee.

No estate tax problems should result because the grantor-insured will not have retained any incidents of ownership in the policy when it was transferred to the ILIT. However, if the grantor-insured does purchase the life insurance policy from the trust, the proceeds will be included in his or her gross estate unless the grantor retransfers all incidents of ownership more than 3 years prior to his or her death.

The practical consequences of this policy acquisition are threefold. First, the grantor-insured must come up with the purchase price to buy the policy. This is an additional expenditure since the grantor-insured has presumably paid the premiums on the policy. If the policy has a significant value, purchasing it may be undesirable to the grantor-insured.

Second, the grantor-insured will have incidents of ownership in the policy when he or she buys it from the ILIT. Consequently, as noted above, the life insurance policy will return to the grantor-insured's estate. A subsequent gift of the policy will be ineffective in removing it from the grantor-insured's gross estate unless he or she survives 3 years following the transfer.

Third, the trustee has to decide independently to sell the policy. The trustee will receive sale proceeds in return that must be reinvested. Unless the sale proceeds are significant, it may not be economically feasible to continue the trust further. The trustee may also be concerned about liability for the sale. If the grantor-insured's health is impaired, an ILIT beneficiary could certainly bring an action for breach of fiduciary duty if the sale proceeds do not take the impaired health into consideration.

Flexibility to Change Beneficiaries

Problem of Divorce

Obviously, the grantor-insured's divorce subsequent to the creation of an ILIT is a concern if the grantor-insured's ex-spouse is a beneficiary of the trust. The grantor-insured cannot reserve the right to change the beneficiaries of the ILIT without causing its inclusion in his or her gross estate. However, when the ILIT is created, the trust can simply stipulate that there be a contingent beneficiary to replace the ex-spouse beneficiary if the grantor is not married at the time of his or her death.

For example, an ILIT could provide for a life income to be paid to the grantor-insured's surviving spouse, but only to the surviving spouse to whom the grantor-insured is married at the time of his or her death. If divorce occurs, the grantor-insured's children would benefit immediately at his or her death. The IRS has ruled privately that allowing a contingent beneficiary to be named in an ILIT in the case of the grantor's divorce is not an incident of ownership in the policy (Ltr. 8819001).

Changing Other Beneficiaries

Since the grantor-insured cannot reserve the right to change trust beneficiaries, what can the grantor-insured do if the named beneficiaries of an ILIT no longer make sense? For example, what if the grantor-insured's children are the beneficiaries, and the grantor is estranged from one or more of them?

What if one or more beneficiaries is in financial difficulty and considering bankruptcy? Or what if a beneficiary is facing long-term care expenses, and trust funds would be exhausted if the trustee is compelled to pay for support and medical needs? The grantor-insured can anticipate such problems by making the trust truly discretionary. Giving the trustee sprinkle powers will not compel the trustee to distribute income or principal currently to any one beneficiary. Thus, the trustee could decide whether distributions to a beneficiary are appropriate at specific points in time.

Unfortunately, this approach, although it provides flexibility, has its drawbacks. The trustee must be relied on to make the correct decisions. There is no guarantee that the trustee will act according to the grantor-insured's preferences. What if the trustee fails to make distributions to beneficiaries who truly deserve them? Or what if the trustee distributes benefits equally and ignores requests from certain beneficiaries despite the fact that unequal distributions are indicated by the circumstances?

If the grantor-insured truly desires to change the beneficiaries of an ILIT, one option he or she has is simply to create a new ILIT. If the grantor-insured is insurable, the existing life insurance policy could be permitted to lapse by failing to make additional premium gifts to the old ILIT. The grantor-insured could then create and fund a new ILIT with the desired beneficiary provisions. The new ILIT would then purchase a new life insurance policy to cover the grantor-insured. Of course, this approach could be costly because the new policy's premium may be substantially higher than that of the lapsing policy. Moreover, the lapsing policy's cash surrender value would essentially be wasted as it would ultimately be used to benefit the beneficiaries of the old trust.

Another alternative is to purchase the policy from the old ILIT and to make a gift of the policy to a new ILIT. The old trust could continue with the sale proceeds of the policy as its principal, or it could distribute the sale proceeds outright to the beneficiaries. The gift of the existing policy to the new ILIT would invoke the 3-year rule of Sec. 2035. Therefore, the life insurance policy would be included in the grantor-insured's gross estate if he or she does not survive the 3-year period.

The 3-year rule cannot be avoided by having the new ILIT purchase the existing policy directly from the old ILIT. If the new ILIT purchases the existing policy from the old ILIT, the transfer-for-value rule would apply to the transaction, and some of the death proceeds would be subject to *income* taxation.

An exception to the transfer-for-value rule is when the grantor-insured purchases the existing policy from the old ILIT. This exception applies when the insured is the transferee of the policy.

Another exception to the transfer-for-value rule is when the transferee takes the transferor's income tax basis in the policy. After purchasing the existing policy from the old ILIT, the grantor-insured can then gift the policy to the new ILIT, which takes the grantor-insured's basis in the policy. Due to the exceptions to the transfer-for-value rule, no adverse income tax consequences will apply to this transaction.

Policy Replacement by Trustee

Competitive forces in the life insurance marketplace will always result in the introduction of new products. Does an ILIT limit the ability of the trustee to replace a life insurance policy with a more competitive product? Fortunately, the answer is no. A trustee typically has broad investment powers and can replace the trust principal with a new investment at any time. Certainly, replacing an existing life insurance policy is within the scope of these powers. (Surrendering a life insurance policy for cash value and investing the proceeds in mutual funds or securities is also within the scope of the trustee's investment powers.) To avoid potential estate tax problems, the replacement process should be performed in the same manner as the initial policy purchase. The trustee, as legal owner of the existing policy, should make the investment decision to replace that policy and should apply for a new policy. The grantor-insured should participate merely as an insured on the application and medical underwriting procedures. The IRS has ruled privately (Ltr. 8819001) that the replacement policy will avoid the grasp of the Sec. 2035 3-year rule under these circumstances.

SPECIAL PLANNING APPLICATIONS FOR ILIT

Generation-Skipping ILITs (Dynasty Trusts)

Planning for the GSTT implications of an ILIT is extremely important. An ILIT can be designed to skip the next generation of the grantor-insured's heirs. Or it can be designed so that the next generation receives benefits that are limited to less than the full principal of the ILIT. For example, at the death of the grantor-insured, his or her children might be given a life income interest. In some cases, the grantor-insured may provide concurrent benefits to be paid to his or her children and grandchildren. The trustee's broad sprinkle powers can provide for benefits at the trustee's discretion to both children and grandchildren. Even if the grandchildren do not benefit other than as remainder beneficiaries, the remainder interests will eventually be available to skip-generation beneficiaries. Under all the circumstances discussed above, the GSTT will be a factor to consider.

The grantor-insured may choose to provide significant benefits for his or her grandchildren (that is, skip beneficiaries) for many reasons. Perhaps the children are financially secure in their own right. Or a life income interest for the children may be sufficient for their support needs. Or the ILIT may be an appropriate vehicle for the grandparent to provide for the educational expenses of his or her grandchildren. Finally, the grantor-insured's children may be expected to be older when a death benefit is received by the ILIT. This is particularly true if the ILIT owns a second-to-die life insurance policy on the grantor and his or her spouse. Providing significant benefits to the grantor-insured's children may increase their estate taxes unnecessarily under these circumstances.

Sheltering ILIT from GSTT

The GSTT is, unfortunately, a particularly burdensome transfer tax. It applies in addition to estate or gift taxes. In fact, it is not invoked unless a transfer is taxable under the estate or gift tax rules. Thus, any transfer subject to the GSTT should also involve careful planning to minimize its estate or gift tax burden. However, the rules for the GSTT are different from those for the unified estate and gift tax system in many respects. First, the GSTT is imposed at the highest estate and gift tax rate, currently 55 percent. It is quite possible for a generation-skipping transfer to cause total transfer taxes in excess of 100 percent of the value of the property transferred.

Second, the $10,000 annual exclusion applicable to generation-skipping gifts is more restrictive than the gift tax annual exclusion. For purposes of the GSTT, the annual exclusion is available only for direct skips. Outright transfers to grandchildren or great grandchildren qualify for the exclusion. But what about gifts to trusts, such as an ILIT? Gifts to trusts qualify for the annual $10,000 GSTT exclusion only if

- the trust benefits one skip beneficiary
- no one else can receive an income or principal distribution during the skip beneficiary's life
- the principal is payable to the skip beneficiary's estate or is subject to his or her general power of appointment if the skip beneficiary dies before the trust terminates

These restrictions typically make the annual $10,000 GSTT exclusion ineffective for sheltering gifts to an ILIT. There is usually more than one beneficiary, and the benefits are generally designed to bypass the beneficiary's estate if he or she dies before the trust terminates. However, the Crummey provisions should still be included in the dynasty trust. Since both the gift tax and the GSTT apply to annual premium gifts, the Crummey powers are necessary to ensure the availability of the annual gift tax exclusion.

Fortunately, an ILIT benefiting grandchildren, a so-called dynasty trust, can avoid the GSTT for annual premium contributions because of another unique feature of the GSTT system. All transferors have a $1 million exemption against the GSTT. This $1 million exemption applies to lifetime gifts or testamentary transfers.

For planning purposes, the allocation of the $1 million GSTT exemption against premium gifts to a dynasty trust is quite beneficial. Since the exemption is applied dollar-for-dollar against the premium gifts rather than against the potentially much larger death proceeds, the allocation of the exemption to gifts to a dynasty trust has the advantage of leverage.

Example: Jennie Generian creates a dynasty trust to benefit her five grandchildren. The trustee applies for and owns a $1 million policy on

Jennie's life. The policy will be paid up with ten $25,000 annual premium contributions. The trust provides for Crummey powers to shelter the premium gifts from gift taxes. In addition, Jennie can shelter the premiums from the GSTT by allocating a portion of her $1 million GSTT exemption each year. If the policy meets its projections and Jennie survives the final required premium payment, she will have used $250,000 of her $1 million exemption. However, the death proceeds of $1 million will be entirely free of the GSTT and estate tax.

Compare this result with allocating the entire $1 million GSTT exemption to a testamentary $1 million bequest to the grandchildren. The leverage would be even greater if Jennie were to die prematurely before the premiums are paid.

Mechanics of $1 Million GSTT Exemption

A portion of the $1 million GSTT exemption must be allocated affirmatively each year to a dynasty trust. It is allocated on the basis of the annual life insurance premium payment transfers to the dynasty trust. Failure to make the annual allocation will make the proportionate share of the death proceeds nonexempt from the GSTT. The allocation is not automatic since the transfers to the dynasty trust are not direct skips. To allocate the exemption, these two steps must be followed:

- The grantor will have to file a timely gift tax return—Form 709—to allocate the GSTT exemption. (It is allocated on Schedule C of the return.) A late allocation is effective only when it is filed; it is not retroactive.
- A notice of allocation must be attached to the return and must contain (1) the trust's tax identification number, (2) the amount of exemption allocated to the gift, (3) the value of the trust principal at the time of the allocation, and (4) the GSTT inclusion ratio of the trust (usually zero if all gifts have been sheltered by the exemption).

ILITs and Employer-Provided Life Insurance

An ILIT is a useful vehicle for sheltering all types of life insurance coverage from estate taxes. Quite often, highly compensated employees receive significant life insurance coverage from their employers. If these individuals have substantial estates, estate planning for the employer-sponsored life insurance becomes critical. The employee can design an ILIT to receive the death benefits and remove the proceeds from his or her gross estate in some circumstances. For example, the employee can assign his or her rights to group term life coverage to an ILIT. If the employee-insured survives for 3 years following the assignment, the proceeds are excluded from his or her gross estate.

In some cases, an ILIT can be used to remove some employer-provided coverage from an employee-insured's gross estate without invoking the 3-year rule. For example, an employee-insured's ILIT can become a party to a split-dollar life insurance agreement with the employer. For executive-bonus insurance (a Sec. 162 life insurance plan), the ILIT can be the initial applicant and owner of the policy, effectively removing the proceeds immediately from the employee-insured's gross estate.

Charitable Wealth Replacement Trusts

Many wealthy individuals' estate plans include charitable contributions. These contributions may be made during the donor's lifetime or at his or her death. In any event, the property contributed to charity lowers the family wealth available to the donor's heirs. However, there are substantial income and gift or estate tax deductions for charitable contributions. An ILIT makes a perfect wealth replacement vehicle for the donor's heirs because it can be funded, at least in part, by the increased cash available to the donor as a result of income and gift tax deductions stemming from his or her charitable contributions. The donor simply creates an ILIT to be funded with sufficient life insurance coverage to replace the value of the property contributed to charity. The beneficiaries of the ILIT are the grantor's heirs who otherwise would have received the donated property.

NOTES

1. Hillery James Gallagher, "Life Insurance for the Liquid Estate," *Journal of the American Society of CLU & ChFC,* vol. XLVI, no. 2.
2. *Estate of Cristofani v. Commissioner,* 97 T. C. 74 (1991).
3. *Estate of Kohlsaat v. Commissioner,* T.C. Memo 1997-212.
4. *Estate of Holland v. Commissioner,* T. C. Memo 1997-302.
5. The ruling, a technical advice memorandum, addressed a couple of interesting issues. First, the grantor retained the right to notify the trustee each year whether or not to make the annual additions subject to Crummey withdrawal powers. Thus the grantor could eliminate the withdrawal right for spendthrift beneficiaries at any time. Since the grantor in this instance never notified the trustee to make the withdrawals available, the annual exclusion was denied.

    In addition, all beneficiaries executed statements indicating their acknowledgment that annual withdrawal notices would be forthcoming but waiving the right to receive such notices. The beneficiaries also retained the right to revoke the waiver and receive actual notice of withdrawal rights at any time. In the author's opinion the IRS may have gone too far since the adult beneficiaries did acknowledge future withdrawal rights. If the same premium is payable every year at the same time, the adult ILIT beneficiaries who execute such waivers certainly have actual knowledge of their annual withdrawal rights. In the recent *Holland* case discussed in the text corresponding to endnote 4 above, the court held that the lack of notice was not fatal to the taxpayer's case. The lack of notice may affect the likelihood of withdrawal, but it does not prevent the legal exercise.
6. Action on Decision (AOD 1996-010).

7. See, for example, TAM 9628004 discussed earlier, where the IRS denied annual exclusions for Crummey beneficiaries who had either extremely remote or no other beneficial interests in a trust.
8. This term refers to ILITs specifically designed to contain limited powers of appointment held by someone other than the grantor. For further discussion, see *Supertrust IV*, Frank B. Weisz, Wisestone Financial Publications, 1989.

4

Valuation Principles Used in the Estate Planning Process

Chapter Outline

VALUATION PRINCIPLES   114
    Decisions about Lifetime Giving   115
    Estate Liquidity   116
    Secs. 303 and 6166   116
    Pegging   116
    Family Business Exclusion   116
SOURCES OF VALUATION RULES   117
    Internal Revenue Code   117
    Treasury Regulations   117
    IRS Rulings   117
    IRS Publications   117
FAIR MARKET VALUE   118
ALTERNATE VALUATION DATE   119
    Procedural Points   119
    Exceptions to Its Use   120
    Summary and Examples   121
VALUATION OF SPECIFIC PROPERTY   121
    Valuation of Life Insurance and Annuity Contracts   122
    Valuation of Real Estate   124
    Valuation of Marketable Securities   132
    Valuation of Closely Held Corporations   132
    Valuation of Personal Property   144
IRC SEC. 7520: RULES FOR VALUING PARTIAL INTERESTS   145
    Valuation of Partial Nonconcurrent Property Interests   145
IRC SECS. 2701–2704: VALUATION OF LIFETIME TRANSFERS WITH
      RETAINED INTERESTS   150

To effectively prepare an estate plan, one of the planner's first objectives is to ascertain the potential size of the client's gross estate for federal estate tax purposes. In fact, the financial services professional cannot properly initiate any meaningful estate planning procedure without knowing the approximate size of the client's estate, which will directly affect the federal estate tax liability.

VALUATION PRINCIPLES

Before the size of the estate can be determined, however, the planner must understand valuation principles. Well-reasoned decisions involving valuation of assets are essential to a well-planned estate. If these vital issues involving specific valuation of assets have not been resolved during the estate owner's lifetime, the executor or administrator of the estate may be faced with unpleasant and potentially protracted struggles with the IRS over values of the estate's assets.

Often the estate's representative values an asset on the low side and the IRS representative values the same asset on the high side. If the two parties cannot agree on a specific issue, costly and time-consuming litigation (valuation litigation) to determine values can result. Even if the estate is ultimately successful in court (which statistics prove is rather uncommon), the family has still lost out because of high attorneys' fees, court costs, and the frustration inherent in such a situation.

Example: The executor of Jonah Tucker's estate placed a value of $225,000 on several acres of raw land that Mr. Tucker had owned in the mountains. The IRS representative, using his own real estate appraisers, placed a value of $472,000 on the land. The two sides have been unsuccessful in reaching an agreement on what value should be affixed to the land. The dispute has now gone to the Tax Court, where it has been pending for well over 4 years. The estate cannot be closed while the litigation is pending. Furthermore, the estate is incurring court costs and attorneys' fees during this period. Even if the estate prevails in court, little will be accomplished because of both the economic and noneconomic aspects of the situation.

Planning point: The competent estate planner must prepare a client for the possibility of a valuation dispute. In the interest of prudent planning, realistic and technically accurate valuation principles must be applied to all estate assets so that future valuation disputes can be avoided.

Life insurance point: If an estate becomes involved in a valuation dispute and must go to court, there are three forums that are available in which to litigate the issue. The estate may use the United States District

Court or the Court of Federal Claims only if the disputed amount of the tax is paid first. If there are not funds available to pay the tax, the Tax Court is the court that must be used. Because there are tactical advantages of choosing one court over another (for example, the District Court will allow a jury trial), it is imperative that the estate have adequate liquidity to pay the tax first. Ample amounts of life insurance on the life of the decedent will remove any liquidity deficit, which will allow the estate to pay any disputed tax and thus litigate tax issues in any forum that the estate chooses.

If possible, questions involving valuation of assets for federal estate tax purposes should obviously be resolved during the lifetime of the estate owner. (Several available methods for the prompt resolution of valuation issues will be discussed in later sections of this chapter.)

In addition to these general considerations, there are specific reasons why it is vital to resolve valuation questions during the estate owner's lifetime. These issues include the following:

- decisions about lifetime giving
- estate liquidity
- Secs. 303 and 6166
- pegging
- family business exclusion

Decisions about Lifetime Giving

Many estate owners may wish to engage in gift-giving programs. The gifting program could include both charitable and noncharitable donees. Even though there is a gift tax that is applied with the same tax rates as the estate tax, there are still many advantages to gifting assets during one's lifetime.

First, if the property in question produces income, the federal and local income tax liability will be shifted to the donee.

Second, future appreciation inherent in the gifted asset will also be shifted to the donee.

Third, there is an annual exclusion for lifetime gifts that is unavailable for transfers at death.

Fourth, charitable gifts both reduce the size of the donor's estate and provide a current income tax deduction.

However, to effectively develop a gifting program and adequately alert the client to all of its implications, the planner must first thoroughly address the valuation issues with respect to the property that will be transferred. The value of the property will determine the use of the annual exclusion or applicable credit amount, the need to file a gift tax return, and the size of any charitable deductions available.

Estate Liquidity

In order to advise a client about anticipated estate tax liability and estate liquidity deficits, the planner must calculate a hypothetical estate. But in order to do that, specific dollar values must be assigned to all estate assets.

Secs. 303 and 6166

If a business interest will be included in the client's gross estate, such estate planning techniques as a Sec. 303 redemption (income-tax-advantaged redemption of closely held stock) or a Sec. 6166 installment payout of federal estate taxes (advantageous 15-year payout of federal estate tax liability) cannot be meaningfully considered until valuation questions are resolved. Because the Internal Revenue Code imposes certain percentage prerequisites before such relief provisions can be taken advantage of, these percentage tests cannot be applied until the value of the adjusted gross estate is determined.

Pegging

Another reason to establish valuation during the estate owner's lifetime is the necessity of "pegging" the value of a business interest for federal estate tax purposes.

The value of a closely held business interest is particularly difficult to determine. Goodwill, dividend-paying and dividend-earning capacity, and trends within the particular industry are among the factors that must be considered in addition to book value.

Often a dispute arises between the estate and the IRS on this valuation question. If an effective buy-sell agreement between a willing buyer and a willing seller has been drafted, and certain technical provisions (which are discussed below) are included as part of the buy-sell agreement, the value of the business interest will be pegged or set. However, to ensure that this arrangement is properly structured, there should be adequate life insurance to fund the buy-out transaction. The starting point in this type of transaction must be to arrive at a value for the business interest.

Family Business Exclusion

Finally, TRA 97 added a new exclusion for qualifying estates of certain family-owned businesses. The rules for this new exclusion are extremely complex, and valuation is a critical component of the various standards that must be met to qualify for the exclusion. For example, the exclusion will not be available unless the value of the family business held by the estate exceeds 50 percent of the adjusted gross estate. Thus, the value of the business included in the estate along with the value of the other estate assets must be determined accurately if the business owner would like his or her estate plan to contemplate the use of the exclusion to reduce taxes. Failure to qualify due to a valuation mistake would result in further liquidity problems.

SOURCES OF VALUATION RULES

Internal Revenue Code

The Internal Revenue Code has several sections relevant to valuation rules. Secs. 2031 and 2511 give basic statements discussing the timing of gift or estate transfers and provide for fair market value as the measure of a taxable transfer. Sec. 2032 gives an alternate valuation date providing that an executor can value assets 6 months after the date of death in some circumstances. Sec. 2032A provides for valuing farm or business real property at its actual use value, if this is less than fair market value, under some circumstances. Sec. 7520 has rules for valuing partial interests, such as term interests, life estates, annuities, or remainders. Finally, Sec. 6662 provides tax penalties for inaccurate valuations resulting in tax underpayments.

Treasury Regulations

The Treasury Regulations give much more extensive guidance for valuing property. Specifically, Secs. 20.2031 and 25.2512 provide rules for valuing estate and gift transfers respectively. Secs. 1.170A-12 and 13 contain rules for valuing and substantiating charitable deductions. Finally, Sec. 1.664-4 has rules for valuing remainder interests in a charitable remainder unitrust. Some of the older regulations concerning the valuation of partial interests in property do not reflect the current requirements of Sec. 7520, but they still provide helpful guidance to the procedures used in valuing such property interests.

IRS Rulings

The IRS has on occasion published rulings, notices, or procedures for valuation issues. Most notably, Rev. Rul. 59-60 deals with the valuation of a closely held business interest. Rev. Rul. 93-12 provides for discounts available for minority interests in a family-controlled business. IRS Notices 89-24 and 89-60 provide guidance for the valuation of charitable remainder trust deductions under the current Sec. 7520 rules. The IRS will generally not issue private rulings with respect to specific property valuation issues.

IRS Publications

The IRS has produced several publications that are useful for valuation of property. Publication 561, *Determining the Value of Donated Property,* gives guidance for valuing and substantiating charitable donations for income tax purposes. IRS Publication 1457, *Actuarial Values Alpha Volume;* Publication 1458, *Actuarial Values Beta Volume;* and Publication 1459, *Actuarial Values Gamma Volume,* provide interest rate and mortality factors for calculating partial interests in accordance with Sec. 7520. These publications can be obtained by contacting the Superintendent of Documents; however, there is a fee for the actuarial volumes.

FAIR MARKET VALUE

The value of an asset for federal estate tax purposes—that is, the specific dollar amount to be included as part of the federal gross estate—is the fair market value of the asset on either the date of death or the alternate valuation date, which is 6 months following death. The value of an asset for federal gift tax purposes is the fair market value of the asset being gifted on the date a completed gift is made.

Although the terms *value* and *fair market value* are mentioned in the Internal Revenue Code, they are not defined. Fortunately, *fair market value* is defined as follows in the Treasury regulations (at Sec. 20.2031): "the price at which property would change hands between a willing buyer and a willing seller, neither being under any compulsion to buy or sell and both having reasonable knowledge of relevant facts." (In *Estate of Gilford,* the Tax Court said, "Property is valued as of the valuation date on the basis of the facts available and the market conditions on the valuation date without regard to hindsight. Postmortem events can be considered by the courts to determine what a willing buyer and seller's expectations were on the valuation date, but only to the extent that the subsequent events were reasonably foreseeable on the valuation date.")

Example: Suppose the decedent, Mr. Jones, was the sole owner of a closely held corporation. At the time of his death, the business was worth $5 million as a going concern. However, $2 million was reasonably attributed solely to his expertise. It is permissible to discount the value of the business to $3 million since the loss of goodwill as a result of his death is reasonably anticipated. However, if his goodwill had no value at the date of death and the drop in value after his death was a result of mismanagement by successors, the value must be determined by the full fair market value at the date of death. (See the discussion below for potential relief under Sec. 2032 .)

Although the fair market value definition is somewhat helpful, it is obvious that there is room for flexibility, depending on who is valuing an asset and other facts of the particular case. Because the definition of fair market value is rather loose, ancillary factors—such as the relationship between the buyer and the seller, options to purchase or sell, and frequency of sales—are used in reaching a decision on valuation questions.

ALTERNATE VALUATION DATE

What is the alternate valuation date for federal estate tax purposes, and how did it become part of the law? Consider the following hypothetical case. Donald Jones died in September 1929 with a gross estate of over $3 million, most of it consisting of marketable securities. After his death but before the final administration of his estate, the stock market crashed, and all the securities in Jones's gross estate became worthless.

This example illustrates the illogical result when there is a rigid date-of-death valuation: The estate was worth less than the amount of the federal estate tax liability, which was based on the value at death.

The possibility of such an occurrence motivated Congress to introduce into the federal estate tax laws a safety provision to guard against such an illogical situation. The alternate valuation date, as provided for in Sec. 2032, is the result.

Sec. 2032 of the Internal Revenue Code allows the executor or administrator of the estate to choose or *elect* the date 6 months after the decedent's death instead of the actual date of death as the date for setting the value of estate assets. However, for the election (which is made by proper notation on the federal estate tax return) to be effective, the estate tax return must be filed within the statutory period established for filing returns.

Procedural Points

There are a few procedural points to bear in mind in electing the alternate valuation date.

First, once the election has been made, it cannot be revoked. This is logical since market fluctuations often take place, and if the election could be revoked, an executor might keep making and rescinding the election to the estate's advantage as asset values keep changing.

Second, if the alternate valuation date is elected, the election applies to *all* assets included in the decedent's gross estate, rather than only part of the estate. In short, there may be no picking and choosing. It is all or nothing, except for two instances that will be discussed below.

Third, the election should be made with not only federal estate tax considerations but also federal income tax considerations in mind. The higher the valuation of the asset, the higher its basis and therefore the *lower* the federal income tax liability at resale. If the alternate valuation date is elected, the basis of a certain asset could be lower than if the date-of-death value had been used and therefore could result in a higher income tax liability when the beneficiary sells the asset. So it is necessary to weigh the federal estate tax implications and the federal income tax implications. If the estate tax bracket is higher than the income tax bracket, the alternate valuation date makes sense if the value is lower on the alternate valuation date. Conversely, if the income tax bracket is higher than the estate tax bracket and if it is likely that assets will be sold at some subsequent time, it is wise to forgo election of the alternate valuation date to get a higher basis.

Fourth, in the event that the alternate valuation method is elected, federal estate tax deductions for estate administration expenses or losses can be claimed only if they are not already allowed by reason of the election. For example, no Sec. 2054 deduction will be permitted for casualty losses for an asset destroyed in the 6 months following death and not compensated for by insurance or otherwise if the asset is included in the gross estate at a zero value as a direct result of electing the alternative valuation approach. This rule prevents an estate from benefiting from both the reduced value and the loss deductions.

Exceptions to Its Use

One final point about electing the alternate valuation date involves the following three circumstances that preclude its use:

- *when there is a sale or exchange of assets during the 6-month period*—If estate assets are distributed, sold, exchanged, or otherwise disposed of during the 6-month period, they must be valued as of the date of disposition, not the date 6 months after death. In essence, the date of disposition fixes the alternate valuation date.

   Example: Bradley Minder died January 14, 1995, with a gross estate of $944,000. The majority of the estate consisted of marketable securities. During the months following Bradley Minder's death, the stocks held by the estate decreased in value and the executor made the decision to elect the alternate valuation date. Three hundred shares of EXXCO, Inc., were sold 2 months following Bradley Minder's death because the estate's advisers urged such a sale. These securities must be valued as of the date of the sale, not as of the date 6 months after death.

- *when the estate involves property whose value is affected by the mere passage of time*—An asset whose value will definitely be affected by the mere passage of time may not be valued 6 months after the date of death. The most frequently used illustration is a patent right, which has a limited life span and will diminish in value as time passes. Therefore it is deemed inappropriate to use the alternate valuation date because it would result in shrinkage in value unrelated to market conditions, which is contrary to the intent of the alternate valuation date. Note that the value of annuities that provide income to another person and are includible in a decedent's estate is affected by the mere passage of time.
- *when the election will not reduce the gross estate and estate tax*—The election is unavailable if its use does not both (1) reduce the gross estate

and (2) reduce the actual estate taxes due. This restriction prevents the executor from gaining income tax advantages on an estate that does not need the relief of Sec. 2032. For example, suppose a taxable estate is under $625,000 and that estate assets have risen in value during the 6 months following the decedent's death, but they still do not exceed $625,000 in value. If the death occurred in 1998, the applicable credit amount will absorb all estate taxes and the Sec. 2032 election will not save estate taxes. However, the use of Sec. 2032, if available under these circumstances, would provide the heirs with a higher stepped-up income tax basis in the estate's assets. The additional step-up in basis would be unjustified under these facts.

Planning point: The estate may not pick and choose when electing the alternate valuation date, applying the date-of-death value to some assets and applying the alternate valuation date to others. Accordingly, the executor must use a balancing test when deciding whether or not to elect the alternate valuation date.

Summary and Examples

In summary, if the alternate valuation approach is elected, it will apply to all assets in the estate. The valuation date will be 6 months from the date of death. However, property distributed, sold, exchanged, or otherwise disposed of during that period will be valued as of the date of disposition.

Example 1: The estate of Doris Sayres owns stock in corporation M, corporation O, and corporation R, each of which is valued at $200,000. Six months later the stock has not been disposed of and the M corporation stock has increased in value to $230,000. Further, the O corporation stock has gone down in value to $30,000, and the R corporation stock has stayed the same. None of the estate's other assets has increased or decreased in value. It is possible to elect alternate valuation because the estate's net value has decreased.

Example 2: Using the same facts as in example 1 except that on the alternate valuation date corporation M has increased in value to $450,000, alternate valuation would not be elected because the estate has increased in value.

VALUATION OF SPECIFIC PROPERTY

We are now ready to focus on the valuation of specific property and will consider the following assets:

- life insurance and annuity contracts
- real estate
- marketable securities
- closely held corporations
- personal property

Valuation of Life Insurance and Annuity Contracts

The value placed on a specific life insurance policy can differ from one context to another. This is not surprising since there are many value components of varying degrees of complexity in a life insurance policy: cash surrender value, interpolated terminal reserve, unused portion of the premium, and of course the face amount of the policy itself. How then should a life insurance policy be valued?

The answer is, it depends. We have seen in chapter 2 that when a paid-up life insurance policy is the subject of a gift, the value will be the policy's replacement value—that is, the cost of similar or comparable policies issued by the same company. We have also pointed out that when the policy is transferred immediately after its purchase (that is, within the first year), the gift will be equal to the gross premium paid to the insurer prior to the time of the transfer. The general rule involving lifetime transfers of life insurance contracts, however, is that the value of the property will equal the interpolated terminal reserve in the policy plus the unearned premiums on the date of the gift. (Interpolated terminal reserve is similar to the cash value of a life insurance policy but is based on end-of-the-year reserves of a life insurance contract.)

For purposes of federal estate taxation, however, a completely different standard is applied. To determine what the actual value of the life insurance contract should be for this tax, the estate planner must refer to Sec. 2042, where rules are given for determining the specific dollar amount to be included in the estate owner's federal gross estate. If the policy is included in the insured's gross estate, the face amount is the relevant value.

> *Example:* Jack Johnson does not have a large estate. He has very little cash and does not own a home, a business interest, or much other property. However, he does own several large life insurance policies on his own life. Because of this life insurance, his gross estate will be large enough to attract a federal estate tax liability.

> *Planning point:* The estate planner should take immediate steps to remove the life insurance from Jack Johnson's gross estate. This can be done either by having Jean Johnson, Jack's wife, own the policies or by transferring the policies to an irrevocable life insurance trust.

Life insurance point: While Jack Johnson's life insurance is being transferred, his overall insurance needs should be reviewed. Whenever life policies are being transferred, it is always an appropriate time to review the amount and type of coverage.

The rule involving valuation of a life policy when the estate owner is not the insured involves a different standard. When the estate owner owns a life insurance policy on someone else's life, the interpolated terminal reserve is used to establish the insurance policy's value. This topic was covered in detail in chapter 2.

For federal estate tax purposes, annuity contracts must be valued in accordance with the standards established by Treas. Reg. Sec. 20.2031-8, which provides that the valuation is to be made according to the cost of "comparable" contracts issued by the company. What this means is that the annuity will be valued at whatever it would cost the survivor (at the date of death) to buy a contract with the same benefits as those contained in the existing annuity contract.

For estate tax purposes and more specifically for determining the annuity amount to be included in the gross estate of the decedent, Sec. 2039(a) controls. This section of the Internal Revenue Code requires inclusion of the annuity in the estate owner's gross estate only when the product involved is a joint and survivor annuity. More specifically, the value of the annuity to be included in the gross estate is the value of amounts receivable by beneficiaries "by reason of surviving the decedent." The value (that is, the fair market value) of the survivor's interest is determined as of the date of death.

If the annuity payments that the surviving beneficiary will receive are not being issued by a "company that regularly engages in such business," a replacement-cost technique for valuation purposes would make no sense, and the valuation of the annuity would have to be determined by specific Internal Revenue Service tables.

Example: Jim Boxner purchased a joint and survivor annuity contract (with his wife, Betty, as the co-owner) from the Apex Life Insurance Company, which rarely sells such products anymore. Jim made payments on the annuity contract for 19 years and then began to receive payments under the contract. Jim died 3 years after he began receiving annuity payments, but his wife, Betty, as surviving beneficiary, began receiving annuity payments that are due to continue for the balance of her life. Since Apex Life Insurance Company cannot be considered to be a company that regularly engages in the annuity business, a replacement-cost technique for valuation purposes would make no sense. Accordingly, the annuity will need to be valued by referring to the rules of Sec. 7520 (discussed later) for the valuation of annuities.

Valuation of Real Estate

Factors in Setting Value

The value of an asset for federal estate tax purposes is its *fair market value* on the date of death or alternate valuation date, but this is not easy to ascertain when it comes to real estate. True, the fair market value is the price that a willing buyer and willing seller agree on, but what are the specific circumstances to look at in order to establish the correct price?

Placing a value on real estate will initially depend directly on whether there is a ready market for the property in question. If there is no actual market for the property, the relevant factor to be applied is either (1) the highest price available or (2) the salvage value of the property, whichever is greater.

If there is a ready market for the real property in question, there are many factors to take into consideration:

- the actual and potential use of the property (often referred to as the "highest and best use")
- economic conditions that might affect the value of the property
- legal restrictions on the property, such as zoning considerations or easements
- the fair market value of other properties in the area
- prices at which similar real property in the area was sold around the same time as the applicable valuation date—provided the sale was an arm's-length transaction (In the 1985 Tax Court case of *Rubish*, an estate's expert witness had valued the decedent's ranch by discounting comparable sales made one year after the date of death back to the date of death. The IRS had computed a higher value based on comparable sales that had been made on dates close to the date of the decedent's death. The court held for the IRS, stating that the estate had not successfully shown the lower value was correct because the expert witness who prepared the valuation did not testify in court. An expert had testified on behalf of the IRS in support of the higher value.)
- the specifics of the property itself, such as location of the realty, unusual physical characteristics, and the like
- any net income received from the property
- the nature and specific condition of the property involved
- any other relevant factors

Even though real property is traditionally thought of as illiquid, there is a fair degree of flexibility in its valuation. For example, if a piece of real property is sold within a reasonable time after the decedent's death and it is clear that the highest possible price has been paid, the amount received will most likely be accepted as the value. Unaccepted offers to purchase real estate will also be taken into account in the valuation process.

Special-Use Valuation

The general rule is that property is valued at fair market value. The implication of this requirement is that a willing and rational buyer would provide a purchase price equal to the value of the property placed in its highest and best economic use. However, it is possible that the decedent and his or her heirs did not, and will not, place the property in its highest and best use.

Consider the following circumstances. Frank Farmer owns 1,600 acres of upper Midwest farmland, which he inherited from his father. Frank actively farms the land and finds it a profitable operation. He feels that the farm property is worth approximately $2,100 per acre, an estimate that he bases on sales of comparable property in the area and on his general knowledge of farmland prices.

Frank dies December 25, 1995. His accountant and other tax advisers preparing his federal estate tax return value the farm property at $2,122 per acre, which they have determined is the actual value of the property when used for farm purposes. Upon examination of the federal estate tax return, however, the IRS decides that the farm property should have been valued at $3,817 per acre. The revenue agent in charge of the case readily admits that for farming purposes the property is worth $2,122 per acre but bases his $3,817-per-acre figure on the highest and best use of the property because it is near a new 25-acre industrial park.

The revenue agent's position is correct as a matter of law. Real estate such as farmland or ranchland or any real estate used in a closely held trade or business may be valued by the IRS for federal estate taxation at the price that its highest and best use, rather than its actual use, would command. Even though Frank Farmer farmed the land and would never have sold the property to the industrial park, the highest-and-best-use price therefore will be the amount included in Frank's gross estate for purposes of federal estate taxation.

Requirements for Qualification. Many farming and real estate groups attacked the obvious inequity in such an arrangement, and in the Tax Reform Act of 1976 a new valuation section—Sec. 2032A—was added to the Internal Revenue Code. The new provision is known as the special-use valuation election. In order to qualify for its benefits, a decedent's estate must meet the following conditions:

- The decedent must have been a citizen or resident of the United States.
- The executor must follow the appropriate procedure to file the special election.

- At least 50 percent of the value of the gross estate must consist of the value of real or personal property devoted to the qualifying use, after certain adjustments (the 50 percent rule).
- A minimum of 25 percent of the adjusted value of the gross estate must consist of the adjusted value of real property that (1) goes to a "qualified heir" and (2) was owned for at least 5 out of the 8 years just before the decedent's death by the decedent or a member of the decedent's family, who used it for a qualified use (the 25 percent rule).

Even if the estate meets the above requirements, the farmland (or other real property) must satisfy certain additional prerequisites before the special-use valuation can be elected. Specifically, the special-use valuation election may be applied only to farmland, ranchland, or real property used in a closely held trade or business.

Finally, the special election is available only if (1) the decedent used the real property in the qualifying use before his or her death and (2) the heirs of the decedent continue the special use of the property.

According to Sec. 2032A, the maximum amount by which the decedent's gross estate may be reduced under special-use valuation is $750,000 (this threshold will be indexed for inflation beginning in 1999).

In summary, therefore, in order to successfully elect under Sec. 2032A of the Internal Revenue Code, (1) the decedent must have owned a working farm or ranch, (2) the decedent or a member of the decedent's family must have been materially participating in the operation of the farm or ranch, (3) the farm or ranch must have been acquired from or passed from the decedent, (4) the interest must pass to a qualified heir of the decedent, and (5) the qualified heir must continue the qualified use of the property.

The real property is deemed in a qualifying use if it is used as a farm or in a closely held business. The property must have been used in the qualifying use 5 or more years of the previous 8 years before the decedent's death. The decedent or his or her family must have materially participated in the use during this period, but material participation is met if they actively managed the land as a rental property used by tenants in the qualifying use.

The requirements after the decedent's death begin with the qualified-heir restriction. The property must be acquired from the decedent by the qualified heir—a group comprising the decedent's ancestors, spouse, lineal descendants, and the spouses of lineal descendants. The requirements are met even if the recipient subsequently transfers the property, providing that the transferee is a qualified heir of the transferor.

The qualified heir or heirs must continue the qualified use. Following a grace period ending 2 years after the decedent's death, the appropriate qualified heir or heirs must materially participate in using the real property in the qualified use 5 or more of the succeeding 8 years. The disposition of the property by the qualified heir or the failure to continue the qualified use results in estate tax recapture, as discussed below.

The Tax Court case *Estate of Thompson* illustrates the difficulty of successfully meeting the qualified-heir requirement. In order to be a qualified heir, a person must be the spouse of the decedent, an ancestor of the decedent, or the lineal descendant or spouse of the lineal descendant of the decedent, the decedent's spouse, or the decedent's parents. In *Estate of Thompson,* the decedent's will had left two farms to a residuary trust that provided for the income to be paid to the decedent's two daughters and an unrelated third party. Upon the death of all three income beneficiaries, the trust corpus was to pass according to the two daughters' appointments in their wills among any of the decedent's issue or any charity. Because the two daughters wanted to be able to make the election under Sec. 2032A of the Internal Revenue Code, they were advised to remove any unqualified heirs. Therefore, they disclaimed their powers of appointment over the trust corpus and paid off the unrelated third party so that she would also disclaim her property rights. The Sec. 2032A election was then made.

When the IRS refused to accept the Sec. 2032A election, litigation in the Tax Court resulted. The court was called upon to decide if the third party was an unqualified heir, thereby defeating the Sec. 2032A election, and if so, if her disclaimer removed the problem. The court found that because the third party had accepted the benefits of the property interest prior to making the disclaimer of her property rights, an interest in the property for which special-use valuation was elected had passed to an unqualified heir such that the requirements of Sec. 2032A were not met. In short, the Tax Court approved the IRS's decision to disallow the special-use election.

> *Life insurance point:* Recapture of the estate tax savings of special-use property will occur if the property is disposed of to a nonqualified heir. To preserve the tax savings, the heirs should enter into a restrictive transfer agreement, such as an insured buy-sell agreement, to prevent the transfer of the property to outsiders.

Procedural Aspects of Its Election. For an estate to take advantage of the special-use valuation election, there are several procedural elements to take into account:

- The executor or administrator of the estate must expressly elect to have Sec. 2032A applied and must file an agreement that is then attached to the federal estate tax return. Once the election has been made, it cannot be revoked.
- The executor or administrator must file a notice of election, which indicates satisfactory compliance with the separate eligibility prerequisites of the decedent's estate and the real property involved.

- The written agreement filed by the executor or administrator must designate the real property to be valued. In addition, all interested parties must consent in writing to the imposition of additional tax should recapture take place. (In PLR 8645004, the IRS took the position that every partner in a partnership that owned real estate must sign this agreement. In this case, the IRS disallowed the special-use valuation treatment because not every partner with an interest in the special-use property had signed the agreement.)
- Special rules permit reformations of incorrect elections if the original election substantially complies with the rules and the reformation occurs within 90 days.

In the *Collins* case, the decedent's estate attempted to elect special use valuation for a farm but forgot to provide the farm's legal description and adjusted value and a separate written appraisal. After the IRS denied the election, the estate claimed substantial compliance and sought to perfect the election as Sec. 2032A provides. The Tax Court held in favor of the IRS. The Court said that because the estate had failed to substantially comply with the procedural requirements of IRC Sec. 2032A, the election was unavailable.

Recapture. The major disadvantage of making the Sec. 2032A special-use election is the possibility that recapture may occur.

Congress enacted the special Sec. 2032A relief provision to aid farm families and to protect them from a distorted valuation of farm property. While Congress enacted this section to encourage the continued use of real property in family farms and other small business operations, it wanted to ensure that if the farm use was not continued for a certain period, the safe harbor of the reduced valuation would be forfeited. The concept of recapture is the result.

Recapture is an additional estate tax that will be imposed (usually within 10 years after the decedent's death) if the qualified heir (1) disposes of an interest in property valued under Sec. 2032A to someone who is not a member of the family or (2) ceases to use the farmland, ranchland, or real property used in a closely held trade or business for the qualified use—that is, for farming or ranching purposes, or in the closely held business. The possibility of recapture will end at the death of the qualified heir or at the end of the 10-year period following the date of the original decedent's death, whichever comes first.

If an estate becomes subject to a recapture tax, the amount of the additional tax will be equal to the federal estate tax that was saved by having successfully elected the special-use valuation in the first place. This approach is logical since it was the intent of Congress that the estate would revert to the position it was in before the special election was made.

The seventh circuit case of *Martin* illustrates how a recapture event may inadvertently result. In this case, a decedent's farm had been valued for federal estate tax purposes using the special-use valuation technique. Subsequently, however, the farm was leased by the decedent's heirs on a net cash lease basis to an unrelated third party. The IRS took the position that the event triggered a recapture tax since the heirs were no longer using the farm for its qualified purpose. The court upheld the IRS's position, holding that the lease made the heirs "passive investors" and not material participants in the actual farming of the land. Accordingly, the court took the position that the farm no longer met the qualified use and upheld the imposition of the recapture tax.

In *Bruch,* a similar case heard in a U.S. District Court in Indiana, the decedent had owned two parcels of farmland that he had leased to a neighbor because the decedent had become ill. The IRS reviewed the special-use election and denied its application, stating that the qualified-use requirement had not been met. The court upheld the IRS's view.

Valuation Issues for Special-Use Property. There have been a number of cases and revenue rulings announced that illustrate quite clearly that the IRS continues to apply the special-use valuation rules in a very stringent and restrictive fashion. For example, in Rev. Rul. 89-30 the IRS took the position that an executor of an estate who makes the Sec. 2032A election must follow certain guidelines. Specifically, Sec. 2032A provides two separate methods for accomplishing the valuation of real property includible in a decedent's gross estate by resorting to current-use value instead of highest-and-best-use value: (1) an objective capitalization-of-rent method as set forth by Sec. 2032A(e)(7) and (2) a more liberal and subjective method using five separate factors as set forth by Sec. 2032A(e)(8).

In Rev. Rul. 89-30 the IRS took the position that an executor may not select one of the five valuation factors as the exclusive basis for valuing real estate used in farming, but rather must apply all five factors in determining the special-use valuation. Furthermore, in Rev. Rul. 89-22 the IRS analyzed the phrase "member of his family" appearing in Sec. 2032A(c)(1). In essence, Sec. 2032A(c)(1) imposes an additional estate tax in the nature of recapture if special-use property is disposed of or stops being used for a qualified use by qualified heirs during the 10-year period. However, the Code further states that when a qualified heir transfers the property to a member of his family, no recapture will be imposed. In Rev. Rul. 89-22 the IRS concluded that the phrase "member of his family" does not include a cousin.

In the Tax Court case of *Estate of Evers,* the court held in favor of the IRS and stated that the Sec. 2032A special-use valuation election is the value of the qualified property for all federal estate tax purposes, including for purposes of the marital deduction. The decedent's qualified heirs had agreed to elect special-use valuation for four tracts of land. However, the estate, although having made the election, used the full fair market value to compute the federal estate tax marital deduction. The IRS argued that the special-use valuation amount must be used for both purposes, and the Tax Court agreed with the IRS position.

The law provides two specific methods for placing a value on real property that qualifies for special-use valuation: the formula method and the multiple-factor method.

Formula Method of Valuation. The formula method can be used only to value qualified real property used for farming or ranching and cannot be applied to other types of real property (such as realty used in a closely held trade or business).

To find the value of the farmland or ranchland in question, the formula takes the average annual gross cash rental of comparable land used for a comparable purpose and then subtracts the average annual state and local real estate taxes for the comparable land. The resulting figure is then divided by the average annual effective interest rate for all new Federal Land Bank loans to give the property's value.

Since the comparable land must actually be rented for farming purposes, obviously the formula method cannot be used if there is no comparable local farmland. (The same piece of comparable land does not have to be rented during the entire 5-year period, but an actual tract of farmland meeting the requirements of Sec. 2032A must specifically be identified for each year.)

An example might best show how the formula method actually operates. Suppose the decedent dies on August 16, 1995, owning 850 acres of farmland. The executor of the estate wants to elect the special-use valuation approach, since the highest and best use of the property will be substantially higher than the actual farm use because the location is excellent for a shopping center. The executor obtains the following data: (1) the gross cash rental per acre of comparable land, $20; (2) the average annual state and local real estate taxes for the comparable land, $3 per acre; and (3) the average annual effective interest rate for all new Federal Land Bank loans, 8.75 percent. This formula can be expressed in the form of a fraction:

$$\frac{\$20 - \$3}{.0875}$$

The formula determines the dollar value per acre for the farmland, $194.2857.

Multiple-Factor Method of Valuation. The law provides for a multiple-factor valuation method as well as the formula method. As mentioned, this is the only special-use valuation method for qualifying real property used for a closely held business other than farming or ranching.

Sec. 2032A(e)(8) stipulates that several factors must be taken into account in order to use the multiple-factor method of valuation:

- the capitalization of income that the property can be expected to yield for farming, ranching, or closely held business purposes over a reasonable period of time
- the capitalized value of the fair rental value based on farm or other actual use
- the assessed land value
- the comparable sales of land in the same geographical area but in locations in which nonagricultural use is not a significant factor in the sales price
- any other factor that tends to establish a value based on the actual use of the property

The advantage of this approach, of course, is that application of these factors results in a valuation that equals the actual value of the asset rather than the highest-and-best-use value. Clearly this could have a significant effect on the size of the decedent's gross estate and, in turn, on the amount of federal estate tax liability.

Is the Election Worthwhile? At first blush it would appear that all estates should elect the special-use valuation provisions of Sec. 2032A and reduce the federal estate tax liability. However, the election presents many potential problems.

The first question that arises is, can the estate even qualify? As mentioned, there are complex and demanding requirements that must be met before an executor or administrator can even begin to think about the election: the 50 percent rule, the 25 percent rule, qualified-use tests, and so on.

Second and more significant is the fact that the property must remain as farmland, ranchland, or real property in a closely held business for many years into the future. If not, the additional tax in the form of recapture will be the result. Since few estate owners know enough about the wishes and plans of the heirs 10 years into the future, incorrect decisions involving the election could be made. For example, assume the special-use valuation election is made, but Junior decides after 7 years to leave the farm and pursue an accounting career in the big city. Recapture would be the result. Yet 7 years earlier the decedent's executor might never have believed it possible.

As a practical matter, the special-use valuation election is burdensome and restrictive. It is chosen to save federal estate tax liability but often causes more trouble than anticipated. The prudent planner may wish to suggest life insurance planning rather than special-use valuation. If additional life insurance dollars are available to pay higher federal estate taxes, the special-use election will not be necessary. Careful and well-thought-out decisions are clearly required before a choice is made.

Example: Ira Harvester owns 2,200 acres of prime ranchland. He dies at a time when the acreage is worth approximately $2,000 per acre. However, at his death the IRS, using a highest-and-best-value standard, values the property at $3,750 per acre. Ira's estate does qualify for the special-use valuation approach, and his executor does consider its use to reduce the federal estate tax liability.

Planning point: Before the executor decides to elect the special-use valuation method, care must be taken to consider the full impact of such an approach. For example, the property must continue to be used for a qualified use (that is, farming) for many years to come. If there is an interruption, recapture may occur.

Valuation of Marketable Securities

Unlike real estate, which usually has no ready market, marketable securities are quite easily valued for federal estate tax purposes. The ready market that already exists offers a point of reference for valuation purposes. According to the Treasury regulations, marketable securities are to be valued by ascertaining the *mean* between the highest- and lowest-quoted selling price on the valuation date. This, of course, may be easily obtained from financial publications. If there were no sales on the valuation date, but there were sales on dates within a "reasonable period both before and after the valuation date," the value of the security is determined by the means between the highest and lowest sales on the nearest date before and the nearest date after the valuation. The average is then weighted by the respective number of trading days between the selling date and the valuation date.

Although valuation of marketable securities is probably the easiest valuation to make because a ready market already exists for these assets, one possible complication involves the practice of "blockage." When there is a large block of stock that would be difficult to market in the usual way because of its size, it may depress the market because it cannot be converted to cash as readily as a few shares could be. The result may well be that selling prices and bid and asked prices will not reflect genuine fair market value. Because of this potential distortion, a *blockage discount* may be applied, based on an estimate of the effect that the block of stock would have had on the market if it had been sold over a reasonable time period rather than in a block.

Valuation of Closely Held Corporations

Marketable securities are easily valued because there is a ready market, but the situation with closely held stock is just the opposite: It has no market at all, making valuation exceedingly difficult and complex. Use of the "willing buyer-willing seller" standard would be appropriate for purposes of establishing value, but there is rarely a ready market.

As a practical matter, valuation of closely held stock creates serious problems for the executor or administrator of the estate, who is generally required by federal estate tax law to file the federal estate tax return (and pay any federal estate tax due) within 9 months of the date of death. (There are several extension provisions available in the Internal Revenue Code that permit a longer period in which to pay the federal estate tax.) Though there will be no problem in filling out the federal estate tax return (Form 706) for assets that are easily valued—for example, cash, marketable securities, life insurance, and other types of assets, such as pension funds, patents, royalty interests, and so on—how does the personal representative go about placing a value on the closely held corporation?

Usually the executor or administrator uses the book value—that is, the net worth of the firm. Although this seems logical in trying to ascertain the value of the company, in Rev. Rul. 59-60 the IRS has stipulated that a series of tests be applied. Certainly book value is one of the factors to be taken into account, but under no circumstances should the determination stop at that point.

Rev. Rul. 59-60 requires all the following factors to be considered when placing a value on a closely held business:

- the nature of the business in question and the history of the enterprise from its inception
- the economic outlook in general as well as the condition and outlook of the specific industry
- the book value of the stock and the financial condition of the business (the Tax Court considers this factor in almost every case)
- the company's earning capacity (for many businesses—especially those that depend heavily on capital to produce profits—this will be the single most important valuation factor)
- the company's dividend-paying capacity
- the existence of goodwill, which can be defined as the economic advantage or benefit that is acquired by a business *beyond* the mere value of the capital invested in it, because of its patronage by habitual customers, its local position, its reputation for skill or punctuality, and similar considerations; in short, a broad term implying that a company has a purchase value exceeding the worth of its tangible assets (a business may have goodwill value even if no amount for goodwill is shown on its accounting statements)
- stock sales and size of the block of stock to be valued
- the fair market value of stock of comparable corporations engaged in the same or a similar type of business if the stock is actively traded in an established market

Valuation Methods Used by the IRS

The specific factors above are considered by the IRS when placing a value on a closely held corporation. As a practical matter, however, the adjusted-book-value method and the capitalization-of-adjusted-earnings method are the most widely used mathematical approaches to valuation.

The adjusted-book-value method involves actively adjusting the asset components of the closely held company to an approximate fair market value for each of the components. This procedure is necessary because accounting statements reflect assets at a specific dollar amount other than the actual fair market value.

In the capitalization-of-adjusted-earnings method, the IRS multiplies adjusted earnings by a specific factor that applies to the industry in question. The capitalization rate varies inversely with the level of risk of the specific industry as well as the rate of return.

Example: Smith-Hall, Inc., a manufacturer of taxicab meters, seeks to have the capitalization-of-adjusted-earnings method of valuation applied to its operations. In 1991, the corporation's adjusted earnings were $80,000; in 1992, $85,000; in 1993, $90,000; in 1994, $95,000; and in 1995, $100,000. Using a weighted-average-earnings formula, we have $93,333 as the average. This is derived as follows:

Year	Earnings		Weight		Product
1995	$100,000	x	5	=	$ 500,000
1994	95,000	x	4	=	380,000
1993	90,000	x	3	=	270,000
1992	85,000	x	2	=	170,000
1991	80,000	x	1	=	80,000
					$1,400,000

$1,400,000 ÷ 15 = $93,333

If an impartial investor wanted to invest in a company that was involved in the same activities as Smith-Hall, Inc., he or she would expect a 9.75 percent return on investment.

Therefore the capitalization factor for Smith-Hall, Inc. would be 100 divided by 9.75, or 10.26. To apply the capitalization-of-adjusted-earnings method of valuation, $93,333 would be multiplied by the capitalization factor of 10.26:

$93,333 x 10.26 = $957,597

The points to bear in mind are that the value of a closely held business will be difficult to establish and that it will be some figure other than mere net worth (book value).

In the case of *Northern Trust Company,* the Tax Court reaffirmed Rev. Rul. 59-60 and set forth the various methods and discounts that are available in an effort to value closely held stock. The court permitted the use of both a discount for lack of marketability and an additional discount for lack of control. Note, however, that the use of the comparable-market approach, even though embraced by the Treasury regulations and Rev. Rul. 59-60, was not accepted by the Tax Court unless the publicly traded comparable company was in the identical business.

There have been many other cases that deal specifically with the issue of valuing closely held stock. For example, in *Estate of Milton Feldmar,* the decedent, who died unexpectedly on March 30, 1982, owned 79.5 percent of the outstanding shares of United Equitable Corporation (UEC), a holding company that owned companies in the business of selling and underwriting several types of insurance coverage. The decedent owned 767,800 shares that were valued on the estate tax return at $10 per share. In its notice of deficiency the IRS determined the stock was worth $46.60 per share. Although individual and family accident and health insurance was the major source of UEC's earnings, the company began emphasizing life insurance sales in 1980. At the decedent's death, each of these lines of business was under pressure. As a result, UEC's net income and profit margin decreased substantially between 1980 and 1981. Experts testified for both the estate and the IRS.

The court determined the UEC stock should be valued based upon a comparative market analysis using (1) price/earnings ratios of similar companies, (2) the relationship of the market price of comparable companies' stock to book value, and (3) the value of UEC stock in prior sales.

As to price/earnings ratios, the 3 full years immediately preceding death were used and weighted, with 1981 given a weight of 7, 1980 a weight of 3, and 1979 a weight of 1. The earnings for 1981 were given primary importance because they were in decline and therefore most indicative of future earnings. A capitalization rate of 5 was used.

Regarding book value, the court said a $2 million insurance policy on the decedent's life should be valued at this amount rather than at UEC's investment in the policy.

In another case on this subject, *Estate of Joseph W. Giselman,* the Tax Court was called upon to determine the value of the decedent's 100 percent interest in J. W. Giselman Corporation. The company's principal business activity was the installation of custom hardwood flooring in residential and commercial buildings. Experts were retained by both the estate and the IRS, and each expert used a capitalization-of-earnings approach. The IRS expert considered the company a growth company and applied a weighted-average method that gave more significance to years shortly before the decedent's death. This was in contrast to the estate's expert, who used a straight arithmetic average. The court agreed with the estate because of the economic outlook for the company's business.

Planning point: If there is a valid buy-sell agreement between a willing buyer and a willing seller (on an arm's-length basis), the specific dollar value that has been stated as the purchase price may peg or set the value of the business interest in question. Such a situation will, of course, remove the need for valuation according to all the factors discussed above.

IRS Ruling Validates Minority Discount

The IRS has had a long-standing policy of aggregating interests held by family members in the same corporation for the purpose of valuing the block of stock transferred for gift or estate tax purposes. The purpose of such aggregation was to deny the application of the minority discount if less than a controlling share of the corporation was transferred. This denial would result in the addition of a control premium to the value of any stock held by family members, regardless of whether the block of stock transferred actually had any power to direct the corporate policy. This treatment would dramatically increase the gift or estate tax cost of a transfer of less than a 50 percent share of a family corporation. Normally such minority interests could be discounted between 10 and 35 percent for tax purposes, reflecting the fact that the minority shareholder's interest is worth less to a buyer due to the inability to control the corporation.

In a somewhat startling reversal of its prior position, the IRS recently issued Rev. Rul. 93-12, 1993-1 C.B. 13, in which it revokes its traditional position and indicates that it will permit discounts for gift tax purposes for gifts of minority interests in a family corporation. In the author's opinion, this change actually brings the position of the IRS more in line with the tax law and economic reality of transfers of business interests.

The gift tax regulations state that if a gift is made in property, its value at the date of the gift will be considered the amount of the gift. The value of the property is the price at which the property would change hands between a willing buyer and a willing seller, neither being under any compulsion to buy or to sell, and both having reasonable knowledge of relevant facts. The regulations further provide that the degree of control of the business represented by the block of stock to be valued is among the factors to be considered in valuing stock when there are no sales prices or bona fide bid or asked prices. Thus an actual minority discount that would give a transferee no significant degree of control should be valued with consideration of the minority discount and without a control premium.

Many parents and grandparents prefer to transfer their family corporations through lifetime gifts. The gift of family corporation stock is quite beneficial for the following reasons:

- *reduced estate taxes*—Lifetime gifts provide an excellent opportunity to reduce the business owner's gross estate. In many cases, the gifts of family stock can be sheltered by the donor's $10,000 annual exclusion. If the donor is married and the donor's spouse elects to split the gifts, the annual exclusion can be increased to $20,000 per donee. If the business owner starts planning early enough, gifts of stock can be made over several years without tax consequences. Even if the gifts exceed the annual exclusion, the donor's applicable credit amount will shelter $625,000 (in 1998) in total gifts. After the gifts of stock are complete, the growth in value of the stock that has been transferred avoids gift or estate taxes.

- *motivation of successors*—One advantage of lifetime gifts of family stock is that the family successors get "a piece of the action" today. The share of ownership will certainly motivate the family successors since they will have a direct reward for their labor.
- *observation and guidance of successors*—Through lifetime gifts, the senior-generation owners can observe and give guidance to the next generation of stockholders.
- *early planning*—By making lifetime gifts of family stock, the business owner becomes focused on a plan for transferring the business; this plan is often otherwise delayed or ignored.

For parents and grandparents who hold interests in family corporations, Revenue Ruling 93-12 represents a tremendous opportunity to make gifts. In fact, lifetime gifts of family stock would be far superior to bequests of stock at death if a controlling interest is to be divided among family successors.

Example: Suppose Mr. McFadden owns 100 percent of the stock in Fameelyco, Inc., and has four children ready to step in. Fameelyco is worth $1 million, including the control premium. He can give 25 percent of the stock to each child and take a discounted gift tax value for each of the shares given to his children. With a reasonable discount for minority interests, the 25 percent interest each child receives might be valued at $200,000 for gift tax purposes. Remember that *each* child will receive a minority interest in Fameelyco even though the entire corporation is given to the children. The total gift tax value of these gifts is $800,000. The value of the power to control (the control premium) is passed free of gift taxes. If Mr. McFadden instead waits until death to transfer his corporation, it will be valued for estate tax purposes at full value ($1 million plus additional growth in the company).

The recent favorable ruling should have similar application to buy-sell agreements for family corporations exercised at the retirement, disability, or death of the family business owner. If the buy-sell agreement is formed with family successors who receive minority (less than 50 percent) shares in the company, the ruling would permit the family buy-sell agreement to appropriately discount the purchase price to successors. This would particularly benefit a parent or grandparent who has more than one family successor who will receive shares in the company. Potentially, a lower purchase price in the family buy-sell agreement provides the family with two benefits. First, the estate taxes of the senior generation are reduced if the agreement establishes the estate tax value of the stock. Second, the lower purchase price makes the agreement more affordable for the junior generation that must purchase life insurance coverage on the senior generation owners.

Impact of Buy-Sell Agreement for a Business Interest

Earlier in this chapter, we indicated the importance of the concept of "pegging" the value of a business interest. One point must be stressed. A buy-sell agreement will not peg the estate tax value of a business interest unless specific rules are followed. The requirements for buy-sell agreements between family members are different from those for agreements between unrelated parties. For buy-sell agreements between unrelated parties, the IRS has generally deferred to the value negotiated by the parties, provided certain requirements were met with respect to the buy-sell agreement. Of course, the agreement must be truly arm's-length between unrelated parties. If family members are involved, the IRS will carefully scrutinize the agreement to see if its intent is to pass the business to heirs at a price discount.

Between the estate tax regulations under Sec. 2031 and case law, the following elements have traditionally been required for the purchase price to establish the estate tax value of the stock:

- There must be a legally binding requirement that the estate of a deceased shareholder must sell the shares of the corporation's stock back to the corporation or to another shareholder for the price stated in the contract.
- If a shareholder wishes to dispose of the stock during his or her lifetime, the stock must be offered back to the corporation or to the other shareholder at the specified offer price before being offered to a nonshareholder.
- The contract must have been made on an arm's-length, bona fide basis. The price as agreed to under the terms and provisions of the agreement must have been fair and adequate at the time the agreement was executed.

If a buy-sell agreement for a business interest between unrelated parties is structured in such a way that these three elements are present, the value of the stock will be effectively pegged for federal estate tax purposes.

For buy-sell agreements between family members, Code Sec. 2703 provides more stringent rules. The Sec. 2703 rules apply to buy-sell agreements either entered into or substantially modified after October 8, 1990. A family buy-sell agreement is defined as an agreement where 50 percent or more of the stock is owned by family members. Family members include spouses, children, grandchildren, parents, siblings, and the children of siblings. If the buy-sell agreement involves family members, the agreement must satisfy all three of the following requirements before the purchase price will peg the estate tax value of the business interest:

- The agreement must have a bona fide business purpose.
- The agreement must not be a device to transfer the business interest to objects of the transferor's bounty for less than full and adequate consideration.
- The agreement must be comparable to similar agreements entered into at arm's length.

The Tax Court examined a family agreement in *Estate of Lauder.* In this instance, stock in a closely held cosmetics company was sold to family members by the decedent's estate pursuant to a buy-sell agreement. The IRS asserted that the formula for determining the purchase price for the stock did not establish its estate tax value. The IRS assessed a $42.7 million estate tax deficiency.

The Tax Court held that the agreement was a device to transfer the stock to the objects of the decedent's bounty for less than full consideration. Since the agreement served the testamentary purpose of the decedent, it did not have a business purpose. Accordingly, the purchase price did not peg the estate tax value of the stock. The appraiser's report the court accepted established an estate tax value that was approximately *double* the actual purchase price the estate received. This result indicates the potentially devastating effect to an estate's liquidity that an ineffective valuation provision in a buy-sell agreement can cause.

In the case of *Estate of Joyce C. Hall v. Comm'r,* the IRS challenged the validity of the executor's valuation of closely held stock that had been included in Joyce C. Hall's gross estate. Specifically, the IRS had attempted to value the majority interest in Hallmark cards at a substantially higher amount and determined an estate tax deficiency of nearly $202 million, due primarily to the higher valuation. The government's contention was that the value of the closely held stock was about 2.5 times greater than that used by the estate. Accordingly, the IRS instructed its valuation expert to completely ignore the transfer restrictions on the decedent's stock, alleging that they were in response to the decedent's estate planning to avoid estate taxation. The Tax Court, however, failed to accept the IRS contention, saying that it was unjustifiable and speculative. The court found the transfer restrictions and the buy-sell and option agreements to be valid and ultimately accepted the value of the decedent's stock as originally set forth on the federal estate tax return.

Life insurance point: We must stress this point. Although a properly drafted buy-sell agreement can peg the value of closely held stock for federal estate tax purposes, it must be adequately funded. The buy-sell agreement is a legally binding contract that requires performance by and between the parties, and if there is inadequate funding to permit the buy-out, serious problems could result. Indeed, lack of adequate funds to accomplish the buy-out is no defense to nonperformance.

Life insurance funding is the safest and most cost-effective method of funding a buy-sell agreement. Since the recent rules of Sec. 2703 make the valuation issues in a family buy-sell agreement more questionable, a conservative approach would be to purchase as much coverage as the parties can reasonably afford to handle estate liquidity problems.

Family Business Exclusion

One critical issue related to valuing closely held businesses is the new family business exclusion. This new provision will permit qualifying estates to exclude up to $1.3 million (including the shelter provided by the applicable credit amount) of the value of a family business from the gross estate. The exclusion will depend upon accurate valuation to meet the qualification rules.

We will discuss these qualification rules in the context of the following four factors:

- limitations on the exclusion
- business interests that qualify
- estates that qualify
- recapture of tax benefits

Limits on the Family-Owned Business Exclusion. When used in combination with the applicable credit amount, the qualified family-owned business exclusion excludes the first $1.3 million of value in qualified family-owned business interests from a decedent's gross estate. In other words, the exclusion is allowed only to the extent that the exclusion for family-owned business interests plus the amount of the business sheltered from tax by the applicable credit amount does not exceed $1.3 million. The effect of this limitation is that the family-owned business exclusion will become less valuable as the applicable credit amount increases according to schedule. (Note: At the time this text was written, Congress was considering technical corrections that would increase the family-owned business exclusion in conjunction with the increases in the applicable credit amount.) The benefits from the exclusion as coordinated with the scheduled increases in the applicable credit amount are indicated in table 4-1.

TABLE 4-1
Business Exclusion Amounts

Year	Exclusion
1998	$675,000
1999	$650,000
2000 and 2001	$625,000
2002 and 2003	$600,000
2004	$450,000
2005	$350,000
2006 and later years	$300,000

The family-owned business exclusion could potentially shelter $2.6 million of a business from estate taxes if qualifying business interests will pass from each spouse's estate in a manner not qualifying for the marital deduction. However, each estate must independently meet the qualification rules discussed below—a potentially difficult task.

Business Interests That Qualify. A qualified family-owned business interest is any interest in a trade or business (regardless of the form in which it is held) that also meets all the following requirements:

- It must have a principal place of business in the United States.
- Ownership of the trade or business must be held at least 50 percent by one family, 70 percent by two families, or 90 percent by three families, as long as the decedent's family owns at least 30 percent of the trade or business.
- The business's (or a related entity's) stock or securities cannot have been publicly traded at any time within 3 years of the decedent's death.
- Not more than 35 percent of the adjusted ordinary gross income of the business for the year of the decedent's death can consist of personal-holding-company income.

In determining the ownership issues, there are specific rules for corporations, partnerships and multi-tiered entities. In the case of a corporation, the decedent and members of the decedent's family must own the percentage (as specified above) of the total combined voting power of all classes of stock entitled to vote and the required percentage of the total value of all shares of all classes of stock of the corporation.

In the case of a partnership, the decedent and members of the decedent's family must own the percentage (as specified above) of the capital interests and the profit interests in the partnership.

In the case of a trade or business that owns an interest in another trade or business (that is, a tiered entity), special rules apply. Each trade or business owned (directly or indirectly) by the decedent and members of the decedent's family must individually meet the requirements of a qualified family-owned business interest.

The exclusion must also be reduced by the amount of certain assets held by the business. The exclusion is reduced if the business contains assets not in the active use of the trade or business. For example, the exclusion is reduced by the amount of cash or marketable securities in excess of the reasonably expected day-to-day working capital needs of the business. Cash accumulated for capital acquisitions is not considered working capital. In addition, the exclusion is reduced by the amount of certain passive assets.

The main purpose behind the family business exclusion is to provide estate tax relief for families that will continue to own and participate in the family business. Thus, there are participation requirements for the family both before and after the death of the business owner. These rules are similar to the participation rules under Sec. 2032A discussed above. First, the decedent or a member of the decedent's family (the decedent's spouse, ancestors, lineal descendants of the decedent or his or spouse, lineal descendants of the decedent's parents, or the spouse of any such lineal descendants) must have owned and materially participated in the trade or business for at least 5 out of the 8 years before the decedent's death. Then, the business must pass to a qualified heir. A qualified heir includes the decedent's family (as defined above) and, interestingly, also includes any individual who was an active employee of the trade or business for at least 10 years prior to the decedent's death. If the business ceases to be owned or run by the qualified heir within the 10 years following the decedent's death, the recapture rules (discussed below) may be imposed.

Estates That Qualify. The new exclusion provision was enacted to prevent the forced sale or liquidation of a small family business due to estate tax liquidity problems. Thus, Congress imposed a threshold to ensure that only estates that really need the provision will qualify. To qualify for the exclusion, the estate must hold a business interest (as defined above) that exceeds 50 percent of the decedent's adjusted gross estate. In determining the 50 percent test, the value of the business included in the gross estate passing to a qualified heir is increased by any lifetime gifts of the business interest made to family members and reduced by certain debts of the estate. Similar adjustments are made to the adjusted gross estate to apply the 50 percent test.

Additional requirements for the estate relate to the citizenship of the decedent or the qualified heir. First, the decedent must have been a citizen or resident of the United States at the time of death. Second, the qualified heir must be a citizen or the business must be placed in a special trust (similar to a qualified domestic trust) for the estate to take advantage of the exclusion.

Recapture of Tax Benefits. The tax benefits of the exclusions for qualified family-owned business interests must be paid back if, within 10 years of the decedent's death and before the qualified heir dies, one of the following recapture events occurs:

- The qualified heir ceases to meet the material participation requirements (that is, neither the qualified heir nor any member of his or her family has materially participated in the trade or business for at least 5 years of any 8-year period in the 10-year period following the decedent's death).
- The qualified heir disposes of any portion of his or her interest in the family-owned business other than by a disposition to a member of the qualified heir's family or through a charitable conservation contribution.
- The principal place of business of the trade or business ceases to be located in the United States.
- The qualified heir loses citizenship. However, recapture can be avoided in this instance by placing the qualified family-owned business assets into a trust that meets requirements similar to a qualified domestic trust, or through certain other IRS-approved security arrangements.

A sale or disposition, in the ordinary course of business, of assets such as inventory or a piece of equipment used in the business (for example, the sale of crops or a tractor) will not trigger a recapture of tax benefits.

If one of these recapture events occurs, an additional tax is imposed on the date of that event. The portion of the reduction in estate taxes that is recaptured is reduced if the qualified heir (or members of the qualified heir's family) materially participated in the trade or business after the decedent's death. Table 4-2 shows the amount of recapture based on the timing of the recapture event.

TABLE 4-2
Percent of Recapture Based on Timing of Recapture Event

Years of Material Participation	Percent Of Reduction Recaptured
Less than 6 years	100%
At least 6 but less than 7 years	80%
At least 7 but less than 8 years	60%
At least 8 but less than 9 years	40%
At least 9 but less than 10 years	20%

Liquidity Problems Created by the Family Business Exclusion. It should be clear now that valuation of the business interest and other assets of the estate is critical for the purposes of qualifying for the family-owned business exclusion. However, the qualification for the provision will be difficult, to say the least. Significant planning could be destroyed by a valuation mistake or an unanticipated change in value of the business or other estate assets. In addition, the recapture potential creates a problem. Each qualified heir is personally liable for his or her portion of the recapture tax. Thus, even nonparticipating heirs are at risk if the estate takes advantage of the exclusion. The failure to qualify or later recapture will result in increased taxes, and the timing of these taxes may be a problem for the estate. Any business owner contemplating using the exclusion should be aware that there is no substitute for the type of liquidity that can be provided by appropriately designed life insurance covering the business owner's life.

Valuation of Personal Property

All personal property owned by a decedent at the date of death must be valued for federal estate tax purposes. Since this could become burdensome, the Treasury regulations permit a single value to be placed on groupings of items if each such item is relatively low in monetary value. Alternatively, the IRS will accept an unitemized figure by an established appraiser.

But what of the more expensive and valuable items? The Treasury regulations suggest that household items or personal effects valued in excess of $3,000 must be appraised by a competent professional.

Example: Joyce James dies owning an antique Model-T Ford. It is one of the first models ever produced by Ford Motor Company and is in fine working condition at the date of her death. Since the value exceeds $3,000, the asset must be appraised by a professional.

Previously we spoke about the concept of blockage and pointed out that this special discount has generally been used in the securities area. However, a recent Tax Court case applies the blockage idea to gifts of artwork. In the Tax Court case of *Calder,* Louisa J. Calder, widow of the famous artist, received 1,226 paintings from her husband's estate. The artwork had been reported on Calder's federal estate tax return at an average value of $735 per painting. The IRS appraiser estimated that each painting had a fair market value of between $2,250 and $2,500. However, because of the large number of paintings in the estate, the IRS appraiser concluded that a 60 percent blockage discount would be appropriate and therefore felt that the estate tax value had been correct.

Following Calder's death, his widow created four irrevocable trusts, transferred some of the artwork into such trusts, and filed a gift tax return using the same value for the artwork that had been used on her late husband's federal estate tax return. The IRS rejected the widow's use of the blockage discount approach, asserting that the transfers should be characterized as separate gifts "with the impact on the market of each transfer being considered separately rather than having all the gifts treated as one block." The Tax Court overruled the IRS and permitted the usage of a blockage discount.

IRC SEC. 7520: RULES FOR VALUING PARTIAL INTERESTS

Until somewhat recently, split interests—such as annuities, life estates, terms of years, remainder interests, and reversionary interests—were valued in a relatively stable and simplistic manner. Specifically, such valuations were done pursuant to IRS tables last published by the Treasury in 1984. These tables were based on table 1 of the *United States Life Tables: 1969–1971* and assumed a 10 percent interest rate.

The Technical and Miscellaneous Revenue Act of 1988 (TAMRA) added Sec. 7520 to the Code. This provision requires that

- annuities, life estates, terms of years, remainder interests, and reversionary interests be valued using an interest rate equal to 120 percent of the federal midterm rate in effect at the time of the transfer
- the IRS prescribe new tables for valuing such types of interests that incorporate the latest available mortality experience
- the tables are to be revised at least once every 10 years in order to reflect the most recent mortality experience

Sec. 7520 became effective for all interests valued on or after May 1, 1989. The provision requires that the value of any annuity, any interest for life or for a term of years, or any remainder or reversionary interest be determined (1) under mortality tables prescribed by the IRS and (2) by using an interest rate equal to 120 percent of the applicable federal midterm rate (AFMR) in effect for the month in which the valuation date occurs.[1] The mortality rates are based on 1980 census data and gender-neutral tables.[2] The phrase "valuation date" is defined as the date as of which the valuation of the interest is made.

Sec. 7520 also provides that if the objective of the valuation is to determine an income, estate, or gift tax charitable deduction, the taxpayer may elect to use the federal midterm rate for either of the 2 months preceding the month in which the valuation date falls. In the event that such an election is chosen and if more than one interest in the sale property is transferred, the same rate must be used with respect to each such interest.

Valuation of Partial Nonconcurrent Property Interests

It is often necessary to value partial interests in property—such as annuities, term interests, and life estates—and remainder interests since these property rights might be transferred to heirs and will become subject to either estate or gift taxes. In addition, certain charitable transfer techniques, such as charitable remainder and lead trusts, must be valued to determine the estate, gift, and/or income tax deductions. As discussed above, the actual factor used to determine the value of a partial nonconcurrent interest involves several calculations and will vary month-to-month according to changes in the AFMR.

The nature of the calculation for such valuations requires a significant degree of mathematic acumen and creates a high possibility for error. As a result, most practitioners will rely on software for making these calculations.[3]

An additional problem is the monthly variation in the interest rate. The tax value of such partial interests must be determined at a specific point in time. For example, gift tax calculations must be made at the time of the transfer. Thus the gift tax imposed on the inter vivos transfer of a partial nonconcurrent interest is based on the value of the interest using the applicable rate for the month in which a completed transfer is made.

The same rule holds true when determining the income or gift tax deduction for a charitable remainder or lead interest donation. The applicable rate for the month in which the decedent dies is used to value the testamentary transfer of these partial interests. Therefore the tax benefits or detriments of the transfer of remainder, term, annuity, or life interests in property will depend on the month of the transfer.

We will give some examples of valuations of partial interests using both the formulas and IRS-provided table factors. The valuation methods in the examples will be used throughout this text to demonstrate the efficacy of various planning techniques, such as private annuities, grantor-retained annuity trusts or unitrusts (GRATs or GRUTs), personal residence trusts, charitable lead trusts, and charitable remainder trusts. All examples are based on a 7 percent interest rate.

Table 4-3, which follows, presents an abbreviated list of 7 percent actuarial factors for term interests, annuities for terms of years, and remainder interests following term interests. Factors for life estates, life annuities, and remainder interests involving single life mortality contingencies are presented in table 4-4, which follows table 4-3. Please be aware that the interest rate needed for calculations in actual practice will vary from month to month and will require either software or a complete volume of tables.

Valuing Remainder Interests following a Fixed Term

Under the Sec. 7520 rules, the value of a remainder interest can be determined by multiplying a "remainder factor" by the value of property placed in a term interest for a period of years. The remainder factor is determined by the following formula:

$$\text{Remainder factor} = \frac{1}{(1+i)^T}$$

$$i = 120 \text{ percent of the AFMR}$$
$$T = \text{the duration of the term interest}$$

TABLE 4-3
Factors for Determining Present Value of Annuities, Term Interests, and Remainder Interests

7.0%

Term of Years	Annuity	Term Interest	Remainder Interest
1	0.9346	.065421	.934579
2	1.8080	.126561	.873439
3	2.6243	.183702	.816298
4	3.3872	.237105	.762895
5	4.1002	.287014	.712986
6	4.7665	.333658	.666342
7	5.3893	.377250	.622750
8	5.9713	.417991	.582009
9	6.5152	.456066	.543934
10	7.0236	.491651	.508349
11	7.4987	.524907	.475093
12	7.9427	.555988	.444012
13	8.3577	.585036	.414964
14	8.7455	.612183	.387817
15	9.1079	.637554	.362446

Valuing Term Interests

The current term and remainder interests in a specific property combine to equal all of the rights contained in the property interest. Thus, the "term factor" is determined by the following formula:

Term factor = 1 − Remainder factor

To determine the value of a term interest, simply multiply the term factor by the total value of the property.

Valuing Annuities for Terms of Years

An annuity interest for a term of years is a fixed amount payment provided to the recipient each year (or more often) for a specified term. The value of the annuity is determined by multiplying an annuity factor by the annual payment. (Adjustments will be necessary for more frequent payments.) The annuity factor is determined by the following formula:

$$\text{Annuity factor} = \frac{\text{Term factor}}{i}$$

$i = 120$ percent of AFMR

Example: Suppose Danny Striker died this month and his estate held an income interest in a trust with a corpus valued at $500,000. The estate's interest in the trust is for 5 additional years. Assuming a Sec. 7520 rate of 7 percent, the value included in the gross estate is determined by multiplying the term factor (.287014) by $500,000. (You could find the term factor by using the formula provided above or by looking up the 5-year term factor in table 4-3.) Thus the estate must include $143,507 for the value of the income interest. The remainder following the term interest is, of course, worth $500,000 minus the term value ($143,507), or $356,493. The remainder value could also be determined by finding the remainder factor for 5 years (.712986) and multiplying the factor by $500,000.

Example: Suppose in the example above that the estate did not hold any income interest but instead had the right to receive $60,000 annually from the trust at the end of the year for the next 5 years. The value of this annuity interest is determined by multiplying the annuity factor for 5 years (4.1002) by the amount of the annual payment ($60,000). Thus the value of the annuity is $246,012. Of course, the remainder value following the annuity interest is $500,000 minus $246,012, or $253,988.

Valuing Nonconcurrent Interests with Life Contingencies

The remaining nonconcurrent property interest valuation methods involve mortality contingencies. For these calculations, the factors involve mortality data and cannot be solved without tables. Table 4-4 gives an abbreviated version of the factors at the 7 percent interest rate in effect at the time this was written and the gender-neutral single-life contingency tables (Table 80CNSMT) used by the IRS. Remember that actual valuations in practice may involve a different interest rate and more than one life contingency. Publication 1457 provides tables for two-life contingencies.

Valuing Life Estates. A life estate in property is valued as an income interest that will continue for the remainder of a measuring life (or measuring lives if the estate is held for more than one life). The Sec. 7520 rules mandate the use of the floating monthly interest rate (120 percent of the AFMR) and the most recent mortality tables. The life estate factor from the tables, based on the age of the measuring life and the appropriate interest rate, is multiplied by the value of the property to determine the value of the life estate.

Example: Suppose Mr. Paternal wanted to provide for his son Wayne, aged 45, for the rest of Wayne's life. He places $500,000 of marketable securities into a trust providing an income interest to Wayne for his life with a remainder to his other children. To determine the value of the gift to Wayne, take the factor for a life estate for an individual aged 45 (.83586 from table 4-4) and multiply this amount by $500,000. Thus the value of the life estate given to Wayne is $417,930.

TABLE 4-4
Factors for Determining Present Value of Life Annuities, Life Estates, and Remainder Interests—Single Life

	7.0%		
Age	Life Annuity	Life Estate	Remainder Interest
45	11.9408	.83586	.16414
50	11.3027	.79119	.20881
55	10.5567	.73897	.26103
60	9.6966	.67876	.32124
65	8.7431	.61202	.38798
70	7.6943	.53860	.46140
75	6.5851	.46096	.53904
80	5.4203	.37942	.62058

Valuing Remainder Interests following a Life Estate. Since a life estate and its remainder interest equal the total value of property, the remainder factor is the inverse of the life estate factor. The value of a remainder interest is determined by multiplying the remainder factor by the value of the property, or it can be determined by subtracting the value of a life estate from the total value of the property.

Example: Assume the same facts as in the previous example. The value of the gift of the remainder interest to Mr. Paternal's other children is determined by multiplying the remainder factor following a life estate for a 45-year-old individual (.16414) by the value of the property placed in the trust ($500,000). Thus the remainder is valued at $82,070.

Valuing Life Annuities. Determining the value of a straight-life annuity has important planning implications. The sale of property in exchange for a private annuity, covered in the next chapter, is a valuable estate planning technique and requires life annuity valuation methods. To determine the value of a life annuity payment, multiply the annuity factor for the annuitant's age by the amount of the annual annuity payment. Time-value-of-money adjustment factors are necessary if the annuity sequence is not annual.

Example: Assume the same facts as in the previous two examples, except that Mr. Paternal provided a fixed annual payment of $40,000 to Wayne for the rest of his life. The value of this annuity is determined by multiplying the factor for a life annuity for a 45-year-old individual (11.9408) by the $40,000 annual payment. The value of the gift to Wayne is $477,632.

IRC SECS. 2701–2704: VALUATION OF LIFETIME TRANSFERS WITH RETAINED INTERESTS

In the Revenue Reconciliation Act of 1990, Congress repealed the estate freeze provisions of IRC Sec. 2036(c) and replaced this concept with a new series of federal gift tax valuation rules contained in chapter 14 of the Internal Revenue Code. One of these rules—Sec. 2703, covering family buy-sell agreements—was covered earlier in this chapter. The remaining provisions of the rules will be covered later in association with estate planning techniques governed by these valuation rules.

NOTES

1. The applicable federal rates are published monthly in the *Internal Revenue Bulletin* and are reprinted in numerous loose-leaf services on tax and financial planning. The actual rate used for Sec. 7520 purposes is 120 percent of the AFMR rounded to the nearest two-tenths of 1 percent. For example, 6.56 percent is 6.6 percent for the purposes of valuing remainder, term, annuity, or life interests.
2. The actual tables are presented in *Actuarial Values Alpha Volume* and *Actuarial Values Beta Volume,* available by writing the Superintendent of Documents, United States Government Printing Office, Washington, DC 20404.
3. For a complete discussion of the calculation methodology and its planning implications, see Robert J. Doyle and Stephan R. Leimberg, "New IRS Valuation Rules: Impact on the Tools and Techniques of Estate and Financial Planning," *TAXES—The Tax Magazine,* May 1990.

5

Gifts to Family Members and Trusts

Chapter Outline

OUTRIGHT GIFTING PROGRAM 152
    Annual Exclusion 154
    Gifts for Educational or Medical Expenses 155
TRANSFERS TO FAMILY TRUSTS 156
    Crummey Accumulation Trusts 157
    Estate Freezes through Family Trusts 158
    Qualified Personal Residence Trusts (QPRTs) 162
    Tangible Personal Property Trusts 170
    Trusts Providing Qualified Retained Interests 171
REMOVAL OF LIFE INSURANCE PROCEEDS FROM DECEDENT-
    INSURED'S GROSS ESTATE 181
    Cross-Ownership 182
    Irrevocable Life Insurance Trust 183

    The larger the taxable estate, the higher the federal estate tax liability will be. It follows, then, that an important objective of the financial services professional, when working in the estate planning context, must be to reduce the size of the taxable estate so that federal estate tax liability can be reduced.

    Before continuing with the discussion of estate reduction, however, it is important to point out that the financial services professional would not be serving the best interest of the client if he or she were to view the estate planning process purely as a method by which *estate taxes* could be reduced. The tax implications must be viewed as secondary and subordinate to the practical wishes of the estate owner. For example, there may be a situation in which transferring a property interest to a family member would result in reducing the gross estate and, in turn, reducing the federal estate tax liability. If the estate planner were to view this result purely from a perspective of *tax reduction,* the transaction would unquestionably be ideal. But there would be nontax overtones to such a transaction, which would involve social considerations and family interrelationships, and neither the estate planner nor the estate owner should make such a decision in a vacuum. The financial services professional must always give higher priority to the client's feelings and personal preferences than to the tax-reduction element. Some clients would gladly incur additional taxes at the estate level rather than cause trouble in the family by making unpopular financial transactions earlier.

Once a financial services professional engages in the process of estate reduction, there are several practical techniques available to him or her. The reduction of the estate tax liability is accomplished either by removing assets from the gross estate, shifting income from family assets to junior-generation family members, or by taking specific steps to substantially reduce the value to be placed on actual estate assets.

This chapter will treat these three specific concepts in this context:

- outright gifts of property to family members
- the gift of property to family trusts
- the removal of life insurance from the decedent-insured's gross estate

Chapter 6 will concentrate on these two estate reduction concepts:

- gifts of family business interests
- estate freeze sale of family business interests to junior-generation family members

Let's explore the first three of these techniques in depth in this chapter.

OUTRIGHT GIFTING PROGRAM

The simplest way to reduce the size of a gross estate is to give assets away. To the extent that the estate owner has made gifts of property to others prior to the date of death, such interests in property are generally not required to be included as part of his or her gross estate for federal estate tax purposes. However, the unified nature of the estate and gift tax system does somewhat diminish the advantage of making lifetime gifts. As we discussed in chapter 3, lifetime gifts do offer significant tax advantages over transfers at death. An understanding of these advantages and the interplay between the estate and gift tax rules is necessary to advise clients about the benefits of the techniques discussed in this chapter and throughout this text. The advantages of lifetime gifts can be summarized as follows:

- The annual exclusion is available for gifts up to $10,000 (to be indexed for inflation beginning in 1999) annually per donee ($20,000 if the spouse of a married donor elects to split gifts). This exclusion

completely removes such gifts from the tax base for the unified estate and gift tax system. No equivalent exclusion exists for transfers at death.
- There is an exclusion for gifts made under the medical and educational expense provisions of Sec. 2503(e). These transfers must be for medical expenses or tuition and must be made directly to the provider of the services. The exclusion has no dollar limit and has no equivalent in the estate tax system.
- An applicable credit amount (formerly known as unified credit) against gift or estate taxes equal to $202,050 exempts the equivalent of $625,000 (in 1998), known as the applicable exclusion amount, of taxable transfers from gift or estate tax. Although this credit is similarly available for both transfer taxes, the posttransfer appreciation on (or future income from) property given away during lifetime avoids estate or gift tax.
- The gift tax system is tax exclusive if gifts are made more than 3 years prior to death; that is, no gift tax is imposed on the gift taxes paid at the time a taxable gift is made. Gift taxes paid avoid later inclusion in the donor's estate if the gifts occur more than 3 years prior to the donor's death. On the other hand, transfers at death (and gifts made within 3 years of death) are tax inclusive since estate taxes are paid not only on the value of the assets transferred at death, but also on the amount of the estate tax paid.
- The gift of income-producing property or business interests to younger or lower-tax-bracket family members will reduce the donor's estate by both the amount of the gift and future income. In addition, the overall family income tax burden may be lowered.
- Lifetime gifts to grandchildren may be beneficial since the annual exclusion and medical or educational expense exclusion have applicability to the generation-skipping transfer tax (GSTT). The other principles, such as the removal of posttransfer appreciation from the GSTT base, also apply. Finally, the $1 million GSTT exemption (indexed for inflation beginning in 1999) applies to lifetime gifts.

Since the federal gift tax was originally enacted to prevent estate owners from avoiding federal estate tax liability, Congress (through enactment of the Tax Reform Act of 1976) unified the gift tax rates and the estate tax rates. Since January 1, 1976, the federal tax rates are the same for estate or gift transfers. Because the same rates apply to either of these transfers, the benefit of lifetime gifts is a legitimate issue. Federal estate tax paid at some future date will most likely be higher than federal gift tax paid today because the asset or assets generating the federal estate tax liability will be worth more than they are today or were at any previous time. However, by reason of the doctrine known as the *time value of money,* the taxpayer may come out ahead economically paying the future estate tax because he or she has the *use of the money* for a longer period by not incurring the federal gift tax liability today. Taxpayers planning lifetime gifts should analyze the potential impact of these principles before making lifetime gifts. Of course, we must reiterate that the nontax reasons should be the primary factor for making a lifetime gift and determining the form in which the gift should be made.

Annual Exclusion

One reason for gifting property to lower estate taxes is that the annual exclusion related to federal gift taxation offers a unique tax advantage in the unified estate and gift tax system. It gives the donor the ability to permanently remove property from the transfer tax base with no adverse transfer-tax implications. The annual exclusion permits the donor to give $10,000 (indexed for inflation beginning in 1999) per year to each selected donee without making a taxable gift.

Further, if the donor is married at the time of the gift and the spouse consents, the amount of the annual exclusion may be doubled to $20,000 per year, per donee. (This doubling of the annual exclusion for a married donor is referred to as a split gift.) As a planning point, bear in mind that the per-year element of the annual exclusion refers to a calendar year and not a 12-month period. Furthermore, if the spouse elects to split gifts for a tax year, such gift splitting applies to all gifts made by either spouse during the year (except gifts between the spouses). If gifts are to be split during the year, Form 709 or 709-A must be filed with the consenting spouse's signature by April 15 of the year following the year the gifts were made.

With outright gifts, qualification for the annual exclusion is ensured because there is no future interest problem (as discussed earlier in chapter 3). The implications of the annual exclusion for the GSTT will be discussed later in the text.

Example: Margaret Lynn, a widow aged 60, has a large estate (currently valued at $3.5 million) and has been advised by her financial planner to seriously consider initiating a gifting program so that some assets may be removed from her gross estate. She has three children and eight grandchildren. She loves all these potential donees and has no reservations about gifting property to any of them. Because the federal gift tax annual exclusion rule allows $10,000 worth of property to be gifted to each donee per year, Margaret can give a total of $110,000 worth of property each year without incurring any federal gift tax liability ($10,000 x 11 donees = $110,000). Assume that Margaret will begin this program next year and continue this pattern of giving for the rest of her life (including gifts made in the year of her death) and that she lives to her tabular life expectancy (24 more years). Thus, she will make 24 years of gifts of $110,000 annually. Also assume that the assets will appreciate at 5 percent per year whether they are retained by Margaret or given away.

Margaret's Projected Estate (no gifts)

Taxable estate	$11,287,850
Tax before credits	$ 5,913,510
Applicable credit amount	–345,800
State death tax credit	–1,272,856
Net federal estate tax	$ 4,294,854
Total death taxes	$ 5,567,710

Margaret's Projected Estate (after gifts)

Taxable estate	$ 6,147,869
Tax before credits	$ 3,022,128
Applicable credit amount	–345,800
State death tax credit	–528,927
Net federal estate tax	$ 2,147,401
Total death taxes	$ 2,676,328

Benefits of Gifting Program

Total gifts	$ 2,640,000
Tax on gifts	-0-
Appreciated value of gifts	$ 5,139,981
Death tax saved	$ 2,891,382

As the numbers demonstrate, Margaret's gifting program was able to save almost $2.9 million in transfer taxes without seriously diminishing her lifestyle (because her gifts are less than the income earned by her assets). The gifting program can be viewed as transferring wealth early to her intended heirs, but at a significant tax discount.

Gifts for Educational or Medical Expenses

Sec. 2503(e) provides an exclusion from taxable gifts for transfers in behalf of a donee for educational or medical expenses. This exclusion applies independently of and in addition to the annual exclusion and thus offers another method of transferring wealth to the junior generation without transfer taxes. The payments must be made directly to the provider of services. In the case of educational expenses, the exclusion is limited to tuition payments; payments for books, meals, and lodging may be taxable gifts. The tuition payments are limited to educational institutions described in the charitable organization rules—that is, schools that normally have a regular faculty and curriculum and enrolled student body regularly engaged in educational activities. In the case of medical expenses, the payments must be for the expenses available for an income tax deduction under Sec. 213. Therefore expenses for the prevention, diagnosis, and cure of illness, including health insurance premiums, are eligible for the exclusion.

The exclusion applies regardless of the relationship of the donor and donee. However, be aware that expenses paid as parental support obligations are not gifts. Thus a parent typically does not incur gift taxes for the payment of medical and educational expenses for children through the college years. For grandparents or other potential donors, however, the exclusion is necessary and extremely useful. With tuition and health insurance costs generally rising at a rate that exceeds normal inflation, the ability to make these payments for grandchildren is both helpful to the children and grandchildren and a pure tax exclusion for the grandparent's estate plan.

> *Example:* Assume the same facts as in the previous example. Suppose that four of Margaret's grandchildren are beginning college and are enrolled at private universities with average annual tuitions of $20,000. In addition, one of her children has been out of work for almost a year and cannot afford health insurance for his family, which costs $6,000 annually. In addition to the $110,000 she is already giving away under the annual exclusion, she can pay her grandchildren's tuitions directly to the universities and pay the health insurance premiums for her son. This allows her to give away an additional $86,000 without transfer taxes each year these expenses are incurred. As other grandchildren enter college or private schools prior to college, she can pay these tuition expenses as well. This plan will keep her estate from growing any larger at the current appreciation rates on her assets. In fact, her estate may contract slightly with these expenditures. Provided that her wealth continues to support her lifestyle, these gifts will significantly reduce her ultimate estate taxes.

TRANSFERS TO FAMILY TRUSTS

Trusts make useful estate planning vehicles for many reasons, including estate reduction goals. They enable a grantor to give assets to donees without giving the donee outright control. The dispositive terms will be provided by the grantor, and the grantor has many choices. The terms under which the beneficiaries receive the income and/or principal can be very strictly spelled out or can be left up to the discretion of a trustee. The appropriately designed trust is a vehicle to accumulate family wealth, protect assets from creditors, use the investment services of a trustee, and reduce estate and gift taxes.

To serve estate reduction goals, a gift—in trust or otherwise—must be truly irrevocable. The gift tax rules clearly require that the grantor part with dominion and control to make a gift of property for gift tax purposes. Therefore the trusts we will be discussing in this context are irrevocable. One trust of this type, the irrevocable life insurance trust (ILIT), was discussed in chapter 3.

The estate and income tax rules also have an impact on irrevocable trusts. In some cases, an irrevocable trust may be treated as complete for gift tax purposes but incomplete for estate or income tax purposes. This is particularly true for trusts in which the grantor has retained interests, either to the trust assets or dispositive controls. Initially we will discuss an irrevocable trust with no strings attached. Later in this section, we will discuss trusts with grantor-retained interests, otherwise known as estate-freezing trusts.

Crummey Accumulation Trusts

The irrevocable trust with Crummey withdrawal powers was discussed in chapter 3 in the context of the ILIT. Although the transfer-tax leverage is greatest if the trust invests in life insurance, Crummey trusts provide transfer-tax advantages with other assets.

Reviewing briefly, a Crummey trust is a trust that gives temporary withdrawal powers to beneficiaries when property is transferred to the trust. The withdrawal power ensures that the annual exclusion is available for gifts to the beneficiaries of the trust even though the trust otherwise delays benefits. Through a consistent pattern of gifting to a Crummey trust, a grantor can use the annual exclusion shelter to accumulate a substantial sum in a family trust without the problems and concerns associated with outright transfers.

Example: Sammy Settlor, a widower aged 65, has two children and five grandchildren. He has a substantial estate and would like to reduce his estate and save transfer taxes. He creates an irrevocable trust with Crummey powers. He feels that he can gift $35,000 to the trust each year. The beneficiaries are expected to lapse the annual Crummey powers. The independent trustee has the discretion to accumulate or pay income annually to Sammy's children during their lifetime. At the death of the survivor of Sammy's children, the principal and accumulated income is to be distributed in equal shares to the grandchildren then living. If Sammy lives to his life expectancy and is not predeceased by any beneficiaries, he will have made $700,000 of tax-free gifts to the trust. If he is in the maximum estate tax bracket, this will save him a minimum of $385,000 in estate taxes (55 percent of $700,000). However, if the postgift income is taken into account (assuming a 7 percent return), the actual estate tax savings is potentially as high as $789,000, because the trust income could accumulate as high as $1,435,000 if no income is distributed to his children.

Planning point: The Crummey accumulation trust is normally associated with ILITs investing in life insurance on the grantor's life.

However, the previous example demonstrates that it can be useful in other situations. The Crummey trust should be used under the following three circumstances:

- The donor wishes to make systematic gifts to family members to reduce his or her gross estate.
- The donor wishes to qualify gifts for the annual exclusion.
- The donor wants the assets held under the protection and dispositive control of a trustee and wants the assets to accumulate for a time before the beneficiaries receive distributions.

Estate Freezes through Family Trusts

An estate freeze is an estate planning technique designed to meet several goals. The primary goal is estate tax reduction. An estate freeze might be defined as any method designed to restrict an asset to its current value for an individual's eventual taxable estate. Following an estate-freeze transaction, the appreciation in property subject to the freeze accrues to someone other than the original owner (presumably his or her heirs). However, an individual considering an estate freeze typically has a second goal—to retain enough wealth to provide for his or her needs until death.

Elaborate schemes have been employed to provide the transferor with an effective estate freeze through the transfer of appreciation rights in property to the next-generation heirs, while leaving the transferor with enough strings attached to the property to provide a substantial current income stream. Therefore an estate freeze can be distinguished from an outright gift by the fact that the transferor does not transfer all interests in the property during his or her lifetime.

The freeze is often accomplished mainly through tools or techniques that lend themselves to valuation manipulations. Since some portion of the "frozen" property is actually transferred, the gift tax value of the transfer must be determined.

Valuation of transfers with retained interests is normally accomplished for gift, estate, and generation-skipping transfer tax purposes through the *subtraction method of valuation.* This method sets the value of the transferred interest at the difference between the value of the entire property interest and the value of all interests in the property held by the donor that are *not* transferred. Stated simply, *the value of the whole minus the value of what is kept equals the gift tax value of what is given away.*

Since substantial transfer-tax revenue is lost if the freeze transaction is effective, the Treasury has always had a jaundiced view of estate freezes. The posttransfer appreciation in the property in a successful freeze escapes both estate and gift taxes. This tax savings is, of course, a goal of lifetime gifting. The concern of both Congress and the IRS is that the typical estate-freeze transaction differs from an outright gift of property because the transferor has not disposed of all interests in the property when the freeze is completed.

The grantor-retained income trust (GRIT) is one type of freeze transaction singled out by Congress as a classic estate-freeze abuse mechanism.

Example: Suppose a parent (P) owns 100 percent of the stock in ABC corporation, valued at $1 million. P transfers the stock to an irrevocable trust and retains an income interest for 10 years with the remainder payable to his children. Using the valuation methods from the previous chapter, the retained income interest is valued at $491,651. (The 10-year income factor is 0.491651 at a Sec. 7520 valuation rate of 7 percent.) Under the subtraction method of valuation, the value of the gift of the remainder interest is $508,349 ($1 million minus $491,651). Thus P can make this transfer at a fixed taxable gift value of $508,349, which is less than P's applicable credit amount. If P survives the term, this is the only transfer-tax implication. If the stock provides no dividends (not unusual for a family corporation) and grows at 6 percent per year, the corporation will be valued at $1,791,000 in 10 years when it is transferred to the trust remainder beneficiaries. If the freeze works, all the growth ($1,282,651) is transferred at no additional transfer-tax cost. Thus the tax base for estate and gift tax purposes was "frozen" at $508,349.

Current Rules Limiting Freezes through Family Trusts

IRC Sec. 2702 drastically changes the applicability of the subtraction method of valuation. We will first discuss the general rule and follow with a discussion of the exceptions that have planning implications. The new valuation rule is stated as follows:

"Solely for the purpose of determining whether a transfer in trust to or for the benefit of a *member of the family* of the transferor (a) is a gift and (b) the value of such gift, the value of any interest in the trust retained by the transferor or any *applicable family member* is generally treated as zero." The rule is applicable to transfers after October 8, 1990.

Now, when the interest held by the grantor or certain "applicable family members" (defined below) after the transfer to "family members" (defined below) of an interest in trust is valued, as a general rule, the value of what the grantor retained is considered to be zero. Thus, if a transfer is made to a trust benefiting a member of the grantor's family, the grantor is deemed to have retained none of the cash or other assets, regardless of the terms of the trust, and is treated as if he or she has given away the entire amount transferred to the trust.

Using the subtraction method of valuation described above, if the actuarial value of the grantor's retained interest is arbitrarily assigned a zero value, the gift tax value of the amount transferred to the beneficiaries of the trust, even if their interest is delayed until the expiration of a retained interest, must equal 100 percent of the gift.

To understand the rules of Sec. 2702, we must define some of its terms. First, what is meant by "a transfer of an interest in trust"? A transfer in trust is defined as a transfer to a new or existing trust and an assignment of an interest in an existing trust but does not include (1) the exercise, release, or lapse of a power of appointment over trust property that is not a transfer for gift tax purposes, or (2) the execution of a qualified disclaimer. Code Sec. 2702 applies only to transfers to trusts that are treated as completed gifts for gift tax purposes. As we discussed above, a completed gift to the beneficiaries is required to result in any potential transfer tax discount.

Code Sec. 2702 applies to transfers that are for the benefit of the grantor's family. Members of the transferor's family include his or her spouse, ancestors, lineal descendants, ancestors or lineal descendants of the spouse of the transferor, brothers or sisters, and the spouse of any of these individuals. So this section applies to transfers to members of the grantor's family who are either junior or senior to the grantor's generation.

The estate-freeze rules apply only if there is a "retained interest" by the transferor or an "applicable family member." Retained interest means a property interest was held by the same individual both before and after the transfer in trust. So even if there were two or more transferees and each was a member of the transferor's family, as long as the transferor or an applicable family member who held an interest prior to the transfer held no interest after the transfer, Code Sec. 2702 would not apply.

Applicable family members include the transferor's spouse, any ancestor of the transferor or the transferor's spouse, and the spouse of any such ancestor. There is no attribution of ownership from one person to another for the purposes of the retained-interest test. An interest is retained only if the same person holds an interest both before and after the transfer in trust. Regardless of the relationships among the transferor, the individuals with a retained interest, and the remainder beneficiaries, Sec. 2702 applies only if the same person held interests before and after the transfer.

For example, these rules would not be applicable to outright gifting techniques, such as the Crummey accumulation trust discussed above, since the grantor retains no interests. The rules of Sec. 2702 apply only if there is a retained interest that would otherwise have value and such value would reduce the gift tax cost of the transfer.

> *Example:* Assume the same facts as the previous example. Under the rules of Sec. 2702, the 10-year income interest retained by P in the GRIT is arbitrarily assigned a value of zero, regardless of the rules normally governing the value of a term income interest. Therefore P will

be treated as making a gift equal to the entire value of the corporation ($1 million) at the time of the transfer to the trust, even though the actual facts indicate that the donees do not receive the property until later. Of course, no transfer taxes are saved under these rules, so the transaction loses much of its appeal.

Example: Suppose Mr. James transfers $1 million worth of mutual funds to an irrevocable trust that provides that all the income from the trust is payable to his wife for life. Upon the wife's death, the trust will end and the remainder will be distributed to their children. It is clear that the transferor (Mr. James) has not retained an interest in the trust after the transfer. Although his wife is an "applicable family member," neither Mr. James nor his spouse held the interest both before and after the transfer; therefore Code Sec. 2702 should not apply. This makes sense because the transfer will not escape transfer tax. The entire transfer will be subject to gift tax at the time it is made. The remainder is a completed future-interest gift, taxable at its present value. The life estate given to his wife will be a taxable gift unless the qualified terminal interest property (QTIP) election is made. If the QTIP election is made, the full trust principal is taxable at the surviving spouse's death because she is treated as the transferor, and the full amount of the trust is included in her estate.

Exceptions to Sec. 2702 General Rule

Fortunately, there are exceptions to Sec. 2702. The statute provides that for some retained interests in trust, the subtraction method of valuation will be used to determine the gift tax value of transfers in trust. The specific exceptions to Sec. 2702 are as follows:

- *personal residence exception*—Sec. 2702 does not apply if the property transferred to the trust is used as the personal residence of the person holding a term interest in the trust. Thus a GRIT can be used with estate tax advantages or gift tax advantages if the trust is limited to a personal residence.
- *tangible personal property exception*—Sec. 2702 does not apply if the exercise or nonexercise of the holder of a *term interest* in tangible property would not affect the valuation of the remainder interests in such property. Therefore certain types of personal property, such as works of art, can be used with GRITs.
- *qualified retained-interest exception*—Sec. 2702 does not apply to the valuation of retained interests that provide "qualified" payments to the holder of the retained interest. Retained interests that qualify are annuity or unitrust interests, which are discussed below.

Qualified Personal Residence Trusts (QPRTs)

Personal residences are specifically excepted from the anti-estate-freeze rules of Sec. 2702. However, the regulations for these rules contain five pages of guidance on the use of personal residence trusts. The rules distinguish between personal residence trusts and qualified personal residence trusts (QPRTs). The use of a personal residence trust that is not qualified is questionable, so our discussion will be limited to QPRTs. The regulations for QPRTs make it clear that the Treasury intends to limit the principal of these trusts to personal residences and only *de minimis* other property.

Estate Planning Uses of a QPRT

A QPRT is a useful estate-freezing technique in certain circumstances. The grantor must have the appropriate real property. It should be real estate that is appreciating and expected to grow substantially in value by the end of the retained-interest term. The grantor should be willing to part with the property at the end of the term or realize that the property must be either repurchased or leased back from the beneficiaries. The term of the trust must be limited to a term that the grantor is reasonably expected to survive.

In the typical QPRT, the grantor (presumably a senior-generation family member) retains the use of the home for a specified number of years. At the termination of the trust, one or more remainder beneficiaries will receive the personal residence. The longer the term of the QPRT, the lower the value of the gift to the beneficiary. The value of the retained interest, measured under Sec. 7520 valuation, is subtracted from the value of the residence placed into trust to determine the value of the gift to the beneficiary. Since Sec. 2702 does not apply, the gift tax value of the transfer is frozen at the present value of the remainder interest.

QPRTs have the following major advantages over other types of retained-interest trusts:

- QPRTs do not require a fixed payout to the grantor during the grantor's retained-interest term. The grantor has merely retained a "personal use" interest in the trust. Therefore the transferor does not retain actual payments that would increase his or her estate, making reduction of the grantor's estate more likely. If the grantor survives the term of the trust, the transfer-tax cost is frozen at the original gift tax cost for transferring the remainder interest.
- Proper planning will enable the grantor to enjoy the home even after the term of the trust expires. For example, the grantor could lease the home at fair rental payments and further reduce his or her estate by making lease payments to the next generation.
- The value of the grantor's retained interest can be increased by including a contingent reversionary interest. For instance, the trust could

provide that the residence will return to the grantor's estate if he or she dies before the end of the selected term. This would solve the liquidity problem that would occur if the grantor dies prematurely. In addition, the reversionary interest would increase the value of the grantor's retained interest, which would thereby reduce the value of the gift to the remainder beneficiary.

Disadvantages of the QPRT can be summarized as follows:

- The transfer involves the grantor's personal residence (defined below), which may be the home the grantor wishes to reside in indefinitely. This may create problems later; the grantor will have to rely on the willingness of the remainder beneficiary to continue leasing such residence under an arm's-length lease, because prearranged agreements to continue the grantor's possession of the home after the term expires could result in adverse transfer-tax consequences.
- The QPRT presents a potentially devastating liquidity problem should the grantor fail to survive the term. If the grantor dies prematurely, the residence will be included in the grantor's gross estate at date-of-death value.
- The QPRT presents some difficulties if the remainder beneficiaries are grandchildren or of a more junior generation. The GSTT rules do not permit the allocation of the grantor's $1 million GSTT exemption to retained interest trusts before the term of the trust ends. Thus the GSTT exemption must be allocated when the trust terminates at the appreciated value of the corpus. In the author's opinion, the GSTT exemption should not be used on the QPRT but allocated instead to an irrevocable dynasty life insurance trust (discussed in chapter 3) providing for the skip beneficiaries.

Qualifying Residences

For the purposes of the Sec. 2702 exception, a personal residence is either the principal residence of the term holder (within the meaning of Sec. 1034, regarding the rollover of gain on a principal residence), one other residence of the term holder (which could be part-personal, part-investment property within the meaning of Sec. 280A(d)(l)), or an undivided fractional interest in either.

Thus the personal residence is defined as the grantor's *principal* residence and a second home. The second home, if also used as an investment, must be used annually for personal use by the grantor 14 days or 10 percent of the time the property is rented, whichever is greater. Therefore a vacation home that is both rented and used by the grantor can be used in the QPRT. In addition, an undivided fractional interest could also be placed in a trust. Thus one spouse can create a QPRT with his or her joint tenancy or community property interest. The

IRS has issued a private ruling permitting the use of one spouse's joint interest in a community property state in a QPRT (Ltr. 9315010).

The QPRT may include a dwelling used as (1) the principal place of the taxpayer's business or (2) a place where the taxpayer sees customers, clients, or patients in the ordinary course of business. Therefore a QPRT could include a home with a qualified home office for income tax purposes as well as a vacation home rented for part of the year.

Permissible Associated Property. A QPRT may also include appurtenant structures used for residential purposes and adjacent land not in excess of that which is reasonably appropriate for residential purposes (taking into account the residence's size and location). The amount of adjacent land permissible is not clear in the regulations. However, the regulations contain examples that indicate that a farmhouse along with the remaining farmland and other structures would not qualify. In private rulings, the IRS has been reluctant to give advance determinations as to the appropriateness of specific tracts of adjacent land. Certainly, the size of permissible plots will vary based on the land typically adjacent to homes within each community or subdivision. The personal residence subject to a mortgage can be contributed to a QPRT, but the regulations will not permit it to include any personal property (for example, household furnishings). Thus, the grantor would continue to own household furnishings individually.

Cash in the QPRT. To pay the essential expenses of the QPRT, the trustee may also hold cash not in excess of the amount required for the following:

- payment of trust expenses (including mortgage payments) already incurred or reasonably expected to be incurred within the next 6 months from the date the cash is added to the trust
- improvements to the residence to be paid for within 6 months from the date the cash is added
- at the creation of the trust, for purchase of a personal residence within the next 3 months; and at any other time, for the purchase of a personal residence within the next 3 months provided the trustee has previously entered into a contract to purchase the personal residence
- purchase by the trustee of a residence to replace another residence within 3 months of the cash addition, provided the trustee has already entered into a contract to purchase the replacement property at the time the addition is made

Effect of a Mortgage. The regulations specifically refer to payments for the mortgage in a QPRT. However, the mortgage on the property does create some complicated income and gift tax issues. The transfer of property with a mortgage greater than the transferor's adjusted basis normally triggers gain for income tax purposes. However, since the QPRT is a grantor trust (as explained below), the gain is not recognized by the grantor until the retained-interest term ends. Furthermore, if the grantor makes additions of cash to pay mortgage principal and interest, such additions could be treated as further gifts to the remainderpersons. Whether or not the payment of such expenses is an additional gift depends on *who* is responsible for such expenses under state law allocating expenses of a trust to income and remainder beneficiaries. If the expense is properly allocated to income, the grantor could pay such expenses without incurring taxable gifts. If the expense is allocated to the remainder beneficiaries, the grantor's payment of such expenses is a gift. The grantor of the QPRT could presumably eliminate these problems by making the mortgage a personal obligation before transferring the residence to the QPRT. Serious tax counsel is obviously needed if mortgaged property is gifted to the QPRT.

Two-Residence Limitation. The regulations limit a taxpayer to being a term holder in only two QPRTs at a time. The IRS presumably takes the position that the definition of a personal residence cannot extend beyond the interest-deduction rules that limit each taxpayer to one primary and one secondary residence.

Failure to Qualify as QPRT

The QPRT is a valuable transfer-tax-saving tool, but the trust must be drafted and administered with extreme care. Any language in the trust that permits or fails to prohibit disqualifying events (for example, standard investment-power language that gives discretionary power to the trustee to invest in nonresidence assets) will disqualify the trust even if the disqualifying act does not take place. The penalty for a drafting error is severe; the full Sec. 7520 value of the grantor's retained interest will be treated as an additional gift at the time the IRS discovers that the trust fails to qualify.

The regulations allow some flexibility, permitting the trustee to sell a residence held by the QPRT. However, to retain the gift tax advantages, the trustee must take one of the following actions:

- replace the residence with another qualifying residence within 2 years
- distribute the cash to the term holder
- convert the QPRT to a qualified grantor-retained annuity trust (GRAT) (discussed later)

Selecting a Residence

The QPRT is not a technique that everyone will find viable. However, this tax-saving device is useful for wealthy taxpayers who wish to reduce their estate, because the subtraction method of valuation may be used to discount the value of the gift for tax purposes. A wealthy taxpayer must own, or be considering the purchase of, an appropriate residence to take advantage of the technique. The rules discussed above limit the residences to the primary and one secondary residence of the grantor. The primary residence should be used only after careful consideration of the effect on the grantor and his or her spouse when the QPRT terminates. The primary residence is, presumably, where the grantor wishes to live into the indefinite future, whereas the remainder interest is irrevocably transferred when the QPRT is created. The primary residence makes a good choice if the grantor knows that he or she will be moving at some predetermined date in the future and the remainder beneficiaries will choose to occupy the primary residence in the future.

If the grantor will wish to occupy the home after the QPRT terminates, he or she will have the following choices:

- *leasing the residence from the remainder beneficiaries on commercially reasonable terms*—The lease cannot be prearranged since this might be deemed a retained right to keep the residence by the grantor. The lease might be beneficial from an estate planning standpoint because the lease payments will be additional transfers to family heirs that avoid gift taxes.
- *repurchasing the residence from the remainder beneficiaries*—This choice would provide cash or other investments to the family heirs in lieu of the residence. The repurchase would allow the grantor to live in the home and receive the income tax basis step up at the time of his or her death. (However, the IRS has issued proposed regulations that prohibit such repurchase.)

Income Tax Consequences of QPRT

A QPRT is a grantor trust for income tax purposes during the retained-interest term. This means that the grantor gets all of the income tax consequences during the term of the trust. Therefore, if there is income from the property (for example, if the home is rented during part of the year), the grantor is taxed on the income. If deductible expenses are incurred, these are also passed through to the grantor.

Gift Tax Consequences of QPRT

The QPRT is irrevocable, and a completed gift of the remainder interest is made for tax purposes when the grantor establishes the trust. The value of the property for gift tax purposes is reduced by the present value of the retained-income interest. This is appropriate enough, although the grantor retains only the *use* of the corpus and not a right to cash payments. The taxable gift at the time of the establishment of the QPRT is merely the present value of the remainder interest. This taxable gift constitutes a future-interest gift that does not qualify for the $10,000 annual exclusion. However, in many cases, the grantor will have applicable credit amount that is available to shelter the entire transfer from any gift tax.

The purpose of the QPRT is to reduce the overall transfer-tax costs of passing the grantor's assets to his or her beneficiaries. Therefore the key to this technique is establishing the highest value possible for the grantor's retained-income interest. This will result in a low present value for the remainder interest, and therefore the total amount subject to gift tax can be minimized.

Under the Sec. 7520 rules discussed in the previous chapter, the value of a remainder interest can be determined by multiplying a "remainder factor" by the value of the residence placed in the QPRT. The remainder factor is determined by the following formula:

$$\text{Remainder factor} = \frac{1}{(1+i)^T}$$

i = 120 percent of the applicable federal midterm rate (AFMR)

T = the duration of the trust in years

Example: Assume a vacation home owned by Tom Taxplanner is valued at $300,000. He transfers the vacation home to a QPRT. He retains the use of the home for 10 years and leaves the remainder interest to his daughter Julia. For gift tax purposes, the taxable amount of the transfer is equal to the present value of remainder interest left to Julia. This is a gift of future interest, and thus the full amount of the remainder interest is subject to gift tax without the benefit of the annual exclusion. The current value of the remainder interest is calculated as follows:

$$\$300,000 \times \frac{1}{(1+.07)^{10}} = \$152,505$$

This calculation is based on an assumed Sec. 7520 rate of 7 percent. If Tom has the full remaining applicable credit amount, this transfer of a future interest worth $152,505 will result in no transfer tax at this time. If Tom survives the term period, the vacation home will pass to Julia with no further transfer-tax costs. If there is no appreciation on the vacation home in that 10-year period, this technique will have saved Tom $81,012 in total transfer-tax costs, assuming a 55 percent estate tax bracket. If the full value of the home was included in Tom's gross estate instead, the tax payable would be $165,000 ($300,000 taxed at 55 percent), whereas the tax payable for the gift of the remainder interest is only 55 percent of $152,505 (or $83,878). Furthermore, if the vacation home appreciates in value after the transfer to the QPRT, the transfer-tax savings will be even larger.

Estate Tax Consequences of QPRT

If the QPRT is properly designed, none of the property will be in the grantor's estate if the grantor survives the term period. Unfortunately, successful use of this technique is not without its tax disadvantages. If the grantor survives the term of the retained interest, no trust property will be included in the gross estate, and therefore the income tax basis step up for the personal residence at the grantor's death will not be available. In addition, the $125,000 capital-gains exclusion for taxpayers over age 55 cannot be used for property placed in the QPRT.

The transfer-tax savings available through the use of a QPRT are realized only if the grantor survives the term of the retained-income interest. You will recall from the estate-inclusion rules that a transfer with a retained interest that does not end before the transferor's death is included in the gross estate under Sec. 2036(a). Therefore the full value of the trust property, not just the value of the remaining term, will return to the grantor's estate if the grantor fails to survive the term. However, the applicable credit amount used on the original transfer, plus any gift tax actually paid, will be allowed as a credit against the estate tax due. Furthermore, the benefit of the income tax basis step up will be available due to the inclusion of the property in the gross estate.

Tax Problems Associated with QPRT

Loss of Income Tax Basis Step Up. One of the problems traditionally associated with the QPRT is the fact that the income tax rules are less favorable for gifts than for transfers at death. If a home is transferred at death, the income tax basis is stepped up to the date-of-death value of the home. If the home has appreciated in value, this basis adjustment will save the heirs income taxes on the subsequent sale of the home. The QPRT provides no such income tax relief if the grantor survives the retained-interest term. Because the QPRT is a completed gift, the remainder beneficiaries receive the residence with a *carryover basis* for income tax purposes; that is, they receive the grantor's basis with an adjustment for gift taxes paid on the transaction. Thus the subsequent sale of the residence by the beneficiaries will result in capital-gain taxes if the property has appreciated since the grantor purchased the residence. This problem has been somewhat mitigated by the new $250,000 ($500,000 for married taxpayers) capital gain exclusion for primary residences. However, the exclusion will be available only if the seller meets the rules for a primary residence. Thus, the capital gain could still be troublesome if the remainder beneficiaries will not use the residence as a primary residence. For example, if more than one child will be a remainder beneficiary, it is unlikely that all will be able to claim the primary residence capital gain exclusion at the time of the sale.

Estate Liquidity Concerns. The unexpired term of the grantor's income interest presents a liquidity problem if the grantor does not survive the term because of the automatic inclusion of the residence in his or her estate. Without dispositive planning for this situation, the *probate* estate will hold an asset equal to the grantor's unexpired term interest. This will prevent the beneficiaries from receiving the residence until the end of the term. It will also create a liquidity problem because the *taxable* estate will include the full date-of-death value of the residence. If the trust property cannot be reached during this time to pay taxes, a liquidity shortfall is likely.

To prevent this problem, the following provisions might be included in the original trust terms:

- *acceleration of the remainder interest to the beneficiaries if the grantor dies before the term expires*—This will prevent delays in getting the property into the hands of the beneficiaries. Unfortunately, this method will increase the value of the remainder interest and the associated transfer costs at the time the trust is established.
- *a general testamentary power of appointment over (or reversionary interest in) the property exercisable only if the grantor dies during the term*—This will help get the funds into the hands of the beneficiaries and will also increase the value of the grantor's interest (thus reducing the transfer-tax costs for establishing the trust). The transfer of the property to a marital deduction trust through the exercise of this power will, at least, preserve the marital deduction if the property is returned to the gross estate.

In addition, the purchase of life insurance to solve this liquidity problem should be seriously considered. Even if the grantor has enough insurance to handle his or her other estate tax problems, the beneficiaries of the QPRT should consider the purchase of coverage on the grantor's life for the term of the QPRT. The death benefit could be used by the beneficiaries to purchase the residence from the grantor's estate if he or she dies prematurely. This would expedite the receipt of the residence by the heirs and add cash to the estate for liquidity purposes. Of course, the grantor could provide the premium payments to the remainder beneficiaries through annual-exclusion gifts.

Term of QPRT. Since the estate and gift tax savings from the QPRT are eliminated if the grantor does not survive the retained-interest term, it is advisable to select a term that the grantor is likely to survive. For this reason, therefore, this technique is not a good planning device for a grantor who is in poor health or at an advanced age. If the term of the QPRT must be kept short due to the health or age of the grantor, the value of the remainder interest increases, thus reducing the potential transfer-tax savings of the technique. However, the downside risk of attempting a QPRT is small because it leaves the grantor's estate with no greater tax liability than it would have had if nothing had been done.

Impact of Sec. 7520 Interest Rate on QPRTs. The value of the gift in the QPRT is determined based on the length of the term and the monthly Sec. 7520 interest rate that is in effect at the time of the transfer. The creation of the trust could be delayed if the interest rate is not favorable. Since Sec. 7520 took effect in May 1989, the interest rate has fluctuated from a high of 11.6 percent to a low of 6 percent.

Because the value of the remainder interest in the QPRT is the inverse of the term-income interest, the effect of the rate on the value of the gift depends on the changes in the income interest. When rates are lower, the income interest is valued lower; therefore the value of the gift is higher. Thus QPRTs are more effective for estate and gift tax planning if interest rates are high at the time of the transfer.

> *Example:* Assume the same facts as the previous two examples. At 7 percent, the gift tax value of the remainder interest following the 10-year retained-interest term for Tom Taxplanner's $300,000 vacation home was $152,505. At the Sec. 7520 rate of 11.6 percent that was in effect in May 1989, the value of the taxable gift would have been $100,110. Thus, at the higher interest rate, $52,395 less of Tom Taxplanner's applicable credit amount would have been used up. (Calculations courtesy of NumberCruncher Software [610-527-5216])

Tangible Personal Property Trusts

Another exception to the general rule of Sec. 2702 is for transfers of certain tangible personal property to a trust. If the transferor's nonexercise of rights under a term interest in tangible property would not have a substantial effect on the valuation of the remainder interest in the property, the term interest retained is not arbitrarily assigned a zero value. However, instead of Sec. 7520 actuarial tables, the retained interest must be valued under the classic "willing buyer-willing seller" method for establishing fair market value. The value of the retained term interest is the amount for which the grantor can prove his or her retained interest could be sold to an unrelated third party.

This tangible property exception is applicable only to certain tangible property. Eligible tangible personal property is defined as *nonwasting assets*—assets for which no deduction for depreciation or depletion would be allowable if the property were used in a trade or business or held for the production of income and for which the failure to exercise any rights under the term interest would not increase the value of the property passing at the end of the term interest. For example, a senior family member can place tangible personal property, such as a painting, into an irrevocable trust that will eventually transfer it to a specified beneficiary but retain the right to keep that painting for a specified period of years. The value of this retained interest will be subtracted from the value of the painting and the balance will be considered a gift to the remainder beneficiary. The retained right to the painting (or other tangible personal property) will be valued at the amount a third party would pay for the term interest.

Example: Tom Taxplanner has a valuable print (current fair market value of $100,000) and would like to reduce his estate taxes. Assume he can prove—through a third-party independent photographic art dealer—that the lease rights on the print for 10 years are worth $40,000. He could contribute the print to a 10-year retained-interest trust with a remainder interest to his daughter Julia. He would receive "credit" for the value of the interest retained in the calculation of the gift tax. So the taxable gift would be $60,000, the $100,000 value of the print minus the $40,000 value of the right to "rent" the print for 10 years, that is, the difference between the fair market value of the print and the amount determined under the tangible property exception. If the print is expected to appreciate in value, the subsequent appreciation passes to Julia free of gift or estate tax provided Tom survives the 10-year term of the trust.

The author has serious reservations about the practical usefulness of a tangible personal property trust. The regulations supply a troublesome example that makes the valuation of a multiyear term trust difficult. They state that a 10-year lease should not necessarily be valued at the going price for a one-year lease multiplied by 10. Thus the lack of a 10-year comparable lease price (which should be nearly impossible to find) makes the value of a 10-year, or any multiyear, tangible personal property trust speculative. The regulations do not adequately explain how the donor should appraise the multiyear value when only one-year comparable leases are available, but the IRS does concede that the 10-year term is not worth *less* than a one-year term. The tangible personal property trust loses its appeal if the gift tax discount (related to the retained-interest term) cannot be valued with the same certainty as for outright gifts, QPRTs, and qualified retained interests.

Trusts Providing Qualified Retained Interests

A *qualified retained interest* in the trust by the transferor or applicable family member will be valued at its full Sec. 7520 table value. A qualified interest is one of the following:

- a right to receive fixed amounts payable at least annually, or grantor-retained annuity trust (GRAT)
- a right to receive amounts payable at least annually that are a fixed percentage of the trust's asset determined annually, or grantor-retained unitrust (GRUT)
- any noncontingent remainder interest if all other interests in the trust are GRATs or GRUTs

Estate Planning with GRATs and GRUTs

Qualified retained-interest trusts provide an excellent opportunity for a wealthy individual to reduce his or her total transfer tax. Property transferred to such a trust will be treated as a current gift for gift tax purposes. Furthermore, the gift tax annual exclusion, the GSTT annual exclusion, the applicable credit amount against estate taxes or gift taxes, and the $1 million GSTT exemption all might be used effectively to reduce the actual current gift tax or GSTT liability to zero.

The estate tax treatment of the transfer to the retained-interest trust depends on the terms and administration of the trust. You will recall from the Sec. 2702 rules discussed earlier that transfers with retained rights for the donor may cause serious estate or gift tax consequences. For example, the wrong retained rights could cause the entire property to be treated as a taxable gift for gift tax purposes. A retained right that does not end before the death of the grantor will cause all, or a portion of, the trust property be included in the donor's gross estate, even if it is currently treated as current gifts for gift tax purposes.

These estate tax rules are very important for designing a successful trust freeze. Quite often the grantor would like to retain some use of the donated property, giving him or her the opportunity to draw on the trust income or principal to receive income payments during retirement. In addition, the retained rights held by the grantor may have value for gift tax purposes, offsetting the gift tax cost of transferring the property to the trust. You will recall that the subtraction method of valuation permits retained rights with "value" to reduce the gift tax cost of transfers subject to grantor-held retained rights.

GRAT Defined. A GRAT is an irrevocable trust in which the grantor retains a right to receive fixed payments (just like a fixed annuity) payable at least annually for his or her life (or the joint lives of the grantor and one or more life tenants) or for a term of years (actuarially similar to a charitable remainder annuity trust). At the end of the term or life interest, the remaining trust corpus is paid to designated remainder beneficiaries. The annuity interest is valued under Sec. 7520 rules, and the gift tax value of the remainder is determined by subtracting the value of the annuity interest from the total value of the principal placed in trust.

> *Example:* Shirley Settlar contributes $1 million in securities to an irrevocable trust. She retains the right to receive $60,000 per year from the trust for the next 10 years. At the end of 10 years, the trust will terminate and the remainder will be paid in equal shares to her grandchildren. The retained interest is a qualified annuity interest and will be given full actuarial value under Sec. 7520 valuation rules. Thus the value of the gift is equal to $1 million minus the value of a 10-year $60,000 annual annuity.

GRUT Defined. A GRUT is an irrevocable trust in which the grantor retains the right to receive amounts payable, at least annually, that are a fixed percentage of the trust's assets as revalued annually (just like a variable annuity). The GRUT is actuarially similar to a charitable remainder unitrust. The term of the trust may extend for the life of the grantor (or joint lives of two or more annuitants) or for a specified term of years. At the end of the term of the trust, all remaining trust assets pass to the designated remainder beneficiaries. The gift tax value of the GRUT may be subtracted from the value of the property transferred to the trust to determine the gift tax value of the remainder interest.

Example: Assume the same facts as the previous example. However, Shirley instead retains the right to receive payments equal to 6 percent of the trust based on its current value each year. The retained interest is a qualified unitrust interest and will be given full actuarial value under Sec. 7520 valuation rules. Thus the value of the gift is equal to $1 million minus the value of a 10-year unitrust interest.

Gift Tax Treatment of GRAT or GRUT

The irrevocable transfer of the remainder interest in a GRAT or GRUT is a current gift for gift tax purposes. Since the gift provides a future interest to the donees, it does not qualify for the annual exclusion. However, the gift is discounted from the full fair market value of the corpus by subtracting the value of the grantor's retained interest as determined under the Sec. 7520 rules. This discounted gift can be sheltered by the grantor's remaining applicable credit amount before any gift taxes must be paid. The regulations require that valuation of the qualified interest be based on the assumption that the term ends on the earlier of the actual termination or the death of the grantor. The assumption for the termination at the premature death of the grantor must be made whether or not the trust terms require termination at the grantor's death. The inclusion of the grantor's mortality contingency reduces the value of the retained interest, thus increasing the value of the gift of the remainder interest. Consistent with the Sec. 2702 restrictions, any retained trust interest other than a GRAT or a GRUT will generally be valued at zero for gift tax purposes.

Example: Suppose Shirley Settlar from the previous two examples was 55 years old when the retained-interest trusts were created. In the case of the GRAT, the retained annuity of $60,000 valued at a term equal to the shorter of 10 years or Shirley's life is worth $400,656, assuming a 7 percent Sec. 7520 rate. Therefore, the remainder is worth $599,344 ($1 million minus $400,656) for gift tax purposes. The entire gift of the remainder can be sheltered by Shirley's applicable credit amount.

The estate planning value of the GRAT should be obvious. Shirley has the right to receive $60,000 each year for 10 years and give away the remainder of the principal (which could be more or less than $1 million depending on the actual investment return) for a gift tax cost limited to the use of $599,344 of her applicable credit amount. If the trust principal is invested in growth assets and appreciates at 9 percent per year, net of taxes, the principal will be worth $1,455,788 when it is transferred to the remainder beneficiaries. (Calculations courtesy of NumberCruncher Software [610-527-5216])

Example: In the case of the GRUT providing Shirley with 6 percent of the annual value of the corpus, the Sec. 7520 rules give a different result. Assuming that the trust principal is valued the time the annual payment is made, the right to receive the 6 percent unitrust amount for the earlier of 10 years or Shirley's death is valued at $438,391. Therefore the taxable gift of the remainder interest is valued at $561,609 ($1 million minus $438,391). Again, the gift can be entirely sheltered by Shirley's applicable credit amount.

The effects of the unitrust payment schedule on the estate plan differ from those of the annuity schedule. The payments vary with the size of the principal; therefore they can never exhaust the principal and will rise if the property appreciates. Suppose again that the principal grows at 9 percent. The payments to Shirley begin at $60,000 and grow to $74,669 by the tenth year. The principal transferred to the remainder beneficiaries is correspondingly less, totaling $1,275,101. (Calculations courtesy of NumberCruncher Software [610-527-5216])

Estate Tax Treatment of GRAT or GRUT

If the grantor survives the retained-interest term in a qualified GRAT or GRUT, Sec. 2036 does not apply and the corpus, including any posttransfer appreciation, is excluded from the grantor's gross estate. In other words, a growing property interest can be transferred to family heirs for a significantly discounted transfer-tax cost.

However, the estate tax benefits are reduced if the grantor fails to survive the term, because some value of the retained rights returns to the gross estate. The amount included is the amount of principal of the trust that would be required under actuarial valuation principles to produce the annuity or unitrust payout. The upper limit on the inclusion is the actual amount of principal at the time of death.

In many circumstances, the includible amount is less than the entire trust principal. The amount includible is based on the annuity or unitrust amount and the Sec. 7520 discount rate at the time of the grantor's premature death. Presumably, the Sec. 7520 rate 6 months after the grantor's death can be used if the alternate valuation date is selected.

Estate Tax Inclusion for the GRAT. The IRS has published a ruling[1] dealing with the estate tax inclusion of a charitable remainder annuity trust. The same valuation principles should apply to a GRAT. Basically, if the grantor dies during the term of the GRAT, the amount included in his or her estate is determined by dividing the retained annuity amount by the Sec. 7520 valuation rate, as shown below:

$$\text{Estate tax inclusion for GRAT} = \frac{\text{Annuity amount}}{i}$$

$$i = 120 \text{ percent of the AFMR}$$

Example: Continuing the previous examples, assume Shirley dies in 5 years, thus failing to survive the term. Assuming the Sec. 7520 rate is the same at the date of death as at the date the GRAT was created, the included estate tax value of the trust is $60,000 divided by .07, or $857,143. Of course, the original gift will be removed from the estate tax computation as an adjusted taxable gift. Note that the amount included is less than the full value of the property and that any posttransfer appreciation avoids both gift and estate tax. In this case, with the assumed 9 percent growth rate, the value of the corpus at the time of Shirley's death would be $1,179,541, whereas the amount included in the estate is only $857,143. The lesson here is that the GRAT could result in transfer-tax savings even if the grantor fails to survive the retained-interest term.

Estate Tax Inclusion for the GRUT. As with a GRAT, the property transferred to a GRUT escapes estate tax includibility if the grantor survives the retained-interest term. The IRS has issued a ruling[2] regarding the estate tax inclusion of a charitable remainder unitrust in the grantor's gross estate when the grantor dies during the term of the trust. Again, there appears to be no reason why this ruling would not apply to a GRUT. According to the IRS ruling, the grantor must compute an "equivalent interest rate" for the unitrust using the following formula:

$$\text{Equivalent interest rate} = \frac{\text{Unitrust adjusted payout rate}}{1 - \text{Unitrust adjusted payout rate}}$$

The fraction of the GRUT included in the grantor's gross estate is computed by dividing the equivalent interest rate by the Sec. 7520 rate at the date of death. Again, the maximum amount included is the amount of the principal at the time of the grantor's death.

$$\text{Estate tax inclusion for GRUT} = \frac{\text{Equivalent interest rate}}{i}$$

$$i = 120 \text{ percent of the AFMR}$$

Example: Assume the same facts from above for Shirley's 6 percent 10-year GRUT. If the Sec. 7520 rate is 7 percent at the time of Shirley's premature death in 5 years, the amount included is the percentage of the trust required to produce the unitrust amount. The equivalent interest rate equals .06 divided by .94, or 6.383 percent. Thus the percentage of the trust principal required to make the unitrust payments, or the percentage included in Shirley's gross estate, equals .06383 divided by .07, or 91.19 percent of the principal.

Zeroed-out GRATs

One type of transaction that has recently gained some attention is the zeroed-out GRAT. *Zeroed out* means that the length of the term and/or the size of the payout is arranged in such a manner that there is no taxable gift under the Sec. 7520 actuarial valuation rules. For instance, by retaining an annuity from a GRAT equal to 50 percent of the initial principal, the grantor could pay almost no gift taxes, even if the term of the trust is only 2 years. However, the principal must appreciate and the income remain high enough to make this practical. Otherwise, the principal will be expended to make the annuity payments, and the grantor's estate will not be reduced. The IRS argues that if the rate of the annuity is inordinately high—so high that the trust will be exhausted before its term ends—the grantor's retained interest should not be based on the full term, but rather on the projected period to exhaustion. Therefore zeroing out the gift may be difficult in any event.

Because GRUT payments decrease as the principal value declines, it is actuarially impossible to completely zero out the gift tax value of the remainder interest in a GRUT.

Choosing Investments for GRATs and GRUTs

Since a major objective of the types of retained-interest trusts described in this chapter is an estate freeze or the intentional reduction of the grantor's estate, the more likely an asset is to substantially appreciate after the transfer, the more desirable it is as a trust investment. So securities and real estate are the best assets to consider. Regular closely held corporate stock is not a good investment because the trustee of the GRAT or GRUT would have to receive taxable dividends to make the annuity payments. S corporation stock can be used as long as the grantor is considered owner of the trust (as discussed below).

A major consideration for the investment of the GRAT or GRUT is the required qualified payments. These payments must be made to the grantor (or applicable family member who holds the retained interest) each year or adverse gift tax consequences will occur. Thus the GRAT or GRUT must have adequate income or liquidity each year or principal will have to be liquidated to make the required payments.

The rate of return produced by the investment should exceed the Sec. 7520 rate for the transfer-tax advantage (gift-tax-free shifting of appreciation to the remainder beneficiaries) to materialize. If the rate actually earned is lower than the Sec. 7520 rate, an outright gift should be considered instead of a GRAT or GRUT. The reason is that if the earnings are insufficient to produce the promised payment, capital that otherwise would have gone to the remainder beneficiaries must be paid to the grantor—defeating the estate reduction goals of the GRAT or GRUT.

Example: Debra Donor, aged 70, creates a 5-year GRAT funded with $1 million that will pay her $70,000 annually for the term of the trust. The principal is invested in a money market fund paying 3 percent. The trustee does not change the investment. At an assumed Sec. 7520 rate of 7 percent, Debra's taxable gift is valued at $734,931; thus her retained interest is worth only $265,069. Furthermore, because her payments and the Sec. 7520 rate exceed the actual income and appreciation of the investment, only $787,635 will be distributed to the beneficiaries at the end of the term unless the money market rates increase. Thus the GRAT provides little gift tax advantage.

Use of S Corporation Stock. Such stock might make an appropriate investment for a GRAT or GRUT because the S corporation can pass through income or cash flow to the trustee without the adverse income tax consequences that a dividend would cause a C corporation. In fact, if the S corporation has adequate cash flow to make the annuity payments and has good appreciation potential, the GRAT or GRUT may be an effective mechanism to retire a family business owner. However, only certain trusts are eligible to hold S corporation stock.

The GRAT and GRUT are not qualified subchapter S trusts (QSSTs), in which all income must be payable annually or more frequently to the beneficiary; a GRAT or GRUT may earn more (or less) income than the amount paid out as a qualified GRAT or GRUT annuity interest. Both trusts can be modified to meet S corporation holding requirements merely by giving the grantor, for the term of the trust, the nonfiduciary right to purchase trust assets in return for cash or other assets of equal value. However, the IRS has issued some troubling private rulings regarding such modification, refusing to rule whether or not the asset replacement power was held in a nonfiduciary capacity until tax returns are filed. Therefore S corporation stock should be placed in a GRAT or GRUT only after careful consideration of the tax ramifications.

Use of Property Subject to a Loan. Several problems may result if such property is transferred to a GRAT or GRUT. The cash flow used by the trust to satisfy a loan against the property could be considered use of trust income for the benefit of the grantor. If the loan is a recourse loan, the grantor will be treated as having his or her obligation satisfied by the trust. This *per se* is not a major problem because the grantor expects to be taxed on trust income. Ironically, the problems begin if and when the grantor makes payments because they are considered additions to the trust, which are permitted for a GRUT but not a GRAT.

Perhaps a more serious problem is that additional payments of the mortgage by the grantor may be viewed as taxable gifts. If the original taxable gift is valued based on the net value of the property (gross value minus encumbrances), the IRS may treat each mortgage payment by the grantor as an additional gift of a future interest. On the other hand, if the property was valued at its gross value (that is, the grantor retained the obligation to pay off the loan), the grantor's additional payments should not be considered taxable gifts to the remainder beneficiaries.

Income Tax Treatment of Grantor

Many commentators believe that a GRAT or GRUT should be treated as a grantor trust for income tax purposes; that is, the grantor should be taxable on all trust income during the retained-interest term. Under the provisions of the grantor-trust rules, some of the income of the trust is distributable to the grantor in the form of the qualified annual payments. At least to this extent, the grantor certainly receives ordinary income from the trust. In many instances, the GRAT or GRUT is intentionally made a grantor trust for other reasons. For example, see the discussion above concerning S corporations as an investment. In summary, the grantor should be treated as receiving the taxable income to the extent of his or her annuity or unitrust payment. Perhaps the grantor may have to report all taxable trust income.

A private ruling on the issue of whether a GRAT can be established with provisions to pay the grantor's resulting income taxes in addition to the specified fixed annuity held that this provision did not disqualify the GRAT for favorable treatment under Sec. 2702, but the retained right to the distributions for taxes could not be assigned value for the purposes of determining the value of the gift of the remainder interest. This result is consistent with Sec. 2702, which states that only the right to the qualified annuity or unitrust payments can be given actuarial value for the purposes of the subtraction method of valuation.

Impact of Sec. 7520 Rate on GRATs and GRUTs

The Sec. 7520 interest rate is used in determining the value of the remainder interest transferred when the GRAT or GRUT is created. The GRAT provides a fixed annuity to the grantor (or other applicable family member who retains an interest). The fixed annuity is valued based on the rules discussed in chapter 4. The value of the gift (the remainder interest) is determined by subtracting the value of the retained annuity from the total value of the principal. Thus, when the value of the annuity is high, the value of the gift is proportionately low. The value of a fixed annuity is higher when interest rates are lower. This makes sense because it should be more difficult to maintain an annuity payment when rates of return drop. Therefore, when the Sec. 7520 interest rate is low, a GRAT is more favorable than when the rate is higher because the gift tax cost of the transfer is reduced. A small time-value-of-money adjustment is required if the annuity is paid more frequently than annually; this adjustment also is based on the Sec. 7520 rate.

Example: Gregory Grantor, aged 65, places $1 million in a GRAT with a retained right to receive $75,000 annually for the next 10 years. At the termination of the GRAT, the remainder is distributed to his daughter, Dawn. At the Sec. 7520 rate of 7 percent, the value of the gift of the remainder interest is $529,202. If the Sec. 7520 rate is 11 percent at the time of the transfer, Gregory's retained annuity is worth less and the gift of the remainder is correspondingly higher ($601,900). Thus the taxable gift increases by $72,698 with the 4 percent increase in the Sec. 7520 rate. (Calculations courtesy of NumberCruncher Software [610-527-5216])

The effect of the Sec. 7520 interest rate is less profound in the case of GRUTs. The value of the retained unitrust interest is based on the unitrust percentage rather than the Sec. 7520 interest rate. This results from the fact that the payment amount will decline or rise with the value of the principal and is not a fixed annuity. The Sec. 7520 rate will have little effect on the valuation of GRUTs in some circumstances. The rate is used for time-value-of-money adjustments if the unitrust payments are made more frequently than annually or if any payments are made at a time other than the annual valuation date of the GRUT assets.

Example: Assume Gregory from the previous example had instead created a GRUT with a 10-year payout of 7.5 percent of the annual value of the trust assets. The payments are made in quarterly installments, and the GRUT is valued at the beginning of the year. Thus 3 months pass between the initial valuation and the first unitrust payment. Under this scenario, the value of the gift of the remainder is $465,969 at a Sec. 7520 rate of 7 percent. If the rate rises to 11 percent, the taxable gift would be $474,037—an increase of only $8,068. If the unitrust amount was paid only once per year at the valuation date of the GRUT, the taxable gift would be unchanged by fluctuations in the Sec. 7520 rate. (Calculations courtesy of NumberCruncher Software [610-527-5216])

Comparing GRATs and GRUTs

When GRATs Are Indicated. In general, GRATs are preferable to GRUTs in most family situations because GRATs still present the opportunity to shift wealth to desired beneficiaries at a gift tax cost lower than the actual economic value of the transfer. This result is much less likely with GRUTs, in which payments to the grantor increase as the value of the trust assets increase. The wealth transfer is most leveraged when the Sec. 7520 rate and the taxable gift are lower. The GRAT transfers relatively more property at a reduced transfer-tax cost when the appreciation rate of the property exceeds the Sec. 7520 rate, because the growth is transferred to the remainder beneficiaries.

The GRAT should also be the choice if zeroing out is the goal. The zeroed-out GRAT provides a tax-free transfer if the appreciation rate on the property is high.

The GRAT is the better choice if the grantor needs steady cash flow during the retained-interest period. The fixed annuity of the GRAT provides a guaranteed payment during the term of the trust regardless of the volatility of the principal investment.

Finally, the GRAT is a better option if the initial contribution of property or the later reinvestment of the GRAT is difficult to value. The GRAT property must be appraised only once, at the time the trust is created. This makes the GRAT a better vehicle to transfer closely held S corporations.

When GRUTs Are Indicated. The GRUT is a better choice under certain circumstances. First, the GRUT should be a better transfer-tax device if the income and growth of the property is less than the Sec. 7520 rate. The variable payment feature of the GRUT prevents the principal from being entirely expended to make the unitrust payments. Thus, even if the investment performs badly, the GRUT will still have valuable property to leave to the remainder beneficiaries.

Second, the GRUT is the only option if the grantor wishes to make additional gifts to the trust. After a GRAT is funded, no subsequent contributions are permitted.

Third, the GRUT is preferable if the grantor wants to "inflation proof" his or her retained interest. The GRUT will provide for increased payments if the principal appreciates. If the grantor is using the GRUT to supplement his or her retirement benefits, he or she may desire to share in the growth of the assets.

Finally, the GRUT is indicated only when the intended investment lends itself to simple valuation. Hard-to-value assets will result in a high appraisal expense each year and, perhaps, a challenge by the IRS as to the validity of the value determined by the trustee.

> *Planning point:* A GRAT or GRUT should be used only after careful consideration of all tax consequences. The term of the trust should be no longer than the grantor is expected to survive. Otherwise,

part of the trust property will be included in the grantor's estate, reducing the transfer-tax advantages. The selection of a GRAT or GRUT depends on many factors.

The planner should run the numbers based on several alternative consequences. For example, the Sec. 7520 rate, the potential growth rate of the assets, the grantor's needs with respect to the retained rights, and the gift tax costs should be examined to determine the optimal choice. Remember, the advantages offered by the GRAT or GRUT could be reduced or eliminated entirely by the grantor's premature death or the assets' unfavorable investment performance.

Life insurance point: The unexpired term of the grantor's retained annuity or unitrust interest presents a liquidity problem if the grantor does not survive the retained-interest term. As discussed above, part of the trust property will be included in the grantor's gross estate in the event of premature death. If the property cannot be liquidated during this time to pay taxes, there will be a liquidity shortfall. This could result from the fact that the grantor did not retain a reversionary interest contingent on such premature death. Or if such reversionary interest was retained, perhaps the principal does not lend itself to a quick sale on favorable terms by the estate.

The purchase of life insurance to solve this liquidity problem should be seriously considered. Even if the grantor has enough insurance to handle his or her other estate tax problems, the beneficiaries of the GRAT or GRUT should consider purchasing coverage on the grantor's life for the term of the trust. The beneficiaries could use the death benefit to purchase the trust principal from the grantor's estate if he or she dies prematurely, expediting the heirs' receipt of the remainder interest and adding cash to the estate for liquidity purposes. Of course, the grantor could provide the premium payments to the remainder beneficiaries through annual-exclusion gifts.

REMOVAL OF LIFE INSURANCE PROCEEDS FROM DECEDENT-INSURED'S GROSS ESTATE

Sec. 2042(2) of the Internal Revenue Code requires the death proceeds of life insurance policies owned by an insured on his or her own life to be included in his or her gross estate. Such a situation may be thought of as the worst of all possible worlds since the estate owner never has the death proceeds to use during his or her lifetime (since the proceeds do not yet exist), yet he or she must be taxed on them after death for federal estate tax purposes. This unfortunate result is even more dramatic when one considers how easily the problem may be resolved.

The test as set forth by Sec. 2042(2) deals with incidents of ownership. If the decedent-insured has had any link with the life insurance policies in question so that he or she is considered to have had these incidents of ownership, the *full* face value of the life policies (the death proceeds) must be included in the gross estate. Because of this doctrine, there are many on-paper millionaires. Since the federal estate tax system is graduated in nature, it is essential that the life insurance be removed from the insured's gross estate. It is often the improper titling of life insurance that pushes a gross estate over the threshold of the applicable exclusion amount ($625,000 of taxable estate in 1998) and ends up making the difference between paying federal estate tax and owing nothing at all! These facts, along with the fact that it is so simple to remove the life insurance from the gross estate, make it shocking and disappointing that more estates have not taken advantage of life insurance removal.

If the death proceeds are to be successfully shielded from federal estate tax liability, the decedent-insured may not possess any incidents of ownership, such as the right to change beneficiaries, the right to borrow against the policy's cash value, the right to pledge the insurance policy as collateral for a loan, and the most basic incident of ownership of all—he or she must not be the named owner of the policy. Mere removal or cessation of these incidents of ownership by the decedent-insured ensures removal of the death proceeds of the policy from the insured's gross estate.

There are two possible ways to remove life insurance from the insured's gross estate:

- *cross-ownership between spouses*—a criss-cross method wherein a husband owns the life insurance on his wife's life and the wife owns the life insurance on her husband's life
- *the irrevocable life insurance trust*—a trust created for the express purpose of holding the life insurance policies involved

Cross-Ownership

Because of the incidents-of-ownership test, cross-ownership is a useful technique and quite easy to achieve. If new life insurance is being acquired on one spouse's life, the other spouse should act as owner and applicant of the policy. This method is preferable because Sec. 2035 (the 3-year, contemplation-of-death concept) still applies to a transfer of life insurance. If the spouse other than the insured spouse owns the policy from the outset, there is *no transfer* and therefore no 3-year problem with which to contend. If the insured already owns his or her own policy, the ownership should be assigned to the spouse. This method is just as effective in terms of removing the death proceeds from the insured's gross estate, except that the transferor must live for more than 3 years after the assignment in order to have effectively removed the insurance from the gross estate.

Although cross-ownership of life insurance is an effective way of defeating the incidents-of-ownership test, there are problems with this particular arrangement. First, should divorce occur, the cross-ownership arrangement would be one more element of an already difficult and anxiety-provoking situation. The life insurance arrangement would have to be restructured and readjusted in accordance with the specifics of the property settlement. If cross-ownership is not involved, the divorce settlement would have one less element of complexity.

An additional reason why cross-ownership is not the best approach is the unpredictability of the order of death of the spouses. In the event that the spouse other than the insured predeceases the insured, it is likely that the insurance would end up back in the insured's gross estate. Cross-ownership would have accomplished nothing.

Although this method will defeat the incidents-of-ownership situation, there are too many potential problems with its use.

Irrevocable Life Insurance Trust

The use of the irrevocable life insurance trust (ILIT) is a popular technique for removing proceeds of life insurance from the insured's gross estate. A trust is created to own the life insurance on the decedent's life. It is intentionally made irrevocable so that the corpus of the trust may not be drawn back into the decedent-settlor's gross estate. If the life insurance involved is newly issued, the trustee should be named as owner and applicant of the policy. Again, this ensures that the 3-year, contemplation-of-death rule of Sec. 2035 is avoided. The named beneficiary of the life insurance is the life insurance trust, and the named beneficiaries of the trust are those family members who are to receive the life insurance proceeds.

If existing life insurance coverage is transferred to a newly created ILIT, there are two potential problems. First, the 3-year, contemplation-of-death rule of Sec. 2035 applies. If the transferor dies within 3 years after transferring the life insurance into the ILIT, the proceeds must still be included in his or her gross estate. The second problem is that the federal gift tax could be triggered if the transferred policy has a value that exceeds the annual exclusion amount.

We have already discussed the fact that the annual exclusion is a very effective way to reduce (or even eliminate) federal gift tax liability. To take maximum advantage of this device, however, a *Crummey* power should be included in the trust. A Crummey power allows each beneficiary of the ILIT to be considered to be receiving a gift of a present interest, which is a prerequisite to taking advantage of the annual exclusion rules. Even with the Crummey power, if the fair market value of the transferred life insurance policy (interpolated terminable reserve and unused portion of the premium payment of the product in a noncash value policy) exceeds the available annual exclusion amount, the federal gift tax could be triggered.

NOTES

1. Rev. Rul. 82-105, 1982-1 C.B. 133.
2. Rev. Rul. 76-273, 1976-2 C.B. 268.

6

Estate Freezes for Family Businesses

Chapter Outline

WHAT IS AN ESTATE FREEZE? 185
    Impact of Chapter 14 187
ESTATE FREEZES THROUGH FAMILY PARTNERSHIPS 192
    Advantages of Family Partnerships 192
    Structuring a Family Partnership 192
    Income Tax Considerations 196
    Protection from Creditors 196
    Family Life Insurance Partnerships (FLIPs) 197
    IRS Attacks on Family Limited Partnerships 200
ESTATE FREEZES THROUGH SALES OF FAMILY BUSINESSES
    TO FAMILY MEMBERS 201
    Installment Sales 201
    Self-Canceling Installment Notes (SCINs) 206
    Private Annuities 207

WHAT IS AN ESTATE FREEZE?

Because business interests have the strongest and most realistic propensity for substantial appreciation in value, estate planners have always attempted to find a way to place a cap or a ceiling on the value of this type of asset. This has traditionally been referred to as an estate freeze. If an estate owner owns all or a portion of a closely held business that has been appreciating in value over the years and he or she has done nothing to place a cap or ceiling on this business interest, the gross estate will be much larger at the date of death than it would have been had a freezing technique been used.

Total removal of the asset from the gross estate prior to the estate owner's death is one way to reduce gross estate size. This in turn proportionately reduces estate tax liability, but such a technique is not an estate-freezing technique *per se*.

Example: Kevin Burns, aged 52, is sole shareholder of Burns Enterprises, Inc., a manufacturer of smoke detectors. Kevin started the business in 1963 in his basement with an initial investment of $2,500. Today there are eight plants in six states, and the fair market value of the company is approximately $2 million. Since Kevin is still the sole shareholder of the stock, the entire value of the business interest would be included in his gross estate if he were to die today. Kevin has recently begun to think of turning control of the business over to his son. Kevin's son Tom, aged 30, has been involved in the business for the last 7 years as senior vice president. Because Kevin wants to retire, has ample assets to do so, and is worried about estate tax liability, he gifts all his stock to Tom. Kevin pays gift tax on $2 million minus the annual exclusion.

When Kevin dies 14 years later, the stock in Burns Enterprises, Inc., has a fair market value of $3.6 million. Kevin has successfully shifted the future appreciation of the business and saved a substantial amount of estate tax.

There are few real situations like the preceding example in which a business owner would make a gift of an entire business interest at one time. A more realistic scenario would not involve a complete, sudden, and abrupt divestiture of the business interest but rather a gradual, piecemeal shifting of the control of the business interest to others. For several reasons, it is unlikely that a senior-generation family member like Kevin Burns would want to pass the entire interest in the family business at one time to junior-generation successors. In many cases, the successors will not be adequately prepared to take over the reins. Moreover, the current owner may wish to retain some control over the activities. Finally, the senior-generation owner may want or need to retain income from business operations.

As we explained in chapter 5 (see "Estate Freezes through Family Trusts"), an estate freeze is an estate planning technique designed to restrict an individual's eventual taxable estate to its current value. The goal of the estate freeze is to retain a business interest that is *frozen* or *capped* in value for tax purposes. Thus, when the retained interest is transferred, it can be done at a predictable estate or gift tax cost.

Also as discussed previously, the Treasury has always been skeptical of estate freezes because the posttransfer appreciation in the property in a successful freeze escapes both estate and gift taxes. As we noted earlier, both Congress and the IRS are concerned because the transferor has not disposed of all interests in the property when the freeze is completed. Congress singled out the preferred-stock recapitalization of a corporation (and the analogous partnership restructuring) as a classic abuse of the estate-freeze mechanism.

Example: Suppose parent P owns 100 percent of the stock in ABC corporation. If ABC recapitalizes by exchanging newly issued preferred stock for 90 percent of P's common stock, P now holds 90 percent of the value of ABC corporation in the form of preferred stock. Preferred stock usually yields fixed income rights (in the form of dividends and a fixed liquidation right) and does not generally share in any growth in the corporation. Thus, following the recapitalization, all of the growth in ABC corporation should accrue to the remaining common stock. In the classic estate-freeze transaction, P would transfer, by sale or gift, the remaining common stock in ABC to P's children, C1 and C2. If the freeze is successful, all future appreciation following the transfer of the remaining common stock to the children accrues to their benefit. The preferred stock held by P until death provides a substantial steady stream of income, but it possesses a date-of-death value that is "frozen" (no greater than its value at the time of the recapitalization). Thus P has retained a substantial current interest in ABC while effectively transferring all of the growth in ABC free of transfer tax to C1 and C2.

Impact of Chapter 14

In the Revenue Reconciliation Act of 1990, Congress established chapter 14 of the Internal Revenue Code (Secs. 2701–2704) to deal with the perceived valuation abuses. These rules are effective for transfers after October 8, 1990. Before this date, the tax value of stock or a partnership interest transferred by gift or by sale to a family member was found by subtracting the value of all other stock or partnership interests held by the transferor from the total value of the interests held prior to the transfer. For these purposes, the value of the other stock or partnership interests took into account the rights to dividends, liquidation, and other distributions, even though such rights might not be enforced due to the family relationships of the stockholders or partners. In other words, the value of the transferred interest could be deflated (and the gift tax liability reduced) by artificially inflating the value of the interests that were retained.

IRC Sec. 2701

Sec. 2701 focuses on proper valuation of assets at the time of transfer for the purposes of determining a gift tax. Thus the purpose of the rule is to place a realistic value of the business interests retained by the senior-generation family member. Only specific rights in the retained interests are deemed to have value for the purpose of determining the gift tax value of the transferred interest.

The general rule under Sec. 2701 provides a harsh result for the estate freeze. For the purposes of determining whether the transfer of an interest in a *controlled* corporation or partnership to (or for the benefit of, such as through a trust) a *member of the family* of the transferor (a) is a gift and (b) the gift tax value of such gift, the value of certain *retained rights* with respect to an *applicable retained interest* held by the transferor or an *applicable family member* immediately after the transfer is generally deemed to be zero. In other words, no valuation credit is given for the value of rights that are retained. The subtraction method of valuation cannot be used (or if it is used, a value of zero is given to what is retained by the transferor), and the gift tax value of the stock transferred is equal to the value of the transferor's entire interest prior to such transfer. You should recognize this rule as virtually identical to the rule applicable to estate freezes in trusts.

Example: A, the sole owner of ACO, Inc., owns 100 shares of common stock valued at $100,000. ACO recapitalizes and issues $90,000 (valued under traditional valuation rules) of noncumulative preferred stock providing a 10 percent dividend to A in exchange for 90 shares of common stock. A then gifts 10 shares of ACO common stock to A's child. A believes the gift of common stock is entirely sheltered by the $10,000 annual exclusion. (Under the subtraction method of valuation, the gift equals the total value of the business [$100,000] minus the value of the retained preferred stock [$90,000], or $10,000.) However, Sec. 2701 applies because A transferred an interest in a controlled corporation to a family member and retains rights (the preferred stock) after such transfer. The value of the gift is actually $100,000, because A's retained preferred stock must be given a zero value under Sec. 2701.

The following definitions are necessary to fully understand the implications of Sec. 2701:

- *member of the family*—This term refers only to the transferor's spouse, the lineal descendants of the transferor or transferor's spouse, and a spouse of any such descendant. Thus the statute is applicable only if a transfer is made to the transferor's spouse or to junior-generation issue (and spouses) of the transferor. This makes sense because "estate freeze" implies a transfer of the growth interests to future generations for a discounted transfer-tax cost.
- *applicable family member*—This term means only the transferor's spouse, an ancestor of the transferor or transferor's spouse, and the spouse of any such ancestor. Thus the retained interest must be held by the transferor, his or her spouse, or senior-generation family members (and spouses) for the statute to apply. Again, this is logical since the freeze involves the retention of frozen rights by the generation whose estate tax concerns are more immediate.
- *applicable retained rights*—For Sec. 2701 purposes, these rights include certain distribution (dividend) rights but only if the transferor and all applicable family members control the corporation or partnership. In determining whether sufficient interest is held within the family, the transferor and any applicable family member are deemed to hold any

interest held by a brother, sister, or lineal descendant. These rights also include "extraordinary payment rights," such as a liquidation, put, call, or conversion rights. Applicable retained rights are valued at zero—unless they are qualified payment rights (described later)—for the purposes of determining the gift tax value of a transferred interest.

- *retained rights not treated as "applicable"*—The harsh rule that pertains to applicable retained rights does not apply to any right that must be exercised at a specific time and at a specific amount. It also typically does not apply to a right to convert into a fixed number (or a fixed percentage) of shares of the same class of stock in a corporation as the transferred stock (or that would be of the same class but for nonlapsing differences in voting power). In other words, if a retained interest carries rights that are not valued at zero under Sec. 2701, the value of these rights is their fair market value determined under traditional valuation methodology.
- *controlled entity*—An entity is controlled if, immediately before the transfer, the transferor, applicable family members, and any lineal descendants of the parent of the transferor (or parents of the transferor's spouse) hold at least 50 percent (by vote or value) of the stock of a corporation or at least 50 percent of the capital or profit interests in a partnership.

The bottom line is that many traditional rights on preferred stock retained by the transferor will not support or further reduce the gift tax value placed on what was given away or sold to a family member. So the general rule of Sec. 2701 is that an estate freeze involving the intrafamily transfer of corporate stock or partnership interests will result in an immediate gift tax based on the entire value of the business held by the senior family member. The transferor gets no credit for the value of the senior business interest retained upon a gift (or sale) of a junior interest to a family member.

The Sec. 2701 rules do not apply to the following retained interests, which can be accorded full fair market value for gift tax purposes:

- *marketable transferred interests*—Sec. 2701 does not apply if there are readily available market quotations on an established securities market for the value of the transferred interest.
- *marketable retained interests*—Similarly, these rules do not apply to any applicable retained interest if there are readily available market quotations on an established securities market for the value of the retained interest.
- *interests of the same class*—Sec. 2701 does not apply if the retained interest is of the same class of equity as the transferred interest. For this purpose, nonvoting common stock is treated as the same class as voting common stock.

- *proportionate transfers*—Sec. 2701 does not apply to a transfer by an individual of equity interests if the transfer results in a proportionate reduction of each class of equity interest held by the transferor.

Qualified Payments Exception. Although the general rule is that applicable retained rights are valued at zero (which under the subtraction method means that the value of what was given away or sold would be assigned a value equal to the entire worth of the business), retained rights to *qualified payments* are valued under general valuation principles.

Qualified payments are dividends payable on a periodic basis under cumulative preferred stock (or comparable payment under a partnership interest) to the extent that such dividend (or comparable partnership payment) is determined at a fixed rate. A payment is treated as having a fixed rate if it is in fact fixed once and for all or if it is determined at a rate that bears a fixed relationship to a specified market interest rate.

Example: P holds all the outstanding stock of X Corporation. Assume the fair market value of X is $1.5 million. X is recapitalized so that P holds 1,000 shares of $1,000 par value preferred stock bearing an annual cumulative dividend of $100 per share (the aggregate fair market value of which is assumed to be $1 million) and 1,000 shares of voting common stock. P transfers the common stock to P's child. Sec. 2701 applies to the transfer because P has transferred an equity interest (the common stock) to a member of P's family and immediately thereafter holds an applicable retained interest (the preferred stock with its distribution and other rights). P's right to receive annual cumulative dividends is a qualified payment right and is valued for purposes of Sec. 2701 at its fair market value of $1 million. The amount of P's gift, determined using the subtraction method of valuation, is $500,000 ($1.5 million minus $1 million).

Minimum Value Rule. Congress wanted to ensure that at least some minimum value was assigned to an equity interest transferred to a family member in an estate freeze. Even if there are actual or deemed qualified payments (or other rights valued under traditional methods), the Code now specifies a minimum valuation for any junior equity interest transferred by gift or sale to a family member. Examples of junior equity interests include common stock or partnership interests with rights to capital and profits junior to other partnership interests. For example, if a father gives common stock to his son while retaining cumulative preferred stock, the minimum value rule requires that the total common stock of the corporation may not be valued at less than 10 percent of the sum of the total value of all stock interests in the corporation *plus* the total indebtedness of the corporation to the transferor or an applicable family member. This means that the gift tax value of common stock gifted to a family member must be at least 10 percent of the total value of stock held by the transferor. A similar minimum value rule applies in the partnership context.

Additional Gift Taxes. These rules also prevent parents from shifting growth to the next generation by failing to make distributions on the retained preferred interest. Any payments not made would accrue to the transferred growth interest. If the qualified payments are not in fact made at the times and in the amounts used in valuing the retained right to the qualified payments, the transferor's taxable gifts (or the transferor's estate if appropriate) may be increased to reflect the value of the preferred stock based on the actual distributions made.

Practical Considerations with Stock Recapitalizations

Valuation Problems. Corporate recapitalizations do provide some estate-freezing potential. However, the valuation of common and preferred stock after a recapitalization presents some difficult issues. The preferred stock must be valued by discounting the expected future dividend and liquidation payments to present value. However, Sec. 2701 and the regulations thereunder do not provide guidance as to the appropriate discount rate. It seems clear that the Sec. 7520 interest rate will not be acceptable. The discount rate selected should reflect the risk of the transaction. Clearly the discount rate will necessarily be high to reflect the risk of receiving such dividend payments in a closely held family corporation. This would reduce the value of the preferred payments and thus the value of the retained preferred stock. Assigning a low value to the preferred stock would reduce the estate-freezing effect of the recapitalization. In any event, the IRS could challenge the valuation of the components of the recapitalization years after it occurs. Preferred-stock recapitalization should be considered only with the advice of competent estate planning counsel.

Gifts of Nonvoting Common Stock. The transfer of the same class of business interest as the interest retained will not be affected by Sec. 2701. Nonvoting common stock is treated as the same class as voting common stock. Both interests will be junior to any preferred interests, but they will reflect the true growth of the corporation. The nonvoting common stock will be valued as a minority interest, reflecting the lack of control inherent in the nonvoting interest. The recapitalization of the family corporation into voting and nonvoting common stock meets the following estate planning goals:

- The nonvoting common stock can be gifted to children. The donor can reduce his or her estate without losing control of the business.
- The nonvoting stock is discounted as a minority interest. The minority discount will reduce the current gift tax cost to the donor.
- Nonvoting common stock is *not* treated as a class of stock for S corporation purposes, and this type of recapitalization is available for

both regular and S corporations. (S corporations are limited to one class of stock and cannot be recapitalized to create preferred stock.)
- The recapitalization transfers some of the corporation's current value and future growth to the nonvoting common stock.
- Nonvoting stock can be given to heirs without giving them a voice in management.

ESTATE FREEZES THROUGH FAMILY PARTNERSHIPS

Advantages of Family Partnerships

The family partnership is a business entity that has both income tax and estate tax planning uses. In addition, many nontax objectives can be met by transferring wealth to family partnerships. Advantages of the family partnership include the following:

- The family partnership can be an estate reduction technique through gifts of partnership interests to junior-generation family members.
- The gift tax issues associated with gifts of family partnerships are fairly straightforward.
- The gift tax value of partnership interests can be discounted below the value of the underlying partnership assets by structuring the partnership interests to provide minority and/or marketability discounts.
- Family partnerships can facilitate income shifting to lower-bracket family members.
- Family partnerships are more flexible than trusts or corporations with respect to distributions and allocations of income.
- The senior generation can maintain control after gifting interests in the partnership to successors.
- Transferring wealth to an appropriately structured partnership provides some protection from creditors.
- Virtually any type of investment or business can be contained in a family partnership.
- Family property located out-of-state can be transferred to a partnership to avoid ancillary administration.

Structuring a Family Partnership

Most family partnerships are established as limited partnerships. Limited partnerships have limited interests held by the limited partners. These partners have limited liability under state law; that is, they may lose the value of their interests, but they do not have their personal assets at stake. The limited partners have fixed "frozen" rights to specified income and liquidation payments. Their rights take precedence over those of general partners. The limited partners have no rights to management control.

Under state law, all limited partnerships have at least one general partner who has management authority and unlimited liability. Depending on the goals for the family partnership, both limited and general partnership interests may be retained by the senior generation or gifted to the next generation.

Traditional Partnership Freeze

Many wealthy individuals create family limited partnerships to operate a business or as an investment vehicle. Senior-generation partners in family partnerships may want to freeze the value of their interests just as older shareholders have attempted to do in family corporation recapitalizations discussed earlier. The partnership may adopt a multiclass partnership capital structure, the analogue of a corporate recapitalization. Recapitalized partnerships have an added advantage over recapitalized corporations in that the preference distributions are not subject to the double tax. (Corporate dividends are taxable income to both the corporation and recipient shareholder.) Preferred interests generally take the form of *guaranteed payments* to the frozen-interest partner, which also reduces the partnership's net income taxable to the other partners. However, guaranteed payments can create taxable income to the recipient, which cannot be deducted by the partnership unless it has sufficient taxable income.

The partnership agreement creates two classes of partners: preferred or "frozen" partners (similar to preferred stockholders) and regular or "common" (or "unfrozen" or "residual") partners (similar to common stockholders). Each class can contain general and/or limited partners. The preferred partnership interest has the right to *cumulative preference distributions* or *guaranteed annual payments*. The unfrozen partnership interest has the right to a proportionate share of the partnership income as reduced by the senior rights of the preferred interests.

The partnership recapitalization is subject to the rules of Sec. 2701 as discussed earlier. The preferred interest is generally disregarded in valuing a transferred junior interest except to the extent it is treated as a right to qualified payments or a liquidation participation right. However, the frozen interests may be considered in valuing the junior interests if they provide *noncontingent* guaranteed payments.

> *Example:* Suppose Mary Matriarch owns a business with a current value of $10 million that is expected to grow by 15 percent annually over the next 10 years. A recapitalization of the partnership capital structure is subject to Sec. 2701. If Mary retains the frozen interest, the unfrozen interest should be provided by gift or sale to her children. Under Sec. 2701, a minimum of 10 percent of the partnership's value (in this example, $1 million) must be attributed to the unfrozen interest

given to the children. Thus a $1 million gift may be incurred to transfer the unfrozen partnership interests to junior-generation family members.

If Mary were to recapitalize the partnership into a multiclass arrangement, the simplest way to do this would be to create a 90 percent preferred interest and a 10 percent junior interest. However, the distribution rights of such an arrangement could be prohibitive. Required cash distributions to preferred qualified interests inject an element of risk as to whether the partnership will be able to make such distributions from available cash flow. This risk reduces the value of the underlying unfrozen interest under ordinary risk-adjusted rates. For example, in order for a 90 percent preferred interest to support a $9 million valuation, it may require a 20 percent ($1.8 million) cumulative return. The 20 percent required return reflects the risk that preferred payments could actually be made to 90 percent of the value of the partnership. On the other hand, a 50 percent preferred interest could be valued at $5 million by carrying only a 12 percent ($600,000) cumulative return. In this example, Mary chooses to recapitalize the partnership at 50 percent each to the frozen and unfrozen interests. A subsequent gift of 20 percent of the 50 percent unfrozen interest (10 percent of the total value of the partnership) is made to her children. Ignoring minority and marketability discounts (which will be discussed later), the transferred partnership interest is worth no more than $1 million.

At the end of 10 years, the children own an interest worth approximately $7.1 million. If Mary dies at that time, $6.1 million ($7.1 million minus the $1 million that was taxable at the time she made the gift) has been removed from her estate, with net tax savings of $3.3 million (assuming a 55 percent estate tax rate). Had she not recapitalized but instead transferred a one-tenth partnership interest in the original single-class partnership, after 10 years the children's interest would have been worth $4 million, thereby removing approximately $3 million ($4 million minus $1 million) from the estate, with net estate tax savings of $1.65 million.

Unfortunately, the result is not quite this good. The required guaranteed payments will increase Mary's income tax and, unless they are consumed, will increase her estate accordingly. Thus the qualified payments required by Sec. 2701 reduce the benefits of the traditional freeze.

Planning point: The rules of Sec. 2701 have somewhat mitigated the benefit of the traditional freeze. However, if the valuation issues can be managed, the plan is still worthwhile for some individuals. Generally the partnership assets should be capable of generating growth and income that exceed the qualified payments. Otherwise, the payments will consume the assets and no growth will be shifted to junior-generation family members. In addition, the senior-generation donor should probably be willing to part with management control and transfer it to the appropriate successor. Thus the plan should be considered at the retirement stage.

Transfers of Limited Interests in Family Partnerships

Since Sec. 2701 went into effect, planners have scrambled to develop new plans to create transfer-tax discounts. One technique currently drawing significant attention is to transfer family assets to a limited partnership structured to take advantage of valuation discounts. One such discount is for marketability. Remember, the value of a gift for tax purposes is based on a willing buyer-willing seller approach. If the partnership can be structured to restrict the limited partners' rights to income or access to the partnership assets, a willing buyer would pay substantially less for the partnership interest than the same buyer would pay for the partnership assets. A discount that is often discussed as appropriate is 35 percent, although aggressive planners have suggested a larger discount may be available. The general partnership interest retains the right to liquidate the partnership under state law; therefore no discount should be available for this interest because the general partner can reach the underlying assets.

> *Example:* Suppose Paul Patriarch has a large, rapidly growing estate and would like suggestions to reduce his estate taxes. Paul transfers $1 million in marketable securities to a family limited partnership. Paul retains a one percent general partnership interest; the 99 percent remaining interest is divided equally among his five children as limited partnership interests. The partnership is structured so that Paul is the general manager and retains investment decisions and controls the distributions to some degree. The preferred limited interests are limited to a payment stream that justifies a 35 percent discount below the value of the securities. No discount is applied to Paul's retained interest.
>
> Paul's interest should be worth $10,000. But what about the gifts to the children? The 35 percent discount should lower the total value to $643,500 (0.65 multiplied by $990,000). Paul can give this amount under his applicable credit amount and annual exclusions. If Paul had transferred a business interest to the partnership that represented a minority interest, a further minority discount could be applicable.
>
> *Planning point:* Gifts of limited partnership interests are generally used in this fashion to transfer family wealth when valuation discounts are important. The senior-generation family donor who wishes to retain control will select this method. The underlying assets are protected from the creditors of the children but not from the creditors of the general partner. If the partnership is a business and family successors are involved, the successors should receive a general partnership interest at

some point. When this controlling element is transferred, some additional transfer taxes will be applicable. If the senior family member's general partnership interest terminates or lapses at some point (for example, at his or her death), the interest is treated under Sec. 2704 (which is not further discussed) as an additional transfer at the time of the lapse.

Income Tax Considerations

Family partnerships will generally be taxable under normal partnership tax rules if the family partnership rules of Sec. 2704 are met. Partnership income is provided to partners as distributive shares of the income. Such shares are determined by the partnership agreement. The ability to shift income to junior generations may have family wealth transfer benefits. First, income shifted to the next generation will avoid inclusion and taxation in the donor's estate. Second, lower family income taxes will result if the donees are in lower tax brackets than the donor.

There are limitations on the ability to shift income. First, the capital of the partnership interests given away must have a "material income-producing factor"; that is, the capital of the partnership must create income. The donor-partner cannot shift income that is developed solely from his or her services. Therefore a service business cannot shift income unless the donee partners provide services. In addition, the donee-partners must have a "real" interest in the capital of the partnership, based on the circumstances of the partnership. The regulations provide that the capital interest of the donee-partners will not be recognized as valid (that is, income shifting will be prohibited) if the donor-partner retains control over the distribution of income and liquidation of capital that extend beyond reasonable business needs.

Protection from Creditors

Asset protection planning has become more vital than ever. A family limited partnership can assist in this goal, which is particularly important if certain partners are in a high-risk occupation or profession. In addition, the senior-generation family members may be concerned about the equitable distribution rights if a donee-child should be divorced.

The creditors of a limited partner are limited to a "charging order" against the partnership interest; that is, the creditors can step into the place of the debtor-partner if income payments will be made. However, the creditors cannot reach the underlying partnership assets unless the partnership is liquidated. Thus the underlying family property is protected against distribution to creditors. It is important to note that the family partnership cannot protect assets if the donor-partner has a known liability and makes a fraudulent conveyance of property to a family partnership.

Family Life Insurance Partnerships (FLIPs)

As discussed in chapter 3, the irrevocable life insurance trust (ILIT) is usually the preferred choice as an entity-owned vehicle for a life insurance policy. The ILIT provides a gift-tax leveraging mechanism if Crummey withdrawal powers are employed.

Recent developments associated with the gift and estate tax considerations of an ILIT have been favorable. However, the ILIT may not be the best choice for every insured seeking estate reduction. Commentators have raised concerns that the tax treatment of the ILIT is too good to last forever; they are concerned that Congress will limit Crummey withdrawal powers in the future. Or Congress may choose to include the policy in the insured's gross estate regardless of the trust's ownership. Such proposals were discussed in the past, but they were never introduced in a bill.

Another concern with the ILIT is the loss of control by the insured; the gift is truly irrevocable, and the ILIT terms cannot be changed by the insured-grantor without adverse tax consequences. This irrevocability would become a problem if the tax laws or the grantor's feelings toward the ILIT beneficiaries change. For many individuals, this loss of control is not a problem, and the ILIT is an appropriate technique. For others, an alternative third-party ownership arrangement must be considered.

One viable estate-planning alternative for entity-owned life insurance that is growing increasingly popular is the family life insurance partnership (FLIP).[1] Family partnerships were discussed for their estate-freezing potential earlier in this chapter. Perhaps the greatest potential estate tax savings in a family partnership occur if the partnership invests in life insurance on the life of a family member.

Structuring a FLIP

Under the FLIP approach, a parent or grandparent who is contemplating a life insurance purchase creates a general business partnership. It is important that the partnership complies with state law as a valid partnership, but this requirement can generally be easily satisfied.

The partnership's ownership interests are held by the insured parent (or grandparent) and the family heirs (the children and/or grandchildren). The partnership applies for, owns, and is the beneficiary of the life insurance policy on the parent's or grandparent's life. The policy premiums are paid for out of partnership assets, or the insured makes additional contributions to the partnership when policy premiums are due.

At the death of the insured, the partnership can continue or be terminated. The proceeds are distributed or allocated to the capital accounts of the partners based on the provisions of the partnership agreement.

Gift Tax Considerations

The heirs receive their partnership interests as a gift from their parent or grandparent. The gifts of the partnership interest qualify for annual gift tax exclusion to the amount of $10,000 per donee, because the partnership interests are current transfers of property creating a present-interest gift. Any value of the gifted interest that exceeds the annual exclusions can be sheltered from tax by the donor's applicable credit amount.

When the insured makes gifts to the partnership to pay premiums on the life insurance policy, these additional gifts will qualify for the annual exclusion to the extent of each child's or grandchild's percentage ownership in the partnership. The heirs' immediate ability to liquidate the partnership through their normal powers as general partners should create a present-interest gift to them for any capital contributed by the insured to the extent of the donee-partner's percentage ownership of the partnership. (See *Wooley v. U.S.*, 736 F. Supp. 1056 [S.D., Ind., 1990].)

Retained Control by Insured

The FLIP's biggest advantage is the insured's ability to control and manage the partnership; compare this to the ILIT, where the insured must *not* act as trustee. As long as the insured retains a general partnership interest, he or she should have adequate control over all transactions with the life insurance policy. In fact, the partnership agreement could name the insured as the managing partner. The heirs should be willing to agree to this control since they had no interest in the partnership prior to the gift. (Remember, these are the same individuals who would be expected to routinely lapse their Crummey powers if the ILIT alternative was chosen instead of the FLIP.) Management control gives the insured the ability to purchase the policy or take a distribution of the policy from the FLIP, provided the insured's partnership capital account is properly adjusted. This control makes a FLIP more appealing than an ILIT if the insured wants considerable future flexibility in handling the life insurance policy.

As an alternative, the insured could place sufficient investment assets into the FLIP to make premium payments out of the partnership income; this method is analogous to the funded ILIT. Although more estate tax savings may result from this large immediate gift, it may require a contribution in excess of the insured-doner's applicable credit amount, immediately creating a gift tax liability. The other choice is to provide the premiums through annual gifts, similar to an unfunded ILIT. However, the unfunded approach might mean that the FLIP would not qualify as a valid partnership under state law.[2] A family partnership funded with significant other assets will offer further estate reduction benefits since the completed gifts to the family partners reduce the insured's estate. The partnership is usually more favorable than a trust under the funded approach because the partnership has more flexibility with respect to distributions.

Estate Tax Considerations

Since the parent makes gifts of the partnership interests (and subsequent gifts of premium contributions), he or she reduces the gross estate by the amount of the gifts. In addition, the full death benefit from the policy is not included in the gross estate. Provided the policy is payable to, or for the benefit of, the family partnership, the insured's estate includes only the estate's percentage of ownership interest in the partnership. (See Rev. Rul. 83-147, 1983-2 C.B. 158.) The parent's ownership interest can be kept to a minimum by making the children the majority interest partners. This, of course, increases the gift tax problems if the parent makes substantial contributions in a given tax year. However, the gift tax results are really no more difficult than if an ILIT was selected.

Unfortunately, any interest held by the parent at the time of death will be enhanced for estate tax purposes by its share of the death benefit payable to the partnership. This is logical because the partnership will increase in value by the amount of the death proceeds. This inclusion is a result of the retained control provided by the partnership approach. (Remember, no amount of the proceeds is included if the ILIT is selected and properly administered.)

The estate tax impact of the inclusion of an FLIP interest in the insured's gross estate can be mitigated through appropriate planning. The partnership interest retained by the insured can be left to the noninsured spouse in a manner qualifying for the marital deduction, or the interest can be left to the surviving partners and be offset by any of the insured's unused applicable credit amount. In addition, inclusion in the insured's gross estate can be avoided if the parent is willing to part with control and make gifts of his or her partnership interest prior to death.

At the insured-parent's death, the proceeds are payable to the partnership. The parent would, presumably, leave any remaining interest through the provisions of his or her will. If the interest is left to the surviving partners, the children then own the partnership outright and can either keep the partnership going as an investment vehicle or terminate it and take the cash proceeds. The surviving partners then become managers of the proceeds, and they can invest or take distributions from them as they see fit. The continued partnership is generally an extremely flexible entity for making necessary distributions to the family heirs.

Example: Suppose Mr. Johnstone, a widower aged 55, has a substantial estate and is contemplating the purchase of life insurance to create liquidity for his estate. The policy that he is considering has a death benefit of $1.5 million and an annual premium of $22,222 for 20 years.

Mr. Johnstone is concerned about the loss of control associated with the gift of a policy to a third party, such as his children or an ILIT. He feels he might want to use the policy in the future as collateral for a business loan.

He has two children, Sarah and Derek, who become partners with him in the Johnstone family partnership. Each of the children receives a 45 percent interest in the partnership as a gift from Mr. Johnstone, while he retains a 10 percent interest and is named managing partner in the agreement. Mr. Johnstone contributes all the premium to the partnership each year as the premium is due.

Ninety percent of the cash contributed by him each year is treated as an annual exclusion gift—45 percent of the premium (or $10,000) each to Sarah and Derek. At Mr. Johnstone's death, 90 percent of the proceeds should escape estate taxes; the cash can be distributed to Sarah and Derek, or it can be held by the partnership for future investment.

Planning point: Compare the FLIP to other third-party ownership arrangements when using life insurance for estate reduction purposes. The FLIP should generally be used for insureds who want to retain maximum flexibility and control. If the insured feels that future access to the policy or changes in the dispositive scheme may be necessary, the FLIP is probably preferable to an ILIT or outright ownership of the policy by the beneficiaries. In addition, the FLIP will be more favorable if the partnership will hold substantial other assets besides a life insurance policy.

IRS Attacks on Family Limited Partnerships

The use of the family limited partnership has garnered a great deal of attention from the IRS. Discounted gifts and estate transfers will attract scrutiny when the estate tax return of the transferor is examined.

The IRS has several approaches to attack the problem. First, the argument could be made that a partnership consisting solely of investments is not a valid partnership for tax purposes. This would be a difficult argument to make since state law determines the legitimacy of the partnership. Second, the argument could be made that the partnership restrictions on the limited partners could be ignored for valuation purposes and that the total proportionate value (without minority or marketability discounts) of the underlying assets is the true value of the transfer for transfer tax purposes. This argument has been used recently in several private rulings involving partnerships established just before the transferor's death in which substantial discounts were taken on the gift/estate tax returns.

One principle is clear: The valuation discount should be substantiated by a complete independent appraisal, and the appraisal should justify the value based on the specific circumstances of the family limited partnership being valued.

ESTATE FREEZES THROUGH SALES OF FAMILY BUSINESSES TO FAMILY MEMBERS

Installment Sales

An installment sale can be a useful technique for financial and estate planning purposes. It is a taxable sale of a property where the income tax reporting of gain is accounted for under the installment accounting provisions of the Internal Revenue Code. An installment sale is any sale in which at least one principal payment is received in a year other than the year of the sale. The installment reporting provisions are typically used when the definition for an installment sale is satisfied. However, the seller can elect to use normal accounting for an installment sale and recognize all gain in the year of sale.

Advantages of Installment Sales

From the seller's standpoint, an installment sale of property can have both income and estate tax benefits. If installment reporting can be used, the taxable gain of the sale of property in exchange for an installment note is delayed and recognized gradually over the installment period. Thus, highly appreciated property can be sold without immediate recognition of the full taxable gain. On the other hand, the ability to elect out of installment reporting gives the taxpayer the opportunity to recognize all gain immediately. For example, a taxpayer may elect to recognize all gain at the time of an installment sale in a year when he or she either has little other income or shows a loss for income tax purposes. Under these circumstances, reporting the gain immediately might prevent the taxpayer from wasting other deductions and tax benefits. The flexibility of an installment sale's reporting rules permits a taxpayer to defer gain recognition and, to some degree, plan the timing of capital-gain taxes from the sale of property.

The installment sale also provides potential estate tax savings for the seller. It is a particularly useful device for family estate planning, which usually occurs when a senior family member wishes to pass property on to a successor in the family. For estate planning purposes, an installment sale is one method of "freezing" the seller's estate and shifting the potential appreciation to a junior family member. If performed properly and if the installment note is equal to the fair market value of the property at the time of the sale, the installment sale shifts the postsale appreciation to the junior family member without any transfer taxes due on the transferred property.

From the buyer's standpoint, the installment sale permits the buyer to defer some or all of the principal payments on the sale. This is particularly important for buyers without the funds for the entire purchase price. In addition, independent financing of the purchase may not be available to the junior family member in normal financial markets. Quite often, the purchase and sale would be impossible without the payment deferral and seller financing provided by an installment sale.

Income Tax Considerations

Income Taxation of Installment Payments. The sale of appreciated property in exchange for an installment note results in some or all of the purchase price being paid at some future date. From the seller's standpoint, the future payments can be broken down into three components for income tax purposes. One component of each annual payment on the installment note is treated as a return of the seller's original basis in the property. This return of basis is not taxable because the seller is merely recovering the cost of the property. A second component of each payment received is treated as taxable gain. The third component of each payment is considered interest, which is taxable to the seller as ordinary income. Under the installment sale rules, the taxable gain component is recognized proportionally over the period in which the installment payments are made. The formula for recognizing gain from any particular installment payment is as follows:*

$$\text{Capital gain} = \text{Payment received during the year} \times \frac{\text{Gross profit}}{\text{Total contract price}}$$

Example: Tom Taxplanner, aged 52, would like to sell his investment real estate to his daughter, Julia. The real estate is valued at $200,000, and Tom's basis in the property is $50,000. Julia proposes an installment sale with a $50,000 down payment and the remaining principal payable in 10 annual installments of $15,000 beginning one year from settlement. Ten percent interest will be payable on any unpaid balance. Tom's gross profit is $150,000 and the contract price is $200,000. Thus Tom will recognize 75 percent ($150,000 divided by $200,000) of each payment as taxable gain. The amounts received by Tom are taxable as follows:

	Return of Cost	Taxable Gain	Interest
At settlement	$12,500	$37,500	—
Year 1	3,750	11,250	$15,000
Year 2	3,750	11,250	13,500
Year 3	3,750	11,250	12,000
Year 4	3,750	11,250	10,500
Year 5	3,750	11,250	9,000
Year 6	3,750	11,250	7,500
Year 7	3,750	11,250	6,000
Year 8	3,750	11,250	4,500
Year 9	3,750	11,250	3,000
Year 10	3,750	11,250	1,500

---

*This formula is simplified to some degree to demonstrate the gain-recognition process without adding federal income tax complexity beyond the scope of this chapter.

Buyer's Income Tax Basis. One critical issue from the buyer's point of view is the cost basis acquired in the purchased property. One advantage of the installment sale is that the buyer gets an immediate cost basis equal to the purchase price. This basis can be used for depreciation purposes (for applicable property), or it can be used to offset gain if the property is subsequently sold by the initial buyer.

Interest on Installment Sale. Interest paid by a buyer on an installment sale is potentially deductible for income tax purposes. Thus it might benefit the buyer to recharacterize some of the purchase payment as interest on the transaction if such interest is deductible. Since there may be little or no rate differential between long-term capital gains and receipt of interest, this recharacterization should not affect the seller.

On the other hand, the buyer may wish to minimize the interest element of the installment sale if the interest is nondeductible. Under these circumstances, it may be more advantageous for the buyer to characterize the payments as principal. The additional amount of principal will give the buyer a higher basis, which may be available for depreciation deductions at a later date. Certainly the interest rate might be a consideration in the negotiation process for the installment sale.

Unfortunately, the tax rules give target rates of interest on installment obligations under either the imputed interest rules (Code Sec. 483) or original-issue-discount (OID) rules (Secs. 1271-1274). These rules minimize the flexibility by specifying a rate of interest that applies to installment obligations falling within these rules. The rules will not be further discussed here; however, the estate planner should be aware that the appropriate tax advice should be sought for determining the rate of interest on an installment obligation.

The deductibility of the interest on the installment sale by the buyer depends on the type of property purchased. Under Code Sec. 163, the interest can be characterized as (1) personal interest, (2) qualified residence interest, (3) business interest, (4) investment interest, or (5) interest from passive activities. Personal interest is nondeductible. Qualified residence interest is deductible on the primary and one secondary residence of the taxpayer; the deduction is limited to interest on $1 million of acquisition indebtedness and $100,000 for home equity loan balances. Business interest is deductible for the purchase of business assets or interests. If a business interest is acquired in an installment sale, the interest incurred to acquire a sole proprietorship, a partnership interest, or S corporation stock is deductible if the taxpayer materially participates in the business. Interest incurred to purchase regular corporate stock is generally treated as investment interest. Investment interest is deductible to the extent of the taxpayer's investment income. Finally, the interest on passive activities usually is deductible only to the extent of the taxpayer's passive income.

Related-Party Installment Sales. Certain transactions can cause the seller to accelerate the remaining deferred gain on the installment sale. One such transaction is the subsequent sale of the property by the initial buyer. This "second disposition" rule applies only if the original installment sale is to a related party. Related parties consist of the seller's spouse, children, grandchildren, parents, grandparents, siblings, and controlled entities (partnerships, corporations, trusts, and estates). The second disposition by the initial buyer causes immediate gain recognition, as if the original seller has received the funds from the second disposition. This rule applies only if the second disposition occurs within 2 years of the first, unless the property sold consists of marketable securities. The second disposition of marketable securities by a related party triggers gain to the original seller if the disposition occurs at any time during the installment period.

Example: Assume the same facts as the previous example. Suppose Julia sold the real estate, 10 months after acquiring it from Tom, for $250,000. Tom is treated as receiving the lesser of his contract price with Julia or the amount received in the second disposition; in this case, the lesser of the two is $200,000. His basis for this "sale" is the sum of the payments he has received to this point (the $50,000 down payment). Therefore Tom would immediately report a gain of $150,000, and Julia would have a gain of $50,000 ($250,000 minus her installment sale contract purchase price of $200,000).

Gain can also be accelerated when the installment note is disposed of or transferred by the seller. For example, if the note is sold for cash by the seller, the gain is accelerated. One exception is the transfer of the installment note to a spouse or pursuant to a divorce. The transfer of the installment obligation by the seller's estate can also result in accelerating the gain to the estate (discussed below).

Estate Tax Considerations

Estate Tax Advantages. The installment sale is particularly useful for estate planning purposes when a senior family member sells property to a junior family member. This transaction is one of the methods of "freezing" the seller's estate and shifting the growth in family property to the next generation to avoid transfer taxes on the growth.

In our previous example, Tom Taxplanner sold a family investment property to his daughter. To avoid any transfer-tax consequences, the real estate was sold for an installment note equivalent to the fair market value of the real estate—$200,000. This transaction is one type of estate freeze. The maximum total value of the installment note received for the real estate is $200,000. Thus the ceiling on the amount included in Tom's estate as a result of owning and selling the real estate will be $200,000. This is, of course, the goal of an estate freeze.

If Tom survives the 10-year installment period, none of the value of the real estate or the installment note will be included in his gross estate. Only the unconsumed amounts of the principal and interest payments received in the installment sale will remain in his estate. If Tom dies during the period of the installment term, the present value of the remaining installment payments will be included in his estate.

In either event, none of the growth on the property following the sale to his daughter will be included in Tom's estate. The growth element has been transferred to his daughter free of transfer taxes. The transfer-tax savings are substantial if rapidly appreciating property is transferred to the next generation in exchange for an installment note.

Seller's Premature Death. The seller's death can result in some serious estate tax implications. First, the value of the remaining installments is includible in the seller's estate at date-of-death value. The installments would be valued as a term interest discounted by the Sec. 7520 interest rate applicable for the month of the decedent's death. Second, the remaining installments are treated as income in respect of a decedent (IRD). IRD items included in the estate do not receive a step up in basis under Sec. 1014; thus the gain on the installment sale is recognized by the estate or beneficiaries as installment payments are received. Since the remaining payments are subject to both income and estate taxes *and* such payments are not available to the estate immediately, a liquidity problem could result. The IRD rules do provide some relief. An income tax deduction is permitted for the estate taxes paid on the IRD items at the time these items are taken into income by the estate or beneficiaries. The deduction is determined by allocating the additional estate taxes created by the inclusion of the IRD items proportionately over the period the installment payments are received.

In some circumstances, the remaining gain on the installment note will be accelerated to the estate. The estate will be treated as making a disposition of the note (which triggers gain recognition) if (1) the note is transferred by bequest, inheritance, intestacy, or otherwise to the obligor of the note (that is, the buyer), or (2) the estate fails to enforce the note. Thus if a parent sells property to a child and dies during the installment term, the remaining gain must be recognized by the estate immediately if the child receives the note as part of his or her inheritance. Similarly, gain is recognized if the decedent's will forgives the remaining balance on the installment note or the executor cancels the buyer's obligation.

Planning point: An installment sale is a useful estate-freezing mechanism. Installment sales are indicated under the following circumstances:

- when the seller has property that has appreciated greatly and would like to spread the capital-gains tax
- when the seller would like to get the future growth in the property out of his or her estate

- when the seller would like to retain a security interest in the property or other collateral (for this reason, the buyer and seller often can be unrelated)
- when the seller can afford to finance the buyer's purchase
- when the seller does not need to retain income from the property for the rest of his or her life
- when the interest on the purchase is deductible by the buyer
- when the buyer needs a certain cost basis in the acquired property

Life insurance point: The seller-financing aspect of the installment sale creates a serious risk for the seller. The buyer's continued success and the value of the collateral offer the only security that the seller will receive the installment and interest payments as they are due. If the seller is relying on these payments to supplement retirement income, for example, it may be critical to protect the seller's interest. It would be prudent under these circumstances to insure the life of the buyer to the extent of the unpaid balance during the term of the note, similar to credit insurance. The benefits payable to the seller would replace the lost income. It is important to note that the collateral may be of dubious value if the buyer dies prematurely. For example, in the case of a business interest, the property may be discounted significantly in value if the buyer was the primary service provider before his or her death.

In addition, the remaining installment payments could cause a liquidity problem for the estate if the seller dies prematurely. As discussed above, the estate will face both income and estate taxes as a result of the inclusion of the note. Compounding this tax problem is the fact that the remaining installments will not be received immediately to pay the estate expenses. The balance may be received over several years or may be canceled by the decedent's will. Insurance on the seller's life would help manage this liquidity problem.

Self-Canceling Installment Notes (SCINs)

One variation of the installment note is an installment note that includes a self-cancellation provision at the seller's death. The SCIN is designed like an installment note and is subject to normal installment sale reporting rules, but it is automatically canceled by the terms of the sale contract if the seller dies before all the remaining principal payments are made. Since the mortality risk is borne by the seller, the buyer will have to pay a higher price for the business. This price includes a risk premium when compared to a normal installment sale; that is, the purchase price is increased by the actuarial value of the contingency that not all installment payments need to be made if the seller dies during the term period. In a family transaction, it is particularly important that the IRS valuation rules under Sec. 7520 (discussed in chapter 4) be followed carefully. The SCIN must be equal in value to the property transferred, or a gift is made to the buyer to the extent that full and adequate consideration is not received in the transaction.

Since the note is canceled automatically at the death of the seller, there is nothing left to be included in the seller's estate if he or she should die during the term. Through the use of a SCIN, a senior family member could transfer property to the next generation for a substantially discounted selling price without any gift or estate taxes.

The SCIN does cause some income tax problems if the seller dies prematurely. The case of *Estate of Frane v. Commissioner* (98 TC 341, 1992, *affirmed*, 8th Cir., 1993) resulted in an unfavorable holding for a taxpayer who died 2 years after selling a family corporation for a 20-year SCIN. The court found that the cancellation-at-death provision caused the SCIN to be disposed of by the estate in a manner that accelerated the remaining gain. Thus, although the estate held no asset and included no value for estate tax purposes as a result of the note, it incurred a sizable immediate capital gain for income tax purposes.

> *Planning point:* The SCIN may still have estate planning uses despite the unfavorable result in *Frane*. The seller still has estate reduction benefits regardless of the income tax problems. Since the seller faces the risk that the payments will terminate upon his or her premature death, the SCIN is virtually always applicable only in family transactions. If the seller lives through the installment period, the SCIN has estate-freeze potential similar to the normal installment sale. The payments the seller receives simply are higher to reflect the mortality risk the seller absorbs. However, if the seller dies prematurely, the property will be transferred at a significant discount. For example, in the *Frane* case, the corporation was transferred to the heirs in exchange for only two of 20 potential installment payments. This discount will not result in additional estate taxes, provided the original contract price was equal to the fair market value of the property, including the mortality factor.[3]
>
> The income tax problem to the estate is a concern only if the property transferred has appreciated substantially prior to the sale and the seller dies prematurely. This risk can be minimized by transferring property without significant capital gain or by purchasing insurance on the seller's life to handle the potential liquidity problem. This cost may be minimal when compared to the estate reduction benefits of a SCIN.

Private Annuities

The private annuity is a variation of the installment sale with particular estate planning benefits. However, the rules and tax advantages are somewhat different. A private annuity is a sale of property, such as a family business, in exchange for the buyer's agreement to make periodic payments of a specified sum for the remainder of the seller's life. The obligor cannot normally be in the business of providing commercial annuities. The amount of the payments is based on the actuarial mortality and interest rate factors determined under the rules of Sec. 7520. A private annuity usually is considered for transfers of family assets from senior family members to successor-generation heirs.

Estate Tax Considerations

The major advantage of the private annuity is its estate tax treatment. In a regular installment sale, some amount is included in the seller's estate if the seller dies holding the installment note. The remaining payments are an enforceable obligation held by the estate, and therefore they are a valuable asset to the estate. As discussed above, the inclusion of the installment note can result in serious adverse income tax consequences in addition to estate taxes. However, in a private annuity, no further payments are due when the seller dies. It is well established that there is nothing to include in the estate of a seller who dies holding a private annuity agreement. Of course, any annuity payments received by the seller and not consumed before the seller's death become part of the seller's estate.

Some of the transfer-tax advantages are lost if the annuity is not equal in value to the property transferred. This raises a series of valuation issues. First, the value of the life annuity obligation must equal the fair market value of the property transferred, or a taxable gift will result. The gift would be equal to the excess of the transferred property's fair market value over the value of the annuity. Certainly the property must be valued carefully. However, as chapter 4 demonstrated, some property interests, such as closely held stock, may be subject to valuation disputes with the IRS years after the transfer.

In addition, once the property is valued appropriately, the life annuity must be valued according to the principles of Sec. 7520. This should be fairly straightforward. However, a life annuity valued under these actuarial tables assumes a normal life expectancy. What is the effect of the seller's impaired health? A shorter life span than predicted by the actuarial valuation tables will have estate tax advantages in a family situation. The estate reduction value of the private annuity is greater if the senior-generation seller dies soon after the sale. A sizable property interest could be transferred at a substantial discount if the seller receives few payments. If the annuity was valued appropriately, the premature death of the seller does not result in additional estate or gift taxes. However, the IRS has issued regulations that the actuarial tables cannot be used if there is a less than 50 percent chance that the seller will survive one year. Thus a private annuity will probably require immediate payment equal to the fair market value of the property if death is imminent. However, normal valuation rules may probably be used if the seller's health is impaired but expert medical testimony can establish a reasonable possibility of the seller's survival for one year.

Income Tax Considerations

Income Taxation of Annuity Payments. Similar to the installment sale, the gain in the property sold in exchange for the private annuity is spread over the remaining portion of the seller's life expectancy. Each annuity payment received over the life expectancy represents part gain and part return of the cost basis of the seller. The amounts received in excess of the gain and cost basis are treated as ordinary interest income. After the seller reaches life expectancy and has recovered all of his or her basis, the remaining annuity payments are ordinary income. However, unlike the installment sale, no part of the purchase payments is deductible as interest by the buyer.

Another distinguishing characteristic of the private annuity is the fact that the seller cannot take a security interest as collateral when receiving the private annuity. A private annuity is an unsecured promise to pay made by the buyer to the seller of the property. Of course, private annuity payments are generally limited to family situations where a senior-family member is transferring property to the next generation.

Example: Suppose Anna Annuitant, aged 65, wishes to reduce her rapidly growing estate. She owns an apartment building that provides a steady stream of income. The building is currently valued at $1 million, and her adjusted cost basis is $250,000. Assume there is no depreciation recapture potential. She would like to sell this property to her daughter, Alice, in exchange for a private annuity. A private annuity to a seller aged 65 for a $1 million property provides an annual payment of $114,376, based on a life expectancy of 20 years and an assumed Sec. 7520 rate of 7 percent. For income tax purposes, the first 20 payments of $114,376 are treated as follows:

Tax-free return of basis	$12,500
Annual capital gain	$37,500
Ordinary income	$64,376

If Anna lives beyond her life expectancy (20 years), the remaining payments are taxable as ordinary income.

For estate tax purposes, the private annuity terminates at Anna's death, and no amount of the annuity is included in her estate. Thus, if Anna dies after one year, the property passes to her daughter for one annual payment of $114,376. However, Alice also bears the risk that Anna will live beyond her life expectancy and the annual payments will continue until her death. Of course, any appreciation in the property after the exchange escapes gift and estate taxation.

Buyer's Income Tax Basis. The buyer's cost basis may be an important consideration in any purchase and sale transaction. The basis will offset the taxable gain if the buyer later sells the property. If the property is depreciable, a larger basis increases the depreciation deduction potential. At the time the sale is transacted, the buyer gets an immediate income tax basis equal to the value of the annuity obligation.[4] This basis is adjusted downward, of course, if the buyer subsequently takes depreciation deductions. But this initial basis assumes payments over the seller's life expectancy. What happens if the seller dies earlier or later than life expectancy or if the buyer sells the property before the original seller reaches life expectancy? In these circumstances, additional basis adjustments are required. If the seller outlives his or her life expectancy, the buyer is allowed to increase the basis by the amount of the additional payments. However, if the seller dies prematurely or the buyer sells the property prior to the seller's life expectancy, the buyer's basis is reduced to the amount of payments actually made minus any depreciation the buyer has already taken.

Impact of Sec. 7520 Interest Rate

As we discussed earlier, the value of a fixed annuity payment goes up when interest rates go down. Thus the private annuity will be a more valuable estate reduction technique when interest rates are relatively low. The estate reduction benefit of the private annuity is enhanced when the junior-generation buyer provides smaller annuity payments. With smaller payments the property is transferred for less, and the income from the property transferred may cover the entire annuity payment. Under these circumstances, the property will be transferred to the next generation without gift tax costs and perhaps no out-of-pocket costs to the junior-generation buyer.

> *Example:* Assume the same facts as the previous example. Suppose the rental income from the apartment building is enough to provide much of the required annuity payments. The $1 million building would be transferred by Anna free of estate and gift taxes and little out-of-pocket costs to Alice. If the Sec. 7520 rate was 11.6 percent—as it was several years ago—the same private annuity would require payments of $154,789, as opposed to $114,376 at 7 percent. Thus Alice would have to make substantial higher annual payments to her mother, undermining the estate reduction goals of the private annuity.

Suitable Types of Property

The private annuity is typically used to transfer property to junior-generation family members. The property selected should generally give the buyer a steady income stream to help cover the annuity payments. It is rarely practical to expect children or grandchildren to have sufficient funds to make the required payments out of other income or accumulated wealth. Thus such property as business interests, investment real estate, or marketable securities may be suitable.

Private annuities have some family corporation application also. Stock of a parent or grandparent can be redeemed by the family corporation in exchange for a private annuity. In this transaction, the corporation has the obligation to provide the annuity payments. If the junior-generation family members own the rest of the stock, the redemption of the senior-generation shareholder's stock effectively transfers the corporation to the successors. To avoid income tax problems, compliance with complex corporate tax provisions under Sec. 302 is necessary, and the annuity term should not exceed 15 years.

Planning point: A private annuity sale is a useful estate-freezing mechanism. It is indicated under the following circumstances:

- when the seller has property that has appreciated greatly and wants to spread the capital-gains tax
- when the seller wishes to remove the future growth on the property from his or her estate
- when the seller does not require a security interest in the property or other collateral (for this reason, the buyer and seller are virtually always related)
- when the seller can afford to finance the buyer's purchase
- when the seller needs to retain income from the property for the rest of his or her life
- when the buyer does not need an interest deduction for the purchase (for example, the interest deduction would otherwise be unavailable to the buyer as a result of the type of property purchased)
- when the buyer is willing to take the risk that the seller outlives life expectancy and payments must continue
- when the buyer is willing to take the risk that the seller's premature death could substantially reduce the buyer's cost basis
- when the seller is willing to take the risk that premature death will greatly reduce the sale proceeds actually received. Again, this characteristic indicates the use of a private annuity between a senior-generation family member and his or her natural heir(s). In this instance, the risk would actually be a significant estate reduction benefit.

Life insurance point: The seller-financing aspect of the private annuity coupled with the prohibition to retain a security interest creates a serious risk for the seller. The buyer's continued success and the income generated by the property may be the only security that the seller will receive the annuity payments. If the seller is relying on these payments to supplement retirement income, for example, it may be critical to protect the seller's right to the annuity. It would be prudent under these circumstances to insure the life of the buyer. The benefits payable to the seller would replace the lost retirement income if the buyer dies prematurely.

Although the annuity is not included in the seller's estate, the loss of the annuity payments at the death of the seller may be a problem for the survivors. Perhaps the surviving spouse will suffer from the lost income, or other heirs may not receive a fair share if the buyer gets the property purchased for the private annuity at a discount. Under these circumstances, the seller's life should be insured to replace the lost annuity payments. With appropriate third-party ownership of the policy and gifts of premium by the seller, the estate can be reduced further.

NOTES

1. For more information, see S. Stacy Eastland, "The Use of Partnerships in Lieu of Irrevocable Insurance Trusts," *Tax Management Financial Planning Journal,* vol. 7, no. 4 (September 17, 1991).
2. At least one private ruling, Ltr. 9309021, found the state partnership law of the state in question to permit a partnership consisting solely of life insurance to be a valid partnership. The author recommends a ruling request based on applicable state law before attempting to treat a similarly funded entity as a partnership for tax purposes.
3. In the *Frane* case, the mortality adjustment consisted of the assessment of an above-market interest rate (12 percent) to create larger payments to the seller. This is not technically the method prescribed by Sec. 7520, which would increase the contract price by the mortality tables used for tax valuation. The sale in question predates the enactment of Sec. 7520, and the IRS did not raise the issue of whether the SCIN's value was less than the fair market value of the stock sold. Such a conclusion would have resulted in a taxable gift of the excess of the value of the stock over the SCIN's value. The report of the case did not specify why this issue was not raised.
4. Rev. Rul. 55-119, 1955-1 C.B. 352.

7

The Basics of Charitable Giving

Chapter Outline

CHARITABLE GIVING IN THE UNITED STATES 214
    Use of Contributions 214
    What Can Be Donated to Charity 214
    Reasons for Making Donations 216
ROLE OF GOVERNMENT IN CHARITABLE GIVING 218
    Availability of Tax Benefits 218
    State Protection of Charitable Organizations 218
GENERAL FEDERAL TAX IMPLICATIONS OF CHARITABLE
      GIVING 218
    Deductible Contributions of Gifts of Property 219
    Transfers of Partial Interests in Property 220
    Selection of Charitable Donee 220
FEDERAL ESTATE TAX TREATMENT OF CHARITABLE GIVING 223
    Requirements of Estate Tax Charitable Deduction 223
    Summary of Key Issues 226
FEDERAL GIFT TAX TREATMENT OF CHARITABLE GIVING 227
    Unlimited Gift Tax Deduction 227
    Qualifying Charitable Organizations 227
    Computing Gift Tax Charitable Deduction 228
    Gift Tax Compliance 229
FEDERAL INCOME TAX TREATMENT OF CHARITABLE GIVING 229
    Limitations on Current Income Tax Deduction—Percentage Limitation
      Rules 229
    Limitations on Current Income Tax Deduction—Reduction Rules 233
    Income Tax Compliance Rules for Charitable Donations 234
ESTATE PLANNING OPPORTUNITIES IN CHARITABLE GIVING 237
    Life Insurance Opportunities 238
    Opportunities Outside of Life Insurance 244

CHARITABLE GIVING IN THE UNITED STATES

For the financial services professional to assist individuals or businesses in planning charitable contributions, it is helpful to recognize who is making donations. According to the American Association of Fund-Raising Counsel Trust for Philanthropy, Americans contributed more than $150 billion to charity in 1996. This represents 1.9 percent of personal income in the United States. Charitable contributions have consistently exhibited steady growth, even during recessionary periods.

In 1996 charitable contributions were almost 2 percent of the gross national product (GNP). The AAFRC also reported that over 86 percent of the total contributions in 1996 were from individuals. As table 7-1 indicates, the majority of individual contributions were given while the individuals were alive rather than by bequests in their wills.

TABLE 7-1
Sources of Donations—1996
($ in Billions)

Source	Donations	% of Total
Individuals	$119.92	79.6
Corporations	8.50	5.6
Foundations	11.83	7.8
Bequests	10.46	6.9
Total	150.70	100.00

Source: AAFRC Trust for Philanthropy

Use of Contributions

Another important factor with respect to charitable contributions is the type of charities to which Americans make contributions. Recent data (see table 7-2) indicate that religious organizations receive more than half of the total charitable donations made in the United States. The purposes of contributions have exhibited some year-to-year variation.

What Can Be Donated to Charity

There are many potential contributions that a person or business can make to a charity. Certainly, anything that confers a benefit to a charity is a donation. The tax implications (discussed below) will sometimes differ, however, based on the type of contribution. Regardless of the tax motivation, the potential donor should be contributing something that he or she sincerely wants to make available to the charity. The contribution should also meet the selected charity's needs.

TABLE 7-2
Purposes of Charitable Contributions—1996
($ in Billions)

Purposes of Contributions	Contributions	% of Total
Religion	$69.44	46.1
Education	18.81	12.5
Health	13.89	9.2
Human Services	12.16	8.1
Arts, Culture, and Humanities	10.92	7.2
Public Society/Benefit	7.57	5.0

Source: AAFRC Trust for Philanthropy

The following are possible types of donations to charity:

- gift of the donor's property. The most common donation is a gift of the donor's property to charity. For example, the donor can give cash, tangible or intangible personal property, or real estate to the charity.
- gift of the donor's income. Another immediate donation is the gift or assignment of the donor's income to the charity. For example, the donor may assign rent or income from his or her property without giving the charity the property itself.
- promises or pledges. Another type of donation is a pledge or a promise of future gifts to a charity.
- the donor's services. A donor may choose to volunteer his or her services to assist a charity. For example, volunteer work in fund-raising activities is very often performed by individuals who feel strongly about the charitable organization.
- expenses incurred on behalf of a charity. When a donor provides services to a charity, he or she often incurs personal expenses such as travel without expecting reimbursement. These unreimbursed expenses represent an additional contribution.
- use of the donor's property by the charity. A donor may permit the charity to use his or her property for a temporary period without permanently contributing the property. For example, the donor may permit the charity to temporarily exhibit his or her valuable artwork free of charge.

- bequests of the donor's property. The donor can leave any of his or her probate property to charity by executing a valid will that includes a bequest to charity.
- designating a charity as beneficiary of death proceeds. A donor can make a charity the designated beneficiary for benefits payable at his or her death. For example, the donor can make the charity a beneficiary of his or her life insurance policy or IRA.
- split-interest transfers. The more sophisticated charitable giving techniques (discussed in greater detail in the next chapter) involve donations where the donor gives up less than his or her full interest in the property. An example of a split-interest transfer is the popular charitable remainder trust. These transfers involve stringent tax limitations and must be planned carefully.

Reasons for Making Donations

There are many reasons why a person would make a charitable donation. One experienced fund-raiser has described three reasons individuals have for making donations. The reasons are based on the theory that donations are made with the expectation of receiving something in return—the *quid pro quo* theory of charitable donations. This theory certainly has merit when the potential economic benefits of various tax deductions are taken into consideration. The expected benefits of the *quid pro quo* theory are as follows:[1]

- souvenirs and symbols. This motivation is the donor's desire to receive recognition in the form of plaques, pens, desk ornaments, or perhaps having his or her name engraved on a permanent plaque or wall figure at the charity's location. The donor hopes to be recognized by his or her peers for such symbols and may be willing to compete to receive higher-status categories of the souvenirs or symbols.
- perquisites and privileges. This type of *quid pro quo* involves the donor's receipt of certain privileges from the charity. For example, receiving preferred seats and parking at sporting events or the local orchestra is often a motivation of donors making substantial contributions to the charity.
- physical and psychic rewards. This motivation involves the receipt of less tangible rewards. The donor may simply feel good that he or she is repaying a "debt" to a charitable institution. For example, someone who has become successful after an educational experience may feel that he or she should repay some of that success to the provider of the educational services. An individual who has received superb medical care may wish to reward a hospital with a charitable donation.

Sometimes the debt that a donor is repaying is not directly to the charitable institution but to honor another individual. Donations to charities are often made by individuals, entities, or groups to honor favored individuals, either living or dead. For example, younger generation family members may make gifts in honor of a parent or grandparent, or the parents of a child who predeceases them may wish to create a legacy to make up for the loss of their beloved child. Many permanent endowments are created for this purpose.

Finally, the psychic reward may be simply to be recognized among one's peers by taking a leadership role in a fund-raising campaign for a favored charity.

The view that a donor is virtually always making a contribution to receive *quid quo pro* is somewhat cynical. Certainly, some large donations are made anonymously and perhaps without the expectation of reward, tangible or intangible. It is hard to deny, however, that every donor is receiving at least some psychic reward for philanthropy.

A significant psychic reward is the "purchase of immortality"—that is, the donor believes that by making a large gift, he or she will be remembered in a positive manner far beyond the event of physical death. His or her name will be remembered kindly and with honor in future generations.[2]

Of course, we agree that many donations are made strictly out of noneconomic motivations—for example, for religious, patriotic, or other altruistic reasons. This is particularly true for smaller gifts. Charitable donations and the very concept of charity existed long before there were any tax or financial incentives for making such contributions.

In addition to pure philanthropy, however, there are economic reasons why charitable donations are made. The federal and state tax laws in this country offer economic incentives for a taxpayer to make donations. Tax deductions for making charitable donations are generally available for federal estate, gift, and income tax purposes. Similar deductions are often available for state income, estate, or inheritance taxes. These incentives have grown in importance over time, particularly for larger and more sophisticated donations. In fact, a recent survey indicated that potential donors of large donations would become significantly less interested in making such donations if a lower tax rate (such as the flat tax concept) were enacted. Obviously, eliminating the tax deductions for donations would also have a devastating impact on the level of contributions from donors motivated by the economic benefits of making charitable donations. How any potential tax changes would actually affect the levels and types of donations is speculative and academic until such changes occur.

The donor's reasons for making charitable donations can be summarized as follows:

- feelings of religious, moral, or ethical obligation
- belief in a specific charitable organization
- aspiration to assist a given group of society

- desire to reduce federal income taxes
- strategy to lower estate taxes and improve the estate's liquidity position

ROLE OF GOVERNMENT IN CHARITABLE GIVING

Availability of Tax Benefits

The federal and state governments have a long-term role in the charitable giving area. The federal income tax charitable deduction was first enacted in 1917, shortly after the enactment of the income tax. The estate tax charitable deduction was enacted in 1921, but it was retroactive to deaths occurring after 1917. The gift tax charitable deduction followed in 1932. Similarly, state tax charitable deductions have been in force nearly as long as most state income taxes. In addition, the government affords tax-exempt status to the "nonprofit" sector of the economy.

Both federal and state governments have, of course, a self-interest in encouraging charitable giving. As table 7-1 demonstrated, Americans have traditionally been generous to charities and have provided unprecedented levels of "public" benefits through the private sector. The standard of living in our society has led to the expectation of at least minimum levels of education, health care, and basic living necessities. To the extent that the private sector does not adequately address these needs, there is pressure on the state and federal government to do so. This makes the government an interested party in the success of private fund-raising efforts.

State Protection of Charitable Organizations

In addition to tax benefits, state law generally offers special contract privileges to charitable pledges. Contract law usually makes mere pledges or promises unenforceable due to the lack of consideration received in exchange for the pledge or promise. In effect, no contract is formed by a pledge or promise. However, the legal principle of promissory estoppel makes pledges to charities enforceable contracts.[3] Moreover, the states' Attorney General Offices, in the legal role of *parens patriae*, generally have the authority to enforce the rights of charitable organizations.

GENERAL FEDERAL TAX IMPLICATIONS OF CHARITABLE GIVING

Regardless of whether the federal income tax, federal estate tax, or federal gift tax is being considered, there are certain basic rules and concepts that apply, including the three that follow:

- A deduction will be available for gifts or contributions of property regardless of tax-avoidance motivation.
- It is essential to carefully consider who the recipient of the charitable gift will be, since the recipient must fall into a certain category before the donor can enjoy a federal tax benefit.
- There are several distinctions in the federal tax treatment of charitable contributions, depending on whether we are considering the estate tax, gift tax, or income tax.

Deductible Contributions of Gifts of Property

The initial threshold for a donation to be eligible for a tax deduction is that a "gift" or "contribution" of property be made. The income tax rules don't adequately define the term contribution. The gift tax regulations, however, clearly define a gift as a transfer for less than full and adequate consideration in money and money's worth. Both the income and gift tax rules do not permit a deduction for the transfer of services.

The gift tax rules indicate that donative intent is irrelevant as long as a transfer is made for less than full consideration. Nevertheless, it is necessary to examine donative intent to some degree for income and gift tax deductions. There is case law that adds this threshold if the donor/transferor has made a contribution with the expectation of some benefit in return. For example, a donor may make a contribution to a college or university with the expectation that a member of the donor's family will be given preferred admissions treatment by that college or university.

The charitable deductions are generally available only if the transferor contributes his or her entire interest in the property to the charitable organization. Certain partial-interest donations, however, will qualify for the income, gift, and estate tax charitable deduction. These donations are discussed in more detail below and in chapter 8.

The income tax regulations state that the deduction is available even if the donation was motivated primarily or solely by tax avoidance. Thus in the area of charitable giving, motivation is not relevant as long as a gift of property is made to a qualifying charity.

Charitable giving can be a powerful financial and estate planning tool because of the various tax benefits. However, the donor and the financial services professional who is advising the donor should not become so enthusiastic about the potential tax savings and other economic benefits that they overlook practical consequences to the donor and the charity. For charitable giving to accomplish the donor's economic and noneconomic goals, it must have substance for both the donor and charity. Although the tax rules affecting donations will be changed or fine-tuned virtually every time broad tax legislation is enacted, the desire to assist worthy charities has survived and will survive changes that reduce the tax benefit of donations.

Transfers of Partial Interests in Property

Generally, the federal tax deduction is denied unless the donor gives up all of his or her interest in the property. However, the tax deductions will be allowed for the value of a partial interest that is transferred or has been transferred for charitable purposes if the partial interest falls into one of the following six special categories:

- the undivided portion of a donor's entire interest
- the remainder interest in a personal residence or farm
- a charitable remainder trust
- the transfer to a pooled-income fund
- a charitable lead trust
- a qualified conservation easement

The charitable deductions available for partial-interest donations are available against federal gift, estate, and/or income taxes depending on the type of donation made. The special partial-interest rules will be discussed in a later chapter.

Selection of Charitable Donee

The primary reason a donor chooses a specific charity is usually not tax related. As a practical matter, a charitable donor wants to help advance the cause and objective of the organization in question. No economic or tax-related factors can change this result. Nevertheless, the tax concerns associated with the choice of a particular charitable donee must not be ignored.

Organizations Eligible for Tax-Deductible Donations

In order for the person making a charitable donation to receive a tax deduction, the recipient of that gift must fall into a specific category as set forth in the law for tax-deductible charitable contributions.[4] Some organizations that appear charitable are not eligible to receive deductible contributions. The IRS publishes a lengthy report each year, known as Publication 78, listing those organizations that will qualify for a charitable deduction. Remember, however, that Publication 78 is only a snapshot at one given point in time. Charities could lose their status as eligible organizations at any time if they fail to meet certain standards. Therefore donors should exercise caution concerning the eligibility of charities, particularly more obscure charities, in planning charitable donations. The IRS also regularly publishes a list of disqualified charities in the Internal Revenue Bulletin. For this reason, donors of deferred gifts often retain, or give to someone else, the power to change the charitable recipient of such donations if the intended charity loses its status as an eligible organization.

Table 7-3 describes categories of various organizations and answers the question of whether the donor (a person or a corporation) may take an estate tax deduction, a gift tax deduction, or an income tax deduction. The table leads to some important observations concerning eligible charities.

First, note that only *organizations* in the specified eligible categories will qualify to receive tax-deductible contributions. Gifts to *individuals* are not deductible, regardless of the merit of their charitable work.

Second, the list of eligible charities does not include every type of organization exempt from the federal income tax. Thus, although the terms *exempt* and *charitable* organization are often used synonymously, the only organizations qualifying to receive charitable contributions are those listed in table 7-3. For instance, a local Chamber of Commerce may be tax exempt and yet may not be an organization to which contributions are deductible as charitable contributions.

Finally, note that the list of qualified donees includes some categories that are not organizations described in Sec. 501(c)(3) of the Internal Revenue Code. Many people have the misconception that Sec. 501(c)(3) defines the only types of organizations that may receive deductible contributions, but this is not correct. For example, contributions to a governmental unit may qualify for an income tax deduction, provided that the contribution is used exclusively for public purposes.

Differing Rules for Various Federal Tax Deductions

The type of organization selected for a donation may have an impact on the federal income, estate, and gift tax treatment of a donation. Other donations will be eligible for deductions against one type of federal tax but not another. For example, note that contributions to foreign charitable organizations are eligible for gift or estate tax deductions but not for the income tax charitable deduction.[5] Further, the amount and extent of certain percentage limitations or reductions imposed on the federal income tax charitable deduction will differ, based on the type of charitable organization. (More detail will be provided later with respect to the impact of the type of charity on these limitations and reductions. As we will see, there are no limitations imposed on the federal estate tax or federal gift tax charitable deductions.)

Example: During 1997 Rod Borrocks makes a $35,000 charitable contribution to DELTA Fund, an organization devoted to improving irrigation techniques in South American countries. He may not enjoy a federal income tax deduction under the current federal income tax laws because the charitable gift will be used outside the United States.

If Rod instead makes a $35,000 testamentary bequest to DELTA Fund in his will, his estate may take a federal estate tax charitable deduction under the current federal estate tax laws.

TABLE 7-3
Categories of Organizations Qualifying for Charitable Deductions

	Federal Estate Tax Deduction	Federal Gift Tax Deduction	Federal Income Tax Deduction
A corporation, trust, community chest, fund, or foundation operating in the United States, exclusively for religious, charitable, scientific, literary, or educational purposes, including the encouragement of art, or to foster national or international amateur sports competition and the prevention of cruelty to children or animals; however, no part of the organization's activities may attempt to influence legislation or involve participation in any political campaign	Yes	Yes	Yes
The United States of America, a state within the United States, any political subdivision of a state, or the District of Columbia, but only if such gift is to be used exclusively for public purposes	Yes	Yes	Yes
A possession of the United States but only if such gift is to be used exclusively for public purposes	No	No	Yes
Religious, charitable, scientific, literary, or educational organizations where the contributions will be used outside the United States	Yes	Yes	No
A post or organization of war veterans, or an auxiliary unit or society of a trust or foundation organized in the United States or in its possessions and chartered by an act of Congress	Yes	Yes	Yes
A post or organization of war veterans, or an auxiliary unit or society of a trust or foundation organized in the United States or in its possessions but not chartered by an act of Congress	No	No	Yes
A cemetery company owned and operated exclusively for the benefit of its members or any corporation chartered solely for burial purposes as a cemetery corporation	No	No	Yes
Contributions to a domestic fraternal society, order, or association operating under the lodge system, but only if such contribution or gift is to be used exclusively for religious, charitable, scientific, literary, or educational purposes, or for the prevention of cruelty to children or animals	Yes	Yes	Yes

FEDERAL ESTATE TAX TREATMENT OF CHARITABLE GIVING

Requirements of Estate Tax Charitable Deduction

Property Must Pass to a Charitable Organization

Sec. 2055 of the Internal Revenue Code provides that the value of a decedent's taxable estate is to be determined by deducting the amount of all charitable contributions to qualifying charitable organizations from the value of the gross estate. The deduction is permitted for the full value of property included in the decedent's gross estate for all bequests or other testamentary transfers by the decedent to an eligible donee. This includes property that passes to the charity by operation of law, by beneficiary designation, as a result of a timely disclaimer by a noncharitable beneficiary, or through either the exercise or nonexercise of a general power of appointment the decedent held at the time of his or her death.

The interpretation of any of these transfers is based on the property law of the state with jurisdiction over the decedent's estate or the state where the property is located. It is clear that the decedent must affirmatively name the charity as a potential recipient of property in some manner.

However, the charitable deduction is available only for transfers that are predictable or "ascertainable" at the time of the decedent's death. For example, any transfers that might be subject to a contingency in the decedent's will do not qualify for a charitable deduction unless the contingency is so remote that the probability that the charity will not receive its bequest is negligible. Any power given to the charity, executor, or beneficiaries to divert property from the charitable bequest will eliminate the deduction even if that property is not so diverted.

A 1993 case[6] demonstrates the painful results that can occur if the charitable bequest is not ascertainable. In the actual facts of the case, the decedent had executed a valid will with the residue left to qualifying charities. He later executed a codicil permitting his executor to benefit any individuals who contributed to his well-being while he was alive but limited the amounts of any bequest to one percent of his probate estate. The amounts that were actually paid to noncharitable beneficiaries under this discretionary power totaled $25,000, whereas the residuary estate that was actually donated to charity exceeded $2.1 million.

Clearly, the loss of the estate tax charitable deduction created a massive liquidity problem for this estate and significantly reduced the charitable bequest. This problem could have been solved in the drafting of the decedent's will. The estate tax charitable deduction would have been preserved if the other bequests had been limited in total dollar amounts or measurable by some ascertainable standard.

Impact of Administration Expenses

Any estate expenses, such as death taxes and administrative expenses, that are apportioned or allocated to the charitable contribution reduce the size of the charitable deduction. These expenses, when paid, reduce the amount actually transferred to the charity and thus the size of the estate tax charitable deduction. These expenses can be allocated to the charitable bequest either by the provisions of the donor's will or, if no such allocation is made by the will, by the terms of the tax apportionment statute in the decedent's state of domicile.

The apportionment of taxes and expenses is a complicated issue and should be discussed with an estate planning attorney whenever a charitable bequest is planned. Failure to apportion taxes could have adverse consequences on the donor's (1) noncharitable heirs, (2) charitable deduction, and (3) marital deduction.

Example: Mary Scott died on June 1, 1998, with a gross estate of $1,544,000. Her funeral and administrative expenses totaled $144,000 and were allocated to her residuary estate. She was unmarried at the time of her death, and her two nieces will receive her residuary estate. Miss Scott had made a specific bequest in her will of $850,000 to the District of Columbia, with the funds to be used in any manner the government saw fit, as long as it was for a public purpose. A deduction in the amount of the full $850,000 is allowable under the current federal estate tax laws. It also represents sound planning since the charitable deduction brings the estate below the unified credit equivalent amount of $600,000 and there will be no federal estate tax liability imposed on her estate.

Miss Scott's estate was computed in this way:

Gross estate	$1,544,000
Less debts, cost of administration	(144,000)
Adjusted gross estate	1,400,000
Less charitable deduction	(850,000)
Taxable estate	$ 550,000
Federal estate tax payable	–0–

Qualifying Charitable Organization

One of the general requirements for all types of charitable deductions is that the recipient organization meet the standard as an eligible charitable organization. Since a bequest to charity is deferred, in some cases for a long period of time until the donor dies, it is not possible to ensure that the selected charity will still qualify for an estate tax charitable deduction at the decedent's death. The donor could mitigate this concern to some degree by selecting a well-known organization that is unlikely to lose its tax-exempt status in the foreseeable future. For example, a bequest to the Red Cross should be fairly safe for the indefinite future. Other more obscure charities may not afford the same assurance to the donor.

One solution to this problem is for the donor to take a more flexible approach in drafting his or her will or charitable trust. The donor could empower the executor or a trustee to replace a disqualified or defunct charity with an organization eligible to receive estate-tax-deductible gifts, and the document should state that the gift be used exclusively for one of the permissible charitable purposes. The will or trust should clearly provide for a charitable intent and a charitable disposition that qualifies for a deduction. If there is any real possibility that the executor could exercise discretion in a manner that makes the bequest pass either to an ineligible charity or for an ineligible purpose, the IRS will take the position that the deduction be denied.

There is some potential relief if the selected charity fails to qualify and the bequest or other testamentary transfer device does not contemplate a replacement. For testamentary transfers that are made prior to the disqualification of a charity, Revenue Procedure 82-39 may offer some relief.[7] Under these circumstances, a bequest made to a charity whose disqualified status has not yet been announced by the Service at the time of the decedent's death should qualify for the charitable deduction.

State law may also provide some help if the charity has ceased to exist at the time of the decedent's death. In this situation, state law will determine the distribution of the decedent's will in the absence of a selected donee. In many cases, the doctrine of *cy pres* has been applied to interpret the decedent's bequest as creating a general charitable intent. If the state court's application of *cy pres* creates a charitable intent to provide the bequest (1) to a charity that qualifies for an estate tax deduction and (2) for a use exclusively for one of the enumerated charitable purposes, the deduction should be preserved to the extent that the donation is actually made by the estate.

It is clear that the relief provisions do not offer a solution in every instance. The donor and his or her advisers should carefully monitor the status of a charity that is named in the donor's will or designated as the beneficiary of the donor's life insurance or employee benefits. In addition, it is prudent to give the donor's executor the discretion to change the recipient of a bequest to an eligible charitable organization.

Estate Tax Charitable Deduction and Incomplete Lifetime Transfers

The federal estate tax charitable deduction can give relief in some cases where the federal estate tax rules create inclusion in the donor's gross estate for an incomplete lifetime gift. For example, the next chapter discusses charitable remainder trusts and gifts of remainder interests in a home or farm. If the donor retains the lifetime noncharitable interest in these transactions, Sec. 2036(a) will cause inclusion of some or all of the remainder interest in the donor's gross estate. Since the remainder interest is transferred to charity, however, there is an offsetting charitable estate tax deduction that effectively eliminates any estate taxes that would otherwise result from this inclusion.

The charitable estate tax deduction will also eliminate similar problems for life insurance benefits left to charity. As we discussed in chapter 2, life insurance is included in the decedent-insured's gross estate if he or she owned any incident of ownership at the time of death or made a gift of the policy within 3 years of death. As a general rule, clients who wish to give their existing life insurance policy to a charitable organization will transfer the ownership of the policy to the charity; presumably, the charity will then be the beneficiary of the policy. If the insured dies within 3 years, the proceeds will be included in his or her gross estate and the charitable deduction will be necessary to eliminate the estate taxes that result.

The charitable deduction is also helpful in cases where the donor-insured desires to retain flexibility. The donor may wish to make the donation revocable by designating the charity as the current beneficiary but retaining ownership of the life insurance policy. Thus the insured could change his or her mind if the policy is needed for another purpose. In these cases, the federal estate tax charitable deduction will be available to eliminate any federal estate tax liability if the insured dies without revoking the beneficiary designation.

Example: Marv Estep wants to benefit The American College and is advised that his existing life insurance policy may be used to accomplish this objective. Marv has a $1 million whole life policy on his life. The policy has substantial cash surrender value, and Marv is unsure about whether he can permanently forgo access to the policy value. He continues to pay the premium and retains ownership; however, The American College is designated as the named beneficiary. He receives no current income or gift tax deductions since the beneficiary designation is revocable.

Marv dies 7 years later with the policy in force. The $1 million of policy proceeds are included in his gross estate. Because The American College is the named beneficiary, however, the federal estate tax charitable deduction is available for the entire $1 million amount.

Summary of Key Issues

The relevant factors for the estate tax charitable deduction include the following key issues:

- The federal estate tax charitable deduction is unlimited in nature. There are no percentage restrictions imposed or adjustments required as there are with federal income taxes.
- Even though there are no restrictions at the federal estate tax level, some states have imposed restrictions on the amount of property a taxpayer

may legally leave to a charitable organization at death. At the very least, the surviving spouse's right to elect against the decedent's will could defeat a charitable bequest. State law must be examined before making a donation.
- The amount of the federal estate tax charitable deduction is limited to the value of property included in the decedent's gross estate and transferred by the decedent by will or other testamentary means to a qualifying charitable organization. Any expenses that reduce the amount passing to charity reduce the charitable estate tax deduction.

FEDERAL GIFT TAX TREATMENT OF CHARITABLE GIVING

Unlimited Gift Tax Deduction

For completed lifetime donations to charity, the primary tax concern is the availability of the federal income tax deduction. However, the donor must also consider the federal gift tax system since the imposition of gift taxes on a donation would be a painful result. Sec. 2522 provides that a completed gift to a qualifying charitable organization will trigger a charitable deduction for federal gift tax purposes. As with the federal estate tax charitable deduction, the gift tax deduction is unlimited.

> *Example:* Ronald Sunworship makes a gift of $1 million in cash to the city of Scottsdale, Arizona, after enjoying a spring vacation there. The recipient falls into one of the categories of a qualifying charity. Although Donald has made a gift, there will be no federal gift tax imposed because of the unlimited gift tax charitable deduction.

Qualifying Charitable Organizations

When planning charitable donations, the major emphasis is usually placed on complying with the rules governing the income tax charitable deduction. Because of some minor distinctions between the income and gift tax charitable deductions, care must be taken in planning large or complex lifetime donations. The small donations that give a present interest to the selected charity will not cause a problem since the federal gift tax annual exclusion of $10,000 is available against gifts to any donees, including charities. Larger gifts or gifts of a future interest, however, will create gift tax concerns. Generally, unless the gift tax return is timely filed, any mistakes with the gift tax charitable deduction will not be discovered until later, perhaps when the donor's estate tax return is audited.

The main distinction between the deductions is that the list of eligible charitable organizations for the charitable gift tax deduction is not identical to the corresponding list for the income tax charitable deduction (see table 7-3). For example, the gift tax charitable deduction permits transfers to foreign charitable organizations that would generally be nondeductible for income tax purposes. On the other hand, the gift tax deduction is denied for foreign-use donations made by nonresident-aliens. Since distinctions do exist between the eligible donees, donors must be very careful when planning any questionable donations. A tax disaster could inadvertently result for a donor who makes an irrevocable donation to an organization eligible to receive an income tax deduction but not a gift tax deduction. This is particularly true if the gift exceeds the amount of the annual exclusion or, in the case of charitable remainder trusts, the gift does not qualify for an annual exclusion.

Computing Gift Tax Charitable Deduction

Gift taxes are computed in a rather unusual fashion because the annual reporting requirement must take into consideration the unified nature of the federal estate and gift tax system. Thus, the gift tax return must cumulate all prior lifetime transfers and determine which of these transfers are taxable in the year currently being reported for gift tax purposes. Once this concept is understood, the computation of the gift taxes is fairly simple, as the example below demonstrates. Note that gifts qualifying for the marital and charitable deduction may first receive a $10,000 ($20,000 if the donor's spouse elects to split all gifts with the donor during the year) annual exclusion (indexed for inflation beginning in 1999). At first glance, it appears that the taxpayer should be indifferent to whether the charitable deduction qualifies for an annual gift tax exclusion or a gift tax charitable deduction. First, most donations made by one donor to a specific charity are less than $10,000 annually. In addition, most donations are immediate outright transfers and qualify for annual exclusions. For gifts to a specific charity in excess of $10,000, the charitable deduction, if the donation qualifies, will eliminate all gift taxes that would otherwise result from the donation. From a mechanical standpoint, however, the charitable deduction must be limited to the amount of the donation included in the donor's taxable gifts (that is, the amount of the donor's gifts that exceed the allowable exclusions).

Example: Dagwood Donor, an unmarried individual, made the following gifts during the previous tax year:

To his nephew	$15,000
To the Salvation Army	$35,000
To his sister	$25,000

Based on these facts, Dagwood's total gifts equal $75,000. Each of these gifts qualifies for a $10,000 annual exclusion. Thus, Dagwood's total taxable gifts equal $45,000. The charitable deduction for the gift to the Salvation Army is limited to $25,000 even though Dagwood's donation totaled $35,000. If the charitable deduction were not limited to the amount of any donation included in taxable gifts, the charitable deduction would shelter taxable gifts made to noncharitable donees from gift taxes. Under the facts of this example, if the full $35,000 charitable deduction were allowable after the reduction from total gifts for the annual exclusions, $10,000 of the charitable deduction would, in effect, be sheltering the gifts made to Dagwood's nephew and sister.

Gift Tax Compliance

Under new rules created by TRA 97, gift tax returns are no longer required for charitable donations in most circumstances. Gift tax returns are still required for donations of less than the donor's entire interest in the donated property unless the donation is a qualified conservation easement. The rules for donations of less than the donor's entire interest are discussed in the next chapter.

FEDERAL INCOME TAX TREATMENT OF CHARITABLE GIVING

Sec. 170 of the Internal Revenue Code explains the tax rules for the federal income tax charitable deduction. The charitable deduction was enacted in 1917, approximately 4 years after the first federal income tax, and has been in place continuously since that time. As we discussed earlier, there are differences in the federal income tax, estate tax, and gift tax deductions for charitable contributions. While the federal gift and federal estate tax laws impose no limitations on the amount of the charitable deduction, the federal income tax law limits the amount of deductions and requires that certain adjustments be made if certain types of property are transferred to a charity.

For federal income tax purposes, transfers of property to qualifying charitable organizations will generate a federal income tax deduction for donors. However, the deduction will be limited to varying degrees depending on the type of organization receiving the charitable donation, the restrictions placed on the donation, and the type property donated.

Limitations on Current Income Tax Deduction—Percentage Limitation Rules

Regardless of how much a donor may give to charity in the form of deductible contributions, there are very strict limitations on the percentage of income that may be deducted in any one taxable year as charitable contributions. These vary according to the nature of the donee organization and the type of property given. As a practical matter, very few donors contribute such a large proportion of their income to charity that they encounter problems under these percentage limitations. Table 7-4 at the end of this chapter serves as a handy quick-reference guide for the percentage limitation rules that apply in this and the next chapter.

Donor's Contribution Base

The contribution limitations described below are stated in terms of a percentage of the donor's *contribution base*. This term is defined as adjusted gross income computed without regard to any net operating loss carrybacks to the year of contribution. For most planning purposes, a donor's contribution base is synonymous with his or her adjusted gross income. Depending on the type of donation, percentage limitations apply to the size of the permissible income tax charitable deduction. The deductions are limited to a percentage of the donor's adjusted gross income (contribution base), *not* a percentage of the donation.

> *CAUTION:* What follows here is an abbreviated summary of the charitable income tax deduction rules that should be sufficient for most planning purposes. However, many details are not included in the material below that may apply to a specific donor's contribution. Please consult with an income tax specialist for the determination of the limitation applicable to a particular donation.

Public versus Nonpublic Charitable Organizations

The percentage limitations permit a larger deduction for donations to public charities. A public charity is supported with public funds; a nonpublic charity does not operate with public funds. Generally, public charities are all Sec. 501(c)(3) organizations that are not private foundations. The greatest permissible charitable income tax deductions are for donations to the following types of public charities:

- churches
- schools with a regular faculty, curriculum, and student body
- organizations providing medical or hospital care or performing medical research or education
- organizations that receive a substantial part of their support from federal and state sources and from the general public, and apply these funds so that educational organizations run by any state agency may continue to operate
- certain types of private foundations

Donations "To" versus "For the Use of" a Charitable Organization

Different percentage limitations exist for gifts "to" versus gifts "for the use of" a charity. A gift made directly to a charity is a gift *to* a charity. A gift *for the use of* a charity refers to a gift in trust, where the charity will receive donations but may never receive the trust property outright. An example of this is a charitable lead trust, discussed in the next chapter. A transfer to a charitable remainder trust is treated as a gift to the charitable remainder beneficiary since the charity will ultimately receive the property outright.

Types of Property Contributions

There are also percentage limitation rules based on the type of property contributed. Distinctions are made between (1) donations of cash, property that would yield ordinary income if sold, or property that would yield short-term capital gain if sold and (2) donations of property that would yield long-term capital gain if sold. There are also rules that permit the donor to elect out of the long-term capital gain property limitation.

Cash or Non-Long-Term Capital Gain Property Contributions. Contributions of cash are subject to the following deduction limitations:

- Cash or non-long-term capital gain property contributions *to* a charity that is a *public charity* are deductible up to 50 percent of the donor's contribution base.
- Other cash or non-long-term capital gain property contributions—that is, contributions *to* a charity that is a *private foundation* and contributions *for the use of* any charity (primarily contributions made via a charitable lead income trust)—are deductible up to the *lesser* of

    (1) 30 percent of the donor's contribution base or
    (2) the excess of 50 percent of the contribution base over all contributions to 50 percent-type charities (determined without regard to the special 30 percent limit for property gifts)

Appreciated Property Contributions. Contributions of appreciated capital gain property[8] are deductible at fair market value (subject to the reduction rules described below) to the extent they do not exceed the following percentage limitations:

- Contributions of appreciated capital gain property *to* a *public charity* are deductible up to 30 percent of the donor's contribution base.
- Contributions of appreciated property *to* a *private foundation* or *for the use of* any charity are deductible up to the *lesser* of

(1) 20 percent of the contribution base or
(2) the excess of 30 percent of the contribution base over all contributions to which the 30 percent limitation applies[9]

Example: Sally Smith's gross income for the taxable year was $162,000. She paid $400 in a penalty for a premature surrender of a certificate of deposit, and she paid alimony of $12,000. Sally's adjusted gross income is computed as follows:

Gross income		$162,000
Less deductions		
CD penalty	$ 400	
Alimony	12,000	
Total		(12,400)
Adjusted gross income		$149,600

That adjusted gross income figure will also be Sally's contribution base for purposes of applying the income tax charitable deduction limitations, as shown in the following example:

Example: During the last taxable year, Sally Smith, who has a contribution base of $149,600, made cash gifts that totaled $17,500 to such public charities as schools and churches. The $17,500 gifts to public charities are fully deductible since they do not exceed 50 percent of Sally's contribution base. If they were to exceed 50 percent of the contribution base, a limitation would need to be imposed.

Example: In addition to the $17,500 Sally Smith gave to public charities during the last taxable year, she also gave $60,000 in cash to a private foundation. Only $44,880 of the gift made to the private foundation, a nonpublic charity, is deductible. The gift to the private foundation exceeded both 30 percent of Sally's contribution base ($149,600 x .30 = $44,880) and the difference between 50 percent of her contribution base ($149,600 x .50 = $74,800) and the amount of her gifts to public charities ($17,500), or $57,300 ($74,800 – $17,500). Since the amount of the deduction is limited to the lesser of $44,880 and $57,300, the allowable deduction will be $44,880.

Special Election for Appreciated Property. A donor may elect to increase a long-term-gain property contribution to a public charity to a 50 percent limitation. However, the election requires the donor to reduce the size of the contribution (for income tax purposes) from its fair market value to his or her adjusted cost basis in the donated property. This election could be valuable when the donated property has appreciated only slightly in value.

Five-Year Carryover of Excess Contributions. If a donor makes contributions of either cash or property in amounts that exceed any of the applicable percentage limitations, the excess donations might not be wasted. That excess may be carried over and deducted (subject to the same percentage limitations) in each of the 5 following tax years. Any amount carried over is treated as a contribution made in the later carryover year, and as such it remains subject to the same percentage limitation in the carryover year.

Reduction in Itemized Charitable Deductions for High-Income Donors. Note that the Revenue Reconciliation Act of 1990 established a new rule dealing with itemized deductions. Specifically, total otherwise allowable deductions, except medical costs, casualty and theft losses, and investment interest, are reduced by 3 percent of the amount of a taxpayer's adjusted gross income in excess of $124,500 (1998 figure). These deductions cannot be reduced by more than 80 percent. The threshold amount is adjusted for inflation.

> *Example:* If Harry Herrick has a contribution base of $127,950 and contributes appreciated property worth $64,500 to a university, only $38,385 is deductible in the year of the gift, since the 30 percent limitation is applicable. In addition, Harry's itemized deduction is reduced by the lesser of (1) 80 percent of the donation or (2) 3 percent of the amount his contribution base exceeds $124,500. Thus his allowable itemized deduction for the year of the gift (assuming 1998 thresholds) is reduced further by $103.5 ([$127,950 – $124,500] x .03).
>
> The excess contribution over the allowable percentage limitation of $26,115 ($64,500 – $38,385) will carry over to the following year (and to the extent not used in that year, to the following year) and will be treated as a contribution of appreciated property made during that year. Thus it will still be subject to the 30 percent limitation, based on Harry's contribution base for the carryover year. In addition, a reduction for the itemized deduction will apply in the later year also with a newly indexed figure for the adjusted gross income threshold.

Limitations on Current Income Tax Deduction—Reduction Rules

In general, the amount that is deductible for a charitable contribution of property is the fair market value of the property on the date that the gift was made. In certain situations, however, the deduction may be limited to the donor's cost basis, depending on the type of property that is contributed and on the type of charitable organization.

Non-Capital-Gain Property (Ordinary Income Property)

As a general rule, the amount of a donor's deduction is reduced by any amount that would *not* have been taxed as long-term capital gain if the property had been sold at its fair market value on the date of the contribution. This rule applies without regard to the type of charitable organization. Some of the types of donated property that are affected by this rule are inventory property, short-term capital gain property, and property that is subject to recapture under Sec. 1245 or Sec. 1250.

Tangible Property/Unrelated Use Rule

A second category of appreciated property donations that are not deductible at full fair market value is certain tangible personal property gifts. If such property is contributed and the charity's use of the donated property is not related to its charitable function, the donor's deduction is limited to the donor's cost basis in the property.

> *Example:* A contribution of construction equipment to a museum would not be deductible at full fair market value. By comparison, a contribution of rare artifacts to the museum would probably be deductible in full; these artifacts, presumably, are related to the museum's regular operations.

Property Gifts to Private Foundations

A third category of appreciated property contributions that are not deductible at full fair market value consists of most contributions to private foundations. With some notable exceptions, contributions of appreciated property to a private foundation will cause the donor's income tax deduction to be reduced to his or her cost basis.

Election of 50 Percent Limitation

The final category of appreciated property contributions that are not deductible at full fair market value consists of contributions that the donor has elected to reduce in amount (to the donor's cost basis). As discussed earlier, this election permits the donor to use the 50 percent limitation generally applicable to cash gifts to public charities, rather than the usual 30 percent limitation governing gifts of appreciated property to public charities.

Income Tax Compliance Rules for Charitable Donations

When Can a Donation Be Deducted?

Generally, only donations that are made in the current tax year and are irrevocable will qualify for the income tax deduction in the current tax year. Thus promises and deferred gifts do not qualify until the actual transfer is irrevocably made. For some deferred gifts, such as charitable remainder trusts, a current deduction is available since the transfer of the remainder interest is irrevocably made and vested. For others, such as designating a charity as the beneficiary of a life insurance policy, no current deduction is available since the designation is revocable and no transfer has been made.

Most donations involve direct transfers and create no disputes. However, donations are sometimes made subject to conditions or have factual circumstances that make delivery unclear.

The timing of the donor's deduction for donations to charities is as follows:

- *Cash* — Deductible when delivered
- *Checks* — Deductible when mailed or delivered (if delivered in person)
- *Credit cards* — Deductible when the charge is made
- *Securities* — Deductible when mailed to the charity if a properly endorsed certificate is mailed; deductible when tranferred on the books of the corporation if the donor transfers the security to his or her broker or to the issuing corporation
- *Tangible personal property* — Deductible when delivered to the charity or when transferred to an agent of the charity
- *Real property* — Deductible when the deed is delivered to the charity *property* (or its agent) or recorded (if recordation is required by state law)
- *Promised gifts* — Do not give rise to a deduction until payment is made (whether or not the promise is enforceable as a charitable pledge)
- *Deferred gifts* — Deductible when the charity's interest is "vested"—that is, can't be forfeited—if the deferred gift qualifies for a deduction (such as charitable remainder trust)

Substantiation and Valuation Rules

Valuation of Charitable Donations. To take a charitable deduction of any kind, it is first essential to determine the value of donated property. If a cash contribution is made to a qualifying charity, calculating the value of the gift is simple. However, when property other than money is transferred to a charity, additional considerations become pertinent. The basic rule is that the amount of a gift of property other than money is the fair market value of the property at the time of the gift (of course, this is subject to the reduction rules discussed above). In general, the fair market value of donated property should be determined no differently than for valuation for estate or gift tax purposes (as explained in chapter 4). The valuation rules for donated property are discussed in the regulations and provided for taxpayers in IRS Publication 561, *Determining the Value of Donated Property.*

Substantiating a Charitable Deduction. The regulations require the taxpayer to substantiate charitable contributions with evidence of the name of the organization and the specific amount, the date, and the value of the contribution. If the taxpayer contributes property with no immediate objective valuation, the law may require an appraisal. (In Rev. Rul. 66-49 the IRS set forth the following guidelines on information to be furnished with an appraisal: [1] a summary of the appraiser's qualifications, [2] the appraiser's valuation and the appraiser's definition of the term value, [3] the restrictions, covenants, and other factors that entered into the appraisal, [4] the date of the appraisal, and [5] the appraiser's signature.)

Regulations under Sec. 170 state the appraisal requirements. A qualified appraisal will be required for a property donation (or a series of donations of similar items) of $5,000 or more. The appraisal threshold is increased to $10,000 for gifts of closely held stock. An appraisal is not necessary for donations of cash or publicly traded securities. The regulations provide rules for choosing a qualified appraiser for the specific property donated. If an appraisal is required, the donor must file an appraisal summary, Form 8283, with his or her income tax return. If the donor is deducting $20,000 or more for donated art, a complete copy of the signed appraisal report must be included with the donor's tax return.

Under a new procedure issued by the IRS, a donor can pay a user fee and request that the IRS issue a statement concerning the donor's proposed deduction. The statement is generally available only for donations of art valued by the donor's appraiser at $50,000 or more. The donor can use the IRS's statement to substantiate the deduction on his or her income tax return. Unfortunately, the donor cannot request the statement unless he or she has already made the donation, and the IRS may disagree with the donor's appraiser.

Charity's Role in Substantiating the Charitable Deduction. A contemporaneous receipt of a donation is now required for donations of $250 or more before the donor can take an income tax deduction. In other words, a cancelled check is not sufficient to substantiate the donor's deduction if the donation meets the $250 threshold. This applies to one-time donations of $250 or more, not to separate donations that add up to $250, even if the separate donations are made by the same donor to the same charity in the same tax year. The charity should give written acknowledgement (for example, a letter, postcard, computer-generated form, or tax form) that provides the following information:

- the amount of cash donated and a description of any donated property
- whether or not the charity provided any goods and services (*quid pro quo*) in return for the donation
- a description and good faith estimate of the value of the *quid pro quo*

The donor should receive the written acknowledgement at the earlier of the date (1) the donor files his or her income tax return taking the deduction or (2) the due date for the return (including extensions).

The IRS has issued proposed regulations concerning the treatment of donations where the donor receives *quid pro quo* in return. In these regulations the deductible amount is limited to the excess of the donor's contribution over the amount of *quid pro quo* received in return from the charity. The donor should receive a written acknowledgment if the donation is $250 or more and can rely on the charity's good faith estimate of the value of any *quid pro quo* received by the donor. In determining the amount of the *quid pro quo* and the required substantiation compliance, the charity and the donor can ignore the following:

- small items or token benefits of insubstantial value. Such items are described in Rev. Proc. 90-12, 1990-1 CB 471 to be "low-cost articles" whose fair market value is less than $7.10 (1998 figure) and the donor has contributed at least $33.50. Other *quid pro quo* benefits can be ignored up to the lesser of 2 percent of the amount of the donation or $71 (1998 figure).
- annual membership benefits offered for a donation of $75 or less that consist of rights or privileges that can be exercised frequently (for example, admission to facilities, parking, preferred access, or gift shop discounts). Members-only events can also be ignored if the cost per person (excluding overhead) is less than the low-cost article threshold. Note that tickets to college athletic events are not included in this exception.

Summary of Income Tax Compliance Issues

Obviously, most donations don't present complex and troublesome timing, valuation, and substantiation problems. Larger donations, however, particularly the sophisticated gifts discussed in the next chapter, will often face these tough compliance rules. The material in this chapter is designed to make the financial services professional aware of the structure of the various tax deductions available for charitable donations. There are also severe tax penalties for a variety of improprieties. For example, there are valuation and appraiser penalties. There are tax penalties for several different potentialities with private foundations. Clearly, sophisticated donations should be planned carefully with the advice of appropriate counsel.

ESTATE PLANNING OPPORTUNITIES IN CHARITABLE GIVING

The taxpayer who is charitably inclined will reap a double benefit from making gifts to charities. First, the gift giving will fulfill a psychological need to help out, which in most cases is far more rewarding than any tax-related benefit. Second, of course, the taxpayer will enjoy tax and economic benefits as a consequence of having made contributions to charities.

Before we review the planning opportunities, we should mention two basic points:

- If a client is not already charitably inclined, no amount of urging, suggesting, or demonstrating tax benefits will make that client want to make charitable gifts.
- The tax benefits of making charitable gifts will usually be secondary to the client's wish to help the recipient, so the tax benefits may be thought of as a bonus.

The next chapter focuses on sophisticated charitable giving in the estate planning process. The remainder of this chapter introduces some estate planning purposes for charitable giving. Our discussion of planning opportunities in the charitable-giving area may be broken down into life-insurance-related and non-life-insurance-related opportunities.

Life Insurance Opportunities

Reasons for Attractiveness

Most observers agree that there are six primary reasons why life insurance is particularly attractive to the client who wants to make charitable gifts. These may be summarized as follows:[10]

- Since the value of life insurance is guaranteed, there can be no doubt that the charity will collect the face amount of the policy. Accordingly, this mode of making a charitable gift is more certain than attempting a bequest funded with marketable securities, for example, which may decrease in value.
- A person can make a significant contribution to a qualifying charitable organization without a substantial out-of-pocket cost during life. Because life insurance operates on the discounted-dollar approach, a small premium will provide a sizable gift to the charity at the insured's death.
- Some clients, although they have an interest in leaving property to a charity, do not want to deprive family members of any estate property. By using life insurance to make a charitable contribution, the estate owner does not impair other assets, which can still be left to loved ones. The only amount of property he or she gives up is the annual premium, reduced by the federal income tax savings generated by the charitable deduction.

- It is very rare that a gift of a life insurance policy to a charity will be challenged by the heirs of the insured, because the proceeds of the policy are not part of the probate estate.
- The face amount of the life insurance policy paid to the charitable organization will not be subject to federal income taxation or probate costs.
- The transfer of a life insurance policy to a qualifying charitable organization, as well as the subsequent payment premiums, will give the donor significant tax benefits, such as having the out-of-pocket cost reduced by the current income tax deduction that is available.

These points can be used in a sales situation to encourage the charitably inclined client to use life insurance as part of his or her charitable gift.

Mechanics of Life Insurance Donations

A client may use a life insurance policy to make a charitable contribution in the following ways:

- designating a charity as the beneficiary of a life insurance policy while retaining ownership of the policy
- naming a charity as the irrevocable beneficiary of a life insurance policy while retaining ownership
- giving an existing life insurance policy to a qualifying charitable organization
- purchasing a new life insurance policy naming the charity as owner and beneficiary
- assigning dividends or other valuable policy rights to a charity

Let's review each of these methods separately.

Designating a Charity as Beneficiary. If a donor designates a qualifying charity as the beneficiary of a life insurance policy while retaining ownership, no completed transfer has occurred. Since beneficiary designations are generally revocable, the transfer is incomplete until the insured under the policy dies. There will be no current income tax deduction and no current gift tax consequences. When the insured dies, however, the transfer will be completed (assuming the charity is still beneficiary of the policy), and gift or estate tax consequences will result. If the insured was the donor, the policy proceeds will be included in his or her gross estate under Sec. 2042(2), and an estate tax charitable deduction will be available for the amount of the proceeds passing to charity. If the policyowner was not the insured, a completed gift will occur when the insured dies, and a gift tax charitable deduction will be available.

Example: Melissa Manfred owns a policy on her life with a cash surrender value of $25,000 and a death benefit of $500,000. The annual policy premium is $5,000. She designates The American Red Cross as beneficiary of the policy but does not transfer ownership. At the time of the beneficiary designation, Melissa does not receive income or gift tax deductions for the value of the policy. Nor may she deduct any subsequent premiums paid. If Melissa dies without changing the beneficiary, her estate will include the $500,000 death benefit but will receive an estate tax charitable deduction of $500,000.

If the policy Melissa owned was on the life of her husband, she would complete a taxable gift of $500,000 at the time of his death. However, she would qualify for a gift tax charitable deduction for the full amount paid to the charity.

Naming a Qualifying Charitable Organization as Irrevocable Beneficiary. If a donor retains ownership of a life insurance policy but names a qualifying charitable organization as the irrevocable beneficiary of the policy, the client will not receive a federal income tax deduction for all the subsequent premiums he or she pays. This is an example of a nondeductible split-interest contribution.

Example: Jeff Starr buys a $200,000 life insurance policy on his own life and names Municipal Hospital as the irrevocable beneficiary. Since Jeff is still the policyowner, the annual premium of $1,170 is not deductible from his federal income tax. At Jeff's death, Municipal Hospital will receive a $200,000 death benefit. Since Jeff owns the life insurance policy at the time of his death, the $200,000 will be included in his gross estate. However, because the death proceeds are benefiting a charity, there will be a $200,000 federal estate tax charitable deduction. Note: There may be some difficult gift tax consequences with this transaction. At the time of the irrevocable beneficiary designation, a completed transfer with some speculative value has occurred. However, no gift tax deduction is available since the charity does not receive all of Jeff's interest in the policy.

Giving an Existing Life Insurance Policy to a Qualifying Charitable Organization. If a donor gives an existing life insurance policy to a qualifying charitable organization, he or she will enjoy both the federal gift tax charitable deduction and the federal income tax charitable deduction. The amount of the deductions will equal the value of the policy (see the discussion in chapter 2)—that is, either the policy's (1) replacement cost or (2) its interpolated terminal reserve plus the pro rata unearned premium. In addition, all subsequent premiums the donor pays will be deductible. Note, however, that the reduction rules may apply to the size of the income tax deduction. If a life insurance policy was sold at a gain, the gain will be taxed as ordinary income. Therefore a gift of life insurance is a gift of ordinary-income property. Assuming the value of the policy (interpolated terminal reserve plus unearned premium on the date of the sale) exceeds the policyowner's net premium payments, the deduction for a gift of a policy is equal to the policyowner's cost basis (cost)—that is, the net premium payments paid by the policyowner.

The percentage limitations may have an impact on the premium payments made by the donor. Premiums the donor pays directly to the insurer will probably be considered contributions for the use of a charity and thus subject to the 30 percent limitation of the donor's contribution base. The donor could avoid this result by sending a check directly to the charity and having it pay the premium to the life insurance company.

Under these circumstances, the estate tax consequences depend on when the donor-insured dies. If the insured dies within 3 years, the proceeds are included in his or her gross estate with an offsetting estate tax charitable deduction. If the donor survives the 3-year period following the donation, the death benefits are excluded from his or her gross estate.

> *Example:* Mary White has had a $100,000 whole life policy with a cash value of $31,522 in force for close to 20 years. Mary, being charitably inclined, makes a gift of the policy to the local youth center, a qualifying charity. She receives a federal gift tax deduction and a federal income tax deduction (subject to the limitations discussed previously) equal to the $31,522 cash value of the policy. If her aggregate net premiums paid were $25,000, this amount would be the limit of her current income tax deduction due to the reduction rules for ordinary-income property.

Purchasing a New Life Insurance Policy Naming the Charity as Owner and Beneficiary. Suppose the donor-insured applies for a policy naming a qualified charity as owner and beneficiary, or the donor contributes funds with the expectation that the charity will apply for insurance on his or her life. All initial payments and subsequent premium payments by the donor should qualify for the gift and income tax charitable deductions. Presumably, this strategy will also avoid the 3-year rule for inclusion of life insurance proceeds in the insured's gross estate.

The IRS recently disallowed this type of deduction in Ltr. 9110016. The case involved a former New York State law that prohibits anyone from obtaining an insurance policy on an individual's life if the person or entity acquiring the policy does not have an insurable interest in the individual's life. The IRS reasoned that the charity would not automatically receive the proceeds since the estate and heirs could, presumably, invoke the insurable interest law and prevent the insurer from paying the benefit to the charity. The IRS was heavily criticized for this ruling and subsequently revoked it (Ltr. 9147040) when New York retroactively amended its insurable interest laws and the donor who requested the ruling backed out of the proposed transaction. Several states have changed their laws as a result of this private ruling.

When planning a transaction of this kind, it is important to examine state law. If there is uncertainty, it is prudent to request a ruling. These concerns should not affect the transfer of an existing policy (as discussed above) that was not purchased to be immediately donated to charity.

Donation of Policy Dividends. Many donors, although charitably inclined and under the impression that the use of life insurance would be an appropriate way to make charitable gifts, may not be in a position to turn an entire insurance portfolio over to a charitable organization. Some donors may not even feel comfortable using a single policy for this purpose. It is still possible, however, for a donor to protect his or her family and at the same time make periodic cash donations to a specific charity by paying annual policy dividends directly to the charity. The donor would be able to retain control over the disposition of the policy proceeds, and the charitable organization's interest would be limited to a right to receive annual cash dividends.

Use of Group Term Life Insurance

There are many situations in which the only life insurance coverage a client owns is his or her group insurance that an employer provides. In addition, many well-insured executives or professionals participate in a group-term life insurance plan provided by their employers. According to Sec. 79 of the Internal Revenue Code, employees must include the cost of group term life insurance coverage in excess of $50,000 in their taxable income. The tax liability generated by this "economic benefit" must be paid with after-tax dollars. The economic benefit is determined by a rate table in the Sec. 79 regulations, and it may be unrelated to the actual cost of the insurance coverage.

This problem is particularly painful to the older executive, professional, or businessowner who has built a large estate. All too often, these individuals find the income tax rates imposed on the excess Sec. 79 coverage to be exorbitant. In fact, the income taxes may exceed the cost of individual term insurance in some cases. To make matters worse, the Sec. 79 benefits are includible in the participant's gross estate unless they have been irrevocably assigned more than 3 years prior to the insured's death.

To avoid this result, the charitably inclined group term life participant may name a qualified charitable organization as beneficiary of the group insurance coverage in excess of the $50,000. With this approach, the donor will be able to give a gift to his or her favorite charity and at the same time eliminate the federal income tax liability on the amount otherwise taxable under Sec. 79. Moreover, the proceeds will either be excluded or deductible from his or her estate.

Planned-Giving Programs with Life Insurance

Many charities have adopted planned-giving programs involving life insurance. These programs generally involve a high-visibility recognition campaign to attract target donors, to encourage them to develop an annual giving habit, and to provide substantial deferred benefits to the charity. Charities are, of course, concerned about deferring all of their receipts, and a life insurance program generally balances some current needs with the long-term deferred-giving program needs.

Usually, the plan is kept simple. There are standard policy sizes (for example, $50,000), and the variations are limited to specific increments such as $25,000 or $50,000. To keep the policies on track with the charity's current needs, there are generally restrictions on the types of policies and the assumptions used in the policy illustrations. If the assumptions are too aggressive, the charity's deferred benefit may be jeopardized. Waiver of premium is also usually included. The charity is the owner and beneficiary of the policies, and generally, an administrator is installed to monitor the program and collect the periodic premiums.

Retaining Flexibility with Donations of Life Insurance

Many donors are concerned with making irrevocable transfers to a selected charity. This concern is magnified for deferred gifts such as life insurance benefits that will not be transferred to the charity until many years in the future. For example, the charity may lose its tax-exempt status or the donor may change his or her feelings toward the charity. The problem with retaining flexibility is that the income tax deduction is unavailable unless the donor gives up his or her entire interest in the policy.

There are some possibilities, which we'll discuss briefly here, that might solve this problem.

Retained Right to Substitute or Add Charitable Beneficiaries. In one private ruling (Ltr. 8030043) the insured entered into a special arrangement with the insurer and the charity to permit the donor to add or substitute charities in conjunction with the original charity. The IRS ruled that the income tax deduction was permissible.

Private Foundations. One method to preserve the right to select charitable recipients is the use of a private foundation. If a policy is contributed to a private foundation, the income tax deduction should be available, subject to the lower percentage limitations applicable to private charities.

Charitable Trusts. The donor may consider creating an irrevocable charitable trust with an independent trustee. The distributions of the trust are limited to qualified charities, but the amounts, timing, and charities can be placed in the discretion of the trustee. The income tax deduction should be available for contributions to the irrevocable trust, subject to the 30 percent limitation for donations for the use of charity.

Substantiation and Valuation of Life Insurance Donations

Most life insurance donations will be relatively straightforward. The charity will generally be given the policy, and the donor will pay the premiums. However, there are some issues that should be addressed. The first is the requirement of a written acknowledgment by the charity for a contribution of $250 or more. The charity should be prepared to do this at the time the policy is donated. The insurance company should provide the charity and/or the insured with Form 712, indicating the policy value on request. (Remember, the insured's income tax deduction is limited to the lesser of the policy's value or his or her cost basis in the policy due to the reduction rules for ordinary-income property.) But what about the acknowledgment of subsequent premiums of $250 or more? If the donor-insured pays these directly to the insurance company, the charity may be unaware of the timing and amount of the payments. A cancelled check will not suffice to substantiate a deduction. It is advisable, therefore, to have the donor make the payment to the charity and let the charity pay the insurance company. The charity will then have knowledge of the payment and can give a contemporaneous receipt to the donor-insured. In a formal life insurance planned-giving campaign, this will generally not be a problem since an administrator will collect and monitor the premiums for the charity.

A second issue arises when the value of the policy claimed as an income tax deduction exceeds $5,000. In this instance, the donation must meet the qualified appraisal rules. Of course, the appraisal should be simple and inexpensive since the insurance company will provide Form 712, indicating the value at the time of the donation. Nevertheless, Forms 8283 and 712 should be included with the donor's return if the income tax deduction exceeds $5,000.

Opportunities Outside of Life Insurance

In addition to the life-insurance-related planning opportunities in the charitable area, there are several other planning techniques available. In this chapter we will examine these two basic concepts:

- the improvement of an estate's liquidity position
- qualification under Secs. 303, 2032A, or 6166

Improvement of an Estate's Liquidity Position

The concept of estate liquidity is important for planners because costs must be paid relatively soon after a decedent's death. Under the tax law the federal estate tax a particular estate owes must be paid (under general circumstances) within 9 months of the date of death. If an estate consists of liquid assets such as cash, marketable securities, or life insurance, the executor or administrator of the estate will have no difficulty meeting payment deadlines. However, liquid assets are often the exception to the rule; many estates are composed of such illiquid

Chapter 7 The Basics of Charitable Giving

assets as real estate or business interests. Often, in order for the personal representative to meet payment obligations, estate assets must be liquidated at a forced sale, usually at a loss.

Making charitable contributions can significantly improve an estate's liquidity position for two reasons:

- Charitable donations can remove illiquid assets from a decedent's estate, which will reduce federal estate tax liability.
- Charitable contributions reduce federal income tax liability, which in turn causes more cash to be available.

Example: Frick and Frack are identical twins, and even though they are adults, they are still very close. Each is in the top income tax bracket for federal income tax purposes, and each has an estate of $900,000, consisting of $100,000 in real estate, $700,000 attributable to a business interest, and $100,000 in XXY, Inc., stock, a publicly traded issue. Frick dies on February 12, 1996, in a domestic air disaster. His federal estate tax liability is $96,450. The XXY, Inc., stock along with some other assets will have to be liquidated by Frack, Frick's executor, in order to pay the federal estate tax due.

Frack learns from Frick's mistake and immediately makes a charitable contribution of the real estate he owns. As a result, he enjoys a federal income tax deduction of $100,000, which in his bracket amounts to $33,000 in cash. Assume Frack dies in 1998. Frack's gross estate has been decreased by $67,000 (that is, the $100,000 fair market value of the real estate minus the $33,000 in extra cash in the estate). His federal estate tax liability is decreased, and his estate liquidity is increased.

The computations in each estate are as follows:

Frick's Estate

Gross estate	$900,000
Final expenses	(45,000)
Adjusted gross estate	$855,000
Federal estate tax (from the tax table)	$289,250
Applicable credit amount	(192,800)
Federal estate tax owed	$ 96,450
Liquid assets available	$100,000
Estate expenses	141,450
Liquidity of estate	($ 41,450)

<u>Frack's Estate</u>

Gross estate	$833,000
Final expenses	(41,650)
Adjusted gross estate	$791,350
Federal estate tax	
(from the tax table)	$264,427
applicable credit amount	(202,050)
Federal estate tax owed	$ 62,377
Liquid assets available	$133,000
Estate expenses	104,027
Liquidity of estate	$ 28,973

Qualification under Secs. 303, 2032A, or 6166

Three provisions in the Internal Revenue Code offer a taxpayer certain relief from tax liability:

- Sec. 303 allows a redemption of stock by a corporation to result in favorable income tax treatment to the person selling the stock.
- Sec. 2032A allows real property used in a trade or business, ranchland, or farmland to be valued for federal estate tax purposes under a formula reflecting actual value, rather than being valued at the "highest and best use."
- Sec. 6166 allows an estate to take a total of 14 years and 9 months to pay the federal estate tax due the IRS.
- Sec. 2033A allows an exclusion for some or all of a family-held business's value from the gross estate.

Before any of these relief provisions may be used, specific percentage prerequisites must be met. For Sec. 303, more than 35 percent of a decedent's adjusted gross estate must consist of a business interest. For Sec. 2032A, at least 50 percent of the value of the gross estate must consist of the value of real property, and a minimum of 25 percent of the adjusted value of the gross estate must consist of qualifying real property. For Sec. 2033A, the value of the business included in the gross estate must exceed 50 percent of the adjusted gross estate. For Sec. 6166, more than 35 percent of a decedent's adjusted gross estate must consist of a business interest.

These special provisions for substantial tax reduction can be tremendously helpful to a taxpayer, but frequently they are not available because the estate cannot meet the percentage tests. If the estate makes charitable contributions of property, which need not be retained by the estate for the percentage test (generally, the donations would have to be made more than 3 years prior to death), then the estate may be brought into compliance.

Example: John Ashford died with an adjusted gross estate of $1 million. This consisted of a business interest valued at $310,000, $300,000 in cash, securities valued on the date of death at $200,000, and real property valued at $190,000. John's executor wants to use the installment payout provisions of Sec. 6166. However, because only 31 percent of the value of the adjusted gross estate represents a business interest, Sec. 6166 will not be available.

If John had provided that lifetime cash gifts were to be made to a qualifying charity, it would have been possible through careful planning to have brought the total value of the adjusted gross estate down to a level so that the business interest represented more than 35 percent of it. In this way, Sec. 6166 would have become available.

NOTES

1. *Charitable Giving and Solicitation,* Stewart et. al., Maxwell MacMillan, 1990, ¶ 510.
2. Stephen R. Leimberg, "Death-Sensitization for the Estate Planner," *Journal of the American Society of CLU & ChFC,* vol. XXX, no. 2 (April 1976).
3. *Restatement of Contracts* 2d, §90.
4. IRC Secs. 170(c), 2055(a), and 2522(a).
5. The only exceptions to this rule would be certain transfers to foreign cemetery companies described in Sec. 170(c)(5) and any special provisions in U.S. treaties with particular foreign nations. The U.S.-Canada income tax treaty, for example, permits U.S. citizens to deduct certain transfers to Canadian charitable organizations.
6. *Estate of Marine v. Commissioner,* 93-1 USTC par. 60,131 (4th Cir. 1993). However, see *Longue Vue Foundation v. Commissioner,* 90 TC 150 (1989) for a case that went against the IRS even though the forced heirship laws of Louisiana could have permitted the children of the donor to claim an interest in the estate, effectively making the charitable bequest voidable. The children did not file timely claims, but the tax court held that the mere voidability of the donation did rise to the level of a contingency that causes the deduction to be denied.
7. Rev. Proc. 82-39, 1982-2, C.B. 759. Ltr. 9005001.
8. These limitations apply only to contributions of property that would produce long-term capital gain. If such a sale would produce anything other than long-term capital gain, (1) the donor's deduction is reduced to his or her cost basis, and (2) the deduction is subject to the 50 percent limitation in the same manner as a gift of cash.
9. While the percentage limitations may seem relatively straightforward when taken separately, they are considerably more complex when they must be applied together in a situation where the donor makes more than one type of donation. Under these circumstances, the donations must be considered in a definite order, as follows:

   Step 1   Consider all cash, ordinary income property, short-term capital gain property, and long-term gain property (for which the election to deduct at the property's basis is made) that is contributed to public (50 percent) charities.

   Step 2   Consider cash and ordinary income property contributions to private charities or donations "or the use of" any charities.

Step 3 Consider long-term capital gain property contributions to public (50 percent) charities.

Step 4 Consider long-term capital gain property contributions to private charities.

10. James D. Percy, "Caritable Giving through Life Insurance," F*inancial and Estate Planners lQuarterly,* no. 419 (spring 1986).

TABLE 7-4
Charitable Giving

Charitable Giving Device	Income Tax (IRC § 170) (General 5-year carryforward for excess)	Gift Tax (IRC §2522)	Estate Tax (IRC §2055)
1. Outright gift during life (subject to 2, 3, and 4 below).	Deductible up to 50% of contribution base for public charities; for other charities up to lesser of 30% of contribution base or the excess of 50% of contribution base over those charitable gifts to public charities that are deductible up to 50%.	Fully deductible.	Not includible in gross estate if completed during lifetime.
2. Outright gift during life of short-term capital gain property or of ordinary income property (including Sec. 306 stock).	Amount of short-term capital gain or of ordinary income not deductible; only tax basis is deductible up to percentage limit under 1 above.	Fully deductible.	Not includible in gross estate if completed during lifetime.
3. Outright gift during life of long-term capital gain property.	Unless gift falls under 4 below, deductible up to percentage limit under 1 above, provided that the 50% limit is allowable only if election is made to reduce deduction by the amount of the long-term capital appreciation; otherwise limit of 30% of taxpayer's adjusted gross income for the year applies (unless contribution is to a private charity to which a 20% limit is applicable).	Fully deductible.	Not includible in gross estate if completed during lifetime.
4. Outright gift during life of tangible personal property to be used by donee-charity in unrelated manner.	Deduction must be reduced by the amount of the long-term capital appreciation; balance deductible up to percentage limit under 1 above.	Fully deductible	Not includible in gross estate if completed during lifitme

TABLE 7-4 (Cont'd.)

Charitable Giving Device	Income Tax (IRC § 170) (General 5-year carryforward for excess)	Gift Tax (IRC §2522)	Estate Tax (IRC §2055)
5. Bargain sale (sale of appreciated property to charity for less than fair market value).	Treated as part sale/part gift. Basis must be allocated between portion sold and portion donated; thus some capital gain tax may result. Donated portion deductible up to percentage limit under 1 above (IRC §1011). Appreciated property rules under 2–4 above apply to donated portion.	Donated portion fully deductible.	Sale portion not taxable, but proceeds of sale portion are taxable to extent found in estate; donated portion is not includible in gross estate if completed during lifetime.
6. Inter vivos lead trust to pay income to charity with remainder to noncharitable donee.	Present value of income interest deductible only if the income is currently taxed to the grantor and only if the income interest is either a guaranteed annuity or a fixed percentage of the fair market value of the property (unitrust); deductible up to the percentage limitations described in 1–4 for the present value of the charitable interest.	Present value of income interest fully deductible if in the form of a guaranteed annuity or is a fixed percentage of the fair market value of the property (unitrust).	Income interest not includible. Remainder not includible in gross estate unless taxable powers or interests are reserved or retained by grantor. No charitable deduction to the extent included.

TABLE 7-4 (Cont'd.)

Charitable Giving Device	Income Tax (IRC § 170) (General 5-year carryforward for excess)	Gift Tax (IRC §2522)	Estate Tax (IRC §2055)
7. Inter vivos trust with remainder to charity.	Present value of remainder interest deductible only if current noncharitable trust benefits are in the form of a charitable remainder annuity trust, a charitable remainder unitrust, or a pooled-income fund; deductible up to percentage limits under 1–4 above.	Present value of remainder interest fully deductible if current noncharitable trust benefits are in the form of a charitable remainder annuity trust, a charitable remainder unitrust, or a pooled-income fund.	Some of principal may be included in donor's gross estate if noncharitable benefits are retained for life under Sec. 2036. Deductible to extent of inclusion.
8. Gift during life not in trust of farm or personal residence to charity with right reserved to donor to live there for life.	Deductible up to percentage limit under 1 above, subject to adjustment for depreciation.	Remainder interest fully deductible.	Remainder interest fully deductible.
9. Testamentary transfer by outright bequest or beneficiary designation to public charity.	N/A	N/A	Fully deductible without percentage limitations.

TABLE 7-4 (Cont'd.)

Charitable Giving Device	Income Tax (IRC § 170) (General 5-year carryforward for excess)	Gift Tax (IRC §2522)	Estate Tax (IRC §2055)
10. Testamentary trust with remainder to public charity.	N/A	N/A	Present value of remainder interest deductible only if noncharitable benefits are in the form of a charitable remainder annuity trust, a charitable remainder unitrust, or a pooled-income fund; fully deductible without percentage limitations.
11. Testamentary lead trust to pay income to charity.	N/A	N/A	Present value of income interest fully deductible if in the form of a guaranteed annuity or is a fixed percentage of the fair market value of the property unitrust); fully deductible without percentage limitations.

8

Sophisticated Methods of Charitable Giving

Chapter Outline

INTRODUCTION 254
DONATIONS OF LESS THAN DONOR'S ENTIRE
    INTEREST IN THE PROPERTY 254
    Undivided Portion of Donor's Entire Interest 256
    Remainder Interest in Personal Residence or Farm 256
CHARITABLE REMAINDER TRUSTS (CRTs) 259
    General Guidelines 259
    Annuity Trust versus Unitrust 265
    Taxation of Annuity or Unitrust Payments 268
    Investment of CRT's Principal 269
    Determining Tax Deduction for CRT 270
PLANNING APPLICATIONS OF CRTs 271
    CRTs and Wealth Replacement Trusts 271
    Using a CRT to Supplement a Retirement Plan 274
    Transferring a Closely Held Corporation through a CRT 280
POOLED-INCOME FUND 281
    Mechanics of Pooled-Income Fund 281
    Ramifications of Pooled-Income Fund 282
CHARITABLE LEAD TRUST 282
    Inter Vivos Charitable Lead Trust 283
    Testamentary Charitable Lead Trust 283
QUALIFIED CONSERVATION DONATIONS 284
    Types of Conservation Donations 284
    Permissible Conservation Purposes 285
    Tax Requirements for Deductible Conservation Donation 285

INTRODUCTION

In the previous chapter we discussed the technical rules for charitable donations that are relatively straightforward. In most instances, the discussion focused on donations that were directly provided to a selected charity, either immediately through an inter vivos donation or at the donor's death by bequest or beneficiary designation. In this chapter we will examine charitable planning techniques that involve more complex designs. Generally, the type of donations discussed in this chapter will include both charitable and noncharitable beneficiaries—often referred to as split-interest donations.

The planning opportunities created by these sophisticated charitable giving methods are exciting to both the donor and charity. The donor may receive a combination of tax deductions that will increase the donor's current cash flow and improve the liquidity position of his or her estate. When combined with the appropriate investment choices, such as life insurance or annuity products, these charitable methods can provide extremely attractive economic forecasts for the donor and his or her family.

However, it is the author's belief that the attractiveness of these charitable giving methods should not lead to their abuse. The donor should have a charitable intent before the donation is considered. There should also be something of real value in the process for the charity. Congress and the IRS are not unaware of the potential abuse of the charitable deduction. There are a myriad of tax penalties for inappropriate actions by the donor and the charity—particularly in the areas of split-interest donations or private foundations. Congress will certainly act again with new legislation if there is a concern that specific charitable giving methods are being abused. The IRS also has the authority to issue rulings on charitable transactions and has taken action to prevent charitable giving methods when the primary purpose is tax avoidance and the benefit to charity is dubious. Finally, the attorney general of the state where the charity is located is also empowered by state law to take action to protect the charity's interest in any given donation. This authority has been used with varying degrees of success to protect the charity in deferred or split-interest donations.

The material in this chapter focuses primarily on the positive aspects of the sophisticated charitable giving methods. The potential tax penalties or other problem areas will be mentioned only as a warning. Please be aware that appropriate tax counsel is essential when planning the types of charitable donations discussed in this chapter.

DONATIONS OF LESS THAN DONOR'S ENTIRE INTEREST IN THE PROPERTY

A donor may wish to donate a portion of his or her interest in a specific property to a charity but also retain an interest in the property. Alternatively, a donor may wish to make a donation to a charity but arrange the transfer in such a

Chapter 8 Sophisticated Methods of Charitable Giving 255

way that there is a private purpose as well. In either of these situations, no federal gift, estate, or income tax charitable deduction will generally be allowed for the value of the interest that is transferred for charitable purposes. In other words, a donor must generally donate *all* of the interests he or she has in the donated property or there will be no charitable deduction. Fortunately, there are exceptions to this general rule and these will be discussed throughout the remainder of the chapter. The art or science of charitable planning is to accomplish the donor's personal and charitable planning goals while preserving the appropriate charitable deduction(s).

No federal tax charitable deductions will be allowed for the value of the interest transferred for charitable purposes unless the transaction falls into one of the following special categories:

- the undivided portion of a donor's entire interest
- the remainder interest in a personal residence or farm
- the charitable remainder trust
- the pooled-income fund
- the charitable lead trust
- the qualified conservation easement

Before examining each of these categories in detail, let's first look at some typical situations in which a taxpayer has made a transfer of property for both charitable and noncharitable purposes, or has made a transfer for charitable purposes but has also retained an interest in the property.

Example: Last year Larry created a trust that, by its terms, was to pay the income to Wilma, his wife, for life. The remainder interest was vested in a charitable organization at the time the transfer was made. Larry has transferred interests in the same property for both charitable and noncharitable purposes. No federal gift or income tax charitable deduction will be permitted.

Example: Randi transferred a tract of income-producing real estate to her brother by gift, reserving the right to the rentals for a term of 25 years. After 6 years, Randi transferred the right to the remaining rentals to a charitable organization. Randi has transferred an interest in the income-producing real estate for both charitable and noncharitable purposes. Accordingly, no federal income or gift tax charitable deduction will be available.

Example: Jim left a qualified terminable interest property (QTIP) trust in his will for the benefit of his wife, Jane. The QTIP provided Jane with a qualifying income interest for life with a remainder to a charitable organization. At the time of Jim's death, the property left to the QTIP will qualify for the estate tax marital deduction if his executor makes the QTIP election. However, the remainder interest left to the charity will not qualify for the estate tax charitable deduction since Jim has left his interest in the property for both charitable and noncharitable purposes.

In spite of the foregoing rules pertaining to the availability of the federal tax charitable deductions, there are special situations that will allow for these deductions even though the donor retains an interest or splits the contribution between both charitable and noncharitable recipients. Let's look at these special situations.

Undivided Portion of Donor's Entire Interest

If a taxpayer transfers his or her entire interest in a property to a charity, the federal income, gift, and/or estate tax charitable deductions will be available. However, if the transfer consists of anything less than this "undivided portion of the donor's entire interest," as the law states, there will be no such deduction available.

Example: Shawn Dobbs owns a valuable art collection consisting of all 33 paintings of a famous European artist. Because the collection is considered a set, it is valued at $1 million. Shawn wants to make a charitable gift of all the paintings to the local museum to be displayed there. If he makes a gift of the complete set, Shawn will enjoy a federal income and gift tax deductions. However, if he transfers fewer than all 33 paintings, it will be considered less than an undivided portion of the donor's entire interest and there will be no federal income or gift tax charitable deductions available.

One type of a partial undivided interest is a joint tenancy. Thus, if the donor makes a charitable organization a tenant in common with said donor, the income and gift tax charitable deductions should be available. The size of the deduction will depend on the percentage ownership transferred to the charity.

Example: Assume in our example above that Shawn gave the museum a 25 percent interest in the entire set of 33 paintings. Provided the museum has the right to display the entire set for 3 months each year, Shawn's contribution will qualify for an income and gift tax deduction to the extent of 25 percent of the value of the paintings.

Remainder Interest in Personal Residence or Farm

We have just discussed the general rule that the federal income, gift, and/or estate tax charitable deductions will not be available if the donor of property retains an interest in the transferred assets. However, one of the special categories we listed earlier is an arrangement in which the donor gives the charity a remainder interest in a personal residence or farm but retains an interest in this asset for life (or for a specific term of years). If this is the case, the value of the remainder interest will be deductible as a federal income, gift, or estate tax charitable deduction. (Note: To receive a deduction in these instances, the personal residence or farm must not be placed in trust.)

Personal Residences

For purposes of this special rule, the term *personal residence* means any property used by the donor as his or her personal residence. This definition includes primary and second homes qualifying as personal residences. Thus, the donor could transfer a remainder interest in his or her vacation home and receive a current income and gift tax charitable deduction.

The deductible portion of the donation includes only the personal residence and not the household effects and other tangible personal property contained in the home. In addition, the donor does not necessarily have to donate all of the real estate adjacent to the personal residence. A remainder interest donation may be limited to the personal residence and a reasonable amount of land necessary to support the residence.

The remainder interest donation works well with property the donor will not need after the retained life estate or term of years. For example, suppose the donor's children have moved away and the donor is the only family member who makes significant use of the vacation home. The transfer of the remainder interest will generate a current income tax deduction and an estate tax deduction later when the vacation home is included in the donor's gross estate. If the donated property is located in a state different from the donor's state of domicile at the time of donor's death, the transfer of the remainder interest will eliminate the need for ancillary probate in the state in which the property is located.

The deductible portion of the donation is the actuarial value of the remainder interest donated to charity. Thus, the valuation rules mandated by Sec. 7520, discussed in chapter 4, must be employed. However, the valuation of the remainder interest in a personal residence must take depreciation (on a straight-line basis) and depletion into consideration. Note that this distinguishes the valuation of the remainder interest in a personal residence from the charitable remainder trust (CRT), discussed later, in which the principal is not depreciated over the noncharitable term.

> *Example:* Marge Hatcher, aged 62, currently domiciled in Pennsylvania, recently donated a remainder interest in her vacation home, located in Ocean City, Maryland, to the state of Maryland for public purposes. The land on which the house is located is worth $60,000 and the house is worth $200,000. Thus, the value of the remainder interest, the nondepreciable portion (the land), is fairly straightforward. Assuming a Sec. 7520 rate of 7 percent, the remainder

factor for a 62-year-old individual is .34726. Therefore, the value of the remainder interest in the land is $20,836 ($60,000 multiplied by .34726). However, the depreciation in the house must be taken into account for these purposes. Assume the house has a useful remaining life of 45 years and no expected salvage value at that time. Using adjustment factors found in *Actuarial Values Gamma Volume*, IRS Publication 1459, the remainder factor in these circumstances after accounting for depreciation is .24794. (Note: The determination of the depreciation adjustment is highly complex and is beyond the scope of this reading.) Thus, the value of the remainder interest in the house is $49,588 ($200,000 multiplied by .24794). The total income and gift tax deduction for the donation of the remainder interest is $70,424 ($20,836 plus $49,588).

Now let's consider what happens later. Suppose Marge dies 4 years after the donation. The value of the home is included in her gross estate for federal estate tax purposes since she has a retained life interest under Sec. 2036(a). However, her estate will receive an estate tax charitable deduction for the value of the property since the property passes to a qualified charity at that time. If she is domiciled in Pennsylvania at the time of her death, most of her estate will be subject to its probate rules. However, the vacation home is located in Maryland and subject to probate under its rules. Normally, her Pennsylvania-based executor would incur ancillary probate costs to hire Maryland counsel to handle this matter. However, the conveyance of the remainder interest through the property's deed is a nonprobate transfer and will avoid the delays, expenses, and publicity associated with probate.

Remainder Interest in a Farm

The same special rule involving a remainder interest in a personal residence applies to a remainder interest in a farm. Specifically, if a donor gives a charitable organization a remainder interest in a farm but retains an interest in that property for life or for a term of years, the value of the remainder interest will be deductible. For purposes of this rule, the term *farm* means any land used by the donor or his or her tenant for the production of crops, fruits, or other agriculture products, or for the sustenance of livestock. Again, the remainder interest donation can include any portion of the farm acreage and does not require the transfer of the entire farm. The rules for valuing the remainder interest in a personal residence also apply to the donation of a remainder interest in a farm.

Example: Thomas Hunt wishes to make a gift of his farm to the Department of Agriculture to be used as an experimental vegetable growth area. Thomas makes the charitable gift today but structures the arrangement in such a way that he may live on the farm until his death.

The value of the remainder interest in the farm will be deductible for federal income and gift tax purposes.

CHARITABLE REMAINDER TRUSTS (CRTs)

If property is given to a trust with a qualifying charity named as the immediate beneficiary, it is logical that a federal income and gift tax deduction, subject to the limitations discussed in the previous chapter, will be available at once to the donor. However, there are many situations in which a donor, although wishing a charity to receive certain property eventually, wants a family member to enjoy the property first.

Example: Harold and Phyllis Johnson are a childless couple with no surviving heirs. Harold wants Phyllis to enjoy his property upon his death but ultimately wants the property to pass to a local charity.

If the charity receives the property either directly or as an immediate beneficiary of a trust, the federal income and gift tax deduction will be equal to the fair market value of the property on the date of the gift. But if there is to be a noncharitable beneficiary in advance of the property's passing to charity, how is the income tax deduction to be determined and when may it be taken?

These situations are known as *split-interest arrangements* and are controlled by Secs. 170(f)(2)(A), 2055(c)(2), and 2522(c)(2) of the Internal Revenue Code. These provisions in the tax law state that gifts of a remainder interest in trust are deductible for federal income, estate, or gift tax purposes only if the trust is a charitable remainder annuity trust, charitable remainder unitrust, or pooled-income fund (discussed later). The valuation rules mandated by Secs. 664 and 7520 must be used to determine the specific amount of the deduction available. The tables of actuarial factors for calculating the deductions are found in *Actuarial Values Alpha Volume* and *Actuarial Values Beta Volume*, IRS Publications 1457 and 1458. The size of the deduction will be based on the length of the noncharitable term or the measuring life of the noncharitable life interest(s), the size of annuity or unitrust payment paid to the noncharitable beneficiary, and the Sec. 7520 rate in effect at the time of the donation.

General Guidelines

A CRT gives either the donor or another noncharitable donee a term interest or a life interest in the property transferred to the trust; the charitable organization receives the remainder interest. Several tax issues arise. For example, does the donor get a current income tax deduction? Is the transfer taxable for federal gift or estate tax purposes?

The donor of the property for an inter vivos CRT is entitled to receive both a federal income and gift tax deduction. Although it is true that the federal gift tax is not subject to any percentage limitations in the same way that the federal income tax is, both the federal income tax and the federal gift tax deduction will be limited to the actuarial value of the remainder interest. The private (noncharitable) donee will receive the right to an annuity or unitrust payment from the property for the rest of his or her life (or for a specified term of years), and at his or her death (or at the end of the noncharitable term of years) the remainder interest will pass to the named charity. If the donor is not the only noncharitable beneficiary, there may be a transfer subject to gift taxes. If the noncharitable beneficiary is the donor's spouse, the marital deduction may be available to shelter this gift from taxes. If other noncharitable beneficiaries are given vested interests in the CRT, a taxable gift will occur. In the event that the underlying property has to be included in the donor's gross estate (perhaps the donor reserved a life annuity or unitrust interest, or the term of years did not end before the donor's death), there will be a federal estate tax charitable deduction for the value of the property included in the gross estate and passing to the charitable organization.

Example: Leonard and Mildred, a married couple, have no children. Leonard transfers assets into a trust naming Mildred as beneficiary of the instrument for the balance of her life, with a local charity named as beneficiary of the property at Mildred's death. Because this is a charitable remainder trust, Leonard will receive both a federal income tax and a federal gift tax charitable deduction but only for the actuarial value of the remainder interest that will pass to the charity. Since Leonard retains no rights to the CRT, no part of the trust principal will be included in his estate at the time of his death. A transfer to Mildred is a gift for tax purposes, but a transfer to the CRT for Mildred's life benefit qualifies for a gift or estate tax charitable deduction.

Example: Ronald wants to provide retirement income to himself, but he has no heirs that he wishes to benefit. He creates a CRT and retains annuity or unitrust rights for the rest of his life. The CRT will terminate at his death, and the proceeds will be paid to a qualified charity. At the time of the transfer, Ronald will receive income and gift tax charitable deductions for the actuarial value of the remainder interest. At the time of his death, some of the principal will be included in his gross estate because of his retained life interest. However, his estate will receive an estate tax charitable deduction for the amount of the property included in his gross estate and transferred to charity.

CRTs can also be created testamentarily through the provisions of the donor's will. The testamentary CRT will provide annuity or unitrust payments to one or more noncharitable beneficiaries for a term of years or for the life of the beneficiary (lives of the beneficiaries). When the noncharitable interests in the CRT terminate, the remainder of the principal will be transferred to a qualified charity. In this instance, the donor's estate must include the assets transferred to the CRT and will receive an estate tax deduction for the actuarial value of the remainder interest.

> *Example:* Ari and Sarah Grey have been married for 40 years but have no children or other relatives. Ari wants Sarah to have full enjoyment of all estate assets for the balance of her life, with the assets passing to the American Cancer Society at her death. Ari creates a testamentary trust under the terms of his will. Sarah is to be life beneficiary with a right to annuity payments from the CRT, with all property passing to the cancer society at her death. Ari's estate may take a federal estate tax charitable deduction for the actuarial value of the remainder interest passing to the cancer society. In addition, the actuarial value of the CRT benefits provided to Sarah will qualify for the estate tax marital deduction.

Permissible Duration of CRT

The term of a CRT must be either of two forms. The trust must terminate after the measuring life or lives of its noncharitable beneficiaries, or it must terminate after a stated number of years.

If the term-of-years approach is selected, the charitable remainder trust may not have a term in excess of 20 years. There is no limitation, however, for the number of years a CRT may last if the life or lives of the noncharitable beneficiaries are used to determine its duration. A qualified charitable remainder trust may be created to make distributions to the donor and the donor's spouse for their lives and then to their children (regardless of the number of children). Thus, CRTs could span several generations. (The longer the actuarial duration of the CRT, the lower the tax deduction, however.)

In some instances, a CRT may have a term that can be altered by specified events. It is permissible for a CRT to terminate and distribute its remaining principal to the charitable remainder beneficiary in the event of a qualified contingency.

> *Example:* Harold creates a CRT under his will to provide an annual annuity to his wife, Sheila, for her life. However, if Sheila remarries, the CRT provides that her interest terminates and the remaining principal will be distributed to the charity. This is a qualified contingency under Sec. 664 and does not disqualify the CRT for the estate tax charitable deduction.

In addition, it is permissible to base the term of a CRT on the shorter of the noncharitable beneficiary's life or a fixed term (not to exceed 20 years).

Finally, Treas. Reg. Sec. 1.664-3(a)(5) permits a donor to retain a power exercisable by means of his or her will to revoke or terminate the interest of any noncharitable recipient. This solves the gift tax problem for transfers to noncharitable beneficiaries who are not the donor or his or her spouse. If the donor retains the power to revoke the transfer or affect the beneficiary's right to the CRT, the transfer is not complete for gift tax purposes, and hence no gift tax is due.

Example: Marge creates a CRT for her life with her children as successor beneficiaries for their lives. The CRT will provide an annual annuity of 7 percent of the initial value of the principal; the remainder will pass to a qualified charity. Technically, the interest of the children is a current future-interest taxable gift. To avoid gift tax consequences (other than the gift tax charitable deduction), the CRT provides that Marge can terminate the children's interest in her will. Because the gift to the children is rendered incomplete by this power, there will be no adverse gift tax consequences. However, unless Marge does revoke the interest to the children in her will, there will be a transfer subject to estate taxes at that time.

Permissible Noncharitable Interests

By definition, CRTs must make specified annual distributions to one or more beneficiaries, at least one of whom is a noncharitable organization. To qualify for federal tax deductions, CRTs must provide only specified annuity or unitrust payments to the noncharitable beneficiaries. A simple income interest or right to enjoy the trust principal will not qualify. Let's review the technical distinctions between the charitable remainder annuity trust and the charitable remainder unitrust.

Charitable Remainder Annuity Trust

A charitable remainder annuity trust (CRAT) must provide for an annual payout of a "sum certain" that is not less than 5 percent of the initial net fair market value of the trust property. The law states that the amount may be expressed as a specified dollar amount or as a percentage or fraction of the *initial* fair market value of the trust assets. The amount of the payments is fixed initially so that the payout may not vary from year to year. Also no additional property may be transferred to the trust.

Example: Suzanne Allan owns stock in EXXTO Corporation, a publicly traded oil company. Her basis in the securities is $10,000, and the stock now has a fair market value of $200,000. Suzanne transfers these securities to a CRAT in which the municipality where she lives is named as the charitable recipient. The trust provides for an annual payment to Suzanne of $10,000 per year for the balance of her life, with the remainder interest to pass to the municipality. The trust is a valid charitable remainder annuity trust because it provides for the minimum 5 percent annual annuity payment.

Charitable Remainder Unitrust

The charitable remainder unitrust (CRUT) must provide for a payout each year of a fixed percentage of at least 5 percent of the annually determined net fair market value of its assets. Therefore the amount of the annual payment in the unitrust situation will vary from year to year depending on the value of the corpus of the trust.

> *Example:* Robert Pine died this year. He wanted to be sure that his wife, Trini, would have adequate income after his death for the remainder of her life. Upon Trini's death, Robert wants his estate assets to pass to a local charity. Robert's will leaves his residuary estate, which is valued at $2 million, to a CRUT. The CRUT will provide Trini with 7 percent of the annual value of the principal held by the CRUT. The estate receives an estate tax charitable deduction for the actuarial value of the remainder interest that is left to charity and a marital deduction for the share that is left to Trini. The CRUT will distribute $140,000 in the initial year to Trini. Thereafter, the CRUT's principal must be revalued annually to determine Trini's distribution. Upon Trini's death, the trust principal then remaining will pass to the charity.

Table 8-1 shows a comparison of the requirements for charitable remainder annuity trusts and charitable remainder unitrusts.

New Limitations on Noncharitable Benefits from CRTs

TRA 97 added new limitations to prevent abuse from the use of charitable remainder trusts. The rules were designed to ensure that the charity will actually receive something when a deductible contribution is made in the form of a CRT. The new rules limit the size of the annual payout under a "50 percent" rule and the size of the charitable remainder under a "10 percent minimum" rule.

50 Percent Rule. A trust can no longer qualify as a CRAT if the annuity payout for any year is greater than 50 percent of the initial fair market value of the trust's assets. The same rule limits a CRUT payout to 50 percent or less of the annual value of the principal. Any trust that fails this 50 percent rule will not qualify for the benefits of a CRT; most important, the income tax deduction will be lost. A trust failing the 50 percent rule will be treated as a complex trust, and all income will be taxed to its beneficiaries or to the trust immediately instead to the beneficiaries through the tier system, discussed below, which would defer taxes until distributions of the annuity or unitrust amounts were actually made to the beneficiaries.

TABLE 8-1
Comparison of Requirements for Charitable Remainder Annuity Trust and Charitable Remainder Unitrust

Annuity Trust	Unitrust
Irrevocable trust	(Same)
Noncharitable life estate or term for up to 20 years	(Same)
Remainder interest passing to an organization described in Code Sec. 2055(a)	(Same)
Beneficiary (noncharitable) must be living at the creation of the trust	(Same)
Income payments to noncharitable beneficiaries must be made at least annually	(Same)
Payout must be at least 5 percent of the value of the trust assets, determined on the basis of the initial fair market value	Payout must be at least 5 percent of the value of the trust assets, determined annually
Annuity amount (and percentage) will not fluctuate with value of assets	Annuity amount (but not percentage) may fluctuate with value of assets
Annuity must be paid out of principal if the income is insufficient	Annuity may, but does not have to, be paid out of principal if the income is insufficient, but deficits must be made up in later years in which there is more than enough income to meet payout requirements
No additional contributions may be made after creation of the trust	Additional contributions may be made on specified terms and conditions
Current income tax deduction for actuarial value of remainder	(Same)
No capital-gains tax on transfer of appreciated property to the trust	(Same)
Trusts are tax exempt, except for unrelated business income	(Same)
If income interest is retained, corpus is included in grantor's estate with charitable deduction	(Same)
If other noncharitable beneficiaries survive the donor, the estate tax deduction (and amount in gross estate) is reduced by value of their interests	(Same)

Source: Howard M. and Martha Altschuller Zaritsky, *New Estate Planning Handbook with Forms and Tables* (Englewood Cliffs, NJ: Prentice-Hall, Inc., 1980), pages 269–270.

10 Percent Rule. The actuarial value of the charitable remainder interest with respect to any donation to a CRAT or CRUT must now be at least 10 percent of the net fair market value of such property transferred in trust on the date of the contribution to the trust. This 10 percent test is measured on each transfer to the CRT. A CRT that meets the 10 percent test on the date of transfer will not subsequently fail to meet that test if interest rates have declined in the interval between the trust's creation and the death of a measuring life. The new law provides some transitional relief and specifically authorizes reformations of testamentary CRTs to meet the 10 percent rule.

Need for Careful Monitoring. These new rules create the need to carefully monitor the numbers for a plan involving CRTs. Unfortunately, the rules may eliminate some planning techniques in which a high payout is desired or a noncharitable benefit would have been provided for the lifetime of a young individual (or joint lifetimes of more than one individual) and the 10 percent rule cannot be satisfied.

Annuity Trust versus Unitrust

Although both the annuity trust and the unitrust are based upon the same provisions in the tax law and exist for the same reasons, there are practical distinctions between the two types of trusts. Which is better for your client?

If a client is particularly concerned with being assured of a fixed payout, the charitable remainder annuity trust is the better choice. The payout will not increase if the value of the trust assets increases during a period of inflation, and the payout will not decrease if the value of the trust corpus falls during an economic downturn.

On the other hand, if the client is more interested in an approach in which the payout depends on the annual value of the trust assets, the charitable remainder unitrust is more appropriate.

Payout Flexibility with CRTs

A typical objection to CRTs is the rigid unitrust or annuity payment structure. A CRAT or CRUT generally must provide an annual payment that must meet the 5 percent minimum threshold. Depending on the trust investment, this could create a situation in which the principal will be expended to make the annuity or unitrust payments.

Payment Reduction at Death of Noncharitable Beneficiary. When there is more than one noncharitable beneficiary, a CRT can provide for noncharitable benefits to be reduced if one of those beneficiaries dies. There are some specific requirements before a reduction will qualify. First, a proportionate amount of the principal must be accelerated to the charitable remainder beneficiary. Second, the reduction must be pro rata with respect to the remaining noncharitable beneficiaries. Finally, the payout after the reduction must continue to meet the 5 percent test.

Example: Paul Patriarch left a testamentary CRAT in his will for the benefit of his three children, Patty, Paula, and Peter, for their lives. The CRAT was initially funded with $900,000 and provided for an annuity of $75,000 to be divided among his children in equal shares. The CRAT further provided that the annuity be reduced proportionately at the death of any of Paul's children. The CRAT meets the minimum 5 percent threshold. Suppose Peter dies; the CRAT will then distribute one-third of the principal to the charitable remainder beneficiary. The annuity payout will be reduced to $50,000 to be shared equally by Patty and Paula.

CRT Payments to Class of Beneficiaries. A CRT can be paid to a class of noncharitable beneficiaries. For example, the donor could provide for annuity payments from a CRAT to be divided among his or her children. However, all members of the class must be alive and ascertainable at the time the trust is created. In addition, if any of the noncharitable beneficiaries receive a stated annuity or unitrust payment, that stated payment must meet the 5 percent threshold.

Can a CRT have "spray" provisions for a group of noncharitable beneficiaries at the discretion of the trustee? The answer depends upon who is exercising the discretion to determine the shares of each beneficiary. A grantor trust (described later in chapter 12) will not qualify as a CRT. Thus, for a trust to avoid grantor trust status, the discretionary power to spray annuity or unitrust payments between beneficiaries can be held only by an independent trustee. The trustee must be someone other than the donor or someone related or subservient to the donor as defined in the grantor trust rules.

Net-Income Unitrusts (NIMCRUTs). The most flexible payout pattern for CRTs is the net-income unitrust, available only for CRUTs. NIMCRUTs are nothing more than a regular unitrust with an additional feature. The payout in a NIMCRUT is limited to the lesser of the stated unitrust payout percentage or the net income earned by the CRUT during the year. For this purpose, "net income" refers to the amount of income realized by the trust under accounting principles and is not limited to taxable income. What is income is determined by the applicable state's principal and income laws as modified by the CRUT document. Tax regulations state that the terms of the CRUT relating to the definition of principal and income will be respected if they do not "depart fundamentally from concepts of local law in the determination of what constitutes income." Normally, income will include rents, interest, dividends, and the like, but not capital gains. If the donor and his or her advisers wish to define income in some extraordinary fashion in the CRUT, it is highly recommended that they request a private letter ruling.

The NIMCRUT is subject to all the usual rules concerning standard CRUTs, but it has one major difference. If the NIMCRUT does not realize enough current income to make the stated unitrust payment, the annual payment is reduced to the amount of the actual income earned. Thus, the NIMCRUT protects the interests of the remainder beneficiary (that is, the charitable beneficiary) against invasion of principal, since the trustee is prohibited from invading principal for the benefit of the noncharitable beneficiaries.

The noncharitable beneficiaries of a NIMCRUT have a less valuable interest than the beneficiaries of a comparable standard CRUT. Beneficiaries of a standard CRUT receive their annual payments, regardless of the income the CRUT realizes, while the beneficiaries of a NIMCRUT might receive smaller payments, depending upon trust income. Despite this result, the NIMCRUT provisions will not increase the charitable deduction even though the charity's rights appear greater.

Fortunately, the IRS has approved NIMCRUTs with a "make-up" feature. Under the make-up feature, the noncharitable beneficiaries can receive payments in excess of the stated unitrust percentage in future years to make up arrearages that might have occurred when the NIMCRUT did not have sufficient income to pay the full stated unitrust amount. As we will discuss later, NIMCRUTs give the donor the ability to provide for a flexible payment structure through a planned investment strategy. The NIMCRUT can offer good flexibility for CRTs that will invest in property that produces little or fluctuating income and/or does not lend itself to be readily converted into cash to make a required payment (for example, an undivided parcel of real estate).

Example: Mary Garner placed $1 million into a standard CRUT. She retained the right to receive 5 percent of the annual value of the CRUT's principal each year for the rest of her life, with the remainder going to The American College. In 1997 and 1998, the trust has the following characteristics:

	1997	1998
Principal	$1,000,000	$990,000
Unitrust payment	$50,000	$49,500
Income of the CRUT	$40,000	$70,500

In 1997 and 1998, the trustee must distribute $50,000 and $49,500, respectively, to Mary. In 1997, this will mean that $10,000 must be taken from principal. In 1998, the unitrust payment can be made entirely out of 1998 income, and the remaining $21,000 of income will be added to principal. At the end of 1998 the following results have occurred:

Total unitrust payments	$99,5000
Principal remaining	$1,011,000

Assume instead that Mary chose a NIMCRUT with a make-up feature. In 1997 the NIMCRUT payment is limited to actual income, or $40,000. Again, assuming a constant market value of principal, the NIMCRUT's income in 1998 is sufficient to cover the full $50,000 unitrust payment. (Note: The principal would have remained at $1 million in this instance since the 1997 payment did not require the invasion of principal.) The 1998 payment to Mary would be $60,000, including the stated $50,000 unitrust payment and the make-up of the $10,000 arrearage for 1997.

Indirect CRT Payments for Benefit of Noncharitable Beneficiary. It is generally required that CRT annuity or unitrust payments be made directly to the noncharitable beneficiaries. This could create a concern for the donor if the beneficiary is a minor or is incompetent. Fortunately, the IRS has ruled in this instance that the CRT is not disqualified from tax deductions if the payments are made to a guardian, conservator, or trustee who is required to make use of the annuity or unitrust payments for the benefit of such donees.

Taxation of Annuity or Unitrust Payments

The CRT is a tax-exempt entity and is not subject to tax unless it has unrelated taxable income. However, the noncharitable beneficiaries will receive distributions, and these distributions will reflect the tax character of the CRT's investments. The noncharitable beneficiary is taxed under a "tier" system provided by Sec. 664(b). To determine the noncharitable beneficiary's tax implications, the trust's income items must be sorted according to the following categories: (1) ordinary income items, (2) capital gains, (3) amounts excluded from gross income (such as life insurance and tax-exempt income), and (4) trust principal. Each of these items is grouped on a net basis; losses from one category cannot offset income from another. Through the tier rules, distributions to noncharitable beneficiaries are first treated as (1) ordinary income, then (2) capital gains, then (3) tax-exempt income, and finally (4) nontaxable distribution of principal. For example, no distributions of capital gain are made until all of the trust's current and accumulated ordinary income is distributed. The amounts of each item distributed are allocated to each noncharitable beneficiary on a pro rata basis if more than one beneficiary exists.

One practical use of a CRT is to avoid capital gains on highly appreciated property by donating that property to a CRT. However, the tier system provides that, although no capital gains tax will be incurred when the tax-exempt CRT sells the property and recognizes the capital gains, the capital gains could eventually be distributed and become taxable to the beneficiaries at the time of distribution.

Investment of CRT's Principal

Tax-Exempt Investments

Tax-exempt investments by a CRT are permitted and are recommended in many instances. This type of investment has the effect of limiting the amount of taxable income distributed to the beneficiaries.

However, the IRS has successfully attacked CRTs when appreciated property is contributed to a CRT followed by its immediate sale and reinvestment in tax-exempt investments.[1] In addition, the state attorney general in at least one state has taken action against certain CRTs for investing solely in tax-exempt property for the failure to provide growth potential for the charitable remainder beneficiary.

Although investing in tax-exempt securities will limit the taxable income received by the noncharitable beneficiaries, caution is recommended. It probably would be prudent to convert the principal of the CRT to such an investment gradually. A balanced investment approach will be more likely to avoid the scrutiny of both the IRS and the state's attorney general.

Deferred Annuities

Annuities could make an excellent investment for a CRT for many reasons. For example, annuities offer a predictable and guaranteed payment pattern. The tax-exempt CRT prevents immediate tax on the buildup inside the annuity policy. (Note that the annuity loses the normal protection of Sec. 72 with respect to the tax-free buildup inside in the policy since the CRT is a nonnatural person.[2])

Deferred annuities can be used particularly advantageously with a NIMCRUT. The terms of the NIMCRUT should define the buildup inside the annuity contract as nonincome and the annuity policy distributions as income.[3] The deferred annuity policy should be designed to permit the flexibility anticipated to turn on or shut off the desired distributions from the NIMCRUT. This type of investment policy works particularly well if the noncharitable purpose of the NIMCRUT is to provide retirement income for the donor.

Closely Held Stock

Generally speaking, any property including closely held stock can be contributed to CRTs. (Note that stock in an S corporation cannot be contributed since a CRT is not an eligible S corporation shareholder.) Some particularly troublesome tax rules that apply to CRTs, however, may have an impact. Therefore, careful planning is necessary prior to considering such a donation of closely held stock.

Life Insurance

In private rulings, the IRS has permitted CRT income to be used to pay premiums on life insurance held by a CRT.[4] This could provide a way to significantly leverage a charitable gift.

Note, however, that the rulings authorizing investment in life insurance are private rulings and cannot be used as precedent. We recommend prudence in selecting life insurance as a CRT investment and, perhaps, asking for a private ruling on the specific issue.

Example: Steve Linbergh would like to ensure a comfortable retirement for his wife, Jeanne. He creates a NIMCRUT and funds it with cash. The NIMCRUT gives Steve and Jeanne the lesser of 7 percent of the annual value of the trust principal or actual trust income for the remainder of their joint lives. The NIMCRUT has make-up provisions. The cash is used to buy a single-premium life insurance policy on Steve's life.

Steve elects to receive a straight-life annuity from his qualified plan, and Jeanne consents to waive her survivor annuity. The NIMCRUT does not have any income while Steve is alive since the buildup inside the life insurance policy is not income for accounting purposes (in fact, it is doubtful that the IRS would accept trust terms defining such buildup as income). At Steve's death, the NIMCRUT's trustee receives the life insurance proceeds, which can be invested in income-producing assets. Thus, provided that the income from the new investments is sufficient, Jeanne's annual payment from the trust will generally equal or exceed 7 percent of the principal for the rest of her life due to the make-up provisions.

Determining Tax Deduction for CRT

For donations after April, 1989, the rules of Sec. 7520 must be used to value split-interest contributions. As discussed in chapter 4, these valuations will be based on updated mortality figures and the Sec. 7520 interest rate. For the purposes of the illustrations below, we will assume a Sec. 7520 interest rate of 7 percent.

For lifetime CRTs, the current income (subject to the limitations discussed in the previous chapter) or gift tax deductions are equal to the present actuarial value of the remainder interest. For testamentary CRTs, the estate tax charitable deduction is valued at the present value of the charity's remainder interest. Note that for the purposes of charitable deductions only, the donor can base his or her tax deduction on the Sec. 7520 rate in the month of the contribution or the interest rate for either of the previous 2 months.

CRATS

The CRAT's permissible deduction is highly sensitive to the Sec. 7520 rate. Generally, the value of the retained annuity is worth more as the interest rate drops. Thus, the deductible remainder interest is directly related to the interest rate.

Example: Suppose a donor transfers $1 million to a CRAT for a term of 15 years and retains an $80,000 annual annuity. Under a Sec. 7520 rate of 7 percent, the income and estate tax deduction for the remainder is $271,368. If the valuation rate is 11.6 percent, as it was in 1989 when Sec. 7520 took effect, the deduction increases to $443,288.

CRUTs

The deduction for a CRUT is generally not that sensitive to changes in the Sec. 7520 rate. The deduction is almost exclusively based on the payout percentage and mortality tables (if applicable). In fact, if payments are made once per year when the trust is valued, no adjustment is necessary for the discount rate. The only time that time-value-of-money adjustments based on the Sec. 7520 rate are required is for payments more frequent than annual and/or payments made at different times than the annual valuation of the trust principal.

Example: Suppose a 65-year-old donor places $1 million in a CRUT paying 8 percent for the donor's life. Payments are semi-annual and occur 3 months after the trust is valued (thus, time-value-of-money adjustments are required). At a 7 percent valuation rate, the deduction is $335,860, while at a Sec. 7520 rate of 11.6 percent, it is $342,210.

PLANNING APPLICATIONS OF CRTs

CRTs and Wealth Replacement Trusts

A CRT allows the donor to take advantage of the tax benefits available to charitable donations while retaining current benefits from the property. A CRT works particularly well if the donor has highly appreciated property that cannot be converted to another investment without significant capital gains taxes. Since a CRT is a tax-exempt entity, the donor can donate appreciated property and avoid the potential capital gains tax. The CRT can sell the appreciated property and convert it to a different investment (perhaps a higher-yield investment) without immediate capital gains tax. However, as we discussed above, the payments to the noncharitable beneficiaries may include this gain for tax purposes—but only as such payments are received by the beneficiaries. Neither the CRT nor the charity will incur a capital gains tax.

Example: Dagwood Donor, aged 62, and his wife Dolores, aged 60, are forecast to be in the maximum 55 percent federal estate tax bracket. Their current estate plan includes an optimal marital-deduction-formula will to take advantage of both of their applicable credit amounts. Nevertheless, they are concerned about the costs of settling their estates. They also want to retain a substantial retirement income. They feel strongly about the charitable needs of their alma mater, State U, but they don't feel wealthy enough to forgo significant wealth currently.

Dagwood and Dolores have a portfolio of securities that have substantially appreciated since they inherited these assets years before from Dagwood's parents. Some of the securities are high growth and low yield. The Donors are anxious about the fluctuations in market value of the securities and want more predictable investments for retirement. Suppose they set aside a portion of these securities for State U. The securities they select have a cost basis of $100,000 and a current market value of $1 million. The Donors are, of course, worried about the built-in capital gains should they choose to sell the securities to convert to higher-yield investments for their retirement.

Suppose Dagwood and Dolores contribute the securities to a CRUT with the remainder interest to State U, and retain a unitrust interest of 7 percent for their joint lives. The CRUT's trustee (who probably would be either of the Donors or a trusted friend or family member) can sell the securities and reinvest the proceeds held by the CRUT. Assume Dagwood has a $300,000 salary and the Donors' total annual investment income of dividends or interest is $250,000.

Result

Adjusted gross income (AGI)	$550,000
Charitable deduction	165,000
Deduction carryover to following year	30,310
Allowable itemized deduction	151,753
Income tax	134,234
Tax without CRUT donation	191,873
Capital gains tax otherwise payable	180,000

The numbers reveal that the CRUT donation creates a potential tax deduction of $195,310 for the remainder interest held by the charity. Thus, over 80 percent of the property contributed is deemed to provide valuable retirement benefits to the Donors. Due to the 30 percent AGI limitation (discussed in the previous chapter) on current contributions of appreciated property, $30,310 of the deduction is carried forward into the Donors' next tax return. The deduction is limited further by the phase-out rules for the itemized deductions.

However, in spite of these limitations, the Donors' current income taxes drop to $134,234. If they didn't make the contribution during the year, their income tax would be $191,873. Thus, the CRUT increases their cash flow by $57,639.

A contribution to a CRT works particularly advantageously with an irrevocable life insurance trust (ILIT). In this instance the ILIT is often referred to as a *wealth replacement trust*. The CRT gives the donor an opportunity to receive an immediate income tax deduction to increase cash flow, avoid built-in capital gains tax on appreciated property contributed to the CRT, and receive annual income (in the form of an annuity or unitrust) from the trust. The donor also reduces his or her estate taxes since the CRT provides an estate tax deduction.

The wealth replacement trust is used to replace the trust principal that is ultimately distributed to charity. If the donor does not wish his or her family to forgo the amount of the principal, the principal can be replaced estate tax free with life insurance benefits. The wealth replacement is funded, at least in part, by a combination of the tax benefits provided by the charitable deductions. The type of policy selected generally depends on the noncharitable benefits chosen for the CRT.

Example: Returning to the facts of our previous example of Dagwood and Dolores Donor, we have a CRUT that benefits the Donors until the death of the survivor. Thus, if the Donors did not want to divest their children of the benefit of the property, they should create a wealth replacement trust, funded with survivorship (second-to-die) coverage with a face amount of $1 million—the amount of the donated property. The policy would have a premium, for example, of $16,000 with a 10-year abbreviated payment illustration. Remember, the donation increases the Donors' current cash flow by $57,639 in the year of the contribution, which amounts to more than three premium payments. In addition, the contribution gives the Donors an estate tax deduction at their second death.

As discussed earlier, some portion of the principal of a CRT will be in the estate of a donor who retains a life interest under Sec. 2036(a). Without the contribution to the CRT, the appreciated securities would be taxable at the Donors' second death without an estate tax deduction. The present value of the premium payments is $123,886. The present value of the estate tax deduction, assuming Dagwood and Dolores live to their joint life expectancy and the securities do not appreciate further, is $129,830. Thus, on present-value terms, the estate tax savings from the donation provide the premium payments to fully replace the donated property to the Donors' children. Of course, the life insurance benefits in the wealth replacement trust are estate tax free.

The benefits of using a CRT in conjunction with a wealth replacement trust are as follows:

- The donor is able to retain a valuable benefit from the CRT for life to provide a stable retirement income.
- The donor's estate receives an estate tax charitable deduction when the donated property is included in his or her estate.
- The charity gets a substantial contribution at the termination of the CRT that the donor may not have been otherwise able to afford.
- The donor and his or her heirs never forgo the value of the donation.
- The appreciated property contributed to the CRT can be sold and converted to another investment without immediate capital gains tax.
- The donor gets valuable tax deductions to help pay for wealth replacement life insurance that is easily excluded from estate and gift taxes.

Using a CRT to Supplement a Retirement Plan

It is often recommended that a CRT be used to supplement or replace a qualified retirement plan for a high-income closely held business owner or professional. There are a number of reasons for this, most of which involve the problems associated with qualified plans.

Problems with Qualified Plans

Funding and Cost Concerns. Qualified plans are an attractive mechanism for tax-advantaged saving for retirement. However, retirement plans can be costly for the closely held business owner or professional practitioner. First, qualified plans must comply with ERISA rules, which subject the plans to reporting, participation, and fiduciary standards for plan administrators and trustees. The owners of small businesses or personal service corporations may find compliance with these rules too expensive.

Second, plan contribution limitations prevent funding unlimited benefits within the tax-deferred scheme for qualified plans. This, more likely than not, has its greatest limitation on the closely held business owner or professional who must make the decision to adopt a qualified plan. These individuals may find it necessary to incur the expense to cover their nonowner-employees, while having their own contributions limited by these rules. Most individuals who would consider the CRT as an alternative to a qualified plan are not eligible to make tax-deductible IRA contributions. In addition, most qualified retirement plan contributions must be made in cash.

Third, the income taxation of qualified plan benefits is severe during the participant's lifetime and can require complex elections. Distributions generally must begin after age 59 1/2 or not later than age 70 1/2, or penalty taxes apply.

There is a 10 percent penalty for benefits taken too early prior to age 59 1/2. Penalties are more severe for the failure to take the minimum distribution after age 70 1/2.

Problems with Transferring Retirement Plan Assets at Death. The death of the retirement plan participant creates additional problems. The tax advantages of qualified plans are designed to be helpful for providing retirement benefits. However, from an estate planning standpoint, retirement plan benefits are probably the least tax-efficient asset to transfer to the next generation. First, the usual federal transfer taxes apply. The remaining account balances of money-purchase plans, profit-sharing plans, 401(k) plans, IRA rollovers, or any survivor annuities are subject to inclusion in the deceased participant's estate at marginal estate tax rates up to 60 percent. The marital deduction defers tax only until the second death, and it is available only if plan accounts or annuities are left to the surviving spouse. In addition, plan benefits could be subject to generation-skipping transfer tax if grandchildren are potential beneficiaries. Depending on the state death tax system, the retirement plan benefits could also be subject to state inheritance or estate taxes.

The particularly disadvantageous feature of retirement plan benefits is that they are also subject to federal and, perhaps, state income taxes at the time of death. The benefits are treated as income in respect of a decedent (IRD) for income tax purposes. Retirement plan assets do not receive a basis step-up at the time of death. Thus, the recipient heir or entity will be taxed on previously untaxed distributions. In some cases, the recipient(s) will have to take the balance in the retirement plan as ordinary income very rapidly.

If the benefits are left to the surviving spouse, he or she might be able to spread the remaining payments over his or her life expectancy. If no surviving spouse exists and the decedent was over age 70 1/2, the beneficiary would have to take the balance into income at least as fast as the decedent had been receiving the payments. This payment structure is, obviously, more rapid than the schedule under which the successor-generation heirs would have to receive the payments if their life expectancies could be used. If the decedent had elected to recalculate life expectancy each year to determine his or her minimum distribution from the retirement plan, the IRD would be income taxable to the beneficiary on an accelerated basis.

There is some relief for the "double" income and estate taxes. There is an offsetting deduction from income tax when the payments are taken into income by the beneficiary under Sec. 691(c) proportionately, and to the extent that the retirement benefits created estate taxes as a result of the includibility of the IRD in the decedent's gross estate.

How a CRT Avoids Many of These Problems

A CRT will avoid most of the problems associated with qualified plans. Individual donors can select and design a plan specifically for the needs of their own families. Donations are limited by the donor's resources and the tax benefits available for the donation. Of course, annually deductible amounts to a CRT are restricted by the 50 (or 30) percent of the donor's contribution base limitation covered in the previous chapter. This will generally exceed the qualified plan contribution limits in any given year for a highly compensated individual. Appreciated property can be contributed to a CRT, while generally cash must be contributed to qualified plans. The appreciated property can be converted into income-producing property without capital gains taxation.

The CRT payments are as restricted as qualified plan distributions. The CRT payments must be 5 percent and the maximum cannot exceed 50 percent. Under the new 10 percent rule, the value of the charitable remainder must be at least 10 percent. Payments and income tax deferral can be accomplished through the NIMCRUT design and investment practice of the CRT.

The income that the noncharitable beneficiary receives is taken into account under the payout scheme selected for the CRT, and it is taxable according to the tier system that we discussed above. As opposed to a qualified plan, a CRT can distribute capital gain or tax-exempt income, depending on the CRT's investment policy.

With respect to transfer taxes at death, the estate and gift tax charitable deductions should eliminate many other transfer tax problems.

Table 8-2 compares qualified plans and CRTs.

Design Considerations for Using CRT as Replacement or Supplement for Qualified Plan

The donor will probably design a CRT with maximum flexibility and choose a NIMCRUT for the trust. He or she will most likely retain the role as trustee. (Note: There are problems with certain types of investments and self-dealing rules for a donor-trustee. These rules can be managed but are beyond the scope of this discussion.)

The NIMCRUT is favorable for several reasons. For example, the unitrust payment scheme permits contributions on a periodic basis. If the donor wants to fund the plan and spread the tax deduction over several years, he or she cannot use a CRAT.

On the other hand, a CRUT has the potential to spread the funding requirements and the related income tax deductions over several years. The contribution pattern and the resulting income tax deduction more closely resemble the funding of a qualified retirement plan.

The NIMCRUT also provides for variable payout patterns. First, any unitrust payout is based on a fixed percentage (at a minimum, 5 percent) that is applied to a fluctuating trust principal. This pattern could be viewed as making the retirement payments "inflation proof" since the unitrust payments to the noncharitable beneficiaries will rise as inflation causes the underlying trust principal to appreciate.

TABLE 8-2
Comparison of CRTs and Qualified Retirement Plans

Characteristic	CRT	Qualified Plan
Current income tax deduction	Permitted to the extent of the actuarial value of the remainder interest. Limited annually to 50 (or 30)% of the donor's AGI.	Employer can deduct contributions subject to IRC Sec. 415 limits.
Taxation of payments to recipient	Income taxable under a tier system. Taxable as ordinary income first to the extent the trust has taxable income to distribute.	Recipient taxable on previous untaxed contributions.
Inclusion in gross estate	Included under IRC Sec. 2036 to the extent the donor retained a life interest. (Actual inclusion is based on the amount of corpus necessary to support required payments.)	Included under IRC Sec. 2039 to the extent of the actuarial value of amounts left to survivors under plan beneficiary options.
Estate tax deduction	Deductible under IRC Sec. 2055 to the extent of the value passing to charity. This generally eliminates estate tax created by the inclusion.	No deduction
Retirement benefits to participant/donor and family heirs	Retirement benefits are provided to noncharitable CRT beneficiaries. Distributions may continue for the lives of the donor, his or her spouse, and successor-generation heirs. Including more heirs lowers the current tax deduction.	Retirement benefits are available under plan options. Inclusion of spouse and successor generations will decrease monthly annuity payments.

Second, the NIMCRUT design can solve the immediate problem that CRTs require the annual noncharitable payments to begin immediately and annuity or unitrust payments to be made every year during the noncharitable period. If the donor is hoping to defer distributions until retirement age, the NIMCRUT option could limit distributions to actual income. You will recall that NIMCRUT distributions can be limited to the lesser of the calculated unitrust percentage or actual trust accounting income. Thus, the NIMCRUT's investment policy could cause little or no income until the trustee chooses to invest in income-producing assets. For example, the trustee could purchase a deferred annuity. Or the trustee could invest in a mutual fund that tends to distribute very little except capital gains. If the NIMCRUT make-up provisions are chosen, higher distributions could be paid out during the retirement years if the investment policy is selected accordingly.[5]

When the donor dies, the CRT will be included to the extent that the corpus is necessary to provide the required annuity or unitrust payments. See Rev. Ruls. 76-273, 82-105.[6] The actual inclusion depends on the Sec. 7520 rate at the time of the donor's death. These rules are applicable only if the donor retained a life annuity or unitrust interest. This generally would be the case if the CRUT is replacing or supplementing a qualified retirement plan. The amount included should be offset totally by an estate tax charitable deduction for the amount passing to charity. If the donor leaves a survivor annuity (for example, the CRUT was retained for two joint lives) to his or her surviving spouse, the marital deduction is available. Inclusion of some portion of the CRT principal will then occur in the surviving spouse's estate, to be offset by an estate tax charitable deduction.

Use of CRT as Beneficiary of Qualified Plan Benefits

As discussed above, qualified plan benefits can be subject to devastating erosion by federal estate tax and income tax at the time of a plan participant's death. A donor who is facing these circumstances and has a charitable intent can provide for his or her heirs and the designated charity, and he or she can alleviate some of the estate and income tax problems. Private letter rulings have approved the use of a CRT as an IRA beneficiary.

With the transfer of retirement benefits to a CRT (actually, the CRT would become the designated beneficiary of the plan assets), the donor receives the following benefits:

- a reduction of some of the estate taxation of the retirement plan benefits since the actuarial value of the CRT remainder interest is available as an estate tax deduction. The amount of the deduction is small if the noncharitable beneficiaries are young and numerous (for example, if the donor named all of his or her children as life beneficiaries of the CRT).
- deferral of the immediate (or rapid) income taxation of the IRD at the donor's death. The income will be spread over the period of the noncharitable term, providing more deferral than might be otherwise available.

- the provision of a life annuity or unitrust interest to his or her children from the retirement plan benefits through the CRT conduit
- the possibility of more net benefits available to heirs from the retirement plan since the taxes are both reduced and deferred
- the ultimate availability of a valuable donation to a selected charity

Example: David Rouse, a widower aged 72, has a retirement plan account balance of $2 million. He is currently taking minimum distributions with maximum deferral by recalculating life expectancy each year. David has two children, currently aged 50 and 47, who will inherit his entire estate valued at $4 million, including the retirement plan account. David's estate faces many problems exacerbated by the large retirement account. If David dies this year, his estate will incur $1,358,350 of federal estate taxes and $280,400 of state death taxes (a typical state). In addition, his entire account balance will be immediately income taxable when distributed to his children. Assuming a combined federal and state income tax rate of 43 percent (not unreasonable when the size of the taxable distribution is considered), the income taxes on the retirement plan IRD are an additional $481,944 (after taking the Sec. 691(c) deduction for the estate taxes caused by the inclusion of the retirement plan in David's estate).

Assume David creates a testamentary CRAT in his will. The CRAT will provide his children with a 6 percent annual annuity ($120,000 every year) until the death of the survivor of his children. His estate would get a charitable deduction of $468,872 (assuming a Sec. 7520 rate of 7 percent) for the remainder interest provided to his chosen charity after the death of the survivor of his children. This lowers his federal estate and state death taxes to $1,248,682 and $232,188, respectively. What's more, the IRD from the retirement plan is based on the tax-exempt CRT. His children, the noncharitable beneficiaries, are taxable on trust income only to the extent of the distributions ($120,000 annually). If the IRD retains its character through the tier system, the IRD income tax deduction should be available to the beneficiaries, but the deduction will be reduced since some of the IRD was removed from estate taxation by the estate tax charitable deduction. Furthermore, since the testamentary CRAT was a probate transfer, David's estate gets the positive publicity associated with a sizable donation.

This arrangement may not be appropriate for every individual with a large account balance. Not every client will be able to assign qualified plan or IRA death benefits to a charity. If the individual is married, the Retirement Equity Act of 1984 (REA) requires (with limited exceptions) the covered participant spouse's consent (in writing) to any beneficiary designations that name someone other than that spouse as the primary beneficiary of some or all of any death benefits. The accrued benefit of a married vested participant who has been married for at least one year at death and who dies prior to the annuity starting date must be paid as a "qualified preretirement survivor annuity"— a survivor annuity payable for as long as the surviving spouse lives. However, widows, widowers, divorcees, and other single individuals are not affected by this rule. Even married individuals may want to consider naming a charity as a secondary beneficiary of retirement plan death benefits. The participant's spouse might be willing to waive his or her rights under the plan to receive the tax benefit and provide the donation to charity. That waiver, which must be in writing, should specify the charity or charities to which the retirement benefits are to be paid. Once made, the designation of the charitable beneficiary generally cannot be changed without the spouse's consent.

Transferring a Closely Held Corporation through a CRT

Earlier in this chapter, we discussed the possibility of using closely held stock as an investment in a CRT. The CRT provides some attractive possibilities with respect to selling the business or passing it on to the next generation. The benefits of the CRT, discussed previously, include the sheltering effect of a tax-exempt trust. Highly appreciated stock in a closely held corporation is ordinarily difficult to transfer while the stockholder is alive, due to the capital gains tax. Even if the stockholder dies and has the basis step-up available for his or her shares, there are income tax dividend problems if the stock is redeemed from the estate and family heirs are stockholders.

One possibility is to contribute the stock to a CRT. The capital gains tax is avoided and the stock can be redeemed by the corporation to provide funds for investment by the CRT. The donor can retain an annuity or unitrust interest for his or her retirement and receive an immediate tax deduction for the contribution.

This transaction has many complexities and should be designed carefully. The donation and the subsequent redemption cannot be prearranged. The redemption must be at fair market value, the CRT cannot be bound to redeem the stock, and the identical redemption offer must be made to all stockholders who own the same class of stock. This is necessary to avoid the self-dealing rules that could provide a 200 percent tax penalty. In addition, there must be an independent cotrustee since the CRT will contain hard-to-value assets. Many donors have applied for a private letter ruling before transferring closely held stock to a CRT.

Example: Harvey Whipple, age 65, owns 60 percent of the stock in ABC, Inc. The remaining stockholders are unrelated to Harvey. The business will have no ongoing value at Harvey's retirement, but he has been remiss in making his retirement plans. Fortunately, ABC owns some hard assets that have significant value. If Harvey sells or liquidates the business, ABC will incur capital gains tax on the corporate assets and the stockholders will incur gain on their stock. Harvey's interest was recently appraised at $1 million, and his basis in the stock is $100,000. Of course, he is unhappy with the prospect of a $900,000 capital gain. Suppose Harvey contributes his stock to a NIMCRUT paying 7 percent of the annual value of the principal each year for the rest of his life. Of course, there will be little dividend income from ABC to generate any current payments to Harvey. The NIMCRUT will provide a current income tax deduction of $366,700. To make payments available to Harvey, ABC can sell some or all of its assets and redeem the ABC stock from the NIMCRUT. Harvey will have avoided or deferred the capital gain on his stock until it is distributed to him and taxable under the tier system applicable to CRT distributions.

POOLED-INCOME FUND

We mentioned earlier that Sec. 170(f)(2) of the Internal Revenue Code will allow a federal income tax charitable deduction in deferred-receipt situations only if the vehicle was either a charitable remainder trust or a pooled-income fund. Let's look at the pooled-income fund more closely now.

Mechanics of Pooled-Income Fund

In a pooled-income fund, which is operated or controlled by a charitable organization and composed of assets donated by many contributors commingled to form one investment pool, the donor retains the right either to receive a share of the fund's income for life, or to select one or more people living at the time of the gift to receive the income. One requirement is that the remainder interest must be donated irrevocably to the charitable organization that maintains the fund. Contributed property is assigned a given number of units of participation in the fund, computed by dividing the fair market value of the donated property by the dollar value of a unit in the fund at the time of the transfer. Payments to the income beneficiary are determined by dividing the net income of the fund for the year by the total number of units of participation outstanding, and multiplying the result by the number of units of participation that are assigned to the beneficiary.

Usually the estimated income of the fund is paid out on a quarterly basis, with a final allocation within 65 days of the close of the fund's taxable year. Beneficiaries (who may enter or leave the fund during the year) receive a proportionate share of fund income based upon the number of days of actual participation in the fund. For purposes of determining the present value of the life-income interest in a pooled-income fund, the first taxable year of a pooled-income fund is the taxable year in which the fund first receives assets.

Sec. 642(c)(5) of the Internal Revenue Code sets forth several basic requirements that must be met before a valid pooled-income fund may be considered to exist:

- The donor who transfers property into the fund must contribute an irrevocable remainder interest in the property to a public charity.
- The donor must retain an income interest for either himself or herself or other noncharitable beneficiaries.
- The property transferred by the donor must be commingled with property transferred by other donors.
- The fund may not invest in tax-exempt securities.
- The pooled-income fund must be maintained by the charitable organization itself.
- The named beneficiaries of the fund must receive annual distributions of the fund's income.

For two reasons, many consider the pooled-income fund to be more convenient than either type of charitable remainder trust. First, a smaller initial gift is generally required. Second, the charity draws up the necessary documents and the donor need only execute an instrument of transfer naming the income beneficiary.

Ramifications of Pooled-Income Fund

A donor making a contribution to a pooled-income fund receives several federal tax advantages. First, there is an immediate charitable income tax deduction for the actuarial value of the charitable remainder interest. Second, gains on fund assets that are sold by the fund are considered to be permanently set aside for the charity and will not be subject to taxation. Third, no gain or loss is realized by the donor on transfers of appreciated property to the fund. Fourth, there is no federal gift tax payable by the transferor because the federal gift tax charitable deduction will be applied.

> *Planning point:* A donor can transfer assets with a low basis to the pooled-income fund and subsequently have the fund sell these assets and reinvest the proceeds at a high rate of return without having triggered any federal income tax liability.

The pooled-income fund offers a viable alternative to a donor who wants to make a charitable gift without incurring the expense of establishing and operating a separate charitable remainder trust.

CHARITABLE LEAD TRUST

The charitable lead trust is an income or estate-tax-saving measure that will enable a taxpayer to reduce his or her tax liability in an unusually high income year or reduce his or her estate taxes.

In an inter vivos lead trust, the taxpayer transfers property to a newly created irrevocable trust. The trust then provides a charitable organization, previously designated by the donor, with a guaranteed annuity or unitrust distribution annually. At the end of an established time period, the property either passes to a noncharitable beneficiary or reverts to the original donor. The time period is not limited to 20 years as in the case of a CRT.

Inter Vivos Charitable Lead Trust

This device is a useful income-tax-saving approach since the transferor is permitted to take a current deduction (subject to the limitation discussed below) for the value of the income interest given to the charity.

Careful planning is involved in an inter vivos charitable lead trust. It must be designed as a grantor trust, and all income tax is taxable to the grantor after the creation of the trust. In addition, there are transfer tax considerations that must be addressed. If the property reverts to the donor, there will be no estate tax benefit since the property will be included in the donor's gross estate. If the property passes to a noncharitable beneficiary at the end of the lead term, this portion of the interest does not qualify for a gift tax charitable deduction. Thus, the remainder interest passing to someone other than the donor will be a taxable gift.

> *Example:* Robert Williams wishes to use a charitable trust to reduce his federal income tax liability during the current taxable year because it was unusually high. He also wishes to ultimately benefit his son, Harry, but this would not be until 12 years from today. Robert creates a trust naming the local community chest as the immediate beneficiary. A $500,000 securities portfolio is transferred into the trust, and the charitable organization is to receive annual payments in an amount equal to 8 percent of the initial fair market value of the trust property. At the end of 12 years, the securities portfolio is to pass to Robert's son, Harry. Robert may take a federal income tax deduction of $317,708 (based on a Sec. 7520 rate of 7 percent) currently for the value of the income interest given to the community chest. The excess amount, $182,292 is a future interest gift to his son that must be sheltered by Robert's applicable credit amount or gift taxes will result.

Testamentary Charitable Lead Trust

A testamentary charitable lead trust is often used to reduce the estate tax burden on large estates in which the testator is charitably inclined and considers his or her family amply provided for from other sources. An example of this is the estate of Jacqueline Kennedy Onassis. Her entire residuary estate was left to a charitable lead annuity trust. The trust provided various charities, to be selected by the trustees, with 8 percent of the initial value of the principal for 24 years. At the termination of the trust, her family will receive the remaining principal. Due to the favorable Sec. 7520 interest rate in effect at the time of her death (6.4 percent), the estate tax charitable deduction totalled 96.8 percent of the value of the residuary estate.

Example: Teddy and Tammy Taxavoider are planning their estate and have become aware of a significant death tax forecast. They have been advised to draft marital formula revocable trusts that will create a marital and credit share at their first death. However, the second death will create an unpalatable tax liability. The Taxavoiders have an interest in benefiting Suburban Children's Hospital, which recently furnished care for their granddaughter. Because their children are very well provided for from existing life insurance and other bequests from the Taxavoiders' estate, they are contemplating a testamentary lead trust. The plan is designed to create a 20-year lead annuity trust out of $10 million of assets from the remainder of the marital trust benefitting the survivor of the Taxavoiders. The annuity trust will provide for an $800,000 annual payment to be made at the end of each year. If the Sec. 7520 valuation rate is 7 percent when the charitable lead trust is created, the estate will receive an estate tax charitable deduction of $8,475,200 for the charitable lead interest. Thus, the estate tax base related to the marital trust principal was reduced by almost 85 percent at the second death without permanently divesting the family of the assets.

QUALIFIED CONSERVATION DONATIONS

A qualified conservation contribution is a split-interest donation involving real property that enables a donor to accomplish three important objectives: First, he or she obtains a meaningful and significant conservation objective. Second, the donor retains an important property right. Third, the donor receives a deduction (even though the charity does not receive the total or in some cases immediate ownership of the property involved). As with the other split-interest donations discussed above, the tax rules for conservation easements are strict and many donors request private rulings before attempting such a donation.

Types of Conservation Donations

There are the following three types of deductible conservation donations:

- The donor can give his or her entire interest in the real estate to the charity except for retained mineral rights.
- The donor can make a gift of a remainder interest in real estate to the charity to preserve the property for one or more of the permissible

conservation purposes. This provision is analogous to the transfer of the remainder interest in a personal residence or farm.
- The donor can agree to perpetually restrict (for conservation purposes) his or her use of the property in favor of a qualified charity, which is granted a perpetual restriction (or easement) to preserve the property for one of the permissible enumerated conservation purposes. A qualified conservation contribution deduction is available to the donor.

Permissible Conservation Purposes

The tax rules limit conservation donations to specific enumerated conservation purposes. The permissible conservation purposes for such a donation include the following:

- the preservation of land areas for outdoor recreation by, or education of, the general public
- the preservation of relatively natural habitats for fish, wildlife (especially endangered or protected species) or plants, or specific ecosystems
- the preservation of open space when the preservation is either for the general public's scenic enjoyment or it is indicated pursuant to a governmental conservation policy and yields a benefit to the public
- the preservation of an historically important land area or historic structure

Tax Requirements for Deductible Conservation Donation

A deductible conservation donation must be made to "eligible charitable organization." This generally includes only governmental units (for example, local, state, federal, and perhaps Indian reservations) and publicly funded charities. In addition, the qualified charitable organization must have a commitment to protect the conservation purposes of the donation. The real property donated or restricted by the easement must be considered a qualifying interest. It must be donated or restricted exclusively for the conservation purposes and donated for the good or use of the general public.

The valuation of the deduction is the sticky point. The subtraction method of valuation is generally applicable. If the property is contributed outright with retained mineral rights, the value of the property in the conservation use less the retained mineral rights is the value of the deduction. If the remainder interest is contributed, the retained right of the donor is subtracted from the total property value (in the conservation use). This calculation should be similar to the deduction for the remainder interest in a home or farm. In the case of the permanent easement, the value before and after the creation of the easement determines the amount of the deduction. The issue here is the amount that the easement reduces the property value from its highest and best use.

The qualified conservation donation is a valuable estate planning device for a family that has an interest in preserving property for a conservation purpose. For example, a family may have an interest in maintaining farmland or other open space for its real estate, or a donor may wish to preserve an important historic structure. The qualified conservation donation may provide a current income or estate tax deduction for preserving the land in the manner that the donor already desired. Of course, the valuation of the donation will be the major problem, and the IRS will not give a private letter ruling on the issue of this value.

NOTES

1. Rev. Rul. 60-370.
2. Sec. 72(u).
3. Ltr. 9009047
4. Ltr. 9227017, March 31, 1992, for example.
5. Note that the IRS has raised concerns about the manipulation of the investment policy of a CRT designed to be used as a retirement plan. Although no formal announcement has been made, informal discussion indicates that the IRS may impose self-dealing penalties on CRTs where the donor manipulates the investment for unusual tax deferral until his or her retirement.
6. 1976-2 C.B. 268 and 1982-1 C.B. 133.

9

Miscellaneous Estate Planning Issues Stemming from the Marital Relationship

Chapter Outline

CONCEPT OF INTESTACY 288
SPOUSE'S RIGHT OF ELECTION AGAINST THE WILL 290
SEC. 2034: DOWER AND CURTESY INTERESTS 292
FEDERAL ESTATE AND GIFT TAX IMPLICATIONS OF TRANSFERS
    INCIDENT TO DIVORCE OR SEPARATION 293
    Safe Harbor of Sec. 2516 294
DIVISION OF THE MARITAL HOME 295
OWNERSHIP OF LIFE INSURANCE 296
ACQUISITION AND MAINTENANCE OF LIFE INSURANCE POLICIES
    PURSUANT TO DIVORCE DECREE OR PROPERTY
    SETTLEMENT 296

It is well established that special planning issues exist when undertaking estate planning for the married client. In fact, there are a number of concepts and techniques that must be considered when planning for the married estate owner. Some of these concepts reduce estate tax liability. Others could result in additional tax liability if not properly handled. Still others (such as the concept of intestacy or a spouse's right of election against a deceased spouse's will) result in increased property interests for the surviving spouse.

This chapter will treat statutory, tax-oriented, and life-insurance-related concepts. It will focus on the planning techniques available to the financial services professional whose client is either married currently or was previously married but is now separated or divorced.

The following specific points will be discussed:

- the concept of intestacy
- the spouse's right of election against the will
- Sec. 2034: dower and curtesy interests
- the federal estate and gift tax implications of transfers incident to divorce or separation in general
- ownership of life insurance
- the acquisition and maintenance of life insurance policies pursuant to a divorce decree or property settlement

CONCEPT OF INTESTACY

The state intestacy provisions apply if an estate owner dies without having executed a valid will. In an intestacy situation, the state law (usually referred to as the *descent and distribution statute*) is applied as a substitute will to establish the distribution of estate property to family members. The state legislature has really written the will for the decedent because he or she failed to draft one during life. Although these descent and distribution statutes do have a common thread, they differ from state to state.

But how do the intestacy statutes affect the surviving spouse? Normally the surviving spouse takes a specified share of the deceased spouse's real property, as well as a specified share of the deceased spouse's personal property.

Although there can be significant differences among the states as to the specific share that the surviving spouse and children are to receive, there is one basic operating rule: The decedent's spouse and children are entitled to estate property before any other relatives in the distribution hierarchy have any rights.

When both the spouse and the children survive a decedent, the surviving spouse's share of the inheritance is generally one-half or one-third of the decedent's real and personal property. This share frequently depends on how many children actually survive. Although this is the majority approach among the states, some states consider the surviving spouse as an additional child and to this extent the surviving spouse receives only a child's share.

> *Example:* James Miller died last week without a will. He left as survivors his wife, Jean, and three children, Nancy, Buddy, and Willie. Since under the state intestacy statute the surviving spouse is considered an additional child when a decedent dies intestate with a spouse and children surviving, Mr. Miller's estate assets are divided equally among four recipients—that is, among Jean Miller and the three children.

When only the spouse survives with no children, the states handle the intestacy result in a variety of ways. In some states, for example, the surviving spouse takes all estate property. In other states the surviving spouse is allowed to take all the estate property only if the total value of the estate does not exceed a certain amount. If the value of the estate does exceed this amount, the estate must then be divided and shared with the decedent's other family members. In many other jurisdictions where the distinction between real property and personal property continues to be applied, the surviving spouse is able to retain all the personal property but must share the real property with relatives of the deceased spouse. Finally, there are some states that apply the intestacy laws in such a way that the surviving spouse receives a specified share of the estate with the balance going to surviving parents or even to surviving brothers and sisters.

Certainly if an estate owner has failed to draft a will, a definite plan for the distribution of estate property is available by state statute. However, this result should not be thought of as a viable alternative to having drafted a will, since intestacy adds unnecessary confusion and complexity to a family's affairs. Intestacy should be avoided at all costs because the disadvantages are too great. In essence, the state intestacy statute will rarely coincide with the wishes of a deceased estate owner. Moreover, the surviving spouse will not (as many incorrectly believe) automatically inherit everything when the spouse dies. In most jurisdictions the spouse will share his or her deceased spouse's estate with the children, and the value of the surviving spouse's share will be directly dependent on the number of children in the family also surviving the decedent.

One major disadvantage of this pattern is that it will result in lost opportunities to reduce federal estate taxes. Specifically the federal estate tax marital deduction, which allows estate property to pass free of any federal estate tax, will be available only to the extent that estate property actually passes to the surviving spouse. When estate property passes intestate to surviving children as well as to the surviving spouse, the tax-reduction opportunities available by using the marital deduction to its fullest extent will be lost.

Example: Wilber Hecker died without a will last June 20. He was survived by his wife, Mildred, and four children, all over age 21. Under the state intestacy statute, Wilber's entire estate is divided into five equal shares, one equal part to each survivor. Wilber's estate will be able to take a federal estate tax marital deduction for only 20 percent of the estate property, since only one-fifth of his estate will pass to his wife under the intestacy law. If Wilber had had a will, he would have been able to leave his spouse, Mildred, enough property to qualify a greater portion of the estate for the federal estate tax marital deduction and reduce or even eliminate federal estate tax liability.

An additional disadvantage of intestacy is the lost opportunity for estate owners to distribute their property in accordance with their exact wishes.

Example: Roger Downs had always intended to leave his jet to his best friend, Ray, and a specific amount of cash to his mother, assuming he predeceased them. Roger died in a plane crash last week without having executed a will. At the time of his death, he was married and had six children. Since Roger died intestate, the state descent and distribution statute operates to dictate the specific distribution of estate property. Roger's wife ends up receiving *all* estate property in accordance with the specific provisions of the intestacy law. The manner in which the intestacy statute distributes the property is totally inconsistent with Roger's wishes.

Planning point: One of the most basic elements of the estate planning process must be to assure the client of the need for a valid will. Not only are there tax benefits to having executed a valid will, but also it will assure the client that his or her estate assets are distributed in exact accordance with his or her wishes.

SPOUSE'S RIGHT OF ELECTION AGAINST THE WILL

One basic right resulting from the marital relationship is the concept of *election against the will*. The effect of this doctrine, which exists under state law and is part of most states' statutory format, is that a deceased spouse is prevented from failing to leave at least a minimum amount of estate property to the surviving spouse. Even though a testator may structure his or her will in such a way that the surviving spouse is cut out of the will, the surviving spouse will still be able, under state law, to assert a claim over a specific share of the estate. The exact extent of any such claim will differ depending on the provisions of the particular state's law. If a state allows such an election, the property that is subject to this right of election will include not only property owned by the testator at the date of death but also certain property given away by the decedent during his or her lifetime, if the decedent had retained the right to any income generated by that property or even the right to use the property until the time of death.

The actual pattern of property distribution differs on a state-by-state basis. But if the surviving spouse does exercise such an election against the will, the spouse generally takes the property according to the intestate distribution rules of that state's descent and distribution statute. Therefore the surviving spouse, when exercising the election against the will, would take the intestate share that he or she would have received if the deceased spouse had left no will at all and had died intestate.

Example: Perry Olson has been married for 23 years to Janet Olson. His estate consists of life insurance (owned by Perry on his own life with Janet named as primary beneficiary), the principal residence (owned jointly), and $750,000 in cash and securities (titled individually in his own name). Perry dies and his will leaves all his estate assets to his brother, Jimmy. Janet Olson may exercise a right of election against the will and thereby receive the approximate intestate share that she would have received if Perry had died intestate. Note, however, that property that passes to a spouse by other means, such as jointly owned property with a right of survivorship or insurance proceeds when the surviving spouse is the primary beneficiary, may not generally be included in computing the spouse's statutory elective share. Therefore, in this example, the statutory election applies only to the cash and the securities since the life insurance and the residence pass to Janet by other means. If the fair market value of the cash and the securities at Perry's death is $750,000 and the statutory election equals one-third, $250,000 will pass to Janet under this concept.

Planning point: The concept of election against the will is a state doctrine and, as such, differs from state to state. In some states, the election appears limited to wives. However, in most states the word *spouse,* not *wife,* is used.

Planning point: The election is governed by a series of state statutes and regulations to which the electing spouse must adhere. For example, most states require that the election be placed in writing and filed with the probate court within a specific period of time. Also the election may be considered waived by failure to comply with the filing deadline or even by a prenuptial or postnuptial agreement.

Relevant case: A Maryland U.S. District Court case, *Hastings*, illustrates the relationship between a spouse's right of election against the will and the federal estate tax marital deduction. The decedent, who died in October 1981, had passed all his property under the terms of his will to a testamentary trust with a life estate for the benefit of his wife. This life estate would not qualify for the federal estate tax marital deduction because it would not be included as part of the surviving spouse's gross estate. If the spouse had elected against the will within the required time period under state law, the marital deduction would have been available. The wife had never been informed of her right to make such an election but did learn of the election after the required election time period had expired. However, the wife was subsequently successful in petitioning a state court to permit the election. The IRS took the position that the late election, even though eventually permitted by the state court, prevented the successful usage of the federal estate tax marital deduction. The court sustained the IRS position.

Relevant case: It is possible that the settlement of a will contest may create a federal gift tax problem. This point is illustrated by the case of *Nelson v. United States.* Here, Anna Nelson married the decedent many years subsequent to his will being executed. When Mr. Nelson died 2 years after his marriage to Anna, she contested the will, which left all of his estate property to his surviving nieces and nephews. North Dakota, the state of domicile here, has an "omitted spouse" statute to protect surviving spouses who find themselves in this type of situation. Specifically the relevant statute says that if a testator fails to provide for his or her surviving spouse who marries the decedent *subsequent* to the execution of the will, the surviving spouse is to receive the same share of the estate such spouse would have received if the decedent had died intestate. Based on this Anna became entitled to the entire estate.

Anna entered into an agreement with the nieces and nephews in which she received one-half of the gross estate and each niece and nephew received one-eighth of the estate. Unfortunately the IRS considered that Anna had received the entire estate (because of the North Dakota statute) and had gifted some of the estate to the nieces and nephews. In short, Anna incurred a federal gift tax liability on the amounts transferred to them.

Relevant case: In the Tax Court case *Estate of Harper* a surviving spouse's election to take against her deceased husband's will did not affect her right to receive distributions as a beneficiary of his inter vivos trust. The Tax Court held that the trust had been created prior to the decedent's death and not under the will. Therefore the Tax Court took the position that the surviving spouse could take under the trust, and any property passing to her under this arrangement would qualify for the federal estate tax marital deduction.

SEC. 2034: DOWER AND CURTESY INTERESTS

In chapter 1 we discussed the concept of required inclusion of assets in the decedent's gross estate. Sec. 2034, more than any other includibility section in the Internal Revenue Code, exists because there are certain inchoate (dormant) property rights between married persons as a result of their marital relationship.

Let's begin our study of Sec. 2034 with a review of the concept of dower and curtesy. Essentially these terms may be thought of as property rights that exist because of the marital relationship. These are common-law concepts that have their roots in the English law and were carried over to the laws of many states today.

The Middle English definition of dower was the provision that the law made for a widow "out of the lands of her husband" for her support and for the support of her children. It has come to be thought of as a type of life estate that a woman is, by law, entitled to claim on the death of her husband in any real property that the husband owned during the marriage.

The Middle English definition of curtesy, on the other hand, was the provision the law made for a man on the death of his wife "out of the lands of his wife" for his support and the support of his children.

Dower and curtesy interests are inchoate or dormant in nature and do not come into existence until after death. (In a sense, an inchoate right may be thought of as a potential right, not an actual right already in existence.) Because of the inchoate character of these rights, many early court decisions held that dower and curtesy rights should not be subjected to inheritance taxation. Courts in many states, for example, held that inheritance tax statutes at the state level could not apply to dower or curtesy rights because at the date of death, no new estate was created in the surviving spouse. Because there was fear at the federal level that the same analysis might be applied in the context of the federal estate tax, Congress enacted Sec. 2034 to ensure inclusion of this property interest in the decedent's gross estate.

Example: James Michael died owning, among other things, a 400-acre tract of real estate in upstate New York. He was married at the time of his death, and under the state dower law James's widow had a right to one-third of that property at her husband's death. James Michael was still required to include the full fair market value of the 400-acre tract in his gross estate, even though at his death a portion of the property was deemed to be owned by his wife. Sec. 2034 prevents the gross estate from being reduced by the value of the dower interest.

In effect, therefore, Sec. 2034 prevents the argument that a decedent's gross estate should be reduced by the value of a surviving spouse's dower or curtesy right. Some commentators have taken the position that the current Sec. 2033 is sufficient in scope and breadth to include the entire value of property owned by a decedent without resulting in any reduction for a surviving spouse's dower or curtesy interest. Therefore many consider Sec. 2034 redundant in character. However, a certain amount of overlap between the statutory provisions is frequently the case with the includibility sections of the Internal Revenue Code.

One additional point must be made when reviewing Sec. 2034. This particular provision should not be thought of as including all property interests involving the marital relationship. For example, jointly titled property between husband and wife is a situation existing because of the marital relationship. Yet it is obvious that this transaction will fall within the terms of a different Internal Revenue Code section—that is, Sec. 2040.

FEDERAL ESTATE AND GIFT TAX IMPLICATIONS OF TRANSFERS INCIDENT TO DIVORCE OR SEPARATION

A major part of a divorce or separation is the transfer of property from one spouse to the other. In addition to dealing with the emotional and other nontax aspects of the divorce, the parties must concern themselves with the federal estate and gift tax implications. The estate and gift tax treatment of these transfers is a confusing area, having endured many changes. We will first concentrate on the effect that a divorce will have on wills and trusts, and then we will look at the federal tax implications of such an event.

When a divorce is taking place, legal instruments such as wills and trusts must be reviewed and, if it is necessary and possible, modified in accordance with the changes the divorce will inevitably bring. Although in some states divorce will not automatically trigger a revocation of an existing will, many jurisdictions have a statutory framework under which a divorce will automatically revoke all provisions regarding the former spouse in the will. Some jurisdictions even have statutes under which a divorce will revoke provisions in an inter vivos trust relating to a former spouse. Regardless of any provisions that are set forth by state law, it is essential for the divorced party to revise his or her will to make the necessary changes. The best illustration of this point is probably that the federal estate tax marital deduction will no longer be available to the taxpayer.

In addition, the divorced individual will need to reconsider the choice of fiduciaries as well as the choice of legal guardian for minor children in the event that the former spouse is uncooperative and refuses to act as guardian. Often, the divorced individual wants the part of the estate that is passed to the children to be controlled by a fiduciary independent of the former spouse. All these considerations should be taken care of as soon as the divorce is final.

To appreciate the current tax implications of a divorce or separation, it will be useful to next explore the legal history of these transfers as far as federal estate and gift taxation is concerned.

Regarding gift taxes, the question is whether a transfer of property made incident to a separation or divorce was supported by "adequate and full consideration in money or money's worth." This is relevant in determining whether a gift had been made. Indeed, in order for a taxable gift to have been made, the transferred property must not have been exchanged for adequate and full consideration. If there had been consideration, no gift would be considered to have been made.

Safe Harbor of Sec. 2516

The issue of whether adequate consideration was received for transfers pursuant to a divorce is clarified by Sec. 2516. The statute provides that if property is transferred pursuant to a valid agreement *and* divorce occurs within a 3-year period beginning one year prior to the agreement, the transferor is deemed to have received adequate consideration. This safe harbor applies even if the transfer was not ordered by the divorce court or incorporated into the divorce decree.

Note: There will be situations when the use of Sec. 2516 is not a good choice for the parties. The best illustration of this is a situation in which a transferor-spouse might be willing to make a transfer in trust with the income to the transferee-spouse followed by a remainder interest to the couple's children. The income interest transferred to the spouse could qualify under Sec. 2516, but the remainder interest would probably be treated as a gift from the transferor to the children, unless the remainder interest in the trust was seen as an integral part of the property and support settlement.

According to another provision of the estate and gift tax law, the obligation to transfer property to a former spouse of the decedent is a valid Sec. 2053 deduction if the transfer of property is made pursuant to an agreement that satisfies the conditions of the gift tax rule under Sec. 2516. Therefore the federal estate tax deduction is available if the transfer is made in accordance with a written agreement between the husband and wife and if the divorce takes place within the 3-year period beginning one year before execution of the agreement.

Example: Jack and Jill Hastings were divorced on December 18, 1990, and on November 22, 1991, they were finally able to agree on the terms of the property settlement and sign the agreement. Under Sec. 2516, there is no gift situation created because the divorce may precede the settlement agreement by as much as one year. If Jack were to die during the 3-year period, an estate tax deduction as a claim against the estate would be acceptable.

Planning point: Sec. 2516 will afford an opportunity for divorced parties to avoid federal gift tax liability in conjunction with property settlements. Further, should a party die during the 3-year period beginning one year before the execution of the agreement, a valid federal estate tax deduction is appropriate. The parties must take care to adhere to the timing restrictions of the 3-year rule and to take advantage of what Sec. 2516 has to offer.

Example: Mike and Lauren Dole are already divorced. As part of the property settlement agreement, Lauren has now agreed to release Mike from any and all claims stemming from her marital rights. The value of these rights, mainly Lauren's right to elect against Mike's estate, is approximately $300,000. Lauren's release of the marital rights is not made a part of any divorce decree, and the agreement is signed approximately 4 years after the date of the divorce decree. Under current tax law the release of the rights worth $300,000 is a taxable gift. It does not trigger gift tax liability *per se,* but it does reduce the unified credit, thus increasing the possibility of federal estate tax liability at Mike's death.

DIVISION OF THE MARITAL HOME

The home owned by the divorcing couple is generally titled either as tenants by the entireties or as joint tenants with right of survivorship. This asset is usually subject to a residential mortgage. In the event that one of the spouses continues to reside in this property, the issues of whether to continue joint ownership and how to structure the continued repayment of the mortgage loan are critical from the perspective of both federal income tax and federal estate tax.

Continued joint ownership of the home is not prudent from an estate planning point of view because upon the death of the first spouse, the property would pass by operation of law to the former spouse even though the federal estate tax deduction would be unavailable. An additional complication arises if the spouse who died was also the spouse who had been making the mortgage payment. The IRS would then assert that the entire value of the residence would have to be included in the decedent's gross estate rather than only 50 percent of the value. Further, because the jointly titled residence would pass by operation of law and thereby bypass probate, the estate could not deduct the amount passing to the former spouse as a claim against the estate. The best solution is probably to transfer ownership of the home to the spouse who is going to live there, with that spouse making the mortgage payments.

OWNERSHIP OF LIFE INSURANCE

In prior chapters, we have treated the federal estate tax implications of life insurance ownership and highlighted the fact that Sec. 2042 requires including face amounts of life policies in the gross estate when the insured owns the insurance on his or her own life. This is known as *incidents of ownership.*

One technique often relied on to avoid the rather harsh result of Sec. 2042 is the cross-ownership approach. This, of course, is an arrangement whereby a wife owns the life insurance on the life of the husband and vice versa. However, there are three basic problems with cross-ownership:

- Existing coverage that is transferred from one spouse to the other may create federal gift tax problems.
- Should a divorce occur, there will be complex questions raised involving property rights.
- If the transferee spouse predeceases the insured, nothing has been accomplished.

The use of the irrevocable life insurance trust will prevent many of the problems created by the spousal cross-ownership technique. Many commentators agree that spousal cross-ownership is not the best approach.

ACQUISITION AND MAINTENANCE OF LIFE INSURANCE POLICIES PURSUANT TO DIVORCE DECREE OR PROPERTY SETTLEMENT

Life insurance must often be transferred to a spouse pursuant to a property settlement agreement. A policy transfer normally triggers taxable gain if the fair market value of the policy exceeds its basis. However, the transfer of a policy pursuant to a property settlement will not cause the transferor to recognize gain.

When one spouse is required by the divorce decree or property settlement to assign an existing life insurance policy to the other spouse, or when a new life policy is acquired on behalf of the spouse pursuant to a divorce decree or property settlement, the premiums paid must be included in the recipient-spouse's gross income and are deductible for income tax purposes by the premium-paying spouse. Indeed this is one of the few factual situations in which premium payments generate a tax deduction.

There are many ramifications of using life insurance in divorce situations. For example, if the insured spouse owns the life insurance policy, it will be includible in his or her gross estate for federal estate tax purposes but will not be subject to the federal estate tax marital deduction. This is the case, of course, because the insured is not passing the estate property to his or her "spouse" as is required by the federal estate tax marital deduction rules. (Think of it as the worst of all possible worlds.) An additional point is that if support payments are increased to an amount required to pay premiums, not only would the insured spouse be entitled to an income tax deduction for federal income tax purposes, but also the owner-spouse would also be able to make certain that the premiums are paid and that the policy does not lapse.

10

Community Property—Its Implications on Estate Planning

Chapter Outline

INTRODUCTION 300
HISTORICAL BACKGROUND 301
THE BASICS OF COMMUNITY PROPERTY 301
    What Is Community Property? 301
    Similarities among Community-Property States 302
    Nature of Separate Property in Community-Property State 302
    Transfers of Property between Spouses 302
    Quasi-Community Property/Personal Property 303
    Real Property 303
    Property Held in Joint Tenancy 303
    Earnings and Management of Spouses 303
    Variations among Community-Property States 304
RESIDENCE AND DOMICILE 305
SEPARATION OR DIVORCE—ENDING THE COMMUNITY 305
    Additional Requirements for California and Washington 306
    Need for Interlocutory Decree 306
DISTRIBUTION OF PROPERTY AT DEATH IN COMMUNITY-
      PROPERTY STATES 306
    Aggregate Theory 307
    Item Theory 307
    Legal Presumption Concerning Bequests 307
    Ancestral Property Rule 307
DISPOSITION OF COMMUNITY PROPERTY IN COMMON-LAW
      STATES FOLLOWING THE UNIFORM DISPOSITION OF
      COMMUNITY PROPERTY RIGHTS AT DEATH ACT 308
PREMARITAL PLANNING 309
LIABILITY PROBLEMS WITH COMMUNITY PROPERTY 309
ESTATE PLANNING CONSIDERATIONS 309
    Trusts 310
    Double Stepped-up Basis 310

Converting Separate Property to Community Property 311
Treatment of Life Insurance 312
Treatment of Retirement Plans 315
Benefit Plans Funded by Taxes 315
SUMMARY 316

INTRODUCTION

Financial services professionals may incur problems with planning and potential liability by not understanding the unique treatment of income and assets either earned or situated in a community-property state. Estate planning texts deal mostly with common-law states, since 41 states are common law, leaving only nine states governed by community-property law. However, all financial services professionals should be familiar with the concepts of community property for three reasons.

First, due to our mobile society and the high population of some of the community-property states, it would be very likely that a financial services professional or tax adviser would be advising clients who acquired some of their property in one of these nine states. Second, certain states adopted community-property laws but later reverted to common-law status. Property acquired during the community-property period may or may not have retained community-property status. Finally, a growing number of common-law states have adopted versions of the "Uniform Disposition of Community Property Rights at Death Act," governing the treatment of community property that is held by their domiciliaries at the time of death.[1]

The treatment of community property will affect the rights of the surviving spouse and other heirs, as well as the federal gift, estate, and income tax results in some instances. The financial services professional will need to understand the nature and historical background of community property to better advise his or her clients as to its implications on taxes and the distribution of assets to clients' heirs.

The nine community property states are Arizona, California, Idaho, Louisiana, New Mexico, Nevada, Texas, Washington, and Wisconsin.[2] Community property is a system of property ownership as a result of a marriage. There is no one set of "community-property law." Each state has a distinct variation of statutory law called community-property law, each influenced by cultural and economic conditions over the centuries.

Several states, including Hawaii, Michigan, Nebraska, Oklahoma, Oregon, and Pennsylvania, enacted community-property laws in the past, but they later repealed them when joint-return provisions allowing income-splitting benefits between spouses were enacted.

HISTORICAL BACKGROUND

Community-property law actually is quite ancient, spanning a history of 2,000 years. Its beginnings can be found in the Code of Hammurabi; in the laws of ancient Egypt, the Byzantine Empire, and ancient Greece; and among the ancient Germanic tribes and the Celts. The modern community-property principles of the United States originated from the nomadic tribes of Spain and France. These nomads realized that both the husband and the wife contributed greatly to the acquisition and conservation of wealth. The marital relationship was considered a partnership in which both spouses contributed and from which both should benefit.

This was a striking dichotomy to the aristocracy developed in England, which passed wealth and estates through the patriarchal line, excluding women of common ancestry. The English law, called common law, was adopted by the 41 non-community-property states. Generally, the community-property states were once territories of Spain, but Florida and Oregon did not retain the community-property system, and Wisconsin converted from the common-law statutes.

THE BASICS OF COMMUNITY PROPERTY

What Is Community Property?

States usually define community property as everything that is not separate property. They generally define separate property as property acquired by either spouse before marriage or after the marriage has been legally terminated, along with property that passes to one or the other spouse individually as a gift, devise, or bequest from a third party during the marriage. Everything else is community property.[3]

Before we describe the many variations of community property, we should explore the common features of this system. Community property refers to the source of assets acquired by a married couple. These are assets acquired while a person is married and living within the domain of one of the community-property states. It may not matter how the property is titled; if it is acquired with community funds (assets while married), it is deemed community property.

Furthermore, in community-property states it is possible to take title to property in the husband's and wife's name as community property. That is, it is possible to title assets acquired during marriage or convert separate property to community property while living in a community-property state. The estate-planning advantage of this change of title will be explained later.

Usually in community-property states, property that cannot be properly traced to its separate property origins will be presumed to be community property. The burden of proof will be on the spouse claiming that the property is separate property.

Similarities among Community-Property States

The basic similarities among the community-property states are as listed below:

- All property a husband and wife acquire during their marriage, while living in a community-property state, is community property.
- Generally, the couple shares all assets acquired during their marriage, including real property, personal property, and wages earned for services rendered.
- Property acquired before marriage or before becoming domiciled in a community-property state is separate property and retains the nature and form of ownership as it had when it was acquired—separate, joint, or other.

Nature of Separate Property in Community-Property States

Besides holding community property, a married couple may own assets of separate property. Separate property in a community-property state is usually acquired by a person prior to marriage or after the dissolution of marriage. Property acquired by one of the parties by gift or inheritance during the marriage is separate property, even though it was acquired during the marriage. In addition, property that was purchased or obtained in exchange for other property retains the same character as the property conveyed. If property is purchased with a combination of community and separate funds, the property is partially community and partially separate property.

Because of the presumption favoring community property, it is necessary to clearly identify the separate-property portion of mixed-character property. This is particularly true for life insurance policies for which separate ownership may be critical to removing the proceeds from the insured's estate. We will discuss the community-property implications of life insurance below.

Transfers of Property between Spouses

A married couple can transfer property between themselves and change its nature if they like. A couple who desires to convert community property to separate property, or vice versa, should adopt a formal agreement, called a *transmutation agreement,* in order to clearly show intent in case a future dispute results.

If they want to acquire new separate property—particularly with community funds—while they are residing in a community-property state, the couple must carefully document the intention to establish separate property. The title and related documents must clearly state the nature of the marital relationship and the intent to establish separate ownership by either spouse.

Quasi-Community Property/Personal Property

Generally, assets retain the same character even after the owners move from state to state. Personal property acquired in a community-property state usually remains community property when the owner moves to a common-law state. The treatment of such property will vary, based on the interpretation of community-property laws in the common-law state. There is a mixed record in common-law states as to the respect given to the community-property rules. The common-law states that have adopted the Uniform Disposition of Community Property Rights at Death Act give specific recognition to community-property rules. In fact, newly acquired property will be treated as community property if it is acquired from the rent, income, or proceeds from community property.[4] Property treated as community property in common-law states adopting the Uniform Act will pass free of any dower, curtesy, or elective-share rights of the surviving spouse under the rules of the state.

What about separate personal property acquired by a couple while they reside in a common-law state? If the couple moves to a community-property state, the property will retain its separate character except in California and Idaho, where the nature of the property is changed into quasi-community property, which is treated like community property.

Real Property

Real property is usually controlled by the law of the situs of the property. It generally retains its nature, no matter where the owners of the property are domiciled. In other words, if the real property is located in Rhode Island, it will continue to be governed by common law, even if the owners live in California, before, during, or after acquiring the property. Likewise, a married couple living in Montana who purchase land in Arizona will own a community-property interest in the land.

Property Held in Joint Tenancy

Since all property not defined as community property is classified as separate property, property held in joint tenancy or as tenants in common by the individual spouses is deemed the separate property of each in a community-property state.[5] Generally, capital gains and rents from separate property during marriage remain separate property, while capital gains and rents from community assets are community property.[6]

Earnings and Management of Spouses

In a community-property state the spouses' earnings during marriage are community property. Property purchased with proceeds from the sale of community property remains community property. Property purchased with separate property remains separate property. Property purchased with commingled community and separate property, in which the two cannot be separated, is community property. Compensation for personal injuries suffered, however, is generally treated as separate property.

In Wisconsin "income" from a person's separate property is community property while that person is married and living in Wisconsin. The asset itself remains separate property.[7]

Generally, in a community-property state both spouses have equal control over the management and disposition of the community property, except when disposing of encumbering real property, which requires the signatures of both parties.

Variations among Community-Property States

The nine community-property states share the general similarities discussed above. The following are some of the major differences among those states, which could affect a client's estate plan.

Regarding life insurance, Louisiana, New Mexico, and Texas follow the *inception-of-title* rule to determine whether property is separate property or community property. The inception-of-title rule retains the nature of ownership of a life insurance policy, whether or not the premiums are paid with community proceeds or separate property. Specifically, if a policy is taken out by one spouse before marriage and premiums are paid from community funds after marriage, according to the inception-of-title rule and in spite of paying premiums with community funds, the proceeds are the separate property of that spouse (presumably subject to a reimbursement claim by the community).

The community-property states that follow the *apportionment* rule or *allocation* rule concerning the ownership of life insurance are California, Nevada, and Washington. The apportionment rule allocates the insurance between separate property and community property in proportion to the ratio of premiums paid with separate funds and premiums paid with community funds. (We will discuss the advantage to this allocation later.)

California and Idaho have a statutory provision that community property transferred to a living trust retains its character as community property if the trust was originally comprised of community property. In addition, California and Idaho have a statute creating a class of quasi-community property, which is generally personal property brought into the state that would have been community property if it had been acquired while the spouses were domiciled in a community-property state.[8]

In Nevada all property is assumed to be community property if the spouses have not filed a record of inventory of separate property and any supplements thereafter.

Texas retains the traditional Spanish rule that the rents and gains of either spouse's separate property are part of the community. The other states allow the income to retain the nature of the property to which it is attached. The exception is income produced by a depletable asset, such as oil, gas, or other minerals. This is because income from a depletable asset is often a return of capital, instead of true income.[9]

RESIDENCE AND DOMICILE

Often residence and domicile are used interchangeably, but they are distinct concepts. *Residence* refers to the physical location where a person resides, except for temporary stays. *Domicile* involves both physical presence in the location and the intention to make the place one's home. It is possible to have multiple residences concurrently; a taxpayer can have only one domicile at a time. A domicile continues until it is replaced by a new domicile.

Generally, an assumption is made that the place where a person lives is his or her domicile. To establish a domicile, a taxpayer must affirm the rights and perform the duties of a citizen in the location, thus making the particular place or state his or her home. In determining a taxpayer's domicile, the following factors are considered:

- location of person's birth
- the state in which taxes are paid
- the place where taxpayer is registered to vote
- location of taxpayer's property
- the place where taxpayer is a citizen
- taxpayer's length of residence
- location of taxpayer's business
- location of taxpayer's community ties[10]

SEPARATION OR DIVORCE—ENDING THE COMMUNITY

A decree of legal separation or of separate maintenance may end the community if the court issuing the decree so specifies.[11]

Spouses must meet the following criteria to qualify for separate property tax treatment:

- The spouses must be married to each other at some time during the calendar year.
- They must live apart at all times during the calendar year.
- They must not file a joint tax return with each other for a tax year beginning or ending within the calendar year.
- One or both taxpayers must have earned income for the calendar year that is community income.
- No portion of community earned income may be transferred (directly or indirectly) between the taxpayers before the close of the calendar year.[12]

Additional Requirements for California and Washington

In California and Washington, more than mere physical separation is required. The spouses must have no present intention of resuming the marital relationship. The IRS has ruled that community-property laws cease to apply when, for all intents and purposes, a marriage is terminated and the spouses show by affirmative action their intent not to maintain community status. The following factors, which are considered in each case, demonstrate intent not to maintain community status:

- The spouses live separately.
- Neither spouse contributes to the support of the other or accounts to the other for income received.
- Neither spouse asserts any claim to any income or property acquired by the other spouse after separation.
- Each spouse manages his or her own affairs free of interference from the other spouse.
- A complaint of divorce is filed.
- The divorce action is uncontested.
- A property settlement is entered into.[13]

Need for Interlocutory Decree

In California a divorce decree or judgment ends the community and makes later earnings separate property. An *interlocutory decree* may provide for a division of community property and adjudicate community-property rights. When the decree does not do so, the spouses' equal interests in the property continue. A spouse's interest in community property is not destroyed by a decree for separate maintenance when no division or settlement of the property is included in the decree.

Taxpayers may alter the status of separate property by mutual agreement after the interlocutory decree is entered. In addition, spouses are taxed on their share of community property up to the date of the decree, despite neither receiving nor enjoying the income.

DISTRIBUTION OF PROPERTY AT DEATH IN COMMUNITY-PROPERTY STATES

At death, a decedent spouse may dispose of the separate estate as he or she desires, subject to liability claims and to statutory protection for the surviving spouse (for example, elective shares). As we discussed earlier, at least one-third of the separate property passing intestate goes to the surviving spouse as the decedent's heir.[14]

For community property, the decedent spouse has testamentary power over his or her half interest in the community property. There are two different methods to determine distribution of community property.

Aggregate Theory

One method of determining the distribution of community property is called the *aggregate theory*.

The aggregate theory is the most often used method in distributing assets. Under this method ownership does not attach itself to any particular asset; instead the entire estate is divided in half in relation to the fair market value of the entire community at the decedent's date of death or the alternative valuation date. The decedent could will his or her community interest to a third party according to this theory.

Item Theory

The other method of determining the distribution of community property is called the *item theory*.

This approach recognizes the surviving spouse as owner of an undivided half interest in every item of community property—a right that the decedent cannot defeat by will even if the latter disposes of no more than half the community estate by value. This means that for the decedent to dispose of an asset, the surviving spouse must "elect" or "allow" the will to dispose of the property to a third party.

Legal Presumption Concerning Bequests

The law presumes that a decedent intends to devise or bequeath only what he or she owns, and that a will cannot be devised to harm the surviving spouse—at least in the distribution of an asset in which the couple holds a community interest. Similarly, the decedent may not restrict the management power that the survivor has unless there is a substantial inter vivos purpose.

Ancestral Property Rule

California has a special rule that applies to a decedent who dies intestate without lineal descendants, and whose spouse died prior to the intestate decedent who never remarried. This rule is called the *ancestral property rule*. The ancestral property rule allows the former in-laws of the surviving spouse to inherit certain property in the survivor's estate. This property is generally the community interest that the former in-laws' son or daughter owned prior to his or her death.[15]

DISPOSITION OF COMMUNITY PROPERTY IN COMMON-LAW STATES FOLLOWING THE UNIFORM DISPOSITION OF COMMUNITY PROPERTY RIGHTS AT DEATH ACT

The disposition of community property in common-law states that follow the Uniform Act clarifies the treatment for couples who are domiciliaries of that state at the time of death. These states respect the community-property status of property acquired in a community-property state. However, the rules illustrate the need to become familiar with community-property laws for the transient client.

There are many parties with potential claims to make to the property. For example, the surviving spouse has rights to his or her share of the community property. The personal representative has interests in the decedent's share of the community property. The other heirs could also have rights in the decedent-spouse's share of the community property by the terms of the decedent's will, intestacy, or otherwise. In addition, new transferees of the community property will have an interest in the status of the property. Finally, the creditors of either spouse will have an interest in the disposition of the property.

The Uniform Disposition of Community Property Rights at Death Act specifically exempts the personal representative of the deceased spouse's estate from liability (provided that there are no claims from the other parties) for the failure to ascertain the community-property status of the property. However, don't feel secure that the couple's other advisers will avoid malpractice for the failure to uncover the facts.

Generally, there is a presumption of community property under the Uniform Act for property the couple acquired while domiciled in a community-property state. New property acquired with community funds or traceable to community funds will normally be treated as community property. The titling of such new assets as tenants by the entireties or joint tenants with rights of survivorship may rebut the presumption of community property.

The surviving spouse's half-interest in the community property is not subject to disposition by the deceased spouse's will or the intestacy laws of the state. If the property is held by the personal representative of the deceased spouse's estate, the surviving spouse can establish his or her half-interest by court order or by a document signed by the personal representative and other heirs. There is a limited time, such as 6 months, for the surviving spouse to make this claim to the property.

The deceased spouse's half-interest in the community property is not subject to the surviving spouse's dower, curtesy, or elective-share rights. If the surviving spouse is holding such property, the personal representative or other heirs can initiate an action to establish their respective rights.

PREMARITAL PLANNING

A financial services professional needs to be aware of the tax and other potential consequences concerning community property to enable him or her to advise a couple prior to their marriage. Most community-property states consider a spouse's earnings community property if a valid marriage exists unless there is clear and satisfactory evidence established otherwise, including an agreement between the spouses changing the status of the property to separate property. This is important if one of the spouses enters into a marriage with prior tax problems, child support problems, spousal support problems, liens, levies, or judgments of any kind.

LIABILITY PROBLEMS WITH COMMUNITY PROPERTY

If the income of either spouse is deemed to be community property, then the courts and various taxing agencies could garnish even the innocent spouse's wages and place liens on his or her property. This would also apply to any of the couple's commingled funds or to assets in which a spouse's separate portion is difficult to ascertain.

The government may attach an asset, especially liquid cash accounts, without asking questions, especially if the liable spouse's name is on the account. It is difficult to get the IRS or the courts to refund the proceeds even if proof can be supplied as to the original separate nature of the assets.

The financial adviser needs to be aware of this provision of the community-property laws in order to warn the couple prior to their marriage. The financial adviser should also warn the couple about the potential problems in not retaining the nature of their separate property in case of a divorce in the future, or in case they desire to control and retain their separate property in their estates after death.

ESTATE PLANNING CONSIDERATIONS

In a community-property state a financial services professional will need to determine how his or her client should hold property—whether the client should hold the property separately or jointly. The tax implications can vary greatly among the choices.

For a married couple, if community property is selected, one-half of the community property will be subject to probate and to estate taxes (unless a qualifying marital deduction bequest is made). If the spouses hold property in joint tenancy with a right of survivorship, upon the death of the first joint tenant, there will be no probate and only one-half of the fair market value of the property will be includible in the decedent's estate. That one-half interest will pass to the survivor and qualify for the marital deduction.

Trusts

Community property must be probated if it is not held in trust. What if the financial services professional recommends holding the community property in a revocable trust while still retaining the nature of the property as community property? The survivor can still benefit from the assets for life, and the decedent's half of estate can escape probate. A revocable trust funded with community property effectively avoids probate in the same manner as a revocable trust in a common-law-property state. The added benefit (and often overlooked provision) accorded to community property is that the entire property—not just one-half, as with separate property of joint tenancy—can get a stepped-up basis.

How can this be done? In community-property states, it is possible to take title to assets in the husband's and wife's names as community property. By holding title as community property a spouse can will away his or her half of the assets at death.[16] This is not possible with assets held in joint tenancy. If these assets are held in a trust as community property, they can also escape probate. Both halves—rather than one-half, as under joint tenancy—of the assets a husband and wife hold with title as community property get a new cost basis.[17]

The trust should contain language stating that any community property contributed to the trust will retain its character as community property both during the existence of the revocable trust and upon any termination of the trust or partial distribution of that property from the trust. California and Idaho now require such a statement in a living trust in order to show the intention to have community property retain its nature.

Double Stepped-up Basis

The general rule is that the basis of property acquired from a decedent is the fair market value of the property on the date of the decedent's death or on the alternate valuation date if the executor so elects. In the case of community property, the surviving spouse is regarded as acquiring his or her own half of the community property from the decedent, provided that at least one-half of the whole community-property interest is includible in the decedent's gross estate.[18] Thus, the surviving spouse gets a stepped-up basis, not only for the decedent spouse's half of the community property, but also for his or her own share of the community interest.

If the heir is not the decedent's spouse, there will be a stepped-up basis on only the decedent's portion of the property. The double stepped-up basis is granted only to the surviving spouse.

If a financial services professional understands this special community-property provision in the tax rules regarding the double stepped-up basis, the heirs could benefit by perhaps not having to pay income tax on capital gains from the sale of the inherited property, since due to the new adjusted basis, at fair market value of the property, all proceeds could be tax free. For individuals holding community property and moving to a common-law jurisdiction, their advisers should be certain to preserve the status of the property as community property. All documentation and actions taken regarding the property should be consistent with its status as community property.

Converting Separate Property to Community Property

What if the client had acquired part of his or her property as separate property before moving to a community-property state? In most community-property states, a couple can change title to assets to make them community property either by registering the assets in both spouses' names as community property or by signing a written agreement, whereby they both agree that all of their assets, or a designated portion, will be community property. The financial services professional must exercise caution when recommending this communal ownership. If the marriage is not strong, costly litigation can occur, particularly if one spouse owns a greater portion of the estate than the other.

If it is the intention of one of the spouses to retain some separate property, it must be itemized in the agreement. Remember, in most community-property states, joint-tenancy property will be deemed to be the separate property of each spouse even though the joint tenancy was created out of community property. This will cause a loss in the double step-up in basis for the survivor spouse.

The technique of converting separate property to community property could save the heirs and/or the surviving spouse thousands of dollars in taxes. If the separate property involved was highly appreciated, the conversion to community property would assure a step-up in basis to the fair market value on the death of either spouse. The unlimited marital deduction, which applies to gifts as well as to estates, has made it possible to transfer property back and forth between spouses at any time with no adverse tax consequences. In a community-property state, the marital deduction will now allow changing separate property into community property so that none of the applicable credit amount is wasted. At the same time it is possible to achieve a step-up in basis for the surviving spouse's community-property interest.

Example: Suppose a married couple, Debbie and Richard Jones, move from a common-law state to a community-property state. They own mutual funds jointly with rights of survivorship; they purchased the funds for $40,000, and they are now worth $200,000. They enter into a community-property agreement that establishes that their property will be community property and will automatically vest in the survivor. Suppose Richard dies immediately thereafter and Debbie sells the mutual funds. If they had not converted the property to community property, Debbie's cost basis in the mutual funds would have been $120,000 and she would have recognized an $80,000 capital gain. Because they converted the funds to community property, the double basis step-up makes the transaction nontaxable.

Treatment of Life Insurance

Life insurance is one of the complex areas of community-property law for the financial services professional. As we've discussed in several previous chapters, third-party ownership, such as an ILIT, is a useful estate planning technique. Financial planners should take particular care to make certain that the transfer of ownership to a third party is not circumvented by the community-property rules. Thus, it is especially important to determine the ownership status of life insurance.

> *Example:* A husband and wife, domiciled in Texas, purchased life insurance policies on each other's life with cross-ownership. They bought the policies with community funds. In a common-law state, the proceeds would be excludible from the deceased insured's gross estate. In Texas, however, the policies are treated as community property and one-half of the proceeds is included in an insured's estate at death. The parties should have established that they desired separate ownership and that they intended to make a gift of the premiums from each spouse to the other. Rev. Rul. 67-228, 1967-2 C.B. 331

Some community-property states treat life insurance proceeds as separate property, and some treat the proceeds as community property. The issue can usually be resolved by determining when, where, and how the policy was acquired, who paid the premiums, and when.

Generally, in a community-property state, as in a common-law state, incidents of ownership will determine whether the life insurance is in the insured's gross estate. In a community-property state, even if the insured is the policyowner, it is possible that only one-half of the proceeds will be deemed part of the decedent-insured's estate. Tax regulations state that if the policy is purchased with community funds and the couple's child is named as beneficiary, the ownership and power of surrender the decedent possessed will be in part as "agent" for his or her spouse. Thus, the decedent will not possess an incident of ownership in the surviving spouse's half of the policy, and only one-half of the policy proceeds will be includible in his or her gross estate.[19] The regulations also state that if the noninsured spouse predeceases the insured spouse, one-half of the policy value will be includible in the noninsured spouse's gross estate.

Nonspousal Beneficiary in Community-Property States

If the policy names a third person as beneficiary on the death of the insured, the noninsured spouse is deemed to have made a gift of one-half of the policy proceeds to the beneficiary.[20] This implies again that the insured was acting as the agent for the spouse. If the noninsured spouse was left out of the inheritance or was denied life insurance proceeds, or if the beneficiary was named without the surviving spouse's knowledge, there could be a violation of fiduciary responsibility and the surviving spouse might be entitled to some of the life insurance proceeds. However, a recent case demonstrates that an insured spouse could make his or her estate the beneficiary of the life insurance proceeds from a community-owned policy on the insured spouse's life and, absent fraud, create an effective beneficiary designation.[21]

Life Insurance Purchased with Community Funds

A financial services professional needs to be aware that in a community-property state there is a presumption that life insurance acquired during marriage is community property. If the intent is to establish separate ownership of the policy in one spouse, the instruments used to accomplish this result should leave no doubt that separate property is intended. Remember, the burden of proof is on the party who asserts separate property status. (Note: The presumption is the opposite in Louisiana if the noninsured spouse is named as policyowner.[22])

Community funds should not be used to pay premiums on insurance the noninsured spouse holds as separate property. If the payment of premiums creates a presumption that the policy is community property or the allocation-of-premium rule (discussed below) applies, as much as one-half of the proceeds of the policy may be includible in the insured's gross estate.[23]

Inception-of-Title versus Allocation-of-Premium Rule

Be aware that the limited case law, the interpretations and rulings of the IRS, and the facts and circumstances of each case make categorizing community-property states and their treatment of life insurance as community or separate property difficult. Commentators on community property differ as to the labels attached to each state's theory.

In most community-property states, as we mentioned earlier, insurance acquired before marriage in a common-law state may retain its character as separate property, with the result that the entire proceeds will be includible in the insured's estate if the insured is the owner. This is known as the *inception-of-title rule*. Even in such states, the later payment of premiums from community funds may create a right of reimbursement for the spouse who is not the policyowner.[24]

However, in California, Nevada, and Washington, a premium test may apply. If any premiums are paid partly from community funds and partly from separate funds, the proceeds of the policy, instead of being includible in full in the insured's estate, are apportioned in the same ratio that the amount of community funds paid bears to the amount of separate funds paid.

Effectively Establishing Third-Party Ownership

Problems Created by Community-Property Rules. The use of third-party ownership of a life insurance policy is an effective estate-reduction technique. For example, cross-ownership of policies between spouses will remove the insurance from the insured spouse's estate. However, the proceeds will be included in the noninsured surviving spouse's estate to the extent that the proceeds are not consumed by the time of the surviving spouse's subsequent death. An ILIT (irrevocable life insurance trust) will remove the life insurance proceeds from the estates of both the insured and the surviving spouse.

However, community-property rules add some danger. Cross-ownership can be circumvented by community-property rules. If the policies are treated as community property, one-half of the proceeds will be included in the insured's gross estate at the time of his or her death.

Example: Alice and Steven Smith apply for and are owners of whole life policies on each other's life. The death benefit for each policy is $500,000. Since the policies were acquired with community funds, a presumption for community property exists. If Alice dies, one-half of the death benefit, or $250,000, is included in her gross estate under Sec. 2042. In addition, one-half of the value of Steven's policy (based on the interpolated terminal reserve and unearned premium) at the time of her death is included in her gross estate for her community interest in his policy.

A problem can also occur with an ILIT if the transfer and gift circumstances are not clearly established. Generally, when dealing with a policy that is separate property in an ILIT, it is customary to provide for income to the surviving spouse and then the remainder to the couple's children.

However, in a community-property state, the income interest might have to be withheld from the surviving spouse to prevent the possibility that the surviving spouse could be deemed to be a grantor who has retained a life interest, causing the proceeds to be drawn back into the surviving spouse's estate. This could occur if the community funds are used to purchase the life insurance policy and the intent to make a gift solely from the insured spouse was not clearly established. If the surviving noninsured spouse is treated as making a transfer of his or her community property to the ILIT, the retained life estate rules under Sec. 2036(a) will create an estate tax problem for the surviving spouse if he or she receives an income interest.

Example: Adam and Martha Jones reside in a community-property state. Martha establishes an ILIT that purchases a $1 million life insurance policy on her life. The trust provides that, following Martha's death, Adam will receive all income for his life with a remainder to their children or grandchildren. The premiums are provided by gifts to the ILIT from community funds. Adam is treated as contributing one-half of the gifts to the ILIT. When Martha dies, Adam will have made a transfer of one-half of the trust principal while holding a retained life estate. One-half of the remaining principal at the time of his death will be included in his gross estate under Sec. 2036(a).

Resolving the Problem. The first step in resolving the problem is to understand when community property applies to life insurance. It could apply if a married couple acquires a policy while they are residing in a community-property state. It could also apply if community-property funds might subsequently be used to pay premiums on the policy. The need for careful investigation and planning is obvious.

First, if separate ownership of the policy is intended, it should be clearly established. This burden will vary from state to state. Apparently, it is not that difficult in Louisiana—it merely requires that the control and incidents of ownership be held by the policyowner.[25] In other states, it may require significant documentation, including (1) a statement of parties' intent to create separate property, (2) a statement of the parties' marital relationship, and (3) the nonowner spouse's intent to make a gift of the community property to the policyowner. We certainly recommend taking all steps necessary to establish separate ownership, even if the steps seem superfluous.

Second, if community funds must be used to pay premiums on a separately owned policy, the nonowner-spouse should make a gift to the policyowner of the community funds prior to the payment of premiums. With the unlimited marital deduction, the gift of one spouse's interest in community property to the other spouse should not have gift tax consequences. Thus, the problem in our previous example could have been resolved if Adam had given Martha his interest in the funds used to pay the premiums prior to Martha's gift to the trustee.

Treatment of Retirement Plans

While the nonparticipant spouse's rights to survivor benefits from the participant spouse's qualified retirement plans is well established by the Retirement Equity Act, a question arises about the nonparticipant's community interest in such plans. What if the nonparticipant dies first? Shouldn't the nonparticipant have the right to dispose of his or her one-half community-property rights in the plan by will or otherwise? The tax rules would seem to include the one-half interest in the nonparticipant spouse's gross estate. However, a recent federal court decision states that ERISA preempts state community-property laws and that the nonparticipant spouse has no dispositive powers in the plan if he or she dies first.[26]

Benefit Plans Funded by Taxes

There is a special provision for the community interest in benefit plans funded by the employee's taxes. The courts have ruled that in a property settlement, the right to receive future social security or Railroad Retirement Act benefits has been held to be separate property of the worker, even though the income and accumulation of the retirement plan were during marriage.[27]

SUMMARY

For the financial services professional to genuinely benefit the client, there must be a basic understanding of the different natures of separate and community property and an understanding of how the properties are treated according to where, when, and how they were acquired, in what jurisdiction the real property is located, and in what state the married individual presently resides. The task is much easier if the financial services professional can memorize the following few basic points:

- The character of real property is generally controlled by the law of the situs of the property (where it is located).
- The character of personal property is usually governed by the law of the state in which the spouses live, and it is usually determined at the time of the purchase.
- Community property is generally that which is accumulated during marriage and purchased by community funds.
- The community-property states have very liberal laws that allow most property to become converted to community property with the approval of both of the spouses. The problems arise when attempting to separate the property or to prove that the property has retained its separate-property character.
- Community-property law has provisions for special double stepped-up basis, which can reduce tax on possible capital gains to the surviving spouse if the assets are sold after the decedent-spouse's death.
- Community-property law allows for simpler planning in equalizing the splitting of the estate between spouses to allow maximum use of the applicable credit amount for each spouse and heirs.

Most estate planning techniques are valid in all states, whether they are common-law states or community-property states. Nevertheless, an enhanced understanding of community-property law is one more tool for the financial services professional who truly has the client's interest at heart. Significant tax savings can be passed along to those clients who qualify for its use. To minimize litigation, however, caution is necessary when recommending converting separate property to community property, in case of future divorce or disgruntled heirs.

NOTES

1. Currently these states are Alaska, Arkansas, Colorado, Connecticut, Florida, Hawaii, Kentucky, Michigan, Montana, New York, North Carolina, Oregon, Virginia, and Wyoming. Note: The versions of the Uniform Act adopted will differ by state and affect certain property dispositions differently.

Chapter 10 Community Property—Its Implications on Estate Planning

2. IRS Pub. No. 555, Community Property (1996). Wisconsin has passed a version of the Uniform Marital Property Act (UMPA) incorporating many concepts of traditional community property.
3. Cal. Civ. Code Secs. 5107, 5108, 5110, and 5118, and IRS Pub. 555, Community Property (1996).
4. Uniform Disposition of Community Property Rights at Death Act, Sec. 1.
5. California Civil Code, Sec. 5104.
6. Arizona Revised Statutes, Sec. 25-214.
7. Wisconsin Statutes 767.29
8. Idaho Code, Sec. 15-2-201; Calif. Civ. Code, Sec. 4803.
9. Vernon's Texas Codes, Sec. 5.01.
10. Community Property and Federal Income Taxes, IRS Pub. No. 555 (1996).
11. Internal Revenue Code Sec. 7703(a).
12. Internal Revenue Code Sec. 66(a).
13. IRS Rev. Rul. 68-88, 1968-1 CB 33.
14. California Probate Code Sec. 221.
15. California Probate Code Sec. 229.
16. California Probate Code Sec. 100.
17. Internal Revenue Code Sec. 1014(b)(6).
18. Ibid.
19. Treas. Reg. Sec. 20.2042-1(c)(5) and IRS Letter Ruling 8928002.
20. IRS Reg. Sec. 25.2511-1(h)(9) and IRS Rev. Rul. 48, 1953-1 CB 392. See also Rev. Rul. 94-69, 1994-2 C.B. 241. In this case it was ruled that the surviving spouse held the property as separate property, but the case demonstrates the inadvertent gift problem since the surviving spouse designated a child as beneficiary of the policy and a completed taxable gift of the full amount of the proceeds occurred when the insured spouse died.
21. *Estate of Street v. Commissioner*, T.C. Memo. 1997-32. Unfortunately, the result was the full inclusion of the proceeds instead of the normal one-half inclusion for a policy that is community property.
22. Id.
23. *Estate of Robert W. Hass*, 51 TCM 453, CCH Dec. 42,874(M). See also *Estate of Meyer*, 66 T.C 41, 1976, and *Kern v. U.S.*, 491 F. 2d 436 (9th Cir. 1974), where the rules for the state of Washington clearly require a statement recognizing the marital status and the intent of the insured spouse to make a gift to the policyowner-spouse. Naming the noninsured policyowner on the application was not sufficient to rebut the presumption for community property for life insurance purchased with community funds.
24. Rev. Rul. 80-242, 1980-2 C.B. 276. In this instance, the Texas resident had acquired the policy prior to marriage, and the policy was treated as separate property. However, the noninsured surviving spouse held a right to reimbursement of one-half of the premiums that were paid from community funds subsequent to the marriage. The amount of the proceeds reimbursable to the surviving spouse will not be included in the insured spouse's gross estate.
25. See Rev. Rul. 94-69, 1994-2 C.B. 241.
26. *Ablamis v. Roper*, 937 F. 2d 1450 (9th Cir. 1991).
27. *Marriage of Nizenkoff*, 65 Cal. App. 3rd 136 (1976).

11

Estate Planning for Non-U.S. Citizens

Chapter Outline

TRANSFER TAXATION OF NONCITIZENS   319
    Distinctions between Citizens, Resident-Aliens, and
        Nonresident-Aliens   320
ESTATE AND GIFT TAXATION OF TRANSFERS BY
        NONRESIDENT-ALIENS   321
    Estate and Gift Taxation of Real Property and Tangible Personal
        Property for Resident-Alien Transferors   321
    Estate Taxation of Intangible Personal Property for Nonresident-Alien
        Decedents   322
    Gift Taxation of Intangible Personal Property for Nonresident-Alien
        Donors   323
    Deductions and Credits for Transfers by Nonresident-Aliens   323
ESTATE PLANNING FOR TRANSFERS TO A
        NONCITIZEN-SPOUSE   325
    Testamentary Transfers to a Surviving Noncitizen-Spouse   326
    Gift Tax Treatment of Transfers to a Noncitizen-Spouse   337
    Impact of Estate and Gift Tax Treaties   339
MINIMIZING THE BURDEN OF QDOT TREATMENT FOR
        SURVIVING NONCITIZEN-SPOUSES   339
    Problems Associated with Taxation of the QDOT   339
    Planning to Reduce the QDOT Burden   340

TRANSFER TAXATION OF NONCITIZENS

    Transfer tax planning techniques differ when the transferee or transferor or both are not U.S. citizens. Failure to ascertain the citizenship of an estate planning client and the client's spouse, the location of their property, and how the property is held by the married couple could result in serious income, estate, gift, and generation-skipping tax consequences. It is important to remember that the citizenship status of a client or the client's spouse is not always obvious from casual observation. A fact-finding process should always include questions about citizenship.

Distinctions between Citizens, Resident-Aliens, and Nonresident-Aliens

Federal transfer taxes (estate, gift, and generation-skipping transfer taxes [GSTT]) are imposed on all transfers, regardless of the location of the property, made by U.S. citizens and resident-aliens. Nonresident-aliens are subject to estate and gift taxes only for transfers of property with U.S. tax situs. The unified estate and gift tax rates are the same, regardless of the citizenship or residence of the transferor. However, as discussed below, many distinctions exist. The GSTT implications for nonresident-aliens are not specified by statute, but they have been clarified by recently released IRS regulations and will not be discussed further here.

Transfer Tax Definition of Residency

For transfer tax purposes a resident-alien is someone who resides in the United States (that is, in the 50 states or District of Columbia) but is not a citizen of the United States. For estate and gift tax—and presumably generation-skipping transfer tax—purposes, residence is synonymous with domicile. Domicile is where the taxpayer lives currently (for even a brief time) as long as the individual has no intention of moving or returning to another location. Simply put, it is where the individual intends to live permanently, for the time being. Thus any individual who has established residency in the United States will be subject to the transfer tax. (Note that the income tax definition of residency is different from the transfer tax definition, generally requiring a green card or a substantial presence in the U.S. during a tax year.)

Transfer Tax Treaties

The United States has entered into estate or gift tax treaties with several foreign countries. These treaties govern the issues concerning the transfer taxes imposed on citizens or residents of either country. The most pertinent provisions for our purposes are those that relate to potential multiple taxation of the same transfers by the two countries, although the treaties may also address important issues such as the availability of the marital or charitable deduction or the applicable credit amount. Because the treaties are not all up-to-date with subsequent changes to either country's estate or gift tax rules that went into effect after the treaty was enacted, there may be ambiguities about the implications of a treaty provision to current law. Please be aware that appropriate counsel should be obtained to determine the tax treatment of transfers that might be addressed by an estate or gift tax treaty. The United States has estate tax treaties with the following countries:

Australia	Italy
Austria	Japan
Denmark	Netherlands
Finland	Norway
France	South Africa
Greece	Sweden
Germany	Switzerland
Ireland	United Kingdom

Gift tax treaties are in effect between the U.S. and these countries:

Australia	Germany
Austria	Japan
Denmark	Sweden
France	United Kingdom

Foreign Death Tax Credit

The federal estate taxes of a citizen or resident of the United States may be reduced in some instances by the foreign death tax credit. The foreign death tax credit, which is available to estates that would otherwise be subject to multiple taxation of the same property, applies against federal estate taxes imposed on property with situs in a foreign country that also imposes death, inheritance, estate, or other death taxes on the same property. The property must be included in the decedent's gross estate, and the credit is limited to the lesser of (1) foreign death taxes paid on the property and (2) federal estate taxes caused by the property taxable in both countries. The credit may be unavailable for estates of resident-aliens unless reciprocity exists for U.S. citizens residing in the foreign country imposing the death tax on the property subject to multiple taxation.

ESTATE AND GIFT TAXATION OF TRANSFERS BY NONRESIDENT-ALIENS

Estate and Gift Taxation of Real Property and Tangible Personal Property for Resident-Alien Transferors

The tax situs of property is its location for the purposes of imposing a tax. It generally requires some nexus or contact with the jurisdiction attempting to impose a tax. As mentioned earlier, for U. S. citizens or residents all property, regardless of location, is subject to gift or estate taxes. For nonresident-aliens only property with tax situs in the United States is subject to tax. This rule applies at the time of the nonresident-alien's death for property included in the gross estate, regardless of how the property is held. Thus both probate and nonprobate items may be subject to tax. For example, community property or property held jointly with rights of survivorship will be taxable if the property has U.S. situs.

Real property has a tax situs wherever it is located. Thus only U.S. real estate held by nonresident-aliens is subject to federal estate or gift taxes. Tangible personal property physically located in the U.S. at the time of a transfer (that is, at the time of the owner's death or when the property is given away) is subject to gift or estate taxes. There is an exception in the regulations for works of art imported into the U.S. solely for exhibition purposes in a museum or gallery (no part of the earnings of which inures to the benefit of a private individual or shareholder).

Estate Taxation of Intangible Personal Property for Nonresident-Alien Decedents

Intangible personal property creates more difficulty for determining tax situs. Intangibles are normally taxed by the domiciliary state of the decedent or donor. For a nonresident-alien, however, the rules are more complex when more than one country is involved. A nonresident-alien's estate is subject to estate taxes on the following intangibles included in his or her gross estate:

- corporate stock issued by a domestic corporation
- bonds or other debt obligations owed by a U.S. individual, domestic corporation, or the United States, a state, a municipality within the United States, or the District of Columbia
- deposits or funds held in a U.S. bank, savings and loan, or similar institution if the deposits or funds are effectively connected with the conduct of a trade or business within the U.S.

The following intangibles are specifically excluded by statute from a nonresident-alien's gross estate:

- life insurance payable at the nonresident-alien's death
- deposits or funds held in a foreign branch of a domestic bank if the branch is engaged in the commercial banking business
- deposits or funds held in a U.S. bank, savings and loan, or similar institution, or funds left with a domestic insurance company under an interest-only settlement option, if the deposits or funds are not connected with the conduct of a trade or business within the U.S.

Life insurance point: Life insurance makes an excellent vehicle to manage the estate liquidity problems facing the estate of a nonresident-alien with property in the United States. The estate liquidity problem will be particularly severe if the U.S.-based property is not sufficiently liquid to pay taxes and other expenses. For example, the nonresident-alien may own vacation real estate or a business interest in the U.S. If the nonresident-alien also owns property that is more liquid but is located and subject to probate in another country, there may be difficulties or delays in receiving probate court approval to pay the U.S. taxes and expenses out of the non-U.S.-based assets. This may result in a forced liquidation of the U.S.-based assets at unfavorable times or terms. Since life insurance benefits are excluded from a nonresident-alien's estate, life insurance is a natural solution to this liquidity problem. Better yet, the rules of Sec. 2042 are inapplicable if the insured-decedent is a nonresident-alien. Thus the nonresident-alien insured can own and control the insurance policy until the time of his or her death without adverse estate tax consequences.

Gift Taxation of Intangible Personal Property for Nonresident-Alien Donors

Transfers of intangible personal property by nonresident-aliens are generally exempt from federal gift taxes. However, the IRS regulations define currency as a tangible personal property item for gift tax purposes. Thus a gift made by a nonresident-alien in the form of a check drawn on a U.S. bank account will be subject to gift taxes. In addition, transfers of intangibles by an expatriate who lost U.S. citizenship within 10 years of the transfer will be subject to gift taxes if the avoidance of taxes was one of the principal reasons for expatriation.

Deductions and Credits for Transfers by Nonresident-Aliens

Nonresident-Aliens' Estates

Funeral Expenses, Administration Expenses, and Claims. A nonresident-alien's estate may deduct normal funeral and administration expenses, claims against the estate, and losses incurred during estate settlement against the value of the gross estate for federal estate tax purposes. These deductions are subject to apportionment between the gross estate located in the U.S. and the nonresident-alien decedent's total gross estate worldwide, regardless of where the deductible expenditures were incurred. The amount deductible from the gross estate is equal to a fraction of the expenses in the proportion that the U.S.-located gross estate bears to the total gross estate. Special substantiation requirements are imposed to verify the deductible expenditures.

Marital Deduction. The normal unlimited marital deduction is available for transfers to a U.S. citizen-spouse, regardless of the the decedent's citizenship or residence. As discussed in greater detail below, the marital deduction is generally not available for transfers to a surviving noncitizen-spouse.

Charitable Deduction. The charitable deduction for nonresident-aliens' estates is more restrictive than that imposed on citizens' estates (as described in chapter 7). Bequests or other qualifying testamentary transfers to charity are deductible only if the donee is a domestic corporation or is a trustee of a fraternal society, order, or association that will use the contributions in the United States. Note, however, that an otherwise disallowed charitable deduction may be authorized by an estate tax treaty between the U.S. and another country.

Estate Tax Credits. A nonresident-alien's applicable credit amount is generally limited to $13,000—the equivalent of a transfer of $60,000. However, the normal applicable credit amount of $202,050 (1998) may apply under some circumstances if addressed by an estate tax treaty. If the treaty permits the resident of the applicable foreign country to claim the credit, the $202,050 credit is available ratably in proportion to the amount of the U.S. gross estate to the worldwide gross estate.

The state death tax credit is available for any state death taxes paid, but the maximum credit is proportionately reduced for the amount of property subject to state death taxes as compared to the total gross estate.

Gifts by Nonresident-Aliens

Excluded Transfers. As discussed above, only gifts by nonresident-aliens of U.S.-situs real and tangible personal property are subject to gift taxes. Fortunately, the $10,000 per-donee annual exclusion is available for these gifts. (Note, however, that this exclusion cannot be increased by gift-splitting between spouses since the gift-splitting rules require that both spouses have U.S. citizenship.) The exclusion for transfers to cover medical expenses or tuition is also available to nonresident-aliens. You will recall from chapter 5 that such transfers have an unlimited exclusion from gift taxes, as long as the donor makes the payments directly to the provider of the services.

Marital Deduction. The normal unlimited marital deduction is available for intraspousal gifts to a U.S. citizen-spouse, regardless of the donor's citizenship or residence. As discussed more fully below, the marital deduction is usually not available for gifts to a noncitizen-spouse. For properly structured transfers, however, the annual exclusion can be increased to $100,000 for gifts to a noncitizen-spouse.

Charitable Deduction. As with the estate tax charitable deduction for nonresident-aliens, the gift tax charitable deduction is also more restrictive than that imposed on donations by citizens or residents (see chapter 7). Donations to charity by a nonresident-alien are deductible only if the donee is a domestic corporation or is a trustee of a fraternal society, order, or association that will use the contributions in the U.S. A charitable deduction otherwise disallowed may be authorized by a gift tax treaty between the U.S. and another country.

Applicable Credit Amount. The applicable credit amount is not available for taxable gifts by a nonresident-alien. Thus it may be advantageous for a nonresident-alien to transfer U.S.-situs property at death unless the annual exclusion can be used to shelter a lifetime gift.

ESTATE PLANNING FOR TRANSFERS TO A NONCITIZEN-SPOUSE

Previously, we discussed the unlimited marital deduction for federal estate tax purposes. It offers a typical married couple an opportunity to avoid federal estate taxes at the death of the first spouse. The marital deduction is not available, however, for property passing to a surviving spouse who is not a U.S. citizen even if he or she resides in the United States. This change, brought about by TAMRA '88 (and further clarified by RRAs '89 and '90), reflects the concern in Congress that a resident-alien-spouse could receive assets in a marital transfer from the citizen-spouse and return to his or her home country with the family wealth. If a marital deduction were allowed under such circumstances, the property transferred to the noncitizen-spouse could completely escape federal estate and gift taxes.

As we discussed above, the United States does not have jurisdiction to tax a nonresident-alien for property located outside the country. Although the statutory rules for the estate and gift tax treatment for transfers were enacted in 1988 and 1989, the IRS issued final regulations on this topic in 1995 and 1996 that add substance to the rules.

Denying the marital deduction for transfers to a noncitizen-spouse follows the overall scheme that was intended for the federal estate and gift tax system—that is, that wealth accumulated by a married couple will, at the very least, be subject to transfer tax at the second death of the spouses. Simply, Congress is preserving its ability to tax the transfer of marital property at some point. The marital deduction is permitted, however, if the noncitizen-spouse is the first to die and transfers property in a qualifying manner to a surviving citizen-spouse. In this instance, the surviving spouse will be a citizen, and the United States will be able to impose a tax whenever the surviving spouse makes a transfer of his or her property.

If a marriage includes a spouse who is either (1) a citizen of or (2) a resident of a foreign country, the transfers to or from that spouse may also be subject to foreign transfer taxes. In addition, property with a foreign situs might be subject to foreign transfer taxes even if transferred by a U.S. citizen. As mentioned at the beginning of this chapter, the United States has entered into foreign estate and gift tax treaties with many countries in an attempt to avoid the double taxation of certain transfers. The actual taxation of these individuals and their foreign property depends on the specific treaty involved. As discussed above, the United States does allow a credit against the federal estate tax for foreign death taxes paid.

Testamentary Transfers to a Surviving Noncitizen-Spouse

The general rule is that transfers to a noncitizen-spouse do not qualify for the unlimited federal estate or gift tax marital deduction. This creates a special concern for marriages that include a noncitizen-spouse because the transfer taxes facing these couples often depend on which spouse survives. If the survivor is the noncitizen, there may be a substantial first-death estate tax. Fortunately, there are some exceptions to this rule, but its harshness can be demonstrated by the following example:

> *Example:* Dr. Ames is a prominent physician who has accumulated a substantial estate valued at $2.6 million. Because he was concerned about some sizable malpractice judgments that were recently imposed against some of his colleagues, Dr. Ames, acting on the advice of his attorney—who was not an estate planning specialist—transferred $1,975,000 in assets into his spouse's name. As part of the planning, a new will was drafted for Dr. Ames, leaving all his remaining assets to a discretionary trust benefiting his spouse first, then his children. He did this to avoid the marital deduction at his death since he believed that his lifetime marital transfers were sufficient for his spouse and that his applicable credit amount was enough to shelter the $625,000 (in 1998) he left in his own name.
>
> Dr. Ames dies and his attorney and executor begin preparing his estate and inheritance tax returns. It is now determined that Mrs. Ames is a citizen of Country B, a jurisdiction that imposes a death tax and does not have a transfer tax treaty with the United States. Upon further investigation, it is discovered that Dr. and Mrs. Ames jointly owned a vacation home in Country B valued at $750,000. He had never disclosed this because he assumed that fairness would prevent the U.S. from taxing assets outside the United States.

The estate examination reveals the following problems:

- First, the lifetime transfer to Mrs. Ames does not qualify for the marital deduction. Only a super-annual exclusion of $100,000 (discussed later in this chapter) and Dr. Ames's applicable credit amount can be used to shelter the gift. Thus, about $1.3 million is subject to gift taxes at marginal rates that reach 45 percent.

- Second, the gift tax return was not filed; interest and perhaps penalties are imposed.
- Third, the discretionary trust left in Dr. Ames's will does not qualify for the marital deduction; nor can the executor make the QTIP election to qualify the trust as a qualified domestic trust (QDOT) (see discussion below).
- Fourth, the jointly held property in Country B is subject to U.S. estate taxes since all worldwide property of a U.S. citizen or resident is subject to estate taxes. Thus one-half of the property located in Country B is included in Dr. Ames's estate. This may be somewhat mitigated by the foreign death tax credit; it may also be resolved if Mrs. Ames contributes this property to a QDOT on a timely basis. However, there is a foreign-source property limitation for QDOTs that might impede this solution.
- Fifth, Dr. Ames has expended his applicable credit amount because of its unexpected mandatory application to the lifetime gift he made to Mrs. Ames, and the entire gross estate is taxable at rates that will reach 53 percent.
- Finally, members of Dr. Ames's planning team are notifying their errors-and-omissions or malpractice carriers for the failure to ascertain the citizenship of Mrs. Ames.

Surviving Spouse Obtains Citizenship

Transfers to a surviving noncitizen-spouse will become eligible for the marital deduction if (1) the surviving spouse becomes a U.S. citizen before the decedent-spouse's estate tax return is filed and (2) the surviving spouse remains a U.S. resident after the citizen-spouse's death.[1]

There are also estate tax benefits to the surviving spouse for obtaining citizenship even after the citizen-spouse's estate tax return is filed. As discussed below, a qualified domestic trust can be used to transfer assets to a surviving noncitizen-spouse while preserving the marital deduction for the transfer. The surviving spouse can avoid some or all of the disadvantages associated with receiving property in a QDOT by obtaining citizenship prior to his or her death.

Qualified Domestic Trust (QDOT)

To alleviate some of the harsh estate tax implications associated with denying the marital deduction for transfers to a noncitizen-spouse, Congress created an exception for transfers to a qualified domestic trust. A QDOT is a unique transfer vehicle for marital deduction transfers to surviving noncitizen-spouses. Unfortunately, the QDOT rules also include a new type of transfer tax (a "deferred estate tax").

Although the QDOT appears to provide all the usual tax benefits of the marital deduction, the discussion that follows shows that it has several disadvantages not applicable to transfers between citizen-spouses. Some of the disadvantages are tax related, and they have to do with the unfavorable methodology behind the imposition of the deferred estate tax. Other disadvantages relate to the compliance requirements for a QDOT, which are generally much more costly and burdensome than complying with the typical marital deduction trust.

A QDOT is a trust that meets the following requirements:

- At least one trustee must be an individual who is a U.S. citizen or domestic corporation. Regulations require the use of a domestic corporate fiduciary or some other security arrangement for large—greater than $2 million—QDOTs. (Note: TRA 97 provided the authority for the Treasury to waive the U.S. trustee requirement if the QDOT is formed in a country that prohibits U.S. trustees.)
- The trust terms must stipulate that no distribution (other than income) can be made from the QDOT unless the U.S. trustee has the ability to withhold tax.
- The trust must be a U.S. trust or created in a foreign jurisdiction but maintained and governed by the laws of a U.S. state or the District of Columbia.
- The QDOT must generally be created in the form of the qualifying types of marital deduction trusts described in chapter 1. (As discussed below, a QDOT created postmortem by the executor of the deceased spouse's estate or by the surviving noncitizen-spouse to be assigned assets inherited from the deceased spouse need not necessarily comply with the marital deduction rules.)
- The executor of the decedent-spouse's estate must make an election to qualify the trust for QDOT treatment.

How Is a QDOT Created? A qualified domestic trust may be created by the decedent-spouse (through the provisions of a will or living trust), the decedent's executor, or the surviving noncitizen-spouse. It must be created prior to the time the return is due, and the QDOT election must be made.

If created by a testamentary device executed by the decedent-spouse, a QDOT is generally eligible to receive any transfer normally qualifying for a marital deduction. The property can either be (1) transferred to the QDOT pursuant to the terms of the decedent-spouse's will or living trust or (2) assigned to the QDOT by the decedent-spouse's executor or the surviving noncitizen-spouse.

A QDOT can be eligible to receive property in the following forms:

- an estate trust
- a general power-of-appointment trust
- a QTIP trust

- a charitable remainder trust payable to charity at the death of the surviving noncitizen-spouse if he or she is the only noncharitable beneficiary
- proceeds of life insurance or retirement plans
- joint property passing by right of survivorship
- transfers of probate property through the decedent's will

It is clear that a QDOT created by the decedent-spouse must take the form of one of the approved marital deduction trusts. If the QDOT does not qualify, however, it can be salvaged by a judicial reformation. The rules for postmortem reformation of a trust to ensure QDOT qualification are complex. If the trust is not reformed pursuant to the terms of the will or actual trust instrument by the estate tax return's due date (including extensions), the executor or surviving noncitizen-spouse must commence a judicial proceeding to reform the trust before that date. To create maximum flexibility and defray potential legal costs of a judicial proceeding, therefore, it is recommended that any trust providing for a surviving noncitizen-spouse authorize the reformation of that trust if QDOT treatment is deemed desirable. Of course, in addition to the normal marital deduction rules applicable to the QDOT, the decedent-spouse's will or living trust should not provide for funding the QDOT with any assets (for example, terminable interests) that do not qualify for the marital deduction.

As noted above, if the QDOT is not created by the decedent-spouse's testamentary device, it can be created by the executor of the decedent-spouse's estate or by the surviving noncitizen-spouse. Under these circumstances, it is not necessary that the trust be structured to qualify as a normal marital deduction trust. All that is necessary is that the tax compliance rules for a QDOT (for example, the U.S. trustee and withholding requirements) be met. In fact, it is advantageous for both tax reasons and administrative flexibility if the QDOT is designed without the normal marital deduction restrictions. For example, the surviving noncitizen-spouse may choose to create a revocable trust retaining all rights to the distribution of principal and income. As discussed below, assets left directly to a surviving noncitizen-spouse can be directly assigned to the QDOT. Since the QDOT is revocable, the survivor will not have made a taxable gift to the trust remainderpersons when assets are assigned to the QDOT. Moreover, the surviving noncitizen-spouse can retain the right to revoke the trust or distribute principal. This gives him or her the flexibility to accelerate the deferred estate tax if it is deemed advantageous to do so by either revoking the trust or distributing principal.

Assignment of Assets to a QDOT. In addition to direct funding of the QDOT through the terms of the decedent-spouse's will or living trust, any property passing to the surviving noncitizen-spouse will be eligible for QDOT treatment if it is irrevocably assigned to the QDOT. Property can be transferred to a QDOT through assignment by the decedent-spouse's executor or by the surviving noncitizen-spouse. For example, any property received directly by the spouse—the proceeds of life insurance on the decedent-spouse's life, tenancy-in-common property transferred to the survivor by operation of law, or direct bequests to the survivor, for example—can be assigned to the QDOT. However, any irrevocable assignment of property to the QDOT must occur before the decedent-citizen-spouse's estate tax return is filed and the QDOT election is made. Generally, the property must be delivered or conveyed before the administration of the estate is completed.

If the decedent-spouse's executor or the surviving noncitizen-spouse can also qualify property transferred directly to the survivor for the marital deduction simply by irrevocably assigning that property to a QDOT, it is irrelevant whether the QDOT was created by the decedent-spouse, the decedent-spouse's executor, or the surviving noncitizen-spouse. Therefore QDOT treatment is available even if the decedent-spouse neglected to include a QDOT in his or her estate plan. The surviving noncitizen-spouse can preserve the marital deduction on property he or she receives by creating a QDOT and irrevocably assigning property received from the decedent-spouse to it in a timely fashion. Thus a surviving noncitizen-spouse can preserve the marital deduction by transferring property he or she received (1) through an outright bequest or intestacy, (2) as proceeds of life insurance on the life of the decedent-spouse, and (3) as survivor annuities[2] to the QDOT.

> *Planning point:* It is important to note that the survivor will be considered the transferor of the property transferred or assigned to the QDOT for all tax purposes (other than qualifying for the QDOT). Thus the surviving spouse should take care to avoid making completed gifts of the remainder interest in the QDOT or immediate gift taxes may result. For example, suppose the QDOT is structured as a QTIP trust giving the surviving noncitizen-spouse all income for life with a remainder to the couple's children. If the surviving noncitizen-spouse transfers property received as an outright bequest or through a beneficiary designation to the QDOT, he or she will be making a taxable gift of the remainder interest to the children. In this instance, it would be preferable for the surviving spouse to create a separate QDOT postmortem, retaining the right to revoke the trust, and to assign these assets to the newly created QDOT. Since the new QDOT would be revocable, no taxable gift would occur when the assets were assigned to the trust.

IRAs and Other Retirement Plan Benefits. Retirement plan assets left to the surviving noncitizen-spouse require special consideration. Planners must therefore be sure to include the client's retirement plan when they are planning the client's estate. The beneficiary designation should be formed in conjunction with the client's wills and trusts and with all the due care that goes into the preparation of those documents. In many instances the beneficiary designation for IRAs and other retirement plan benefits is even more important than for wills

Chapter 11 Estate Planning for Non-U.S. Citizens

and trusts because retirement plan assets may dwarf the size of the probate estate.

The QDOT regulations give special treatment to retirement plan accounts or annuities. Although individual retirement annuities are generally not assignable, the regulations provide for QDOT treatment if certain complex compliance requirements are met. Thus retirement assets will be treated as passing in the form of a QDOT, notwithstanding that the spouse does not irrevocably transfer or assign the annuity or other payment to the QDOT. The regulations also permit assignable retirement plan accounts to be treated as nonassignable and thus qualify for QDOT treatment under the same rules applicable to the nonassignable annuities.

The nonassignable annuities will receive QDOT treatment if one of two requirements is met: (1) The surviving spouse could pay the deferred estate tax on any principal distributions (the taxation of principal from QDOTs is discussed below) from the IRA, or (2) he or she could roll over the principal portion of an annuity payment to a QDOT. The procedure for meeting the first requirement is as follows:

- The surviving noncitizen-spouse agrees to pay on an annual basis the deferred estate tax imposed on the principal (except for distributions on account of hardship) from the nonassignable annuity or other payment received under the plan or arrangement.
- The executor of the decedent's estate files an information statement providing details of the retirement annuity or account with the estate tax return.
- The executor files the agreement to pay deferred estate tax with the estate tax return and makes the QDOT election for the retirement annuity or account.

Alternatively, rolling over the principal portion of an annuity payment entails the following:

- The surviving noncitizen-spouse agrees to roll over and transfer, within 60 days of receipt, the principal portion of each annuity payment (except principal that could be distributed for hardship) to a QDOT.
- The executor of the decedent's estate files the information statement with respect to the retirement annuity or account with the estate tax return.
- The executor files the agreement to roll over annuity payments and makes the QDOT election with respect to the nonassignable annuity or other payment.

The regulations use complex formulas to determine how each payment from the retirement annuity or account must be divided between principal and income.

Remember, the principal (other than for hardship) portion of any distribution is subject to deferred estate tax unless the rollover election is made. These rules for determining the principal and income portion of each payment apply in addition to the normal minimum distribution rules applicable to retirement plans.

Other QDOT Funding Issues. Assets transferred to a QDOT must be included in the decedent-spouse's gross estate (or be the proceeds of the sale of such assets). The survivor cannot transfer substitute property to a QDOT. In addition, the survivor can choose to assign property to a QDOT through pecuniary or other marital formula transfers. This gives the executor and the surviving noncitizen-spouse the opportunity to do optimal postmortem marital deduction planning with assets assigned to the QDOT. Typically, they would choose to fund the QDOT with just enough assets to defer the estate tax but use the decedent-spouse's applicable credit amount. However, if the assignment is expressed in the form of a pecuniary amount (such as a fixed-dollar amount or a formula designed to reduce the decedent's estate tax to zero), the regulations have rules for assigning a fair value to the QDOT. This prevents the postmortem technique of funding the QDOT with heavily depreciated assets.

Taxation of QDOT Distributions. The transfer to a QDOT is unlike the typical marital deduction transfer in many respects. Although the tax treatment applicable to the QDOT delays the estate taxation until the noncitizen-spouse's death, this second-death taxation depends on a unique theory. The taxation of property distributed from a QDOT is based on the estate situation of the first spouse to die. The first spouse to die is treated as the transferor of distributions from the QDOT, and the QDOT estate tax is calculated with the QDOT property included in the first spouse to die's tax base. Because of the marital deduction, however, the estate tax for property transferred to a QDOT is deferred until the QDOT corpus is distributed either (1) during the life of the surviving noncitizen-spouse or (2) at his or her death. The following events will trigger the QDOT tax (the deferred estate tax):

- distributions of QDOT property to the surviving spouse except distributions of (1) income[3] or (2) on account of hardship
- distributions of QDOT property at the surviving spouse's death
- the trust's failure to meet the QDOT requirements
- payment by the QDOT of the tax imposed (or the U.S. trustee's withholding of such tax) upon the first of any of the above triggering events (which is considered a taxable distribution that sets off yet another tax). In other words, the QDOT's payment of the deferred estate tax on a distribution is itself a distribution (equal to the amount of the tax) subject to a further estate tax. Thus the deferred estate tax is tax inclusive just like the regular estate tax. (However, there is a specific exemption for reimbursement for income taxes if the surviving

noncitizen-spouse takes a lump-sum distribution from the decedent's retirement plan.)

Similar to other transfer taxes, the deferred estate tax, which is imposed on any of the above taxable events, is determined cumulatively. That is, each additional QDOT taxable event will be added to previous taxable transfers to form the QDOT tax base, and each transfer may be subject to a higher marginal estate tax bracket. The notable distinguishing characteristic between the deferred estate tax and the tax on a typical marital deduction trust is that the deferred estate tax is referenced to the decedent-spouse's transfer tax base rather than the survivor's. The deferred estate tax is calculated by adding the property to the decedent-spouse's taxable estate and by computing the tax based on the rate applicable to that estate after the QDOT property is added.

This unusual tax treatment causes the deferred estate tax imposed on a QDOT distribution to be different, perhaps substantially, from the second-death tax imposed on the normal marital-deduction trust. If the spouse leaving assets to the noncitizen-spouse has substantially more assets, the overall estate tax paid will be greater. This is because the deferred estate tax paid on the QDOT distribution will be based on the wealthier spouse's estate tax bracket. Under these circumstances, the spouses will not receive the benefit of the surviving noncitizen-spouse's lower marginal transfer tax rate. Conversely, this special tax treatment could be beneficial if the noncitizen-spouse is the wealthier spouse.

Calculating the QDOT Tax. The tax payable on the occurrence of any of the four triggering taxable events discussed above is computed (in a cumulative manner similar to the tax on taxable gifts) as follows:

Step 1: State the amount of property that is involved in the taxable event.

Step 2: Add all previous taxable events.

Step 3: Compute the federal estate tax on the estate of first spouse to die if the total of steps 1 and 2 is included in the decedent's gross estate.

Step 4: Compute the federal estate tax on the estate of first spouse to die if only the amount of previous taxable events is included in the decedent's gross estate.

Step 5: Subtract the tax computed in step 4 from the tax computed in step 3.

Result: Tax imposed as result of current taxable event

Hardship Distributions. As discussed above, there is an exemption from the deferred estate tax for distributions to the surviving spouse on account of hardship. According to the regulations, a distribution of principal from the QDOT is treated as being made on account of hardship if it is in response to an immediate and substantial financial need relating to the surviving noncitizen-spouse's health, maintenance, education, or support, or to the health, maintenance, education, or support of any person whom the survivor is legally obligated to support. A distribution is not treated as made on account of hardship if the amount distributed may be obtained from other sources that are reasonably available to the surviving spouse—for example, by selling his or her personally owned, publicly traded stock or by cashing in a certificate of deposit he or she owns. However, assets such as closely held business interests, real estate, and tangible personal property are not considered sources that are reasonably available to the surviving spouse.

The preamble to the new regulations indicates that the trustee has the obligation to determine independently whether or not the surviving spouse has other assets available and cannot rely merely on the surviving spouse's statement of hardship. This places an additional burden on the U.S. trustee who is liable for the deferred estate tax if a mistake is made. Although a hardship distribution of principal is exempt from the deferred estate tax, it must be reported to the IRS on the deferred estate tax return (Form 706-QDT) even if it is the only distribution that occurred during the filing period.

Applicable Credit Amount. The applicable credit amount is generally available to shelter an individual's taxable transfers up to $625,000 (in 1998) from gift or estate taxes. Under an optimal scenario, a married couple could leave assets of up to $1.25 million free of federal estate tax by fully utilizing each spouse's $625,000 exclusion amount. However, the QDOT transfer might eliminate the possibility of taking full advantage of the applicable credit. Since the ultimate distribution of the QDOT corpus at the death of the surviving noncitizen-spouse is treated as if the decedent-spouse made the transfer, the surviving noncitizen-spouse's applicable credit is unavailable to shelter this transfer from QDOT tax. Thus the noncitizen-spouse will waste his or her credit unless he or she owns sufficient assets (approximately $625,000) outside the QDOT.

> *Example:* Suppose Tom, a U.S. citizen, is married to Sheila, a noncitizen. Tom has $1.5 million of individually owned assets, while Sheila has accumulated no personal wealth. Tom dies this year (1998), and his will leaves $625,000 to a credit shelter trust to benefit his children from a prior marriage. The remaining amount, $875,000, ignoring taxes and other estate settlement expenses, is left outright to Sheila. If Tom dies this year, Sheila can qualify the transfer of the $875,000 for the unlimited marital deduction by transferring those funds irrevocably to a QDOT before Tom's estate tax return is filed. The

remaining $625,000 left in trust to his children will be sheltered from tax by Tom's applicable credit. If Sheila dies later this year, the $875,000 in the QDOT will be subject to tax as if it were included in Tom's estate—that is, at a marginal bracket of 43 percent—and will incur an additional estate tax of $353,750. If the $875,000 were instead subject to Sheila's tax rate, only $95,000 of tax would be due because her estate would be in only a 39 percent marginal bracket and would, in this case, have the benefit of her applicable credit—leaving only $275,000 subject to estate tax. (As discussed below, the QDOT actually *is* in Sheila's estate. Any tax due as a result of its inclusion in Sheila's estate will be avoided, however, since her estate will receive a credit for the QDOT tax paid on the same distribution.)

State Death Tax Credit. Because the surviving spouse has the benefit of the QDOT for the remainder of his or her life, the transfer of the QDOT corpus at his or her death will, most likely, be subject to state death taxes. Since the federal tax—the deferred estate tax—is treated as if the original decedent-spouse is making the transfer, there is a question about the state death taxes the surviving noncitizen-spouse pays. The regulations provide for the state death taxes the surviving noncitizen-spouse's estate pays to be included in the computation for the deferred estate tax. Thus the surviving noncitizen-spouse's state death tax credit can be used against the deferred estate tax payable at his or her death.

Credit for Tax on Prior Transfers. A QDOT, similar to any typical marital deduction trust, is included in the surviving spouse's gross estate at his or her death. Will the QDOT property be subject to both a QDOT tax and a federal estate tax imposed on the surviving spouse's estate? Fortunately, there is a credit for a transfer tax paid on prior transfers of the same property, and it applies liberally to the QDOT taxable distribution. The net effect of this credit is that when the surviving spouse dies, no federal estate tax will be due to the extent that the same property transfer incurs a QDOT tax.[4]

Credit for Foreign Death Taxes. Since the assets of the QDOT are included in the surviving noncitizen-spouse's gross estate for federal estate tax purposes, these assets may be subject to both U.S. and foreign death taxes. In computing the deferred estate tax, the taxes paid by the surviving noncitizen-spouse's estate with respect to the QDOT are creditable to the extent normally allowable. Foreign death taxes previously paid by the decedent-spouse's estate are also creditable to the extent normally allowable.

New Compliance and Security Requirements for QDOTs

The QDOT rules were created by Congress to prevent the loss of estate tax dollars if assets left to a noncitizen-spouse could be transferred out of the U.S. and away from the jurisdiction of the Treasury. As discussed earlier, the statute imposed requirements that a U.S. trustee be named and that the trustee have the power to withhold deferred estate taxes on any taxable distribution. Also as discussed above, the final regulations necessitate voluminous compliance filings by the U.S. trustee to report a QDOT's activities.

New regulations offer additional security requirements to ensure the collection of the deferred estate tax. The regulations impose different and more stringent standards on large (greater than $2 million) QDOTs and generally add more volumes to the filing requirements. Until the values are finally determined on an estate tax return, a will or other testamentary device creating a QDOT should include the requirements of both large and small QDOTs if there is any question about whether the trust will meet the threshold for large QDOTs.

Small QDOTs. For QDOTs containing under $2 million, an individual U.S. trustee is sufficient. This is desirable if the family wishes to avoid the expense of having a corporate fiduciary and wants the personal touch of a family-friendly trustee.

Large QDOTs. According to the regulations, a large QDOT must meet one of three alternative security requirements. (The regulations also suggest that other arrangements will be considered in a request for a private ruling.) The three specified alternatives are as follows:

- The QDOT must require that at least one trustee be a U.S. bank or a U.S. branch of a foreign bank (provided a U.S. trustee with a tax home in the U.S. serves as cotrustee).
- The QDOT must require an individual U.S. trustee to post a bond in favor of the IRS equal to 65 percent of the value the trust assets.
- The trust instrument must require that the individual U.S. trustee furnish an irrevocable letter of credit issued by a U.S. bank, a United States branch of a foreign bank, or a foreign bank, and confirmed by a U.S. bank in an amount equal to 65 percent of the fair market value of the trust assets.

The regulations give rules for determining the size of the QDOT for the purposes of the $2 million threshold. First, the fair market value of the assets passing, treated, or deemed to have passed to the QDOT (or in the form of a QDOT) is determined without reduction for any indebtedness of QDOT assets. Second, the value of the surviving noncitizen-spouse's personal residence placed in the QDOT (up to $600,000 attributed to real property and related furnishings) may be excluded in determining whether the $2 million threshold is met. Finally, the trust instrument must require that no more than 35 percent of the fair market value of the trust assets can consist of real property located outside of the United States, or the trust must meet the bank trustee, bond, or security requirements required for QDOTs greater than $2 million.

Of course, substantiating valuation issues demands meeting significant annual filing requirements, and penalties can be applied to understatements of value. Trust assets require careful monitoring since the QDOT could easily slip above the $2 million threshold. Therefore the trustee's investment policy should cautiously control the amount of principal in the QDOT. In some instances, the family might prefer investments that are less productive or distributions of principal (an event causing the deferred estate tax) to hold down the growth of principal and avoid the higher compliance cost of a large QDOT.

Gift Tax Treatment of Transfers to a Noncitizen-Spouse

The discussion that follows concerns the gift tax treatment of lifetime marital transfers to a noncitizen-spouse. The status of the donor-spouse is immaterial for this portion of the discussion. What is relevant is that the donee is a noncitizen; the donor can be a citizen, resident-alien, or nonresident-alien. Although the unlimited marital deduction shelters all qualifying marital transfers to a citizen-spouse, no gift tax marital deduction is available for transfers to a noncitizen-spouse. However, there is some special relief in the tax rules for marital transfers to a noncitizen-spouse. The gift tax annual exclusion is raised for such transfers to $100,000 (a so-called super-annual exclusion). The citizenship status at the time of the transfer is controlling for these purposes. The normal marital deduction cannot be salvaged by having the noncitizen-spouse obtain citizenship after the transfer is completed.

Present-Interest Gift Requirement

The super-annual exclusion creates some new complexity since both the annual exclusion and marital deduction rules apply. First, the normal annual exclusion rules requiring a present-interest gift are applicable. Reviewing briefly, a present-interest gift requires (1) an outright transfer in property, (2) a current income interest in a trust, or (3) a future-interest trust with current Crummey withdrawal powers given to the beneficiary for any new additions to the trust.

If the present-interest requirement is not satisfied, no exclusion will apply to the gifts; neither the regular nor super-annual exclusion will be applicable, and the donee-spouse's applicable credit amount will be wasted. Of course, wasting a noncitizen-spouse's credit for such lifetime gifts would be a serious mistake. When one or both spouses are noncitizen-residents of the U.S., the applicable credit amount is even more critical since transfers at death to a noncitizen-spouse meet the unfavorable rules discussed above. The applicable credit amount offers some relief from the necessity to fund a QDOT.

Marital Deduction Requirement

Transfers in Trust. Lifetime super-annual exclusion gifts to a noncitizen-spouse made after June 29, 1989, must follow a revised version of the normal marital deduction rules. Certainly, outright transfers to the noncitizen-spouse will qualify. Transfers to the noncitizen-spouse in trust are a more complex issue because they depart from the normal marital deduction rules described in chapter 1. A life income interest coupled with a testamentary general power of appointment (a general power-of-appointment trust) will qualify for the super-annual exclusion to the extent of the actuarial value of the income interest given to the noncitizen-spouse. A lifetime QTIP trust will not qualify. Since the donee-spouse is not a citizen, the donor-spouse cannot make the QTIP election for such transfers. This will be a problem if the donor-spouse wants to provide for the noncitizen-spouse but has children from a prior marriage and wants to preserve principal for those children. An estate trust will not qualify either; although it meets the normal marital deduction rules, it fails the present-interest test for the annual exclusion.

Joint Tenancies. The creation of a joint tenancy with rights of survivorship (or a tenancy by the entireties) is slightly more complicated. (Believe it or not, the regulations refer to old rules from a repealed code section.) Because of the unlimited marital deduction, the creation of a joint tenancy with rights of survivorship between spouses will not usually cause problems even if the contribution to the purchase price is unequal. However, the marital deduction will be denied when the donee-spouse (who contributes less than one-half the purchase price of the property) is a noncitizen. According to the regulations, the creation of a joint tenancy in real property after August 13, 1988, that would otherwise be a gift will not be treated as a gift if the donee-spouse is a noncitizen. The termination of that joint tenancy in real property, however, may result in a gift if the donee-noncitizen-spouse gets a disproportionate share (based on the initial contributions) of the proceeds. The gift on the termination of the joint tenancy should be eligible for the super-annual exclusion since the transfer is an outright present interest in property when the joint tenancy in real property is terminated.

Example: Suppose Mrs. Krandall, a citizen of the U.S., gave $150,000 to help purchase a $200,000 home in 1989. The home is held in tenancy by the entireties with her husband, a noncitizen, who provided the remainder of the purchase price ($50,000). The home is sold this year for $300,000, and the proceeds are divided equally. Mrs. Krandall makes a gift of $75,000 when the proceeds are divided equally since she should have received her proportionate share of the proceeds, which is $225,000 ([$150,000/$200,000] x $300,000), when the home was sold. However, the $100,000 super-annual exclusion shelters the entire gift from tax at that time (presuming Mrs. Krandall had not made earlier gifts exceeding $25,000 to her husband this year).

The creation of a joint interest in personal property will create an immediate gift if either spouse contributes more than one-half of the acquisition price. If the donee-spouse is a noncitizen, the marital deduction is denied. The super-annual exclusion should be available, however, since joint interests in personalty would be severable under state law and create a present interest.

Retirement Plans. Transferring a qualified survivor annuity (the required default election under the qualified plan rules) from a qualified retirement plan will qualify for an unlimited marital deduction despite the general prohibition of these rules. Presumably, it makes no difference in this instance whether the nonparticipant-surviving-spouse is a citizen or not.

Impact of Estate and Gift Tax Treaties

The countries that have estate and gift tax treaties with the United States were identified earlier. These treaties must be considered in the tax issues facing transfers to noncitizens.

To the extent that they are inconsistent with a treaty provision relating to estate, inheritance, or gift tax marital deductions, the new marital transfer rules discussed in this chapter do not apply. Effectively, this permits the donor or the estate to choose either the statutory deduction under the QDOT rules or the marital deduction allowed under the treaty. However, the estate may not avail itself of both the marital deduction under the treaty and the marital deduction under the QDOT provisions with respect to the remainder of the marital property that is not deductible under the treaty.

As cautioned earlier in this chapter, please be aware that many of these treaties were formed prior to the current rules, and there will be some ambiguities in the interpretation of the provisions. Appropriate counsel is essential for planning to use a specific treaty provision.

MINIMIZING THE BURDEN OF QDOT TREATMENT FOR SURVIVING NONCITIZEN-SPOUSES

Problems Associated with Taxation of the QDOT

The deferred estate tax imposed on QDOT distributions creates a unique system of taxation for transfers to noncitizen-spouses. The deferred estate tax is payable as if the taxable distributions from QDOT property were included in and distributed from the decedent-spouse's estate. This bunching of assets into the tax base of the decedent-spouse's estate has the following disadvantages over the normal unified estate and gift tax system:

- The noncitizen-spouse's applicable credit amount cannot be used against the deferred estate tax payable on taxable QDOT distributions, regardless of when it is imposed. Making unlimited marital transfers to a QDOT for the benefit of a noncitizen-spouse, therefore, may waste the

surviving noncitizen-spouse's applicable credit. This is most significant if the noncitizen-spouse does not have enough individual wealth to use his or her full credit.
- The couple's total taxes may be higher since bunching results in the application of higher progressive estate tax rate brackets to the QDOT distributions. Again, if the noncitizen-spouse is less wealthy, his or her lower estate and gift tax brackets may be underutilized.
- All nonhardship distributions of principal from a QDOT will be subject to immediate taxes. Normal marital deduction trusts often permit the surviving spouse to consume or give away principal to reduce the estate taxes payable at the second death.

In addition to the tax disadvantages of a QDOT, complying with the regulations means veritable full-time employment for compliance professionals. This will increase the nontax expenses for transfers to a noncitizen-spouse.

Planning to Reduce the QDOT Burden

As this chapter points out, the QDOT tax creates a problem for a married couple if one spouse is a noncitizen. This problem is exacerbated if the noncitizen-spouse is the less wealthy spouse and he or she is expected to be the second spouse to die.

Planning in these circumstances focuses on either (1) avoiding the transfer tax when distributions are made from a QDOT or (2) minimizing the use of the QDOT to transfer wealth to the noncitizen-spouse. Techniques to minimize the QDOT burden are summarized as follows:

- The noncitizen-spouse could obtain citizenship prior to his or her death and thus avoid QDOT treatment for subsequent distributions from the marital deduction trust.
- To the extent that they qualify as hardship distributions withdrawals could be made from the QDOT without tax during the surviving spouse's lifetime.
- The remainder interest in the QDOT could be transferred to a charity. The charitable deduction will eliminate such transfers from the transfer tax base.
- The surviving spouse could remarry. If the new spouse is a U.S. citizen, the surviving spouse could transfer QDOT property to the new spouse and qualify for the marital deduction. Of course, this technique is available only in limited circumstances and to the extent that the surviving noncitizen-spouse has the ability under the terms of the trust to transfer the QDOT corpus.
- Making lifetime super-annual exclusion gifts to the noncitizen-spouse could minimize the need to fund the QDOT.

- Life insurance could be particularly advantageous for estate planning in this situation. There are advantages for insuring either spouse under these circumstances.

The discussion below focuses on three of the techniques above—the noncitizen-spouse's obtaining U.S. citizenship, the making of lifetime gifts to the noncitizen-spouse, and the use of life insurance to mitigate the QDOT tax burden.

Obtaining Citizenship Status

If it is feasible and desirable, the noncitizen-spouse could obtain U.S. citizenship and thereby reduce or eliminate the QDOT tax. If this is accomplished while both spouses are alive, subsequent lifetime gifts will qualify under the normal unlimited marital deduction rules. Furthermore, the QDOT problem will be avoided at the death of either spouse.

While citizenship that a surviving noncitizen-spouse attains on a timely basis eliminates the QDOT requirements entirely, even if the surviving noncitizen-spouse attains citizenship later, it will help reduce the QDOT burden. If the surviving noncitizen-spouse becomes a citizen prior to his or her own death, the QDOT rules can be avoided by treating all QDOT distributions made before he or she became a citizen as gifts by the survivor. The QDOT's trustee must notify the IRS that the surviving spouse has attained citizenship, and under these circumstances there is a general residency requirement for the surviving spouse. Special adjustments will be necessary for treating precitizenship taxable transfers as gifts by the survivor.[5]

Lifetime Gifts to the Noncitizen-Spouse

Annual gifts to the noncitizen-spouse over a number of years will increase his or her individually owned property. There are three benefits to this pattern of gifting. First, the donor-spouse's gross estate will be reduced. Second, the wealth transferred to the noncitizen-spouse will lessen the need to fund a QDOT. Finally, the assets transferred to the noncitizen-spouse through lifetime gifts will be included in his or her gross estate and can be sheltered by his or her applicable credit amount.

> *Example:* Suppose Mrs. Haynes, a citizen of the U.S., has individually owned wealth that totals $1,625,000. She is married to Mr. Haynes, who is not a U.S. citizen and has no significant wealth. If Mr. Haynes is expected to survive Mrs. Haynes, the normal optimal marital deduction planning would indicate placing Mrs. Haynes's estate into a marital formula arrangement leaving a QDOT and a credit shelter trust. Ignoring estate expenses, the QDOT would be funded with $1 million and the credit shelter trust with $625,000. The credit shelter trust would

bypass estate taxes at the death of either spouse. However, the QDOT remainder would be subject to a second-death tax at Mr. Haynes's subsequent death as if it were included in Mrs. Haynes's estate. Thus the marginal bracket payable on this deferred estate tax would be 45 percent (the bracket for taxable estates between $1.5 and $2 million) since the total transfers would be bunched in Mrs. Haynes's estate for the purposes of the deferred estate tax on QDOT distributions. It could be worse if the principal of the QDOT grows over the time of Mr. Haynes's survivorship. We can assume that the access to all income of the two trusts would prevent Mr. Haynes from qualifying for nontaxable hardship distributions of principal from the QDOT.

Suppose instead that Mrs. Haynes made super-annual-exclusion gifts of $100,000 per year to Mr. Haynes over the last 6 years of her life. At her death, her estate would be divided between a $400,000 distribution to the QDOT and a $625,000 distribution to her credit shelter trust. If Mr. Haynes lived off the income of the QDOT (assume it is invested to maximize income and hold down growth) and his own assets, the tax picture at Mr. Haynes's subsequent death would be much more attractive. The credit shelter trust created by Mrs. Haynes would escape tax, as would the $600,000 Mr. Haynes held individually since he could now use his full applicable credit amount. What's more, the deferred estate tax paid on the QDOT would probably be paid with 39 or 41 percent as its highest marginal tax bracket.

Using Life Insurance to Minimize the QDOT Burden

Life insurance can be used effectively to mitigate or even avoid the QDOT tax. First, the noncitizen-spouse could purchase life insurance on the other spouse's life. Since the death proceeds would not be included in the insured spouse's gross estate, the noncitizen-spouse would receive the proceeds free of the necessity of a QDOT. These proceeds might be useful later in creating a fund to use the noncitizen-spouse's applicable credit amount at his or her subsequent death. If the noncitizen-spouse will have other assets against which to use his or her applicable credit amount, the couple should consider alternative ownership arrangements. For example, if an irrevocable life insurance trust (ILIT) owned the life insurance, the proceeds would escape estate taxation in both spouses' estates.

Survivorship (second-to-die) life insurance policies are particularly useful in these circumstances. The deferred estate tax on the QDOT is usually payable at the death of a surviving noncitizen-spouse and is usually more onerous than the typical second-death estate tax. For these reasons, survivorship life insurance is especially suitable for a marriage in which one spouse is a noncitizen. If an ILIT is undesirable, the couple's children could own the life insurance policy and the proceeds would escape taxation in either spouse's estate.

NOTES

1. For purposes of determining when a return is filed, an early return is considered filed on the last date that the return is required to be filed (including extensions), and a late return filed at any time after the due date is considered filed on the date that it is actually filed. Treas. Reg. Sec. 20.2056A-1(b). Of course, under the naturalization statutes there are some additional requirements to obtain citizenship. An applicant for citizenship must maintain a residence within the United States and have continuous residence and physical presence in the United States for 2 1/2 out of the 5 years prior to application. It has been suggested that it may be practically impossible to attain citizenship within the 15 months following the decedent's death. One solution would be to file late and apply "reasonable cause" relief from late filing and payment penalties for the purposes of Sec. 6651 if the survivor decides to begin naturalization proceedings. Another choice is to qualify the transfers to the survivor under the QDOT rules and then begin (or continue) naturalization proceedings.
2. The Treasury regulations provide for QDOT treatment for a joint-and-survivor annuity. These rules are necessary to permit such treatment since distributions from a qualified retirement plan or an IRA often cannot technically be assigned to a QDOT.
3. Income distributions are defined to be the actual income of the trust for accounting purposes; taxable income and accounting income are not necessarily the same. The regulations limit the flexibility of the trust terms with respect to the definition of *income* to prevent the abuse of the QDOT tax. For example, income does not include capital gains. In addition, income does not include any other item that would be allocated to corpus under applicable local law governing the administration of trusts, irrespective of any specific trust provision to the contrary. In cases where there is no specific statutory or case law regarding the allocation of such items under the law governing the administration of the QDOT, the allocation will be governed by general principles of law (including but not limited to any uniform state acts, such as the Uniform Principal and Income Act, or any restatements of applicable law).
4. However, if the noncitizen-spouse is the wealthier spouse, the credit for the QDOT tax paid may be less than the noncitizen-spouse's estate tax liability with respect to the same transferred QDOT property. The credit for tax paid on prior transfers will not eliminate the surviving spouse's estate tax under these circumstances.
5. A QDOT is no longer subject to the imposition of the deferred estate tax if the surviving spouse becomes a citizen of the United States and the spouse is a United States resident at all times after the death of the decedent and before becoming a United States citizen, or no taxable distributions are made from the QDOT before the spouse becomes a United States citizen (regardless of the residency status of the spouse). If the spouse fails the residency requirement and taxable QDOT distributions have already occurred, a special election by the surviving spouse will eliminate future QDOT treatment if the following occur:
    - The spouse elects to treat any taxable distribution from the QDOT prior to the spouse's election as a taxable gift made by the spouse for the purposes of determining adjusted taxable gifts on the survivor's estate tax return and for the purposes of determining the amount of the gift tax imposed on actual taxable gifts made by the spouse during the year in which he or she becomes a citizen or in any subsequent year.
    - The spouse elects to treat any previous reduction in the deferred estate tax by reason of the decedent's unified credit as a reduction in the surviving spouse's unified credit for purposes of determining the amount of the credit allowable with respect to taxable gifts made by the surviving spouse during the taxable year in which he or she becomes a citizen or in any subsequent year.

12

Taxation of Trusts

Chapter Outline

REVOCABLE TRUSTS 346
TRANSFERS TO TRUSTS WITH RETAINED POWERS; EFFECT
    OF GRANTOR TRUST RULES 348
  Income Tax Consequences under Grantor Trust Rules 348
  Prohibited Powers and Controls 349
  Permissible Powers and Controls under Sec. 674 353
  Relinquishment of Retained Powers 354
  Estate Tax Consequences of Transfers to Trusts with Retained Powers
      or Control 354
COMPARISON OF INCOME, GIFT, AND ESTATE TAX
    CONSEQUENCES OF TRANSFERS TO TRUSTS WITH
    RETAINED POWERS OR CONTROL 355
  Transfers with Retained Powers to Alter, Amend, Revoke,
      or Terminate 355
  Transfers to Trusts or Custodial Arrangements for Benefit of Minors 357
  Transfers with Powers to Invade Corpus 359
  Reciprocal Transfers 361
IRREVOCABLE LIVING TRUSTS WITH NO RETAINED POWERS
    OR CONTROLS 362
  Advantages 362
  Disadvantages 363
  Tax Consequences 364
  Tax-Advantageous Trust Provisions for Life Income Beneficiary
      of Irrevocable Trust 365
GENERATION-SKIPPING TRANSFER TAX 366
  Taxable Distributions 367
  Taxable Terminations 367
  Direct Skips 368
  Overlapping Definitions 369
  Taxable Amounts 369
  Exemptions and Exclusions 370
  Rate of Tax 370

Deductions, Credits, and Special Provisions 371
Planning Implications 371
POWERS OF APPOINTMENT 372
Terminology and Definitions 372
Taxation of Powers 372
Lapse of Powers 374
5-and-5 Rule 374
Increased Flexibility with No Adverse Tax Consequences 375

Since the taxation of trusts is so complex, it is helpful to start with the concept of the least complicated types of transfers to trusts in terms of how much of the property interest the grantor (transferor) actually gives away. If one considers transfers to trusts in this way, the least property interest that a grantor can transfer is bare legal title, reserving for himself or herself the beneficial enjoyment of the transferred property and the power to change any part of the arrangement at any time. This is an example of a revocable trust. Since the grantor has not really transferred any significant property interest, the federal tax law for income, gift, and estate tax purposes treats the transfer as if it had never occurred. That is to say, the income from the trust is taxed to the grantor, no gift tax liability arises, and all the property in the trust is includible in the grantor's estate for estate tax purposes. For a revocable trust there is no question that these are the tax results.

On the other hand, if the grantor transfers property to an irrevocable trust and retains no power over the trust and no beneficial interest in the trust either for himself or herself or his or her estate, the tax consequences are again certain: A gift tax liability will arise if the amount transferred to the trust exceeds (or does not qualify for) the $10,000 per donee annual exclusion, the income from the trust property will be taxed to the trust or its beneficiaries, and generally the value of the property transferred will be excluded from the grantor's gross estate for estate tax purposes.

The uncertainties and complexities arise when transfers to trusts are made by grantors who wish to retain certain benefits from or control over the property. In those cases the tax consequences of each transfer depend on the powers or benefits retained, and the results may be surprising. For example, it is possible to have a transfer to a trust that is complete for gift tax purposes and yet will still be includible in the grantor's gross estate for estate tax purposes.

REVOCABLE TRUSTS

A truly revocable trust is a neutral tax tool. No gift tax is incurred on the creation of a revocable trust because there has been no completed gift. All the income will continue to be taxed to the grantor whether it is actually paid to the grantor or to someone else. This is because the grantor has the right to get the property back at any time. Indirectly, the grantor has control over the income for this reason. Because no completed gift has been made, there will be no gift tax to pay. However, when income is actually paid out to a beneficiary other than the grantor, the gift of the income paid out is complete and is subject to tax. When the grantor dies, the trust property will be included in his or her gross estate.

Although the revocable trust does not offer some of the tax advantages available to the irrevocable trust during the grantor's lifetime, there are many other reasons for recommending it. The revocable trust is often adopted as the vehicle for passing either all or a portion of an individual's estate at death. The following are some of its advantages:

- A revocable living trust will become irrevocable at the death of the grantor and it will avoid probate, thus eliminating the expenses, publicity, and delays of probate. Moreover, in contrast to a will and testamentary trust, court supervision can generally be avoided.
- If the trust is funded during lifetime, the grantor has an opportunity to observe the trust in operation as well as to make any necessary changes.
- A funded trust can provide investment management and a steady flow of income with no interruption at the death, disability, or incompetency of the settlor.
- The revocable living trust can be used as a pour-over device to which assets are transferred, such as death benefits from qualified employee plans and life insurance kept outside the estate.
- Assets that are located in more than one jurisdiction can be consolidated in a revocable trust, thereby reducing the need for administration of the decedent's property in more than one jurisdiction.
- A revocable trust may be a way to safeguard assets against the spouse's right of election against the grantor's will.
- The grantor may select the situs of a revocable trust, thereby allowing him or her to choose the law that will govern the operation and interpretation of the trust instrument. By selecting the law of one state over another, it may be possible to accomplish particular objectives that would be prohibited by the law of the grantor's domicile.
- The revocable trust may offer immunity from the claims of creditors in a number of states.
- The revocable trust may be useful in avoiding statutory restrictions on gifts. Some states have enacted laws specifically limiting or prohibiting gifts to charities made shortly before the estate owner's death. The revocable trust may be able to bypass this restriction and make gifts to charitable beneficiaries.
- If the grantor has a going business in operation, placing it in a revocable trust may enable the business to continue without interruption at the grantor's death.

- Although there are no tax benefits with regard to income or estate taxes, revocable trusts may be set up so that the estate tax is avoided on the death of the income beneficiaries.

TRANSFERS TO TRUSTS WITH RETAINED POWERS; EFFECT OF GRANTOR TRUST RULES

Although there is the possibility of both income and estate tax saving through the creation of a living irrevocable trust, there are potential problems in achieving these desired tax results if the grantor has retained some interest or control over the transferred property. It is not sufficient that an irrevocable trust be created to obtain the benefit of separate taxpayers. Every effort should be made to avoid the taxation of trust income to the grantor and to eliminate the possibility that the property will be included in the grantor's gross estate when he or she dies. Although the grantor gave the property away completely during lifetime and did not retain any direct benefits, care must be taken to comply with a set of income tax rules called the grantor trust rules as well as with certain estate tax provisions to accomplish maximum results. Congress enacted this series of complex rules to prevent grantors from giving away property to avoid taxes when in reality they retained some interest or control over the property.

Be acutely aware that the income, gift, and estate tax rules and concepts are separate units that are not necessarily integrated. They often do not work in synchronization. For example, a gratuitous transfer may be complete for gift tax purposes but will be incomplete for estate tax purposes because of some retained interests. Although a gift tax has been paid on a transfer, there is no assurance (1) that the property will avoid taxation in the donor's estate or (2) that the donor can successfully shift the income tax burden of the property from himself or herself to the trust or beneficiaries. Savings in estate and income taxes through lifetime gifts are possible only if the donor is willing to completely sever any prohibited interest and control over the property and to eliminate the possibility of obtaining personal benefits (whether direct or indirect) from the trust. Through an irrevocable trust it may be possible to make less than absolute transfers and still avoid negative estate and income tax consequences. However, the trust must be so designed as to avoid all the potential tax traps both for income and estate tax purposes.

Income Tax Consequences under Grantor Trust Rules

Although the grantor has created an irrevocable trust with no chance of the property's being returned to him or her and has filed a timely gift tax return, the income may be inadvertently taxed to the grantor if he or she retains any of the proscribed powers and controls enumerated in a series of income tax provisions (Secs. 671–678) in the Internal Revenue Code, commonly referred to as the grantor trust rules. These prohibited powers or types of control must be avoided if the grantor of a trust wants to successfully shift the income tax burden to the trust or its beneficiaries.

A concept that is very important to an understanding of the grantor trust rules is that of an adverse party or a party having an adverse interest. An adverse party is defined under these Code sections as someone having a substantial beneficial interest in the trust, including a general power of appointment over the trust property. In other words, an adverse party for these purposes is someone who stands to benefit from the trust, either as an income beneficiary, remainderperson, or both. Note that an independent trustee who is presumably objective is generally considered a nonadverse party. The terms *adverse interest* or *adverse party* as used in these sections imply that consent is needed from someone who stands to lose by the grantor's exercise of the power.

Prohibited Powers and Controls

The following are forbidden powers and controls:

- The right to acquire the trust property for less than full and adequate consideration is forbidden. This prevents the grantor from shifting the income tax while simultaneously retaining the power to regain the property. The prohibition is broad; even if a nonadverse party (any person who does not have a beneficial interest in the trust property) has a power to acquire the trust property for less than full and adequate consideration, the income of the trust will still be taxable to the grantor, regardless of who the nonadverse party is. Additionally, income will be taxed to the grantor if the trust property can be sold to any person for an inadequate consideration. The reason for these restrictions is that such a power would enable the grantor to control beneficial enjoyment of the property. In other words, it would be possible for the grantor to deprive the named beneficiary of part of his or her interest and transfer it to another person by bargain sale.
- The power to borrow trust assets or trust income without adequate interest or security is a prohited power. This rule is not applicable if the consent of a person with an adverse interest is required. Note again that the trustee typically does not have an adverse interest. However, the trust instrument may contain a general lending power that authorizes a trustee (other than the grantor) to make loans to any person without regard to interest or security without creating adverse income tax consequences for the grantor (Sec. 675(2)).

Technical Advice Memorandum 8802004 addresses certain issues involving Sec. 675. The IRS stated the chief issue this way:

> If a grantor transferred to himself as trustee of a trust a promissory note that had been made by a partnership in which

he was a partner, and if, after the transfer of the note in trust, the partnership terminated and the grantor became the sole obligor on the note, then is the grantor treated as the owner of the trust under Section 675(3) of the Internal Revenue Code if he fails to make required payments on the note as they become due?

The ruling continues by saying:

> "A," as trustee, failed to enforce the terms of the mortgage note. The note calls for monthly payments of principal and interest, and the note requires that interest be computed by reference to a specified index. Moreover, the note provides that if the obligor does not make payments on the note according to its terms, the holder may, at the holder's discretion, accelerate the entire principal due on the note. "A," in his capacity as the obligor on the note, did not make the payments required under the terms of the note, but rather, passed through to the trust the net cash flow from the encumbered property. "A," in his capacity as trustee, never sought to collect a greater amount.
>
> By failing to enforce the terms of the note, "A," in effect, extended credit to himself on terms different from those contained in the mortgage note. This new extension of credit was the economic equivalent of a transaction in which a borrower renegotiates a loan with a lender and substitutes a new note for a preexisting one. In each instance, there is a new borrowing for purposes of Section 675(3) of the Code.

- The power to borrow corpus or income and not repay it completely before the end of the current tax year is also proscribed. This provision complements the prior one, and both are concerned with preventing the grantor from recapturing trust assets or income. An exception to this rule exists for a loan that bears adequate interest rates and is adequately secured, if the loan is made by a trustee that is not the grantor or a related or subordinate trustee subservient to the grantor (Sec. 675(3)). Related and subordinate trustees are defined in Sec. 672(c) and include the grantor's spouse if living with the grantor, and any of the following: the grantor's father, mother, issue, brother, or sister; the grantor's employees; a corporation or any employee of a corporation in which the stockholdings of the grantor or the trust are significant from the standpoint of voting control; and a subordinate employee of a corporation in which the grantor is an executive.
- If any one of the general administrative powers discussed below can be exercised by any person in a nonfiduciary capacity or without the consent of a person in a fiduciary capacity, the grantor will be treated as the owner of the income and thus be taxable on it:

- the power to vote or direct the voting of stock, in cases where the grantor and the trust have significant voting control
- the power to control investments, to the extent trust funds consist of stock in which the grantor and the trust both have significant voting control interests
- a power to reacquire the trust corpus by substituting other property of equal value

Where a person is acting as trustee, the presumption is that powers are exercised by that person in a fiduciary rather than personal capacity. Therefore it would be presumed that when a power is exercised by a trustee, it will be primarily in the beneficiaries' interest. Clear and convincing evidence is needed to rebut this presumption. However, if the power is vested in a person other than the named trustee, the IRS and the courts will examine the terms of the trust as well as the actual way in which the trust is being operated in order to determine if the power is exercised in a fiduciary or nonfiduciary capacity.

- The retention of a reversionary interest in either the corpus or the income is forbidden if, at the inception of the trust, the value of the reversionary interest exceeds 5 percent of the value of such portion of the trust, or there is more than a 5 percent possibility that any administrative powers or interests that would cause the trust's income to be taxed to the grantor will be revested in the grantor or the grantor's spouse. This effectively eliminates the Clifford trust approach, which was popular prior to the enactment of the Tax Reform Act of 1986.
- The grantor will be treated as owner of the trust and taxable on all trust income if he or she has the power alone or in conjunction with a nonadverse party to revoke the trust and have the property returned to the grantor (Sec. 676(a)). This power would make the trust a truly revocable trust and therefore neutral for tax purposes. However, this provision will not apply if the power to revoke is exercisable only after 10 years have passed from the time the property was transferred to the trust (Sec. 676(b)).
- If the right to control the beneficial enjoyment of the principal or income is exercisable by the grantor, a nonadverse party, or both, without the approval or consent of an adverse party, income will be taxable to the grantor (Sec. 674(a)).

However, income will not be taxable to the grantor under the above mentioned prohibited powers if the powers to alter beneficial enjoyment are exercisable by an independent trustee (not the grantor) acting alone. Under this exception the independent trustee may have the right to distribute, allocate, or accumulate income to or for beneficiaries or within a class of beneficiaries, or to pay out principal to or for beneficiaries or a class of beneficiaries whether or not they are income beneficiaries. The trustee may also apportion income among named beneficiaries or a class of beneficiaries if the power to do so is limited to a reasonably definite external standard by the trust instrument (Secs. 674(c) and (d)).

There is a sister provision to Sec. 674(a) providing that income will be taxable to a person other than the grantor if such an individual has the power to invade the trust to receive either principal or trust income for himself or herself. Generally this is a power of a beneficiary to withdraw principal or income for his or her own benefit without the consent of any other party. In this case the income would be taxable to the beneficiary. However, if the grantor is already taxable on this income for some reason under the grantor trust rules, it will not be taxable to the beneficiary. Also if the beneficiary renounces or disclaims this power within a reasonable time after he or she becomes aware of its existence in the trust instrument, the beneficiary will not be taxable on the income (Sec. 678).

- The grantor will also be treated as owner of any portion of a trust whose income may be distributed to the grantor or the grantor's spouse without the approval of an adverse party. This rule also applies to income that is held or accumulated for future distribution to the grantor or his or her spouse. Also if income from the trust may be used to pay premiums for life insurance policies on the life of the grantor or the grantor's spouse (unless the insurance proceeds are irrevocably payable to a qualified charitable organization), the income will be taxed to the grantor (Sec. 677(a)). Note that income will be taxable to the grantor under this section regardless of whether it is actually used for these purposes. The law provides that any income that could be distributed or spent for these purposes without the consent of an adverse party will be taxable to the grantor and not to the trust or its beneficiaries.

    Despite the income tax consequences, a transfer where trust income may be applied to the payment of insurance premiums may possibly benefit the donor. Note that it is only for income tax purposes that the grantor is treated as owner. The proceeds will not be includible in his or her gross estate for estate tax purposes merely because the grantor paid or provided the funds for the payment of the premiums.

    It should also be stressed that income will not be taxed to the grantor if the life insurance purchased by the trust or transferred to the trust is on the life of someone other than the grantor or the grantor's spouse. It is totally permissible for the trustee to use trust income to pay life insurance premiums on the life of a trust beneficiary without adverse income tax consequences to the grantor.

- Income will also be taxed to the grantor if it is used to discharge his or her own legal obligation. Under this provision the income must *actually be used* to discharge his or her support obligation to cause the grantor to be taxed. It is not sufficient that the trust contain a statement that income may be used for such purposes. Also it is only the amounts of income actually used to satisfy the support obligation, and not the entire income from the trust, that will be taxed to the grantor (Sec. 677(b)).

Permissible Powers and Controls under Sec. 674

There are important exceptions to the rule that the grantor will be treated as owner of trust income and therefore taxable on trust income for income tax purposes if he or she retains the power to control the beneficial enjoyment of either income or corpus. Regardless of the person who possesses them, the following powers will not cause income to be taxed to the grantor:

- the power to apply income, except to the extent actually applied, for the support of the grantor's dependents (Sec. 674(b)(1))
- the power to effect the beneficial enjoyment of the income only after 10 years from the time the property was transferred to the trust. However, the grantor may be treated as the owner and taxed after the 10-year period unless the power is released (Sec. 677(b)(2)).
- the power to allocate the beneficial enjoyment of corpus or income among charitable beneficiaries, provided that the corpus or income is irrevocably payable for a charitable purpose (Sec. 677(b)(4))
- the power to invade corpus for the benefit of a designated beneficiary or class of beneficiaries if the power is limited by a reasonably definite standard contained in the trust instrument (Sec. 677(b)(5))
- the power to postpone the payment of the income to the beneficiary for a reasonable time (Sec. 677(b)(6))
- the power to withhold income and postpone payment during the beneficiary's minority or legal disability (Sec. 677(b)(7))
- the power to apportion receipts and disbursements between income and principal (Sec. 677(b)(8))

A power can even be given to an independent trustee (a person neither related nor subordinate to the grantor) to apportion income and principal among a class of beneficiaries in a sprinkle-type trust without causing the grantor to be taxable on trust income (Sec. 674(c)). Furthermore, the power to apportion among a class can be given to a related or subordinate trustee (one presumably subject to influence by the grantor) other than the grantor or the grantor's spouse, if that power is limited by an ascertainable and external objective standard such as payments for health, education, support, or maintenance (Sec. 674(d)).

Obviously, a great deal of flexibility is possible even with the grantor functioning as a trustee or cotrustee, although most estate planners advise that the grantor name someone other than himself or herself as trustee so that the possibility of having the income taxed to the grantor will be more remote.

Relinquishment of Retained Powers

What happens if a donor has retained a prohibited power and then later gives up that power? Where a transfer is incomplete because of a reserved power, a later release of that power will constitute a taxable event (that is, a completed gift made at the time the grantor relinquishes the power). The amount of that gift is measured by the value of the interest subject to the power at the time the power is released.

It is very important for the financial services professional to keep in mind that, in general, grantor trust rules have no effect for income tax purposes if the powers are exercisable by the grantor only in conjunction with an adverse party. In other words, having a power to effect beneficial enjoyment only with an adverse party will not make income from the trust taxable to the grantor. On the other hand, as we will see for estate tax inclusion, the exercise of certain powers by the grantor alone or in conjunction with any other party (including an adverse party) will have no effect on the negative impact of the rule requiring inclusion in the gross estate if the grantor retains certain powers. A discussion of the estate tax consequences of transfers to trusts with retained powers will follow.

Estate Tax Consequences of Transfers to Trusts with Retained Powers or Control

The creation of an irrevocable trust will remove the transferred property from the grantor's estate only if the grantor irrevocably relinquishes all control and powers over the property. Assets that are subject to incomplete transfers where the decedent retained certain rights or powers will be included in the decedent's gross estate for federal estate tax purposes. We will discuss the estate tax provisions that will cause property given away during lifetime to be brought back into the gross estate further when we study the gross estate.

Because they constitute important tax traps that the financial services professional should be familiar with, incomplete transfers will be listed here; they were discussed in detail in chapter 3 as property that will be included in the gross estate because of retained powers.

The following types of incomplete transfers will create insidious, negative estate tax consequences that should be avoided unless they serve some lifetime purpose of the grantor:

- retention of the right to possess, enjoy, or receive income from the transferred property for life (Sec. 2036)
- a reversionary interest (the right to have the property returned to the grantor) worth more than 5 percent of the value of the property at the time of the grantor's death (Sec. 2037)
- the right to alter, amend, terminate, or revoke the trust (Sec. 2038)
- possession of a general power of appointment over the trust property (Sec. 2041)

- retention of any incidents of ownership of life insurance policies (Sec. 2042)
- proceeds of a life insurance policy transferred within 3 years of the grantor's death (Sec. 2035)

If the grantor retained any of the above rights or powers (except a general power of appointment) over the property transferred and did not release them (give them up) more than 3 years before his or her death, the value at the time of the grantor's death of the property subject to prohibited powers will be included in his or her gross estate (Sec. 2035).

COMPARISON OF INCOME, GIFT, AND ESTATE TAX CONSEQUENCES OF TRANSFERS TO TRUSTS WITH RETAINED POWERS OR CONTROL

Transfers with Retained Powers to Alter, Amend, Revoke, or Terminate

An incredible amount of confusion occurs because of the differences in the estate and income tax languages. For example, the estate tax provisions relating to revocable transfers require the inclusion of property in a grantor's gross estate if the grantor, alone or in conjunction with *any* other person, has the power to alter, amend, revoke, or terminate a trust. A corresponding income tax provision in the grantor trust rules speaks of a power to revoke exercisable by the grantor, a nonadverse party, or both. Therefore the estate tax provision is much broader.

Example: Suppose Mary Blakely creates a trust. The trust provides that income is to be paid to her children as long as they live, and the remainder will then go to their issue. Assume that Mary retains a power to revoke the trust, but the agreement provides that the power is exercisable only with the consent of her children (all of whom are adults). The trust is not revocable for income tax purposes. The income will be taxed to the beneficiaries and not to Mary, because Mary's power to revoke requires the consent of those persons who have a substantial interest. However, for estate tax purposes, the trust is revocable since Mary has retained the power to revoke in conjunction with other persons. Even though the other persons who must give their consent have substantial adverse interests, the assets in such a trust will be includible because the estate tax law is written so broadly.

A slight change in facts could produce the opposite result.

Example: Suppose Ray Bernard created the same trust but provided that the trustee was authorized in the trustee's own discretion to return the corpus to the grantor at any time. In this case the trust is revocable for income tax purposes, since the trustee is a nonadverse party. However, since Ray does not have the power either *alone or in conjunction* with the trustee, for estate tax purposes the property will not be included in Ray's estate. The power in this case is vested exclusively in a third party.

Clearly the arbitrary lines that have been drawn by the tax law sometimes yield what seem to be unfair, harsh, or unrealistic results. But the strict interpretation given to these provisions by the courts generally makes it advisable that (1) the donor relinquish all voice in the administration of the trust and (2) the trustee be independent from and unrelated to the donor, and not associated with him or her in business.

There are also gift tax implications to transfers with retained powers to alter, amend, or terminate.

Example: A donor might create an irrevocable trust and expressly provide that the property will never return to him or her under any circumstances but reserve the right to change the beneficiaries or to vary the respective interests. For example, the trust might state, "The trustee is to provide income equally to my three daughters, but I retain the power to vary the percentage interest of any daughter at any time or wholly exclude any daughter from sharing in the income or principal of the trust." For estate tax purposes the right to amend, revoke, or terminate will cause the corpus to be includible in the grantor's estate. This is because the grantor could revise what he or she has given to each of the donees by taking away one donee's share and giving it to another. Furthermore, the income will be taxable to the grantor (even though irrevocably payable to others). However, there is a completed gift for gift tax purposes.

Where a transfer is incomplete for income tax purposes and also incomplete for estate tax purposes, it will generally be incomplete for gift tax purposes. A primary exception to this general rule is illustrated by the preceding example (that is, where a donor makes a transfer but reserves a right to designate who will enjoy the property or the income from the property). This type of transfer does not shift income taxes to the trust or its beneficiaries; furthermore, it does not remove the property from the grantor's estate. In spite of this, a gift tax is incurred. The grantor has achieved the worst of all possible worlds.

By a slight change in wording, the grantor could obtain a slightly more favorable result.

Example: If the grantor transfers property to a trust but retains the power to revoke with the consent of the trustee, the gift will be considered incomplete for both gift and income tax purposes. The property will be includible in the grantor's gross estate because of the power to revoke *in conjunction with* another. The income will be taxed to the grantor because the trustee does not have an adverse interest. But no gift tax should result.

Transfers to Trusts or Custodial Arrangements for Benefit of Minors

The estate tax implications of a retained power to alter, amend, revoke, or terminate extend to gifts made in trust or under custodial arrangements to minors.

> *Example:* A grantor, Michael Nathan, named himself trustee of certain securities for his son. As trustee he had the right to accumulate income during his son's minority. Income that was accumulated was to be paid to the son at age 21. The trust was to terminate and the principal was to be distributed to the son at age 25. The sole right that Michael retained as trustee was the power to pay out principal at an earlier date if he saw fit. But the court held that this was sufficient to subject the property to federal estate tax at the donor's death. The holding of this case is particularly important, since there are literally thousands of trusts and custodial accounts in which the donor is trustee (or one of several trustees) or custodian. Any one of the usual absolute discretionary powers given to such fiduciaries will cause inclusion of the transferred property in the donor's estate.

Can the problem be avoided by giving an independent trustee such powers but having the grantor retain the right to remove that trustee and appoint a substitute, including himself or herself? The answer is that the grantor will be considered to have retained the powers for himself or herself if the grantor has the right to substitute himself or herself as trustee. Furthermore, if an independent trustee dies and the grantor becomes the successor trustee (or custodian), the property will be includible at the grantor's subsequent death.

One important exception is where a power to pay out, accumulate, or distribute principal may be exercised only at the occurrence of a specified future contingency. For example, in one case the power that was retained allowed the donor to accelerate payments of interest or principal "in case of need for educational purposes or because of illness or other good reason." In another case the retained power allowed the donor to make payments "for the support, maintenance, and education of our daughter." In neither case did the contingency actually occur by the date of the grantor's death. In these cases the courts have held that because of the objective standards and the absence of conditions warranting the exercise of the powers, the transfers were not subject to inclusion. Thus it is possible for a grantor to be one of the trustees, provided that all discretionary powers relating to the enjoyment of the property are limited by substantial external and objective standards.

But complex questions are posed. On the one hand, the estate tax inclusion can be avoided if discretionary powers are limited by objective standards. On the other hand, to the extent discretionary powers are limited, flexibility is lost or severely restricted. Perhaps a viable alternative is to give an independent trustee absolute discretionary power and thus increase flexibility without generating any adverse estate tax consequences.

As a parenthetical, it should be noted that the advantageous tax implications of using a custodial arrangement for the benefit of minors have been significantly eroded by the Tax Reform Act of 1986. This act imposes a provision, which has come to be referred to as the "kiddie tax," whereby all net unearned income of a child who has not attained age 14 before the close of the taxable year and who has at least one parent alive at the close of the taxable year will be taxed to the child. This tax applies to all net unearned income; the source of the assets creating the income or the date the income-producing property was transferred is irrelevant.

The tax payable by the child on net unearned income is essentially the additional amount of tax that the parent would have had to pay if the net unearned income of the child was included in the parent's taxable income. If parents have two or more children with unearned income to be taxed at the parent's marginal tax rate, all the children's applicable unearned income will be added together and the tax calculated. The tax is then allocated to each child based on the child's pro rata share of unearned income.

The intent of the law is to create the following three stages:

1. There will be no tax on the first $700 (1998 figure) of unearned income because of the child's standard deduction. (The standard deduction offsets unearned income first, up to $700. Any remaining standard deduction is then available to offset earned income.)
2. The next $700 of unearned income will be taxed to the child at the child's bracket.
3. Unearned income in excess of the first $1,400 will be taxed to the child at the parent's appropriate rate.

The Treasury has now issued regulations that define what unearned income is subject to the kiddie tax and that also explain how the tax is to be computed. These regulations, which are in question-and-answer form, also treat the determination of the parent's taxable income and the effect of subsequent adjustments to the parent's income or to the net unearned income of any of the children. The highlights of the regulations are as follows:

- Unearned income is all income not attributable to wages, salaries, or other amounts received as compensation for personal services.

- The kiddie tax applies to unearned income received during taxable years beginning after 1986, regardless of when the assets producing the income were acquired by the child and regardless of whether the child acquired the assets by gift (from a parent, grandparent, or any other person) or purchased the assets with earned income.
- The kiddie tax applies to interest received on earned income deposited in an interest-bearing account owned by the child.
- Unearned income also includes social security or pension benefits to the extent such items are includible in the child's gross income.
- The amount of the kiddie tax will be the greater of (1) the tax that would have applied without the application of the kiddie-tax rules or (2) the sum of the tax on the child's income, reduced by the child's net unearned income, by using the child's brackets, plus the child's share of the allocable parental tax. The allocable parental tax is defined by the new regulations as the excess of the tax on the parent's taxable income plus the unearned income of all the parent's children subject to the tax over the tax on the parent's taxable income.

An additional problem area in the context of custodial accounts consists of a proliferation of the parent's support obligation and the corresponding restrictions imposed on custodian funds to fulfill support obligations. In *Sutliff v. Sutliff,* for example, the Pennsylvania Superior Court clearly stated that a financially able parent may not use the existence of custodian funds to reduce his or her obligation of support to minor children, even though the state statutes under which the funds were established would otherwise permit such a use of the funds. *Sutliff* emphasized the limitations imposed on the parent-custodian's discretion to use such funds.

Transfers with Powers to Invade Corpus

The following discussion relates specifically to trusts in which the grantor has retained the power to alter, amend, or terminate the trust alone or in conjunction with another person or to trusts in which a nonadverse party can exercise that power. The discussion directly below will consider the tax consequences when the grantor has the absolute power to recapture trust assets and when a third party has a comparable power. Note the effect of the income tax doctrine of constructive receipt in each case.

Where a *grantor* retains the right to regain property at any time, essentially he or she has the power to revoke the trust. But if a *beneficiary* has the power or right to withdraw trust assets at any time, this power is called a power of invasion. If the beneficiary has an absolute power to invade at any time, the beneficiary is treated as the owner of the property for income, gift, and estate tax purposes.

Example: In one case a father transferred property to a trustee. The trustee was instructed to pay income to the son until the child reached a specified age, at which time the trustee was to distribute the entire corpus to the son. However, the grantor's wife was given an absolute power to withdraw any or all of the trust assets at any time she desired, purely for her own use and benefit. When the mother failed to exercise her power, the trustee paid income to the grantor's son. But the IRS argued that the mother could have withdrawn trust income and assets at any time; therefore she had constructive receipt of both. To the extent that she did not exercise her power, she was making taxable gifts each year to her son. Therefore the corpus was part of her estate when she died. She had the equivalent of a general power of appointment. To the extent of her right to invade, she was treated as owner of the trust for income, gift, and estate tax purposes. (Under current law, if trust beneficiaries are under age 14, the income would be taxed to the minor at the parent's rate of tax.)

There are limitations on these seemingly harsh rules. One limitation is that a person other than the grantor will be treated as owner for income tax purposes only if no one else can exercise that power. Likewise, the power of invasion will not subject the property to federal estate tax in the beneficiary's estate unless the power is exercisable only by the decedent (or by the decedent together with a person who does not have an adverse interest). Note, however, that for federal income tax purposes under current law, if a trust beneficiary has not yet attained age 14, all income is taxed to the minor at the parent's rate of tax.

If a decedent cannot exercise the power without the joint action of another person, only a fractional interest must be includible. In other words, if joint action is required with a person in whose favor the power can be exercised, only a fractional portion of the property subject to the power is includible. This portion is determined by dividing the value of the property by the number of such persons in whose favor it may be exercised.

Example: Assume three beneficiaries—Steve, Rob, and Lee—are given the right to withdraw principal but only if all three execute a written request. None of the three can convey without the consent of the others, and each is a person in whose favor the power can be exercised. Therefore the tax law presumes that each of the three can influence the others only to the extent of a one-third right to withdraw principal. Thus, for estate tax purposes, each of the beneficiaries is considered the owner of one-third of the corpus.

These third-party rules regarding power of invasion make it possible to incorporate extremely flexible trust provisions without adverse tax consequences. A very different result occurs where there has been a retention of powers exercisable in favor of the grantor.

Reciprocal Transfers

Reciprocal transfers involve so-called cross trusts. Essentially the rule in this area provides that whenever trusts are interrelated in an arrangement established by two or more grantors that leaves them in the same economic position they would have been in if each had created the trust that bears the name of the other, tax consequences will be imposed accordingly.

Example: Stewart Chane would like to transfer property but retain the right to the income from that property for life. Upon being told that this would not avoid the federal estate tax on the property transferred, he asks if he could transfer $150,000 in trust and provide income to his brother for life, with the remainder going to his brother's children but with the stipulation that his brother must act in an equally *brotherly fashion* by creating a similar trust for him and his family. The first brother would enjoy the income from the trust his brother created, and his children would receive the corpus of that trust when he died. Since the economic effect of such an arrangement is the same as if Stewart had set up a trust for himself and retained the income from property he transferred to it, the tax effect would be the same (that is, property subject to the transfer would be in his estate).

This cross-trust technique has been tried in many different ways.

Example: Assume an estate owner, Brad Davis, is primarily concerned with retaining the right to control the beneficial enjoyment of the property he places in trust. When he asks his attorney, he is told that this cannot be accomplished without having the income taxed to him and the corpus and trust includible in his gross estate.

To avoid this adverse tax treatment, Brad devises a reciprocal arrangement. First, he transfers property in trust for his three children. He gives his wife a special power of appointment by deed or by will over the trust property. Second, he has his wife create an identical trust that gives him an equivalent special power. Each trust is in the exact same amount. The net result is that his position and his wife's position are the same as they would have been had each retained the power over the trust he or she created. Therefore the court treats Brad as the real grantor of the trust nominally created by his wife. For estate tax purposes it is as if Brad had created a trust in which he had reserved the right for his life to alter the beneficial enjoyment. Therefore this estate owner technically would be treated as the grantor of the trust that his wife ostensibly created.

The essence of the cross-trust or reciprocal-trust doctrine is the *quid pro quo*. The transfer by the decedent's brother (or some other individual), having been paid for and brought about by the decedent, is in substance a transfer by the decedent. In other words, when there is a reciprocal arrangement and the terms are essentially identical, leaving both parties in the same economic position they were in before the transfers occurred, each will be treated as the grantor of the other's trust.

However, in a recent case the existence of a special (limited) power of appointment in one trust that was not in an otherwise identical trust was ruled sufficient to defeat the reciprocal trust doctrine.

IRREVOCABLE LIVING TRUSTS WITH NO RETAINED POWERS OR CONTROLS

An irrevocable living trust with no retained powers or controls can offer many advantages as an estate planning tool. It is a trust to which the grantor has permanently transferred property. The transfer of the property is considered a completed gift unless it has been transferred, in whole or part, for full and adequate consideration (that is, sold to the trust).

With regard to general trust purposes (such as protection, flexibility, security, as well as prudent and capable management of trust property), the irrevocable trust functions like most other trusts do. Many of the purposes discussed earlier that trusts can serve generally pertain to irrevocable living trusts.

Advantages

Irrevocable trusts generally function as a separate taxpayer and can provide a vehicle through which the family can save income taxes. Because it becomes a separate taxpayer, this type of trust can be used to allocate income to more than one taxpayer (the trust and its beneficiaries) with the result that the income may be taxed at lower tax brackets.

The trust can be used to maximize the value of the trust property through accumulation and investment appreciation. Generally there are two financial objectives that are applicable to the irrevocable trust. One is to provide safety of principal and diversification of assets with a minimum of risk. The second objective is to achieve appreciation in the value of the underlying assets over time.

The trust offers security and protection to the beneficiaries. Since it is created and the property is transferred during the grantor's lifetime, there will be a saving in estate taxes, particularly if the property transferred to the trust appreciates in value between the time of transfer and the grantor's death. If the trust is structured so that there are life income beneficiaries, there can be estate tax savings both in the estate of the grantor and the estates of any life income beneficiaries. In all cases the trust will avoid probate. Therefore there will be a reduction in administration costs.

Example: A grantor's estate may be left in trust for his or her spouse for life and then for the lives of the grantor's children, with the principal eventually to be distributed to the grantor's grandchildren. There will be no estate taxation at the death of the spouse or the grantor's children because only life interests have been created. Since neither the grantor nor the grantor's children have the right to control or pass the principal of the trust at death, the assets of the trust will not be includible in the estates of any life income beneficiary. This may result in a substantial reduction of administrative costs and estate taxes.

Since the trust will avoid probate, it will also have the advantage of privacy. A trust that does not pass under a will does not become part of the public record. This will ensure that the decedent's financial matters and named beneficiaries are kept private. However, if the trust becomes subject to question with regard to one or more of the trust provisions, it will become open to public scrutiny as a matter of court record. Clearing title to real estate transferred to the trust at death may also require some disclosure. Otherwise the grantor can be assured of privacy regarding the contents and other provisions of the trust.

In addition, since an irrevocable living trust has been in existence prior to death, there is no delay in funding the trust or providing income to the beneficiaries, which might occur if the assets were subject to probate. Furthermore, the costs of being included in the probate estate, such as additional executors' and attorneys' fees, will be eliminated. Remember, however, that drafting and executing irrevocable trusts does involve legal fees. There will also be trustees' fees on a continuing basis for the management of trust property, administrative services, and preparation of fiduciary income tax returns.

Another advantage in setting up an irrevocable trust may be to shelter property from the spouse's right of election against the grantor's will. The irrevocable trust may also allow the grantor to protect his or her assets for children of a prior marriage.

Disadvantages

What are the disadvantages of an irrevocable living trust? The major disadvantage is that the trust is irrevocable. Basically it cannot be changed or terminated. Once the trust is created, the grantor has lost control over his or her property. Many people are reluctant to permanently part with their assets, unless they are people of substantial means who will never require income from the property for their support and maintenance, or are very elderly and, again, will not need the property for their own use. Of course, if the irrevocable trust is a life insurance trust, it is true that the grantor will lose control over the assets, including all incidents of ownership over the policy. On the other hand, the actual value of the policy to the grantor as an asset during lifetime is small relative to other assets that could have been transferred to the trust. Only the grantor can decide whether creation of an irrevocable trust is a sensible and desirable planning vehicle in light of his or her total financial and personal circumstances and goals.

Tax Consequences

The transfer of property to an irrevocable trust always carries with it a potential gift tax liability depending on the amount of assets transferred. Although the irrevocable trust carries with it gift tax consequences, the trust property will be removed from the grantor's gross estate when he or she dies unless the grantor retained certain rights over the trust property or trust income for life.

Remember that the gift and estate tax system is a unified one. Therefore any post-1976 transfers to an irrevocable trust will be brought back into the estate tax computation as adjusted taxable gifts. However, the property will be brought back at its value on the date of the gift. Any appreciation in the property after the transfer will avoid taxation. Furthermore, if the trust is a life insurance trust, the value of the property for gift tax purposes will probably be minimal compared with the policy proceeds, the value of which will be removed from the gross estate. As a matter of fact, if the policies transferred or purchased by the trust consist of term insurance or a newly purchased policy, the gift tax consequences will be either nil or negligible.

To summarize the tax consequences, there is potential gift tax on the creation of an irrevocable trust. The annual gift tax exclusion of $10,000 per donee is available for post-1981 transfers of a present interest. The annual exclusion does not apply to transfers of remainder interests that are future interests. Unless the property transferred is a gift of a life insurance policy and the grantor dies within 3 years of the transfer, the property will avoid estate taxation in the grantor's estate. Appreciation in the value of the property will not be brought back into the gross estate. If the grantor survives more than 3 years after transferring the property to the trust, the gift tax payable will be excluded from the gross estate. If the trust property was transferred after 1976, it will be included in the estate tax computation as an adjusted taxable gift valued at the time of the transfer and any postgift appreciation will avoid gift or estate taxation.

Also remember that the applicable gift and estate tax credit must be applied against all taxable gifts first. Therefore, depending on the number of beneficiaries and the value of the property transferred to the trust, it is possible to transfer sizable amounts without requiring an immediate gift tax payment.

Tax-Advantageous Trust Provisions for Life Income Beneficiary of Irrevocable Trust

In creating a trust to provide income and some principal for a life income beneficiary, the grantor can achieve considerable tax leverage as compared with an outright gift. It is possible to arrange the trust to give significant flexibility and to provide substantial access to both income and principal for the benefit of the income beneficiary without incurring estate taxes in that person's estate.

The financial security of the life tenant can be enhanced by all the following types of provisions without causing the trust property to be includible in the life tenant's gross estate:

- The trust may require all income to be paid annually, or more frequently, to the income beneficiary.
- The income beneficiary may be given a noncumulative power to withdraw the greater of $5,000 or 5 percent of the trust corpus annually for a limited time each year.
- The life income beneficiary may be given a power to demand principal in unlimited amounts to enable the beneficiary to maintain his or her accustomed standard of living. Note that these withdrawals of principal may be made in excess of the greater of the 5 percent or $5,000 limited withdrawals described above. However, if the powers to invade principal for this purpose are not made according to an ascertainable standard (that is, for health, education, support, or maintenance), all trust income may become taxable to the beneficiary (unless the income is already taxable to the grantor under the grantor trust rules discussed previously).
- A trustee may be given discretionary powers to invade principal for the benefit of the life income beneficiary in any amount or for any reason that the trustee determines is reasonable and appropriate.
- The life income beneficiary may be given a special power of appointment—either by deed or by will—that may be used during the grantor's lifetime, at his or her death, or both to appoint trust assets to and among a specific class of persons who do not include the beneficiary, the beneficiary's creditors, the beneficiary's estate, or the creditors of the beneficiary's estate.

The use of any or all of the above powers builds a great deal of flexibility into the trust while at the same time protecting the assets from estate taxation in the life income beneficiary's estate.

It is also possible to reduce overall family income taxes by the following methods:

- Separate trusts may be created or trusts may be divided into separate shares for each beneficiary so that there will be more than one taxpaying entity, including the trust.
- The trustee may be given the discretionary power to either accumulate or distribute income earned by the trust.

- The trustee may also be given the discretionary power to sprinkle income among beneficiaries in different income and estate tax brackets according to their needs.
- The trustee may receive the power to allocate receipts and disbursements between income and principal. This power makes it possible for the trustee to enhance or diminish the financial security and the potential tax liability of various beneficiaries within the bounds of local law.
- The trustee may also be given the authority to purchase life insurance on the life of any individual, including the grantor or the grantor's spouse. While this may cause the income of the trust to be taxed to the grantor, it can be arranged in such a manner that the proceeds will not be taxable in the grantor's estate or his or her spouse's estate.
- The trustee may be given the authority to purchase life insurance on the life of a beneficiary or some individual in whom the beneficiary has an insurable interest. This would make it possible for a trust to make an outright purchase, or to *split-dollar* an insurance policy on the life of a business associate or a personal beneficiary. Likewise, the authority to purchase life insurance on a life income beneficiary can provide security for that beneficiary's family at his or her death when the income stream ceases.

Example: The family of a life income beneficiary who receives $40,000 a year from trust income would be left with a substantial reduction in income when that beneficiary dies. Life insurance proceeds purchased by the trust that are payable to the trust's beneficiaries can be used to replace that income.

GENERATION-SKIPPING TRANSFER TAX

The Tax Reform Act of 1986 made sweeping revisions to the way generation-skipping transfers will be taxed. One of the main reasons for these changes was that the prior statutory materials dealing with generation-skipping transfers were felt to be so complex and difficult to apply that there was a perceived need for Congress to totally repeal the former approach and replace it with a new method for taxing these types of transfers.

Unlike the former law regarding generation-skipping transfers, there is no longer any requirement that there be a splitting of benefits between an income-receiving generation and a principal-receiving generation. Under the current approach it is possible for direct skips to be characterized as generation-skipping transfers.

The current law breaks generation-skipping transfers into one of three categories:

- taxable distribution
- taxable termination
- direct skip

We'll describe each one separately.

Taxable Distributions

Sec. 2652(c)(1) of the Internal Revenue Code provides that a person has an "interest" in a trust if that person has a right (other than a future right) to receive income or trust principal from the trust or if that person is a recipient of income or corpus.

A taxable distribution is any distribution of either income or principal from a trust to a person two or more generations younger than the transferor's generation who is not otherwise subject to estate or gift tax. Those individuals who receive property as part of such an arrangement are referred to as *skip beneficiaries.*

Example: John Marks transferred income-producing property to a trust naming his three great-grandchildren as beneficiaries. If the trustee makes distributions of either trust income or trust principal to these named beneficiaries, this will be classified as a taxable distribution, which will trigger generation-skipping transfer tax.

Taxable Terminations

A taxable termination occurs if there is a termination of an existing arrangement by reason of death, lapse of time, or release of a power, or in situations where the property interest held in trust passes to a skip beneficiary.

Example: James Pennell's last will and testament contained a provision that created a testamentary trust. Mr. Pennell's son, Peter, was to receive all income generated by the trust for life, with the principal to pass to Peter's son, Paul, at Peter's death. If Peter dies and Paul receives the trust property, a taxable termination has taken place, which will trigger generation-skipping transfer tax.

Sec. 2612(a)(2) provides that if, upon the termination of an interest in property held in a trust, a specified portion of the trust assets is distributed to skip persons who are lineal descendants of the holder of that interest (or to one or more trusts for the exclusive benefit of such persons), the termination constitutes a taxable termination with respect to that portion of the trust property. The exception under Sec. 2612(a)(2) would appear to apply to a trust established for the benefit of a transferor's children from which, upon the death of a child, a portion of the trust is distributable to the deceased child's descendants.

A consequence of treating this event as a taxable termination rather than a taxable distribution is that deductions may be available under Sec. 2622(b) that are not available for taxable distributions. In addition, a full basis adjustment would be made under Sec. 2654(a), rather than a basis adjustment under Sec. 2654(a)(1) limited to GSTT attributable to appreciation.

Direct Skips

The approach to the taxation of direct skips as introduced by the Tax Reform Act of 1986 confirms a Congressional belief that it was unfair to allow those who are ultrawealthy to avoid the prior GSTT system by bypassing their children's generation with a portion of their estates. Therefore, under current GSTT law, a transfer that completely bypasses the children's generation is to be taxed as though it had, in fact, passed through that generation.

Outright transfers of property that skip a generation will, under the current law, trigger the application of the generation-skipping transfer tax. This is a substantial departure from the previous approach where there had to be a splitting of benefits between two younger generations before the generation-skipping tax could be imposed. Direct skips may take place either during lifetime or at death.

> *Example:* In 1997, Clara Belle made a gift of income-producing property to her granddaughter, Sharon. This is a direct skip, which will attract generation-skipping transfer tax in addition to the application of federal gift tax.

Sec. 2612(c)(2) of the Internal Revenue Code sets forth an exception to what would otherwise be treated as a direct skip. If an individual is a grandchild of the transferor (or even the transferor's spouse or former spouse) and if at the time of the transfer, the parent of that individual who is a linear descendant of the transferor (or the transferor's spouse or former spouse) is dead, the individual is to be considered a child of the transferor and all that individual's children are to be treated as if they were grandchildren of the transferor.

> *Recent development*: TRA 97 expanded the predeceased parent rule to other heirs besides grandchildren if the transferor has no living lineal descendants and the parent of the transferee is not living at the time of the transfer. In addition, the predeceased parent rule will now apply to taxable terminations and distributions. The rule will apply if the parent of the transferee is dead at the earliest time the transfer was subject to estate and gift taxes.

Example: Grandpa Smith transfers $1 million to an irrevocable trust. The trust will distribute income to his children and grandchildren in shares determined by an independent trustee. At the death of Grandpa Smith's children, the trust will terminate and will be distributed to his grandchildren.

Since the trust is irrevocable and Grandpa Smith does not retain any controls, the transfer is subject to gift taxes when the trust is created. If one of his children predeceased the creation of this trust, the children of the predeceased child would not be treated as skip persons and distributions to such grandchildren would not be taxable distributions or terminations for GSTT purposes. If all Grandpa Smith's children were alive at the time the trust was created, a later death of a child prior to the termination of the trust would not give rise to the predeceased parent exception because the child was alive at the first time the transfer became subject to gift taxes.

Overlapping Definitions

It is important for the taxpayer and the planner to ascertain whether a specific generation-skipping transfer is a taxable distribution, a taxable termination, or a direct skip in order to plan for such concepts as basis adjustments, the amount of tax liability, when the return will be due, when the tax will be due, and which party is liable for the tax. The generation-skipping transfer tax provisions assume that taxable terminations, taxable distributions, and direct skips are integrated in such a way that a transfer that constitutes one of these three events cannot include another. However, as a practical matter, there is a significant degree of overlap in these three definitions, and it can be unclear what type of GSTT event has taken place.

Sec. 2612(b) of the Internal Revenue Code does eliminate taxable terminations and direct skips in the definition of taxable distributions. Nonetheless, this area has great potential for confusion, and the planner will need clarification from either the Revenue Service or Congress.

Taxable Amounts

The amount considered to be taxable in a generation-skipping transfer transaction directly depends on whether the transfer is a taxable distribution, a taxable termination, or a direct skip.

If the transaction is a taxable distribution, the taxable amount will be the net value of the property received by the distributee less any consideration he or she may have paid in order to receive the property.

If the transaction is a taxable termination, the taxable amount is the value of all property transferred less a deduction for any expenses, debts, and taxes generated by the property, and any consideration paid by the transferee.

If the transaction is a direct skip, the taxable amount is the value of the property or interest in property received by the transferee reduced by any consideration paid by the transferee.

Exemptions and Exclusions

Although the law regarding generation-skipping transfers may subject transactions to new tax liability, the statute does include several exempted categories. We'll touch on each one separately.

Per-Donor Exemption

The law provides that every individual is permitted to make aggregate transfers of up to $1 million, either during lifetime or at death, which will be wholly exempt from the generation-skipping transfer tax.

Per-Grandchild Exemption

All transfers involving direct skips to grandchildren made prior to January 1, 1990, were considered not to meet the definition of a direct skip and therefore escaped the generation-skipping transfer tax to the extent that aggregate transfers did not exceed $2 million. Unfortunately, this safe harbor expired on December 31, 1989.

Transfers Subject to Estate or Gift Tax

A transfer from a trust—other than a direct skip—to the extent the transfer is subject to federal estate tax or federal gift tax with respect to a person in the first generation below that of a transferor is excluded from the definition of a generation-skipping transfer.

Transfers Qualifying as Gift Tax Free

Transfers that, if made by gift, would qualify as gift tax free because they are direct payments made for the donee's educational or medical expenses, or some transfers that pass federal gift tax free under the annual exclusion rules, are excluded from the definition of a generation-skipping transfer.

Rate of Tax

The current law imposes a flat-rate tax set equal to the highest current estate or gift tax bracket—55 percent. The transferor is responsible for payment of the generation-skipping transfer tax for direct skips. The trustee is liable for the tax on taxable terminations, while the transferee is liable for GSTT on taxable distributions.

Deductions, Credits, and Special Provisions

The Tax Reform Act of 1986 added several provisions to the Internal Revenue Code that make the operation of the GSTT system analogous to the federal estate and gift tax areas. These provisions include the following:

- Sec. 691(c)(3) of the Internal Revenue Code was amended to permit a federal income tax deduction for GSTT attributable to items of gross income that were not properly includible in gross income prior to the GSTT. Bear in mind that this particular deduction will be available only on a taxable termination or direct skip taking place as a result of the death of the transferor.
- Sec. 303(d) of the Internal Revenue Code was amended to permit closely held stock to be redeemed in payment of generation-skipping taxes.
- Sec. 2013(g) of the Internal Revenue Code was repealed so that the credit on previous transfers subject to federal estate tax within a 10-year period will not be available for generation-skipping taxes.
- Sec. 6166(i) of the Internal Revenue Code was added to permit an extension of payment of generation-skipping tax attributable to a decedent's interest in a closely held business.
- Sec. 2604 of the Internal Revenue Code was added to the Code to allow a credit for state death taxes on GSTT situations, not to exceed 5 percent of the amount of tax imposed by the GSTT system. Note that the Sec. 2604 credit is available only if a generation-skipping transfer—other than a direct skip—occurs at the same time as and as a result of an individual's death.

Planning Implications

The financial services professional must constantly remain cognizant of the dangers of inadvertently triggering the current generation-skipping transfer tax. This tax could be triggered in situations involving outright cash transfers or even in more subtle circumstances. For example, in Rev. Rul. 89-3 an exchange of stock in a generation-skipping trust was held to inadvertently trigger the GSTT. Caution must always be exercised in the planning context to avoid this problem.

An additional issue involves reformation of "grandfathered" trusts subject to the generation-skipping transfer tax. For example, the GSTT is generally effective for transfers after October 22, 1986, with certain exceptions. One exception applies to generation-skipping trusts in existence and irrevocable on or before September 25, 1985, but only to the extent that a transfer under such a trust is not made out of corpus added to the trust after September 25, 1985. In PLR 8927026 the IRS considered whether a proposed modification of such a "grandfathered" trust would create an addition to corpus and thereby cause the GSTT to apply to transfers under the modified trust provisions. The IRS held that if the proposed modifications are made to the trust, any generation-skipping transfers made under that trust will be subject to the GSTT. The financial services professional must be aware of these issues.

POWERS OF APPOINTMENT

Terminology and Definitions

A power of appointment may be defined as a right or power with respect to property that is created by the property owner, by which he or she gives to another to designate, within the limits prescribed by the property owner, who will receive the property subject to the power.

The creator of the power (that is, the grantor or estate owner) is known as the donor of the power. The donee of the power is the person who is given the power to designate who will receive the property subject to the power. The class of persons who are the ultimate recipients of the property is known as the *appointees*. Generally the donor specifies that if the donee of the power does not appoint the property to an eligible appointee, certain takers in default will receive the property. For example, the grantor might state, "On my death, the property is to be held in trust with the income payable to my daughter for life and at her death to such children of hers as she may designate but if she fails to designate, then equally to all her children." In this case the children are not only the possible appointees but also the takers in default.

For purposes of trust law, if the power can be appointed to anyone without limitation, including the donee or the donee's estate, the power is *general*. If it is exercisable only during the donee's life, it is a *general power by deed*. If it is exercisable only at death, it is a *general power by will*. If it may be exercised at either time, it is called a *general power by deed or by will*. If the class of possible appointees is limited (such as to the children of the daughter in the example above), the power is called a *special or limited power* because the class of potential appointees is restricted.

Taxation of Powers

As a general rule, if a power is given to a person other than the grantor, it is possible to make the power quite broad without attracting any adverse tax consequences. Conversely, if a grantor reserves powers, it is likely that the consequences will be adverse even if the powers retained have been quite limited.

For federal tax purposes a general power is one that is exercisable by the donee of the power in favor of anyone, provided that the right can also be exercised in favor of the donee or the donee's creditors, or the donee's estate or creditors of the donee's estate. Note that to be a general power for federal tax purposes, it is not necessary that the power be exercisable for all four categories or in favor of any other person. The donee's unfettered right to withdraw corpus (unless limited by an external, ascertainable standard pertaining to the donee's health, education, support, or maintenance) is always a general power (Sec. 2041 (b)(1)(A)). Thus a power permitting a widow to withdraw all or part of the corpus at any time for any reason is a general power. (But if the widow is given the right to invade corpus to the extent necessary to enable her to maintain her accustomed standard of living, the power is not general.)

The tax law recognizes that in many respects a general power of appointment is the equivalent of outright ownership. Effectively, the donee can exercise this ownership right by merely calling on the trustee for conveyance of the title to the property and the trust. If a general power is exercised or completely released (formally given up) by the donee during the donee's lifetime, the donee is making a taxable transfer of the property subject to the gift tax. The mere possession of a general power subject to the exceptions noted below will result in the inclusion of a property in the donee's estate whether or not the power is exercised.

There are some exceptions to the rule that the mere possession of a general power will result in the inclusion of the property in the donee's estate whether he or she exercises the power or not. The first exception applies where the consent of the donor is required in order to exercise the power (Sec. 2041(b)(1)(C)(i)).

A second instance in which a general power will not be treated as such is where the consent of a person having a substantial adverse interest is required (Sec. 2041(b)(1)(C)(ii)). For example, assume a wife is given a general power of appointment and her children are named as takers in default in the absence of her exercise of that power. If the donor has required that the wife's children must consent in writing to her exercise of the power, the power would not be considered (or taxed as) a general power. This is because the children have a substantial amount to lose if the donee, their mother, exercises the power in her own favor to the exclusion of the children.

If the consent of a person in whose favor the power might be exercised is required, the power will be considered general only in part (Sec. 2041(b)(1)(C)(ii)). For example, if two children are given the power to appoint jointly to any person or persons, including themselves, on appointment each will really be making a gift of one-half. Therefore it is only proper that each be treated as having a general power over one-half. In this case the power is treated as general only as to that half.

Property will be subject to estate tax if the exercise or release results in a disposition coupled with a reserved life estate, reversionary trust, or retained powers to alter, amend, revoke, or terminate. For example, assume a husband is entitled to the income for life of a trust established by his late wife. Assume that he is also given a general testamentary power over the trust corpus. If he releases (gives up) that general testamentary power, the effect is equivalent to a transfer to the parties who take in default of his exercise. However, since he has the right to the income from all of the trust property for life, he has given away the property but retained an income interest. In other words, the property subject to the power might be includible in the donee's estate if he (1) does nothing and dies possessing an unexercised general power or (2) has transferred the power in such a way that it will be includible in his estate despite the conveyance.

Lapse of Powers

A power lapses when it is allowed to expire and is not exercised. For federal tax purposes the lapse of a power is the same as a formal release. If the lapse occurs during the lifetime of the donee, a gift is made to the takers in default. If the lapse occurs because the power is unexercised at the donee's death, the property subject to the power is includible for estate tax purposes in the donee's estate. For example, suppose the income beneficiary of a trust has the power to withdraw all or a portion of the $100,000 corpus at any time up to his or her 50th birthday. If none of the $100,000 is withdrawn by that date, a gift has been made to the remainderpersons. This is because one day before the donee's 50th birthday he or she could have taken the $100,000 capital of the trust. But one day after the 50th birthday, the donee—by doing nothing—has enriched the remainderpersons by $100,000.

Quite often a life tenant of a trust will be given a noncumulative right ("use it or lose it") to withdraw a given amount annually. If no withdrawal is made, the interest vests in the remainderpersons. Assume, for example, that a donee is given the noncumulative right to withdraw $10,000 a year. If the fund amounts to $100,000 and the life tenant has allowed 10 years to pass without making a withdrawal, he or she has made gifts in each of those years. The gifts, of course, do not amount to $10,000 times 10 since the life tenant, by definition, retains the right to the income produced by the trust assets. So the gift was one of only the remainder interest; that is, it is as if the donee gave away the $10,000 each year but retained the right to the income produced by that $10,000. Therefore each gift would be treated as a transfer with the income retained for life. At the end of the 10th year the entire property would be includible in the estate of the life tenant.

5-and-5 Rule

There is an important exception to the rule that a lapse of a power is the same as a gift with a retained life interest. This is known as the *5-and-5 rule*. In essence this rule provides that the power to withdraw 5 percent of the corpus or $5,000, whichever is greater, can be allowed to lapse each year with no adverse gift or estate tax consequences (Secs. 2041(b)(2) and 2514(e)). Amounts transferred either by lifetime *gift* or at death that fall within this limit will be gift and estate tax free. In other words, the lapse of a power will be considered a release (and therefore a taxable gift) only to the extent that the property that could have been appointed exceeds the greater of $5,000 or 5 percent of the assets subject to appointment. For example, if the assets subject to appointment are worth $500,000, the donee can be given the power to withdraw up to $25,000 a year without adverse taxes.

Increased Flexibility with No Adverse Tax Consequences

There are significant estate tax savings possible through special powers. For example, assume a woman has inherited a substantial amount of money from her husband. At her death she could leave the property to her son outright; alternatively, she could give him a life estate coupled with certain rights and powers that would make the bequest more economically beneficial to the son. If the special power is properly arranged, the property subject to that power will not be includible in the son's estate. The savings could be substantial.

What are the powers or rights that can be given to a beneficiary that would increase the flexibility yet not cause property subject to a power to be taxable in the beneficiary's estate? Such rights and powers include the following:

- The beneficiary can be given, in addition to all the income from the trust, the right in any year or years to withdraw the greater of $5,000 or 5 percent of the value of the corpus in that year. This can be done at the beneficiary's whim and pleasure; no explanation to the trustee is necessary. At worst this right will cause the amount the beneficiary could have withdrawn (but did not) in the year of death to be includible in his or her estate.
- The beneficiary can also be given the right to demand funds in addition to the income from the trust and the *5-and-5 powers* mentioned above. A beneficiary can be given an enforceable right to demand capital to maintain his or her accustomed standard of living or to meet extraordinary medical expenses.
- It is permissible to give a trustee a power in his or her (or its) sole and absolute discretion to distribute principal to the beneficiary for any reason satisfactory to the trustee. Note that in this case the beneficiary has no right to funds but must persuade the trustee to disburse them. For example, if the beneficiary wanted to go into a business, he or she would have to persuade the trustee to advance the appropriate amount of capital.
- A beneficiary can be given a special power by deed to appoint the corpus of the trust to his or her spouse and/or children. This in essence enables the donee of the power to make gift-tax-free transfers to his or her children. For example, if a donee's son is about to marry, the donee can appoint money to him for the purchase of a car, home, or any other reason. The donee may also be given a special power to appoint principal to and among his or her family by will. Since the class is limited, the power will not be considered general and therefore will not cause inclusion of the assets in the donee's estate. The only

qualifications are that the donee may not be given the dubious privilege of appointing trust assets to his or her personal creditors and may not tie up assets indefinitely because of the rule against perpetuities.

Powers of appointment are among the most commonly used tools of estate planning. They have both tax and nontax utility. Flexibility is the key to their usefulness: A power of appointment enables an estate owner to control the devolution of his or her property through two or more generations. By using a special power, for example, an estate owner can provide the major guidelines and still leave to succeeding generations the implementation of the objectives to which the property is to be devoted. For instance, a father may leave property to his daughter for life and then to his daughter's children as his daughter shall appoint. This might make it possible for his daughter to determine the distribution among her children in light of the events occurring even 25 or 30 years after her father's death.

Another example is where a husband leaves his wife a life estate but gives her the power to appoint the corpus among their children. If one son has married a wealthy woman, another is a college professor with limited finances, and a third child has a physical or mental handicap that calls for special consideration, the mother can appoint corpus among the children as is most appropriate under the changing circumstances.

13

Estate Planning Implications of Employee Benefits

Chapter Outline

ESTATE PLANNING FOR DISTRIBUTIONS FROM QUALIFIED PLANS AND IRAs   379
    Federal Tax Treatment of Qualified Plans and IRAs   380
    Retirement Plan Assets—Inefficient Inheritances   382
    Planning for Qualified Retirement Benefits   384
NONQUALIFIED DEFERRED COMPENSATION   396
    Advantages of Nonqualified Plans   396
    Federal Income Tax Implications   397
    Federal Gift Tax Implications   398
    Federal Estate Tax Implications   398
    Use of Life Insurance   399
DEATH-BENEFIT-ONLY PLANS   400
    Definition of DBO Plan   400
    Federal Estate Tax Implications   400
    Federal Gift Tax Implications   401
    Federal Income Tax Implications   402
    Use of Life Insurance   402
GROUP TERM LIFE INSURANCE (SEC. 79) PLANS   402
    Income Tax Implications   402
    Estate Planning for Group Term Life Benefits   403
SPLIT-DOLLAR LIFE INSURANCE PLANS   405
    Basic Split-Dollar Arrangements   405
    Reverse Split-Dollar Plans   407
    Estate Tax Considerations of Split Dollar   408
SEC. 162 BONUS LIFE INSURANCE PLANS   410
    Basic Design of Sec. 162 Plan   410
    Estate and Gift Tax Planning Considerations   410

Employee benefits are often a sizable component of an individual's estate. Unless a person is individually wealthy and has chosen not to work, earnings from employment and employee benefits will enhance his or her estate. This is true even if the individual owns a business entity or is self-employed. Owner-employees of corporations will often choose employee benefits to the maximum extent permissible due to the tax advantages available for employee benefits. Even individuals who are self-employed[1] will have significant employee benefit issues since retirement plans, such as Keogh plans or simplified employee pensions (SEPs), represent an excellent method for self-employeds to reduce current taxes and plan for retirement.

Employee benefits create many estate planning problems and opportunities. The planner's failure to carefully analyze this relationship and to take advantage of many of the planning techniques available can have an extremely negative impact on the client's estate and on his or her survivors' lives.

In this chapter we will study six important employee benefits and then see what estate planning techniques and opportunities are available. Let's first get an overview of each of these areas:

- *qualified plans and IRAs*—One of the most important topics in employment is the treatment of distributions from qualified plans. There have been many significant changes concerning federal estate taxes that affect the way qualified plan benefits are to be included as part of a decedent-employee's gross estate. We will look at these changes, as well as current planning opportunities. We will also discuss federal income tax issues as they relate to the overall estate planning process in this area.
- *nonqualified deferred compensation*—One of the most popular employee benefits today is nonqualified deferred compensation, which is basically a promise an employer makes to pay an employee at a future time for services rendered and work-related duties performed currently. There are many tax and non-tax-related issues that must be examined when studying such a deferred-compensation arrangement. First, what are the federal income tax overtones of a nonqualified deferred-compensation package? What income, if any, is taxed currently to the employee? Second, what are the federal estate tax rules? Are compensation payments that have been deferred included, in whole or in part, in the decedent-employee's gross estate? Third, what are the non-tax-related considerations for the employee? What is the best payout approach? We will treat these and other questions in detail.
- *death-benefit-only plans*—Many employment contracts offer benefit payments to named survivors of an employee. The best example of this situation is an arrangement in which an employer is contractually obligated to make specified payments to members of the employee's family (who had been named previously) if the employee dies while

actively employed. We will examine the many complex estate tax issues raised by using such an approach, and we will discuss the planning opportunities involved.

- *group term life insurance*—Many employers offer group term life insurance plans sheltered from current income tax by Sec. 79. This coverage is an inexpensive and tax-efficient method to provide income-replacement insurance for workers. However, it is not a permanent solution for retired employees' estate planning problems.
- *split-dollar life insurance*—Split-dollar life insurance is perhaps the most frequently used form of permanent life insurance as an executive compensation benefit. Although split-dollar arrangements are not limited to the employer-employee relationship, they traditionally have almost always been used as an employee benefit. In recent years, a new form of split dollar, *reverse split dollar,* has become increasingly popular. Our focus for this chapter will be the use of split dollar as a permanent solution in the estate plan.
- *Sec. 162 bonus life insurance plans*—One type of employee compensation arrangement that is currently advantageous for shareholder-employees is the Sec. 162 life insurance plan. Its primary advantage is the ability to avoid the nondiscrimination rules applicable to other fringe benefits while providing permanent and fully portable coverage to the selected executives and shareholder-employees. Since permanent coverage is provided, the Sec. 162 plan can be used for estate planning purposes when the participant retires.

ESTATE PLANNING FOR DISTRIBUTIONS FROM QUALIFIED PLANS AND IRAs

Almost every estate owner who is an employee or is self-employed needs to consider the tax and estate planning overtones stemming from distributions from qualified plans or individual retirement accounts (IRAs). Studies have shown that since Congress enacted the Employee Retirement Income Security Act of 1974 (ERISA), many Americans are covered by some form of qualified plan. The American Council of Life Insurance recently reported that over 65 million Americans were covered by pension plans with life insurance companies in 1995; reserves for these plans totaled over $972 billion. Assets in qualified retirement plans not funded with life insurance companies totaled over $2.6 trillion in 1995. Individual or self-employed retirement plans, such as IRAs, SEPs, or Keogh plans, are also used extensively as tax-advantaged retirement savings vehicles. The 1996 tax changes generally created more opportunities to establish and fund private retirement plans.

The distributions from such plans must be considered as part of the overall planning process. This point is even more crucial in light of the several legislative changes in this area in the last few years. Planners must examine the way distributions from qualified plans and IRAs are treated as a matter of federal estate and income taxation. Failure to consider the implication of these transactions will result in an incomplete and distorted estate plan. What makes the estate planning problems for individuals even more troubling is that retirement plans often represent a large percentage of their estates. As we will discuss below, retirement plan account balances are not a comfortable fit with the normal estate planning techniques for wealthy individuals. Over the last couple of years, the most frequent comment we've heard from financial services professionals is that they need guidance with respect to estate planning for clients with large retirement plans.

Federal Tax Treatment of Qualified Plans and IRAs

Federal Estate Tax Treatment

As we discussed in chapter 1, the amounts left to survivors from a qualified plan or IRA are subject to federal estate taxes under the provisions of Sec. 2039. The amounts left to survivors could be in the form of a survivor annuity or account balance to be distributed at some point(s) in the future. All that is required under Sec. 2039 is that some amount be left to survivors and that the decedent or the decedent's employer contributed the funds that are subject to estate taxes. In other words, something will be included in the decedent's gross estate unless he or she had elected a single-life annuity distribution option that terminated with his or her death. Of course, the estate tax marital deduction will often make the qualified plan or IRA funds deductible if the surviving spouse is the beneficiary.

Federal Income Taxes

All funds in a qualified retirement plan or IRA that were previously untaxed are subject to income taxes, regardless of whether the funds are withdrawn while the plan owner is alive or after his or her death. The funds in a qualified plan or IRA are treated as income in respect of a decedent (IRD) and do not receive a basis step-up to date-of-death value. There is, however, a deduction available under Sec. 691(c) for any estate taxes caused by including the qualified plan or IRA in the decedent's gross estate. Note that this is a tax *deduction* and not a tax credit. Thus, it does not eliminate all income taxes even if the qualified plan or IRA was subject to the maximum federal estate taxes.

How quickly the income taxes are payable by the survivors depends on a particular decedent's circumstances. Factors that determine how fast the income taxes are incurred include (1) who the decedent named as designated beneficiary, (2) whether or not the decedent has reached age 70 1/2, and (3) how the decedent had chosen to take his or her distribution while alive. The discussion that follows is an attempt to briefly summarize the income tax options available to survivors. For more information, the reader should seek a thorough discussion of the distribution rules for retirement plans.

Death Occurs before the Required Beginning Date (RBD). If the qualified plan participant or owner of the IRA dies before the RBD (that is, before April 1 of the year following attainment of age 70 1/2), the following options are available even if distributions have already begun:

- For income tax purposes the entire balance in the qualified plan or IRA must be distributed by December 31 of the 5th year following the participant's or IRA owner's death. Under this option, there are no minimum distribution requirements for any year other than the 5th year.
- If the participant had named a qualified designated beneficiary other than his or her surviving spouse, distributions can be made over that beneficiary's life expectancy for income tax purposes. If there are multiple beneficiaries of a single account, the designated beneficiary with the shortest life expectancy will be used to determine the distribution period for all beneficiaries. Under these circumstances, distributions must commence by December 31 of the year following the participant's death.
- If the beneficiary is a surviving spouse who is eligible for rollover treatment, distributions may commence on April 1 of the year following the year the surviving spouse attains age 70 1/2. If rollover treatment is unavailable or the surviving spouse has already reached his or her RBD, distributions must commence by December 31 of the year following the participant's death. Only the surviving spouse has the option to recalculate his or her life expectancy annually for determining the minimum distribution. (Recalculation will provide the maximum deferral for taking distributions, but as we will discuss below, it will result in a tax burden for survivors at the distributee's death.)

Death Occurs after the Decedent's RBD. If the participant or IRA owner dies after the RBD, the individual would have already chosen a distribution pattern. For example, the individual may have selected a joint-life payout over his or her lifetime and his or her spouse's lifetime. A designated beneficiary generally must have been selected at the RBD. If the participant or IRA owner dies after his or her RBD, distributions must usually continue at least as rapidly as required under the distribution plan in effect at death. However, the following are some notable exceptions based on the participant's distribution choices and designated beneficiary:

- single-life payout without recalculation. In this instance, distributions must generally continue for the heirs or the estate at least as rapidly as required under the distribution plan in effect at death.

- single-life payout with recalculation. This is the worst-case scenario for postmortem income taxes. The survivors must take the distribution for income tax purposes by the end of the year following the year of the participant's death.
- joint-life payout with surviving spouse as designated beneficiary—no rollover. The surviving spouse must continue the current pattern of distribution over his or her remaining lifetime. If recalculation has been elected, the surviving spouse's death creates the worst-case scenario discussed above.
- joint-life payout with surviving spouse as designated beneficiary—rollover. If the rollover option is available, the surviving spouse can treat the amount rolled over as his or her IRA and make independent elections. This option, which we will discuss further below, provides the best income tax deferral. Be aware that the rollover option is not always available. For example, if the IRA is left to a QTIP trust benefitting the surviving spouse, rollover is not available and the payout must continue over the joint-life expectancy.
- joint-life payout with nonspouse beneficiary. If the joint-life payout is made with a beneficiary other than the spouse, the beneficiary can take the balance over his or her life expectancy. Note that this could significantly defer income taxes if the beneficiary is much younger.

State Death Taxes

The state death tax treatment of qualified plan and IRA accounts depends upon the type of inheritance tax or estate tax in place. States that have individual inheritance taxes will sometimes exempt or limit taxes on these assets. However, all states have some form of credit estate tax or "sponge" tax that imposes a tax equal to the maximum state death tax credit allowable on the federal estate tax return. In these instances, the credit estate tax is based on the federal taxable estate and will impose a tax on all assets comprising the federal estate tax base, including qualified plan assets or IRAs. Thus, we need to be concerned with state death taxes on these retirement assets in all taxable estates (above $625,000 in 1998) unless these assets will be left to the surviving spouse in a manner that qualifies for the federal estate tax marital deduction.

Retirement Plan Assets—Inefficient Inheritances

The tax treatment of retirement plan assets left to heirs is as follows:

- These assets do not receive an income tax basis step-up to date-of-death values and are treated as income in respect of a decedent (IRD). Therefore survivors will pay the income taxes lurking in retirement plan funds (in some cases very soon after the plan owner's death).

Chapter 13 Estate Planning Implications of Employee Benefits

- These assets are also subject to federal estate taxes, generation-skipping taxes, and state inheritance taxes in some cases. The federal estate taxes paid on the retirement assets will be deductible from federal income taxes under IRC Sec. 691(c).

This tax treatment is often called a "double tax" on retirement plan assets held by a decedent. The bottom line: Retirement plan assets are income tax efficient for funding retirement benefits but overall tax inefficient for funding inheritances.

Example: Mrs. Adams, aged 75, owned her own business for many years prior to her retirement. She named her husband as beneficiary of her IRA when she reached age 70 1/2, and they elected to take a joint and survivor payout from the IRA, recalculating life expectancy to determine the required minimum distribution. Her husband predeceased her 2 years ago. Mrs. Adams dies this year with an estate of $6 million, with $2 million remaining in her IRA payable to her two children, aged 51 and 46. Assume the remainder of her estate contains no other income-in-respect-of-decedent items. The taxes for her estate and her IRA are:

Federal estate tax	$2,237,200
State death tax (taxes equal to the maximum state death tax credit allowable)	510,800
Income tax on the IRA (assuming a 39.6% marginal rate after the Sec. 691(c) deduction)	447,638
Estate remaining after taxes	$2,804,362
Percentage of estate passing to heirs	47

Let's take a closer look at what happens to the IRA account. The IRA was $2 million at the time of Mrs. Adams's death. If we assume the federal estate and state death taxes are divided proportionately between the IRA and the remainder of her estate, the death taxes attributable to the IRA are $745,733 and $170,266. The income tax is payable in the tax year following the year of the decedent's death (the result of the recalculation method for determining the IRA minimum distribution that Mrs. Adams chose). The following demonstrates the inefficiency of the IRA as an inheritance:

IRA balance at death	$2,000,000
Less	
Federal estate tax	(745,733)
State death tax	(170,266)
Income tax on IRA	(447,638)
Total reduction	$1,363,637
Net value of IRA for heirs	$636,363
Percentage of IRA passing to heirs	31.8

Mrs. Adams's estate shrinks by just over 53 percent, but her IRA shrinks by more than 68 percent (with taxes fairly proportioned). What's more, her IRA account balance will be subject to income taxes (compressed into the highest marginal bracket) in the year following her death since she elected to recalculate life expectancy when determining her minimum required distribution.

At first glance, this result looks horrible. However, we need to remember that Mrs. Adams probably accumulated far more in her qualified plan account than she would have been able to accumulate in a taxable investment alternative. She probably took advantage of years of before-tax contributions and tax-deferred buildup in her qualified plan. Her family is probably better off in spite of the triple tax. Her heirs, however, may not view the final result as a victory.

For clients to appropriately fund their own and their spouses' retirement the estate planning decisions for qualified retirement plans will generally be subordinate to the retirement distribution decisions. Clients' decisions will be based on their financial needs and, for wealthier individuals, will generally focus on income tax deferral. Unfortunately, while the tax rules applicable to retirement plans are extremely efficient for accumulating retirement assets, the rules are very complex for planning distributions for the retiree. The tax treatment for transferring retirement plan assets to heirs could be viewed as confiscatory.

Planning for Qualified Retirement Benefits

General Guidelines for Retirement Distributions and Estate Planning

Although the estate planning implications for qualified retirement plans create some complex choices, there are several general rules to follow. The good news is that the standard choice of naming the surviving spouse as designated beneficiary and selecting a joint-life payout will probably be the optimal choice in more than 90 percent of the cases.

In most retirement plans, a participant will be given annuity options. An annuity is a form of payout guaranteed for life or, in the case of a qualified joint and survivor annuity (QJSA), for the joint lives of a husband and wife. In other plans, the participant may have the choice of a lump-sum option or have an account balance that can be rolled over to an IRA. If income tax deferral is the goal, the rollover option is usually the best alternative.

Generally, an individual must begin drawing from a pension plan or IRA no later than April 1st of the year following the tax year in which he or she attains age 70 1/2. The beneficiary designation for the account balance must also be made at this time. In advising your clients on how to take retirement plan distributions and select a beneficiary for their retirement plan, keep in mind the following general rules:

- Check the retirement provisions of the specific plan. Not all options are available in every plan.
- The financial needs of the participant, his or her spouse, and other heirs should be the primary concern.
- The income tax issues regarding the type of distribution option selected are more immediate and usually outweigh the estate planning issues. Thus, when in doubt, defer as long as possible or practical.
- The best choice for income tax deferral (annual recalculation of life expectancy) while the participant and/or his or her spouse is alive will create the worst income tax result after their deaths, since the remaining life expectancy will be zero after the second death. Thus, as in the earlier example of Mrs. Adams, the income tax problem is immediate.
- A designated beneficiary should be selected. This will usually provide the longest income tax deferral. The participant's spouse or other family members can be designated beneficiaries; the individual's estate or trust cannot be unless some special planning (discussed later) has been performed.
- Decisions about the retirement plan are extraordinarily complex (even in the context of the tax laws) and should not be made without appropriate professional advice.

Factors That Affect the Choice of Beneficiary

Most married individuals designate their spouses as beneficiaries of their retirement plans. Many retirement plan participants will need to provide for the nonparticipant spouse from the retirement plan since the other family assets will be insufficient to afford them a comfortable retirement. Furthermore, there may be no choice in many types of qualified retirement plans. The Retirement Equity Act (REA) stipulates in many instances that a married individual covered by a qualified pension plan must provide his or her spouse with a qualified joint and 50 percent survivor annuity. This survivor annuity can be avoided only with the nonparticipant spouse's consent. The REA rules do not apply to IRAs, SEPs, or Sec. 403(b) plans. For qualified plans that permit rollovers to an IRA, the participant's spouse must generally consent to a rollover. The IRS recently released Notice 97-10, which gave much needed explanations of a plan participant spouse's rights in a qualified plan, along with sample language for waiving a QJSA.

A married individual's decision to consent to a distribution different from a QJSA will depend on several factors. First, the surviving spouse must have sufficient funds outside of the retirement plan to provide for the remainder of his or her retirement. Quite often, these funds could come from life insurance, a far superior vehicle for funding inheritances than the retirement plan account balance. *Pension maximization* employs the technique of choosing a larger single-life payout from a retirement plan and using some of the extra cash to buy life insurance for the surviving spouse as a replacement fund.

Second, the participant could have another beneficiary who would be the appropriate choice from a personal and tax standpoint. For example, the plan participant may have children from a prior marriage who would be his or her first choice as designated beneficiary.

Third, the income and estate tax consequences of a retirement distribution choice must be carefully considered. The selection of the designated beneficiary has the following important tax consequences:

- The choice of designated beneficiary will affect the size of the minimum distribution if a joint and survivor option is selected.
- The income tax deferral available to the heirs depends on the selection of the designated beneficiary.
- The availability of the marital deduction and the ability to defer the excess accumulations tax until the second death depends on the selection of the spouse or the appropriate marital trust as the designated beneficiary.

Unique Tax-Deferral Options of Naming the Spouse as Designated Beneficiary

Income Tax Issues. Naming the spouse as designated beneficiary of an IRA offers income-tax-deferral options. First, the minimum distribution requirements at age 70 1/2 provide for a longer payout period if the married couple's joint life expectancy is used. The required payout period is 16 years for one life at age 70 but much longer if two lives are used. For example, it is 26.2 years if the participant's spouse is 10 years younger and a joint-life payout is selected. Thus, the income taxes on the account balance are spread over a longer period. In addition, if the surviving spouse is the designated beneficiary, he or she can roll over the account balance to his or her own IRA and delay distributions until he or she attains age 70 1/2. This gives more flexibility for deferral, particularly if the beneficiary-spouse is significantly younger. Better yet, the surviving spouse can name a new designated beneficiary of the rollover IRA (such as the couple's child or children). This permits the family to further defer the income taxes since the minimum required distributions can be taken over a new joint-life payout.

Example: Suppose Mr. Jones, aged 68, is married to Mrs. Jones, aged 55, and has a large account balance in his IRA rollover. They have one child, Mitch, aged 35. If Mr. Jones dies this year and has designated Mrs. Jones as the beneficiary of the IRA, she can create her own IRA and roll over his account balance to her IRA. She will not have to take distributions from this IRA until she is age 70 1/2, or in about 16 years. She could then designate her child as sole beneficiary of the IRA and choose a joint-life payout. Her minimum required distributions would then be based on the joint life expectancy of herself and her child. However, the minimum distribution rules permit only a maximum 10-year differential between joint life expectancies if the beneficiary is not the participant's spouse. Thus, a 26.2 year payout can be chosen. If Mrs. Jones dies before the balance is withdrawn and has not recalculated life expectancy, Mitch can spread the remaining payments over his actual life expectancy. Of course, this wonderful flexibility to defer income on the IRA presumes that the Jones family will not need sooner or larger distributions.

Estate Tax Issues. For estate tax purposes, the estate tax marital deduction will defer estate taxes until the second death (on any plan assets remaining at that time) if the designated beneficiary of the retirement plan is the surviving spouse. In addition, the participant's estate can elect to defer the excess accumulations tax until the second death under these circumstances.

Marital Trust as Potential Beneficiary

Generally, a marital trust should be designated as the beneficiary only when the plan participant has an asset-protection goal. That is, the participant either (1) desires a trustee of the marital trust to control the management of the retirement plan account or (2) wants to preserve as much as possible of the principal of the retirement plan account for the next generation. For example, the participant may have children from a prior marriage. Using a marital trust as the designated beneficiary of the retirement plan will provide retirement income for the new spouse, but it will also guarantee that the remaining retirement account balance will be distributed to the children at the surviving spouse's death.

The use of the marital trust adds significant complexity and may remove flexibility. In a pure QTIP trust, the principal will be protected from unlimited invasion by the surviving spouse. Thus, the participant will be able to name the remainder beneficiaries of the IRA and preserve as much principal as possible for these heirs. However, the surviving spouse will not be able to roll over the account to his or her IRA. The rollover potential is foreclosed unless the surviving spouse has sufficient control over the IRA to treat it as his or her IRA for rollover purposes. This type of control is not normally provided in a QTIP trust. In fact, such control is contrary to the asset-protection goal. For example, a recent private ruling (Ltr. 9608036) permitted rollover if the surviving spouse has a general power of appointment over the marital trust. Other private rulings (most recently, Ltrs. 9703036 and 9620038) have permitted rollover treatment when the IRA was payable to the estate, which could include testamentary trusts not qualifying for rollover, but the surviving spouse as executor had the power to allocate the IRA balance to an outright marital bequest. In either of these instances, the surviving spouse could invade the IRA at his or her discretion.

Thus, the participant had to forego the asset-protection goal to achieve the rollover potential.

A QTIP trust as beneficiary of the IRA will qualify for the marital deduction if the requirements of Rev. Rul. 89-89, 1989-2 C.B. 231, are met. The trustee must be able to compel distribution of all income from the IRA, and the marital trust should receive the greater of the actual income or the minimum required IRA distribution. The annual distribution to the QTIP must be paid to the surviving spouse. Of course, the actual income that an IRA with a large account balance earns may be greater than the minimum required distribution under the normal IRA rules. Thus, the QTIP requirement to distribute actual income may cause a larger annual distribution, and some income tax deferral may be lost if the QTIP trust is used as a beneficiary. In addition, the income-tax-deferral potential of a rollover is unavailable.

To some degree, the investment policy for the IRA could control the amount of annual income. For example, dividends, interest, or rent is normally allocated to income, while capital gains are normally allocated to principal. The IRA forms should be adapted to provide for the determination of principal and income.

If the surviving spouse is not a citizen of the United States, the qualified domestic trust rules must be followed, and the amount of the IRA distribution treated as principal must be determined to calculate the deferred estate tax applicable (see chapter 11 for a discussion of the deferred estate tax for a qualified domestic trust). In any event, significant additional compliance complexity and costs are associated with the selection of the marital trust as beneficiary if the beneficiary is a noncitizen.

Estate or Credit Shelter/Bypass Trust as Beneficiary

Naming the participant's estate or credit shelter trust (CST) as the designated beneficiary of the retirement plan account balance is generally not recommended because of adverse income tax treatment. The estate and any testamentary trust (including the CST) created under the participant's will cannot be designated beneficiaries for retirement plan purposes.

Therefore the minimum required distributions at age 70 1/2 must be based solely on the participant's life if his or her estate or testamentary trust is the named beneficiary. This causes the income tax to be incurred over a shorter period since payout cannot be made over a surviving designated beneficiary's life expectancy. Depending on the age of the participant at his or her death or the type of distribution selected, the beneficiaries would take the remaining balance either (1) at least as fast as the participant was taking distributions, (2) in five installments beginning in the year following the year of the participant's death, or (3) all in the year following the year of the participant's death (if the participant chose recalculation).

In addition, the CST should generally be designed with a goal of maximum growth since it is a bypass trust and estate taxes are not imposed on this trust until the next generation. Funding the trust with retirement plan assets will shrink its growth by the amount of the income taxes that the CST will incur on these retirement assets. Thus, it is usually recommended that the CST be funded with retirement plan assets only if there are no other estate assets available and only if the estate tax savings outweigh the adverse income tax consequences. One option may be to use the CST as a disclaimer option if the surviving spouse and his or her advisers think this would be an appropriate postmortem choice.

Living Trust as Designated Beneficiary

It is possible to designate a living trust, perhaps designed to use the marital deduction or applicable credit amount, as beneficiary of retirement plan assets. If the requirements of proposed Treas. Reg. Sec. 1.401(a)(9)-1 (Q&A D-5(a)) are met, a trust beneficiary can qualify as a designated beneficiary. Thus, the beneficiary's life expectancy can be used to determine the payout after the participant's death. Of course, if the trust is a marital trust, the greater of the minimum distribution or the actual income must be paid to the spouse.

The proposed regulations give the following requirements for the living trust:

- The beneficiaries of the trust who are beneficiaries of the participant's retirement benefits must be identifiable from the trust document.
- The trust is a valid trust under state law.
- The trust can be revocable until the death of the participant.
- A copy of the trust or a description of the beneficiaries must be given to the plan administrator or custodian of the IRA.

Several private rulings have approved variations of this living trust beneficiary designation. Thus, a living marital trust or UCST can be named as the designated beneficiary and the age of one of the trust beneficiaries can be used to determine the minimum distribution under a joint-life payout option. Some recent private rulings seem to permit the change of beneficiary designation to a revocable trust after the required beginning date, but the payout must continue as initially determined.

Charitable Giving and Retirement Plan Benefits

A charity can be the beneficiary of a retirement plan, even though the plan account or an IRA is generally nonassignable. The charity makes an appropriate beneficiary if two circumstances coincide:

- First, the participant has a desire to benefit a charity.
- Second, the income and estate tax benefits from the charitable gift are important to the client.

The designation of a charity or a charitable remainder trust (CRT) solves several of the tax problems discussed above, and for this reason it will probably be better to fund a charitable gift with retirement plan assets than with other family assets. If these tax problems are mitigated, the family, the charity, or both will receive greater net inheritances than if non-IRD assets are used to fund the charitable bequest.

If a charity or CRT is the named beneficiary, the following tax consequences occur:

- The estate receives a charitable deduction for the amount passing to charity.
- The charity or CRT is tax exempt, and the IRD may be avoided (or deferred if a CRT is the beneficiary). The excess accumulations tax is not avoided.

Example: Suppose Mrs. Adams, from our previous example, would like to leave $2 million to The American College. You will recall that her $6 million estate consisted of a $2 million IRA account balance and $4 million of non-IRD items. If she designates The American College as the beneficiary of her IRA and apportions all taxes and expenses to her residuary estate, The American College will get $2 million and her heirs will receive $2,261,250. If she leaves the IRA to her children and makes a bequest of $2 million of non-IRD items to The American College, the College will still receive its $2 million; however, her children will receive only $1,917,413. This result is far worse since the income tax on the IRA is not avoided.

The use of a CRT solves a problem created by the recalculation method of determining the minimum required distribution. Suppose a participant named his or her surviving spouse as the beneficiary and elected a QJSA with recalculation. At the second death, the entire remaining balance will be subject to estate taxes within 9 months and income taxes on the IRD in the year following the survivor's death. By naming a testamentary CRT as the remainder beneficiary, the retirement assets will be payable to a tax-exempt trust. Thus, the IRD will not be immediately taxable.

If the married couple names their children as the CRT's noncharitable annuity or unitrust payment recipients, the IRD can be spread over the lifetime(s) of the noncharitable beneficiaries, an alternative not available without the charitable donation. What's more, an estate tax deduction is available for the remainder interest passing to charity.

Example: Suppose Mrs. Adams, from our earlier examples, did not want to deprive her children of the use of the IRA during their lifetimes, but she still wanted to make a substantial gift to The American College. Mrs. Adams could designate a testamentary charitable remainder trust as the beneficiary of the IRA. Her children would receive an annual distribution equal to 6 percent of the annual value of the CRT's principal (payable at the end of the year) for the remainder of their lives. The American College would receive the balance of the principal at the death of the survivor of her children. In this scenario, her estate would receive a charitable deduction of $252,700, saving her estate $138,985 in state and federal death taxes. Moreover, the income taxes on the IRA would not have to be taken until her children received their annual payments from the CRT. The actuarial value of their payments would be $1,708,860, assuring them of substantial funds for the remainder of their lives.

Life Insurance within Qualified Plans

Most of the discussion above has focused on qualified plan or IRA benefits left to survivors. It is possible to supplement these benefits in a qualified plan with life insurance. In fact, life insurance may be the only method to provide a substantial benefit to survivors in the early years of plan participation. Life insurance gives the plan significant funds at a participant's death, which is particularly important in the early years of his or her employment when the amount contributed on the participant's behalf is still relatively small.

Life Insurance Limited by Incidental Benefit Test. An insured preretirement death benefit can be provided in either a defined-benefit or defined-contribution plan. Contributions to the plan by the employer may be used to pay life insurance premiums as long as the amount qualifies under the tests for incidental benefits.

In general the IRS considers that nonretirement benefits—life, medical, or disability insurance, for example—in a qualified plan are incidental and therefore permissible as long as the cost of providing these benefits is less than 25 percent of the cost of providing all the benefits under the plan. In applying this approach to life insurance benefits, the 25 percent rule pertains to the portion of any life insurance premium that is used to provide current life insurance protection. Any portion of the premium that is used to increase the policy's cash value is considered to be a contribution to the plan fund that is available to pay retirement benefits, and it is not considered in the 25 percent limitation.

Following its general 25 percent test, the IRS has ruled that if a qualified plan provides death benefits using ordinary life insurance (life insurance with a cash value), the death benefit will be considered incidental if either (1) less than 50 percent of the total cumulative employer contributions credited to each participant's account has been used to purchase ordinary life insurance, or (2) the face amount of the policy does not exceed 100 times the anticipated monthly normal retirement benefit or the accumulated reserve under the life insurance policy, whichever is greater. In practice defined-benefit plans using ordinary life insurance are usually designed to take advantage of the 100-times rule, while defined-contribution plans, including profit-sharing plans, that use ordinary life contracts generally make use of the 50 percent test.

If term insurance contracts are used to provide the death benefit, then, because the 25 percent test will be applied to the entire premium, the aggregate premiums paid for insurance on each participant should be less than 25 percent of the aggregate additions to the employee's account. Term insurance is sometimes used to fund death benefits in defined-contribution plans but rarely in defined-benefit plans.

The IRS has not yet ruled on the use of universal life insurance and similar products in qualified plans, but it informally takes the position that the total premiums for such products must meet the same 25 percent limit as that for term insurance. This is almost certainly incorrect, however, since a substantial part of the premium for a universal life policy, as for an ordinary life policy, goes toward increasing the cash value. The limit in theory therefore should be higher than 25 percent.

The discussion so far is somewhat simplified because insurance can be used in qualified plans in many ways and because the IRS has issued numerous rulings, both revenue rulings and private letter rulings, applying the basic 25 percent test to a variety of different fact situations. Thus, there is considerable room for creative design of life-insurance-funded death benefits within qualified plans.

Life Insurance Opportunity in Profit-Sharing Plans. We should note an additional planning opportunity in *profit-sharing plans*. In profit-sharing plans, the incidental benefit tests described above do not apply. Generally, all funds that have been in the plan for at least 2 years can be used for life insurance premiums. In addition, once the participant has been in the plan for 5 years, all funds can be used for life insurance premiums. To accomplish this goal, the profit-sharing plan must contain a directed investment provision allowing participants to direct the plan trustee to purchase life insurance or other investments with their accounts. The purchase of survivorship (second-to-die) coverage on the participant and the participant's spouse provides excellent tax leverage. First, the income taxes on the life insurance premiums (discussed below) are based on lower Table 38 rates measuring the annual taxable cost of insurance coverage. Second, the delay of the death benefit until the second death offers an opportunity to later remove the policy from the plan and transfer it to a third-party owner to eliminate the death benefits from the gross estate of the participant or the participant's spouse.

Taxation of Participant. If life insurance is provided for a participant through a qualified plan (that is, by using employer contributions to the plan to pay insurance premiums), part or all of the cost of the insurance is currently taxable to the participant. Life insurance provided by the plan is not considered part of a Sec. 79 group term plan (discussed later in the chapter), and consequently the $50,000 exclusion under Sec. 79 does not apply.

If life insurance with a cash value is used, and if all the death proceeds are payable to the participant's estate or beneficiary, the term cost or cost of the "pure amount at risk" is taxable to the employee. The term cost is the difference between the face amount of insurance and the cash surrender value of the policy at the end of the policy year. In other words, the cost of the policy's cash value is not currently taxable to the employee because the cash value is considered part of the plan fund to be used to provide the retirement benefit. As discussed earlier, the term cost is calculated using either the PS 58 table of rates provided by the Internal Revenue Service or the insurance company's rates for individual one-year term policies at standard rates, if these are lower and if the insurance company actually offers such policies.

If the plan uses term rather than cash-value insurance to provide an insured death benefit, the cost of the entire face amount of insurance is taxable to the employee.

If the plan allows employee contributions, the nondeductible employee contributions can be used to offset taxable income resulting from including any form of insurance in the plan. Unless the plan provides otherwise, however, insurance will be considered to have been paid first from employer contributions and plan fund earnings, so this offset is not available unless the plan makes specific provision for it.

Taxation of Beneficiaries. The following points summarize the taxation of an insured death benefit that a beneficiary receives:

- The pure insurance element of an insured plan death benefit (the death benefit less any cash value) is income tax free to a participant's beneficiary.
- The total of all PS 58 costs paid by the participant can be recovered tax free from the plan death benefit (if it is paid from the same insurance contracts that gave rise to the PS 58 costs).
- The remainder of the distribution is taxed as a qualified plan distribution. This taxable portion of the distribution may be eligible for 5- or 10-year averaging if the plan participant was over 59 1/2 at death. If the decedent participated in the plan before 1987, there are also some favorable "grandfather" tax provisions that may apply.

Compared with the tax treatment of life insurance personally owned or provided by the employer outside the plan, there is usually an economic advantage to insurance in a qualified plan, all other things being equal. Insurance outside the plan is paid for entirely with after-tax dollars, so there is no tax deferral. Although the death benefit of nonplan insurance may be entirely tax free instead of partially tax free, the deferral of tax with plan-provided insurance can result in a measurable net tax benefit.

Furthermore, the pure insurance amount of a qualified plan death benefit is not subject to the 15 percent excess accumulations tax. PS 58 costs can also be recovered free of the excess accumulations tax. Finally, although qualified plan death benefits are, in general, included in a decedent's estate for federal estate tax purposes, it may be possible to exclude the insured portion of the death benefit if the decedent had no incidents of ownership in the policy.

Use of a Qualified Plan Subtrust. One technique that has received some attention is the use of a subtrust in a qualified plan to hold the life insurance purchased on the participant's life.[2] The goal of the subtrust is to use "lightly taxed" qualified plan dollars to provide life insurance without estate taxation of the proceeds. The subtrust is used to avoid incidents of ownership by the participant-insured. Although there are not any rulings or authority on this technique at this point, there is a reasonable argument to be made under the tax laws that properly created subtrusts will be excluded from the participant-insured's estate at the time of his or her death.

The first step in the process is for the qualified plan to contain language to permit the creation of the subtrust and appointment of a special subtrustee (and successors to the subtrustee). As with the typical irrevocable life insurance trust, the trust should be created and in place within the plan before the insurance is purchased. Next, the trustee must be selected. The trustee of the subtrust should be independent of the participant and his or her survivors, such as a corporate fiduciary. The trust should have successor trustee provisions and prevent the participant from being involved in the selection process if a trustee resigns after the plan is in effect.

The selection of the beneficiary of the proceeds is always an important step with life insurance. Under the subtrust approach, the beneficiary is either irrevocably elected at the time the trust is set up, or the beneficiary selection is under the control of the subtrustee. This is to prevent the participant-insured from exercising this incident of ownership after the insurance is purchased. The subtrust should also be drafted carefully to prevent the participant-insured from exercising any other incidents of ownership. For example, the cash value of the policy should not be distributable to or controlled by the participant-insured.

Each year, the participant will be taxed on the cost of the insurance measured by the PS 58 rates, Table 38 rates, or the insurer's term rates, as appropriate. The amount of the annual cost of the insurance is also treated as a taxable gift from the insured to the subtrust each year.

Life Insurance Solutions outside of the Qualified Plan

A relatively simple method for planning to mitigate the triple tax on qualified plan accounts or IRAs is to set up an ILIT outside of the qualified plan or IRA. The proceeds of the ILIT will replace the taxes imposed on the retirement assets. The plan owner can use withdrawals from the plan to fund the life insurance purchase. This plan has particular appeal for three reasons. First, it

Chapter 13 Estate Planning Implications of Employee Benefits

is simple to design and explain to clients. Second, its results are predictable and based on established tax laws. Third, the life insurance proceeds are received income tax free by the trustee and are not subject to estate taxes.

Example: Let's look at a married couple—Dr. and Mr. Richard, both aged 62. They have accumulated an estate of some $4 million. Half that amount is in a qualified retirement plan or rollover IRA and the balance in other assets. They have three children and mistakenly believe that the children and not the tax collectors should get the majority of their wealth at their second death. Assume the second-to-die of the Richards lives to age 75 and the estate at that time is as follows:

Retirement assets	$2 million
Other property	2 million
Total estate	$4 million

Taxes Payable from Estate of $4 Million

Federal estate tax (after applicable credit amount and state death tax credit)	$1,367,600
State death tax (a typical figure)	$ 280,400
Income tax on IRA distributions to children after income in respect of a decedent tax deduction assuming a 40% federal and state income tax bracket	$ 448,232
Net estate available for children's benefit after payment of all taxes	$1,903,768
Percentage of total estate remaining after payment of all taxes	47.5%
Percentage of IRA remaining after subtracting taxes directly related to IRA (excise and income tax) and equitably apportioning taxes related to entire estate (federal and state estate tax)	36.4%

After payment of all taxes, the amount inherited per child is $634,589. Instead of the current arrangement, Dr. and Mr. Richard can make up for the triple tax through the purchase of a $2 million second-to-die (survivorship) life insurance policy. Since they are both aged 62 now, the premium would be about $45,000 for 10 years. Thereafter, premium payments could come from policy values without any further out-of-pocket expense. If the three children or an ILIT is designated as the policyowner(s), the death benefit will pass to the children entirely free of income tax and all death taxes at the couple's second death.

Where will the premium dollars come from? One source of funds is the retirement plan. For example, because Dr. Richard's annual income is more than $120,000, her maximum annual contribution to a money-purchase pension or combination pension and profit-sharing plan is $30,000. If she does not have other cash available, the premium can be funded by eliminating her annual contribution to the retirement plan and withdrawing $10,000 each year from the plan account. This will create more income tax for the couple; however, an additional withdrawal can be made from the plan to cover the income tax burden. Thus, the couple can give a $2 million death benefit (more than they would receive in total under the current tax picture) to their children in addition to the remainder of their estate without any out-of-pocket costs. All premium dollars are provided by the retirement plan funds. By reducing their funding of the retirement plan and taking current withdrawals, the couple is also reducing their exposure to the triple tax on the plan at their deaths.

NONQUALIFIED DEFERRED COMPENSATION

Advantages of Nonqualified Plans

A nonqualified deferred-compensation plan is an employer-provided retirement plan that does not meet the qualified plan rules. The nonqualified approach may be advantageous for a closely held corporation if it has the following objectives:

- to exceed the maximum benefit and contribution levels applicable to qualified plans for selected employees
- to provide a retirement plan for owners and other key employees without including rank-and-file employees in the plan
- to avoid the administrative compliance standards applicable to qualified plans
- to permit shareholder-employees or other key executives to temporarily defer taxes on income into a later tax year

Types of Nonqualified Deferred-Compensation Plans and Salary Reduction Arrangements

Most nonqualified plans fit into the broad category of salary continuation plans. Salary continuation plans can be designed to provide deferred-compensation benefits at the participant's death, disability, and/or retirement. These arrangements have no current cash option available to the employee. The death or disability benefits are a percentage of the employee's compensation and are provided to the employee or his or her designated beneficiary. A salary reduction plan, which is also called an *in lieu of* plan, is an agreement between the employer and the participating employee either to reduce the employee's salary or to defer an employee's anticipated bonus and provide that such amounts be received in future tax years.

Salary continuation plans designed to provide retirement benefits can be categorized as *excess-benefit plans* or *supplemental executive retirement plans (SERPs)*. An excess-benefit plan is a retirement plan in which selected participants, generally shareholder-employees and key executives, will receive retirement benefits in excess of those possible under the qualified plan limitations. That is, these plans have (1) benefits in excess of the 100-percent-of-salary or $120,000 (for 1997) limitation in defined-benefit plans or (2) contributions in excess of the 25-percent-of-salary or $30,000 limitation in defined-contribution plans.

A SERP generally complements the qualified plan benefits for a selected group of participants. SERPs offer benefits to a corporation's key executives and, unlike excess-benefit plans, supplement the retirement benefits at levels both above and below the qualified plan limitations. These plans meet the goal of providing discriminatory benefits to shareholder-employees and other key executives.

Federal Income Tax Implications

The taxation of nonqualified deferred-compensation benefits links the timing of the corporation's deduction to the participant's receipt of benefits. The key to success is deferring the income tax liability until the receipt of the benefit. To avoid current taxation on the deferred benefit, the employee cannot (1) be in *constructive receipt* of the income or (2) receive a current *economic benefit* from the deferred amounts.

To avoid constructive receipt the employee's receipt of the income must be as follows:

- subject to *substantial limitation or restriction*. This requirement is met if the employee simply has to wait a certain time period (for example, until retirement) for the benefits.
- deferred by binding agreement prior to the time the employee earns the compensation. The employee cannot have the choice of taking cash when the income is earned. In a salary reduction agreement the employee and employer agree to defer the receipt of the salary or bonus before the related services are performed.

Any economic benefit the participant currently receives from the nonqualified plan is immediately taxable to the participant even if the benefit is not constructively received. The participant receives an economic benefit if funds are vested or set aside for the employee outside the claims of general corporate creditors. The economic benefit exists under these circumstances because the employee has a cash equivalency in the form of a secured and funded promise.

Of course, the income tax deferral is eliminated when benefits are paid (or when the constructive receipt or economic benefit tests are failed). Thus, the participant is subject to income taxes as the nonqualified plan benefits are distributed. Unfortunately, the income tax payable upon receipt of the nonqualified deferred-compensation benefits is not extinguished with the death of the participant. These benefits, if payable to survivors, are treated as IRD and remain subject to income taxes

Federal Gift Tax Implications

Since a nonqualified deferred-compensation arrangement generally involves no completed transfer of property, in most situations there are no federal gift tax implications.

Federal Estate Tax Implications

It is well established that the fair market value of a nonqualified deferred-compensation benefit payable to an employee or an employee's named beneficiary will be includible in the employee's gross estate for federal estate tax purposes. This result is based on a position taken by the IRS that under Sec. 2039, the decedent-employee had an interest during his or her lifetime in the nonqualified plan benefits payable at some future point in time. Thus, nonqualified benefits will generally result in both income and estate taxes if left to survivors.

> *Example:* Jane McFadden is employed by TAC Enterprises, Inc. As an inducement to Jane, the company agrees to give her a nonqualified benefit of $50,000 per year for 10 years after she reaches age 65. If she dies prior to receiving all of the benefit, the remainder is payable to her designated beneficiaries. Jane dies at age 66 after receiving two payments of the nonqualified benefits. The present value of the remaining eight payments is included in her gross estate under Sec. 2039. The payments are also subject to income taxes as they are received. The amount of estate taxes created by the inclusion of the nonqualified benefits (an IRD item) is deductible from the income tax return of the recipient of the payments.

Benefits from a nonqualified plan are generally eligible for the estate tax marital deduction if left to the surviving spouse. Since these benefits are taxed by both the income and estate tax systems, they are probably best used to provide for the retirement of the participant and his or her spouse. They are inefficient from a tax standpoint as inheritances. Thus, once the deferral option is no longer available, the participant is best served by taking the funds and providing for his or her retirement.

Use of Life Insurance

The employer can finance its obligation in a nonqualified plan through corporate-owned life insurance. This type of financing is attractive since life insurance as a corporate asset is a good match for the type of liabilities created by the various nonqualified arrangements. The accumulation in an ordinary life insurance policy or the benefits of an annuity policy can be useful in the participant's retirement years to provide for any salary continuation benefits offered by the plan. Of course, the primary benefit of the life insurance financing is its ability to meet the employer's death benefit obligation if the participant dies prematurely. The life insurance financing is particularly appropriate to provide benefits in a DBO plan, as discussed below.

Nonqualified plan policies are owned by and payable to the employer. As such, they avoid constructive-receipt or economic-benefit problems because general creditors have access to the funding policies. The premiums are, of course, nondeductible; however, the cash surrender value builds up tax free, and the proceeds will be nontaxable when received (the corporate alternative minimum tax [AMT], discussed later in this chapter, may create an alternative tax liability under these circumstances). The corporation receives a deduction when the benefits are actually paid to the participant.

> *Example:* Ringo Corporation, a manufacturer of pet toys, enters into a nonqualified deferred-compensation agreement with Ringo Square, a key employee. Under the terms of the agreement, Ringo Square has agreed to defer $15,000 per year in bonuses. The agreement further states that if Mr. Square dies prior to retirement, $15,000 per year will be paid to Mrs. Square for the same number of years that her husband was covered by the plan. If Ringo remains employed by the corporation until the retirement age of 65, he is to receive $28,500 per year for a 10-year period. Ringo Corporation buys cash-value life insurance on Ringo Square's life. The corporation is the premium payer and beneficiary of the policy. If Ringo dies, the death proceeds are available to the corporation to make payments to Ringo's widow. The corporation receives the proceeds tax free, and it can deduct amounts paid to the beneficiaries. If Ringo retires, the cash value of the life insurance is available to make payments to Ringo.

DEATH-BENEFIT-ONLY PLANS

One employee benefit that has become increasingly popular recently is the *death-benefit-only (DBO) plan* (sometimes referred to as a *naked death benefit*). Because it is a specialized arrangement with unusual federal tax implications, it is necessary to study it in detail as part of the overall estate planning process. Since there are many client situations in which this technique would be very useful, the estate planner must become familiar with this plan.

Definition of DBO Plan

A DBO plan is an employee benefit in which an employer becomes contractually obligated to make specified payments to previously designated members of the employee's family if the employee dies while actively employed.

Example: On the day that Don Marker becomes employed at the home office of a nationally known cosmetics company, his employer enters into a contract with Don's wife, Jean, who Don indicates should be the beneficiary of all Don's benefits. This contract states that if Don dies while he is an employee, Jean will receive a lump-sum payout of $25,000. This is an example of a death-benefit-only plan.

Federal Estate Tax Implications

The death benefit paid to the employee's beneficiary under a death-benefit-only plan is *not* included in the employee's gross estate. Many have called this an estate tax loophole. However, because the contract creating the plan is between the employer and the employee's previously named beneficiary, the Internal Revenue Code cannot include the death benefit in the employee's gross estate. Sec. 2039 covers the federal taxation of annuities for federal estate tax purposes and would normally apply to a plan providing retirement benefits to survivors. Sec. 2039 cannot reach a death-benefit-only plan because Sec. 2039 applies only to contracts or agreements under which the decedent was, or might become, entitled to receive an annuity or other lifetime benefit. In essence, a death-benefit-only plan is a contractual provision for payment of salary—not for payment of an annuity. Sec. 2039 therefore cannot reach the death benefit in a death-benefit-only program. However, Treas. Regs. Sec. 20.2039-1(b)(1) states that when determining whether a contract or agreement meets the conditions for estate inclusion as set forth in Sec. 2039 of the Internal Revenue Code, separate employee benefit plans maintained by the employer must be aggregated. The regulation defines "contract or agreement" as including "any arrangement, understanding or plan, or any combination of arrangements arising by reason of the decedent's employment." Thus, the financial services professional must take an inventory of other employer-provided benefits available to the employee to determine if any of them will be aggregated with the death benefit to bring such benefits into the employee's gross estate.

Federal Gift Tax Implications

In 1981 the IRS announced the release of Rev. Rul. 81-31, 1981-1 C.B. 475, which states that the employee makes a completed gift of the amount of the death benefit at the time of his or her death when the gift first becomes susceptible to valuation. The revenue ruling is based on a line of reasoning that is regarded as illogical by many tax commentators and is a complete departure from traditional principles of federal gift taxation. For example, the position of the IRS that the employee's gift of the death benefit to his or her named beneficiary was not completed until the employee died (because that is the first point at which the gift became subject to valuation) is totally inconsistent, according to many tax observers, with the basic thrust of the federal gift tax that has always been based on lifetime principles. In Rev. Rul. 81-31, it takes the death of the taxpayer to trigger a taxable gift!

> *Example:* Jan Howell is employed by the Aardvark Corporation of Beverly Hills, California. As part of her employment package, she has been asked to designate a beneficiary who is to receive a $20,000 death benefit if Jan dies while employed by Aardvark. She names her husband, Norman, as beneficiary. Eight years later Jan dies while still employed by Aardvark, and the $20,000 death benefit is paid to Norman. Although this $20,000 death benefit is not subjected to federal estate tax for the reasons previously discussed, it is considered by the IRS to be a taxable gift made by Jan to Norman at Jan's death.

In the Tax Court case of *Estate of DiMarco,* the point was made that a lack of control over a death-benefit-only plan will keep the benefit from being taxable. In this case, the taxpayer, an employee of IBM, worked for the company until the time of his death in 1979. IBM had as part of its benefits package a noncontributory "group term life insurance and survivor's income benefit plan" for all regular employees. The plan consisted of group term life insurance coverage and an uninsured, unfunded DBO plan. This benefit was payable only to an employee's surviving spouse, certain minor children, and dependent parents. It is clear from the facts of the case that the decedent had no ability to select or modify the beneficiaries of the survivor's income benefit, to change the amount of the survivor's income benefits, to terminate the coverage, or to exert any other degree of control. The IRS took the position that an adjusted taxable gift of the present value of the survivor annuity had been made by the decedent upon his death. The court agreed with the estate's position that the decedent had never made any taxable gift of any property in the survivor's income benefit since there had never been any act by the decedent that could logically be characterized as a transfer. The Tax Court disagreed with the IRS's contention that the decedent's act of going to work for IBM amounted to a transfer for federal gift tax purposes.

Federal Income Tax Implications

The IRS position on the proper federal income tax result of a DBO plan is straightforward and simple. The IRS position is that a payment under a DBO plan is taxable (for federal income tax purposes) to the named beneficiary as IRD. Therefore the death benefit is required to be included in the named beneficiary's gross income when received.

Use of Life Insurance

DBO plans are nonqualified plans designed to provide death benefits to a participant's heirs. While DBO plans can provide a lump sum to the participant's survivors, they generally pay installment benefits at the participant's death.

The DBO plan is an effective way for an employed person to provide additional benefits for his or her survivors. Because the death benefit is not subject to federal estate taxation, the plan is even more attractive.

An employer that makes a DBO plan available to its employees would be wise to consider using life insurance as a funding technique for the death benefit. This is the case since the concept of premium payments allows the employer to make a small periodic investment currently to provide dollars at a later time—that is, at the employee's death.

A DBO plan can be tricky and, if not properly drafted, can create federal estate and gift tax problems. In the estate tax context, the planner must be careful to avoid inclusion of the benefits in the participant's estate. However, in the gift tax area, since *DiMarco,* the Tax Court's analysis would present a problem if the IRS wanted to argue that federal gift tax may be applied to death benefits.

GROUP TERM LIFE INSURANCE (SEC. 79) PLANS

Income Tax Implications

Group term life insurance is a benefit plan provided by an employer to a group of participating employees. Such plans, also known as Sec. 79 plans, allow the employer a tax deduction for premium payments on behalf of a participant unless the premium amounts cause the reasonable compensation limit to be exceeded (an unlikely event).

If the coverage under the plan is nondiscriminatory, the first $50,000 of coverage is provided tax free to all plan participants. These tax benefits make group-term life insurance an attractive benefit for employees, even owner-employees, of a regular corporation. Note: The tax benefits under Sec. 79 will not be available for sole proprietors, partners of a partnership, members of an LLC (limited liability company), or greater-than-two-percent shareholders of an S corporation. It is important that the plan qualify as nondiscriminatory under Sec. 79 to avoid the adverse tax treatment of shareholder-employees. Otherwise, it is usually better for the employer to adopt an informal bonus plan (discussed below) and permit the shareholder-employees to purchase individual coverage (assuming all selected employees can be underwritten on an individual basis), while permissibly discriminating against other classes of employees.

The taxable amounts of coverage (that is, amounts above $50,000) are taxed according to a rate schedule—the so-called Table I—provided by IRS regulations. Recent changes to the regulations increased the Table I cost for coverage over age 64 to appropriate actuarial costs in 5-year age brackets. The effect of these rate changes is to increase the taxable costs of Sec. 79 coverage in excess of $50,000 (or the full amount for key employees if the plan is discriminatory), particularly for the older participants. Thus, significant coverage for older employees will become expensive from a tax standpoint and probably will not represent a cost-effective estate planning use of life insurance for the rest of the insured's life.

Although not technically a nondiscrimination rule, the welfare benefit plan rules apply to postretirement group term life insurance provided through retired lives reserves (RLR) plans. These rules make it generally infeasible to fund postretirement group term life coverage to retired shareholder-employees in excess of $50,000. This is unfortunate since most of these individuals have substantial estates and desire permanent postretirement coverage of higher face amounts.

Estate Planning for Group Term Life Benefits

Reducing Income Taxes

Although group term life generally does not represent a solution for permanent estate planning needs, it should not be ignored in the process of planning a client's estate. First, the planner should consider the rising income tax implications an older employee. In many cases, the income taxes will just have to be paid. In other cases, something can be done. As discussed in chapter 7, the taxable amount of coverage (coverage in excess of $50,000) can be assigned to a qualified charity. The charitable income tax deduction will offset the taxes created by the group term life coverage.

> *Example:* Ted Taxavoider, aged 70, has $500,000 of coverage from his corporation's group term life insurance plan. Each year, the cost of $450,000 of the coverage will be subject to federal income taxes. The monthly Table I rate for $1,000 of coverage is $3.76 at age 70 and beyond. Thus, Ted will incur $20,304 of taxable income as a result of

the excess group term benefit. If Ted assigns the excess $450,000 of death benefit to The American College, he will receive an offsetting deduction of $20,304 from his income tax base.

Fortunately, the death benefits received from a group term life insurance plan at the employee-insured's death are not subject to income taxes, similar to most other types of life insurance benefits.

Avoiding Inclusion in the Insured's Gross Estate

The death benefits received from a group-term life insurance plan will normally be included in the employee-insured's gross estate. Although these plans will not generally have cash value or other living benefits available to the insured, the insured's ability to name and change the designated beneficiary of the proceeds is an incident of ownership. To remove the proceeds from his or her gross estate, the employee-insured must assign all incidents of ownership in the life insurance plan to a third-party owner and survive 3 years to satisfy Sec. 42035(d).

Some issues could arise following the assignment of the policy. For example, it is quite possible that the insurer will change several times during the employee's period of coverage. Does the change in carrier cause a new assignment and 3-year rule? In a private ruling (Ltr. 9436036) the IRS ruled that the taxpayer's execution of a new document with the successor insurer confirming the assignment was not a new assignment and a new 3-year rule did not have to be satisfied. What about the incidents of ownership held by a majority shareholder-employee who could control the master group contract through his or her control of the corporation? This right was held to not give rise to an incident of ownership.

In Rev. Rul. 84-130, 1984-2, C.B. 195, the IRS said that the right to convert the policy to permanent insurance upon termination of employment is not an incident of ownership if the insured had previously assigned all incidents of ownership. However, in TAM 9141007, the IRS held that the proceeds were includible in the gross estate of an insured who converted his group term coverage at retirement and had the trustee of his ILIT apply for and own the new permanent contract. The decedent had not previously assigned the underlying group coverage and died within 3 years of the inception of the converted coverage.

Gift Tax Implications

Once the insured has assigned all rights to his or her group insurance coverage to a third-party owner, a gift will occur. This is an obvious transfer of property.

The gift tax problem is generally minimal. There is no cash value to transfer. The value of the gift is the annual value of the coverage measured by the Table I rates. Thus, the annual gift is small unless the death benefit is relatively large and the insured is old. However, a revenue ruling[3] held that the annual value of the gift in a group term life insurance plan after the assignment is not eligible for the gift tax annual exclusion.

SPLIT-DOLLAR LIFE INSURANCE PLANS

Split-dollar life insurance plans split a life insurance policy's premium obligations and policy benefits between two individuals or entities—normally an employer and employee. The two parties share the premium costs while the policy is in effect, pursuant to a prearranged agreement. At the death of the insured or the termination of the agreement, the parties split the policy benefits or proceeds in accordance with their agreement. Plans must meet minimal reporting and disclosure compliance requirements. Most of the administration is handled by the insurer.

Split-dollar plans are an excellent fringe benefit option for a closely held corporation since the plans can be limited to a select group of shareholder-employees and other key personnel. As we will discuss, proper design and planning could result in the avoidance of estate taxes on the employee's share of the death benefit.

Split-dollar life insurance plans have a long and varied history. The first IRS rulings on such arrangements were issued in the 1950s, but many new types of split-dollar arrangements have been developed since then to adapt to changing tax laws and the needs of the insured executives.

We must remember that all authority for the taxation of split-dollar plans is based on published and private rulings by the IRS and some infrequent case law. Thus, the tax treatment that we will discuss is based on factual circumstances addressed by the IRS and the courts.

Planners must often extrapolate the reasoning from these limited opinions when addressing new forms of split dollar. The ultimate danger is that the IRS could revoke its rulings at any time.

The following discussion summarizes the basic forms of split-dollar arrangements. However, it is important to note that there are numerous variations within each arrangement and that the general rule is almost the exception in actual practice.

Basic Split-Dollar Arrangements

Policy Ownership

The owner of the underlying policy in a split-dollar plan can either be the employer or the insured-employee. Under the *endorsement* method the employer owns the policy and has primary responsibility for premium payment. The employer's share of the benefits is secured through its ownership of the policy.

The insured designates the beneficiary for his or her share of the death proceeds, and an endorsement is filed with the insurer stipulating that the beneficiary designation cannot be changed without the insured's consent.

Under the *collateral assignment* method the insured is the policyowner and has premium payment responsibility. The corporation loans the employee the corporation's share of the annual premium, and the corporate amounts are secured by the assignment of the policy to the corporation. The corporation receives its benefits as assignee of the policy at the earlier of the employee's death or the termination of the split-dollar plan.

As we will discuss, the collateral assignment method is the method that is used when the goal is to remove the policy proceeds from the employee's gross estate, particularly if the insured is a controlling shareholder-employee. In this instance, the policyowner will be a third party, such as the employee's child or an ILIT.

Income Taxation of the Split-Dollar Plan

Since a split-dollar plan is most often provided as a fringe benefit, the taxation of split-dollar life insurance varies depending on the type of split-dollar plan, but it is based on the general premise that the employee is taxed on the economic benefit that he or she receives annually from the plan.

In Rev. Rul. 64-328, C.B. 1964-2, the IRS ruled that the tax consequences of the basic split-dollar plan are the same, regardless of whether the plan is designed under the endorsement or collateral assignment method. The economic benefit is the pure insurance element, measured by the cost of one-year term life insurance conferred on the insured during the year. The term cost is the employee's share of the amount of protection in a given year multiplied by the term rate for the employee's attained age.

In Rev. Rul. 66-110, C. B. 1966-1, the IRS has also ruled that the term cost is the lesser of the PS 58 rates (see table 13-1) or the insurance company's standard rates for a one-year term policy. Any contributions made by the employee to the split-dollar plan can be applied against the economic benefit to reduce the taxable cost of the plan.

> *Example:* Suppose the XYZ Corporation offers a split-dollar plan to its sole shareholder and company president, Mr. Joffe, aged 55. If the policy has a $100,000 face amount death benefit and the corporation has the rights to the cash surrender value of $40,000, Mr. Joffe's share, which is the pure amount at risk, is $60,000.
>
> For the tax year Mr. Joffe received an economic benefit of $824 (60 multiplied by the PS 58 cost per $1,000 of $13.74). If Mr. Joffe makes no contributions to the split-dollar plan, the taxable benefit to him for the year is $824.

TABLE 13-1
PS 58 Rates
One-Year Term Premiums for $1,000 of Life Insurance Protection

Age	Premium	Age	Premium	Age	Premium
15	$1.27	37	$ 3.63	59	$ 19.08
16	1.38	38	3.87	60	20.73
17	1.48	39	4.14	61	22.53
18	1.52	40	4.42	62	24.50
19	1.56	41	4.73	63	26.63
20	1.61	42	5.07	64	28.98
21	1.67	43	5.44	65	31.51
22	1.73	44	5.85	66	34.28
23	1.79	45	6.30	67	37.31
24	1.86	46	6.78	68	40.59
25	1.93	47	7.32	69	44.17
26	2.02	48	7.89	70	48.06
27	2.11	49	8.53	71	52.29
28	2.20	50	9.22	72	56.89
29	2.31	51	9.97	73	61.89
30	2.43	52	10.79	74	67.33
31	2.57	53	11.69	75	73.23
32	2.70	54	12.67	76	79.63
33	2.86	55	13.74	77	86.57
34	3.02	56	14.91	78	94.09
35	3.21	57	16.18	79	102.23
36	3.41	58	17.56	80	111.04
				81	120.57

These rates are used in computing the cost of pure life insurance protection that is taxable to the employee under qualified pension and profit-sharing plans. The rate at the insured's attained age is applied to the excess of the amount payable at death over the cash value of the policy at the end of the year.

Of course, the many variations of split-dollar life insurance may cause other taxable benefits to be conferred on the employee. For example, the employer might pay all or part of the employee's share of the premium. In addition, policy dividends that benefit the employee by providing cash, additional insurance, or reduction of the employee's premium will be taxable to the employee.

Reverse Split-Dollar Plans

As an alternative to traditional split-dollar arrangements, which provide a significant death benefit, reverse split-dollar (RSD) plans have achieved recent popularity as a method of giving substantial retirement benefits to executives. In the RSD variation, the corporation and executive roles are reversed.

The basic form of RSD involves the payment of the pure insurance portion of the premium by the corporation. The measure of the corporation's premium share depends on the variation of RSD selected. The executive pays the balance of the premium. The corporation's share at the employee's death is the pure insurance proceeds.

The plan is designed for individual ownership of the policy by the executive (or a third party), and the executive retains all rights in the policy other than the corporation's death benefit. At some point in the future, usually the executive's retirement, the plan is terminated and the executive receives the policy unburdened by the employer's right to the death benefit.

The RSD plan is designed to meet some specific goals and should be used only when circumstances indicate. First, there should be a corporate need for the pure insurance on the executive's life. For example, the corporation may use the death proceeds as key person indemnification, to fund a stock redemption, or to fund a death-benefit-only (DBO) plan. Since the corporate need ceases when the executive retires, the temporary nature of the RSD plan is appropriate. Of course, the split-funding nature of the policy helps hold the cost down for the executive who receives a substantial cash surrender value (CSV) benefit at retirement when the corporation's interest terminates.

Income Tax Considerations of RSD

There are many variations of RSD. Most base the corporation's share of the premium payment on the annual PS 58 costs. The theory behind this approach is that the IRS has held in traditional split dollar that the PS 58 costs can be used to measure the economic value of the pure death benefit payable to the corporation.

The concern that arises is that if the corporation's share of the premium contributes to the growth of the employee's CSV, some income tax consequences might arise. To date, there have been no rulings on the income tax consequences of RSD.

Estate Tax Considerations of Split Dollar

Traditional Split Dollar

The estate tax implications of traditional split-dollar life insurance plans are well established. If estate liquidity will be a concern for the employee who is participating in a split-dollar plan, some kind of third-party ownership—the employee's spouse, child, or an irrevocable life insurance trust (ILIT)—should, in lieu of the insured, enter into the split-dollar arrangement with the employer at its inception.

The majority shareholder in a split-dollar arrangement faces a more difficult problem. It is imperative for the majority shareholder to avoid corporate incidents of ownership in the split-dollar policy since these will be attributed to him or her if the proceeds are not deemed payable to the corporation. IRS rulings have made it clear that corporate incidents, such as the ability to borrow from the policy, should be avoided in a traditional split-dollar arrangement between the corporation and a majority shareholder. If corporate incidents of ownership are attributed to the majority shareholder, the death proceeds will be includible in the insured's gross estate, regardless of whether or not a third party actually held the insured's interest in the split-dollar agreement. Practitioners therefore generally recommend collateral assignment of the policy if a majority shareholder is involved.

One solution to avoid inclusion in the majority shareholder's estate is for the participant to create an irrevocable trust to enter into the split-dollar agreement with the corporation. The trust would collaterally assign the policy to the corporation to secure the corporation's share of the death benefit. In drafting the split-dollar contract care should be taken to avoid giving any incidents of ownership to the corporation. For example, the corporation should not be given access to the CSV. The contract should limit the corporation's interest to merely being repaid by the trust.

Fortunately, we have some new and positive authority for this collateral assignment split-dollar arrangement since the last edition of this book. In a recent private ruling, Ltr. 9511046, the IRS held that the death benefit payable to the insureds' ILIT was excludible from the insured's gross estate when the trustee of the ILIT entered into a collateral assignment split-dollar agreement with the insured's employer.

> *Example:* Mr. and Mrs. Jones each hold 50 percent of their S corporation in separate living revocable trusts. The revocable trusts become irrevocable at the death of the grantor and become a marital deduction trust. Thus, the surviving spouse effectively becomes the sole owner of the corporation. Mr. and Mrs. Jones create an ILIT with an independent trustee. The trust purchases a $1 million survivorship (second-to-die) policy covering their lives and enters into a collateral assignment split-dollar agreement with the corporation. The corporation will pay the entire premium for the policy and retain the right to be repaid by the trust, but it will hold no other rights. Although the surviving spouse will effectively own all of the S corporation, the corporation will hold no incidents of ownership in the policy, and the death benefits paid to the trust will not be included in the surviving spouse's gross estate.

Reverse Split Dollar

Estate tax concerns about RSD plans—designed for the insured-executive to own the policy from its inception—have been alleviated somewhat by a private letter ruling. The existing law requires the entire proceeds to be includible in the insured's estate at his or her death, including the death proceeds payable to the corporation. Thus, RSD has the potential for creating a huge estate liquidity problem for a participant. However, the IRS has ruled that the amount payable to the corporation is a deductible claim against the estate and will not create additional estate tax. That is, the corporation's death proceeds share will be included in the insured's gross estate for tax purposes, but the estate will receive a deduction for the amounts payable to the corporation.

SEC. 162 BONUS LIFE INSURANCE PLANS

Basic Design of Sec. 162 Plan

Sec. 162 plans have the advantage of simplicity, which holds down their administrative costs. Shareholder-employees and executives who participate in the plan apply for, own, and name the beneficiary on permanent life insurance policies covering their lives. The personally owned nature of the policies gives them maximum flexibility. The premiums for such policies are provided through bonus payments by the employer-corporation. The corporation either pays the premium directly to the insurer or gives the amount necessary to pay the premium as a bonus to the employee, who is then billed directly by the insurance company.

The income taxation of the plan is also easy to illustrate to clients. The premium amount paid directly to the insurer (or bonus to the employee) is treated as gross compensation income to the employee under Sec. 61(a)(1). This compensation is treated as ordinary income subject to the employee's normal individual income tax rate. If the bonus along with the employee's other compensation represents reasonable compensation, the corporation can deduct the amount of the bonus as an ordinary business expense under Sec. 162(a)(1)—thus the origin of the name *Sec. 162 plans*.

Estate and Gift Tax Planning Considerations

The Sec. 162 bonus life insurance plan involves ownership of an individual life insurance policy by an insured-employee. As such, the life insurance proceeds will be included in the insured-employee's gross estate for federal estate tax purposes under the provisions of Sec. 2042. This may not be a desirable result, particularly since the highly compensated plan participants are probably accumulating substantial estates irrespective of the bonus life insurance plan.

If the gross estate inclusion is a concern to the participating executive(s), the plan can be designed with third-party ownership of the individual life insurance policy. For example, the life insurance can be owned by the insured-employee's spouse or by an irrevocable trust created by the insured-employee. If the third party is the initial applicant and owner of the policy, the proceeds should be excludible from the insured's gross estate even if the insured dies immediately after the coverage becomes effective.

If estate tax problems become a concern at a later date, a plan participant could gift an existing life insurance policy to a third-party owner. In this event, the insured must survive the 3-year period following the policy transfer in order to remove the insurance proceeds from his or her gross estate for federal estate tax purposes (Sec. 2035).

The gift tax consequences of such a transfer depend on the circumstances of the transfer. If an individual third-party owner, such as a spouse, is selected as the donee of the life insurance policy, the original transfer of the policy plus any premiums paid by the employer will be treated as a gift from the insured-employee to the third party. The gift, in this case, will qualify for the $10,000 annual gift tax exclusion as a gift of a present interest. Of course, any premiums paid by the employer will still be treated as taxable income to the insured-employee and as gifts from the insured employee to the policyowner.

If the policy is transferred instead to an irrevocable trust created by the insured, the transfer of the policy and any premiums paid subsequently by the employer will be treated as a gift from the insured-employee to the beneficiaries of the trust. However, the gifts under these circumstances will qualify for the annual exclusion only if the beneficiaries are given current withdrawal rights to premiums added to the trust.

NOTES

1. These individuals include sole proprietors, partners of a partnership, members of a limited liability company, or greater-than-two-percent shareholders in an S corporation.
2. For a thorough discussion of this technique, see "Planning with Plans: Qualified Plans and Life Insurance," *The Practical Tax Lawyer,* summer 1994.
3. Rev. Rul. 79-47, 1979-1 C.B. 312. The ruling involves the assignment of the group term life insurance policy to an ILIT. The gift was treated as a future-interest gift not eligible for the gift tax annual exclusion. The ruling made no mention of Crummey powers for the beneficiaries. Even if the ILIT did permit Crummey powers, what could the beneficiaries withdraw? The gift tax annual exclusion should be available to a group term interest assigned directly to an individual since a present-interest property would be transferred under these circumstances.

14

Procedural Principles of Estate Planning (Including a Case Study)

Chapter Outline

EFFECTIVE ORGANIZATION OF WRITTEN ESTATE PLAN   413
    Excessive Transfer Costs   415
    Estate Liquidity   418
    Patterns of Distribution   422
    Adequate Future Income   424
CASE STUDY   424
    Case Narrative   424
    Written Estate Plan   427

Throughout this book, we've focused on specific estate planning principles and techniques. We've explored both the tax and nontax overtones of these planning methods, illustrated the effects of these planning concepts, and reviewed the practical advantages and disadvantages of each technique. At this point it would be useful to move away from the substantive aspects of estate planning and to focus instead on the procedural aspects of the actual planning process. To accomplish this, we'll first look at the actual organization and proper categorization of estate planning topics, and then we'll apply both these procedural principles and the substantive materials covered in the previous chapters to a case study.

EFFECTIVE ORGANIZATION OF WRITTEN ESTATE PLAN

The actual estate planning process can be complex because, as we've seen in previous chapters, the specific facts and circumstances of a client's case may be voluminous and complicated. Because of this, effective organization of the written estate plan is critical. One way to help accomplish this is to break the written estate plan down into the following four broad categories:

- *excessive transfer costs*—In this section the estate planner looks at the client's current estate situation. This overview should include a valuation of current estate assets, possible use of special valuation procedures (such as the alternate valuation date or the special-use-valuation concept), and an ascertaining of the client's gross estate for federal estate tax purposes. Once the estate planner and client have discussed and commented on the current situation, planning techniques are introduced. Emphasis in the category of excessive transfer costs is, of course, placed first on identifying those areas that have unnecessarily created excessive estate taxation and then on finding the techniques available to reduce these unnecessary costs.
- *estate liquidity*—The federal estate tax laws require that under ordinary circumstances the federal estate tax must be paid within 9 months of the date of death. If the estate is sufficiently liquid, no estate liquidity problem will exist because the executor or administrator of the estate will have ample cash with which to meet the 9-month deadline. However, many estates, although large in value, are illiquid. The result is often that the executor or administrator will not have ample funds on hand with which to pay the federal estate tax due. We'll discuss the problems in this situation and the available solutions to an estate liquidity deficit.
- *patterns of distribution*—The manner in which an estate owner chooses to distribute property interests is a vital part of the estate planning process. Is the current dispositive arrangement in accordance with the estate owner's wishes? Is his or her will up-to-date? If the client owns a business interest, have all necessary steps been taken and implemented to be sure that the interest passes exactly in compliance with the client's wishes? Does the manner in which the estate owner's assets are distributed coincide with intelligent and prudent tax planning? These are the types of questions that must be asked in the category of patterns of distribution.
- *adequate future income*—One of the key elements in the estate planning process is making decisions regarding the standard of living for the decedent's survivors. "Will the surviving spouse be in a position to enjoy the same standard of living he or she enjoyed prior to the decedent's death?" is one question that must be addressed. If a client has children who have not yet reached college age, there are also questions involving adequate funding of college costs.

Let's now begin a detailed study of each of these broad estate planning categories.

Excessive Transfer Costs

The most critical problem facing the unplanned or poorly planned estate is in the area of unnecessarily excessive transfer costs. In most cases even a basic and unsophisticated estate plan will have the effect of reducing certain costs. Because the cost problem is the most common one in estates, and because it is of the greatest interest to estate owners and their families, it is treated first in the written estate plan.

Present Plan versus Modified Plan

To alert the estate planning client to possible problems in the cost area and to illustrate to the client how planning can reduce costs, the written estate plan should emphasize the current versus the modified arrangement. This approach allows the client to see exactly what the costs are under the present plan and to appreciate how much those costs can be reduced by using certain estate planning techniques.

> *Example:* A thorough review of Edward Becker's current estate situation reveals that if he were to die today, there would be a federal estate tax liability of $167,464. You point out that by the prompt initiation of a concerted gifting program (using the annual exclusion), removal of the life insurance (currently owned by Edward Becker on his own life) from his estate, and effective use of the federal estate tax marital deduction, Mr. Becker can reduce his federal estate tax liability to zero. The entire excessive-transfer-cost portion of your written estate plan should emphasize the distinction between Mr. Becker's current arrangement and the modified arrangement, including reference to the specific reduction in costs, with tables and charts highlighting the differences.

Specific Topics to Treat

There are four specific topics that should usually be treated in the excessive-transfer-costs area:

- valuation of assets in general
- ascertaining the exact size of the client's gross estate
- the federal estate tax marital deduction
- reduction of the gross estate

Let's review each of these subcategories in depth.

Valuation of Assets in General. We've already seen that the federal estate tax liability that an estate may face is directly based on the size of the decedent's taxable estate. We've also seen that the size of the taxable estate is determined by ascertaining the gross estate and then taking various deductions from it.

A prerequisite to the successful and accurate determination of an estate owner's gross estate is the use of proper and appropriate methods of valuing estate assets. The basic rule is that the fair market value of an asset on the decedent's date of death will be used for placing a value on estate assets. However, we've observed that a provision exists in the federal estate tax law permitting the use of an alternate valuation date of 6 months after the date of the decedent's death. We've also seen that Sec. 2032A permits a special-use-valuation approach to be used in those cases involving farmland, ranchland, or real property used in a closely held business. These topics must be addressed in the excessive-transfer-costs category of the estate plan.

> *Example:* Glenn Roth is preparing a written estate plan on a client, Walter Joyher. In the excessive-transfer-costs portion of the plan, Glenn has reviewed the current fact pattern and drawn specific conclusions about how the assets Mr. Joyher owns should be valued for purposes of the estate plan. For example, since the client owns no farmland, ranchland, or other real property used in a closely held trade or business, the special-use-valuation provisions of Sec. 2032A will not be appropriate.

Many clients who seek estate planning advice have interests in closely held businesses. Often, ownership of these assets will be the largest single property interest in the client's gross estate. As mentioned above, the client's interest in various assets must be accurately valued for an estate plan to be effective. When dealing with a closely held business interest, however, an estate planner must take special valuation considerations into account. This is the case because mere book value and other tangible examples of economic value will not be the sole determining factors in arriving at the fair market value of the business interest. Many intangible factors such as goodwill and earning capacity must also enter into the overall valuation process. If the estate planner is to perform a comprehensive and accurate job, he or she must place a value on the business interest that corresponds to the value the IRS would use in the estate tax context. The planner's failure to do so will distort the tax liability computations.

> *Example:* Lucille Learner is preparing a written estate plan on a client, Wayne Johnston. Mr. Johnston is president and sole shareholder of Johnston Wax Company, which manufactures over 400 different wax-related products. Lucille must apply sophisticated methods of valuation in order to accurately ascertain the value of Mr. Johnston's stock interest in the wax company. Lucille's failure to do so will distort the value of Mr. Johnston's gross estate.

Determination of Size of Gross Estate. Once basic valuation principles have been established, the estate planner should consider the issue of which of the client's assets would be required to be included as part of his or her gross estate for federal estate tax purposes. As a practical matter, the estate planner will be unable to determine whether there are any excessive transfer costs unless and until the actual size of the client's gross estate has been ascertained. This can be accomplished only by applying the basic includibility provisions as they are set forth in Secs. 2033–2042 to the specific facts and circumstances of the client's case.

Example: Paula Pinter is preparing a written estate plan on a client, Janelle Moore. In the excessive-transfer-costs portion of the plan, Paula has analyzed every asset Janelle owns and has made a determination whether each asset will be required to be included in her gross estate for federal estate tax purposes. Paula made the determination by relying on Secs. 2033–2042.

Federal Estate Tax Marital Deduction. If used properly, the federal estate tax marital deduction may be the *most* dramatic technique available to the estate planner as a means of reducing unnecessarily excessive transfer costs. Conversely, if the federal estate tax marital deduction is not taken advantage of effectively, excessive transfer costs will invariably be the result. Accordingly a critical component of the estate plan in general, and of the excessive-transfer-costs portion of the plan in particular, will be the specific treatment in the client's plan of the use of the federal estate tax marital deduction.

Planning in this area is complex since the federal estate tax marital deduction is unlimited and the applicable credit amount is wasted if all assets are transferred in a manner qualifying for the marital deduction. This problem will grow even more significant as the applicable credit amount increases. For example, is it prudent to use the full and unlimited marital deduction, or should some equalization effect be used? Furthermore, has the applicable credit amount been used in conjunction with the marital deduction? These are some of the questions that this portion of the estate plan must address.

Example: David East is preparing a written estate plan for a client. In the excessive-transfer-costs portion of the plan David devotes a substantial amount of time to the analysis of the client's current will arrangement. He does this primarily so that the client can understand how his current situation relates to the federal estate tax marital deduction, and so that he can see that a modification of his current situation must be made at once to take maximum advantage of the benefits of the federal estate tax marital deduction. This approach will result in reduced costs for the client's estate.

Methods to Reduce Taxable Estate. Previously, we've emphasized that the prudent estate planner should attempt to find ways to reduce the taxable estate since such a reduction will in turn reduce the federal estate tax liability. A critical portion of the excessive-transfer-costs segment of the estate plan must address these issues. As a practical matter, the use of certain estate reduction techniques is one of the most important ways that excessive transfer costs can be eliminated or at least reduced. Therefore the planner will need to discuss such estate reduction techniques as

- a gifting program
- the removal of life insurance from the insured's gross estate
- estate freezing techniques

Example: Georgia Sanders is preparing a written estate plan for a client, Raquel Webb. In the excessive-transfer-costs portion of the plan, Georgia has reviewed the current fact pattern and has concluded that Mrs. Webb *must* consider specific estate reduction techniques so that her current projected federal estate tax liability can be reduced. Accordingly, Georgia recommends that Mrs. Webb initiate a gifting program, remove the life insurance on her own life from her gross estate, and consider some form of estate freezing technique.

Estate Liquidity

The concept of estate liquidity becomes pertinent in the analysis of an estate because of the rules under the federal estate tax laws usually requiring the payment of all federal estate tax within 9 months of the date of the decedent's death. In the event that the estate is composed of sufficient liquid assets, the executor or administrator of the estate will not confront any estate liquidity deficit. However, in many situations an estate will face a liquidity deficit because the assets making up the federal gross estate for federal estate tax purposes will not be liquid. In these situations the executor or administrator will usually be required to liquidate certain illiquid estate assets so that he or she will have ample cash with which to pay the estate tax within the 9-month deadline. Since these liquidation activities take place under a time pressure, there will often be a loss taken on the actual sale of the assets.

Example: Bruno Brinks is executor of the estate of his late brother, Barry, whose gross estate, consisting of real estate and a closely held business interest, totals $2.4 million. The federal estate tax on this property equals $643,950. Bruno is required to pay the tax within 9 months of the date of Barry's death, but the estate does not have the funds in liquid form. To meet the deadline, Bruno is compelled to sell some of the real estate to raise the cash. Unfortunately, at the time the property is sold it's a soft market and the estate has to take a loss.

Example: Diane Black is the executor of the estate of her late brother, Bob. His gross estate, which consists of cash, securities, and life insurance, totals $2.4 million. The federal estate tax on this property equals $634,950. Diane Black is required to pay the tax within 9 months of the date of her brother's death. There is no liquidity deficit since there are ample liquid assets in the estate with which to pay the tax due.

Time-Extension Provisions

There are two provisions in the federal estate tax laws that allow an estate an extension beyond the 9-month tax payment deadline. Let's review each of these.

Sec. 6161. Sec. 6161 of the Internal Revenue Code allows the secretary of the Treasury, *for reasonable cause,* to extend the time for payment of any part of the federal estate tax for a reasonable period not to exceed 10 years from the date on which the federal estate tax was originally due. In practice, the district director of the IRS for the district in which the decedent lived will make the decision on the extension. Although such extensions are often granted, the estate must be prepared to successfully meet its burden of proving that there is reasonable cause for granting the extension. We must emphasize that the existence of a liquidity deficit that would compel the executor or administrator of the estate to liquidate illiquid assets, even at a loss, does *not* constitute reasonable cause.

Sec. 6166. Many times, the reason an estate faces an estate liquidity deficit is directly attributable to the fact that the decedent owned a prosperous and valuable business interest and that this business interest accounted for a large portion of his or her estate. Because this valuable asset is required to be included in the gross estate, it generates a federal estate tax liability—a liability for which ample liquid assets may not be available.

Example: Lauren Leroux is the executor of the estate of her late husband, Theodore. Approximately 64 percent of her husband's adjusted gross estate (gross estate reduced by costs of administration, debts, and so forth) is composed of his 96 percent interest in Leroux Enterprises, Inc., a closely held corporation that manufactures rear-view mirrors for motor vehicles. Lauren does not have ample liquid assets with which to pay the federal estate tax because so much of her late husband's estate is made up of the illiquid business interest.

Because of the situation described in the above example, Congress saw fit to enact Sec. 6166. This provision allows those estates composed of a closely held business interest to elect to pay out the federal estate tax over a 15-year period. As a prerequisite to being allowed to use this special relief provision, the law provides that the business interest must consist of greater than 35 percent of the decedent's adjusted gross estate (that is, the gross estate reduced by expenses incurred by the estate for administration costs, debts, casualty losses, and the like). If the estate can meet this 35 percent requirement, the executor or administrator of the estate may elect the 15-year payout provisions.

Example: James Worthington passed away on June 9, 1998, after a long illness. His gross estate consisted of the following assets:

Cash	$ 40,000
Marketable securities	20,000
Real estate (principal residence)	200,000
100% of the stock of Worthington Enterprises	900,000
Personal property	60,000
Gross estate	$1,220,000

The executor of the estate wishes to make the payout election under Sec. 6166. In order to do so, however, greater than 35 percent of the decedent's adjusted gross estate must be composed of a closely held business interest. In this case the estate's costs of administration, debts, and final expenses are $220,000, so the adjusted gross estate is $1 million. Therefore the 35 percent test is successfully met since $900,000 (the value of the closely held business interest) is more than 35 percent of the adjusted gross estate of $1 million. Accordingly, the estate may elect to pay the federal estate tax attributable to the business interest on an installment basis.

Example: Lois Jamison passed away suddenly on June 9, 1998. Her gross estate consisted of the following:

Cash	$ 25,000
Marketable securities	25,000
Real estate (principal residence)	655,000
100% of the stock of Jamison Enterprises	325,000
Personal property	70,000
Gross estate	$1,100,000

The executor of the estate wants to make the payout election under Sec. 6166. To do so, of course, more than 35 percent of the decedent's adjusted gross estate must be composed of a closely held business interest. The estate's costs of administration, debts, and final expenses are $100,000 in this case, making the adjusted gross estate $1 million. Since the business interest in Jamison Enterprises is $325,000, the 35 percent test is *not* met and the estate may not elect to pay federal estate tax over a 15-year period.

By way of procedure, the election of Sec. 6166 will permit the executor or administrator of an estate to pay estate tax triggered by the inclusion of a closely held business interest in the estate owner's gross estate. During the length of the deferral period, interest of 2 percent on the estate tax that is directly attributable to the first $1 million of estate property must be paid to the IRS on an annual basis. The maximum amount of tax eligible for the 2 percent rate, therefore, will be $345,800. Any tax on the business value in excess of $1 million will incur interest at 45 percent of the federal interest rate imposed on the underpayment of tax. In either event, the interest is nondeductible by the payer.

The first installment of the actual tax must be paid not more than 5 years after the normal due date for the tax, and the time during which installments may be paid may not be longer than 10 years. Therefore we have a 15-year deferral (actually, the length of the deferral is 14 years 9 months).

Although the use of Sec. 6166 may seem like an attractive and prudent choice, there are many disadvantages associated with it. The main objective of the executor or administrator of the estate has traditionally been to settle the estate as quickly as possible, but this becomes impossible if Sec. 6166 is elected. This is the case since election of this provision guarantees that the estate will remain open for as long as the deferral period continues.

Furthermore, the Sec. 6166 approach often creates problems with banks and creditors, because when the election is made, a federal lien is lodged against the business interest. This, of course, may discourage lenders. The use of the election will also generate additional attorneys' fees, accountants' costs, probate costs, and the like.

In conclusion, although Sec. 6166 does exist as a method for making the payment of the federal estate tax somewhat more manageable, this provision should be used only after all its potential pitfalls have been considered thoroughly. Because Sec. 6166 results only in the deferral of the estate tax owed, not in the discharge of the obligation, it is not as desirable a method of meeting obligations in the estate liquidity planning context as is the use of life insurance. It is, of course, preferable to selling assets at a loss to raise cash.

Court Cases Involving Sec. 6166 Disputes. We have seen that Congress enacted Sec. 6166 of the Internal Revenue Code in order to provide relief to those estates that are composed mainly of an interest in a closely held business. Of course, the justification for this approach was that families of decedents who owned a closely held business would often be compelled to sell the business to raise the cash to pay federal estate tax due 9 months following the date of death. Because Sec. 6166 contains no definition of "trade or business," the IRS has issued many rulings in an attempt to clarify this point. This issue was raised in the case of *Schindler*.

At the time of the decedent's death, Mrs. Schindler owned two farms that she did not personally operate because she had made an arrangement with an unrelated person to operate them. Upon Mrs. Schindler's death, her estate attempted to use Sec. 6166 treatment, asserting that the two farms were interests in a "trade or business." The IRS took the position that because of the specific arrangement with a manager, these farms were not available for Sec. 6166 treatment. The court held that the decedent's activities were "passive" in nature and not the type of active participation envisioned by Sec. 6166. The court was very emphatic in its view that a business interest held by a decedent for investment purposes alone will not be appropriate for Sec. 6166 treatment. Rather, according to the court, the decedent must have been an active participant in the business interest.

In another case, *Estate of Green,* a United States District Court in Texas held in favor of the IRS in a Sec. 6166 dispute. Specifically, an estate had paid a portion of the federal estate taxes due and elected to defer the remainder of the tax liability under Sec. 6166. The IRS initially accepted the election and sent the estate a notice of interest due, which the executor of the estate paid. Subsequently, however, the IRS concluded that the estate did not qualify for the election. The court held that even though the IRS had at first accepted the election, the IRS was not prevented from later denying it to the estate.

Use of Life Insurance

We've seen that the Internal Revenue Code does give estate owners alternatives to the requirement that the federal estate tax liability must be paid in full within 9 months of the estate owner's date of death. We've also seen that often these are not practical alternatives to the prompt discharge of estate tax obligations.

Life insurance, however, is particularly well suited to resolve many estate liquidity deficit problems. For example, the availability of life insurance proceeds at the death of the insured will enable the executor or administrator of the estate to pay the federal estate tax within the 9-month deadline, rather than having to rely on the conditions and inflexible restrictions of the time-extension provision of the Code.

Patterns of Distribution

The third broad category in the properly organized estate plan, patterns of distribution, will address the specific manner in which the estate owner has arranged the actual distribution of estate assets at the time of his or her death. Once an analysis of the present situation is performed, suggested modifications should be emphasized as part of the estate plan so that the estate owner's specific dispositive wishes may be carried out.

Example: In the patterns-of-distribution section of the estate plan, Henry Hope has pointed out his client's current arrangement involving the distribution of his estate assets. After reviewing this current arrangement, Henry suggests specific modifications that should be made to ensure compliance with his client's actual dispositive wishes. These suggestions are written into the estate plan.

We'll study the following two aspects of patterns of distribution separately:

- current will arrangement
- distribution of business interest

Current Will Arrangement

Examining the client's legal will arrangement is the clearest way for the estate planner to ascertain the current distribution of estate assets. The provisions in the will make an excellent starting point for the estate planner and client to talk about the patterns of distribution in the client's written estate plan. Such a discussion will serve as a clear summary of the client's present dispositive scheme and will lead in a smooth manner to a discussion of proposed changes in this area.

Example: Claire Bunting has been working with her client, Dawn Burns, a widow with no heirs, to develop an effective estate plan. Although in the fact-finding interview Dawn has emphasized her desire to make large cash contributions to several charitable organizations, neither her current will nor any other portion of her present plan addresses this wish. In the patterns-of-distribution portion of the written estate plan, Claire reviews what the current will provides, mentions that it ignores the charitable concerns and wishes of the client, and makes recommendations for specific modifications of the will to allow Dawn Burns to meet her charitable objectives.

Distribution of Business Interest

The second important component of the patterns-of-distribution section deals with how the client's business interest will be distributed under the current arrangement. (This, of course, presupposes that the client in question has an interest in a business.) Just as with the will, the estate planner and client should initially discuss the current scenario, with recommendations for modifications of the plan treated subsequently if necessary under the facts and circumstances of the client's case.

Example: Cecil Manhardt has been working with his client, Randall Marshall, to develop an effective estate plan. Although in the fact-finding interview Randall Marshall has emphasized his desire to leave his business interest to his partner, Elaine Souderton, neither his current will nor any other portion of his present plan addresses this wish. In fact, his current will leaves all probate property to his adult son, Charles. Furthermore, there is no buy-sell agreement or other document that would allow Randall Marshall to leave his interest in the business to Elaine Souderton. In the patterns-of-distribution portion of the written estate plan, Cecil reviews how the current arrangement handles the distribution of the business interest, mentions that it will not effectively transfer Randall's portion of the business interest to Elaine, and makes recommendations for specific modifications of the arrangement to meet the client's wishes.

Adequate Future Income

The final broad category in the properly organized estate plan, adequate future income, will address the issue of whether the estate owner-client has taken effective steps to be sure that his or her surviving family members will be in a position to enjoy the same standard of living they enjoyed prior to the estate owner's death. The written estate plan needs to answer such questions as "Will the surviving spouse be adequately provided for upon the decedent's death?" and "Will the surviving children be adequately provided for upon the decedent's death, as far as college funding is concerned?"

CASE STUDY

Now that we've described the procedural steps that a well-organized written estate plan should follow, let's next turn to a case study. First, we'll set forth the facts of our hypothetical case, and then we'll present a full and comprehensive estate plan that addresses all the pertinent issues that need to be treated in the plan.

Case Narrative

Mark and Barbara Hillman retain you to provide them with a comprehensive estate plan. Last week, they both came to your office so that you could develop a comprehensive fact finder on them. This, of course, is a crucial prerequisite to the accurate development of the estate plan.

The data-collection process yields the following information:

- Mark and Barbara Hillman have been married for 16 years. Mark, aged 42, is the owner of a closely held corporation that manufactures computer software. Barbara, aged 41, owns a small baby clothing shop in partnership with her next-door neighbor.

- The clients live in a suburb of Anytown, Anystate. Mark is a native of the area but Barbara is originally from Othertown, Otherstate. She had attended college in Anytown and decided to remain in the area following graduation.
- The clients have two children, Jennifer Hope Hillman, aged 7, and Scott Cory Hillman, aged 8 months.
- The children are currently enrolled in private schools, and the total annual educational cost is $20,000.
- Mark Hillman's will, drafted on October 20, 1995, is a "simple will," which leaves all estate property to his wife, Barbara.
- Barbara Hillman's will, also drafted on October 20, 1995, is also a simple will, which leaves all estate property to her husband, Mark.
- Neither will names guardians for the children.
- Mark and Barbara Hillman are both in favor of making some form of inter vivos gifts to their two children as a way to reduce federal estate tax costs.
- Mark and Barbara Hillman have ranked their financial objectives in the following order:

    - Maintain their standard of living.
    - Continue the private school education of their children.
    - Provide college education for their children.
    - Take care of the family in the event of death.
    - Take care of both self and family during a period of long-term disability.
    - Enjoy a comfortable retirement.
    - Invest and accumulate wealth.
    - Reduce their estate tax burden.
    - Develop an estate distribution plan.

- The clients' sources of income are as follows:

    - Mark Hillman takes a salary of $104,000 per year. Last year he received a bonus of $46,000 in addition to this base salary.
    - Barbara Hillman, who shares equally in the partnership earnings, received $40,000 last year.
    - The Hillmans had investment income of $14,000 last year.

- The clients' inventory of estate assets is as follows:

    - money market funds, mutual funds (jointly titled) $ 46,551
    - money market funds, mutual funds (Mark individually)   80,000
    - money market funds, mutual funds (Barbara individually) 32,500
    - marketable securities (jointly titled)   200,000

– marketable securities (Mark individually)	2,400
– marketable securities (Barbara individually)	21,000
– principal residence (jointly titled, net of mortgage)	175,000
– investment property (jointly titled)	79,900
– Hillman Enterprises, Inc. (Mark individually)	440,000
– Kid's Shoppe partnership interest (Barbara individually)	100,000
– personal property (jointly titled)	85,000
– current vested benefit from Mark's pension plan	155,822

- Mark also tells you during the fact-finding process that he used to own a joint interest in a farm with a fair market value of $599,000. He had inherited the farm jointly with his sister from his father's estate but had made a gift of his interest to his sister, Hillary Browner, who owned the farm jointly with him, 2 1/2 years ago. The farm does generate income from the sale of crops, and Mark says that although he gave the property to his sister, he retains the right to receive 10 percent of the earnings per year derived from the farm operation.
- Both Mark and Barbara also have universal life insurance policies on their own lives. However, after reading up on the subject of estate planning last year, Mark and Barbara have transferred their policies into life insurance trusts that they drafted themselves with commercial living trust software that they purchased at an office supply store. Mark's policies total $300,000. Barbara's total $325,000. The policies have minimal cash value since the Hillmans have been paying the minimum premiums.

    They leave the trusts with you for review. You learn that the trusts are not irrevocable and can be revoked by Mark and Barbara at any time. A particularly disturbing point is that the trustees are the owners of the life insurance policies, but the policy beneficiary designations are the estates of the insureds.

    So much for do-it-yourself estate planning.
- Mark advises you that he is particularly aware of the fact that his business interest is appreciating in value at a rate that is surprising to him, and he asks if something can be done to stop this problem as a matter of estate planning.
- Barbara advises you that there is no provision in her partnership agreement as to how to handle the death, disability, or retirement of a partner in Kid's Shoppe. She requests information on the tax and estate planning implications of such an arrangement.
- Mark and Barbara have been thinking about moving out of the suburbs and into downtown Metrogopolis, Anystate. They ask you for information about the tax and estate planning implications of making such a move.

Written Estate Plan

As mentioned previously, the well-organized estate plan should be divided into the following four broad categories: excessive transfer costs, estate liquidity, patterns of distribution, and adequate future income.

Let's now begin the actual written plan by first discussing the excessive-transfer-cost area.

Excessive Transfer Costs

In the excessive-transfer-costs area, there are six separate issues that must be treated:

- valuation of estate assets in general
- inclusion of assets in the gross estate
- marital deduction considerations
- hypothetical probate computations
- special valuation provisions and considerations
- reduction of the gross estate

We'll review each one separately.

Valuation of Estate Assets. All estate assets that end up being included in the gross estates of Mark or Barbara Hillman will be valued in accordance with the principles set forth in Sec. 2031 or Sec. 2032. Essentially, the value to be affixed to each asset will be the fair market value of the asset either on the date of death or on the alternate valuation date (which is 6 months following the date of death).

The written estate plan should emphasize that the executor of the estate must make a decision as to which valuation date should be used. Since it is not possible to pick and choose between the two dates, with the date-of-death value applying to some assets and the alternate valuation date applying to others, the executor must examine all assets before making a choice as to which valuation date should be used for all the assets. The written estate plan cannot make this decision since asset values do change. The decision is the responsibility of the executor.

Inclusion of Assets in Gross Estate. The next portion of the written estate plan within the excessive-transfer-costs section will involve the question of which specific assets are to be included as part of the decedent's gross estate. As a result of the data given by Mark and Barbara Hillman during the fact-finding interview, you develop two tables summarizing their assets and include them in the written estate plan (tables 14-1 and 14-2).

> **TABLE 14-1**
> **Summary of Assets—Mark Hillman**
>
> Jointly Titled Assets[a]
>
> | | | |
> |---|---|---|
> | Cash | $23,276 | |
> | Marketable securities | 100,000 | |
> | Principal residence | 87,500 | |
> | Investment property | 39,950 | |
> | Personal property | 42,500 | |
> | Total jointly titled assets | | $ 293,226 |
>
> Individually Titled Assets
>
> | | | |
> |---|---|---|
> | Cash | $ 80,000 | |
> | Marketable securities | 2,400 | |
> | Hillman Enterprises, Inc. | 440,000[b] | |
> | Pension proceeds | 155,822[c] | |
> | Farm property | 298,000[d] | |
> | Life insurance proceeds | 300,000[e] | |
> | Total individually titled assets | | $1,276,222 |
>
> Gross estate $1,569,448
>
> a. Sec. 2040 provides that if the property is held jointly between husband and wife, one-half the fair market value of these assets at the date of death will be included in the gross estate of the decedent.
> b. Based on what Mark Hillman believes the business interest is worth. The IRS, by applying Rev. Rul. 59–60, could arrive at a higher figure. A buy-sell agreement could peg the value and remove any doubts with respect to valuation.
> c. Under current tax law there are no provisions that would permit the exclusion of these funds from the gross estate.
> d. This represents Mark's former tenancy-in-common interest in the farm owned jointly with his sister. Sec. 2036 will require inclusion of the full fair market value of the 1/2 interest in the farm because of the decedent's retained interest over the property.
> e. Mark's life insurance trust is not irrevocable. Therefore the proceeds of the life insurance policies are included as part of Mark Hillman's gross estate. Since the policy is payable not to the trustee but to the estate of the insured, the proceeds will pass according to the will provisions.

Effective Use of Federal Estate Tax Marital Deduction. You now know that Mark Hillman's gross estate for federal estate tax purposes is $1,569,448 and that Barbara Hillman's gross estate is $771,726. Without proper estate planning, these large gross estates will trigger excessively high transfer costs since the larger the size of the estate, the higher the federal estate tax liability will be. The use of the federal estate tax marital deduction has traditionally been one of the most effective methods available to married estate owners for reduction of excessive transfer costs. However, bear in mind that the marital deduction will operate to reduce federal estate tax liability only to the extent that wills, which incorporate the estate tax marital-deduction concept, are drafted properly. In the Hillman case there are wills, but the wills totally ignore not only the marital-deduction concept but also methods for reducing federal estate tax liability.

TABLE 14-2
Summary of Assets—Barbara Hillman

Jointly Titled Assets[a]

Cash	$ 23,276	
Marketable securities	100,000	
Principal residence	87,500	
Investment property	39,950	
Personal property	42,500	
Total jointly titled assets		$293,226

Individually Titled Assets

Cash	$ 32,500	
Marketable securities	21,000	
Partnership interest	100,000[b]	
Life insurance proceeds	325,000[c]	
Total individually titled assets		$478,500
Gross estate		$771,726

a. Sec. 2040 provides that if the property is held jointly between husband and wife, one-half the fair market value of these assets at the date of death will be included in the gross estate of the decedent.
b. Based on what Barbara Hillman believes her share of the business interest is worth. The IRS, by applying Rev. Rul. 59-60, could arrive at a higher figure. A buy-sell agreement could peg the value and remove any doubts with respect to valuation.
c. The life insurance trust is not irrevocable. Therefore the proceeds of the life insurance policies are included as part of Barbara Hillman's gross estate. Since the proceeds are payable to her estate as the designated beneficiary, the proceeds pass according to the provisions of her will.

You know from the facts as related by the Hillmans that both Mark and Barbara currently have simple wills. Each will leaves all estate property to the surviving spouse. Although in a rudimentary and simplistic way this may comply with the client's dispositive wishes, it is not a wise approach from the perspective of eliminating excessive transfer costs. Let's now see why this is the case.

The federal estate tax marital deduction is permitted by Sec. 2056. As the wills and property ownership are currently designed, the full amount passing to either spouse at their first death will be deductible to determine the taxable estate.

In order to take advantage of this provision, the decedent and his or her estate must meet these basic tests:

- At the date of death, the decedent must have been married.
- The estate property to be subjected to the federal estate tax marital deduction must pass from the decedent to his or her surviving spouse.
- The estate property passing to the surviving spouse must pass in such a way that it will be included and taxable as part of his or her subsequent estate, unless expended or given away.
- The surviving spouse must be a citizen of the United States.

Regarding the third test, the estate planner must realize that the federal estate tax marital deduction must never be regarded as a complete forgiveness of federal estate tax liability, but rather as a mere deferral of such tax liability. In other words, the estate tax laws will permit a deferral of estate tax liability at the death of the first spouse, but since this mechanism is merely a deferral and not a total forgiveness of the tax, the IRS *must* be given the opportunity to impose federal estate tax at a subsequent time (that is, at the death of the second spouse). The only legal manner in which such tax may be imposed at the second death is to have estate assets of the first spouse to die included as part of the gross estate of the second spouse to die.

It is this requirement that estate property must be included in the gross estate of the second spouse to die that will create a problem for the Hillmans and cause excessive costs. Under the current arrangement wherein all Mark's estate property passes to Barbara and all Barbara's estate property passes to Mark, the tax liability *at the second death* will be excessive. This is the case because at the death of the second spouse, not only will his or her own estate property be subject to estate taxation, but the property received from the deceased spouse will be taxed as well. Because the federal estate tax is progressive in nature, such an approach pushes the estate of the second spouse to die into a much higher bracket. Table 14-3 illustrates the estate costs if Mark were to predecease Barbara, and table 14-4 shows the estate costs if Barbara were to predecease Mark. Both tables reflect the current situation with the simple wills in effect and assume a state death tax that is equal to the federal state death tax credit and administrative expenses equal to 8 percent of the estate. The illustrations assume both deaths occur in 1998 and that the value of the assets remains constant.

A careful study of tables 14-3 and 14-4 will reveal that Mark and Barbara Hillman's combined estates do face significant excessive-transfer-cost problems. If Mark were to predecease Barbara under the current arrangement, the total costs of both estates, including Anystate's estate tax and administrative expenses, would be $900,356. If Barbara were to predecease Mark under the current arrangement, the total costs of settling both estates would be $870,413. Clearly, you must find ways to reduce these excessive costs for your clients.

TABLE 14-3
Estimated Estate Costs—Mark Hillman Predeceases Barbara Hillman (With Simple Wills)

At Mark's Death

Gross estate	$1,569,448	
Less costs of administration, final expenses, debts (8%)	(125,556)	$ 125,556
Adjusted gross estate	1,443,892	
Less marital deduction	(1,443,892)	
Taxable estate	-0-	-0-
Federal estate tax		-0-
Total costs at first death		$125,556

At Barbara's Death

Gross estate	$2,215,618[a]	
Less costs of administration, final expenses, debts (8%)	(177,249)	$177,249
Adjusted gross estate	2,038,369	
Less marital deduction	(-0-)	
Taxable estate	2,038,369	
Federal estate tax (precredits)	799,601	
Less applicable credit amount	(202,050)	
Less state death tax credit	(102,363)	
Federal estate tax (postcredits)	495,188	495,188
Total costs at second death		$774,800
Combined costs at both deaths		$900,356

a. Barbara's separate gross estate of $771,726 plus $1,443,892 received by Barbara under the terms of Mark's last will and testament.

As outlined above, properly drafted wills that take advantage of the federal estate tax marital-deduction laws will be very helpful in your effort to reduce estate tax liability. This is because of the applicable credit amount, which may be used *in conjunction with* the federal estate tax marital deduction. Let's explore this in detail.

Sec. 2010 provides that for all decedents who die in 1998 a credit against federal estate tax liability in the amount of $202,050 will be available (for a complete list of the applicable credit amounts for the appropriate years, see table 1-3 in chapter 1). A credit, of course, is a below-the-line computation that results in a dollar-for-dollar reduction in estate tax owed. This applicable credit amount of $202,050 translates into a taxable estate of $625,000. Since every taxpayer has the right to use this credit, it would be foolish and poor planning to waste it and to not take advantage of its benefits.

TABLE 14-4
Estimated Estate Costs—Barbara Hillman Predeceases Mark Hillman (With Simple Wills)

At Barbara's Death

Gross estate	$ 771,726	
Less costs of administration, final expenses, debts (8%)	(61,738)	
Adjusted gross estate	709,988	$ 61,738
Less marital deduction	(709,988)	
Taxable estate	-0-	
		-0-
Federal estate tax		
Total costs at first death		-0-
		$ 61,738

At Mark's Death

Gross estate	$2,279,436[a]	
Less costs of administration, final expenses, debts (8%)	(182,355)	$182,355
Adjusted gross estate	2,097,081	
Less marital deduction	(-0-)	
Taxable estate	2,097,081	
Federal estate tax (precredits)	828,370	
Less applicable credit amount	(202,050)	
Less state death tax credit	(106,590)	
Federal estate tax (postcredits)	519,730	519,730
Total costs at second death		$808,675
Combined costs at both deaths		$870,413

a. Mark's separate gross estate of $1,569,448 plus $709,988 received by Mark under the terms of Barbara's last will and testament.

In the Hillman case, the credit is not being taken advantage of under the current arrangement. Instead of using it, the present will arrangement leaves all estate property to the surviving spouse. Because the estate property ends up being included in the surviving spouse's gross estate outright, there is a stacking effect wherein one estate is stacked on top of the other. This has the result of creating unnecessarily excessive costs.

You as the estate planner must urge the Hillmans to have their wills redrafted to take advantage of the applicable credit amount in conjunction with the federal estate tax marital deduction. This technique, often referred to as a *credit shelter trust,* eliminates the federal estate tax liability at the first death. Any estate property over and above the applicable exclusion amount will then be subjected to the estate tax marital deduction. This approach prevents the excessive stacking effect and reduces estate tax liability dramatically. An overqualification of the federal estate tax marital deduction, such as in the Hillmans' present arrangement, is avoided.

To effectively use the credit-shelter-trust approach, at least the amount of estate property equal to the applicable exclusion amount ($625,000 for 1998) should be directed by an effectively worded will to a trust that gives the surviving spouse access to the funds without the assets contained in this trust being subjected to federal estate tax liability.

An appropriate design for a new will for Mark Hillman that will contain these provisions and a credit shelter trust will read substantially as follows:

1. Any interest I (Mark Hillman) own in my personal residence at my death I leave to my wife, Barbara, outright, subject to any indebtedness secured thereby.
2. Any interest in household furnishings, automobiles, and personal effects that I own at my death I leave to my wife, Barbara, outright.
3. If my wife, Barbara, survives me (and if we die under such circumstances that it is difficult or impossible to determine who died first, it shall be presumed that she survives me and that this bequest shall be effective), I give, devise, and bequeath to my wife an amount determined as follows:
   a. Ascertain the maximum marital deduction allowable in determining the federal estate tax payable by reason of my death, taking into account any election my executor makes for tax purposes.
   b. Deduct therefrom the value of any and all other property that passes or has passed to my wife either outside this will or under any other item of this will in such manner as to qualify for the marital deduction.
   c. From that figure deduct that amount, if any, needed to increase my taxable estate to the largest amount that, after allowing for the applicable credit amount (unified credit), will result in no federal estate tax being imposed upon my estate. The resulting amount shall be the amount bequeathed in this item. No reduction shall be made in this bequest, however, and no charge shall be made against any bequest or the beneficiary thereof because of any estate or inheritance tax imposed on my estate or this bequest.

4. All the rest, residue, and remainder of my property of every kind and description and wherever located, including any lapsed or void legacy or devise (but not including any property over which I may have a power of disposition or appointment), I give, devise, and bequeath to the First National Bank of Anytown, as trustee.

The residuary trust should provide that the net income from the trust will be paid to Barbara, Jennifer, and Scott, as necessary in the sole discretion of the trustee during the period the children are minors. In addition, the trustee should be empowered to invade the principal of this residuary trust for the same beneficiaries as long as the children are minors.

Table 14-5 illustrates the estate costs if Mark were to predecease Barbara with a modified will arrangement using the credit-shelter approach. Table 14-6 illustrates the estate costs if Barbara were to predecease Mark, again using the credit-shelter approach.

Using the credit-shelter-trust approach, assuming Mark predeceases Barbara saves $333,414. Using the credit-shelter-trust approach, assuming Barbara predeceases Mark saves $209,764.

The fact that the savings are less if Barbara dies first reveals another planning opportunity for the Hillmans. Barbara does not have enough individually titled assets to fund a full credit shelter trust. This problem exists even though the improperly structured insurance beneficiary designation leaves her life insurance proceeds to her estate.

As we will demonstrate later, this becomes a larger problem if the insurance is removed from the estate. In 1998, $625,000 would be required and the figure would rise each year as the applicable credit amount increases. It should be immediately recommended that some of the joint property, particularly the securities, be moved into Barbara's name only.

As the Hillmans acquire new wealth, they and their planners should be cognizant of the amount of individual property needed by each spouse to use a full applicable exclusion amount if either spouse should die. The newly acquired assets could then be titled appropriately. This will be an ongoing monitoring responsibility for the Hillmans' advisers.

Special Valuation Provisions and Considerations. The Hillman case has three possible situations that could be appropriate for application of special valuation considerations. The first is a general matter involving possible use of the alternate valuation date. The second is more specific and deals with the concept of special-use valuation. The third deals with valuation of the business interests.

The valuation of the business interests leads us to two key issues: the potential to use the family-held business exclusion and the need to set up a succession plan. Let's look at each of these separately.

TABLE 14-5
Estimated Estate Costs—Mark Hillman Predeceases Barbara Hillman (Using the Credit Shelter Trust)

At Mark's Death

Gross estate	$1,569,448		
Less costs of administration, final expenses, debts (8%)	(125,556)	$ 125,556	
Adjusted gross estate	1,443,892		
Less marital deduction	818,892[a]		
Taxable estate	625,000[b]		
Federal estate tax (precredits)	202,050		
Less applicable credit amount	(202,050)		
Federal estate tax (postcredits)	-0-	-0-	$125,556
Total costs at first death			

At Barbara's Death

Gross estate	$1,590,618[c]		
Less costs of administration, final expenses, debts (8%)	(85,196)	$ 85,196	
Adjusted gross estate	1,505,422		
Less marital deduction	(-0-)		
Taxable estate	1,505,422		
Federal estate tax (precredits)	555,800		
Less applicable credit amount	(202,050)		
Less state death tax credit	(64,747)	64,747	
Federal estate tax (postcredits)	291,443	291,443	
Total costs at second death			$441,386
Combined costs at both deaths under current arrangement[d] (assuming Mark predeceases Barbara)			$900,356
Combined costs at both deaths with the credit shelter trusts			$566,942
Savings by using the credit shelter trust			$333,414

a. This figure represents a proper coordination between the applicable exclusion amount of $625,000 (for 1998) and the federal estate tax marital deduction. Since $625,000 worth of taxable estate is the maximum amount of value that may be left in Mark's estate without attracting federal estate taxation, $818,892 is the amount that would need to qualify for the federal estate tax marital deduction.
b. The exact amount of the applicable exclusion.
c. Barbara's separate gross estate of $771,726 plus $818,892 received by Barbara under the terms of the credit-shelter-trust-type will.
d. See table 14-3.

TABLE 14-6
Estimated Estate Costs—Barbara Hillman Predeceases Mark Hillman (Using the Credit Shelter Trust)

At Barbara's Death

Gross estate	$ 771,726	
Less costs of administration, final expenses, debts (8%)	(61,738)	$ 61,738
Adjusted gross estate	709,988	
Less marital deduction	(293,226)[a]	
Taxable estate	416,762[b]	
Federal estate tax (precredits)	127,499	
Less unified credit	(127,499)	
Federal estate tax (postcredits)	-0-	-0-
Total costs at first death		$ 61,738

At Mark's Death

Gross estate	$1,862,674[c]	
Less costs of administration, final expenses, debts (8%)	(149,014)	$149,014
Adjusted gross estate	1,713,660	
Less marital deduction	(-0-)	
Taxable estate	1,713,660	
Federal estate tax (precredits)	651,947	
Less applicable credit amount	(202,050)	
Less state death tax credit	(78,984)	78,984
Federal estate tax (postcredits)	370,913	370,913
Total costs at second death		$598,911
Combined costs at both deaths under current arrangement[d] (assuming Barbara predeceases Mark)		$870,413
Combined costs at both deaths with the credit shelter trusts (assuming Barbara predeceases Mark)		$660,649
Savings by using the credit shelter trust		$209,764

a. This figure represents the coordination between the applicable credit amount and the federal estate tax marital deduction on the facts of this case. In 1998, $625,000 worth of taxable estate is the maximum amount of value that may be left in Barbara's estate without attracting federal estate taxation. However, Barbara owns substantial assets jointly with Mark. These assets pass automatically to Mark (this represents a transfer to Mark of $293,226). Her individual assets are the only assets available to fund the credit shelter trust. Thus, the credit shelter trust will be funded with $416,762 after expenses.
b. The amount of the assets available to fund credit shelter trust, after expenses.
c. Mark's separate gross estate of $1,569,448 plus $293,226 joint property received by Mark. Total is $1,862,674.
d. See table 14-4.

Chapter 14 Procedural Principles of Estate Planning

The value to be affixed to estate assets, of course, will be the fair market value of the specific asset either on the date of death or on the alternate valuation date (which is 6 months following the date of death). Since at this point you cannot predict what the value of estate assets would be on a date 6 months following the date of Mark and/or Barbara's death, it is not possible for your written estate plan to advocate one valuation date over another. However, the written estate plan must discuss the fact that two separate valuation processes are available and must emphasize that it will be the duty of the executor or administrator of the estate to make such decisions at the appropriate time.

With regard to the second valuation point, the farm property included as part of Mark Hillman's gross estate at $298,000 should be examined within the context of special-use valuation. In chapter 4 we studied the fact that the IRS has traditionally placed the highest-and-best-use value on farm property. Because the highest-and-best-use value can often be much higher than the actual farm value, Congress enacted Sec. 2032A in 1976 to allow a more realistic value to be placed on farmland, ranchland, and/or real property used in a trade or business. As stated previously, however, before an estate can successfully take advantage of this concept, there are several prerequisites that must be met. One of these requirements is that the estate owner or a member of his or her immediate family must have materially participated in the operation of the farming or ranching operation. This is not the case in the Hillman fact pattern. Another of these requirements is that at least 50 percent of the value of the decedent's gross estate must consist of the value of the land in question. Again, this is not the case in the Hillman fact pattern. Therefore the relief provisions as set forth in Sec. 2032A will not be available to Mark Hillman's estate. However, to be considered well written, your estate plan should first mention the concept of special-use valuation under Sec. 2032A and then explain why it would not be available under the particular facts and circumstances of the Hillman case.

The third point involving special valuation considerations deals with the value to be placed on the two closely held business interests in the Hillman case. We have seen from the fact pattern that Mark Hillman has a 100 percent interest in the stock of Hillman Enterprises, Inc. (valued at $440,000), and that Barbara Hillman has a one-half interest in Kid's Shoppe, which is a partnership. Her one-half interest is valued at $100,000.

The values placed on the two business interests as reflected in tables 14-1 and 14-2 are based on best estimates of what both Mark and Barbara concluded their respective interests would be worth if death were to happen at once. However, the IRS uses specific valuation principles that could result in the government's placing a much higher value on these interests. If this were to transpire, hypothetical federal estate tax computations would be distorted and could render prior estate planning decisions useless and ineffective.

In chapter 4, where there was also a detailed study made of Rev. Rul. 59-60, we said that the IRS will apply eight separate factors in the decision-making process to arrive at a value for a closely held business. We also said that the IRS will use such mathematical methods as the adjusted-book-value method and the capitalization-of-adjusted-earnings method to arrive at a specific dollar value for a closely held business interest. You should review these provisions at this time.

One of the issues that could be of importance with respect to valuation is the family-held business exclusion discussed in chapter 4. To qualify for an estate tax exclusion that would exempt the first $1.3 million (including the amount sheltered by the applicable credit amount) of a closely held business from estate taxes, many tests have to be satisfied. Let's take a look at the Hillman facts. (Note that the following discussion grossly oversimplifies the rules for the Sec. 2033A family-held business exclusion. The rules are provided in more detail in chapter 4.) The business would have to be held by a qualified heir who would materially participate for 10 years after the decedent's death. A qualified heir for this purpose would also include a key employee who worked for the business for 10 years. In addition, the value of the business held by the decedent must be greater than 50 percent of the adjusted gross estate. In the Hillman case, neither spouse is close to the necessary threshold. Mark's interest is worth $440,000 out of a $1,569,448 gross estate. Barbara's partnership interest is worth $100,000 out of a $771,726 gross estate. Of course, this presumes that all the values are correct as presented in the fact-finder. If the business interest is closer to the threshold for the Sec. 2033A exclusion, the valuation of the business will be critical.

Chapter 4 also pointed out that an effectively drafted buy-sell agreement can peg the value of a closely held business interest for federal estate tax purposes. Your written estate plan must emphasize that the execution of such a buy-sell agreement will eliminate potential valuation problems, and if possible it should be seriously considered for use in this case. In the Hillman case, neither business interest has a succession plan. In Barbara's partnership, the agreement does not handle the potential of premature death or disability. With two partners, a natural buy-sell opportunity exists and should be considered. For Mark's business, discussion should begin about the options for a business succession plan.

Reduction of the Gross Estate. One key element in your attempt to eliminate, or at least reduce, excessive transfer costs involves reducing the size of the decedent's estate. If the estate size can be reduced, the federal estate tax liability can be dramatically reduced. You know from an analysis of the Hillmans' fact pattern and summary of assets that each of their estates definitely faces an excessive transfer cost problem. Proper use of the federal estate tax marital deduction in conjunction with the applicable credit amount has already been recommended in the written estate plan, and we have seen how dramatic some of the cost savings have been.

However, the planner can do even more to reduce excessive costs. Such methods as removal of the life insurance proceeds from both Mark and Barbara's respective estates, a concerted gifting program, or some form of estate freeze must all be discussed in the written estate plan. We'll review each of these separately.

Chapter 14 Procedural Principles of Estate Planning

Gifting Program. Sec. 2503(b) permits $10,000 worth of cash or property to be gifted free of any federal gift tax liability. The provision permits the $10,000 exclusion to be used for each donee (recipient) of gifted property. This exclusion exists each year, and to the extent that the donor's spouse joins in the gift, the amount of the exclusion may be doubled to $20,000 per year.

Because the Hillmans have two children, they should begin a gifting program today. The $20,000 annual exclusion per year, per donee can become meaningful over the years. Since the Hillmans are both relatively young, a full annual exclusion gift of $40,000 over a period of years can result in a sizable reduction of the gross estate. We will illustrate a gifting program to provide maximum annual exclusion gifts of the insurance premiums and cash totaling $40,000 annually. The results of the gifting program are demonstrated in tables 14-7 and 14-8.

Removal of Life Insurance Proceeds from Respective Estates. Table 14-1 (Summary of Assets—Mark Hillman) shows that $300,000 of life insurance proceeds are included in Mark's gross estate; table 14-2 (Summary of Assets—Barbara Hillman), shows that $325,000 of life insurance proceeds are included in Barbara's gross estate. In both cases, the reason for the inclusion is that the life insurance trusts that hold these life insurance policies are *not* irrevocable, but rather may be revoked by either Mark or Barbara at any time. In addition, the policies remain payable to the insured's estate through the beneficiary designations.

In your written estate plan you must emphasize that the Hillmans have accomplished nothing from a tax planning point of view by having a revocable trust hold their life policies. As we have seen in earlier chapters, a transfer of property into a revocable trust will not allow the transferred property to escape federal estate taxation. Only an irrevocable life insurance trust would allow such a result here. (In the alternative, of course, cross-ownership of the life insurance policies would be possible as another method for preventing federal estate taxation of the life insurance proceeds.) Your written estate plan should therefore suggest that the current arrangement in which a revocable trust owns the life insurance policies be changed to an irrevocable life insurance trust approach. (The Hillmans must be advised, however, that Sec. 2035 would bring the proceeds of the policies back into the gross estate of the insured if either spouse were to die within 3 years of the change in the trust from revocable to irrevocable.) Again, we will demonstrate the effect of the gift of the life insurance policies and subsequent premiums and assume the Hillmans die in 4 years (2001). This time frame will allow for the removal of the insurance from their gross estates and $80,000 of annual exclusion gifts from both Mark and Barbara. The impact of this prograkm is illustrated for both orders of death in tables 14-7 and 14-8.

Estate Freezing Techniques. Chapters 5 and 6 devoted a great deal of attention to the concept of the estate freeze. We know that this technique is used in conjunction with a business interest that is appreciating. The attractive and useful feature of the estate freeze method is the ability of the client to retain some form of control over the business interest while shifting future appreciation in the asset to others, usually children.

Your written estate plan must emphasize that the Hillmans should consider an estate freeze since their business interests will have a propensity to appreciate. In addition, their other assets will grow in value. Since Barbara Hillman's business interest in Kid's Shoppe is a partnership arrangement with an unrelated third party, no estate freeze technique is available. This is true since the only estate freeze available for partnerships is the family partnership, and this will not operate properly with a nonfamily member as one of the partners. However, since Mark Hillman's operation is a corporation, a recapitalization along with a gifting program should be considered to accomplish an estate freeze. This type of recapitalization will make more sense if one or both of the children will become involved in the business. It's certainly too early to make this call. Another possibility is to take business assets and investment assets to form a family limited partnership (FLP) to reduce the cost of shifting wealth to the next generation. Again, with the ages of the Hillmans and their children and the size of the couple's current estates, it may be a bit premature to do anything irrevocable. However, one of the benefits of the FLP is that the Hillmans would retain general partnership interests and control the FLP's activities for as long as they retain the general partnership interests.

Conclusion. The excessive transfer costs portion of the written estate plan is probably the most important component of the report since it deals with costs the estate would incur unnecessarily. If left alone, dollars that could and should be passing from a decedent to his or her surviving spouse or children would instead pass to taxing authorities. Basic estate planning techniques such as gifting, removal of life insurance proceeds from the estate, or effective use of the federal estate tax marital deduction can dramatically reduce estate costs. We have seen this in the Hillman case. Tables 14-7 and 14-8 reflect a savings of $730,862 if Mark were to predecease Barbara and a savings of $445,665 if Barbara were to predecease Mark. Savings like these will certainly interest your clients, and you must bring the savings to their attention. Again, the most immediate problem to implement the optimal marital deduction/credit shelter trust plan is the lack of sufficient assets in Barbara's name to fund a credit shelter trust. In fact, after removing the life insurance and cash gifts from her estate, she will have only $44,162 remaining at her assumed death in 2001 to fund a credit shelter trust that would require $675,000 to be fully funded in 2001.

Estate Liquidity

The concept of estate liquidity becomes pertinent in the analysis of an estate because the federal estate tax laws require that all tax the estate owes must be paid within 9 months of the date of death. If an estate is especially liquid in

Chapter 14 Procedural Principles of Estate Planning   441

character, with ample amounts of cash, marketable securities (which are a near-cash equivalent) or life insurance proceeds, then the executor or administrator will have no problem meeting the 9-month deadline. However, since most estates in reality consist of valuable assets and interests that are illiquid, liquidity problems are quite prevalent.

TABLE 14-7
Estimated Estate Costs—Mark Hillman Predeceases Barbara Hillman
Modifications:
- **Credit Shelter Trust**
- **Gifting Program for 4 Years**
- **Removal of Life Insurance**

At Mark's Death

Gross estate	$1,189,448[a]	
Less costs of administration, final expenses, debts (8%)	(95,156)	$ 95,156
Adjusted gross estate	1,094,292	
Less marital deduction	(419,292)[b]	
Taxable estate	675,000[c]	
Federal estate tax (precredits)	220,550	
Less applicable credit amount	(220,550)	
Federal estate tax (postcredits)	-0-	-0-
Total costs at first death[d]		$ 95,156

At Barbara's Death

Gross estate	$ 786,018[d]	
Less costs of administration, final expenses, debts (8%)	(52,796)	$ 52,796
Adjusted gross estate	733,222	
Less marital deduction	-0-	
Taxable estate	733,222	
Federal estate tax (precredits)	242,092	
Less applicable credit amount	(220,550)	
Less state death tax credit	(19,595)	19,595
Federal estate tax (postcredits)	1,947	1,947
Total costs at second death		$ 74,338

Combined costs at both deaths under current arrangement[e] (assuming Mark predeceases Barbara)	$900,356
Combined costs at both deaths with these modifications (assuming Mark predeceases Barbara)	$169,494
Savings by using these modifications	$730,862

(Table continued on next page)

> a. The gross estate was $1,569,448 in the current arrangement (see table 14-1). Assume gifts of $20,000 for 4 years (that is, $80,000). Assume removal of life insurance proceeds of $300,000. Therefore $1,569,448 minus $80,000 minus $300,000 equals $1,189,448.
> b. This figure represents a proper coordination between the applicable exclusion amount of $675,000 for 2001 and the federal estate tax marital deduction. Since $675,000 worth of taxable estate is the maximum amount of value that may be left in Mark's estate without attracting federal estate taxation, $419,292 is the amount that would need to qualify for the federal estate tax marital deduction.
> c. The exact amount of the applicable exclusion amount.
> d. Barbara's separate gross estate under the current arrangement is $771,726 (see table 14-2). Assume gifts of $20,000 for 4 years (that is, $80,000). Assume removal of life insurance proceeds of $325,000. Therefore $771,726 minus $80,000 minus $325,000 equals $366,726. To this figure $419,292 received by Barbara under the marital deduction trust must be added. Total is $786,018.
> e. See table 14-3.

Let's look at the Hillmans' estates in terms of liquidity. Tables 14-1 and 14-2 list the Hillmans' estate assets. The total combined estate (under the current arrangement) is $2,341,174. Of this amount, the following assets are liquid in nature:

Cash	$126,552
Marketable securities	223,400
Pension proceeds	155,822
Life insurance proceeds	620,000
Total liquid assets	$1,130,774

Since $1,130,774 exists in liquid assets out of a total combined estate of $2,341,174, this means that 48.3 percent of the combined estate is liquid.

If tables 14-3 through 14-8 are examined, the maximum settlement costs for both estates under any scenario is $900,356. Therefore, regardless of which approach is used, there will be no estate liquidity deficit at either death since the family will have $1,130,774 available in liquid form to pay the expenses. However, the estate liquidity situation should be monitored regularly. The composition of the Hillmans' estate could change in the future. Perhaps their business interests will grow in value faster than other assets. They could acquire illiquid assets by expending liquid assets, such as the purchase of a vacation home or other real estate. Another possibility is that their liquid assets could be drained by their children's educational costs or some unforeseen expense. A regular check-up on the composition of their estates and the relative value of their assets should reveal liquidity concerns.

Chapter 14 Procedural Principles of Estate Planning 443

TABLE 14-8
Estimated Estate Costs—Barbara Hillman Predeceases Mark Hillman
Modifications: • **Credit Shelter Trust**
 • **Gifting Program for 4 Years**
 • **Removal of Life Insurance**

At Barbara's Death

Gross estate	$ 366,726[a]	
Less costs of administration, final expenses, debts (8%)	(29,338)	$ 29,338
Adjusted gross estate	337,388[b]	
Less marital deduction	(293,226)	
Taxable estate	44,162	
Federal estate tax (precredits)	9,199	
Less applicable credit amount	(9,199)[c]	
Federal estate tax (postcredits)	-0-	-0-
Total costs at first death		$ 29,338

At Mark's Death

Gross estate	$1,482,674[d]	
Less costs of administration, final expenses, debts (8%)	(118,614)	$118,616
Adjusted gross estate	1,364,060	
Less marital deduction	-0-	
Taxable estate	1,364,060	
Federal estate tax (precredits)	497,346	
Less applicable credit amount	(220,550)	
Less state death tax credit	(55,700)	55,700
Federal estate tax (postcredits)	221,096	221,096
Total costs at second death		$395,410
Combined costs at both deaths under current arrangement[e] (assuming Barbara predeceases Mark)		$870,413
Combined costs at both deaths with these modifications (assuming Barbara predeceases Mark)		$424,748
Savings by using these modifications		$445,665

(Table continued on next page)

> a. Her gross estate ;is $771,726 under the current arrangement (see table 14-2). Assume gifts of $20,000 for 4 years (that is, $80,000). Assume removal of life insurance proceeds of $325,000. Therefore $771,726 minus $80,000 minus $325,000 equals $366,726.
> b. Because the adjusted gross estate is far less than the applicable exclusion amount of $675,000 (for 2001), it normally would not be necessary to pass property to Mark through the federal estate tax marital deduction. However, since their jointly held property passes automatically, some marital deduction will be taken and further waste some of Barbara's applicable credit amount.
> c. Amount of Barbara's separate assets available to fund the credit shelter trust.
> d. Gross estate is $1,569,448 under the current arrangement (see table 14-1). Assume gifts of $20,000 for 4 years (that is, $80,000). Assume removal of life insurance proceeds of $300,000. Therefore $1,569,448 minus $80,000 minus $300,000 equals $1,189,448. Added to this is the amount of joint property received directly from Barbara ($293,226) to leave a gross estate of $1,482,674.
> e. See table 14-4.

Earlier in this chapter, we discussed Sec. 6166 and pointed out that it is available to an estate if certain prerequisites are met. This is one possibility for liquidity relief if a problem develops. We mentioned that if greater than 35 percent of a decedent's adjusted gross estate is made up of a closely held business, then the estate may elect to pay out federal estate tax liability over a 15-year period. Table 14-1 shows that the corporation is valued in the estate at $440,000. Table 14-3 shows that Mark Hillman's adjusted gross estate (under the current arrangement) is $1,443,892. Therefore, under the current arrangement, the estate will not qualify for the Sec. 6166 election, since 35 percent of $1,443,892 is $505,362 and the value of Hillman Enterprises, Inc., is only $440,000. Given these circumstances, the advisers should watch the liquidity picture carefully since 6166 will be a possibility for Mark's estate if he holds his business until death and it grows faster than the rest of his estate.

Patterns of Distribution

The third portion of the Hillman estate plan will deal with the exact manner in which your clients currently have arranged their estate assets and how such assets will pass at the respective deaths of Mark and Barbara. Once these facts have been analyzed and discussed, proposed changes should be highlighted.

The four specific areas that you should address separately in the Hillman case (based on its particular facts and circumstances) are

- current will arrangement
- life insurance arrangements
- property ownership
- distribution of business interest

Current Will Arrangement. The written estate plan must first focus on the current will arrangement and subsequently discuss what the actual dispositive wishes of Mark and Barbara Hillman are. Finally, as estate planner you must draw conclusions regarding whether the current will arrangement adequately handles the dispositive wishes of the Hillmans; if necessary, you should recommend corrective action. Since the subjects of the current wills and the use of a marital-deduction credit-shelter-trust-type will were already covered in depth in the excessive-transfer-costs area, it will not be necessary in this portion of the written estate plan to spend much time going over the same facts and issues. However, it is still a good idea to *briefly* summarize the facts, issues, and recommendations in this portion of the plan. Therefore you should mention that (1) both Mark and Barbara Hillman currently have simple wills in which all estate property is left outright to the surviving spouse, (2) such an arrangement will result in a higher federal estate tax liability because of the loss of the unified-credit-shelter approach, and (3) both Mark and Barbara should draft credit-shelter-type wills. Refer to the excessive-transfer-costs portion of the plan for further details on the subject.

Life Insurance Arrangement. Under the current plan the insurance is owned by revocable trusts but payable to the insured's estate. This creates a couple of problems. First, the insurance is unnecessarily included in the insured's gross estate. Second, the insurance could be included in probate under the laws of some states. This might subject the proceeds to the claims of creditors or increase state death taxes. The solution is to transfer the policies to irrevocable trusts and designate the trustee as the beneficiary of the policy. This immediately removes the insurance from the probate estate, solving the second problem. If the insured survives for 3 years following the transfer, the insurance proceeds will be removed from the insured's gross estate, solving the first problem. In the Hillman case, the surviving spouse will probably need significant access to the death benefits to meet the family's needs. As we discussed in chapter 3, it is possible to give the spouse limited access without causing inclusion in the surviving spouse's gross estate. The spouse could receive all income from the trust, have the noncumulative right to receive annually the greater of $5,000 or 5 percent of the principal, and have principal distributed if necessary for health, maintenance, or support. Some estate planners are concerned about the reciprocal trust doctrine becoming a problem if each spouse transfers life insurance to an irrevocable trust benefiting the other spouse. It may be prudent to have the terms of each trust drafted somewhat differently to avoid this problem. (See chapter 12 for a discussion of the reciprocal trust doctrine.)

Another problem is the significant death costs for the Hillmans' estates. Although there is not an immediate liquidity problem, the Hillmans should consider additional insurance, perhaps second-to-die coverage, to handle the settlement costs for their estates.

Property Ownership. It has been demonstrated that Barbara has a shortfall in individually titled assets to fund a credit shelter trust to its maximum amount. The couple own significant amounts of property in joint name. This property passes automatically to the survivor and is eligible for the marital deduction. Unfortunately, this property disposition wastes some of Barbara's applicable credit amount. Some or all of the joint property should be severed and titled in Barbara's name only.

Distribution of Business Interest. Since both Mark and Barbara are involved in a business interest, this portion of the written estate plan will become very important to your clients. Here, you should undertake a review of the current situation involving your client's business interests. Following this you should emphasize some of the issues and problems that may arise if adequate planning is not considered.

With regard to Mark Hillman, the written plan should reflect that he is currently the sole shareholder of Hillman Enterprises, Inc., but that he has taken no action to ensure smooth business transition or continuity in the event of his death. The plan at this point should remind the client that the excessive-transfer-costs component of the report touched on this topic previously within the context of reducing unnecessarily high costs. There, the subject of a buy-sell agreement was explained to show the Hillmans that if such an agreement were drafted in accordance with certain principles as set forth by the IRS, the value of the business interest could be pegged for federal estate tax purposes.

Discuss the subject of the buy-sell agreement again here. However, at this point in the report, emphasize that if something were to happen to Mark Hillman (that is, death or disability), the stock in the corporation would all pass to Barbara under the provisions of Mark's current will. Given that Barbara has no experience in or knowledge about Mark's business, she would have to sell Hillman Enterprises, Inc., following Mark's death or disability, probably at a loss. A buy-sell agreement (drafted and executed during Mark's lifetime) with a willing buyer will not only resolve valuation problems by pegging the value of the business interest but will also ensure that Mark's business interest is disposed of exactly in accordance with his wishes.

You should apply the same principles involving the use of a buy-sell agreement to Barbara's one-half interest in the Kid's Shoppe partnership. In one sense it will be even easier for Barbara to have such a buy-sell agreement executed than it will be for Mark, since Barbara already has a partner with whom the agreement may be drafted. Mark, of course, must locate a willing buyer. In both Mark's and Barbara's cases, the written estate plan should emphasize that the buy-sell agreement should be funded with life insurance. Furthermore, the plan should raise other issues, such as whether the agreements should be entity or cross-purchase types, and should provide for the annual update of the agreements regarding valuation of the business.

Miscellaneous Points. Based on the facts you learned about the Hillmans' case during the initial fact-finding interview, the written estate plan will need to discuss two other points within the patterns-of-distribution category:

- Neither Mark Hillman nor Barbara Hillman has named a guardian for their two children, Jennifer and Scott, in the current wills. When the wills are revised to incorporate the marital-deduction credit-shelter-trust approach, guardians should be named. Of course, guardians are only necessary if both parents die during the children's minority.
- Although Mark Hillman had advised you during the fact-finding process that both he and Barbara were in favor of becoming involved in some sort of charitable giving program, both their wills are silent on this point. When the wills are revised to incorporate the marital-deduction/credit-shelter-trust approach, charitable bequests should be considered. It is also conceivable that the Hillmans could make lifetime charitable bequests. These options should be discussed at this point in the written estate plan.

Adequate Future Income

The adequate-future-income portion of the estate plan is different from the other three categories in the report since it deals exclusively with postmortem planning and with income questions. Because this portion specifically addresses questions involving the ability of the decedent's surviving family members to maintain their current lifestyles, it is one of the most vital components of the entire project.

Based on the following facts of the Hillmans' case, the concept of adequate future income should not present a major problem for your clients:

- Mark and Barbara each have sizable gross estates.
- The estates do not currently show a liquidity shortfall.
- Mark and Barbara currently have adequate incomes. In the event that one dies, however, the surviving spouse will not have adequate income to maintain the current lifestyle and the educational costs that are anticipated.
- The life insurance coverage on the lives of both Mark and Barbara should be evaluated. In light of the ages of the children and the lack of a succession plan for either business, a problem could develop if either spouse dies. At least in Mark's case, his individual coverage should be doubled to $600,000 at a minimum. If Barbara's death would cause Mark to take time away from his growing business for child-raising responsibilities, his income could suffer from her premature death. Combined with the loss of Barbara's income at her death, the additional

burdens on Mark would probably indicate the need for Barbara to have additional coverage.

You should discuss all these points in detail in this portion of your written estate plan.

Index

Editor's note: A lowercase *n.* following a page number refers the reader to a note on said page; a lowercase *t.* indicates a table. Thus "249 *n.* 15" refers to note 15 on page 249, and "5 *t.*" refers to a table on page 5.

Actuarial Values
    Alpha Volume, 118, 150 *n.* 2, 259
    Beta Volume, 118, 150 *n.* 2, 259
    Gamma Volume, 118, 258
Adjusted gross estate, 16
Adjusted-book-value method, 134
Administrative expenses
    estimating in estate settlement, 8
    of nonresident-alien estate transfers, 323
Adverse interest, 349
Adverse party, 349
Aggregate theory, 307
Allocation rule, 304
Allocation-of-premium rule, 313
Alternative minimum tax, 399
Alternative valuation date, 119–21
    examples of, 119
    exceptions to use of, 120–21
    procedural points of, 119–120
American Association of Fund-Raising Counsel Trust for Philanthropy, 214
Ancestral property rule, 307
Annual gift tax exclusion
    advantages of, 80–81
    Crummey withdrawal powers and, 82–94
    doubling of, 154
    for large-premium ILITs, 90–94
    for outright gifts, 152–55
Annuity
    benefits from, 10
    deferred, 269
    factors determining present value of, 146–47
    private, 207–12
    valuation of, 145, 50
    valuing for terms of years, 147–48
Annuity contracts, 122–24
Applicable credit amount, 18 *t.*
    estate settlement work sheets and, 27–37
    for nonresident-alien gifts, 325
    for QDOT transfer, 334–35
    in case study, 431–44
    in conjunction with marital deduction, 25, 417, 431–44
    in determining estate tax payable, 17–18
    property ownership and, 446
    taxable transfers sheltered by, 17
    with credit shelter trust approach, 433–34
    with family-held business exclusion, 16, 438
Applicable exclusion amount, 18 *t.*
    in case study, 431–44
    making full use of, 25
    state death taxes for estates with assets less than, 8
    with family-held business exclusion, 16
Applicable federal midterm rate (AFMR), 145, 147
    calculation of, 150 *n.* 1
Appointees, 372
Appointment, general powers of, 11
Apportionment rule, 304
Appraisal
    fees, 6
    reports, for valuing estate assets, 13
    requirements for, 236
Appreciated property contributions, 231–32
    to private foundations, 234
    special election for, 232
Appurtenant structures, 164
Assets
    assignment to QDOT, 329–30
    power to loan to insured's estate, 100–101
    purchase of by ILIT, 101–2
    valuation of, 415–16, 427

Beneficiary
    charitable organizations as, 239–40
    CRT as, 278–80
    estate or unified credit shelter/bypass trust as, 388–89
    flexibility to change, 105–6
    marital trust as, 387–87
    powers or rights of, 375–76
    of qualified plan
        choice of, 385–86
        tax-deferral options of, 386–87
    skip, 367
Benefits, retirement plan, 10
Bequests, legal presumption concerning, 307
Blockage discount, 132
Bonus life insurance plan, 379, 410–11
Bruch case, 129
Burial costs, 3
Business interest
    buy-sell agreement impact for, 138–40
    capped, 186
    distribution of, 423, 446
    pegging value of, 116
Business owner, incidents of ownership attributed to, 49–50
Buy-sell agreement, 138–40

Calder case, 144
California
    ancestral property rule in, 307
    community property in, 304
    divorce and separation in, 306
    life insurance premium test in, 313
    living trusts in, 310
    statutory fees and commissions for executors and attorneys, 4, 5 *t.*
Capital gain
    from CRT, 271–72, 273, 274, 276
    property contributions, 231–32
    property gifts producing, 247 *n.* 8
Capitalization-of-adjusted earnings method, 134
Case study
    narrative of, 424–26
    written plan, 427–48
Cash surrender value benefit, 408, 409
Catchall provision, 9–10
Chapter 14, 187–92
Charitable contributions
    administrative expenses apportioned to, 224
    deductible, 219
    five-year carryover of excess, 233
    income tax compliance rules for, 234–37
    of less than donor's entire interest in property, 254–59
    percentage limitations on, 247–48 *n.* 9
    purposes of, 215
    reasons for making, 216–18
    rules for tax deductions for, 221
    tax benefits for, 218
    timing of deduction for, 234–35
    types of, 214–16, 249–52
    use of, 214
    valuation of, 235–36
Charitable deductions
    categories of organizations qualifying for, 220–21
    charity's role in substantiating, 236–37
    estate tax requirements for, 223–27
    incomplete lifetime transfers and, 225–26
    limitations on, 226–27
    limited to property value, 227
    for nonresident-alien estate transfers, 324
    for nonresident-alien gifts, 324–25
    reduction for high-income donors, 233
    substantiating, 235–37
Charitable donee, selection of, 220–21
Charitable giving
    basics of, 213–52
    estate planning opportunities in, 237–47
    federal estate tax treatment of, 223–27
    federal gift tax treatment of, 227–29
    federal income tax treatment of, 229–37
    federal tax implications of, 218–22
    government role in, 218
    retirement plan benefits and, 389–91
    sophisticated methods of, 253–86
    in United States, 214–18
Charitable lead trust, 282–84
    inter vivos, 283
    testamentary, 283–84
Charitable organizations
    as beneficiary, 239–40
    conservation donation to, 284–86
    donations to versus for use of, 231
    eligible for tax-deductible donations, 220–21
    giving existing life insurance policy to, 240–41
    as irrevocable beneficiary, 240
    property passing to, 223
    public versus nonpublic, 230

Index

purchasing new life insurance policy naming, 241–42
qualifying for estate tax deduction, 224–25
qualifying for gift tax deduction, 227–28
role in substantiating donations, 236–37
state protection of, 218
Charitable remainder trust, 259–71
  annuity, 260, 262–63
    as beneficiary of qualified plan benefits, 278–80
    versus charitable remainder unitrust, 265–68
    payout flexibility of, 265–68
    as retirement plan replacement, 276, 278
    tax deduction for, 270–71
    taxation of payments, 268
  as beneficiary of qualified plan benefits, 278–80
  determining tax deduction for, 270–71
  distribution of payments of, 275–76
  guidelines for, 259–65
  investment of principal of, 269–70
  manipulation of investment policy of, 286 *n.* 5
  payout flexibility with, 265–68
  permissible duration of, 261–62
  permissible noncharitable interests in, 262
  planning applications of, 271–81
  as retirement plan beneficiary, 389–90
  to supplement retirement plan, 274–80
  taxation of payments, 268
  transfer taxes at death, 276
  transferring closely held corporation through, 280–81
  wealth replacement trusts and, 271–74
Charitable remainder unitrust, 259, 263
  versus CRAT, 264 *t.*, 265–68
  payout flexibility of, 265–66
  as retirement plan replacement, 276–78
  tax deduction for, 270–71
  taxation of payments, 268
  wealth replacement trusts and, 271–74
Charitable wealth replacement trusts, 110
Claims, against nonresident-alien estate transfers, 323
Client goals, 1
Clifford trust approach, 341
Closely held corporations, 132–44
  transfer through a CRT, 280–81
  valuation of, 132–44

Closely held stock, 269
Common stock gifts, 191–92
Community property, 300
  converting separate property to, 311
  definition of, 301
  disposition of in common-law states, 308
  earnings as, 303–4
  estate planning considerations for, 309–15
  held in joint tenancy, 303
  historical background on, 301
  liability problems with, 309
  premarital planning and, 309
  quasi, 303
  real property, 303
  residence and domicile, 305
  separation or divorce and, 305–6
Community-property laws, 300, 301
Community-property states, 300
  distribution of property at death in, 306–7
  similarities among, 302
  transfers of property in, 302
  variations among, 304–5
Conservation donations
  permissible purposes of, 285
  tax requirements for deduction of, 285–86
  types of, 284–85
Constructive receipt of income, 397–98
Contributions. *See* Charitable contributions; Charitable giving
Controlled entity, 189
Conversion privileges, 43
Corporate-owned life insurance, 49–50
Corpus, powers to invade, 359–62
CRATs. *See* Charitable remainder trust, annuity
Credit estate tax, state, 7–8
Credit shelter trust, 388–89, 433–34
Creditors, protection of family partnerships from, 197
Credits, net deferral estate tax payable after, 17–20
Cristofani v. Commissioner, 84–86, 91, 92
  extension of, 92
Cross trusts, 361–62
Cross-ownership, 181–82
CRT. *See* Charitable remainder trust
Crummey accumulation trusts, 157–58
Crummey beneficiaries, 110 *n.* 7
  eligible, 84–86
  gift tax consequences to, 88–90

providing notice to, 86–87
stacking, 91–92
Crummey v. Commissioner, 82–94
Crummey withdrawal powers, 82, 110 *n.* 5, 411 *n.* 3
   application to ILITs, 83–94
   duration of, 87
   in dynasty trust, 107
   establishing validity of, 84–90
   hanging, 93–94
   ILITs and, 183
   in large-premium ILITs, 90–94
   limited, 92–93
   permanent, 90–91
   size of, 88
CRUT. *See* Charitable remainder unitrust
Curtesy interests, 292–93
Custodial arrangements, to benefit minors, 357–59
Cy pres doctrine, 225

DBO plan. *See* Death-benefit-only plans
Death
   costs of wealth transfer at, 3–8
   removal of proceeds from decedent-insured's gross estate, 181–83
Death tax, 7–8, 41
   credit for, 20 *t.*
     for QDOT transfer, 335
   estate liquidity and, 41–42
   payment reduction for noncharitable beneficiary, 265–66
   on qualified plans and IRAs, 375
Death-benefit-only deferred-compensation plan, 50
Death-benefit-only plans, 378–88, 400–402
   definition of, 400
   federal estate tax implications of, 400–401
   federal gift tax implications of, 401–2
   federal income tax implications of, 402
   life insurance in, 402
Debt, of decedent, 3
Decedent
   final costs of, 3
   life insurance on, 11
   property interests transferred by gift, 10
   property owned outright by, 9–10
Deferred compensation, 396–400
Deferred-compensation plan, death-benefit-only, 50

Descent and distribution statute, 288
Determining the Value of Donated Property, 117–18, 235–36
DiMarco case, 401–2
Direct skip, 368–69
Direct-skip transfer, 57
Dispositive discretion, 97–102
Distribution patterns, 414, 422–24
   in case study, 444–47
Divorce
   changing ILIT beneficiaries with, 105
   division of home at, 295–96
   ending community, 305–6
   estate and gift tax implications of transfers incident to, 293–95
   life insurance policy acquisition and maintenance pursuant to, 296–97
Domicile, as community property, 305
Donations. *See* Charitable contributions; Charitable giving
Donor of the power, 372
Donor's contribution base, 230
Double stepped-up basis, 310–11, 316
Dower, 292–93
Dynasty trusts, 107–9

Earnings, as community property, 303
Educational expenses gifts, 153, 155–56
Employee benefits
   in estate planning, 377–411
   types of, 378–79
Employee Retirement Income Security Act, 379
   rules of, 274
   state community-property laws and, 315
Employer-provided life insurance, 109–10
Equity of inheritance, 67–68
ERISA. *See* Employee Retirement Income Security Act
Estate
   enhancement of with life insurance, 40–41
   keeping ILIT proceeds out of, 94–97
   life insurance payable to, 45–47
   liquidity of, 41–42
   transfer of by nonresident-aliens, 323–24
   value of policy includible in, 54–56
Estate assets
   current value of, 13
   impact of inflation on, 13–16
   valuing, 14–16

Index

Estate freeze
  current rules limiting, 159–61
  definition of, 185–87
  for family businesses, 185–212
  impact of Chapter 14 on, 187–92
  techniques of, 439–40
  through family partnerships, 192–200
  through family trusts, 158–61
  through sales of family business to family members, 201–12
Estate liquidity, 414
  in case study, 440–44
  charitable donations to improve, 245–47
  creating, 99–102
  in estate planning, 418–22
  life insurance in, 64–67, 445
  QPRT and, 169
  time-extension provisions and, 419–22
  in valuation, 116
Estate of Evers case, 129
Estate of Joyce C. Hall v. Commissioner case, 139
Estate plan
  adequate future income in, 424
  case study of, 424–48
  effective organization of, 413–24
  patterns of distribution in, 422–24
  present vs. modified, 415
  topics to treat in, 415–18
Estate planning
  charitable giving and, 237–47
  community property in, 299–317
  for distributions from qualified plans and IRAs, 379–96
  employee benefits and, 377–411
  with GRATs and GRUTs, 172–73
  issues stemming from marital relationship, 287–97
  life insurance in, 39–73
  for non-U.S. citizens, 319–43
  practical uses for life insurance in, 62–73
  procedural principles of, 413–48
  QPRTs in, 162–63
  steps in, 1
  valuation principles used in, 113–50
Estate settlement costs
  calculation of
    for married client, 22–25
    for single client, 21–22
  forecasting, 1–38
    issues in, 8–21
  forecasting final, 21
  sample work sheet for, 27–29
  work sheet for, 30–37
Estate tax
  advantages of ILIT in, 77
  on bonus life insurance plan, 410
  charitable giving and, 223–27
  on DBO plan, 400–401
  federal, 6
    calculating, 16–19
    forecasting, 9–21
    on life insurance, 45–56
    paid by insurance beneficiaries, 56
  FLIPs and, 199–200
  forecasting, gross estate inclusion rules and, 12
  with GRATs and GRUTs, 174–76
  on installment sales, 204–6
  marital deduction in, 417
  on nonqualified deferred-compensation plan, 398–99
  on private annuities, 208
  QPRT and, 168
  on qualified plans and IRAs, 379
  on split-dollar life insurance plans, 408–10
  state, 7–8
  of transfers by nonresident-aliens, 321–25
  on transfers incident to divorce or separation, 293–95
  trust transfers subject to, 370
  unified rate schedule for, 19 *t.*
Estate tax credits
  on irrevocable living trust, 364
  for nonresident-alien estate transfers, 324
Estate trust, as qualified plan beneficiary, 388–89
Excessive transfer costs, 414
  in case study, 427–40
  present plan vs. modified plan, 415
Excluded transfers, for nonresident-alien gifts, 324
Executor
  commission of, 4
  fee schedule for, 5 *t.*

Fair market value, 118
  willing buyer-willing seller method of establishing, 170
Family business
  estate freezes for, 185–212
  installment sales of, 201–6

sale to family members, 201–12
Family corporation, 211
Family estate settlement costs, 23–24
Family life insurance partnerships, 197–200
    estate tax considerations of, 199–200
    gift tax considerations of, 198
    retained control by insured, 198
    structuring, 197
Family limited partnerships, 440
Family members, 188
    applicable under Sec. 2701, 188
    gifts to, 151–84
    sales of family business to, 201–12
Family partnerships
    advantages of, 192
    estate freezes through, 192–200
    income tax considerations in, 196
    life insurance, 197–200
    limited, 192–93
    protection from creditors, 196
    structuring of, 192–96
    traditional freeze of, 193–95
    transfer of limited interests in, 195–96
Family trusts
    Crummey accumulation, 157–58
    estate freezes through, 158–61
    providing qualified retained interests, 171–81
    qualified personal residence, 162–70
    tangible personal property, 170–71
    transfers to, 156–81
Farm, remainder interest in, 258–59
Federal government, in charitable giving, 218
Federal taxes
    charitable giving and, 218–22
    on qualified plans and IRAs, 380–82
    valuation of life insurance for, 122
Feldmar case, 135
Fiduciary capacity, incidents held by insured in, 48
Fifty percent limitation, 234
5-and-5 rule, 374–75
Fixed-price premium life insurance, 43
Flexible-premium life insurance policy, 43–44
FLIP. *See* Family life insurance partnerships
FLP. *See* Family limited partnerships
Foreign death tax credit, 18, 321
    for QDOT transfer, 335
Formula valuation method, 130
Frane case, 212 *n.* 3
Frane v. Commissioner, 207

Friedberg v. Commissioner, 46, 54
Funeral expenses, of nonresident-alien estate transfers, 323
Future income, adequate, 414, 424
    in case study, 447–48

General power by deed, 372
General power by will, 372
Generation-skipping ILITs, 107–9
Generation-skipping transfer
    deductions, credits, and special provisions in, 371
    estate planning implications of, 371–72
    exemptions and exclusions of, 370
    tax on, 6–7, 56–58
        advantages of ILIT in, 77–78
        on life insurance, 56–58
        mechanics of $1 million exemption, 109
        rate of, 370
        sheltering ILIT from, 108–9
        on trusts, 366–72
    taxable amounts in, 369–70
Gift tax, 2–3
    additional, 191
    advantages of ILIT in, 76–77
    annual exclusion in, 80–81
    on bonus life insurance plan, 410–11
    charitable giving and, 227–29
    for Crummey beneficiaries, 88–89
    on DBO plan, 401–2
    versus estate tax savings, 60–61
    FLIPs and, 198
    with GRATs and GRUTs, 173–74
    on group term life insurance plans, 404–5
    on irrevocable living trust, 364
    on life insurance, 58–60
    on noncitizen-spouse transfers, 337–39
    on nonqualified deferred-compensation plan, 398
    planning for ILITs, 80–94
    QPRT and, 166–67
    of transfers by nonresident-aliens, 321–25
    on transfers incident to divorce or separation, 293–95
    trust transfers subject to, 370
    unified rate schedule for, 19 *t.*
    unlimited marital deduction for, 68
Gift tax deduction
    computing, 228–29

unlimited, 227
Gifting programs
   outright, 152–56
   valuation of, 115
   in written plan, 439
Gifts. *See also* Charitable contributions; Gifts
   advantages of, 60–62
   of corporate stock, 136–38
   for educational or medical expenses, 153, 155–56
   to family members, 151–84
   to family trusts, 156–81
   inadvertent, 59–60
   by nonresident-alien, 324–25
   of policies to trusts, 62–63
   present-interest, 81
   qualifying to ILIT for annual gift tax exclusion, 80–81
Gift-splitting, 59, 86
   by nonresident-aliens, 315
Gilford case, 118
Giselman case, 135
Giving. *See* Charitable contributions; Charitable giving; Gifting programs
Grandparent-grandchild trusts, 63–64
Grantor trust rules
   effect of, 348–55
   income tax consequences under, 348–49
   permissible powers and controls under, 353
   prohibited powers and controls under, 349–53
   relinquishment of retained powers, 354
Grantor-retained annuity trust, 146
   choosing investments for, 176–78
   compared with GRUTs, 180–81
   defined, 172
   estate planning with, 172
   estate tax inclusion for, 175
   estate tax treatment of, 174–75
   gift tax treatment of, 173–74
   impact of Sec. 7520 rate on, 178–79
   income tax treatment of, 178
   indication of, 180–81
   use of property subject to loan, 178
   zeroed-out, 176
Grantor-retained income trust, 159
   estate-freeze rules and, 159–61
Grantor-retained unitrust, 146
   choosing investments for, 176–78
   compared with GRATs, 180–81
   defined, 173

estate planning with, 172
estate tax inclusion for, 175–76
estate tax treatment of, 174–76
gift tax treatment of, 173–74
income tax treatment of grantor in, 178
indication of, 180–81
use of property subject to loan, 178
Sec. 7520 rate impact on, 178–79
GRATs. *See* Grantor-retained annuity trust
Green case, 422
GRIT. *See* Grantor-retained income trust
Gross estate
   adjusted, 16–17
   determining, 9–16
   determining size of, 417
   inclusion of assets in, 427
   inclusion rules, 12
   reduction of, 438
Group term life insurance plans, 379, 411 *n.* 3
   as charitable donation, 242
   estate planning for, 403–5
   exempt from attributed-incidents rule, 50
   gift tax implications of, 404–5
   income tax implications of, 402–3
   reducing income tax with, 403–4
   Sec. 2035 and conversion of, 52
GRUTs. *See* Grantor-retained unitrust
GSTT. *See* Generation-skipping transfer tax

Hanging Crummey powers, 93–94
Hardship distribution, QDOT, 334
Harper case, 292
Hass case, 317 *n.* 23
Hastings case, 291
Headrick case, 51–52, 96–97
Health insurance costs, 156
Highest and best use, 125

Idaho
   community property in, 304
   living trusts in, 310
ILIT. *See* Irrevocable life insurance trusts
Inception-of-title rule, 313
Incidental benefit test, 391–92
Incidents of ownership, 47–50
   attributed to business owner, 49–50
   held by insured in fiduciary capacity, 48
Income distributions, defined, 343 *n.* 3

Income in respect of decedent, 10
   qualified plan funds as, 373
   retirement plan assets as, 275
   rule of, 205–6
Income tax
   charitable giving and, 229–37
   on DBO plan, 402
   on family partnerships, 196
   under grantor trust rules, 348–49
   on group term life insurance plans, 402–3
   on ILIT, 79
   on installment sales, 202–4
   loss of basis step up, 168
   on nonqualified deferred-compensation plan, 397–98
   on private annuities, 209–210
   QPRT and, 166
   on qualified plans and IRAs, 380–82
   reduction with group term life insurance plans, 403–4
   on split-dollar life insurance plans, 406–7
Income tax deductions
   compliance rules for charitable donations, 234–37
   limitations on, 229–34
   reduction for high-income donors, 233
Individual retirement accounts, 378
   benefits from, 10
   choosing beneficiary of, 385–86
   distributions from, 379–96
   federal tax treatment of, 380–82
   QDOT regulations and, 330–32
   rollovers of, 275
Inflation
   impact on estate assets, 13–16
   rate of, 15
Inheritance
   equity of, 67–68
   inefficient, 382–84
   state tax on, 7
Installment note, self-canceling, 206–7
Installment sales, 201–6
   advantages of, 201
   buyer's income tax on, 202
   estate tax considerations of, 204–6
   income tax considerations of, 202–4
   interest on, 203
   related-party, 203–4
   seller's premature death and, 205–6
Intangible property
   for nonresident-alien decedents, 322–23
   for nonresident-alien-donors, 323
Inter vivos charitable lead trust, 283

Interest
   on installment sales, 203
   of same class, 189
Interest rates
   impact on QPRTs, 170
   monthly variation in, 146
   of private annuities, 210
Interlocutory decree, 306
Internal Revenue Code
   Sec. 170(c)(5), 247 *n.* 5
   Sec. 170(f)(2), 271
   Sec. 213, 156
   Sec. 280A(d)(1), 163
   Sec. 303
      qualification of donation under, 246–47
      in valuation, 116
   Sec. 303(d), 371
   Sec. 501(c)(3), 221, 230
   Sec. 642(c)(5), 281–82
   Sec. 672(c), 350
   Sec. 674, 351–52
      permissible powers and controls of trusts under, 353
   Sec. 675(3), 349–50
   Sec. 676, 351
   Sec. 677, 353
   Sec. 677(a), 352
   Sec. 677(b), 353
   Sec. 678, 352
   Sec. 691(c)(3), 371
   Sec. 2010, 431–32
   Sec. 2013(g), 371
   Sec. 2031, 55, 117, 138, 427
   Sec. 2032, 119, 121, 427
      alternate valuation date in, 119–20
   Sec. 2032A, 117, 125–26, 127–32, 437–38
      qualification of donation under, 246–47
   Sec. 2033A, 438
   Sec. 2034, 292–93
   Sec. 2035, 45, 50–52, 54, 77, 355
      ILITs and, 95–97
   Sec. 2036, 174, 354–55
   Sec. 2037, 354
   Sec. 2038, 354
   Sec. 2039, 380, 398, 400–401
   Sec. 2039(a), 125
   Sec. 2041, 354
      on taxation of powers, 373
   Sec. 2042, 46, 54, 80, 94, 122, 355
   Sec. 2042(2), 48, 181, 182

Sec. 2206, 56
Sec. 2503(b), 439
Sec. 2503(e), 153, 155–56
Sec. 2511, 117
Sec. 2514, 88–89
Sec. 2516, 294–95
Sec. 2604, 371
Sec. 2612(a)(2), 367–68
Sec. 2612(b), 369
Sec. 2612(c), 368
Sec. 2652(c), 367
Sec. 2701
    Chapter 14 and, 187–92
    implications of, 188–89
Sec. 2702, 159–61
    exceptions to, 161
Sec. 2703, 138–39
Sec. 6161, 419
Sec. 6166, 419–21
    court cases involving, 421–22
    qualification of donation under, 246–47
    in valuation, 114, 116
Sec. 6166(i), 371
Sec. 6662, 117
Sec. 7520, 117, 118, 123
    impact on QPRTs, 170
    private annuities and, 208–9, 210
    rules for valuing partial interests, 145–50
Secs. 2033–2046, 45
Secs. 2701–4, 150
Internal Revenue Ruling
    59-60, 117, 133
    83-147, 50, 199
    89-22, 129
    89-30, 129
    79-47, 1979-1 C.B. 312, 411 *n.* 3
    80-242, 1980-2 C.B. 276, 317 *n.* 24
    81-31, 1981-1 C.B. 475, 401
    84-130, 1984-2 C.B. 404
    93-12, 1993-1 C.B. 13, 136–38
    64-328 C.B. 1964-2, 406
    66-110 C.B. 1966-1, 406
Internal Revenue Service
    in Crummey case, 82, 84–86
    Notice 89-24, 117
    Notice 89-60, 117
    publications of, 117–18
    validating minority discount, 136–38
    valuation of closely held corporation of, 132–36
    valuation rules of, 117

Interpolated terminal reserve, 55–56
Intestacy, 288–90
    advantages of, 288
    disadvantages of, 288–89
Investments
    of CRT principal, 269–70
    for GRATs and GRUTs, 176–78
IRAs. *See* Individual retirement accounts
IRC. *See* Internal Revenue Code
IRD. *See* Income in respect of decedent
Irrevocable beneficiary, 240
Irrevocable life insurance trust, 63
    advantages of, 76–80
    concerns about, 102–7
    Crummey case and, 82–94
    dispositive provisions of, 97–102
    employer-provided life insurance and, 109–10
    family, 156–81
    versus family life insurance partnerships, 197
    flexibility to change beneficiaries in, 105–7
    gift tax planning for, 80–94
    irrevocability of, 79, 102–7
    keeping proceeds out of grantor's estate, 94–97
    to mitigate triple tax on qualified plans, 394–96
    policy replacement by trustee, 107
    purchase of estate assets by, 101–2
    removal of proceeds from, 181–84
    retrieving life insurance policy from, 103–5
    Sec. 2035 3-year rule and, 95–97
    special planning applications for, 107–10
    third-party ownership of in community-property states, 313–14
Irrevocable living trusts
    with no retained powers or controls
        advantages of, 362–63
        disadvantages of, 363–64
        tax consequences of, 364
        tax-advantageous provisions of, 364–66
    taxation of, 362–66
Item theory, 307

Joint life insurance, 44
Joint tenancy, 256
    assets of in trusts, 310

noncitizen-spouse transfers to, 338
property held in, 303
Jointly titled property with rights of
survivorship, 10–11

Keogh plans, 378, 379
Kiddie tax provision, 358–59

Lauder case, 139
Legal fees
associated with lifetime gifts, 2
probate, 4
Liability, with community property, 309
Life annuities, valuing, 149–50
Life estates
factors determining present value of, 149
valuation of, 145–50
valuing remainder interests following, 149
Life income beneficiary, 364–66
Life insurance
beneficiaries of
responsibility for paying federal estate taxes by, 56
taxation of, 393–94
bonus, 379
as community property, 304
cross-ownership of, 314
in DBO plan, 402
on decedent's life, 11
in equity of inheritance, 67–68
in estate enhancement, 40–41
in estate liquidity, 41–42, 64–67, 422
in estate planning, 39–72
federal estate taxation of, 45–56
generation-skipping transfer taxation of, 56–58
gift taxation of, 58–60
gifts of to trusts, 62–63
group term plans, 379, 402–5, 411 *n.* 3
held by CRT, 270
inception-of-title versus allocation-of-premium rule, 313
limited by incidental benefit test, 391–92
marital deduction and, 52–54
to minimize QDOT burden, 342
multiple life coverage, 44
in nonqualified deferred-compensation plan, 399

nonspousal beneficiary in community property states, 312–13
of nonworking spouse, 68–69
outright gifts of, 60–62
outside qualified plans, 394–96
ownership of, 296
payable to decedent's testamentary trust, 47
possession of incidents of ownership of, 47–50
practical uses for in estate planning, 62–72
products, 42–44
in profit-sharing plans, 392
purchased with community funds, 313
purposes of, 40–42
in qualified plans, 391–94
removal of proceeds
from decedent-insured's gross estate, 181–84
from estate, 439
return to insured, 61–62
second-to-die policy, 69–72
single life coverage, 43–44
split-dollar, 379
taxable termination of, 57–58
taxation of participant of, 392–93
third-party ownership of, 313–15
transfer tax implications of, 45
treatment of in community-property states, 312–15
valuation dispute over, 114–15
valuation of, 122–23
Life insurance donations
group term, 242
mechanics of, 239–42
planned-giving programs with, 243–44
reasons for, 238–39
retaining flexibility with, 243
substantiating and valuation of, 244
Life insurance policy
of decedent, 54
gift taxation of, 58–59
owned by decedent on lives of other, 54–56
purchasing from ILIT, 104–5
pursuant to divorce, 296–97
replacement of by trustee, 107
retrieving from ILIT, 103–5
right or option to repurchase, 48–49
transfers of within 3 years of death, 50–52
value includible in gross estate, 54–56

Index

Lifetime gifts
   costs of, 2–3
   to family, 152–54
   to noncitizen-spouse, 341–42
   with retained rights, 10
Lifetime giving decisions, 115
Lifetime transfer
   incomplete, 225–26
   valuation of, 150
Limited partnership interest gifts, 195–96
Liquidity, 414
   in case study, 440–44
   charitable donations to improve, 244–46
   enhance by ILIT, 80
   in estate planning, 418–22
   of ILIT proceeds, 99–102
   of life insurance coverage, 41–42, 64–67, 422
   needs for, 42
   QPRT and, 168–69
   shortfall in GRAT or GRUT, 181
   time-extension provisions and, 419–22
   in valuation, 116
Living trust
   as designated beneficiary, 389
   reducing probate estate by, 78
Loaning powers, 100–101
Longue Vue Foundation v. Commissioner, 247 *n.* 6
Louisiana
   community property in, 304
   life insurance ownership in, 315

Marine case, 247 *n.* 6
Marital deduction
   denial to noncitizen-spouse, 325
   effective use of, 428–34
   in federal estate tax, 417
   for gift taxes, 68
   life insurance and, 52–54
   on noncitizen-spouse transfers, 337–39
   for nonresident-alien estate transfers, 323–24
   for nonresident-alien gifts, 324
   as tax deferral, 69
   unlimited, 98
Marital deduction trust, as qualified plan beneficiary, 387–88
Marital home, division of, 295–96
Marital relationship
   issues stemming from, 287–97

   ownership of life insurance and, 296
Marketable retained interest, 189
Marketable securities, 132
Marketable transferred interest, 189
Married client
   calculating estate settlement costs for, 22–25
   goals of, 22–23
   two mortality contingencies for, 23–24
Martin case, 128–29
Medical expense gifts, 153, 155–56
Membership benefits, 237
Minimum value rule, 190–91
Minority discount, 136–38
Minors, trust transfers or custodial arrangements to benefit, 357–59
Modified endowment contract (MEC) rules, 79
Money, time value of, 153–54
Mortality contingencies
   forecasting with, 23–24
   in interest valuation methods, 146, 149
Mortgage, 164–65
Multiple life coverage, 44
Multiple-factor valuation method, 130–31

Naturalization statutes, 343 *n.* 1
Nelson v. United States, 291–92
Net federal estate tax payable after credits, 17–19
Net-income unitrusts, 266–68
Nevada
   community property in, 304
   life insurance premium test in, 313
New Mexico, community property in, 304
NIMCRUT, 266–68
   investment of principal of, 269–70
   as retirement plan replacement, 276–78
   transfer of closely held corporation through, 280–81
Non-capital-gain property contribution, 233–34
Noncitizens
   estate planning for, 319–43
   transfer taxation of, 319–21
Noncitizen-spouse
   estate planning for transfers to, 325–39
   minimizing burden of QDOT treatment of, 339–42
   obtaining citizenship status, 327, 341
   testamentary transfers to, 326–37

Nonconcurrent interests, 145–50
Noncontingent guaranteed payments, 193–94
Nonqualified deferred-compensation plan, 378
    advantages of, 396–97
    federal estate tax implications of, 398–99
    federal gift tax implications of, 398
    federal income tax implications of, 397–98
    life insurance for, 399
    types of, 396–97
Nonresident-alien estate transfer, 323–24
Nonresident-alien gifts, 324–25
Nonresident-aliens, 320
    estate and gift taxation of transfers by, 321–25
Nonworking spouse insurance, 68–69
Northern Trust Company case, 135

Optimal marital deduction, 25
Ordinary income property, 233–34
Original issue discount (OID) rules, 203

Partial interest gifts, 254–59
Partial interests
    deductible transfer of, 220
    nonconcurrent property, 145–50
    undivided, 250
    valuation of, 145–50
Partnerships
    family, 192–200
    recapitalized, 193–94
    state laws on, 212 *n.* 2
Pegging, 116, 138
Pennsylvania inheritance tax, 8
Pension maximization, 385–86
Percentage limitation rules, 229–33
Per-donor exemption, 370
Per-grandchild exemption, 370
Permanent life insurance, 43–44
Permissible associated property, 164
Personal property
    intangible
        for nonresident-alien decedents, 322–23
        for nonresident-alien-donors, 323
    tangible, for nonresident-alien transferors, 321–22
    valuation of, 144

Planned-giving programs, 242–44
Policy dividend donation, 242
Pooled-income funds, 281–82
Power by deed, 372
Powers
    of invasion rules, 359–60
    lapse of, 374
    taxation of, 372–74
Powers of appointment, 372–76
    5-and-5 rule and, 374–75
    increased flexibility of, 375–76
    lapse of, 374
    taxation of, 372–74
Predeceased parent exception, 58
Premarital planning, 309
Premium payment test, 51–52
Present-interest gift, 81
    with minors, 82
    in noncitizen-spouse transfers, 337
Private annuities, 207–12
    buyer's income tax on, 209–10
    estate tax considerations in, 208
    income tax considerations in, 209–10
    Sec. 7520 interest rate impact on, 210
    suitable types of property for, 210–12
Private foundations
    life insurance donations to, 243
    property gifts to, 234
Private letter ruling (Ltr. 9030005), 93
Private letter ruling (PLR) 8712014, 85–86
Probate
    expenses of, 3–6, 41
        avoiding, 78
Profit-sharing plans, 385–86
Property. *See also* Property gifts; Real estate
    as deductible contribution, 219
    disposition of in common-law states, 308
    distribution at death in community-property states, 306–7
    right to regain, 349, 359
    separate and mixed-character, 302
    subject to loan, 178
    transfer of partial interests in, 220
    transfers between spouses, 302
    value affected by time, 120
Property gifts
    partial, 254–59
    to private foundations, 234
    producing long-term capital gain, 247 *n.* 8
    types of, 231–33
Property interests transferred by gift, 10
Property owned outright by decedent, 9–10

Index   461

Proportionate transfers, 190
Publicity, avoidance of, 78

QDOT. *See* Qualified domestic trust
QJSA. *See* Qualified joint and survivor annuity
QPRT. *See* Qualified personal residence trust
QSST. *See* Qualified subchapter S trust
QTIP. *See* Qualified terminable interest property
Qualified conservation donations, 284–86
Qualified domestic trust
  administration of, 343 *n.* 3
  assignment of assets to, 329–30
  applicable credit amount and, 334–35
  calculating tax on, 333
  creation of, 328–29
  death tax credit and, 335
  distributions of
    planning to reduce burden of, 340–42
    problems associated with taxation of, 339–40
    taxation of, 332–33
  foreign death tax credit for, 335
  funding issues of, 332
  hardship distributions of, 334
  new compliance and security requirements for, 335–37
  prior transfer tax credit and, 335
  problems associated with taxation of, 339–40
  regulations of retirement benefits in, 330–32
  requirements of, 328
  rules of, 343 *n.* 1
  for surviving noncitizen-spouse, 326–37
  taxation of, 343 *n.* 4, 343 *n.* 5
  Treasury regulations for, 343 *n.* 2
Qualified joint and survivor annuity, 384–86
Qualified payments exception, 190
Qualified personal residence trust, 162–70
  disadvantages of, 163
  estate planning uses of, 162–63
  estate tax consequences of, 168
  failure to qualify as, 165
  gift tax consequence of, 166–67
  income tax consequences of, 166
  permissible associated property, 164
  qualifying residences for, 163–65
  selecting residence in, 165–66
  tax problems associated with, 168–70
  term of, 169
Qualified plan subtrust, 394
Qualified retained interests trust, 171–81
Qualified retained-interest exception, 161
Qualified retirement plans, 378
  CRT as beneficiary of, 278–80
  death after decedent's required beginning date of, 381
  death before required beginning date of, 380–81
  distributions from, 379–96
  federal tax treatment of, 380–82
  funding and cost concerns of, 274–75
  mitigating triple tax on, 394–96
  planning for benefits of, 384–96
  problems with, 274–75
  transferring assets of at death, 275
Qualified subchapter S trusts, 177
Qualified terminable interest property, 11–12
  election of, 53–54
  estate-freeze rules and, 161
Qualified terminable interest property trust, 255–56
  as qualified plan beneficiary, 387–88
Quasi-community property/personal property, 303
Quid pro quo
  donations, 237
  in reciprocal-trust doctrine, 361–62
  theory, 216, 217

Railroad Retirement Act, 315
Real estate. *See also* Property
  community, 303
  as community property, 303
  conservation donation of, 284–86
  factors in setting value on, 124–25
  for nonresident-alien transferors, 321–23
  special-use valuation of, 125–32
  valuation of, 124–32
Recapitalization
  of family partnerships, 193-95
  stock, 191–92
Recapture, 128–29, 132
Reciprocal transfers, 361–62
Remainder factor, 146
Remainder interest
  acceleration of, 169
  factors determining present value of, 146–47
  in farm, 258–59

in personal residence, 257–58
    valuing following life estate, 149
    valuing of, 145
Repurchase rights, life insurance, 48–49
Residence. *See also* Personal residence
    as community property, 305
    leasing, 166
    for QPRTs, 163–66
    repurchasing from remainder
        beneficiaries, 166
    selecting for QPRT, 165–66
    transfer tax definition of, 320
Resident-aliens, 320
Residuary trust, 434
Retained interest
    estate-freeze rules and, 160
    not under Sec. 2701, 189–90
    Sec. 2701 and, 187–88
    trust providing, 171–81
Retained powers
    to alter, amend, revoke, or terminate,
        trust transfers with, 355–57
    estate tax consequences of trust transfers
        with, 354–55
    relinquishment of, 354
    transfers to trusts with, 348–55
        income, gifts, and estate tax
            consequences of, 355–62
Retained rights, Sec. 2701, 188–89
Retired lives reserves plans, 403
Retirement Equity Act (REA), 279–80, 315, 385
Retirement plans. *See also* Individual
        retirement plans; Qualified
        retirement plans
    assets left to heirs, 382–84
    benefits from, 10
        guidelines for distributions and estate
            planning of, 384–85
        planning for, 384–96
        QDOT regulations and, 330–31
    in community-property states, 315
    CRT to supplement, 274–80
    distributions from, 379–96
    noncitizen-spouse transfers to, 339
    problems with, 274–75
    tax-funded, 315
Revenue Reconciliation Act, Chapter 14 of, 187–92
Reverse split-dollar plans, 407–8, 409–10
Revocable trusts
    advantages of, 347–48
    taxation of, 346–48

Rubish case, 124

S corporation stock, 191–92
    for GRATs and GRUTs, 177
Safe harbor, 294–95
Salary reduction arrangements, 396–97
Schindler case, 421–22
SCINs. *See* Self-canceling installment notes
Sec. 162 bonus life insurance plans, 379, 410–11
Sec. 7520 interest rates, 212 *n.* 3
Sec. 79 plan, 402–5
Sec. 170 regulations, 236
Second disposition rule, 204
Second-to-die policy, 69–72
    ILIT, 99
Security requirements, 335–37
Self-canceling installment notes, 206–7, 212 *n.* 3
SEP. *See* Simplified employee pension
Separation
    ending community, 305–6
    estate and gift tax implications of
        transfers incident to, 293–95
Simplified employee pension, 378
Single client, estate settlement costs for, 21–22
Single life coverage
    permanent, 43–44
    term, 43
Skip beneficiaries, 367
Special-use valuation, 125–32
    election of, 131–32
    formula method for, 130
    multiple-factor method for, 130–31
    procedural aspects of, 127–28
    recapture of, 128–29
    requirements for qualification of, 125–27
    valuation issues of, 129–30
Split-dollar life insurance, 366, 379, 405–10
    basic arrangements of, 405–7
    estate tax considerations of, 408–10
    income taxation of, 406–7
    policy ownership of, 405–6
    reverse, 407–8, 409–10
Split-interest donations, 254, 259, 284–86
    charitable, 216
Sponge tax, state, 7–8
Spouse
    noncitizen

estate planning for transfer to, 325–39
minimizing QDOT burden on, 339–42
surviving
ILIT provision for, 98–99
intestacy and, 288–90
leaving property to, 25
right of election against will, 290–92
tax-deferral options of naming as beneficiary, 379–80
Spray provisions, 266
State death tax, 7–8
credit for, 18, 20 *t.*
on qualified plans and IRAs, 375
Stock recapitalizations
practical considerations with, 191–92
valuation problems of, 191
Stocks
nonvoting, 191–92
private annuities and, 210–11
valuation of, 136–37
Street case, 317 *n.* 21
Supertrust, 111 *n.* 8
Supertrust powers, 103–4
Survivorship
jointly titled property with, 10–11
life insurance for, 44
Sutliff v. Sutliff, 359

Tangible personal property exception, 161
Tangible personal property trusts, 170–71
Tangible property/unrelated use rule, 234
Tax. *See also* Estate tax; Federal taxes; Generation-skipping transfer, tax on; Gift tax; Income tax; State death tax; Transfer tax
credits for QDOT distribution, 334–35
deductions
for charitable giving, 218–19
for CRTs, 270–71
for qualified plan, 380
on QDOT distribution, 332–33, 339–40, 343 *n.* 4, 343 *n.* 5
reduction with family gifts, 152–56
on trusts, 345–76
Tax preparer fees, 4–5
Tax Reform Act, 351
generation-skipping transfer and, 366–67
"kiddie tax" provision of, 358–59
on taxation of direct skips, 368–69

valuation section of, 125–27
Taxable distributions, generation-skipping, 57–58
Taxable estate
determining, 17
methods of reducing, 418
Tax-exempt investments, 269
Technical Advice Memorandum 8802004, 349–50
Technical and Miscellaneous Revenue Act (TAMRA), 325
Temporary withdrawal powers, 157–58
Tentative federal estate tax, 17
Tentative tax base, 17
Term interests
factors determining present value of, 147
valuation of, 145–50
Term life insurance, 43
Testamentary charitable lead trust, 283–84
Testamentary power of appointment, 169
Testamentary transfer, to noncitizen-spouse, 326–37
Testamentary trust, 47
Texas community property, 304–5
Thompson case, 127
Three-year rule
on existing policies, 95–96
ILITs and, 95–97
on newly acquired policies, 96–97
Time value of money, 153–54
Time-extension provision, 419–22
Transfer costs, excessive, 414, 427–40
Transfer tax
on CRTs, 276
definition of residency, 320
federal generation-skipping, 56–58
on life insurance, 45
for noncitizens, 319–21
on qualified retirement plans, 275
sheltering ILIT from, 108–9
treaties, 320–21
Transmutation agreement, 302
Treasury Regulation
Sec. 1.664-4, 117
Sec. 20.2031, 117
Sec. 20.2031-8, 123
Sec. 25.2512, 117
Sec. 1.664-3(a)(5), 261–62
in valuation rules, 117
Trustee
distribution of ILIT by, 104
ILIT policy replacement by, 107

Trusts
- administrative powers of, 350–51
- beneficial enjoyment of principal of, 351–52
- borrowing assets of, 349–50
- borrowing corpus or income from, 350
- charitable, life insurance donations to, 243
- charitable wealth replacement, 110
- community property and, 310
- dynasty, 107–9
- family, 156–81
- generation-skipping transfer tax of, 366–72
- gifts of life insurance policies to, 62–63
- gifts to, 151–84
- giving grantor dispositive flexibility, 78–79
- grandparent-grandchild, 63–64
- income distributed to grantor, 352
- income to discharge grantor's legal obligations, 352–53
- irrevocable life insurance, 75–111
- irrevocable living, 362–66
- noncitizen-spouse transfers to, 337–39
- power to revoke, 359–60
- powers of appointment in, 372–76
- reciprocal transfer of, 361–62
- reversionary interest in corpus or income of, 351
- revocable, 346–48
- taxable distributions of, 367
- taxable terminations of, 367–68
- taxation of, 345–76
- transfers of
    - for benefit or minors, 357–59
    - with powers to invade corpus, 359–60
    - with retained powers to alter, amend, revoke, or terminate, 355–57
- transfers to with retained powers
    - income, gift, and estate tax consequences of, 355–62
    - taxation of, 348–53
- wealth replacement, 271–74

Tuition payment gift, 155–56
Two-residence limitation, 165

UCST. See Unified credit shelter trust
Undivided portion of donor's entire interest, 256
Unearned premium value, 55–56
Unified credit. See Applicable credit amount; Applicable exclusion amount
Unified gift credit on irrevocable living trust, 364
Unified rate schedule, 19 t.
Uniform Disposition of Community Property Rights at Death Act, 300, 303, 308, 316 n. 1
Uniform Marital Property Act, 317 n. 2
United Equitable Corporation, 135
United States Life Tables: 1960–1971, 145

Valuation
- of assets, 415–16
- of charitable donations, 235–36
- of estate assets, 427
- fair market, 118
- of life insurance donations, 244
- of lifetime transfers with retained interests, 150
- of partial interests, 145–50
- preparing for dispute over, 114–15
- principles of, 114–17
    - alternate valuation date and, 119–21
    - fair market value and, 118
- provisions, 434–38
- sources of rules for, 117–18
- for specific properties, 121–44
- of stock recapitalization, 191

Variable life insurance, 44

Washington
- community property in, 304
- divorce and separation in, 306
- life insurance premium test in, 313

Wealth replacement trusts, 271–74
Wealth transfer costs
- at death, 3–8
- during lifetime, 2–3

Will
- current arrangement of, 423, 445
- failure to draft, 289
- spouse's right of election against, 290–92

Willing buyer-willing seller standard, 132–33, 170
Wisconsin, Uniform Marital Property Act of, 317 n. 2

Index 465

Zeroed-out GRATs, 176